D1710534

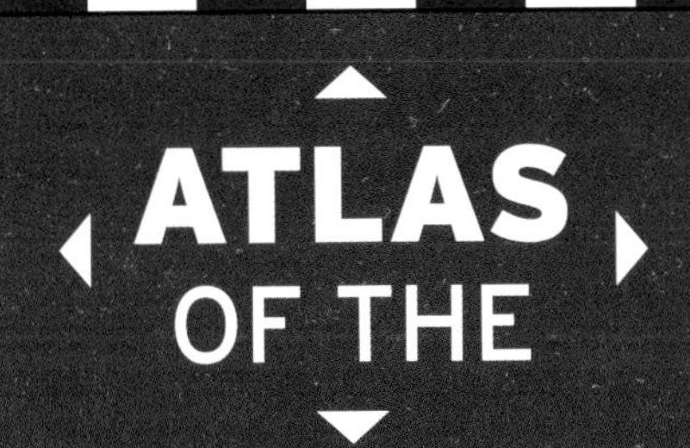

2016 ELECTIONS

EDITED BY Robert H. Watrel
Ryan Weichelt
Fiona M. Davidson
John Heppen
Erin H. Fouberg
J. Clark Archer
Richard L. Morrill
Fred M. Shelley
Kenneth C. Martis

CARTOGRAPHY BY Robert H. Watrel and J. Clark Archer

ROWMAN & LITTLEFIELD
Lanham • Boulder • New York • London

Published by Rowman & Littlefield
A wholly owned subsidiary of The Rowman & Littlefield Publishing Group, Inc.
4501 Forbes Boulevard, Suite 200, Lanham, Maryland 20706
www.rowman.com

Unit A, Whitacre Mews, 26-34 Stannary Street, London SE11 4AB, United Kingdom

British Library Cataloguing in Publication Information Available

Library of Congress Cataloging-in-Publication Data Available

ISBN 978-1-5381-0422-4 (cloth : alk. paper)
ISBN 978-1-5381-0423-1 (electronic)

∞™ The paper used in this publication meets the minimum requirements of American National Standard for Information Sciences—Permanence of Paper for Printed Library Materials, ANSI/NISO Z39.48-1992.

Printed in the United States of America

CONTENTS

FIGURES AND TABLES

FIGURES

TABLES

PREFACE

The Atlas of the 2016 Elections offers a spatial perspective of the presidential primaries and campaigns of the major party candidates leading up to the presidential election on Tuesday, November 8, 2016, in the United States. The pivotal 2016 presidential election was one aspect of a snapshot of national, state, and local elections and ballots held in 2016 and analyzed in this atlas.

The editors working on this atlas span several generations, which brings an incredible wealth of political and geographic knowledge to our final product. On behalf of our fellow editors, we recognize several of our current and past editors: Dick Morrill (University of Washington, emeritus), Stan Brunn (University of Kentucky, emeritus), Ken Martis (West Virginia University, emeritus), J. Clark Archer (University of Nebraska–Lincoln), Fred Shelley (University of Oklahoma), Jerry Webster (University of Wyoming), and our late friend Steve Lavin (University of Nebraska–Lincoln). Each of these political geographers has served as teacher, mentor, role model, and friend. They are unselfish and always willing to aid in the professional development of young geographers, as evidenced by the many PhD students and new faculty who have contributed to the three atlases in this series. We were welcomed into the fold of political geographers through their kindness and guidance, and we hope to emulate and return the favor to future geographers.

Finally, we would like to recognize financial assistance from the Department of Geology and Geography at West Virginia University, the Department of Geosciences at the University of Arkansas, University of Wisconsin–Eau Claire Department of Geography and Anthropology's George Simpson Geography Fund, the Department of Geography and Geographic Information Science at the University of Wisconsin–River Falls, and the Thomas A. Daschle Research Fellowship at South Dakota State University.

Robert H. Watrel and Erin H. Fouberg

1 INTRODUCTION

ROBERT H. WATREL AND ERIN H. FOUBERG

Republican nominee Donald Trump won the 2016 presidential election by carrying thirty states that gave him 306 of the 538 votes in the Electoral College.[1] Democratic nominee Hillary Clinton won almost 2.9 million more popular votes than Trump, with a surplus of votes in a few of the more populous states she carried, including a surplus of more than 4.2 million votes in California. The election came down to a few key swing states where the race was incredibly tight: Michigan (Trump won by 10,704 votes: 47.6 percent to Clinton's 47.4 percent), Wisconsin (Trump won by 22,748 votes: 47.8 percent to Clinton's 47 percent), and Pennsylvania (Trump won by 44,292 votes: 48.8 percent to Clinton's 47.6 percent). These three states had gone to the Democratic presidential candidate since Bill Clinton won them in 1992, but on November 8, 2016, they went to Republican Donald Trump.

Clinton swayed fewer voters to get out and vote than Barack Obama did in swing states in 2012 and 2008. While the election shocked many pundits and rattled pollsters, it came down, as every election whether national, state, or local does, to voter turnout. Trump's campaign rallies inspired and compelled voters to the polls, and Clinton's campaign did not as effectively compel voter turnout where she needed it most.

County scale analysis of the map shows the stark contrast between rural Republican areas mapped in red and urban Democratic areas mapped in blue. Trump is proud of how much acreage he won on the county scale map, having passed out color copies of the county scale map to reporters in April and bringing a framed color poster-sized map into the West Wing in May (Bowden 2017). While Trump won the rural vote, careful inspection of the county scale map shows Clinton carried counties with large minority populations, including Native Americans living on reservations in the Southwest and Great Plains, along the Mexican border, and in the Mississippi Delta. While the acreage Clinton won was much smaller than Trump's, Clinton won huge numbers of votes in acreage mapped in blue, winning more than 80 percent of the vote in the cities of Boston, New York, and San Francisco and more than 90 percent of the vote in Washington, DC.

THE 2016 UNITED STATES ELECTIONS

Contributors to this atlas analyze the primaries leading up to the US presidential election, the campaigns, and the US presidential election from a political geography perspective. Analysis of the geography of primaries votes reveals splits within both major parties. Hillary Clinton ran as a moderate Democrat relative to Democratic Socialist Bernie Sanders. Trump ran as an outsider in the Republican primaries relative to career politician and party loyalist Ted Cruz.

Both parties had contentious primaries that revealed the geographies of the splits within the parties. Sanders found success in states with open primaries, where independents (and in some cases Republicans) could vote in Democratic primaries, and in states with caucuses, where voters are inspired enough by their candidate to attend a caucus. Sanders carried progressive states and counties and fared well in university towns and counties. Clinton won consistently in closed primaries and among the traditional Democratic base, including urban and minority voters.

Trump emerged from a crowded field of seventeen candidates in the Republican primary, having received massive amounts of free media for his well-attended rallies and provocative tweets. As primaries passed, the field narrowed to Trump, Ted Cruz, and John Kasich. Cruz received strong support from Republican evangelical voters. Kasich carried college-educated Republicans across several primaries and won his home state of Ohio.

As shown by the maps of the general election, Clinton's campaign strategy focused largely on states with larger urban populations. Polls were so favorable in the states of Wisconsin, Michigan, and Pennsylvania that she largely ignored them until the end, and she paid dearly for it. The Trump campaign focused on the swing states of Ohio, Florida, Pennsylvania, and North Carolina, appealing to many white voters who felt left behind and whose jobs were lost or threatened by globalization and illegal immigrants. In the end, Trump flipped six states into the Republican category that were usually in the Democratic column (Brownstein 2016).

The election results reveal an ever-increasing urban and rural divide in the electorate. Clinton won many of the cities with populations over one million and related suburbs. Meanwhile, Trump won most smaller urban and rural areas by large margins. Clinton's only wins in rural counties were those with minorities, especially African Americans, Native Americans, and Hispanics. As in 2012, millennial voters supported the Democrat, while older white voters supported the Republican.

The November 2016 elections included races for 34 Senate seats and 435 seats in the House of Representatives. Going into these contests, pundits talked about Democrats winning the Senate and possibly coming close to winning a majority in the House. In the end it never happened, Democrats only gained two seats in the Senate and six in the House. As shown by maps in this atlas, similar to the presidential vote, most urban House districts elected Democrats and most rural districts elected Republicans.

ORGANIZATION OF THE ATLAS

The atlas is divided into nine chapters, each, except for this introduction, containing maps and accompanying narratives. Contributors to the atlas analyze more than 150 maps of voting patterns and demographics at the national, state, county, and local precinct scales.

Chapter 2 addresses the primary election process that led up to the nominations of Trump and Clinton by the Republican and Democratic parties, respectively. Trump was one of seventeen major candidates who vied to become Republican Party nominee. After hotly contested and often contentious caucuses and primaries, by March 6, 2016, only three candidates remained: Donald Trump, Ted Cruz, and John Kasich. Trump sealed his nomination by the Indiana primary on May 3, 2016. Trump became the official Republican candidate for president during the Republican National Convention in Cleveland. In a much longer and contested Democratic primary, Hillary Clinton and Bernie Sanders fought for delegates until June 7, 2016, when Clinton secured a majority of pledged delegates after winning the California and New Jersey primaries. She became the first female presidential candidate nominated by any major party in US history. Maps and analyses of the primary elections show deep spatial and ideological divides within both parties.

Chapter 3 focuses on the electoral process and the campaign, illustrating the campaign itself. Each party raised and spent millions of dollars from campaign donors. Candidates concentrated campaign funds in places where party leaders believed they would make a difference in the Electoral College. The chapter also examines the pattern of daily newspaper endorsements of the two major candidates. Even a casual reading of the maps reveals some distinct geographic variations in campaign contributions, newspaper endorsements, and campaign stops in the months following the party conventions. Campaign efforts during the last week and month of the campaign reveal some interesting patterns, especially when comparing candidate appearances with actual votes of individual counties and states.

Chapter 4 examines the outcome of the election itself. Of particular interest are election results mapped at the county level. Although the 2016 election was historic in its upset and seeming revolt against party establishment, the geographical patterns were similar to past elections. Maps in this chapter identify the voting patterns of major and third parties, the Electoral College, the popular vote by county, and comparisons of state- and county-level results with past elections. The maps in this chapter show the partisan divisions between larger metropolitan areas and the micropolitan and rural areas of the Great Plains and Midwest.

When comparing the 2012 to the 2016 elections, maps reveal a significant swing toward the Republican Party at the county level, especially in areas of the Midwest. Trump effectively flipped 221 counties that Obama won in 2012, largely in this region. The remainder of this chapter examines the issues of voter turnout, historical patterns of the Republican vote, polarization of the electorate, and absolute margins of victory.

In chapter 5, we examine the 2016 election returns at a regional level, again with reference to recent and past electoral history. The seven regions discussed include the Northeast, Appalachia, the Southeast, the Midwest, the Great Plains, the Mountain West, and the Pacific Coast states. Contributors analyze electoral patterns in each of these regions. The Northeast and the Pacific Coast regions, which Democrats had dominated in recent years, remained heavily Democratic, although with an increase in the Republican vote in rural areas. Appalachia and the Southeast remained predominantly Republican, although the Democratic vote was strong in many urban areas and in the Black Belt.

In the central part of the country, the Midwest was an especially significant swing region. Trump outperformed Clinton throughout the region, especially in rural counties and smaller urban cities. The Great Plains remained Republican, although Clinton won some urban counties in Texas and counties with larger Native American and Hispanic populations. The historically Republican Mountain West states remained predominantly Republican, although Clinton won Colorado, New Mexico, and Nevada.

The maps and narratives in chapter 6 examine the distribution of demographic indicators, including measures of ethnicity, gender, religion, occupational structure, population growth and decline, income and wealth, education, and mobility. For this atlas, we created a new set of bivariate maps that compare the Democratic vote to demographic variables at the county scale. The essays in this chapter use these maps to discuss possible associations of population subgroupings to provide unique interpretations about the 2016 election.

In chapter 7, we focus on the congressional election, party affiliation, and selected roll call votes in the 114th Congress. The maps and essays focus on change in party membership in both the Senate and House and the congressional races in the Arizona First, Minnesota Second, and the Wisconsin Senate. Several maps of contentious roll call votes of the 114th Congress reveal the strong ideological divide among representatives over issues such as sanctuary cities, the Keystone pipeline, repeal of the Affordable Care Act, nuclear proliferation in Iran, and LGBT antidiscrimination.

In chapter 8, contributors focus on selected campaigns for statewide and municipal elections and referenda. Analyses of gubernatorial elections include Montana, Missouri, and North Carolina. Essays on municipal elections focus on Seattle's vote on the election of city council member by district and the Cook County sheriff's election after the Laquan McDonald shooting. Contributors also analyze votes on marijuana legalization and minimum wage.

Chapter 9 concludes the atlas with some final thoughts about the election of 2016. Contributors discuss how the current geography of voting and demographic patterns could affect the major parties in the highly anticipated 2020 presidential election.

REFERENCES

Bowden, John. 2017. Trump to Display Map of 2016 Election Results in the White House: Report. *The Hill: Blog Briefing Room*.

Brownstein, Ronald. 2016. Is Donald Trump Outflanking Hillary Clinton? *The Atlantic*. November 2, https://www.theatlantic.com/politics/archive/2016/11/trump-clinton-electoral-college/506306 (last accessed July 11, 2017).

NOTE

1. The final Electoral College vote was 304–227 because seven electors refused to vote for their party's candidate in the Electoral College.

2 PRIMARY ELECTIONS

THE 2016 PRESIDENTIAL PRIMARY CAMPAIGNS

FRED M. SHELLEY AND ASHLEY M. HITT[1]

After a spirited, vigorous, sometimes contentious, and often controversial pair of primary campaigns that lasted more than a year, both major parties chose their presidential and vice presidential nominees for the 2016 presidential election to replace outgoing president Barack Obama. The Democrats selected former secretary of state and former US senator Hillary Clinton of New York for president, and Senator Tim Kaine of Virginia for vice president. The Republicans chose business executive Donald Trump, also of New York, for president and governor Mike Pence of Indiana for vice president.

In 2012, Democrats nominated incumbents President Obama and Vice President Biden for president and vice president without opposition, and so only the Republican Party held contested primaries for their nomination. In 2016, however, Barack Obama was ineligible for a third term and Joe Biden declined to run for the presidency. The unsuccessful Republican candidates for president in 2008 and 2012, John McCain and Mitt Romney, also declined to contest the 2016 Republican nomination. The 2016 presidential contest was set to have new faces nominated by both political parties.

Over the past fifty years, Republicans have tended to nominate insiders for president, while Democrats have been most successful when selecting outsiders for their party's nomination. The last three Democrats to win the party's nomination and the general election—Jimmy Carter, Bill Clinton, and Barack Obama—went into the primary election campaigns that year without strong initial support of party leaders. In contrast, Republicans have usually selected a candidate who had significant initial support among the party's leadership. The last Republican presidential candidate nominated without the strong initial support of party insiders was Barry Goldwater in 1964.

In 2016, however, the traditional roles of the two major parties reversed: Clinton, who had been a national figure in politics for twenty-five years, enjoyed the very strong and nearly unanimous support of her party's leadership throughout the Democratic primary campaign before fighting off a spirited challenge from Sanders. On the other hand, Trump was a political outsider who had virtually no support from the party's leadership before his nomination. Although the public knew Trump well for his business activities and appearances as a reality television star, he had never before run for public office and had not been associated previously with the Republican Party.

The two parties have different rules for selecting delegates, who are formally responsible for selecting their parties' nominees, to their national conventions. On the Republican side, Republican primary voters select all of the delegates. However, each state has different rules for choosing these delegates. In some states, the party allocates delegates by congressional district. In others, primary elections select delegates on a statewide basis.

On the Democratic side, primary voters do not select all of the Democratic Party's delegates. Rather, about 15 percent of the party's delegates are elected governors and members of Congress, members of the Democratic National Committee, and other important party leaders and functionaries. These delegates, known informally as "superdelegates," are free to support whatever candidate for the Democratic nomination they wish. The other 85 percent of the party's delegates are pledged delegates who are chosen on a proportional basis in each state based on the primary election vote or caucus results in that state. A state Democratic Party allocates a percentage of the state's pledged delegates proportional to the percent of a state's primary ballots. A candidate winning 60 percent of the primary ballots receives 60 percent of the state's pledged delegates. In contrast to the Republican procedure, the Democratic Party requires every state to allocate its pledged delegates using the proportional representation system. Unlike superdelegates, pledged delegates are obligated to support their candidates for at least one ballot at the Democratic Party National Convention.

States can choose open primaries, closed primaries, or caucuses to elect delegates. The majority of states hold primary elections. Some states use an open primary, where any voter can request the ballot of either party at the polls. Other states used closed primaries, restricting participation to registered party members. Still other states select their national convention delegates via caucuses. In most states, both major parties use the same system, although there are a few exceptions. For example, in Kentucky, Republicans hold caucuses while the Democrats hold a primary. In most states, both parties hold their primaries or caucuses on the same day, but in other states, the two major parties hold their primaries or caucuses on different days.

THE REPUBLICAN PARTY CAMPAIGN

In 2015, seventeen candidates formally entered the race for the Republican presidential nomination for president. In addition to Trump, these candidates included (in alphabetical order): former governor Jeb Bush of Florida, retired neurosurgeon Ben Carson of Maryland, governor Chris Christie of New Jersey, Senator Ted Cruz of Texas, businesswoman Carly Fiorina of California, former governor Jim Gilmore of Virginia, Senator Lindsey Graham of South Carolina, former governor Mike Huckabee of Arkansas, governor Bobby Jindal of Louisiana, governor John Kasich of Ohio, former governor George Pataki of New York, Senator Rand Paul of Kentucky, former governor Rick Perry of Texas, Senator Marco Rubio of Florida, former senator Rick Santorum of Pennsylvania, and governor Scott Walker of Wisconsin. Unlike Trump, the majority of these candidates had extensive experience in public office. Early on, many political pundits predicted that Bush, who is the son of former president George H. W. Bush and brother of former president George W. Bush, and Walker, who had gained national attention for his strong opposition to public-sector unions, would be the strongest contenders for the nomination.

The Early Republican Primaries

Even before the nomination race began with the Iowa caucuses on February 1, 2016, low polling numbers and/or difficulties in raising campaign funds induced Graham, Jindal, Pataki, Perry, and Walker to withdraw. Walker's support in particular dropped quickly during the summer of 2015, at the beginning of which he led some public opinion polls. The remaining twelve candidates contested the Republican caucuses, which are mapped in figure 2.1. Cruz won 27.7 percent of the Iowa Republican caucus vote, followed by Trump with 24.3 percent and Rubio with 23.1 percent. Carson got 9.8 percent of the vote, and none of the other candidates got as much as 5 percent.

Cruz's campaign had strong appeal to evangelical voters, who represent a significant share of the Republican electorate in Iowa. Evangelical voters in Iowa are concentrated in rural areas, in which Cruz's support was highest. Statewide, Cruz won fifty-six of Iowa's ninety-nine counties while Trump won thirty-seven counties and Rubio won five (Cruz and Trump tied in Adair County in the southwestern part of the state). All of Rubio's counties were urban, relatively upscale counties, including Polk County (Des Moines), Dallas County (Des Moines suburbs), Story County (Des Moines suburbs and Iowa State University), Johnson County (University of Iowa), and Scott County (Davenport). Trump's victories included most of Iowa's other urban counties, including those containing the cities of Council Bluffs, Dubuque, and Sioux City.

Exit polls taken in Iowa showed no significant differences among the candidates on the basis of age and gender. However, they revealed substantial differences among them with respect to voters'

FIGURE 2.1

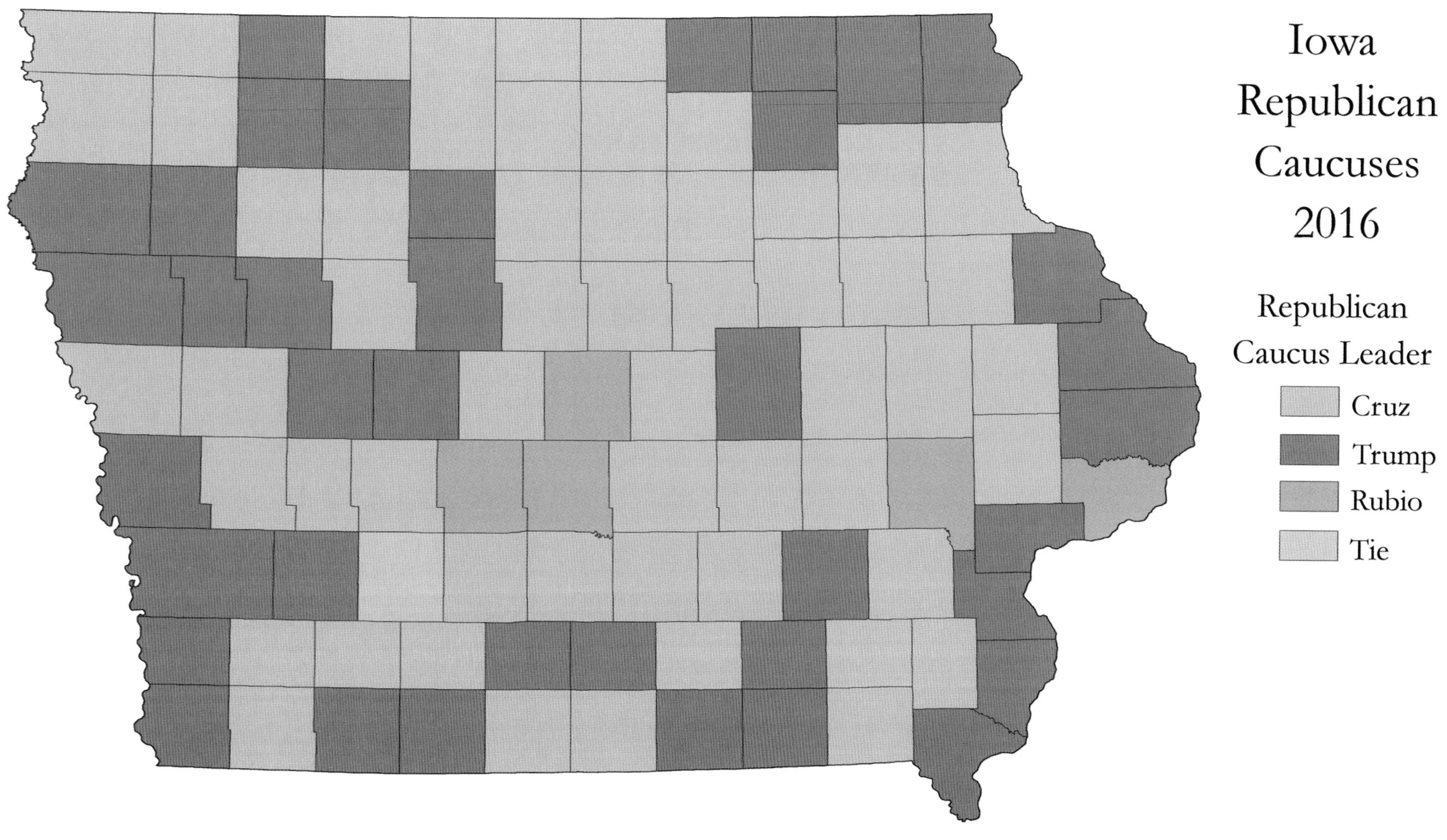
Iowa
Republican
Caucuses
2016
Republican
Caucus Leader
Cruz
Trump
Rubio
Tie

levels of education. College graduates were most likely to support Rubio, those with some college were more likely to support Cruz, and those who had not attended college were more likely to support Trump.

Having received little support in Iowa, Huckabee, Paul, and Santorum left the race. The following week, Trump won the New Hampshire primary by a substantial margin and Christie, Fiorina, and Gilmore withdrew. On February 20, 2016, South Carolina held its primary. Trump won with 32.5 percent of the vote, followed by Rubio with 22.5 percent, and Cruz with 22.3 percent. Following the pattern established in Iowa, Rubio carried the counties containing the state's two largest cities and Trump carried the others. Bush, with 7.8 percent of the vote, finished in fourth place and dropped out shortly thereafter.

March Primaries

During the month of March, Trump moved steadily closer to the nomination. Eleven states held primary elections or caucuses on March 1, "Super Tuesday." Trump was victorious in seven of these contests, winning Alabama, Arkansas, Georgia, Massachusetts, Tennessee, Vermont, and Virginia. These wins added a great number of delegates to his pledged delegate count, placing him significantly ahead of his fellow Republican candidates. Cruz won Alaska, Oklahoma, and his home state of Texas, and Rubio won Minnesota, the first win of his campaign. Neither Kasich nor Carson won any primaries or caucuses on Super Tuesday, but Kasich was very close to being victorious in the state of Virginia, where Trump beat him by a margin of 32.7 percent to 30.4 percent. Carson announced the suspension of his campaign on March 4, three days after Super Tuesday, leaving only Cruz, Kasich, Rubio, and Trump in the running.

Eight states and the District of Columbia held Republican primaries or caucuses between March 5 and March 12. During this period, Trump won Hawaii, Kentucky, Louisiana, Michigan, and Mississippi. Cruz prevailed in Idaho, Kansas, and Maine, and Rubio won in the District of Columbia. This set the stage for critical primaries on March 15 in Florida, Illinois, Missouri, North Carolina, and Ohio. The Florida and Ohio primaries were particularly critical because both states selected delegates on a winner-take-all basis, and they were the home states of Rubio and Kasich, respectively.

In the March 15 primaries, Kasich won Ohio by a margin of 46.8 percent to 35.6 percent over Trump, while Trump won the other four states. Trump won 45.7 percent of the votes in Florida, 38.8 percent in Illinois, 40.9 percent in Missouri, and 40.9 percent in North Carolina. Trump defeated Cruz by only 0.2 percent in Missouri, 3.6 percent in North Carolina, and 9 percent in Illinois. However, he defeated Rubio decisively in Florida by a margin of 46 percent to 27 percent, with Cruz finishing in third place with 17 percent. After having lost his home state, Rubio withdrew from the race. By this point, Trump had a substantial lead in the delegate count.

Analyzing Early March Republican Primaries

The geography of support for major Republican candidates in the March primaries can be discerned through examination of county-level results in and exit polls from Mississippi, North Carolina, and Ohio. In Mississippi, Trump won seventy-six of the state's eighty-two counties, while Cruz won the remaining six. However, Cruz won his largest margin in DeSoto County, which is located just south of the Tennessee border and contains upscale suburbs of Memphis, and Oktibbeha County, which contains the city of Starkville and Mississippi State University. Both of these counties have substantially more college graduates than the statewide percentage. Lee County, containing the city of Tupelo, also has a relatively high proportion of college graduates. In these counties, support for Cruz could be interpreted in terms of opposition to Trump's nomination among more upscale Republican voters. However, according to exit polls, Cruz won more than half of the ballots of voters who described themselves as "very conservative." Despite Cruz's explicit appeals to Mississippi's numerous evangelical Christians, exit polls also showed that he ran even with Trump among these voters, in contrast to Iowa, in which a majority of evangelicals supported Cruz. Trump also did best among voters who had not attended college. The median income of Trump voters in Mississippi, according to exit polls, was $62,000, which was lower than the median income of Kasich voters ($94,000) and Cruz voters ($64,000) in Mississippi (Silver 2016).

A similar pattern prevailed in North Carolina two weeks later. In defeating Cruz by a margin of 40.9 percent to 37.3 percent, Trump carried seventy-seven of the state's one hundred counties, as shown in figure 2.2. Many of the counties carried by Cruz are located in central North Carolina, including those containing the state capital of Raleigh and the university communities of Durham and Chapel Hill. He also carried counties containing Asheville, Greensboro, and

FIGURE 2.2

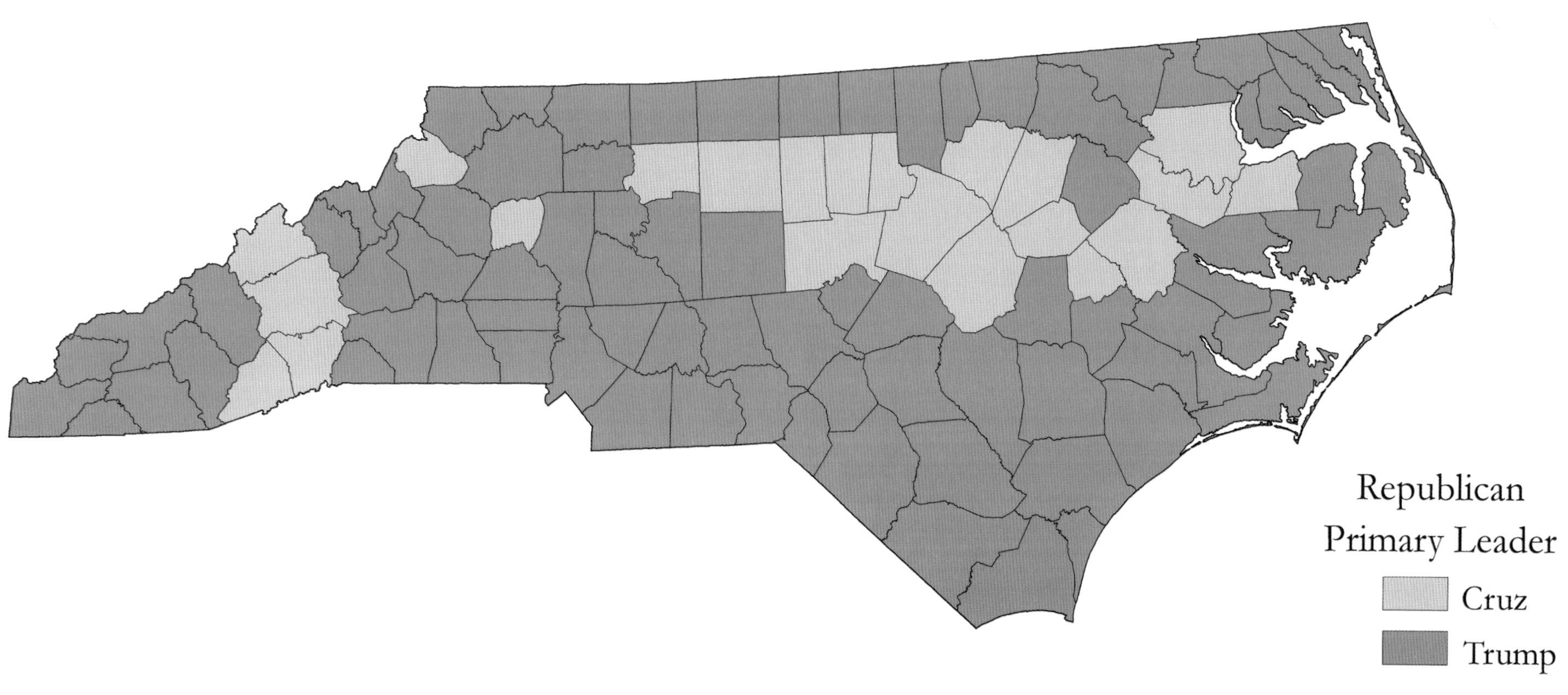
North Carolina Republican Primary
2016
Republican
Primary Leader
Cruz
Trump

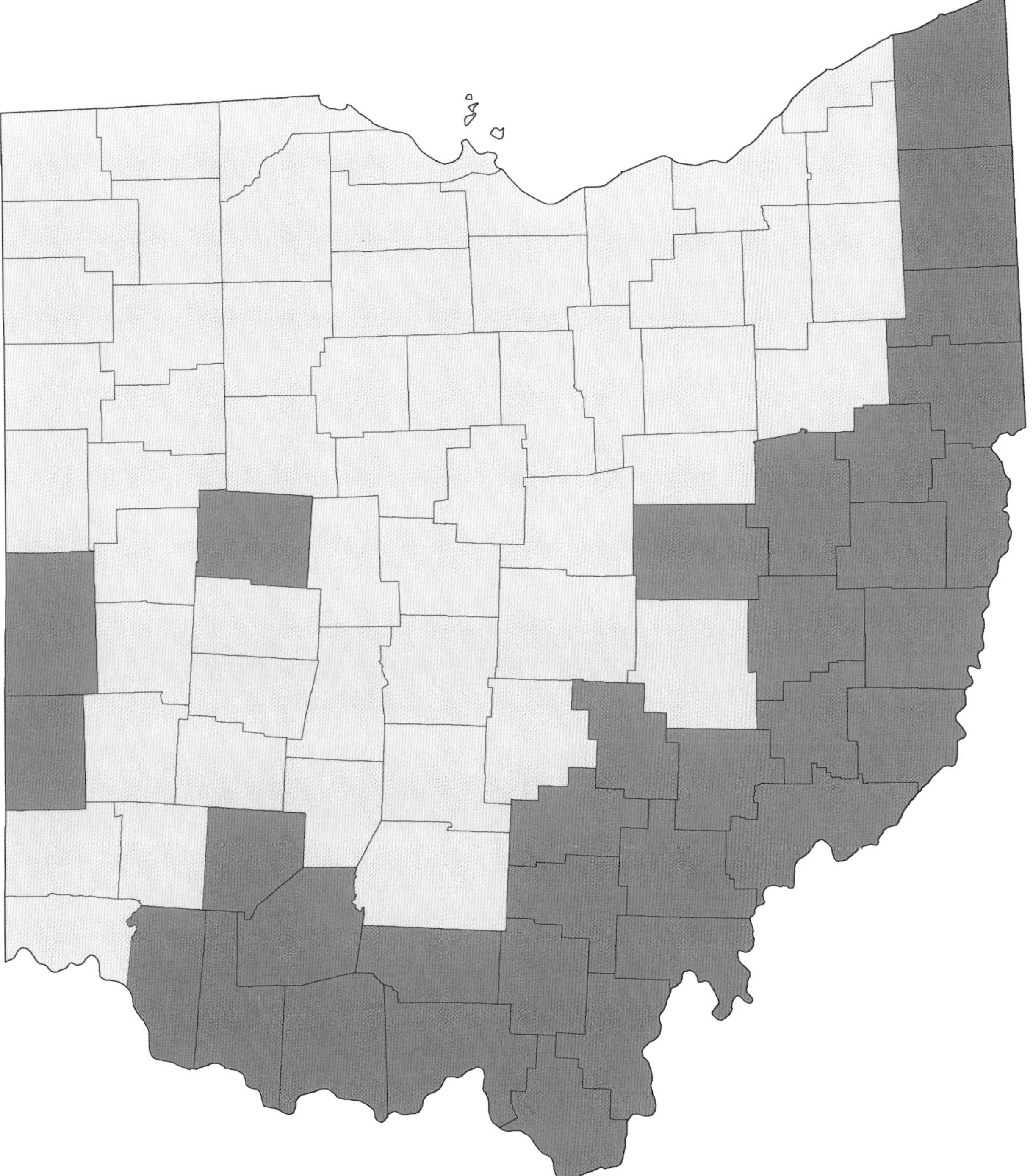

FIGURE 2.3

Ohio Republican Primary 2016

Republican Primary Leader

Kasich

Trump

Winston-Salem and barely lost Mecklenburg County, which includes Charlotte. As in Mississippi, Trump's strongest counties were those containing more older, lower-income, and less-educated Republican voters. Cruz and Kasich both did better among college graduates. Kasich's strongest county was Orange County (Chapel Hill), where he finished a close third behind Cruz and Trump. Statewide, Cruz's support appeared to combine anti-Trump voters with evangelicals and very conservative voters.

In Ohio, Kasich carried fifty-five counties to thirty-three for Trump. Kasich won the state by piling up substantial margins in the state's major cities and their suburbs, as shown in figure 2.3. Kasich achieved his largest vote percentage of 63.9 percent in Delaware County, which contains suburbs of Columbus and has the highest per capita income in the state. Trump, on the other hand, carried eastern and southern Ohio, including old industrial cities such as Youngstown, Warren, Steubenville, Belmont, and Ironton. Southeastern Ohio, in which Trump also did very well, is also part of Appalachia. Trump's largest vote percentage was in Trumbull County, which contains Warren and part of Youngstown and in which he got 52.6 percent of the vote. Almost a third (32.7 percent) of Delaware County's adult residents hold college degrees, as compared with 12.1 percent in Trumbull County. Statewide, exit polls showed a substantial difference between more highly educated and less highly educated voters. Kasich won about 54 percent of the vote among college graduates, as compared to 38 percent among those who did not graduate from college. On the other hand, 29 percent of college graduates and 43 percent of voters who were not college graduates supported Trump in Ohio.

The Later Republican Primaries and Analysis of the Republican Race

Between March 22 and April 19, 2016, Trump added to his delegate lead over Cruz and Kasich. Trump's biggest prize was his home state of New York, in which he received 59 percent of the vote. He also won the Arizona primary. Meanwhile, Cruz won caucuses in Colorado and Wyoming and primaries in Wisconsin and Utah, where many Mormons strongly opposed Trump's candidacy. By this time, Cruz had emerged as Trump's main rival, and prominent Republican leaders including Romney and Walker endorsed him. However, on April 26, Trump won five Northeastern states—Connecticut, Delaware, Maryland, Pennsylvania, and Rhode Island—in what was called the "Acela Primary" after the high-speed Amtrak train that runs between Washington and Boston. Among these five states, Trump won 111 delegates, while Kasich won 5 and Cruz only 2. A week later, Trump won the Indiana primary decisively, beating Cruz by a 53 percent to 37 percent margin. In doing so, Trump clinched the nomination with more than half of the delegates supporting him.

Figure 2.4 shows that nationwide, Trump won thirty-seven of the fifty state primaries and caucuses. Cruz won ten, Kasich won his home state of Ohio, and Rubio won Minnesota and the District of Columbia. Voters in the North Dakota caucuses selected an uncommitted slate of delegates. Trump swept the South and the Northeast. Cruz did best in the Southern Plains and the Rocky Mountain states along with Wisconsin, Iowa, and Maine. With the exception of his home state of Texas, Cruz's states were relatively small, whereas Trump won several large states, including California, Florida, New York, Illinois, Georgia, and North Carolina.

Exit polls taken in various states and nationwide showed a consistent pattern of support for Trump. Trump supporters tended to be white, non-evangelical, lower-income, and less-educated voters. He won a majority of Republican ballots from voters with annual incomes of less than $50,000. He also did better among voters over fifty as compared to younger voters. Cruz, on the other hand, tended to get more support from evangelical voters although he and Trump split the evangelical vote in some states. Commenting on this pattern, journalist Shane Goldmacher (2016) wrote, "Cruz has topped 30 percent among non-evangelicals in only one of the 20 states with exit polls." In general, a key to Trump's victory was that Trump got much more support among evangelical voters than did Cruz among non-evangelical voters.

THE DEMOCRATIC PARTY CAMPAIGN

In mid-2015, most observers expected that Clinton would have little trouble winning her party's nomination. Having served for eight years as First Lady, eight years as a US Senator from New York, and four years as Secretary of State, Clinton was one of the best-known public figures in the United States. She had also run unsuccessfully for the Democratic Party's nomination in 2008. Clinton's status as the favorite for the Democratic nomination was cemented when Biden along with popular Senator Elizabeth Warren of Massachusetts declined to run for the nomination.

As 2015 continued, Clinton was challenged by four other candidates, including Sanders,

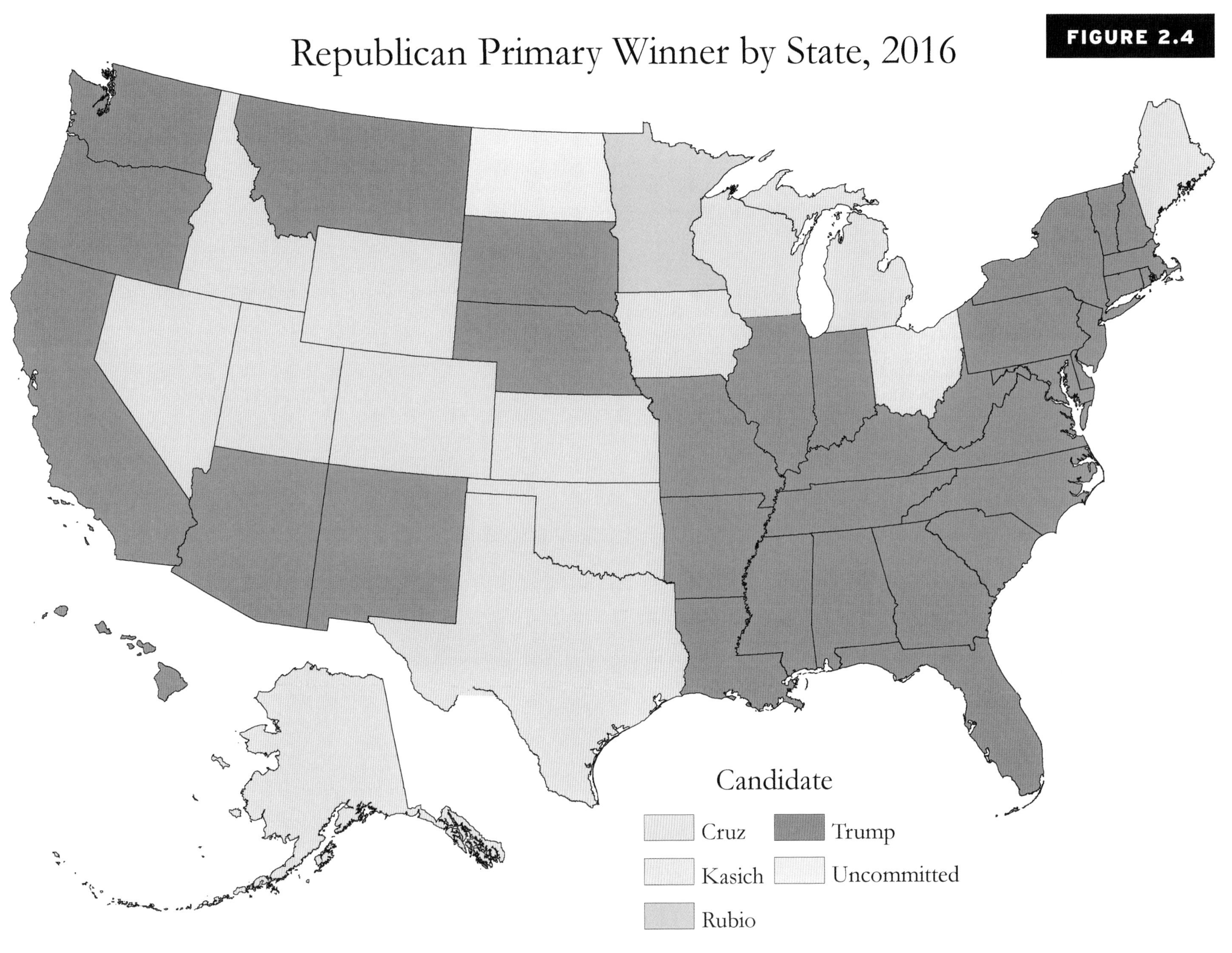
FIGURE 2.4
Republican Primary Winner by State, 2016
Candidate
Cruz
Trump
Kasich
Uncommitted
Rubio

former governor Martin O'Malley of Maryland, former US Secretary of the Navy and US Senator Jim Webb of Virginia, and former governor Lincoln Chafee of Rhode Island. O'Malley, Webb, and Chafee received very little support among the Democratic Party electorate and dropped out quickly.

By February 2016, when the primary and caucus season began, it had become clear that Sanders was Clinton's major challenger. Although Sanders had been a member of Congress for nearly twenty-five years, as a senator from a small state he was not well known nationally. Moreover, Sanders was seventy-four years old and described himself as a Democratic Socialist. He was also a political independent who was not a formal member of the Democratic Party. However, Sanders ran on an unabashedly progressive program. He attacked corporate greed and called for redistribution of wealth by increasing corporate taxes and taxes on wealthy persons. Sanders' campaign caught fire among many Democrats, particularly political progressives and young voters. Many of Sanders' supporters were skeptical of what they regarded as Clinton's excessively moderate views, her ties to Wall Street, and her history of controversial actions. Investigations of Clinton's use of a private e-mail server to send and received classified e-mails reinforced these perceptions. Meanwhile, Clinton's strongest constituencies included African Americans, other minorities, and older voters, particularly older women. This pattern was consistent throughout the campaign.

Early Primaries and Caucuses and Super Tuesday

Going into the February primaries and caucuses, public opinion polls of Democratic voters nationwide showed Clinton with a lead over Sanders. For example, a Reuters poll taken between January 30 and February 3 gave Clinton a lead of 54 percent to 39 percent, with 2 percent supporting O'Malley, who dropped out shortly thereafter. The first state to vote was Iowa, which held its caucuses on February 1. Here Clinton and Sanders fought to a virtual tie. Clinton won 49.84 percent of the votes of caucus participants to 49.59 percent for Sanders. Here Clinton carried sixty of ninety-nine counties. Sanders carried thirty-seven counties, with the other two reporting ties, as shown in figure 2.5. Clinton did relatively better in rural counties with smaller populations. Given his strength among young voters, it was not surprising that Sanders carried Iowa's two major university counties: Johnson County (University of Iowa) and Story County (Iowa State University), by margins of 60 percent to 40 percent. However, Clinton carried Polk County, which contains Iowa's largest city of Des Moines, by a margin of 55 percent to 43 percent, giving her enough votes to win the state very narrowly.

The campaign moved to New Hampshire, the first state to hold a primary election as opposed to a caucus. Here Sanders, from neighboring Vermont, won handily. However, Clinton then won an even larger landslide in South Carolina. Next, Clinton won a small majority of votes in the caucuses of Nevada.

The stage was then set for "Super Tuesday" on March 1 when eleven states held primaries and caucuses. Clinton won landslide victories in primary elections in Alabama, Arkansas, Georgia, Tennessee, Texas, and Virginia and defeated Sanders narrowly in Massachusetts. Sanders won primary elections in Oklahoma and his home state of Vermont along with caucuses in Colorado and Minnesota. In most of these states, the winning candidate won most of these states' counties. For example, Clinton won each of the 67 counties in Alabama and all but one of Georgia's 159 counties. On the other hand, Sanders won seventy-five of Oklahoma's seventy-seven counties. Nationwide, these results gave Clinton a lead that she would retain for the remainder of the campaign. Clinton's strength in the South was evident again when she won Louisiana by a landslide on March 5. She won Mississippi by an even larger margin on March 8.

On the same day as the Mississippi primary, Sanders won the primary in Michigan in what was considered an upset by many observers given that Clinton led in public opinion polls in that state. On March 15, however, Clinton added to her lead by winning decisive victories in Florida (64.4 percent to 33.3 percent), North Carolina (54.6 percent to 40.8 percent), and Ohio (56.5 percent to 42.7 percent), and narrow victories in Illinois (50.5 percent to 48.7 percent) and Missouri (49.6 percent to 49.4 percent). In general, Clinton did relatively better in states with closed primaries, for example, Florida, as opposed to states with open primaries. This trend indicates Clinton's relative strength among long-term party

FIGURE 2.5

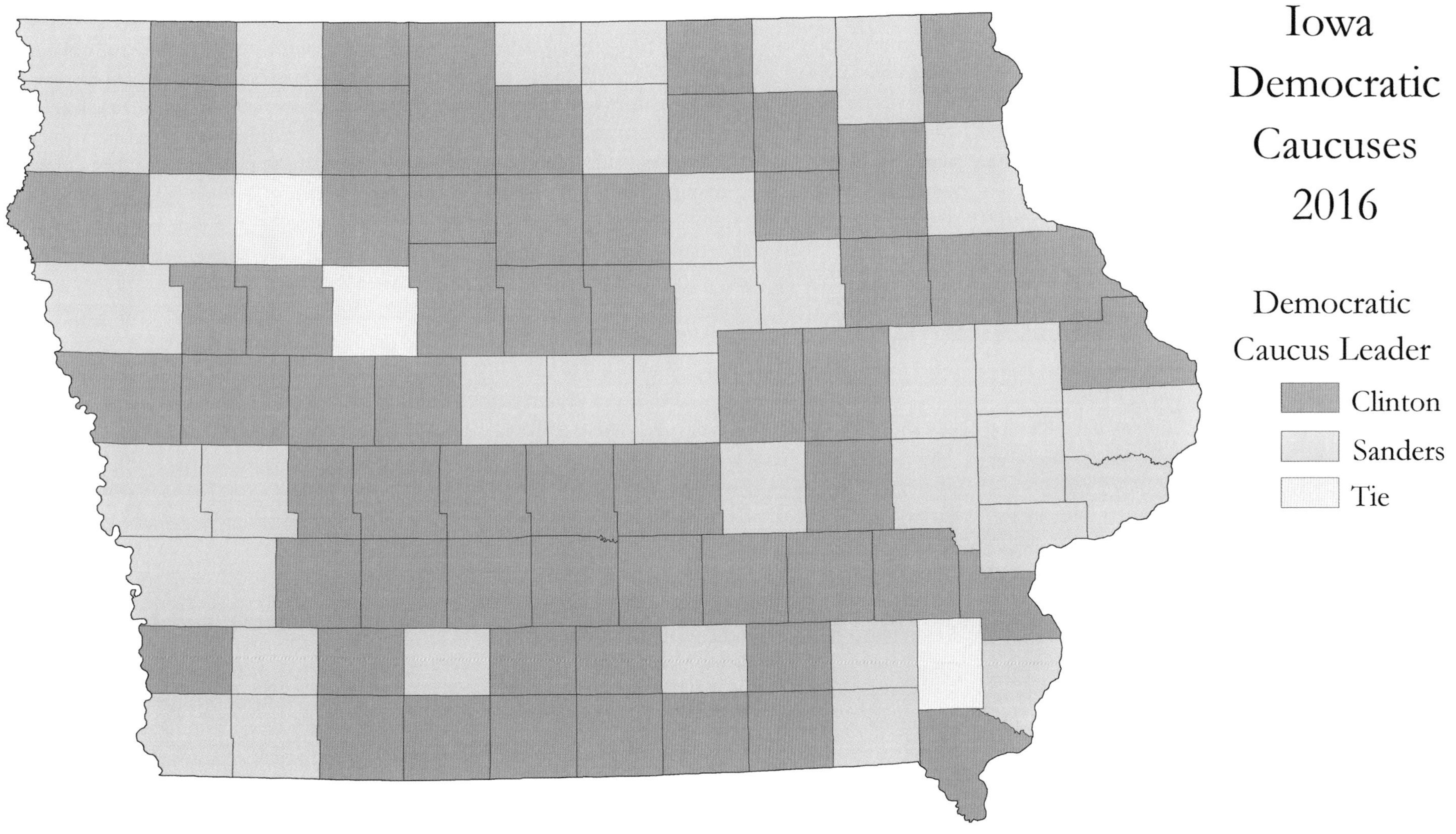
Iowa
Democratic
Caucuses
2016
Democratic
Caucus Leader
Clinton
Sanders
Tie

members compared to Sanders' strength among independents.

Analysis of the Early Democratic Primaries and Caucuses

Throughout the early primaries and caucuses, Clinton did best consistently among older voters and among minority voters, especially African Americans. Sanders, on the other hand, won very strong support among millennial voters under thirty years of age. On or before March 15, exit polls in 15 of the 21 states that had had Democratic Party primaries or caucuses revealed Clinton won a majority of millennial votes only in Mississippi. Sanders won majorities among millennials in the other fourteen states, topping 80 percent in Iowa, Michigan, Nevada, New Hampshire, Oklahoma, and Vermont.

Journalists and political analysts have identified several reasons why Sanders was so popular among millennial voters. They noted that Sanders' consistent attacks on Wall Street and corporate power, his strong support for decisive action on climate change and environmental degradation, and his strong advocacy of free college education at a time when the cost of higher education continues to skyrocket were issues particularly appealing to millennials. Some millennials regarded Sanders as authentic and trustworthy while regarding Clinton as insincere, tepid, inconsistent, and tied too closely to corporate interests. Another reason for her low numbers with young voters is that they felt that she was talking down to young people, and did not take them seriously. For example, according to journalist Kevin Gosztola (2016) of an online progressive newspaper, Clinton stated in April that she "feel[s] sorry for the young people who believe the lies" that Sanders told about her and the fossil fuel industry, and that young people "don't do their own research." Millennials criticized Clinton for ignoring them while concentrating on winning support from large donors.

Significantly, all of the states in which Sanders won more than 80 percent of the millennial vote except Nevada have relatively few minority voters. Clinton did best among millennials in the South, where many Democratic voters are African Americans. Sanders' support among millennial voters was especially prevalent among white millennials and was much weaker among non-white millennials. The degree to which non-white voters were more likely to support Clinton relative to white voters is evident in examining Mississippi. Here, Clinton won 82.6 percent of the vote and carried all of Mississippi's eighty-two counties. However, Sanders exceeded 25 percent of the vote in northeastern Mississippi, with its relatively small African American population. He got less than 10 percent of the vote in several counties in the Mississippi Delta region, a majority of whose residents are African American.

The gender gap between Clinton and Sanders supporters is not as prominent as was expected. Before exit poll data became available, pundits predicted that Clinton's support among women would be much greater than Sanders' support among women, due to the anticipation of electing the first female president. However, according to exit polls, the difference in percentage between the men and women who voted for Clinton was not that large. According to journalist Ben Geier (2016), 46 percent of female Democratic voters preferred Clinton while 35 percent preferred Sanders. Meanwhile, the two candidates nearly tied among men.

The size of the gender gap varied by age and was larger among older voters and smaller among younger voters, who tended to be less enthusiastic about electing the first female president. Journalists Eric Bradner and Dan Merica (2016) wrote, "Older women who waged the wars against sexism don't understand why the prospect of the first female president doesn't excite their younger counterparts; younger women see presidential politics as open to their gender now, so electing a woman in this election—as opposed to any that follow—doesn't seem pressing." Millennial journalist Shiva Bayat (2016) wrote in an online feminist newspaper, "Feminism is a worldview that understands and critiques power. Women should join movements that align with economic justice, environmental protections, and basic human rights, while still maintaining the perspective of our lived experiences as women. I see this happening with the wide support for Bernie Sanders among young female voters." The gender gap in the early 2016 primaries and caucuses was less than expected, and was considerably less than gaps based on age and race.

Arkansas, Oklahoma, and Texas

Of the Super Tuesday primaries, perhaps the most significant and meaningful comparison was among the states of Arkansas, Oklahoma, and Texas. The three states are adjacent to one another. The demographics of Arkansas and Oklahoma are similar and overlap with the demographics of those portions of Texas located near the shared borders. Demographically, one might expect that the voting patterns in the three states would be similar. Clinton carried Texas by a margin of 65.2 percent to 33.2 percent and Arkansas by a margin of 66.3

percent to 29.7 percent. However, Sanders carried Oklahoma by a margin of 51.9 percent to 41.5 percent. At the county level, Sanders won only 1 of Arkansas' 75 counties and only 13 of Texas' 254 counties (two were tied). On the other hand, he won 75 of Oklahoma's 77 counties. Sanders carried all of Oklahoma's counties located along its boundaries with Arkansas and Texas, whereas Clinton carried all but one of the counties on the Arkansas and Texas sides of the border. Also, Clinton lost by a larger margin in Oklahoma in counties along the Texas border than she did relative to the whole state; she received about 30 percent or less of the vote in the far southern counties in Oklahoma, while she received 41.5 percent of the vote in Oklahoma as a whole. What might account for these differences, mapped in figure 2.6?

Campaign strategy may offer part of an explanation. Prior to the Super Tuesday primaries, the Sanders campaign aired advertisements only in five states: Colorado, Minnesota, Oklahoma, Vermont (all of which he won), and Massachusetts (which he lost to Clinton in a close race). Sanders did not campaign in Arkansas or Texas, but he held a large rally in Tulsa several days before the election. Although public opinion polls in Oklahoma showed Clinton with a lead, the gap began to narrow before the election and so Sanders decided to hold a second rally in Oklahoma City shortly before the election. By March 1, public opinion polls showed the race in Oklahoma as a toss-up but to the surprise of many observers, he carried the Sooner State by a 10 percent margin. Clinton's association with Arkansas might also have been a factor, given that Clinton had lived in the state for more than twenty-five years, including twelve years during which her husband served as the state's governor. She was Arkansas Woman of the Year in 1983, and she was associated with organizations including the Arkansas Education Standards Committee and Arkansas Children's Hospital Legal Services. Hillary Clinton's heavy involvement with Arkansas' politics and her past residence could be a reason why she won the state's primary election by such a wide margin while losing Oklahoma.

Other factors might also be in play. Tulsa media are accessible in northwestern Arkansas, including Washington County along the state border that contains the University of Arkansas. Oklahoma has a rich history with socialism. Writing shortly before the Oklahoma primary, journalist Clare Malone (2016) stated that Sanders' support in Oklahoma "is a return to the state's historic political roots." She went on to quote University of Oklahoma political science professor Keith Gaddie: "Oklahoma is where your Southern agrarian populism and Nebraska prairie populism collided in America." According to Malone, Gaddie noted also that "we at one point had five socialists in the state legislature." Socialism in Oklahoma in the early twentieth century came from poor farmers leasing land and borrowing too much money; farmers did not receive enough profits from their crops and most ended up in debt. Many farmers regarded this situation as unjust, moved to socialism, and demanded land redistribution. While the socialist movement in rural Oklahoma collapsed after World War I, this brand of socialism left a huge mark on Oklahoma. A residual populism in Oklahoma may have compelled voters to cast their ballots for Bernie Sanders, who identifies himself as a Democratic Socialist.

The sense of Bernie Sanders as an outsider may also explain the abrupt split between ballots casted in Texas and Oklahoma. Journalist John Cassidy (2016) described Oklahoma's modern-day populism as "a deep suspicion of political, corporate, and media élites." Sanders' message emphasizing a shift in political power away from large corporate interests to poor and middle-class Americans may have responded to shift political power from super PACs, and other political positions/organizations that hold a lot of money, to the average citizens of the United States. Journalist Nicole Gaudiano (2016), writing shortly before the Oklahoma primary, pointed out that Oklahoma has "a tremendous amount of outsider, antiestablishment sentiment in the electorate and the electorate at large." Gaudiano (2016) contended that a recently populist and historically socialist state like Oklahoma would vote for a progressive socialist such as Senator Sanders over Hillary Clinton.

Eastern Oklahoma's historic association with socialism extended across the border into northwestern Arkansas. The only Arkansas county carried by Sanders was Newton County, which is one of the state's poorest counties. Many of Newton County's voters were sympathetic with agrarian socialism before World War I. Sanders lost neighboring Madison County, with similar demographics and history, by only seven votes. Orval Faubus, who was born in Madison County, is best remembered today for his opposition to integrating Little Rock's schools as governor of Arkansas in 1957. However, Faubus' father, Sam, was editor of a socialist newspaper in Madison County, and Orval Faubus was given the middle name of Eugene after Socialist Party leader Eugene Debs.

An additional contributing factor to this result could be that the overall population of African American voters is higher in Arkansas than in Oklahoma—7.4 percent of the population of

FIGURE 2.6

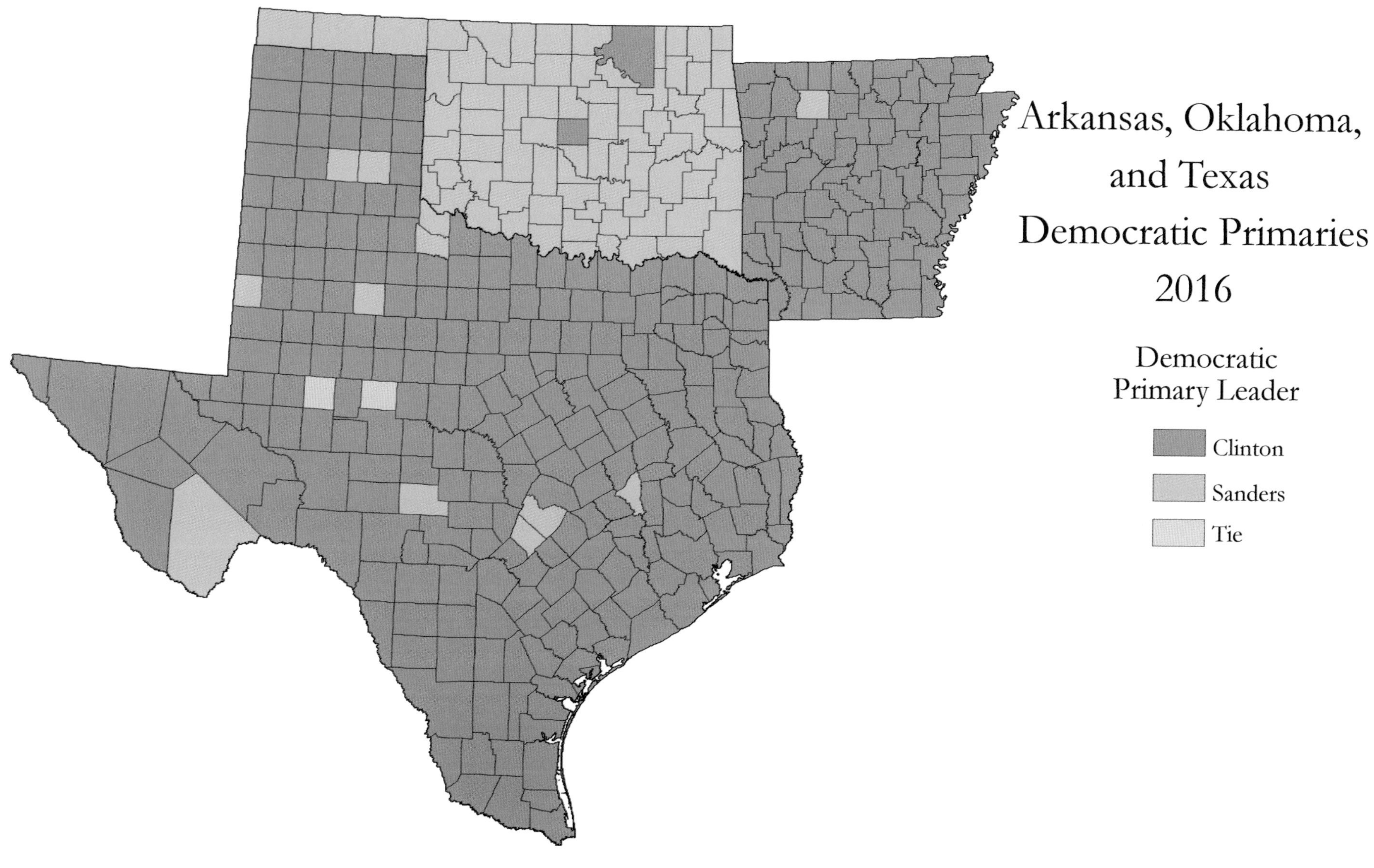
Arkansas, Oklahoma, and Texas Democratic Primaries 2016
Democratic Primary Leader
Clinton
Sanders
Tie

Oklahoma is African American, while African Americans make up 15.6 percent of Arkansas' population. This could have impacted how the state as a whole voted in the primary election, for the core of Hillary Clinton's support throughout the South included African Americans. In Arkansas, the counties that have a larger population of African Americans were counties in which she had larger leads. In counties with a higher percentage of African Americans than the statewide percentage, she won an average of 69.9 percent of the vote, whereas her average vote in those counties with lower percentages of African Americans was 60.8 percent.

Texas has a much larger percentage of minorities than either Arkansas or Oklahoma, and Clinton swept the areas of the Lone Star State that contain the largest percentage, of African Americans and Mexican Americans. She won large majorities in South Texas, with a significant Mexican American population. For example, she carried Starr County on the Rio Grande with 77 percent of the vote. Of the thirteen counties carried by Sanders, ten are small, predominantly white counties in western Texas. In fact, only five voters cast ballots in the Democratic primary in Armstrong County (population 1,901) in northwestern Texas, and Sanders received four of these votes. (Donald Trump would carry Armstrong County by a margin of 91 percent to 7 percent in November.) The other three counties carried by Sanders were Travis, Brazos, and Hays Counties, which contain the University of Texas at Austin, Texas A&M University, and Texas State University–San Marcos, respectively. That Sanders carried these three counties was consistent with his success among young voters throughout the country. However, his margins in these three counties were narrow, with 51.8 percent of the vote in Hays County, 51.4 percent in Travis County, and 49.4 percent in Brazos County, which he carried by only twenty-one votes.

LATER DEMOCRATIC PRIMARIES AND CAUCUSES

In late April and early May, Sanders won seven of eight contests. He lost the primary in Arizona to Clinton, but he won the Wisconsin primary and won caucuses in six Western states. Significantly, the Arizona primary was a closed primary in which only registered party members could participate, and the Wisconsin primary was an open primary in which anyone could vote regardless of party affiliation. The difference between the outcomes in Arizona and Wisconsin was typical of differences between outcomes in closed and open primaries across the United States. Clinton continued to do best in closed primaries, and Sanders maintained his success in open primaries, indicating his relative strength among political independents and comparable weakness among party regulars.

Despite these victories, Sanders cut only slightly into Clinton's delegate lead because most of the states that Sanders won are small, and because of the Democratic Party's proportionality rule in primaries. The campaign moved to the Eastern Seaboard in mid-April. Here, Clinton got a large boost by winning five of six primaries, including Connecticut, Delaware, Maryland, New York, and Pennsylvania. Sanders won only in Rhode Island, the smallest of these states. Of the five states that Clinton carried during this period, only in Connecticut did she fail to win at least 55 percent of the vote.

After Clinton's decisive wins on the East Coast, Sanders' chances of overtaking her delegate lead became very slim. In May, Sanders won primaries in Indiana, West Virginia, and Oregon while Clinton won primaries in Washington, Nebraska, and Kentucky. Thus, during this stretch, the two candidates divided the pledged delegates about evenly. Time was running out on the Sanders campaign.

The final primaries of the campaign took place in California, Montana, New Jersey, New Mexico, and South Dakota on June 7. A few days earlier, the news media announced that Clinton had clinched the party's nomination. The media arrived at this conclusion by adding the number of pledged delegates won by Clinton to the number of superdelegates who had stated their support for her in public. Some in Sanders' camp were irate and found this announcement premature in that superdelegates were free to change their minds before the national party convention. They also expressed concern that the announcement would discourage Sanders' supporters from voting in the June 7 primaries. However, Clinton left no doubt about the outcome of the campaign by winning a landslide in New Jersey and a comfortable victory in California. She carried New Mexico and South Dakota narrowly, while losing Montana to Sanders. Clinton clinched the party's nomination, which she accepted formally at the Democratic National Convention in Philadelphia in July.

Washington State

An unusual opportunity for political geography research occurred in Washington State in 2016 when the Democratic Party opted to allocate delegates to the state and national Democratic conventions based on caucus meetings, even though a statewide primary was also scheduled. The caucus results are binding, and the primary votes are used here only as a source of interest and comparison.

The caucuses took place on March 26, 2016, in each of the state's 7,100 precincts. Over 230,000 voters "elected approximately 27,000 precinct delegates" (Washington State Democrats 2017). Although it was quite difficult to get information on where and how to participate, voters overran many of the caucus sites, creating high levels of chaos and confusion. Senator Bernie Sanders (VT) did very well in the caucuses, easily defeating Secretary of State Hillary Clinton. The Democratic Party only released countywide data on the caucuses, which figure 2.7 maps. In April and May, precinct delegates elected 1,400 legislative district delegates, who in turn elected 67 district-level national delegates at congressional district caucuses on May 21, 2016. In addition to these 67 national delegates chosen through the caucus process, the Washington State Democratic Party sent 34 at-large national delegates, including state party leaders, and 17 national superdelegates, "comprised of DNC members, members of Congress, and the Governor" to the Democratic National Convention (Washington State Democrats 2017).

Two months later on May 24, 2016, the state held separate primaries for registered Democrats and Republicans. The state required a statement of party affiliation to prevent voters from casting ballots in both primaries. Although the State of Washington Democratic Party completely ignored the votes in the state's Democratic primary, the results were fascinating. In contrast to the caucuses held in March, Clinton easily won the primary in May. In fact, her share of the vote by registered Democrats doubled from 26 to 53 percent. The primary results by county are shown in figure 2.8, and are not just a little different, but astoundingly so. The Sanders partisans claim that this was because Sanders' supporters did not bother to vote in the primary. This argument is difficult to support because 800,000 voters cast ballots in the Democratic primary, compared to only 230,000 ballots in the Democratic caucuses. A more compelling argument for Sanders' success in the Washington caucuses is that "Caucuses reward highly motivated and ideologically devoted voters, a dynamic which has tended to favor Sanders" (Foran 2016).

The geography of strength of support for Senator Sanders was similar in both the caucuses and the primary. Sanders fared best on the northern and eastern edges of the state, as well as in the area influenced by Portland, Oregon. Support for Sanders was also strong in several less-populated counties with colleges or universities. Secretary Clinton found the highest levels of support in the greater Seattle metropolitan core, and in Hispanic areas in eastern Washington.

The City of Seattle, home of the 1919 General Strike, elector of communist Anna Louise Strong to the school board in 1916 and of socialist Kshama Sawant to the city council in 2012, favored Clinton by a margin of 58,705 to 42,170 in the 2016 primary. Precinct results are shown in figure 2.9, showing Clinton's dominance in older, more educated, professional, and affluent areas, testimony to decades of gentrification and displacement of the poor and of minorities, and the simultaneous shift of more liberal Republicans to the Democratic fold.

How did eventual Republican nominee Donald Trump fare in Washington's primary? In the May 2016 Democratic primary, 802,754 voters participated, with Clinton garnering 420,461 votes. In the May 2016 Republican primary, 602,998 voters participated, with eventual nominee Donald Trump winning 455,023 votes. Although more Washington voters cast ballots in the Democratic primary than the Republican primary, Trump won a larger share of votes in the Republican primary than Clinton won in the Democratic primary. Trump won an absolute majority in eighteen counties, including four metropolitan counties in eastern Washington, and pluralities in sixteen more counties, including Seattle's three suburban counties. Sanders had a plurality in two ultra-environmental counties and in two college-dominated counties. Clinton had a plurality in only one county—King, which is home to Seattle.

California

Clinton carried California on June 7, defeating Sanders by a margin of 53.1 percent to 46.0 percent. The county-level geography of the California primary illustrates divisions within the state, as shown in figure 2.10. Patterns of support for each candidate in California were consistent with outcomes in other states that had held their primaries and caucuses earlier.

Clinton won California by sweeping the state's biggest cities, including Los Angeles, San Diego, San Jose, Sacramento, Fresno, San Francisco, and Oakland. Her margin throughout urban Southern California was consistent across counties, with 57 percent in Los Angeles County, 55 percent in San Diego County, and 54.6 percent in Orange County. She swept the inland agriculture-oriented counties in the Imperial, San Joaquin, and Sacramento Valleys.

Clinton's margins in Southern California and in the central valleys were unsurprising. However, some observers were more surprised that Clinton

FIGURE 2.7

Washington Democratic Caucuses, 2016

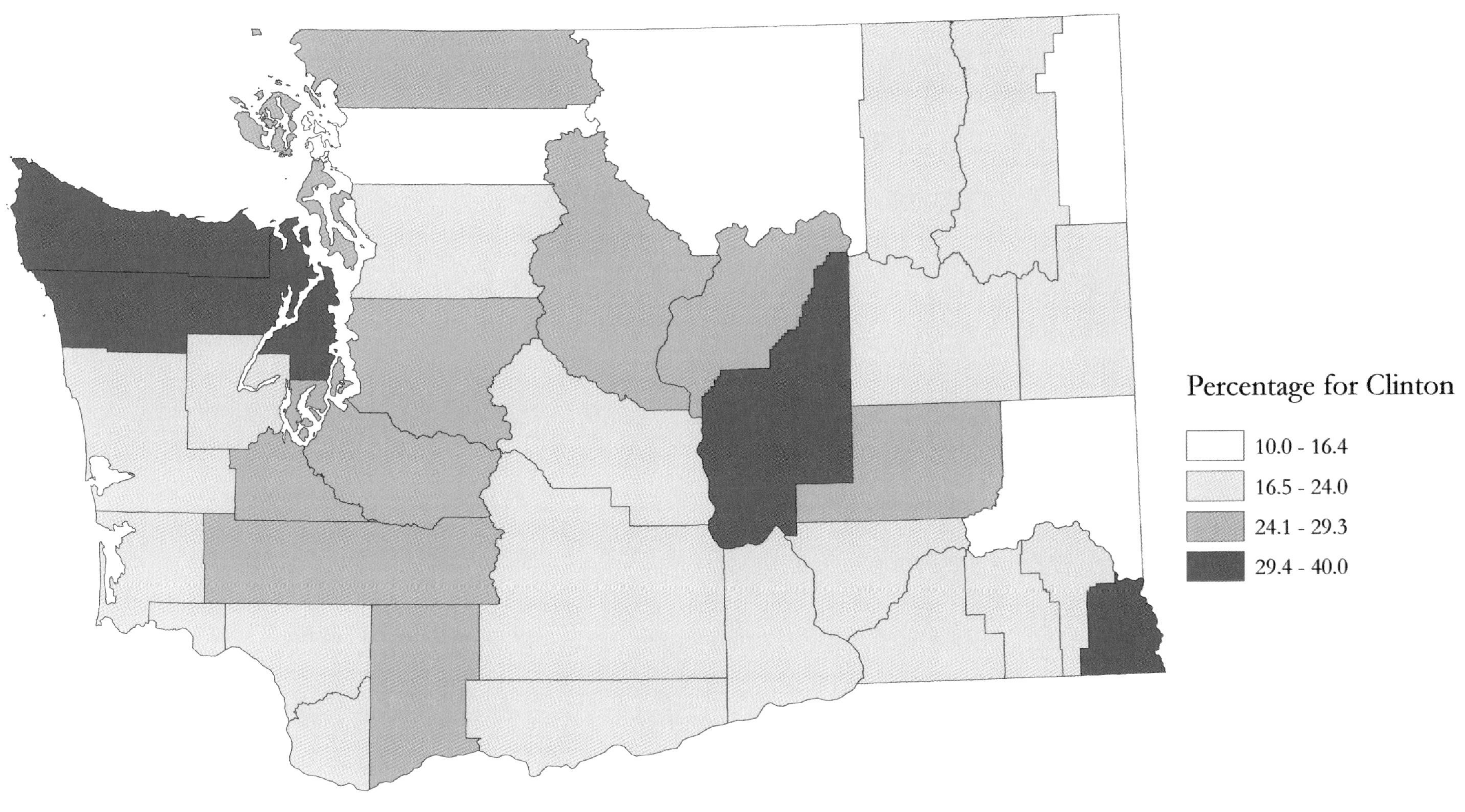

Washington Democratic Primary Election, 2016

FIGURE 2.8

Seattle (precincts)

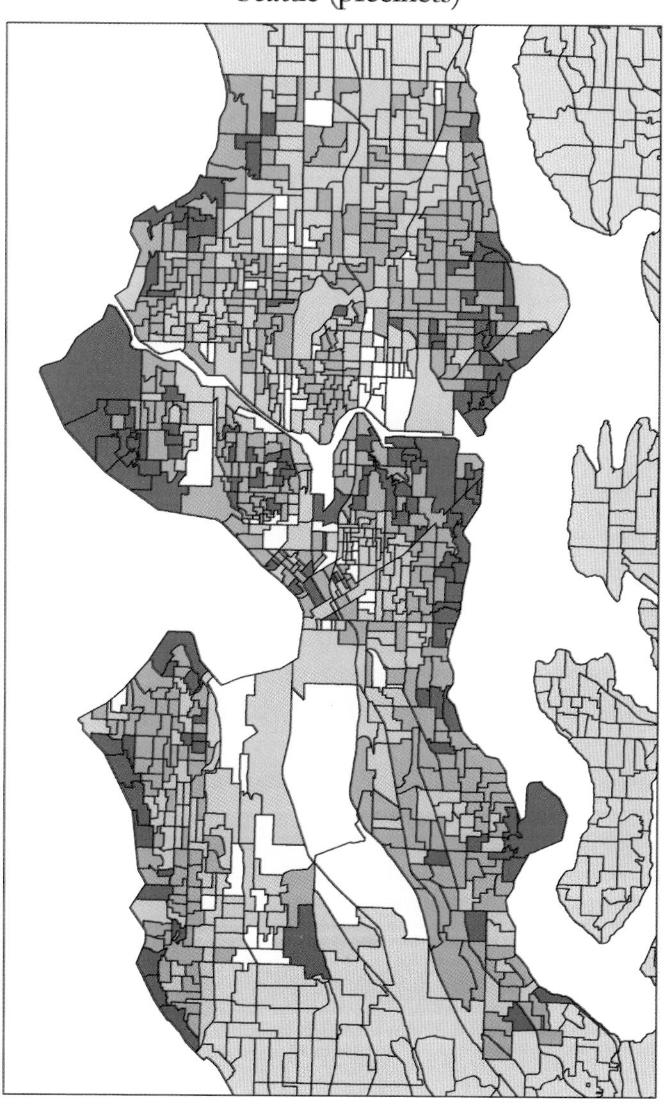

Percentage of Vote for Clinton

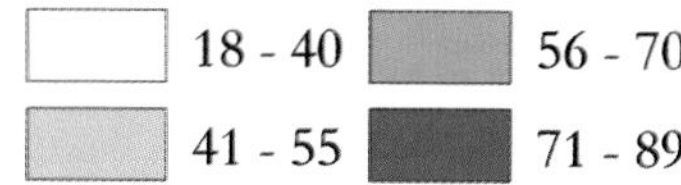

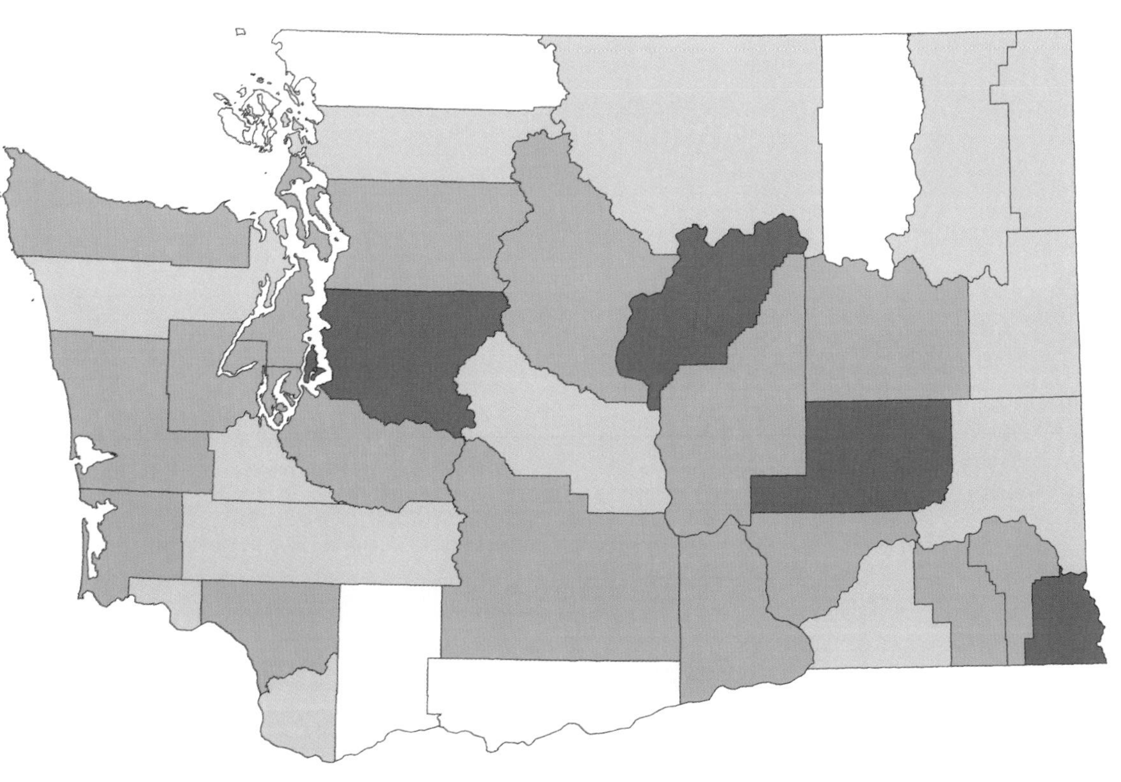

Percentage of Vote for Clinton

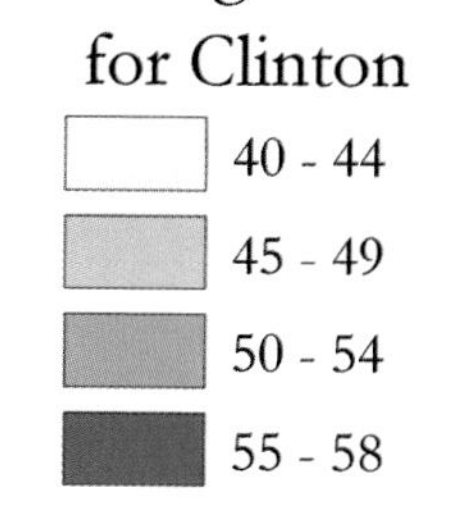

Democratic Popular Vote 2016 Presidential Election

Seattle Area

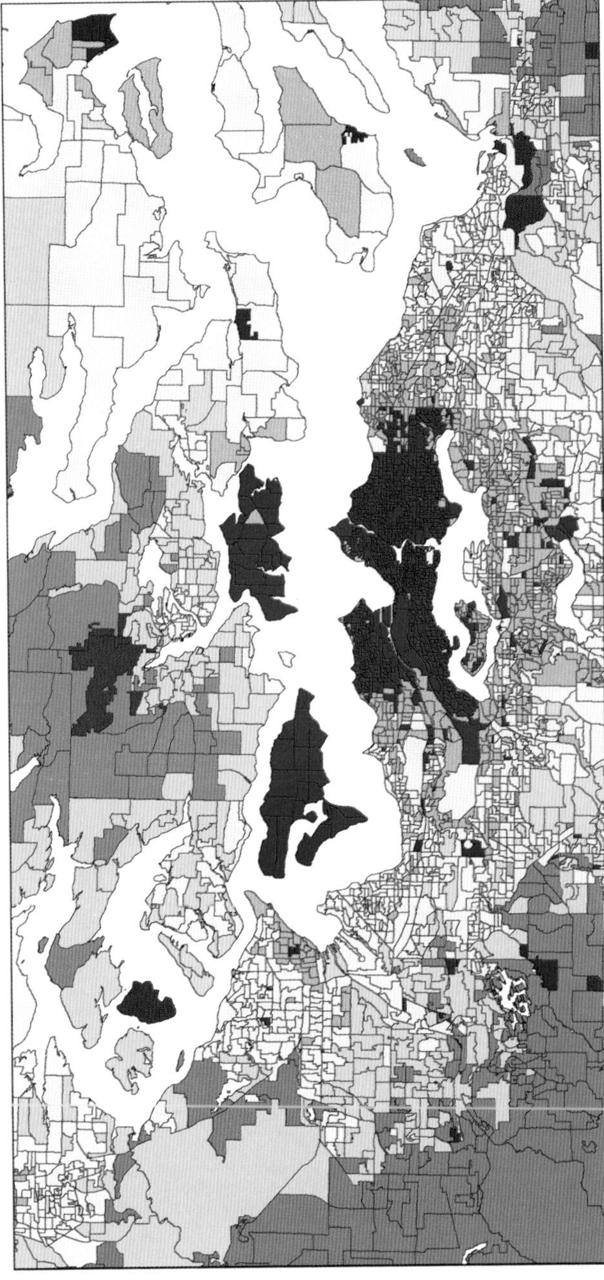

Democratic Percentage of the Popular Vote

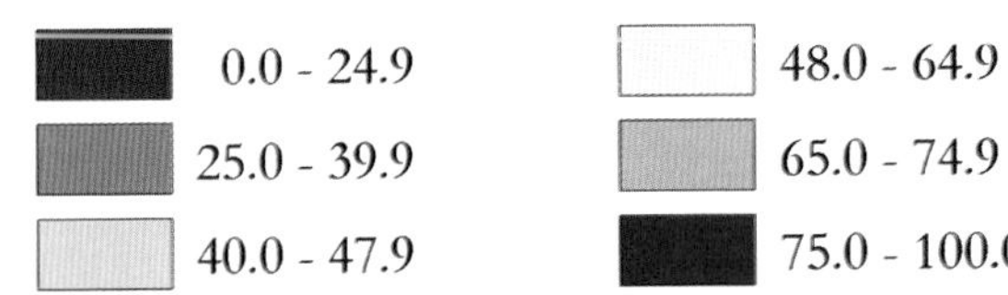

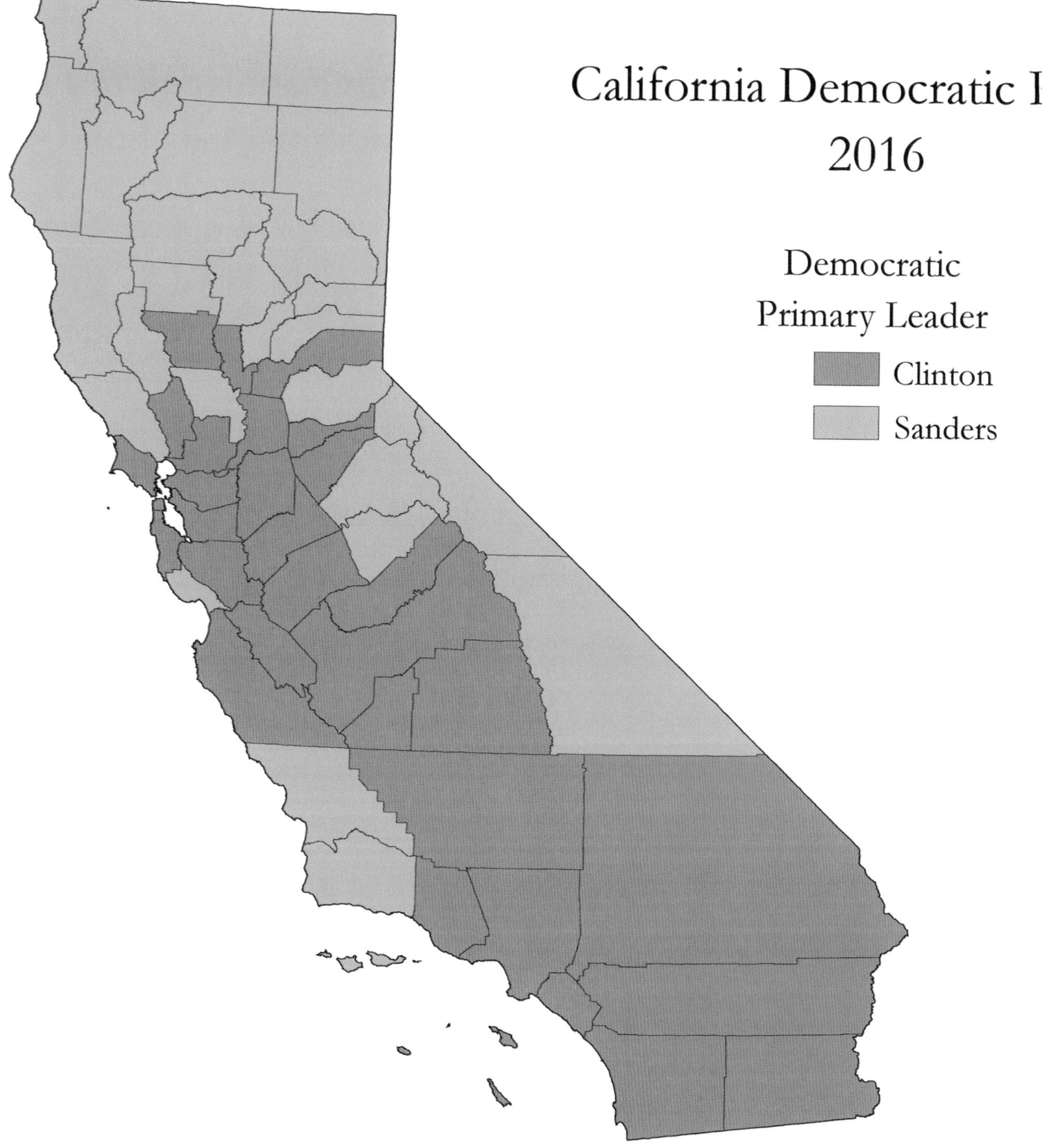

FIGURE 2.10

California Democratic Primary 2016

defeated Sanders in the Bay Area, including San Francisco, along with the counties extending southward along the Pacific coast toward Los Angeles. Although San Francisco is one of the country's most liberal cities, its voters nevertheless supported Clinton with 55.6 percent of the vote. She won larger margins in suburban areas east and south of San Francisco. She also won Alameda County, which contains the cities of Oakland and Berkeley, with 53.9 percent of the vote. These wins, perhaps associated with votes from the region's substantial minority populations, were key to Clinton's win in California. Sanders swept the northern part of California along with several counties on the Nevada border. However, most of these counties have relatively small populations and Sanders' margins in these counties were by no means large enough to overcome Clinton's lead elsewhere.

Given the Democratic National Committee's requirement to assign pledged delegates proportionally within each state, the outcome in California made no difference in the overall result of the Democratic nomination process. However, the California primaries were marred with confusion because of differences in how Democrats and Republicans handled independents. California classifies registered independents as having "no party preference" (NPP) (Myers 2016). The California Democratic Party allowed NPP voters in its primary, but the California Republican Party did not. Voting became even more confusing within the California Democratic primary because counties did not handle registered NPP voters consistently. In the Democratic primary, the party required NPP voters to use a special ballot called a crossover ballot to cast their votes. The crossover ballot only included the Democratic presidential primary candidates and did not include the election for the California Democratic Party's governing committee. Confusion ensued at polling places because NPP voters had to request a crossover ballot to vote in the Democratic primary in California (Myers 2016).

Many described voting in the Democratic primary as confusing, especially new voters. In some counties, election officials gave NPP voters provisional ballots even though they should have given NPP voters crossover ballots. The California Secretary of State explains a provisional ballot is "a regular ballot that is placed in a special envelope prior to being put in the ballot box." Provisional ballots are cast by voters who believe they are registered to vote but are not listed on the official voting roll and by voters who requested votes by mail but either did not receive the ballot or forgot to take the ballot to the polling place. Crossover ballots were guaranteed to be counted, but provisional ballots are handled on a case-by-case basis and were not guaranteed to be counted. In some counties, election officials considered provisional ballots cast by NPP voters who did not request or receive crossover ballots as invalid.

This led to reports that many voting ballots in California were not counted. Examining this situation, journalist John Myers (2016) reported that "In Contra Costa County, 88 percent of provisional ballots were successfully counted, [and] in Los Angeles County, where more than 268,000 provisional ballots were cast, 87 percent were ultimately counted." However, these figures imply that more than 10 percent of the provisional ballots were not counted. Another journalist, Judy Frankel (2016), writing for the online *Huffington Post*, noticed that many provisional ballots were separated into a box for "snagged votes." These votes were cast by NPP voters who, for whatever reason, were given Democratic ballots instead of the crossover ballots and may not have been counted. Although there is no evidence that a majority of these uncounted ballots had been cast for Sanders, throughout the country Sanders polled consistently better among independents than among registered Democrats and thus many Sanders supporters argued that the confusing process of casting crossover ballots was biased against the Sanders campaign. Unfortunately, no exit polls were conducted in California, so it is impossible to speculate with any certainty the extent to which age, race, ethnicity, or other characteristics were correlated with the percentages of votes cast for the two candidates.

Analysis of the Democratic Campaign

Results of the Democratic Party campaign at both the national and the state level showed a large degree of consistency. Throughout the country, Clinton did best among older voters, women, political moderates, party regulars, and non-white voters. Sanders did best among millennial voters, political progressives, and independent voters. In general, Sanders did well in the North, and Clinton did well in the South, as mapped in figure 2.11. Gender was a significant factor, although not to as great an extent as some observers had predicted. Rather, the age and race of voters differentiated Sanders and Clinton supporters to a larger degree than did gender.

The results highlighted important ideological differences between supporters of Clinton and those of Sanders. Although Clinton's supporters were often quick to point out that the two candidates had few differences with respect to policy ideas and proposals, Clinton came across as much more moderate, perhaps because of her ongoing

FIGURE 2.11

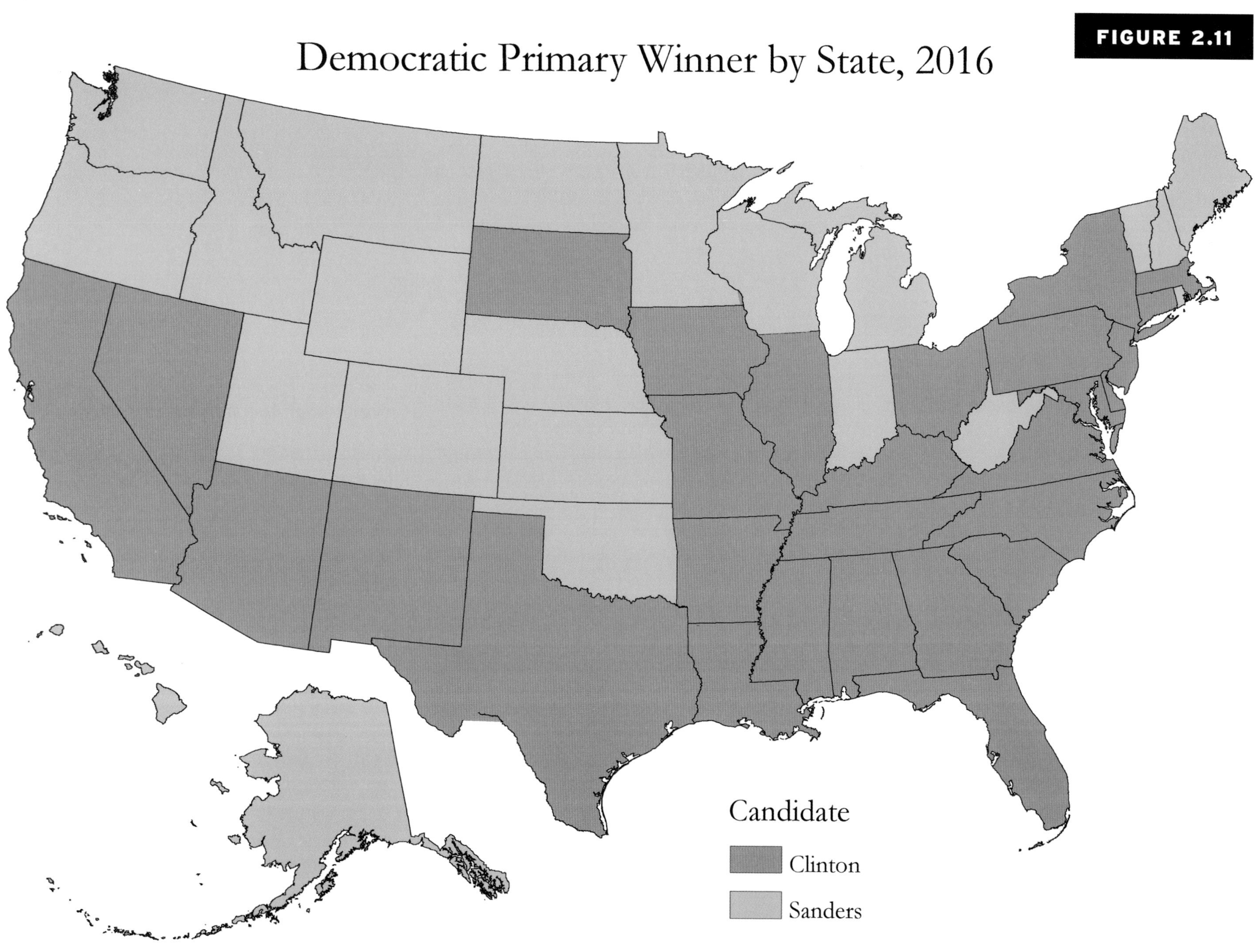
Democratic Primary Winner by State, 2016
Candidate
Clinton
Sanders

ties to Wall Street. After Clinton lost in November, tension between the progressive wing and the more moderate wing of the Democratic Party intensified although leaders on both sides recognized the value of party unity looking ahead to the 2020 presidential election.

NOTE

1. Richard Morrill and Ben Anderstone contributed the section on Washington State.

REFERENCES

Bayat, Shiva. 2016. A Vote for Bernie is a Feminist Act. *Doublex*. February 19, http://www.slate.com/articles/double_x/doublex/2016/02/voting_for_bernie_sanders_is_a_feminist_act.html (last accessed June 1, 2017).

Bradner, Eric, and Dan Merica. 2016. Young Voters Abandon Hillary Clinton for Bernie Sanders. *CNN*. February 10, http://www.cnn.com/2016/02/10/politics/hillary-clinton-new-hampshire-primary (last accessed June 1, 2017).

California Secretary of State. 2017. Provisional Voting. http://www.sos.ca.gov/elections/voting-resources/provisional-voting (last accessed July 4, 2017).

Cassidy, John. 2016. Bernie Sanders and the New Populism. *New Yorker*. February 3, http://www.newyorker.com/news/john-cassidy/bernie-sanders-and-the-new-populism (last accessed June 1, 2017).

Foran, Clare. 2016. An Awkward Reality in the Democratic Primary. *The Atlantic*. May 25.

Frankel, Judy. 2016. Snagged Votes in Los Angeles. *Huffington Post*. July 5, http://www.huffingtonpost.com/judy-frankel/snagged-votes-in-los-angeles_b_10794718.html (last accessed June 1, 2017).

Gaudiano, Nicole. 2016. Why Bernie Sanders Could Win Oklahoma. *USA Today*. February 29, https://www.usatoday.com/story/news/politics/elections/2016/02/29/oklahoma-primary-bernie-sanders-super-tuesday/81088324 (last accessed June 1, 2017).

Geier, Ben. 2016. Poll: More Men Support Hillary Clinton Than You Might Think. *Fortune*. May 13, http://fortune.com/2016/05/13/poll-more-men-support-hillary-clinton-than-you-might-think (last accessed June 1, 2017).

Goldmacher, Shane. 2016. Ted Cruz's Evangelical Problem. *Politico*. April 1, http://www.politico.com/story/2016/03/ted-cruz-christian-evangelical-vote-221349 (last accessed June 1, 2017).

Gosztola, Kevin. 2016. "Get a Life": Clinton Bashed Anti-Fracking Activists During Private Labor Meeting. *Common Dreams*. October 17, https://www.commondreams.org/views/2016/10/17/get-life-clinton-bashed-anti-fracking-activists-during-private-labor-meeting (last accessed June 1, 2017).

Malone, Clare. 2016. If You Want to Understand What's Roiling the 2016 Election, Go to Oklahoma. *Five Thirty Eight*. February 29, https://fivethirtyeight.com/features/if-you-want-to-understand-whats-roiling-the-2016-election-go-to-oklahoma (last accessed June 1, 2017).

Myers, John. 2016. "Confusing" California Primary Ends on Sour Note. *Los Angeles Times*. July 11, http://www.latimes.com/politics/la-pol-ca-california-primary-results-confusing-20160711-snap-story.html (last accessed June 1, 2017).

Silver, Nate. 2016. The Mythology of Trump's "Working Class" Support. *Five Thirty Eight*. May 3, https://fivethirtyeight.com/features/the-mythology-of-trumps-working-class-support (last accessed June 1, 2017).

Washington State Democrats. 2017. 2016 Democratic Caucuses. http://www.wa-democrats.org/page/2016-democratic-caucuses.

2016 PRESIDENTIAL PRIMARIES: MICHIGAN

LISA M. DECHANO-COOK

The 2016 presidential primary election in Michigan drew over 2.5 million voters to the polls, roughly 34 percent of registered voters in the state. Voter turnout for the presidential primaries was the largest in history, eclipsing the previous record of 1.9 million ballots cast in 1972 when George Wallace won 51 percent of the Democratic vote. One of the many reasons for this high turnout may be that this was the first time since 1992 that both parties held a primary instead of a caucus. Moreover, both parties held their primaries on the same day.

Republican residents in Michigan overwhelmingly voted for Donald Trump in the 2016 presidential primaries. He won seventy-two of the eighty-three counties, including the highly populous counties of Wayne (Detroit), Oakland, and Macomb, Ingham County (Lansing), and all but one county in the Upper Peninsula. Nine counties went to Ted Cruz, with the majority of these counties being in western Michigan, including Allegan, Kent (Grand Rapids), Ottawa, Muskegon, Oceana, and Newaygo Counties. Many of them are located in western Michigan along Lake Michigan, an area with a large Dutch American population. Cruz was the only other candidate to win a county in the Upper Peninsula—Houghton County, which is home to Michigan Technological University. Kalamazoo County in southwest Michigan (home of Western Michigan University) and Washtenaw County (home of the University of Michigan) in southeast Michigan were the only counties that John Kasich was able to win in Michigan. Kasich beat Cruz and Trump in Kalamazoo County by less than 1 and 2 percent, respectively. In Washtenaw County, Kasich won over Trump and Cruz by over 4 and 10 percent, respectively.

Trump's victory may be attributed to many variables. One of these variables is the fact that he garnered larger-than-historical averages for Republicans in rural areas He was also able to sway many working-class voters to vote for him who were dissatisfied with perceived political elites. He confronted Michigan's auto industry and discussed a plan for more domestic jobs. Another variable of his win was the lower-than-expected turnout in Wayne County.

On the Democratic side, Bernie Sanders had a stellar showing in Michigan. His win was dubbed "one of the greatest upsets in modern political history" (Enten 2016). He won the Democratic primary with the same overwhelming results as Donald Trump on the Republican side. Aside from Grand Rapids, the second largest city in the state, Sanders' supporters were mainly rural and suburban. Hillary Clinton was able to secure the Detroit metropolitan area, including Wayne, Oakland, and Macomb Counties in southeast Michigan, all of which have a high population. She added Genesee and Saginaw Counties that are adjacent to those near Detroit. The other counties that she earned the most votes from are spread throughout the state, including Berrien County in the southwest, Osceola County in the northwest, Alcona and Montmorency Counties in the northeast, and Menominee County in the Upper Peninsula. As was the case elsewhere, Sanders did better among males, younger voters, white voters, and in areas with large populations of college students (Ann Arbor, East Lansing, Kalamazoo), whereas Clinton succeeded with women and older voters and African American voters. Seventy percent of independents voted for Sanders (Gray and Spangler 2016). Thus, the geographical and demographic profile of the Michigan Democratic primary was highly consistent with those of earlier primaries, but Sanders' numbers were unexpectedly high and contributed to his surprising victory.

Bernie Sanders' win in Michigan caught everyone by surprise. Every poll prior to the primaries had Clinton winning the state by a margin of 13 to 27 percent (Gray and Spangler 2016). These polls suggested demographics would be the deciding factor (Gray and Spangler 2016). Clinton's policies on trade, which Sanders claimed ultimately hurt employment in the United States, were one such issue that resonated with residents voting for Sanders, as did his generally antiestablishment outlook that may have resonated with many persons, especially young voters, throughout the state.

REFERENCES

Enten, Harry. 2016. What the Stunning Bernie Sanders Win in Michigan Means. *FiveThirtyEight*. https://fivethirtyeight.com/features/what-the-stunning-bernie-sanders-win-in-michigan-means.

Gray, Kathleen, and Todd Spangler. 2016. How Bernie Sanders Won Michigan. *Detroit Free Press*, March 9.

3 THE CAMPAIGN

THE 2016 CAMPAIGN

JOHN HEPPEN

The 2016 presidential election began when Republican Donald Trump won the Indiana Primary on May 3 and Ted Cruz conceded. Until Election Day experts and polls had former secretary of state Hillary Clinton winning the presidency but they were all wrong. Trump's historic campaign broke all rules during the Republican primaries and general election. The Democratic side was equally as historic. Bernie Sanders did not concede until July though the media anointed Hillary Clinton the nominee in late April after she won the New York Primary. Democratic Socialist and Vermont Senator Bernie Sanders battled Hillary Clinton with energetic support from younger voters and the most liberal and progressive wing of the party. He took *socialist* from a term of derision to a term of pride among his followers and brought socialism back into the American political discourse as a challenge to capitalism.

Clinton began the fall campaign with what many considered an insurmountable lead in electoral votes based on Obama's electoral map in 2012. Clinton counted on the Northeast, Great Lakes, West Coast, Colorado, New Mexico, and Florida. That supposedly gave her 332 electoral votes to 206 for Trump. Trump made a play for manufacturing states Ohio, Pennsylvania, Michigan, and Wisconsin based on his opposition to the North American Free Trade Agreement (NAFTA) and Trans-Pacific Partnership (TPP). He stated that he would bring manufacturing jobs back by making better trade deals and cracking down on illegal immigration by building a wall on the Mexican border and having Mexico pay for it. Trump counted on a base of the South, Great Plains, and the Interior. Trump ran a different campaign and after the Republican National Convention, some polls showed him tied or in the lead nationally and within striking distance in battleground states. Despite his statements and actions that would derail any other candidate, the theory was that enough white working-class Americans fed up with the country voted for him despite the accusations of racism, sexism, and xenophobia. Even with faithless electors for both sides, Trump won the Electoral College 304 to 227, showing that the nature of the Electoral College produces a bias in favor of a candidate regardless of the popular vote, bringing back memories of the 2000 election and calls once again for Electoral College reform (see Johnston, Rossiter, and Pattie 2006).

The campaign began when the Republican National Convention was in Cleveland, Ohio, from July 18 to 21, with Trump formally accepting the nomination on July 21. Texas Senator Ted Cruz's speech, which did not endorse Donald Trump, slightly spoiled Trump's coronation on the third night as Trump supporters booed Cruz. The Democratic National Convention took place in

Philadelphia from July 25 to 28 with little controversy as Sanders endorsed Clinton with no hesitation and enthusiastically.

Third-party candidates, Jill Stein of the Green Party, Gary Johnson of the Libertarian Party, and Evan McMullin of Utah running as an independent conservative, had hoped to reach 15 percent in a combination of public opinion polls to be allowed to participate in debates. However, no third-party candidate reached that threshold despite waging national campaigns to the best of their ability beyond occasional cable news appearances.

In late July and early August, Trump's campaign ran into trouble with his attacks against the family of US Army Captain Humayun Khan. Khan, a Muslim, died in Iraq in 2004. His father, Khizr Khan, addressed the Democratic National Convention and criticized Donald Trump for his statements on Muslims. Trump responded by suggesting that the mother was not allowed to speak because the family is Muslim and Khizr Khan did not write the speech. The outrage over attacking the family was short-term with no lasting damage. Trump also refused to endorse House Speaker Paul Ryan in his Republican primary in August, which caused another media storm. Clinton began the campaign with her neverending theme of portraying Donald Trump as personally unfit for the presidency, confident in the lead most polls gave her going into the debates.

The debates were potentially turning points for Trump, but the media generally crowned Clinton the winner of all three debates. The first debate, on September 26 at Hofstra University in Hempstead, New York, was a Clinton victory according to most observers, but did little to change public attitudes. The vice presidential candidates had a debate on October 4 at Longwood College in Virginia that did nothing to change the dynamics of the race though most observers crowned governor Mike Pence of Indiana the winner. On October 7, Trump was hit with allegations of sexual harassment and was caught on audio making crude comments about women to reporter Billy Bush of the television show *Access Hollywood*. The comments, made eleven years previously, caused a firestorm and yet did not cause any lasting damage. During the fall campaign, Trump faced accusations of sexual harassment, unwanted attention, sexual assault, walking in on teenage beauty pageant contestants while they were changing, making inappropriate comments about teenage girls, and shaming former Miss Universe Alicia Machado over her weight (*New York Magazine* 2016). Trump was owner of beauty pageants.

The second debate on October 9 in Saint Louis had the same result as most saw Clinton winning on substance and performance but did little to change polling numbers. Clinton did not really push the issue of sexual harassment during the debate. The final debate on October 19 at the University of Nevada Las Vegas also did little to change the polling numbers even with Trump calling Clinton a "nasty woman." In summary, his debate performances in September and October were deemed subpar by most of the media; his refusal to say he would accept the results of the election if he lost and allegations of sexual harassment were considered mortal blows to his candidacy. Polls showed Clinton with leads in Pennsylvania, Michigan, and Florida that made Trump's task look very difficult on election eve.

Hillary Clinton had her own campaign issues of trust and likability. She was hit by allegations of improper use and storage of e-mails on her personal server while secretary of state. FBI director James Comey became a prominent player in the election by his announcements of opening and closing investigations in regards to Clinton's e-mail server issue within nine days of the election. He announced on October 28 that the FBI was investigating the e-mails and then on November 6 he announced that the FBI would not pursue any criminal charges.

Additionally, Russian hackers hacked the Democratic National Committee (DNC) computers and released embarrassing e-mails from DNC staffers regarding the Sanders campaign. This led to the WikiLeaks revelations as that website published the hacked e-mails. Clinton campaign chief John Podesta was the victim of embarrassing e-mails. The e-mails were released on July 23, but the sheer volume of e-mails made them a story throughout the campaign. Despite being embarrassing, there is little evidence that they made a difference in the vote. However, Debbie Wasserman Schultz resigned as chair of the Democratic National Committee since the leaked e-mails indicated a bias toward Clinton. Clinton campaign staff blamed the WikiLeaks controversy and Comey for her defeat and stalled momentum late in the campaign (Chozik 2016).

During the campaign, Trump concentrated on Florida, Pennsylvania, and Ohio as swing states and visited Wisconsin, Michigan, and Minnesota, ignored by Clinton until the end when it was too late. Trump swept traditional Republican strongholds of the South, the Plains, and Northern Rockies. Clinton won Democratic strongholds in the Northeast and West Coast but lost Pennsylvania, Florida, and vital Great Lakes states. Trump made, in hindsight, smart moves in campaigning in Michigan and Wisconsin whereas Clinton ignored those states, convinced that polling data were correct. Florida, Michigan, Ohio, and Pennsylvania and their eighty-three combined electoral votes swung the election to Trump.

Before midnight Eastern Time, it was becoming clear that Donald Trump was going to be president. Clinton, convinced that she would win every Obama state and be competitive in North Carolina and Arizona, miscalculated. The overarching narrative is that Trump won on the strength of white working-class voters angry over their economic position caused by bad trade deals, immigrants, and repression by political correctness. Republicans since 2008 have done better in regions with more conservative, white voters in Southern and Western states (Warf 2011). Polling and election data do reveal Trump improving among working-class whites over Romney, but he also won with the traditional Republican coalition of wealthier whites and Christian Conservatives combined with a lower turnout among traditional Democratic voters as the Obama coalition collapsed under Clinton (Cohn 2016a). The switch of Florida, Pennsylvania, Ohio, Michigan, Wisconsin, and Iowa proved pivotal as the Electoral College weighs heavily toward the candidate who wins battleground states (Cohn 2016b). On Wednesday morning, many people asked themselves, How did polling and conventional wisdom end up being so wrong? In the end, the election came down to the geographical nature of the Electoral College, which validated Trump's strategy despite his losing the popular vote by about 3 million votes.

REFERENCES

Chozik, Amy. 2016. Clinton Says "Personal Beef" by Putin Led to Hacking Attacks. *New York Times*. December 16, https://www.nytimes.com/2016/12/16/us/politics/hillary-clinton-russia-fbi-comey.html (last accessed May 30, 2017).

Cohn, Nate. 2016a. How the Obama Coalition Crumbled, Leaving an Opening for Trump. *New York Times*. December 23, https://www.nytimes.com/2016/12/23/upshot/how-the-obama-coalition-crumbled-leaving-an-opening-for-trump.html (last accessed May 30, 2017).

———. 2016b. Why Trump Had an Edge in the Electoral College. *New York Times*. December 19, http://www.nytimes.com/2016/12/19/upshot/why-trump-had-an-edge-in-the-electoral-college.html (last accessed May 30, 2017).

Johnston, Ron, David Rossiter, and Charlies Pattie. 2006. Changing the Scale and Changing the Result: Evaluating the Impact of an Electoral Reform on the 2000 and 2004 US Presidential Elections. *Political Geography* 25:557–69.

The Cut. 2016. An Exhaustive List of the Allegations Women Have Made Against Donald Trump. *New York Magazine*. October 27, http://nymag.com/thecut/2016/10/all-the-women-accusing-trump-of-rape-sexual-assault.html (last accessed May 30, 2017).

Warf, Barney. 2011. Class, Ethnicity, Religion, and Place in the 2008 Presidential Election. In Barney Warf and Jonathan Leib, eds., *Revitalizing Electoral Geography*, 133–55. Burlington, VT: Ashgate Publishers.

DONORSHEDS: INDIVIDUAL CONTRIBUTIONS TO CLINTON AND TRUMP

CARL T. DAHLMAN

An estimated $2.4 billion was spent on the 2016 presidential race. This total includes $466 million spent primarily by corporations and special interests to influence the election. Such "dark money" entered politics following the Supreme Court's 2010 *Citizens United* decision; the identities of these donors are not reported to the Federal Election Commission (FEC). The far larger source of campaign funding comes from US citizens donating to candidates. These donations are capped at $2,700 per person and all donations over $200 require disclosure of the donor's name and address to the FEC. In the 2016 election cycle, individual donations to presidential candidates totaled about $1.4 billion. Overall, the race cost the candidates approximately $1.5 billion, about 12 percent less than the record spent in 2008.

Individual donors in this election cycle gave Hillary Clinton $629 million, the largest sum among all candidates. Clinton also received the highest proportion of large donations: 28 percent of all donations to her campaign were in amounts of $2,000 or more. Bernie Sanders received the second largest sum, $232 million, from individual donors during his primary run against Hillary Clinton. Notably, 87 percent of contributions to Sanders were small donations of $200 or less, compared to 50 percent for Clinton. Donald Trump publicly swore off campaign contributions yet he raised $213 million from individual contributors, of which 58 percent were small donations. Donations provide some indication of candidates' popular support among voters.

Mapping "donorsheds" of where campaign contributors live reveals a pattern similar to a map of the US population weighted by income. The most important donorsheds are the wealthier neighborhoods of major metropolitan areas. These donors are a key part of national political campaigns yet they represent a small fraction of the population and an even smaller cross-section of American communities. In fact, watchdog groups estimate that 1/1000th of all donors were responsible for 30 percent of all campaign funding in 2016, including dark money and congressional campaigns (Sultan 2016).

What is, perhaps, more interesting is to compare the donorsheds of the parties' presidential candidates. The FEC website allows users to build their own maps of its data at the level of ZIP-3 postal regions (FEC 2016). More detailed data mapping reveals that while candidates seem worlds apart politically, their largest donors often live quite near one another. Smaller donors, on the other hand, are spread across the country and are important as a whole for presidential campaigns, but individually they do not attract special attention from candidates. Fundraising dinners in Silicon Valley can raise more money than mailers to a thousand farming communities.

Donors in California, New York, Texas, and Florida contributed the largest sums to both presidential candidates in 2016. The donorsheds for Trump and Clinton sometimes contrasted sharply at the state and local level, however. Repeating a pattern from earlier elections, donations to conservatives generally come from suburban and rural areas, while liberals do better in urban areas and wealthy suburbs. This largely reflects voting patterns, although the largest donors to either party often live in the same exclusive neighborhoods.

Texas was the largest source of individual donations to Donald Trump, totaling $15.7 million, yet Clinton did better in Texas, raising more than $22 million. She also raised more than Republican Ted Cruz, who gathered $19.7 million from his fellow Texans. In the famously liberal city of Austin, Clinton raised $4.2 million, almost twice as much as Cruz and Trump combined. In the border city of El Paso, Clinton raised only $284,000 yet that was roughly equal to the combined donations to Trump and Cruz. Cruz dominated a few cities, such as Fort Worth, while Trump tallied modest sums from across the state.

In California, Clinton raised $93.7 million, six times more than the state's donations to Trump. While Trump did better than Clinton in the midsized cities and rural towns of California's central valleys, she dominated metropolitan areas, the far wealthier donorsheds. Clinton raised $31 million in Los Angeles and Long Beach, about thirteen times more than Trump. Donors in San Francisco sent her $22 million compared to $622,000 for him.

FIGURE 3.1

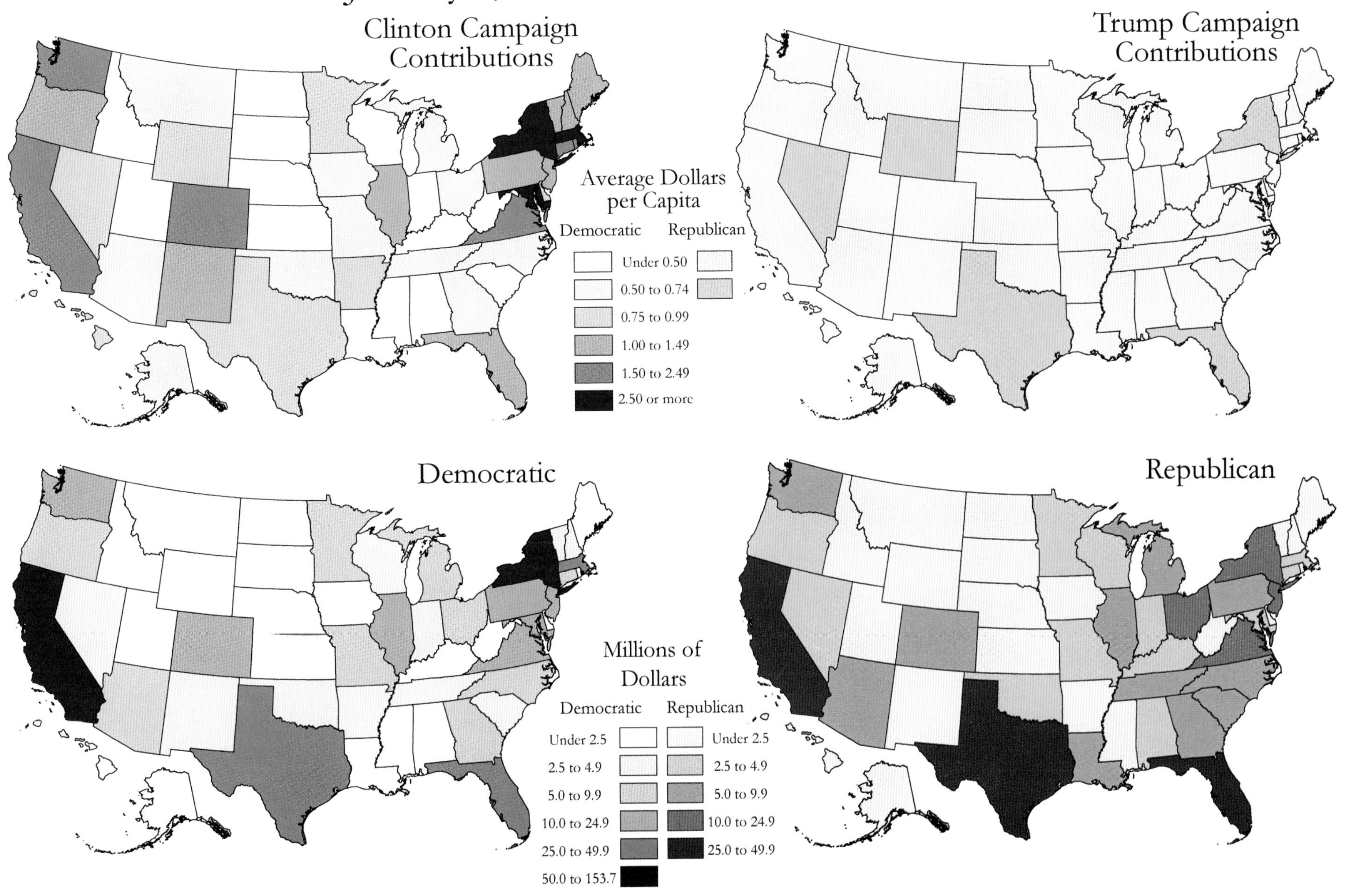
Donorsheds: Reported Campaign Contributions
January 1, 2015 to December 31, 2016
Clinton Campaign Contributions
Trump Campaign Contributions
Average Dollars per Capita
Democratic
Republican
Under 0.50
0.50 to 0.74
0.75 to 0.99
1.00 to 1.49
1.50 to 2.49
2.50 or more
Democratic
Republican
Millions of Dollars
Democratic
Republican
Under 2.5
2.5 to 4.9
5.0 to 9.9
10.0 to 24.9
25.0 to 49.9
50.0 to 153.7
Under 2.5
2.5 to 4.9
5.0 to 9.9
10.0 to 24.9
25.0 to 49.9

Clinton was clearly the better fundraiser. She received $17 million from donors in Washington, DC, compared to $233,000 for Trump. In Trump's hometown of New York City, he raised $2.2 million but Clinton raised $50 million. Yet while the largest fundraiser and spender in 2016 was the winner of the popular vote, neither total donations nor total votes equated to success in the Electoral College.

REFERENCES

Federal Election Commission. 2016. Presidential Campaign Finance (Map of disclosed data). Washington, DC. http://classic.fec.gov/disclosurep/pnational.do (last accessed May 25, 2017).

Sultan, Niv. 2016. Election 2016: Trump's Free Media Helped Keep Cost Down, But Fewer Donors Provided More of the Cash. Washington, DC: Center for Responsive Politics. https://www.opensecrets.org/news/2017/04/election-2016-trump-fewer-donors-provided-more-of-the-cash (last accessed May 25, 2017).

CAMPAIGN EXPENDITURES IN THE 2016 ELECTION

CHRIS MAIER

Over the past few years, campaign spending has played an important role in presidential elections. After all, candidates need money to communicate with voters and volunteers, and to fund other aspects of their campaign. Nonetheless, the 2016 presidential election was different from recent presidential elections as Donald Trump, the Republican nominee for president, ran one of the more unorthodox presidential campaigns in recent history.

During the 2016 presidential election, former secretary of state and Democratic nominee Hillary Clinton and Republican challenger Donald Trump combined to spend $340,070,199 during the primary season and another $580,193,408 during the general election. Thus, in total, the two candidates spent $920,263,607 on the 2016 presidential campaign (Federal Election Commission, Trump 2016; Federal Election Commission, Clinton 2016). The calculated expenditures in this essay do not include each candidate's itemized deductions, nor do they include outside spending on the presidential election from organizations such as super PACs (Political Action Committees).

Donald Trump spent $86,607,699 during the highly competitive 2016 Republican presidential primaries and caucuses, which saw seventeen major candidates vie for the Republican nomination (Federal Election Commission, Trump 2016). While $86 million is a significant amount of money, Mr. Trump spent considerably less than Secretary Clinton as well as the 2012 Republican nominee Mitt Romney (Maier 2014). Even though much of Trump's spending was in Virginia, New York, and Texas, he spent money in forty-seven of the fifty states, ranging from nothing in Hawaii, North Dakota, and South Dakota to a high of $21,922,609 in Virginia. Most of his spending in Virginia went to Rick Reed Media, which produced place-based media advertising for the Trump campaign.

During the primary season, Secretary Clinton's campaign vastly outspent the Trump campaign. Clinton spent $253,462,500 during the 2016 Democratic presidential primaries and caucuses, which pitted her against the upstart campaign of Senator Bernie Sanders from Vermont (Federal Election Commission, Clinton 2016). Unlike the Trump campaign, Clinton spent money in all fifty states, ranging from a low of $2,500 in North Dakota to a high of $119,027,868 in Washington, DC. Clinton spent nearly half of her money ($119,027,868) in Washington, DC, which is home to GMMB. GMMB is a political consulting group that consulted, produced media, and bought media time for the Clinton campaign during the primaries, caucuses, and general election. Clinton also spent a significant amount of money in New York and New Jersey. New York was home to her campaign headquarters and the state she represented in the US Senate.

Figure 3.2 shows the expenditures for Donald Trump's 2016 general election campaign, which totaled $254,668,640 (Federal Election Commission, Trump 2016). The geographic pattern of Trump's largest general election expenditures was similar to the pattern seen in the primaries and caucuses, with the largest expenditures occurring in Virginia and Texas. Many of the expenditures in Virginia and Texas had national implications as they funded national media buys, including online advertising and political consulting (Federal Election Commission, Trump 2016). Trump also spent a significant amount of money in New York, which was home to his campaign headquarters. Along with Virginia, Texas, and New York, Trump also spent a substantial amount of money in "battleground" or "toss-up" states, including Arizona, Florida, Iowa, Michigan, Missouri, New Hampshire, North Carolina, Ohio, and Wisconsin.

Figure 3.2 also shows the expenditures for Hillary Clinton's 2016 general election campaign, which totaled $325,524,768 (Federal Election Commission, Clinton 2016). Clinton's general election expenditures were similar to those during the primaries and caucuses, with well over half of the money spent in Washington, DC. Like the primaries and caucuses, during the general election, Clinton spent money in all fifty states, ranging from a low of $4,290 in South Dakota to a high of $233,700,146 in Washington, DC. Clinton, like Trump, spent a significant amount of money on battleground states, including Colorado, Florida, and Pennsylvania. Unfortunately for Clinton, the battleground states decided the 2016 presidential

FIGURE 3.2

Reported Primary and General Election Expenditures

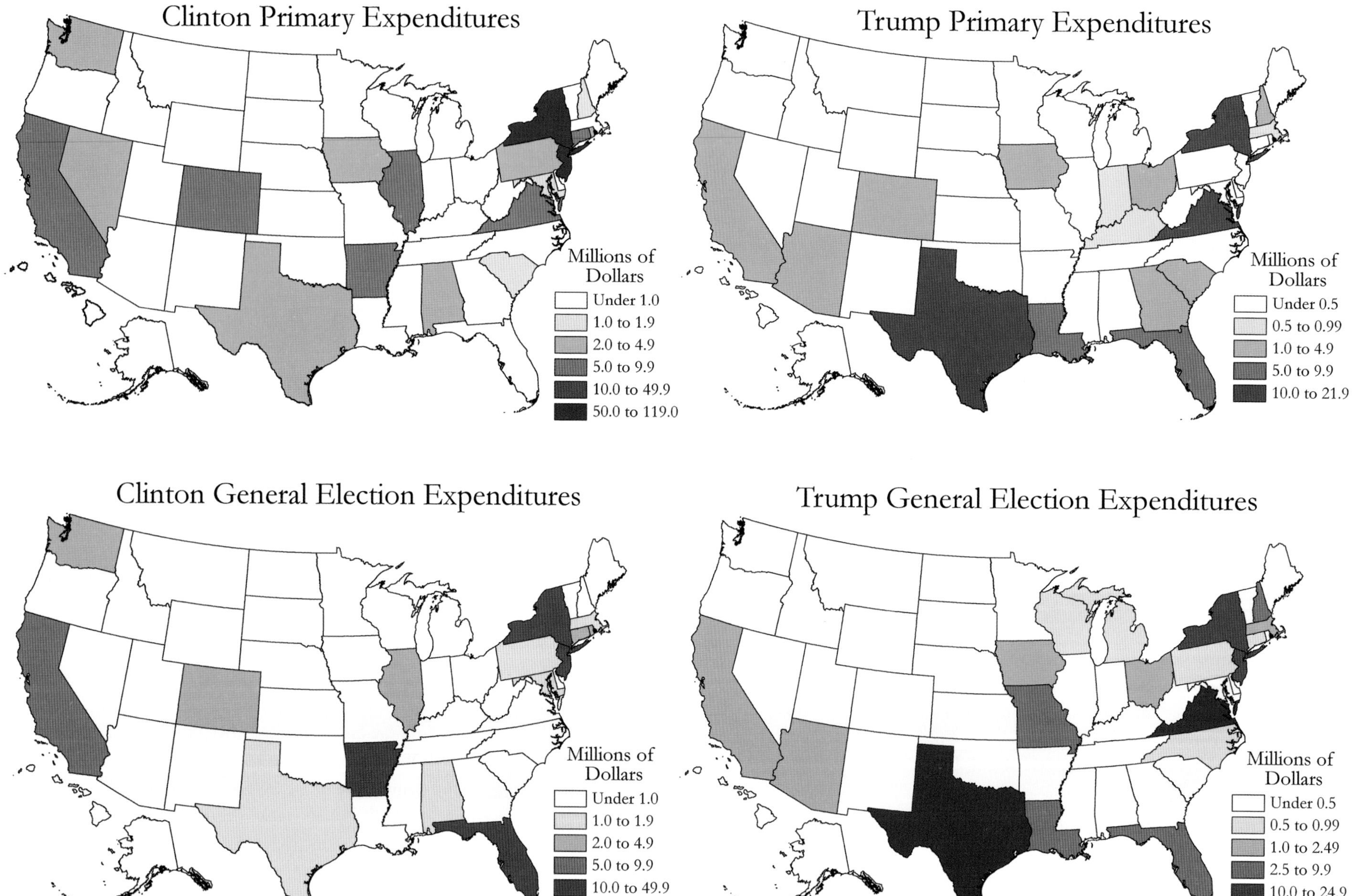

election. Unlike the 2012 presidential election, the candidate who spent the most money in the 2016 presidential election did not win. In terms of campaign expenditures, Clinton's campaign outspent Trump's campaign by $237,710,929. In the end, the spending advantage for Secretary Clinton was not enough as Trump's campaign received a significant amount of free media attention, which helped propel his unorthodox campaign to victory.

REFERENCES

Federal Election Commission, Clinton. 2016. Two-Year Campaign Expenditures. http://www.fec.gov/fecviewer/CandidateCommitteeDetail.do (last accessed June 15, 2017).

Federal Election Commission, Trump. 2016. Two-Year Campaign Expenditures. http://www.fec.gov/fecviewer/CandidateCommitteeDetail.do (last accessed June 15, 2017).

Maier, Chris. 2014. Campaign Expenditures in the 2012 Election. In J. Clark Archer, Robert H. Watrel, Fiona Davidson, Erin H. Fouberg, Kenneth C. Martis, Richard L. Morrill, Fred M. Shelley, and Gerald R. Webster, eds., *Atlas of the 2012 Elections*, 52–54. Lanham, MD: Rowman & Littlefield.

CAMPAIGN STOPS

J. CLARK ARCHER AND JILL A. ARCHER

On November 19, 1863, in his famous Gettysburg Address, the nation's first Republican President, Abraham Lincoln, described the American federal democracy as "government of the people, by the people, for the people." A general presidential election campaign is unquestionably the most visible and important mechanism for maintaining and renewing links between government and the people. In the most recent election cycle, considerably more than one billion dollars was spent by major and minor party candidates for president to organize their campaign efforts and to convey their pleas for requested electoral support to the citizens of the United States as potential voters in the general election contest of November 8, 2016. In addition, over 135 million citizens did indeed respond to these requests for support by taking the time to cast their ballots. However, a presidential election is an indirect contest in which in 2016 the candidate who received the most popular ballots did not win the White House as a result. Many voters are only vaguely aware that their presidential ballots are actually cast for slates of electors who are expected to and in some states legally bound to vote for the presidential and vice presidential candidates to whom they have been pledged. A presidential election is thus a federal election and not a national election.

Presidential candidates and their campaign organizations tend to be keenly aware that the ballots of only some of the people are likely to weigh heavily in the decisive Electoral College tabulation. While the identification and assessment of which potential voters are most likely to influence election outcomes is contingent on many demographic, economic, and geographical factors, virtually all campaign models and election strategies prioritize the boundaries of states far above all other possible considerations. In a US presidential election, popular votes are counted and Electoral College seats are won or lost state by state, usually on a "winner-take-all" basis. Hence, two citizens of voting age with otherwise identical characteristics in terms of education, ethnicity, income, social status, and so on who live in two different states are very unlikely to be of equal importance in a federal presidential election. One of those citizens may have his or her mailbox flooded with election flyers and television screen inundated by campaign advertisements, while the other similar but differently located citizen has to struggle to glean enough information from mass media sources to try to decide whether and how to vote.

In deciding where and how to allocate campaign assets, the attentions of presidential candidates and their strategists tend to focus on two questions: How many electoral votes does each state possess? And what has been the recent electoral history of each state? Under Article II, Section 1, of the US Constitution, each state receives one elector for each of its seats in the US Senate and in the US House of Representatives. Less populous states, such as Alaska or Wyoming, each have a minimum of three electoral votes; California, which is the most populous state, has fifty-five electoral votes. However, voters in big states, including California, New York, or Texas, do not always receive the most attention in an election campaign, especially if they have voted consistently for the candidates of one or another party in recent elections. Everything else being equal, a state with a greater number of electoral votes and a more volatile election history will get more campaign attention and effort than one with fewer electoral votes and a less volatile election history.

An Electoral College–based cartogram that codes recent election history is an effective way of cartographically showing the likely relative importance of each state in a presidential election campaign. Figure 3.3 depicts each state not in terms of its actual geographical area but rather in terms of the number of electoral votes it was apportioned following the US Census of 2010. Two states with the same area are thus equal not in actual geographical extent but rather in the number of certified electoral votes that they were required to report to the president of the US Senate and the US national archivist following the December 19, 2016, meetings of their respective Electoral Colleges. Shadings show the numbers of elections won by candidates of each major party in the eight elections held from 1984 to 2012. Nationally, Republican candidates won in the elections of 1984, 1988, 2000, and 2004; and Democrats won in the elections of 1992, 1996, 2008, and 2012. States where one party or the other won

FIGURE 3.3

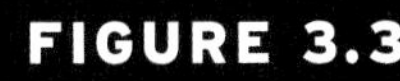

Electoral Vote Wins by State for the 1984 to 2012 Elections

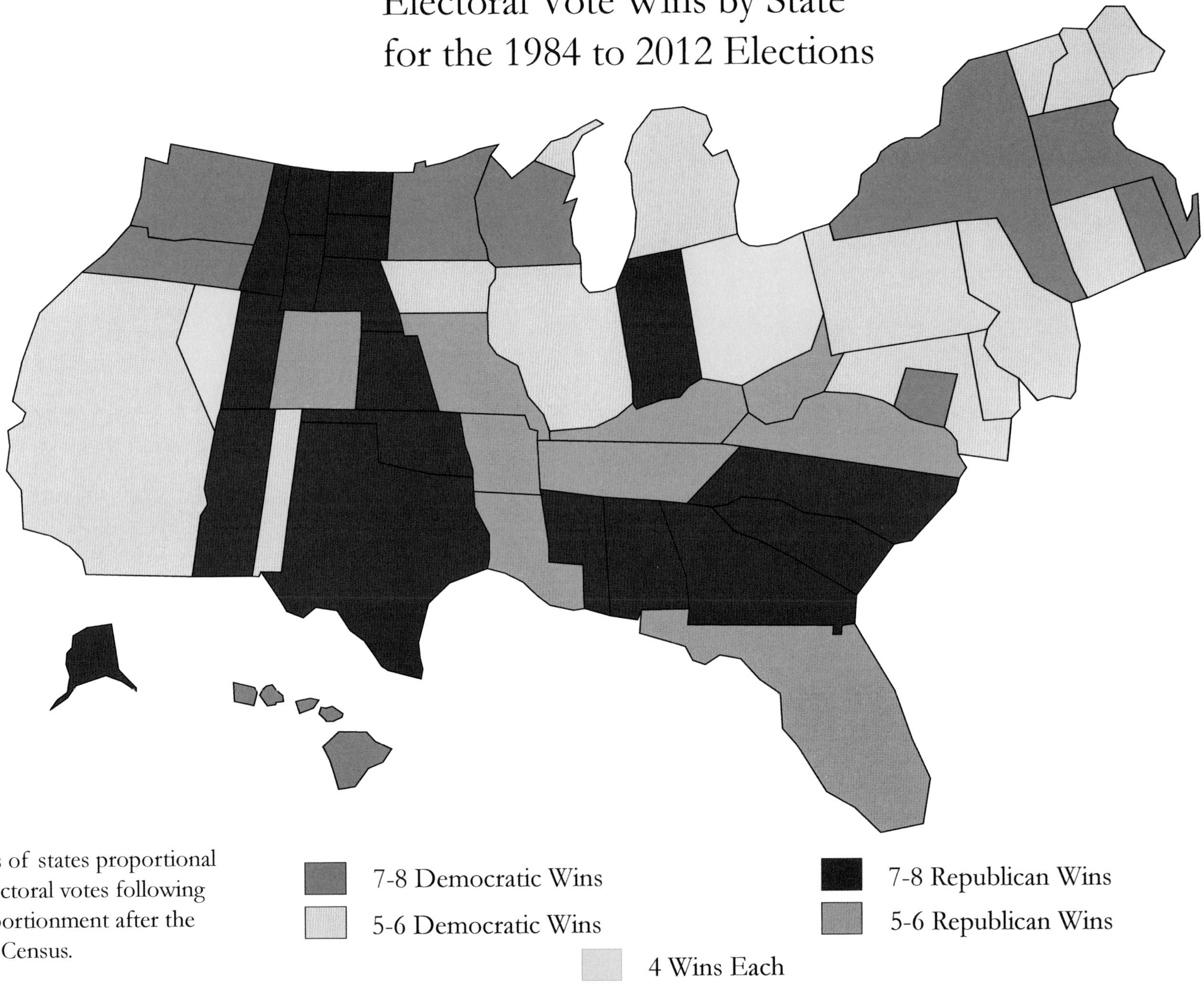
7-8 Democratic Wins
5-6 Democratic Wins
4 Wins Each
7-8 Republican Wins
5-6 Republican Wins

Areas of states proportional to electoral votes following reapportionment after the 2010 Census.

seven or more times during this period were not likely to be "battleground states" in 2016. These "deep blue" or "deep red" states were concentrated in New England, the inner South, and the inner West. Whether campaign strategists actually made such a map is not known, but numbers of electoral votes and election history were undoubtedly important variables in their campaign resource allocation models.

The largest allocations are probably for paid television campaign advertisements and "get-out-the-vote" efforts by campaign staffs. But the scarcest resources of any presidential campaign are the campaign efforts of the candidates themselves. In addition, these tend to be highly visible and widely publicized, since no candidate ever wants to arrive at a "campaign stop" to find only a few potential voters there to witness the event. Actual dollar amounts spent by state and locality would be enlightening about campaign strategy, but such information is not generally available. Fortunately, campaign stops can be publicly identified, geocoded, and counted.

Figure 3.4 shows the numbers of campaign stops by the Democratic and the Republican presidential and vice presidential candidates in each state from late July following the nominating conventions until November 7, 2016, the day before the election (National Popular Vote 2016). The degree of geographical concentration is obvious. There were no campaign stops at all in twenty-four states, and merely one to four stops in another fifteen states. Eight states received ten to twenty-three stops by at least one presidential or vice presidential candidate, including Arizona (10), Wisconsin (14), Nevada (17), Colorado (19), New Hampshire (21), Iowa (21), Michigan (22), and Virginia (23). Four states received many more stops, including Ohio (48), Pennsylvania (54), North Carolina (55), and Florida (71). In other words, of the 399 total campaign stops identified, 158 or half were concentrated in just four states, and over nine out of ten were concentrated in only twelve states. A glance back at the Electoral College cartogram demonstrates that most of the states won by one or the other party seven or more times from 1984 to 2012 received very little campaign attention in the 2016 contest.

When comparisons are made by party affiliation, it is obvious that Democrats Clinton and Kaine, and Republicans Trump and Pence had similar but not entirely identical campaign travel itineraries. Florida, North Carolina, Pennsylvania, and Ohio show up very conspicuously on both party-based maps, so it is obvious that these were the most heavily contested battleground states. The pivotal role of Florida in the 2000 election between George W. Bush and Al Gore may have been behind the fixation that both presidential candidates had on Florida in the 2016 campaign. Several other states, including Michigan, New Hampshire, and Nevada, also received a fair amount of attention from the candidates of both parties. However, there were differences in the travel itineraries of the Democratic and the Republican candidates. Especially notable is that there are conspicuously more states shaded on the Republican map than on the Democratic map; indeed, Trump and Pence's total of 248 campaign stops was more than one-and-one-half times greater than Clinton and Kaine's 151 campaign stops.

The specific campaign stops made by Clinton and by Trump from October 30 until November 8 were gleaned from each of their campaign websites (Clinton 2017 and Trump 2017) and then geocoded by nearest city in order to depict campaign travel patterns during the last ten days of the campaign. Trump's much more peripatetic campaign style was again obvious during the last ten days of the campaign, during which he made a total of thirty-three stops (see figure 3.5), compared with a total of only eighteen stops by Clinton (see figure 3.6). Essentially, Trump clearly out-hustled Clinton by making almost twice as many campaign stops during the last ten days.

Most important, perhaps, is that Clinton's campaign appears partly to have missed late signals of electoral weakness in Wisconsin, Michigan, and Pennsylvania. Clinton's late travel itinerary focused on the southern states of North Carolina and Florida but entirely missed Wisconsin and was relatively light in Michigan and Pennsylvania during the last ten days of the campaign. In contrast, Trump made nine stops in Wisconsin, Michigan, and Pennsylvania during the last ten days of the campaign. Trump's narrow victories in these states were pivotal in the final Electoral College tally.

Unfortunately, there may also have been a very dark shadow over the election campaign in these states late in the campaign. There appears to be some evidence that fake news stories and anti-Clinton stories, perhaps emanating from Russia, were particularly targeted at swing districts in these states (Calabresi 2017). The situation may not be as serious as it was when Abraham Lincoln first gave the Gettysburg Address, but it is worth completing the opening quotation by noting Lincoln's wish, "That this nation, under God, shall have a new birth of freedom, and that government of the people, by the people, for the people, shall not perish from the earth."

FIGURE 3.4

Post-Convention General Election Campaign Visits July–November 2016

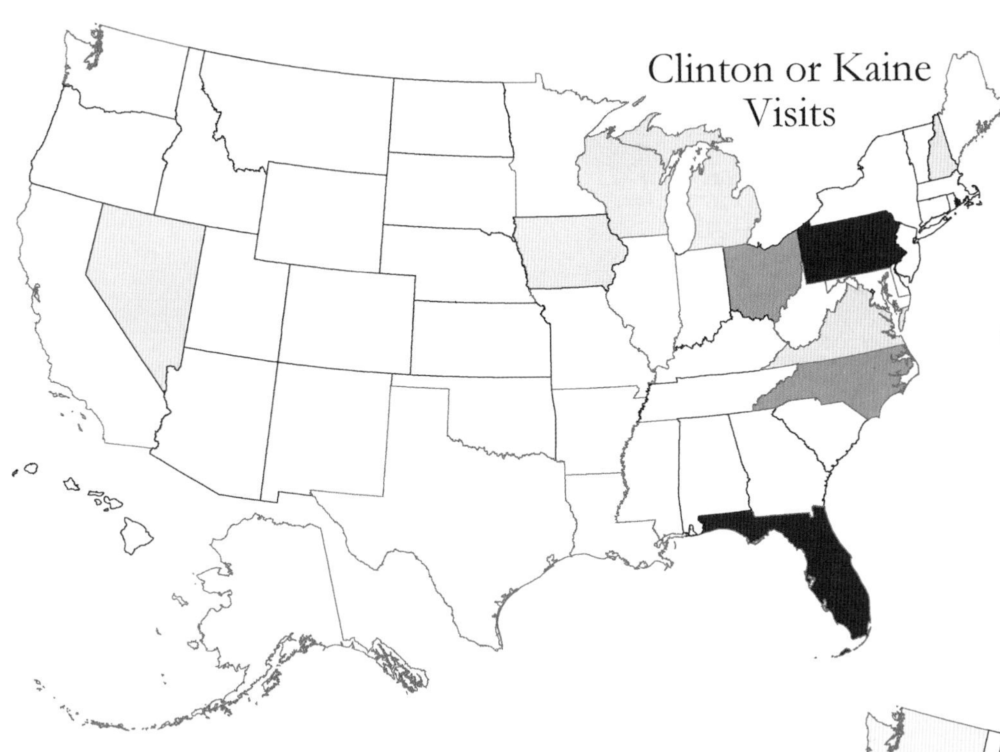

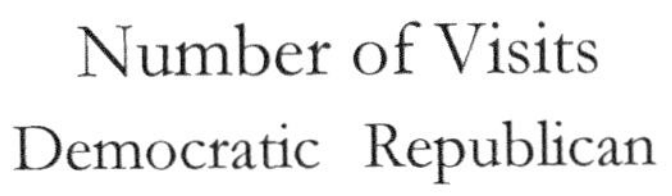

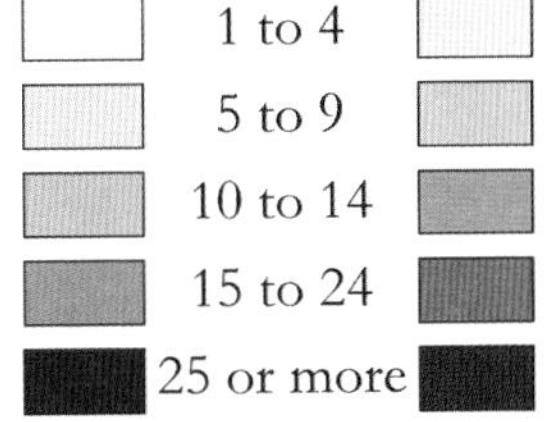

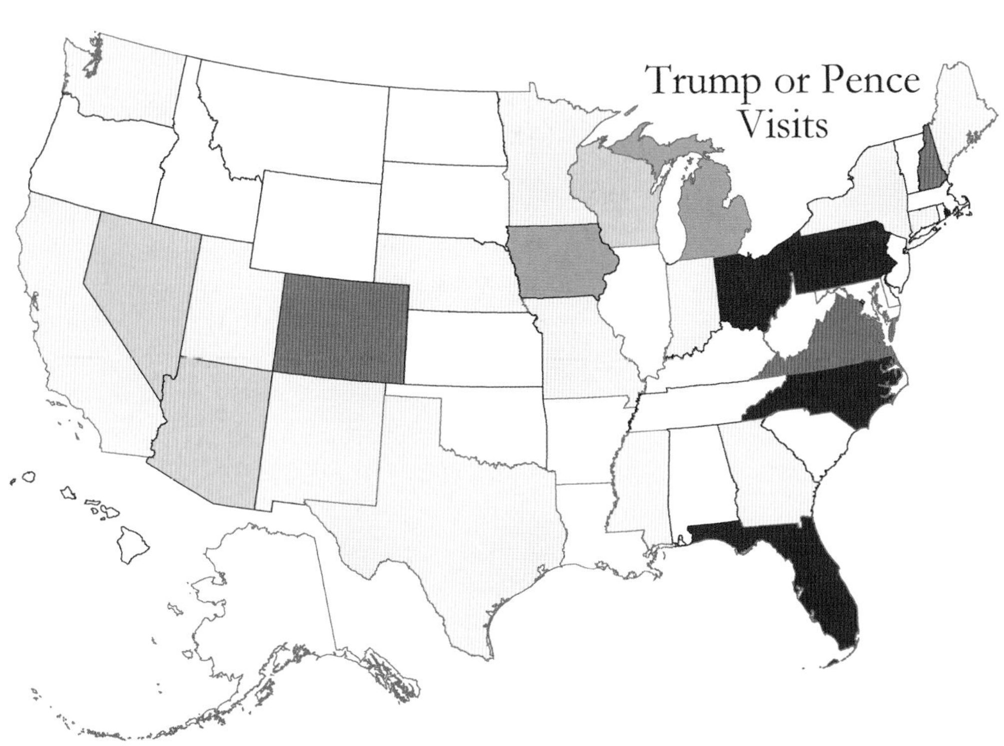

FIGURE 3.5

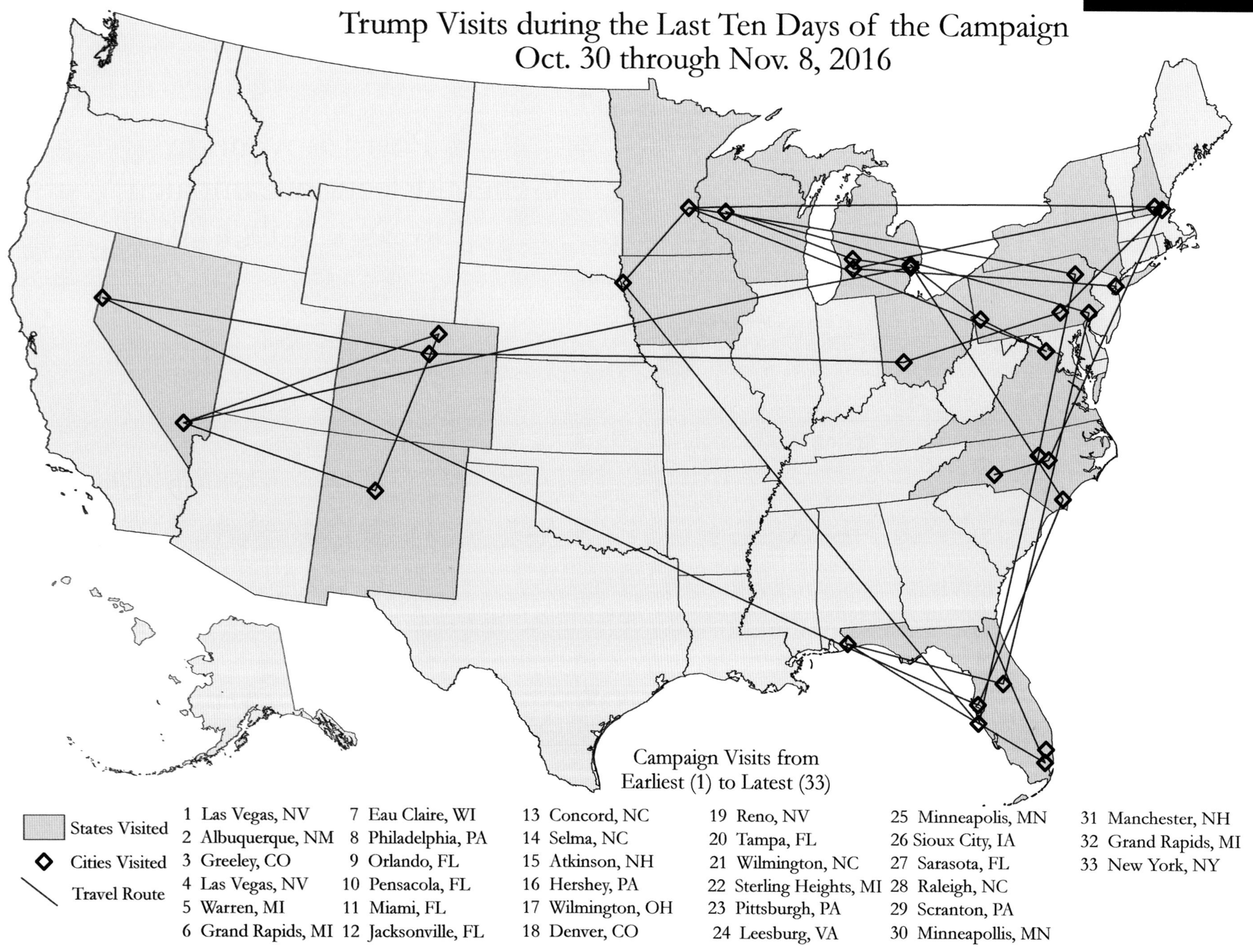

Trump Visits during the Last Ten Days of the Campaign
Oct. 30 through Nov. 8, 2016
Campaign Visits from
Earliest (1) to Latest (33)
States Visited
Cities Visited
Travel Route
1 Las Vegas, NV
2 Albuquerque, NM
3 Greeley, CO
4 Las Vegas, NV
5 Warren, MI
6 Grand Rapids, MI
7 Eau Claire, WI
8 Philadelphia, PA
9 Orlando, FL
10 Pensacola, FL
11 Miami, FL
12 Jacksonville, FL
13 Concord, NC
14 Selma, NC
15 Atkinson, NH
16 Hershey, PA
17 Wilmington, OH
18 Denver, CO
19 Reno, NV
20 Tampa, FL
21 Wilmington, NC
22 Sterling Heights, MI
23 Pittsburgh, PA
24 Leesburg, VA
25 Minneapolis, MN
26 Sioux City, IA
27 Sarasota, FL
28 Raleigh, NC
29 Scranton, PA
30 Minneapollis, MN
31 Manchester, NH
32 Grand Rapids, MI
33 New York, NY

FIGURE 3.6

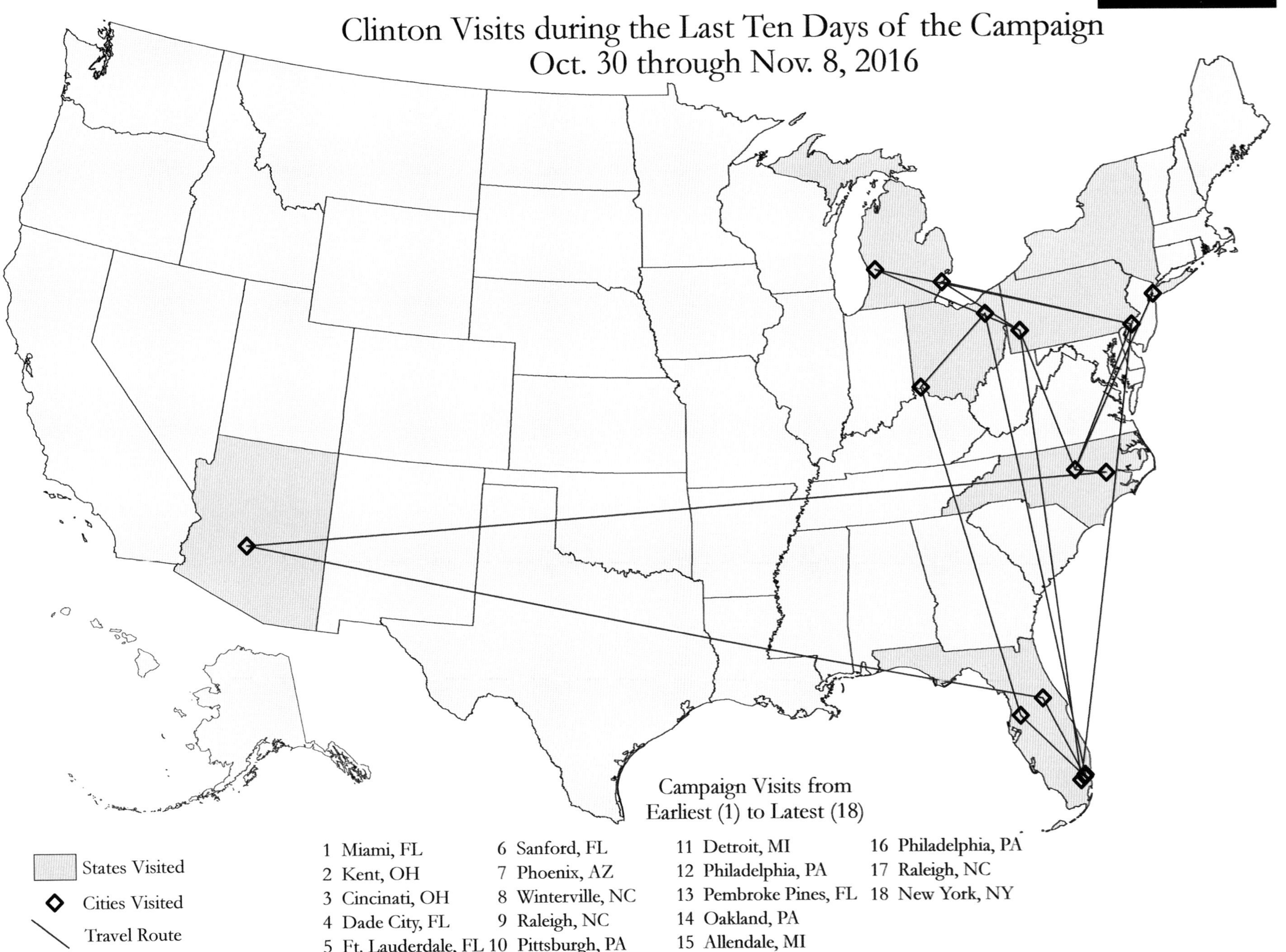
Clinton Visits during the Last Ten Days of the Campaign
Oct. 30 through Nov. 8, 2016
Campaign Visits from
Earliest (1) to Latest (18)
States Visited
Cities Visited
Travel Route
1 Miami, FL
2 Kent, OH
3 Cincinati, OH
4 Dade City, FL
5 Ft. Lauderdale, FL
6 Sanford, FL
7 Phoenix, AZ
8 Winterville, NC
9 Raleigh, NC
10 Pittsburgh, PA
11 Detroit, MI
12 Philadelphia, PA
13 Pembroke Pines, FL
14 Oakland, PA
15 Allendale, MI
16 Philadelphia, PA
17 Raleigh, NC
18 New York, NY

REFERENCES

Calabresi, Massimo. 2017. Special Report: Hacking: Inside Russia's Social Media War on America. *Time* 189(20): 30–35.

Clinton, Hillary. 2017. *Hillary Speeches*. https://hillaryspeeches.com (last accessed June 15, 2017).

National Popular Vote. 2016. Two-thirds of Presidential Campaign Is in Just 6 States. http://www.nationalpopularvote.com/campaign-events-2016 (last accessed June 15, 2017).

Trump, Donald J. 2017. https://www.donaldjtrump.com (last accessed June 15, 2017).

PLACE NAME USE IN THE 2016 PRESIDENTIAL DEBATES

MATTHEW BALENTINE AND GERALD R. WEBSTER

The 1960 presidential debates between Democrat John F. Kennedy and Republican Richard M. Nixon were the first face-to-face debates between major party nominees during a general election. While there were no presidential debates in 1964, 1968, or 1972, since the 1976 debates between Republican Gerald R. Ford and Democrat Jimmy Carter, presidential campaigns are expected to include debates (Sutherland and Webster 1994). Presidential debates warrant geographic analysis because policy discussions are often geographically compartmentalized. This is evidenced by efforts from moderators to categorize and guide debate topics with respect to one of two geographic domains: foreign versus domestic issues. Past presidential debate moderators have sometimes stated explicitly that questions were intended to focus on one of these domains. There is also a strategic component to the use of geographic language in debates with candidates emphasizing one geographic domain over the other if they conclude it provides an advantage (Balentine and Webster forthcoming). For example, incumbents often emphasize foreign place and policy knowledge because of prior experience. Similarly, challengers lacking such experience may emphasize economic and domestic concerns. Finally, geographic language may be strategically important in light of the US electoral system, which places a premium on swing states. Place names can demonstrate candidate familiarity with these important places. Thus, we might expect candidates to mention swing states more often than electorally noncompetitive states.

The 2016 presidential election contrasts starkly with past contests. First, Donald Trump was the first Republican nominee without prior military or political experience at any level of government. Second, the campaign had voluminous amounts of bellicose rhetoric, especially from the Trump campaign, most notably on Twitter. Third, the election cycle included several alleged scandals. While there was no shortage of controversy from the Trump campaign, future experts will remember Clinton's inability to shed public perceptions of impropriety surrounding her time as Secretary of State. Finally, in 2016, there was suspicion of foreign meddling in a US election. American intelligence experts concluded there was Kremlin involvement in the leaking of Democratic National Committee ≤members' e-mail exchanges in the run-up to the election.

Some of the campaign's unusual events occurred during the presidential debates, two of which stand out. The first occurred during the second debate, at Washington University in St. Louis, when candidate Trump threatened legal action against Clinton if he won the election. The threat related to allegations of Clinton's mishandling of sensitive e-mails. The second and possibly even more shocking incident occurred during the third debate, at UNLV, when Trump refused to confirm whether he would accept the election's outcome. The following day Trump again cast doubt as to whether he would honor the election results, stating, "I will totally accept the results of this great and historic presidential election—if I win" (Rappeport and Burns 2016).

TABLE 3.1. Swing State References in the 2016 Debates as a Percentage of All Domestic References

	Clinton Percentage	Trump Percentage
Debate 1	50	50
Debate 2	No swing state references	44
Debate 3	70	70

Source: Calculated by authors. States meeting one of the following criteria were classified as a swing state: margin of victory ≤6%; mean of state polls before first debate ≤6%; inclusion in RealClearPolitics.com list of swing states.

Note: Only specific references at or below the state level were included in the analysis. References to Washington, DC, and candidates' home state were excluded from the analysis.

2016 Presidential Debates

FIGURE 3.7

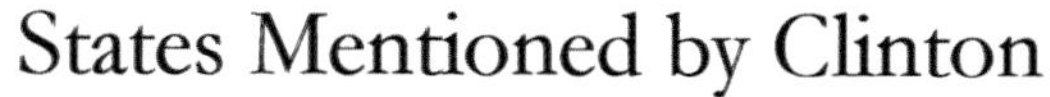

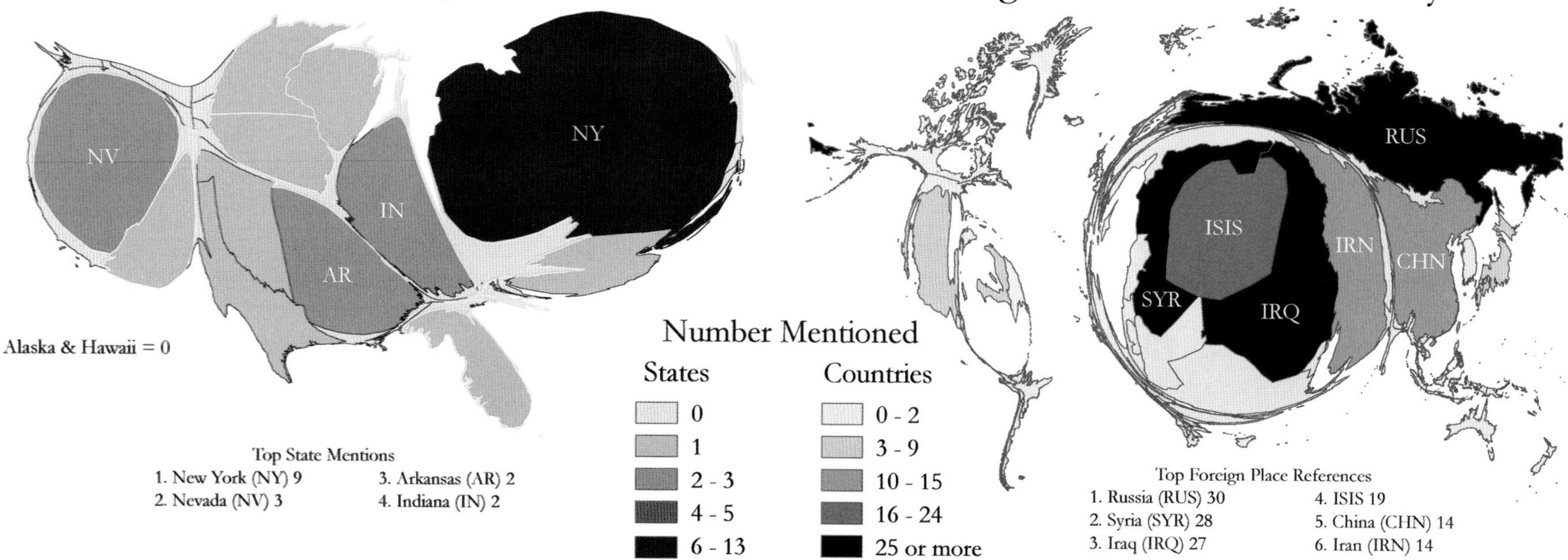

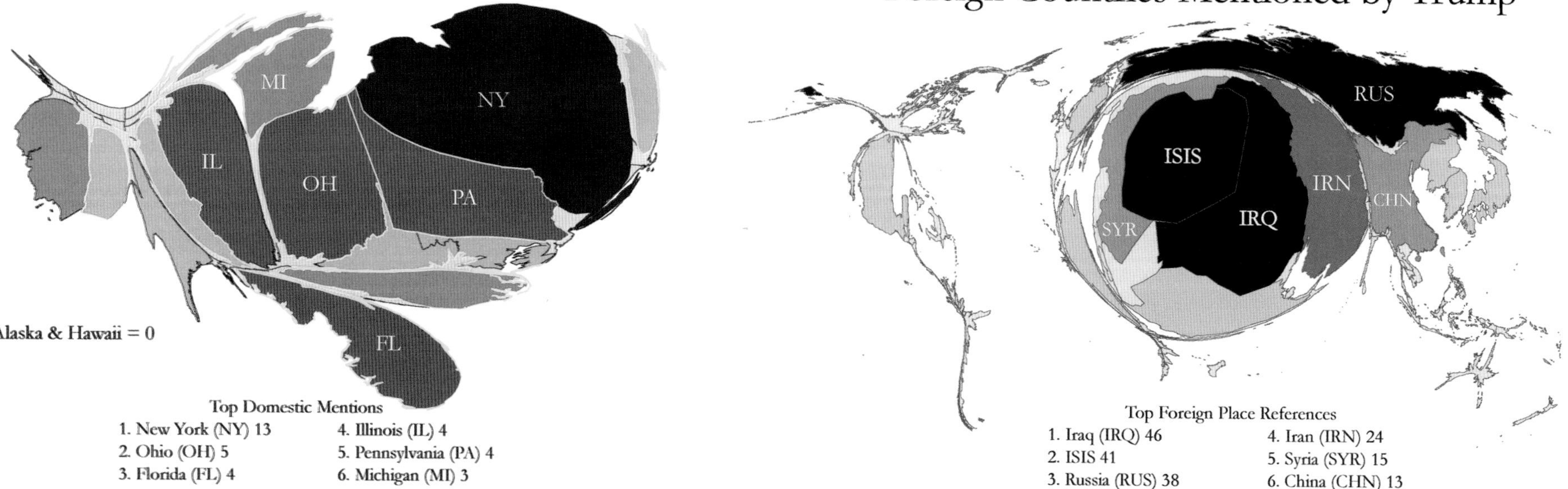

As noted in table 3.1, candidates may emphasize discussions of swing states in order to connect with strategically important constituencies. The 2016 election included sixteen swing states. Excluding the candidates' home state of New York, this amounted to 34 percent of the lower forty-eight qualifying as swing states (16/47 = 34 percent). If candidate references to swing states exceeded 34 percent of all state references, it may reflect strategic intent. Notably, both candidates exceeded the 34 percent mark in all but one of the debates. The reference proportions suggest similarities between the candidates' debate behavior. On the other hand, numeric counts reflect a lack of domestic references from Clinton, and an abundant and diverse number from Trump. Clinton referenced six swing states, of which only Nevada was referenced multiple times. Trump mentioned eight swing states and made multiple references to five of them (see table 3.2). Trump's abundance of swing states references is possibly associated with his penchant for salesmanship tactics. For example, marketing efforts utilize targeting, word repetition, and vague exposition, which are better suited for cultivating brand recognition than substantive discussion (Grunwald 2017).

Unsurprisingly, both candidates mentioned their home state of New York the most. More surprising was Clinton's lack of emphasis on important constituencies of the Upper Midwest and Rust Belt regions. Failing to highlight areas that have been impacted by deindustrialization may have hurt her campaign. Trump referenced Ohio, Michigan, and Pennsylvania twelve times while Clinton failed to reference them at all. These states have reeled from declines in manufacturing jobs and are arguably symbolically important to voters disenchanted with the globalizing economy.

TABLE 3.2. Top Domestic References for Trump and Clinton in the Debates

Trump's Top Domestic References	Clinton's Top Domestic References
New York–13	New York–9
Ohio–5	Nevada–3
Pennsylvania–4	Arkansas–2
Illinois–4	Indiana–2
Florida–4	Arizona–1
Michigan–3	Texas–1
North Carolina–2	Iowa–1
California–2	Wisconsin–1
Maryland–1	Florida–1
Missouri–1	Minnesota–1
Texas–1	
Arizona–1	
West Virginia–1	
New Hampshire–1	

Source: Calculated by authors.

Note: Only specific references at or below the state level were included in the analysis. References to Washington, DC, were excluded from the analysis.

Each candidate's most-referenced foreign countries suggest similar foreign policy concerns. Russia, Syria, and Iraq were among the candidates' five most-referenced foreign states (see figure 3.7 and table 3.3). The Islamic State of Iraq and Syria (ISIS), a terrorist group that has claimed de facto territorial sovereignty in the wake of the Syrian Civil War, was also among the candidates' top five referenced countries.

TABLE 3.3. Top Foreign References for Trump and Clinton in the 2016 Presidential Debates

Trump's Top Foreign References	Clinton's Top Foreign References
Iraq–46	Russia–30
ISIS–41	Syria–28
Russia–38	Iraq–27
Iran–24	ISIS–19
Syria–15	China–14
China–13	Iran–14
Mexico–9	Mexico–8
Japan–8	Haiti–6
Saudi Arabia–7	Japan–3
North Korea–5	Saudi Arabia–2
Libya–5	South Korea–2
South Korea–4	Afghanistan–1
Germany–3	Ethiopia–1
Haiti–2	Korea–1
Canada–1	Libya–1
France–1	
Vietnam–1	
Qatar–1	

Source: Calculated by authors.

Note: Only specific references at or below the national level were included in the analysis. References to regions and regional organizations were excluded from the analysis.

The ratio between foreign and domestic references can indicate candidate emphasis toward one of the two geographic domains, with a value of 1.0 indicating proportional balance (see table 3.4). Given Clinton's experience as secretary of state,

TABLE 3.4. Ratio of Foreign and Domestic References in the 2016 Presidential Debates

	Clinton			Trump		
	Foreign	Domestic	F/D	Foreign	Domestic	F/D
Debate 1	57	33	1.73	80	37	2.16
Debate 2	54	35	1.54	81	42	1.93
Debate 3	79	56	1.41	104	56	1.86
Totals	190	124	1.53	265	135	1.96

Source: Calculated by authors.

it was unsurprising foreign terms accounted for a higher proportion of her geographic references. More interesting was Trump's even greater emphasis on foreign places despite having no diplomatic experience. Accounting for this disparity requires a multifaceted explanation. First, even though Clinton's foreign/domestic place name ratio was comparable with previous experienced candidates, Trump's ratio may have been higher because his campaign perceived Clinton's time at the State Department as a weakness. Indeed, Clinton was plagued by the multiple Republican-led investigations into her time at State, including charges of security failings leading up to the 2012 Benghazi attacks and negligent use of a private e-mail server. Negative perceptions may also have prevented her from highlighting her foreign policy experience at the State Department.

Second, Clinton emerged as the Democratic nominee from a hard-fought primary against Vermont Senator Bernie Sanders, who focused on domestic economic concerns. Arguably, had Clinton run unopposed, there would have been little need to shore up doubts over economic issues among working-class Democrats during the general election. The Trump campaign highlighted Clinton's connection with transnational economic partnerships, which were portrayed as harmful to middle-class workers. During the debates Trump and Clinton referenced trade agreements nine and two times, respectively. This may also explain Clinton's unwillingness to reference the Upper Midwest and Rust Belt regions, a critical mistake as Ohio, Pennsylvania, Wisconsin, and Michigan ultimately swung the electoral vote total in Trump's favor.

REFERENCES

Balentine, Matthew, and Gerald R. Webster. Forthcoming. Place Names as a Form of Strategic Political Communication: An Analysis of Geographic Language Used in US Presidential Debates from 1976–2012. In S. Brunn, ed., *Changing World Language Map*. Springer.

Grunwald, Michael. 2017. Salesman-in-Chief. *Politico*. March 1, http://politi.co/2lcbLH0 (last accessed June 15, 2017).

Rappeport, Alan, and Alexander Burns. 2016. Donald Trump Says He Will Accept Election Outcome ("if I Win"). *The New York Times*. 20 October, https://www.nytimes.com/2016/10/21/us/politics/campaign-election-trump-clinton.html (last accessed June 12, 2017).

Sutherland, Cynthia L., and Gerald R. Webster. 1994. The Geography of the 1992 US Presidential Debates. *The Geographical Bulletin* 36(2): 83–93.

VOTE FRAUD OR VOTE SUPPRESSION: THE DEBATE BEFORE AND AFTER THE 2016 ELECTION

RICHARD L. ENGSTROM

For a little over a decade, Republicans have asserted that elections in the United States are infected with massive voter fraud and have advocated new election laws that will allegedly minimize, if not eradicate, the problem. Front and center among their remedy proposals for the alleged problem are new voter identification requirements, the strictest of which require people to show government-issued identification cards with their pictures on them to vote. Only photo ID cards from specified government sources satisfy the requirement, while other government-issued photo ID cards do not count. People who fail to show one of the required cards at the polls may, under these laws, cast provisional ballots while at the polls, but have to take additional steps later, at another location, to verify who they are before their provisional ballot will be counted.

Democrats respond that the widespread voter fraud alleged by Republicans does not in fact exist. They point to the absence of credible evidence of such fraud, and refer to the Republicans' so-called remedies for it as solutions in search of a problem. This is especially the case with strict photo ID requirements that are designed to stop voter impersonation at the polls, which has been "exceedingly rare" in contemporary elections (Waldman 2016). Democrats maintain that the purpose of these laws is not to prevent fraud, but rather to impede certain types of people from voting, such as members of minority groups, especially African Americans and Latinos, and poor people and young people, especially college students. All of these groups are known to vote disproportionately for Democratic candidates. These people are less likely than others to possess the required photo ID cards and less likely than others to have the means, in terms of time, money, and transportation, to acquire them. These battles play out primarily at the state level of government, where most election-related laws are adopted. It is well documented that strict photo ID laws, as well as others that selectively restrict people's access to the ballot, are adopted in states under the political control of the Republican Party, in terms of members of that party constituting majorities in both chambers of the state legislature and holding the governor's office. Indeed, all twelve of the states that adopted strict photo identification laws since 2005 have been states under Republican Party control (Biggers and Hanmer 2017; Highton 2017).

This was the situation in North Carolina when the state adopted its Voter Information Verification Act in 2013 (VIVA). The Republican-controlled legislature passed it on strict party line votes, and the state's Republican governor signed it. It contained a new strict photo identification requirement and more. The additional provisions had nothing to do with voter verification, but were intended to impede African Americans from voting.

Five provisions of that law were challenged in federal court. The case, *North Carolina State Conference of the NAACP v. McCrory*, was decided in July 2016, before the presidential election, by a three-judge panel of the Fourth Circuit Court of Appeals. The panel voted unanimously to invalidate each of the provisions for violating the United States Constitution and the federal Voting Rights Act (see 831 F.3d 204). One was the state's new strict photo ID provision. The state, according to the court, had "failed to identify even a single individual who has *ever* been charged with committing in-person voter fraud in North Carolina" (at 235, emphasis added). Yet the state not only felt the need to require photo ID to vote at the polls, it required it to be types that African Americans were less likely to possess than white people, such as a driver's license (at 216). Apparently the state had no concern about voter impersonation when it came to absentee voting, which the evidence showed whites engaged in disproportionately more than African Americans (at 230). The state did not make the photo ID provision applicable to absentee voters.

In addition, the state reduced the number of days that people may vote early, before Election Day itself. The evidence showed that African Americans were about fifteen percentage points more likely to vote early than whites in recent presidential elections, and were especially more likely to do so during the first week of the early voting period (at 216). In VIVA, the state chose to eliminate the first week of early voting. In so doing, it reduced the number of Sundays in which early voting could occur from two to one. Sunday was

FIGURE 3.8

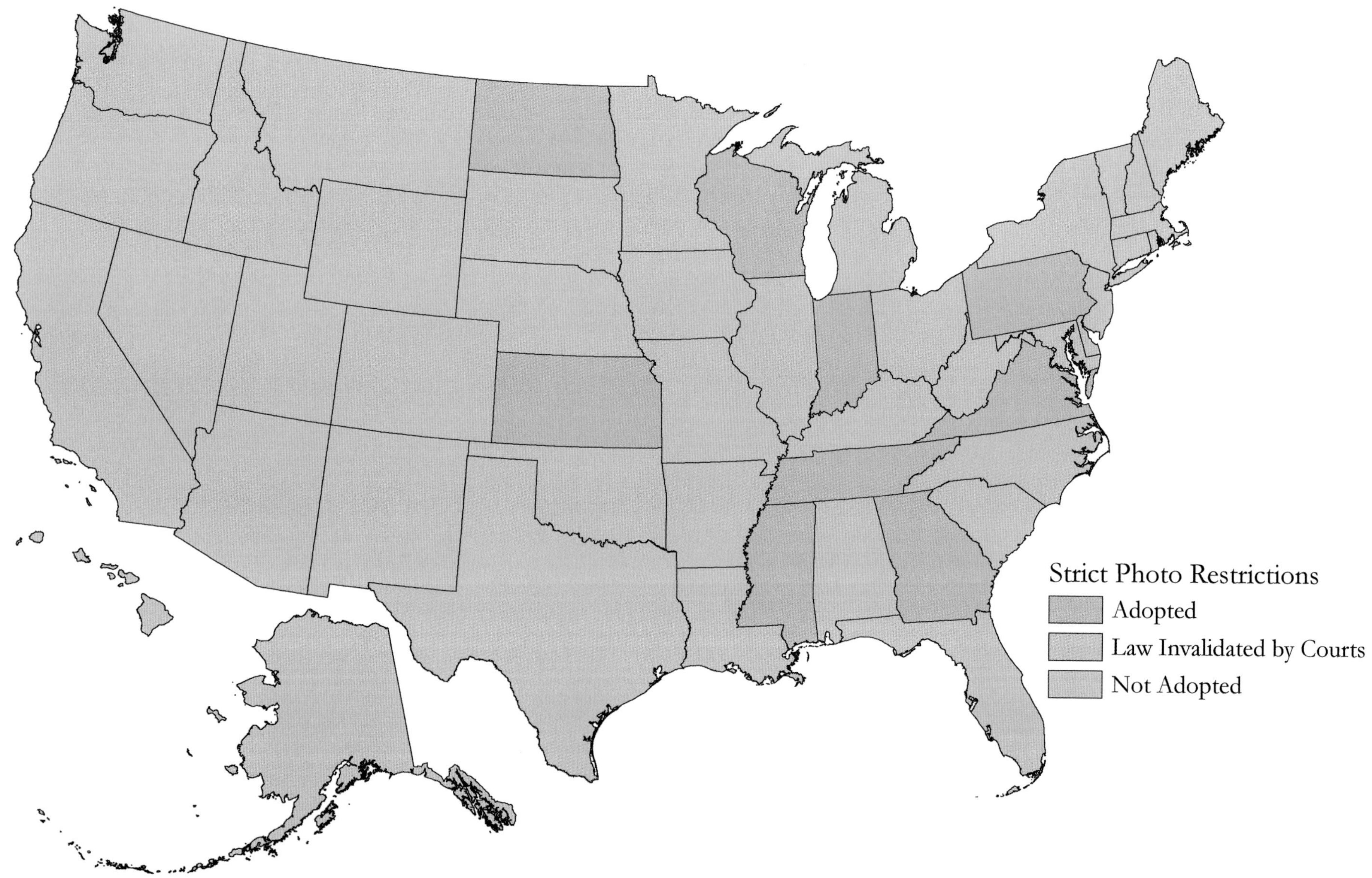
Strict Photo Identification Requirements
Strict Photo Restrictions
Adopted
Law Invalidated by Courts
Not Adopted

a day when many African American churches provided their members with transportation, after the services, to early-voting sites, a voter mobilization practice known as "Souls to the polls" (at 217).

Three other features of voting in North Carolina that African Americans had used disproportionately in past elections were eliminated completely in the VIVA. One was same-day registration, in which people could both register to vote and then cast their ballots the same day at an early-voting site (217). Another was "out-of-precinct voting," in which a registered voter who went to the wrong precinct in his or her county to cast their vote was allowed to cast a provisional ballot in that precinct, which the county Board of Elections was directed to count in their proper precinct (at 217). The third feature eliminated the preregistration of sixteen- and seventeen-year-olds who indicated their intention to vote during registration drives held at their high school, or while obtaining driver's licenses. When they turned eighteen, they would be automatically registered to vote by their county Board of Election after their eligibility was verified (at 217). The three-judge panel, not surprisingly, found the legislature had employed "almost surgical precision" in crafting a law designed to impede African American voting (at 214). The parts of the law invalidated were found, by the court, to be the product of intentional racial discrimination. The United States Supreme Court, in 2017, declined to review the panel's decision.

Following the 2016 presidential election, President Trump stoked debate further. He claimed that three million to five million people voted illegally in that election, and that each of them voted for Hillary Clinton. If not for this fraudulent voting, he claimed, he would have won the popular vote rather than Clinton, in addition to his decisive Electoral College vote. Trump has yet to offer any credible evidence for this assertion. Clinton, in response, has asserted that she lost the Electoral College vote because of voter suppression in Michigan, Pennsylvania, and Wisconsin, states in which she lost to Trump by less than a single percentage point. Wins in those states, the latter two with strict photo ID laws, would have given her a majority of the Electoral College vote. Her claim of vote suppression, while more plausible than Trump's of voter fraud, also needs evidentiary support.

Trump's claim is the basis for his creation, through an executive order (EO), of a Presidential Advisory Commission on Election Integrity in May 2017. The purpose of the order, he states, is "to promote fair and honest elections." But judging from the text of the EO, the president's concern for fair and honest elections is limited to eradicating voter fraud. While the commission is explicitly tasked by the president to study fraudulent voter registration and fraudulent voting, there is no mention whatsoever in the EO of eradicating vote suppression. In conclusion, the Fourth Circuit panel of judges in the North Carolina case made it crystal clear, "intentionally targeting a particular race's access to the franchise because its members vote for a particular party, in a predictable manner, constitutes discriminatory purpose" (at 222), and is therefore unconstitutional.

REFERENCES

Biggers, Daniel R., and Michael J. Hanmer. 2017. Understanding the Adoption of Voter Identification Laws in the American States. *American Politics Research* 45:4.

Highton, Benjamin. 2017. Voter Identification Laws and Turnout in the United States. *Annual Review of Political Science* 20:149–67.

North Carolina State Conference of the NAACP v. McCrory, 831 F.3d 204 (4th Cir. 2016).

Voting Rights Act of 1965 (PL 89–110, August 6, 1965), 79 United States Statutes at Large, 437–446. http://www.gpo.gov/fdsys/pkg/STATUTE-79/pdf/STATUTE-79-Pg437.pdf (last accessed May 22, 2017).

Waldman, Michael. 2016. *The Fight to Vote*. New York: Simon and Schuster.

NEWSPAPER ENDORSEMENTS OF PRESIDENTIAL CANDIDATES IN THE 2016 ELECTION

LINDY WESTENHOFF AND GERALD R. WEBSTER

Newspaper endorsements of presidential candidates have historically served to both direct and reflect public opinion. As a result, in previous election years the candidate receiving the largest number of newspaper endorsements commonly won the presidential election. In 1980, for example, Ronald Reagan received 50 percent more newspaper endorsements than incumbent Democrat Jimmy Carter and easily won the election. Further, the candidate winning the most newspaper endorsements in seven out of the ten most recent presidential elections won the Electoral College, and the candidate with the largest number of newspaper endorsements won the popular vote in nine out of the last ten elections. The one case not fitting the popular vote pattern was Democrat John Kerry. He had a substantially larger number of newspaper endorsements in 2004, but lost both the Electoral College and the popular vote to incumbent Republican president George W. Bush.

FIGURE 3.9

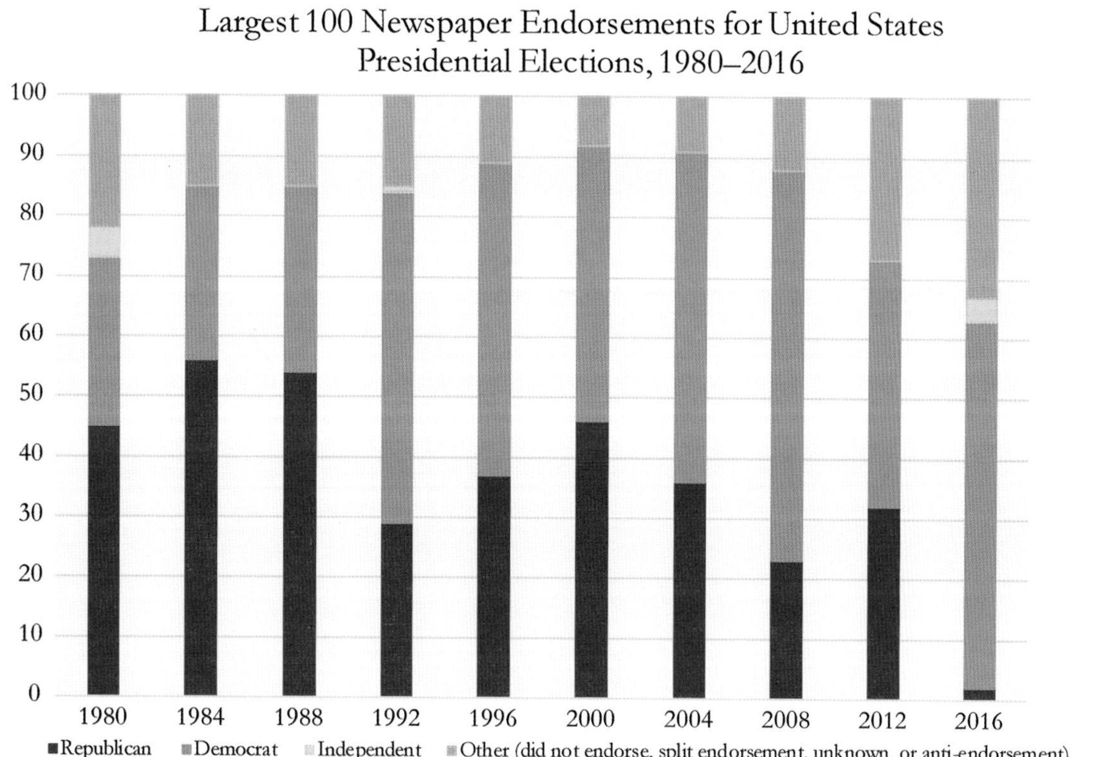

Some newspapers consistently endorse only the Republican or Democratic candidate for president. The *New York Times*, for example, has never endorsed a Republican, while the *Las Vegas Review-Journal* has never endorsed a Democrat. Other newspapers have variable records of endorsing candidates of either party, or of not endorsing any candidate. While historically rare, there are a few newspapers that have endorsed independent candidates in the past, likely reflecting dissatisfaction with the nominees of the two major parties. Thus, some newspapers endorsed independents John Anderson in 1980, Ross Perot in 1992, and Gary Johnson in 2016.

There are no national schedules or traditions for when newspapers make their endorsements. The *New York Daily News*, for example, endorsed Democrat Hillary Clinton in late July 2016, the day the DNC ended. In contrast, twenty-one newspapers did not make their endorsements until November 6, just two days prior to the election. Among these endorsements were seven for Republican Donald Trump, five for Hillary Clinton, two for Libertarian Gary Johnson, and two anti-Trump endorsements, with the remaining five newspapers announcing they were not going to make any endorsement. Given the growth in early voting

FIGURE 3.10

Daily Newspaper Endorsements: Trump, Johnson, McMullin, and Non-Endorsements, July to November 2016

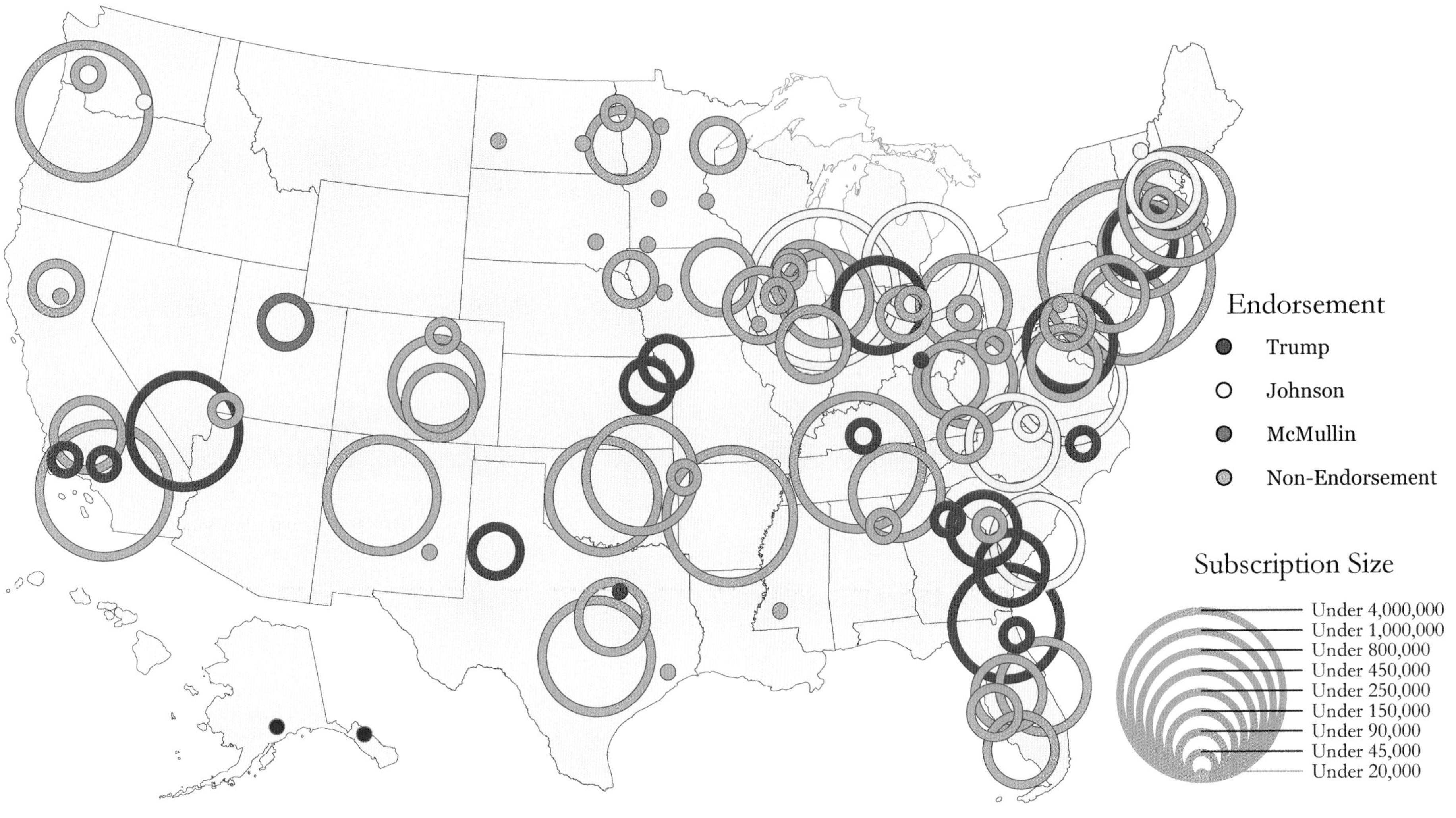

FIGURE 3.11

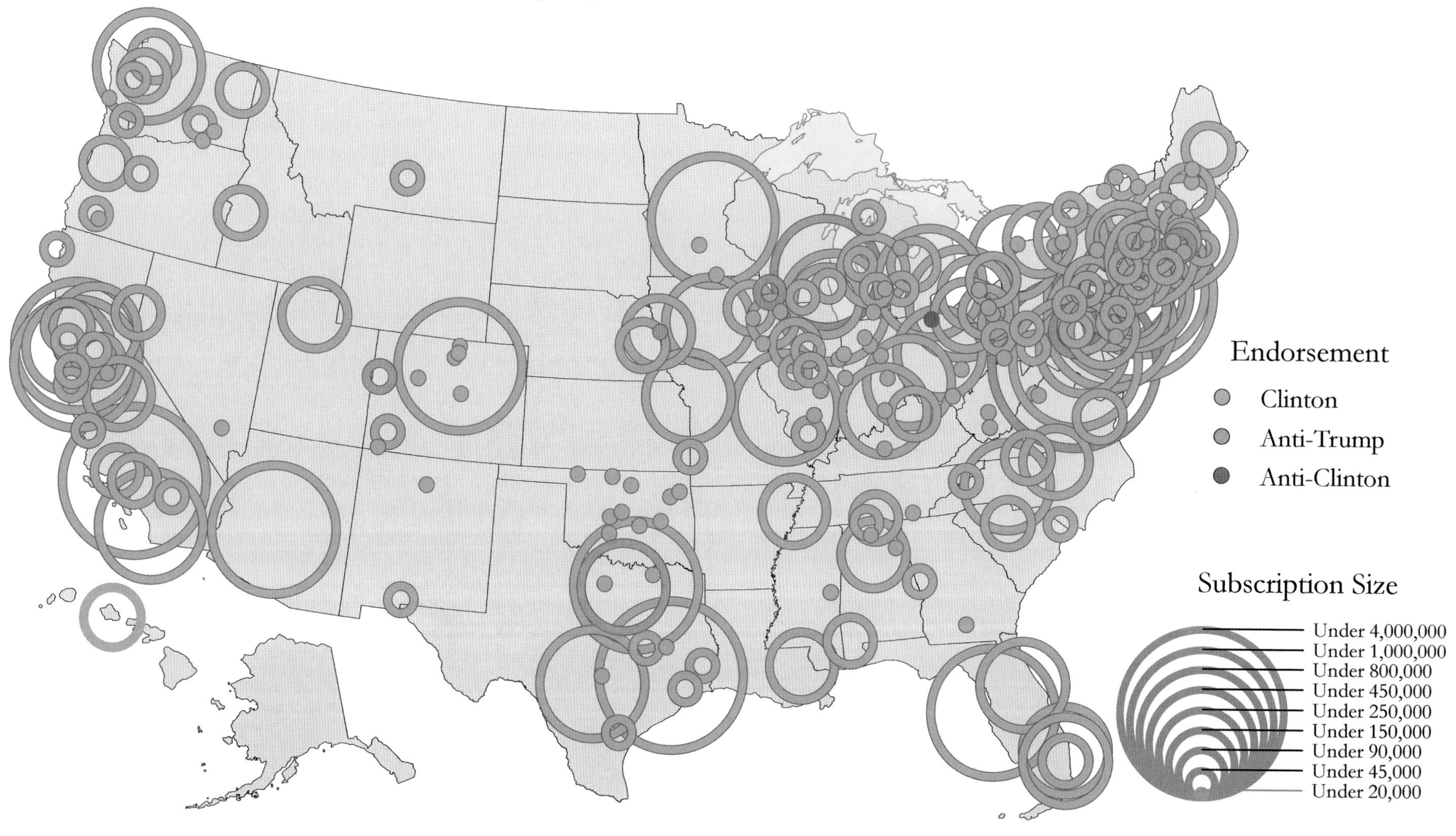

Daily Newspaper Endorsements: Clinton, Anti-Trump, and Anti-Clinton
July to November 2016
Endorsement
Clinton
Anti-Trump
Anti-Clinton
Subscription Size
Under 4,000,000
Under 1,000,000
Under 800,000
Under 450,000
Under 250,000
Under 150,000
Under 90,000
Under 45,000
Under 20,000

around the United States, the potential effect of newspapers making endorsements just prior to the election is demonstrably quite limited.

During the 2016 United States presidential election campaign, 241 newspapers endorsed Hillary Clinton, 20 newspapers endorsed Donald Trump, 9 newspapers endorsed Gary Johnson, and 1 newspaper, the *Daily Herald* in Utah, endorsed independent candidate Evan McMullin. Notably, the number of newspapers endorsing Trump was by far the lowest number for a major party candidate in recent history, providing Clinton a landslide of endorsements.

Of the twenty newspapers that endorsed Donald Trump, eleven waited until the fifth and sixth of November to make their endorsements. Of these newspapers, only the *Florida Times-Union* and the *Las Vegas Review-Journal* have circulations above 100,000. Even with the inclusion of the two largest papers, the average circulation of the twenty newspapers endorsing Trump was under 37,000, indicating limited public reach. Further, there is no clear regionalism in the locations of the papers endorsing Trump. Two of the twenty newspapers are located in Florida and three are based in Georgia, for example, but two are in Alaska, and the largest is in Nevada. Interestingly, the newspapers that waited until the final hours to endorse are largely concentrated in the Southeast, including papers in Georgia, Texas, and Kentucky.

All of the newspapers endorsing Donald Trump had previously endorsed the 2012 Republican nominee, Mitt Romney. In contrast, not all of the newspapers endorsing Hillary Clinton were traditionally Democratic-leaning newspapers that had endorsed President Barack Obama in 2008 and 2012. The editorial board of the *Houston Chronicle*, the largest newspaper in terms of circulation that endorsed Romney in 2012, stated that Trump was "totally lacking in qualifications to be president" and "a danger to the Republic" and endorsed Hillary Clinton (Editorial Board, *Houston Chronicle* 2016). Similarly, the editorial board of the *Dallas Morning News* also endorsed Hillary Clinton, stating that she was the "one serious candidate on the presidential ballot." Significantly, this was the first time since World War II that the *Dallas Morning News* endorsed a Democratic candidate for president (Editorial Board, *Dallas Morning News* 2016).

The *Chicago Tribune*, one of the few newspapers to endorse Gary Johnson, had previously endorsed Barack Obama in 2012. The editorial board selected Johnson not for any better or demonstrated qualities, but because Trump "has neither the character nor the prudent disposition" and Clinton had "[raised] serious questions about honesty and trust" (Editorial Board, *Chicago Tribune* 2016). Several other papers indicated similar attitudes—choosing Johnson not because he was *better*, but because he provided an alternative to endorsing Clinton or Trump.

A study by Ansolabehere, Lessem, and Snyder (2006) found that since 1940 newspapers have shifted from a strongly Republican stance in their endorsements to a more even distribution of endorsements between the Republican and Democratic Party nominees. The study also found, perhaps more importantly, that newspapers tend to favor incumbents in their endorsements. If one classifies Clinton as a pseudo-incumbent due to her close ties to President Obama, we would expect her to have more endorsements than Trump, though her much greater number of endorsements is clearly unprecedented in recent history and does not indicate an even distribution. Only 6 percent of all newspaper endorsements were for Trump, with 69 percent for Clinton and 2 percent for Johnson. The disparity in endorsements between Clinton and Trump might have less to do with partisanship and more to do with Trump's combative relationship with the media; even before his inauguration he repeatedly labeled news agencies critical of him as "fake news" via his Twitter account (Trump 2016/2017).

An interesting side note to this election was the rejection of traditional endorsements in favor of what might be termed "anti-endorsements." These did not endorse Clinton or Trump, but advocated "anyone but him/her." Eight newspapers anti-endorsed Trump. *USA Today*, which had not endorsed any presidential candidate in its history, broke with that tradition and stated that the Republican candidate "has demonstrated repeatedly that he lacks the temperament, knowledge, steadiness and honesty that America needs from its presidents" (Editorial Board, *USA Today* 2016). One newspaper in Ohio additionally anti-endorsed Clinton, citing her promises to "accelerate the government's assault on" coal mining and Second Amendment rights (Editorial Board, *Tiffin Advertiser-Tribune* 2016).

REFERENCES

Ansolabehere, Stephen, Rebecca Lessem, and James M. Snyder. 2006. The Orientation of Newspaper Endorsements in US Elections, 1940–2002. *Quarterly Journal of Political Science* 1(4): 393–404.

Editorial Board, *Chicago Tribune*. 2016. A Principled Option for US President: Endorsing Gary Johnson, Libertarian. September 30, http://www.chicagotribune.com/news/opinion/editorials/

ct-gary-johnson-president-endorsement-edit-1002-20160930-story.html (last accessed May 19, 2017).

Editorial Board, *Dallas Morning News*. 2016. We Recommend Hillary Clinton for President. September 7, http://www.dallasnews.com/opinion/editorials/2016/09/07/recommend-hillary-clinton-us-president (last accessed May 19, 2017).

Editorial Board, *Houston Chronicle*. 2016. These Are Unsettling Times That Require a Steady Hand: That's Hillary Clinton. November 3, http://www.chron.com/opinion/recommendations/article/For-Hillary-Clinton-8650345.php (last accessed May 19, 2017).

Editorial Board, *Tiffin Advertiser-Tribune*. 2016. Eager for Change? Don't Vote for Clinton. October 23, http://www.advertiser-tribune.com/opinions/editorials/2016/10/eager-for-change-dont-vote-for-clinton (last accessed May 19, 2017).

Trump, Donald J. 2016/2017. Twitter account @realDonaldTrump. Archived. December 10, 2016; January 10, 2017; January 11, 2017; January 28, 2017; February 4, 2017; February 6, 2017; February 12, 2017; February 15, 2017; February 16, 2017 (last accessed February 17, 2017).

Editorial Board, *USA Today*. 2016. USA TODAY's Editorial Board: Trump Is "Unfit for the Presidency." September 29, http://www.usatoday.com/story/opinion/2016/09/29/dont-vote-for-donald-trump-editorial-board-editorials-debates/91295020 (last accessed May 19, 2017).

Veltman, Noah. 2017. Newspaper Presidential Endorsements, 1980—Present. GitHub, http://noahveltman.com/endorsements (last accessed May 19, 2017).

MISOGYNY, TWITTER, AND THE RURAL VOTER

MONICA STEPHENS, LI TONG, SCOTT HALE, AND MARK GRAHAM

The 2016 US presidential election was the first election with a female candidate as a major contender for one of the two main political parties. Gender attitudes played a substantial role in the campaign as Hillary Clinton was both celebrated and reviled for her gender. Donald Trump was critiqued for his regressive remarks toward and about women. At the same time both candidates used social media to attract and connect with constituents. Donald Trump regularly received substantial press coverage for controversial statements made on Twitter and controversial statements made toward women. This essay examines the role of Twitter, misogyny, and the rural voter in the 2016 presidential election.

In Andi Zeisler's (2016) *New York Times* essay, she highlights how "bitch" was used as "both an epithet and an honorific for Mrs. Clinton." As much as this derogatory term has been used to silence women, it was also partially reclaimed by the Clinton campaign as her supporters implied that "Bitches get stuff done" (Zeisler 2016; Horowitz 2016). Donald Trump supporters also applied the term to Hillary Clinton as they purchased merchandise and tweeted phrases like "Trump That Bitch," "Lock the bitch up," "take the bitch down," "devilbitch," and simply "bitch" (Bellstrom 2016; Rozsa 2016; Horowitz 2016). The official Trump campaign never overtly tweeted these phrases or produced any of the alt-right memes targeting the Clinton campaign. However, Trump did harness the language and the ideologies of the Internet subgroups creating this misogynistic content.

Trump's surprising wins in states like Pennsylvania, Michigan, and Wisconsin were in part a result of the Trump campaign's strategy to target particular rural electoral areas to swing states away from Clinton. Since 2008, rural voters have increased their support for Republican candidates, and in 2016 the more rural the county, the stronger the support for Trump (Kurtzleben 2016). As Cramer (2016) explains, rural voters resent the attention and resources paid to cities as rural areas fall behind socially and economically.

In social media, a similar rural/urban divide exists. Hecht and Stephens (2014) determined that even when normalized, Twitter, Flickr, and Foursquare are biased toward urban perspectives. Cities have more social media users, more posts, and more relevant information than rural counterparts. Hecht and Stephens argue that this is in part because the social structure of these networks does not appeal to rural populations. Nevertheless, there are substantially more tweets per capita in urban areas than in rural areas, as content on Twitter is not evenly distributed (Graham, Stephens, and Hale 2013). Many of the maps made by the FloatingSheep collective to identify patterns of Twitter usage have identified cultural practices or perceptions as "maps of the digital world are a reflection of the material world" (Zook 2015). The presidential election was no different.

In 2016, Twitter was a part of constructing and reproducing the misogynistic rhetoric of the presidential election. Figure 3.12 identifies tweets for the phrase "bitch" that were geotagged in the United States in 2016. Geotagged tweets represent a small sample of all tweets where the user has opted for their device to capture their location. The data for this map were harvested from the Twitter API onto servers in real time (throughout 2016), indexed by the archive at Oxford Internet Institute, and supplemented with DOLLY, the Twitter aggregator from the University of Kentucky. In order to capture the tweets, we used the Twitter API with a 180 x 360 bounding box (covering the whole planet) to collect a subset of tweets with geolocation information (Graham, Hale, and Gaffney 2014). We then filtered the data to find all tweets containing the word "bitch" (case insensitive). We experienced rate limiting and people who geolocate their tweets are known to differ from the general Twitter population (Hecht and Stephens 2014; Stephens and Poorthuis 2015), so we cannot say these data are fully representative of Twitter users. After some cleaning, this created a dataset of 2.2 million geotagged tweets in the United States containing the word "bitch."

Tweets for "bitch" do not primarily reference Hillary Clinton. We did not conduct a sentiment analysis on the target of this term, as algorithmic sentiment analysis frequently miscategorizes hateful terms and sarcasm. However, we did track a general pattern of misogynistic speech in the

FIGURE 3.12

Misogynist Tweets during the 2016 Presidential Election

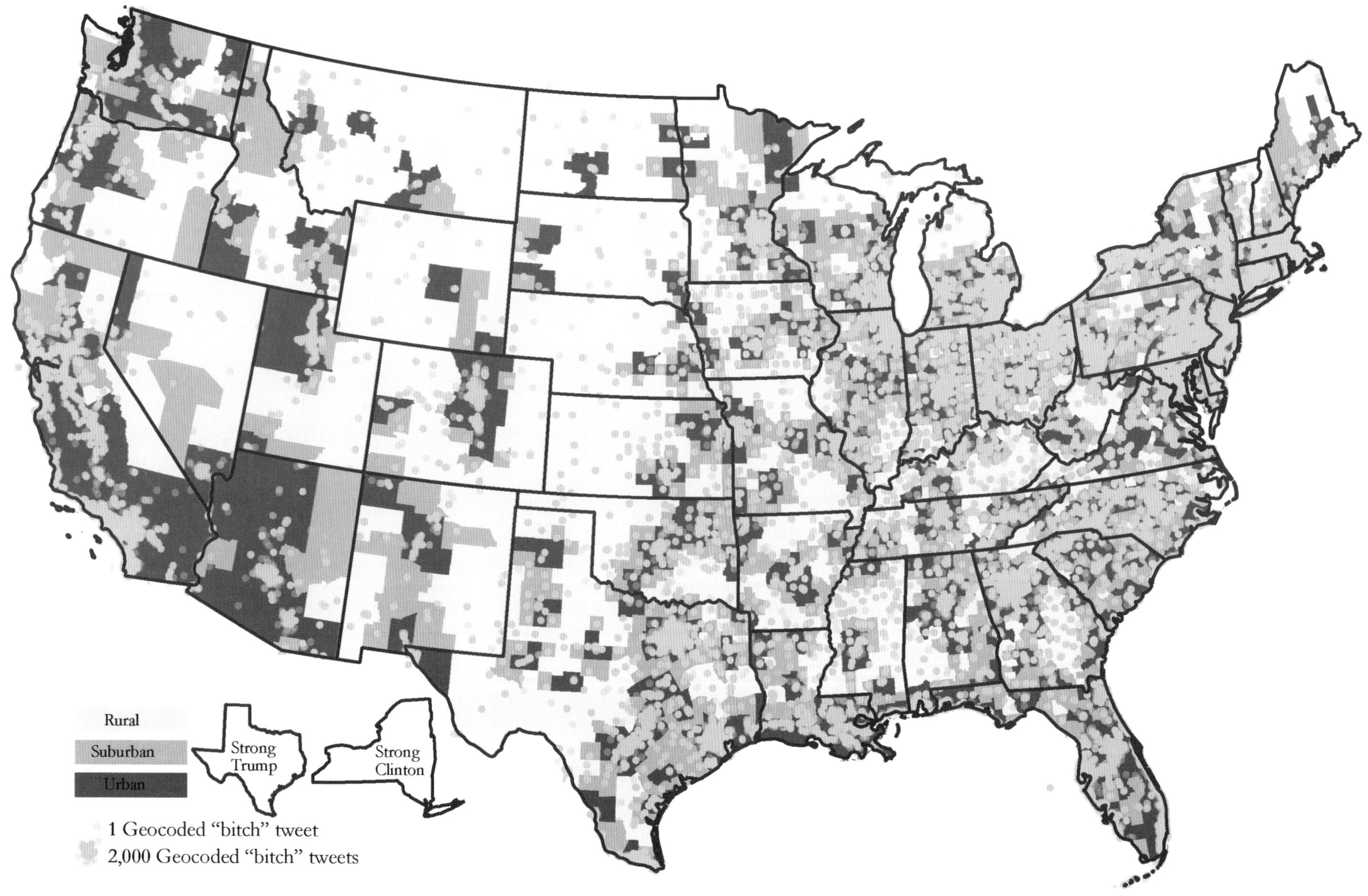

United States. We divided the counties based on their rural-urban continuum code (United States Department of Agriculture 2013), and grouped counties based on "metropolitan," "adjacent to a metro area" (e.g., suburban) or "rural." Within these categories we used a Spearman's rank correlation coefficient as a measure of the association between counties containing a tweet for "bitch" and the percentage of votes cast for Hillary Clinton. In the rural areas and small towns (USDA Rural-Urban Continuum Codes 5, 7, 8, and 9), this returned a correlation coefficient of 0.5, in the suburbs (codes 4 and 6) it was 0.139, and in the metropolitan areas (codes 1, 2, and 3) it was 0.57.

The 2.2 million tweets for the word "bitch" are largely located in urban (dark gray) and suburban (medium gray) areas. Each yellow point represents one geotagged tweet. Individually each tweet has little meaning, but en masse they represent spaces of misogyny. The tweets appear to cluster east of the Mississippi, but this is simply a result of population density. The county with the most "bitch" tweets was Los Angeles County, California. This was followed by Harris County, Texas (Houston), and Cook County, Illinois (Chicago). When normalized per capita, small communities with one or two people tweeting derogatory terms pop out—Concho County, Texas; Wilkinson County, Georgia; and a density spread among the parishes around New Orleans, Louisiana.

Unfortunately, the overwhelming numbers of tweets from urban areas drown out the voices of rural communities. As this map demonstrates, the conversations on Twitter, even potentially misogynistic conversations, maintain a pattern specific to densely populated areas. In an election year fueled by rural resentments and xenophobia, the content of tweets can provide a lens into the daily conversations people have over social media. However, creating meaning from Twitter data requires looking at the sentiment of each tweet and understanding conversation at the scale of the individual.

REFERENCES

Bellstrom, Kristen. 2016. Trump Supporters Are Selling "Trump That Bitch" T-Shirts Featuring Hillary Clinton. *Fortune*, Election 2016: Fortune Magazine. April 25, http://fortune.com/2016/04/25/trump-clinton-misogynistic-merch (last accessed July 8, 2017).

Cramer, Katherine J. 2016. *The Politics of Resentment: Rural Consciousness in Wisconsin and the Rise of Scott Walker*. Chicago: University of Chicago Press.

Graham, Mark, Scott A. Hale, and Devin Gaffney. 2014. Where in the World Are You? Geolocation and Language Identification in Twitter. *The Professional Geographer* 66(4): 568–78.

Graham, Mark, Monica Stephens, and Scott Hale. 2013. Featured Graphic. Mapping the Geoweb: A Geography of Twitter. *Environment and Planning A* 45(1): 100–102.

Hecht, Brent J., and Monica Stephens. 2014. A Tale of Cities: Urban Biases in Volunteered Geographic Information. *ICWSM* 14:197–205.

Horowitz, Nitzan. 2016. What It Means When Hillary Clinton Is Called a "Bitch." *Haaretz*. September 14, http://www.haaretz.com/opinion/.premium-1.741952 (last accessed July 8, 2017).

Kurtzleben, Danielle. 2016. Rural Voters Played a Big Part in Helping Trump Defeat Clinton. *Politics*, NPR. November 14, http://www.npr.org/2016/11/14/501737150/rural-voters-played-a-big-part-in-helping-trump-defeat-clinton (last accessed July 8, 2017).

Rozsa, Matthew. 2016. Ted Nugent: Hillary Clinton is a "Devilbitch" Who "Hates Everything Good about America." *Salon*: Salon.com. October 27, http://www.salon.com/2016/10/27/ted-nugent-hillary-clinton-is-a-devilbitch-who-hates-everything-good-about-america (last accessed July 8, 2017).

Stephens, Monica, and Ate Poorthuis. 2015. Follow Thy Neighbor: Connecting the Social and the Spatial Networks on Twitter. *Computers, Environment and Urban Systems* 53:87–95.

United States Department of Agriculture. 2013. Rural-Urban Continuum Codes, ed. Economic Research Service.

Zeisler, Andi. 2016. The Bitch America Needs. *New York Times*. September 10, https://www.nytimes.com/2016/09/11/opinion/campaign-stops/the-bitch-america-needs.html (last accessed July 8, 2017).

Zook, Matthew, Taylor Shelton, Ate Poorthuis, Rich Donohue, Matthew Wilson, Mark Graham, and Monica Stephens. 2015. What Would a Floating Sheep Map? In *FloatingSheep*. Lexington, KY: Oves Natantes Press.

4 OUTCOMES

RESULTS OF THE 2016 PRESIDENTIAL ELECTION AT THE STATE AND COUNTY LEVELS

FRED M. SHELLEY, JOHN HEPPEN, AND RICHARD L. MORRILL

Although Democratic nominee Hillary Clinton won nearly 2.9 million more popular votes nationwide than her Republican opponent, Donald Trump, Trump won the 2016 presidential election by carrying thirty states containing 306 electoral votes. Hillary Clinton carried the remaining twenty states and the District of Columbia for a total of 232 electoral votes (see figures 4.1 and 4.2). Although Clinton won a majority of the electoral votes of Maine, Maine law grants an electoral vote to the candidate carrying each House of Representatives district, and Trump carried Maine's Second District. Thus, Maine's electoral votes were split, with three going to Clinton and one going to Trump. The actual vote in the Electoral College was 304–227 in favor of Trump because seven electors, two Republicans and five Democrats, refused to vote for their respective parties' nominees and instead voted for other persons.

At the state level, the pattern of popular vote support for Trump and Clinton paralleled patterns of support for Republican and Democratic candidates in recent elections, with Clinton carrying the Northeast and the Pacific Coast states while Trump carried the South, the Great Plains, and the Rocky Mountain states. However, Trump succeeded in 2016 by carrying several states that had given their electoral votes to his predecessor, Barack Obama, in 2012. These states included Florida, Iowa, Michigan, Ohio, Pennsylvania, and Wisconsin. Michigan, Pennsylvania, and Wisconsin were especially crucial to Trump's victory because all three had gone Democratic in the previous six elections and because Trump carried them by narrow margins—10,704 popular votes in Michigan, 44,292 in Pennsylvania, and 22,748 in Wisconsin. Thus, if about 39,000 voters in these states had voted for Clinton instead of Trump, or if an additional 78,000 persons who did not vote had instead voted for Clinton, Clinton would have carried these states and would have won the election. In addition to Michigan, Pennsylvania, and Wisconsin, Trump carried Florida by a margin of less than 2 percent. Thus, had Clinton gotten an additional 1 percent of the vote and Trump had gotten 1 percent fewer votes than he did, Clinton would have won all four of these states.

Although presidential elections are won and lost at the state level in the Electoral College, examination of state-level results obscures the important additional insights that can be gained by examining the results of the election at the county level. Figure 4.3 shows which candidate

FIGURE 4.1

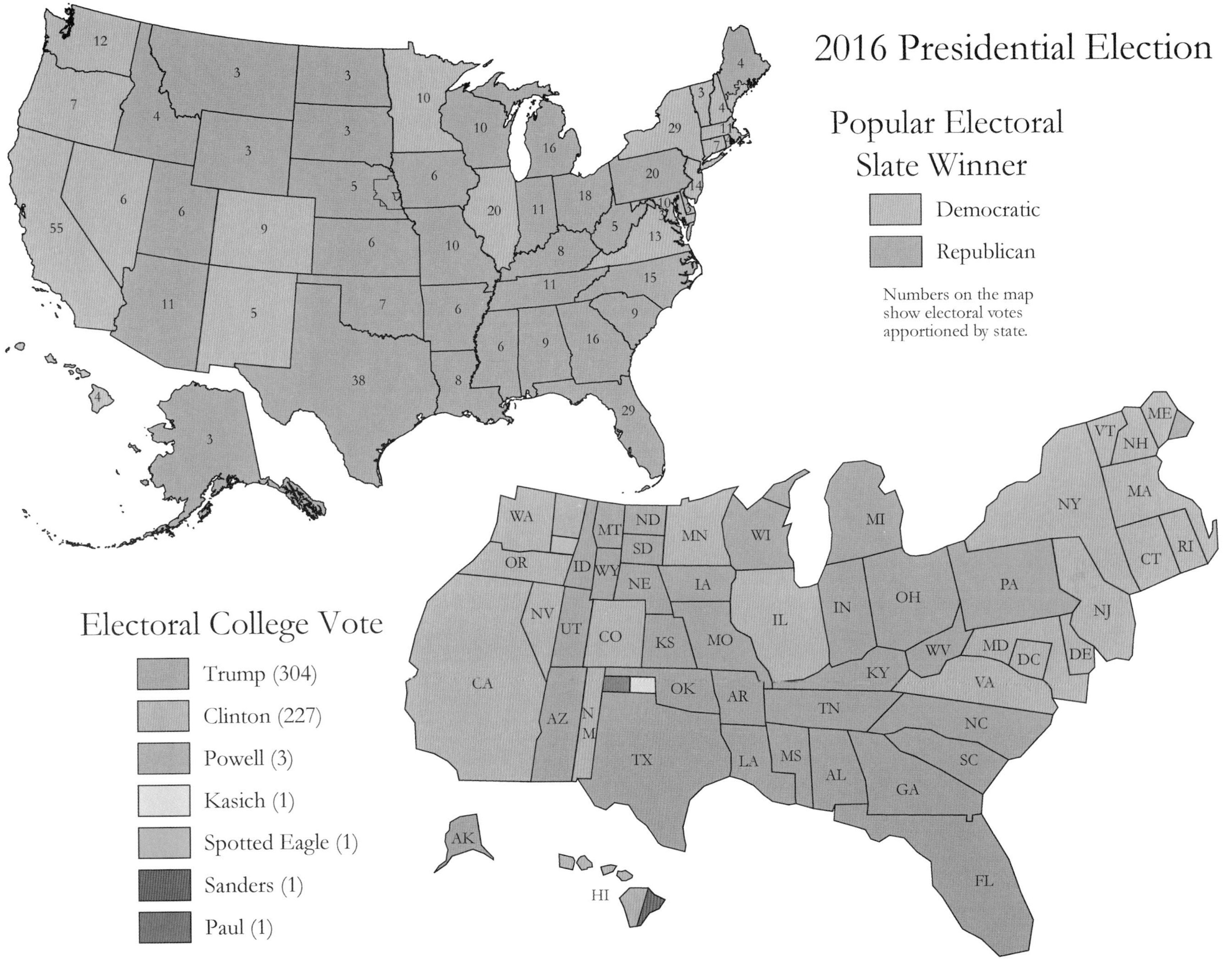
2016 Presidential Election
Popular Electoral Slate Winner
Democratic
Republican
Numbers on the map show electoral votes apportioned by state.
Electoral College Vote
Trump (304)
Clinton (227)
Powell (3)
Kasich (1)
Spotted Eagle (1)
Sanders (1)
Paul (1)

FIGURE 4.2

Percentage of Popular Vote 2016 Presidential Election

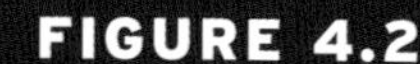

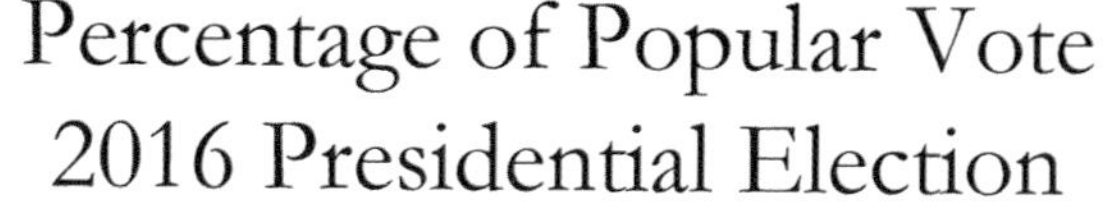

Democratic
Republican
Third Party
Percentage of Total Popular Vote
Democratic
Republican
Under 30
30 to 39
40 to 49
50 to 59
60 or over
Percentage of Popular Vote
1.9 to 2.4
2.5 to 4.9
5.0 to 7.4
7.5 to 9.9
10.0 to 26.9

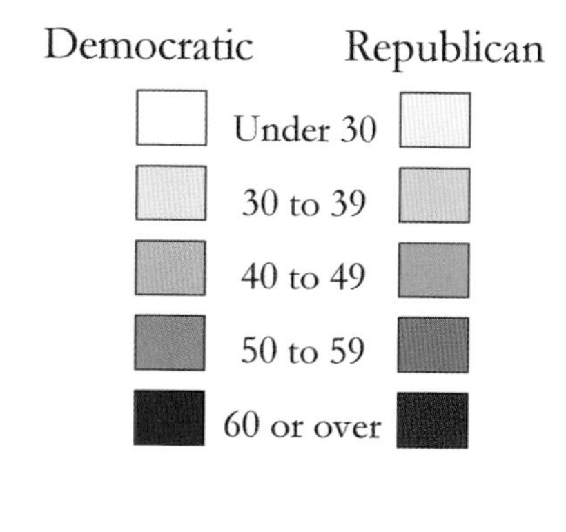

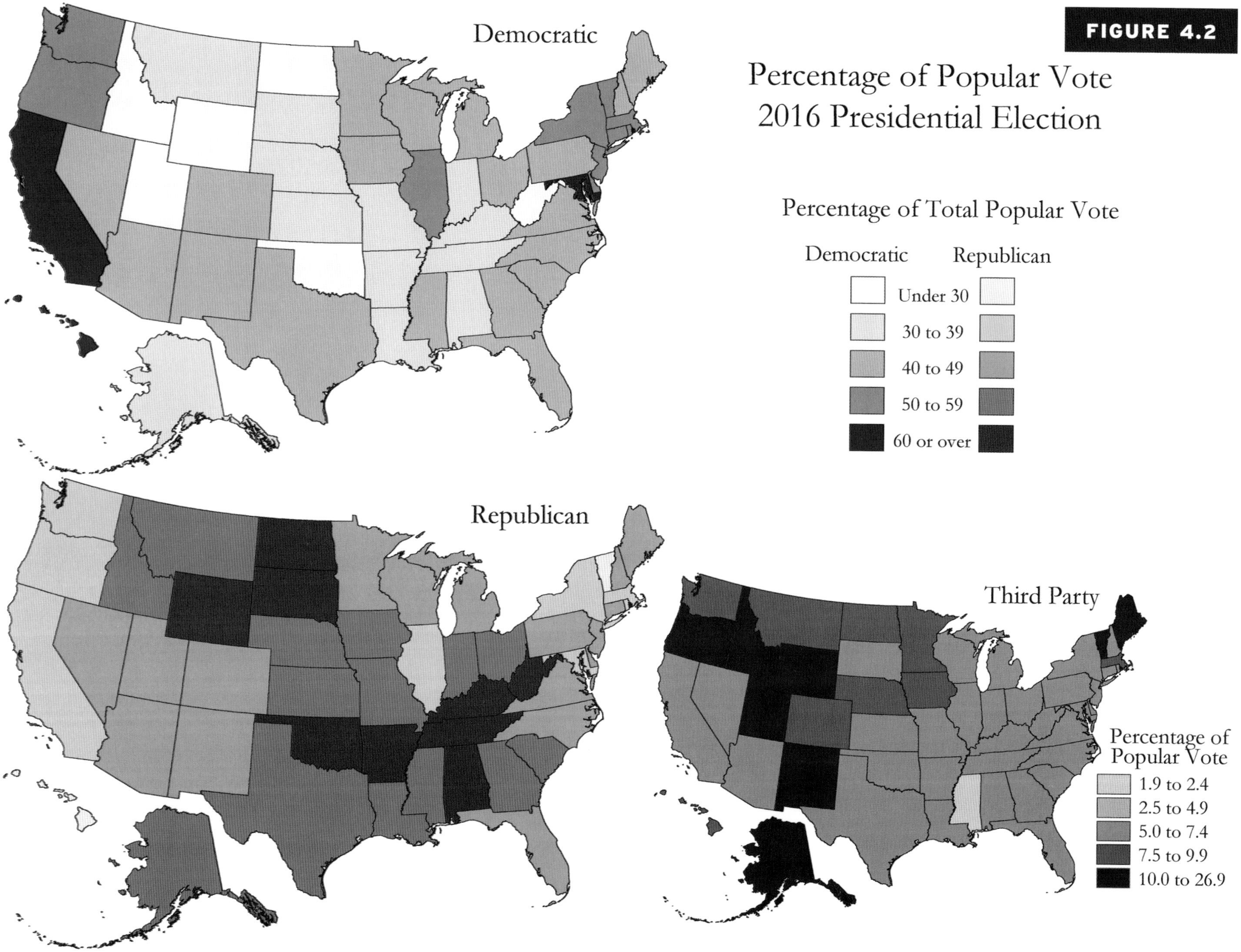

FIGURE 4.3

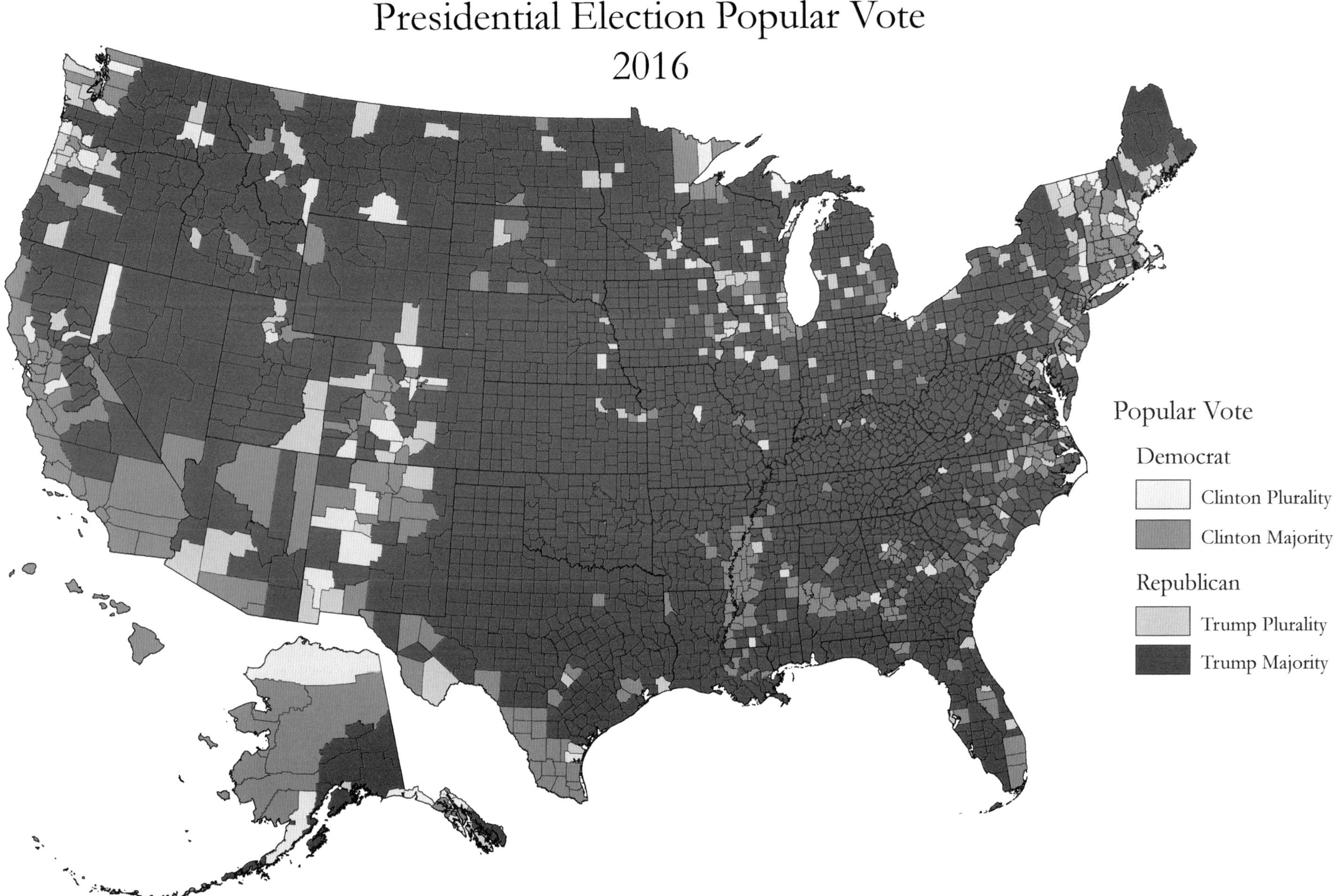
Presidential Election Popular Vote
2016
Popular Vote
Democrat
Clinton Plurality
Clinton Majority
Republican
Trump Plurality
Trump Majority

got the most votes in each county and illustrates the sharp divide between urban and rural places. This gap had been evident in previous elections, but intensified in the 2016 election as rural voters tended to support Trump strongly. However, Clinton did carry many rural counties containing large minority populations. Examples included African American majority counties in the Mississippi Delta, central Alabama, and northeastern North Carolina, heavily Hispanic counties in South Texas, and counties containing American Indian reservations.

Otherwise, Clinton's support was confined largely to metropolitan areas. She won Illinois and Minnesota by carrying the Chicago and Twin Cities metropolitan areas, respectively, while losing most of these states' nonurban counties. She carried Detroit, Philadelphia, and Milwaukee in Michigan, Pennsylvania, and Wisconsin, respectively, but her margins in these cities were outweighed by Trump's margins in less-populated counties. Elsewhere, urban-rural differences are evident, particularly in Texas, where Trump won most counties but lost Harris County (Houston), Dallas County (Dallas), Bexar County (San Antonio), and Travis County (Austin) to Clinton. Similarly, Clinton won Cleveland, Columbus, and Cincinnati but lost most other counties in Ohio, and she won Kansas City and St. Louis but lost most other counties in Missouri.

Nationwide, according to the US Census of 2010, about 80.7 percent of Americans lived in urban areas. Of the eighteen states with less than 70 percent urban residents, fifteen gave their electoral votes to Trump. The only exceptions were the northern New England states of Maine, Vermont, and New Hampshire. On the other hand, of the eighteen states with more than 80 percent urban populations, Clinton carried fourteen while losing only Florida, Utah, Arizona, and Texas. In states that Trump carried, Clinton also did very well in counties containing large college towns such as Clarke County, Georgia (Athens), Douglas County, Kansas (Lawrence), Johnson County, Iowa (Iowa City), and Washtenaw County, Michigan (Ann Arbor). These counties contain the Universities of Georgia, Kansas, Iowa, and Michigan, respectively.

Even more insights can be gained by looking at levels of intensity of vote for Trump and Clinton, as shown in figures 4.4, 4.5, and 4.6, respectively. On a percentage basis, Trump won his largest margins in rural and generally sparsely populated counties in the Great Plains. For example, he won 91.3 percent of the popular vote in Wallace County, Kansas, along the Colorado border, while winning Sherman County to the north with 80.5 percent and Cheyenne County, north of Sherman County, with 83.6 percent. Cheyenne County borders both Nebraska and Colorado and Trump did equally well in counties in these states adjacent to Cheyenne County, with 86.7 percent in Dundy County, Nebraska, and 80.4 percent in Yuma County, Colorado. Trump also exceeded 80 percent of the vote in many rural Appalachian counties, with 86.6 percent in Clay County, Kentucky, and 83.5 percent in DeKalb County, Alabama.

Clinton, who won the metropolitan vote nationwide, did especially well in large central-city places. She won 92.8 percent in Washington, DC, 87.4 percent in New York County, New York (Manhattan), 85.6 percent in San Francisco County, California, and 81.8 percent in the City of Boston, Massachusetts. All of these places are small in land area and very densely populated. However, her margins in some urban counties with larger land areas and containing suburbs were almost as large, with 82.5 percent in Philadelphia County, Pennsylvania, 74.8 percent in her native Cook County, Illinois (Chicago), 72.0 percent in Los Angeles County, California, and 71.9 percent in King County, Washington (Seattle). Outside of metropolitan areas, her largest percentages were concentrated in rural areas with large minority populations, with 86.8 percent in Claiborne County, Mississippi, 79.1 percent in Starr County, Texas, along the Rio Grande, and 86.4 percent in Oglala Lakota County, South Dakota.

Because third-party candidates won about 5 percent of the popular vote nationwide, neither Trump nor Clinton won majorities in dozens of counties. Examples include Scott County, Iowa (Davenport), Washoe County, Nevada (Reno), Broome County, New York (Binghamton), and Frederick County, Maryland (Frederick). Clinton won pluralities in Scott and Washoe Counties, whereas Trump won pluralities in Broome and Frederick Counties. Throughout the country, many of these evenly divided counties contain medium-sized or smaller cities and/or are located on the outskirts of major metropolitan areas, as is the case with Frederick County, located at the edge of both the Washington and Baltimore metropolitan areas, and with Dutchess County, New York, north of New York City.

These trends are evident also from examination of Trump's margin of victory at the county level, as illustrated in figure 4.7; Trump's margin of victory exceeded 40 percent in several hundred counties. These counties included many in Appalachia, from central and western Pennsylvania southward and westward to northern Georgia and Alabama. He also won many counties in the Upper South states of Kentucky, Tennessee, Arkansas, Missouri,

FIGURE 4.4

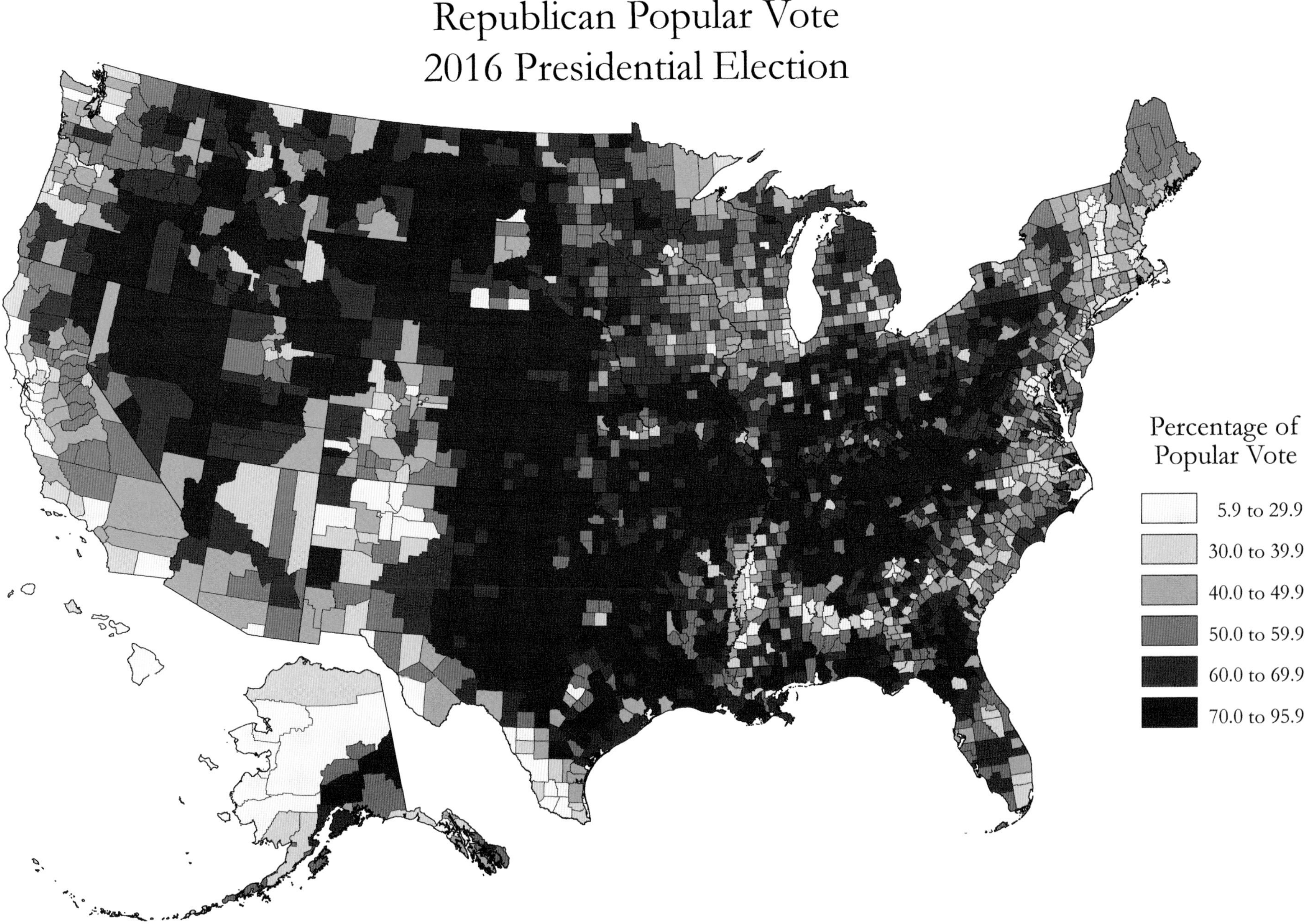
Republican Popular Vote
2016 Presidential Election
Percentage of Popular Vote
5.9 to 29.9
30.0 to 39.9
40.0 to 49.9
50.0 to 59.9
60.0 to 69.9
70.0 to 95.9

FIGURE 4.5

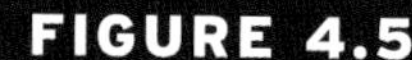

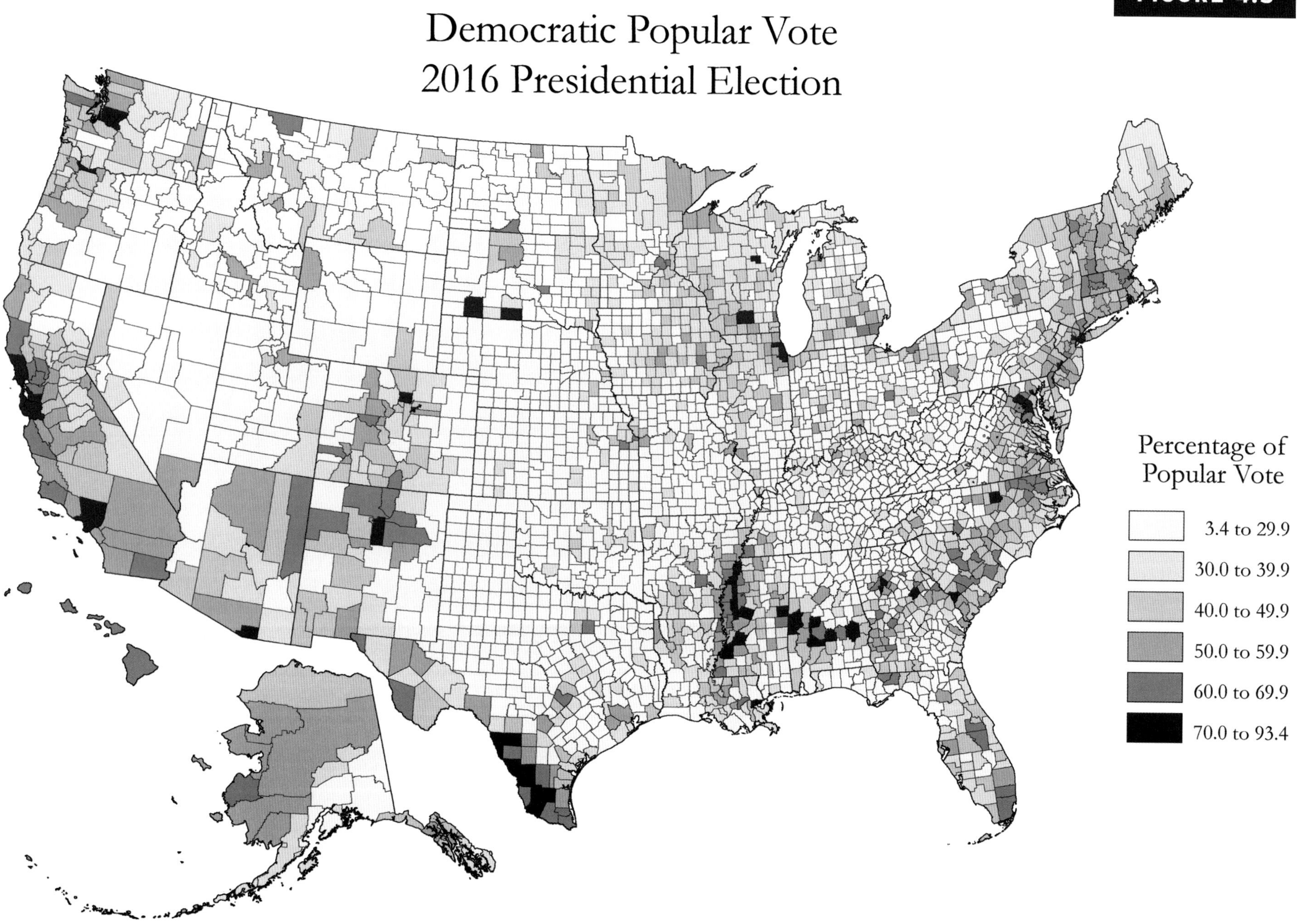
Democratic Popular Vote
2016 Presidential Election
Percentage of
Popular Vote
3.4 to 29.9
30.0 to 39.9
40.0 to 49.9
50.0 to 59.9
60.0 to 69.9
70.0 to 93.4

FIGURE 4.6

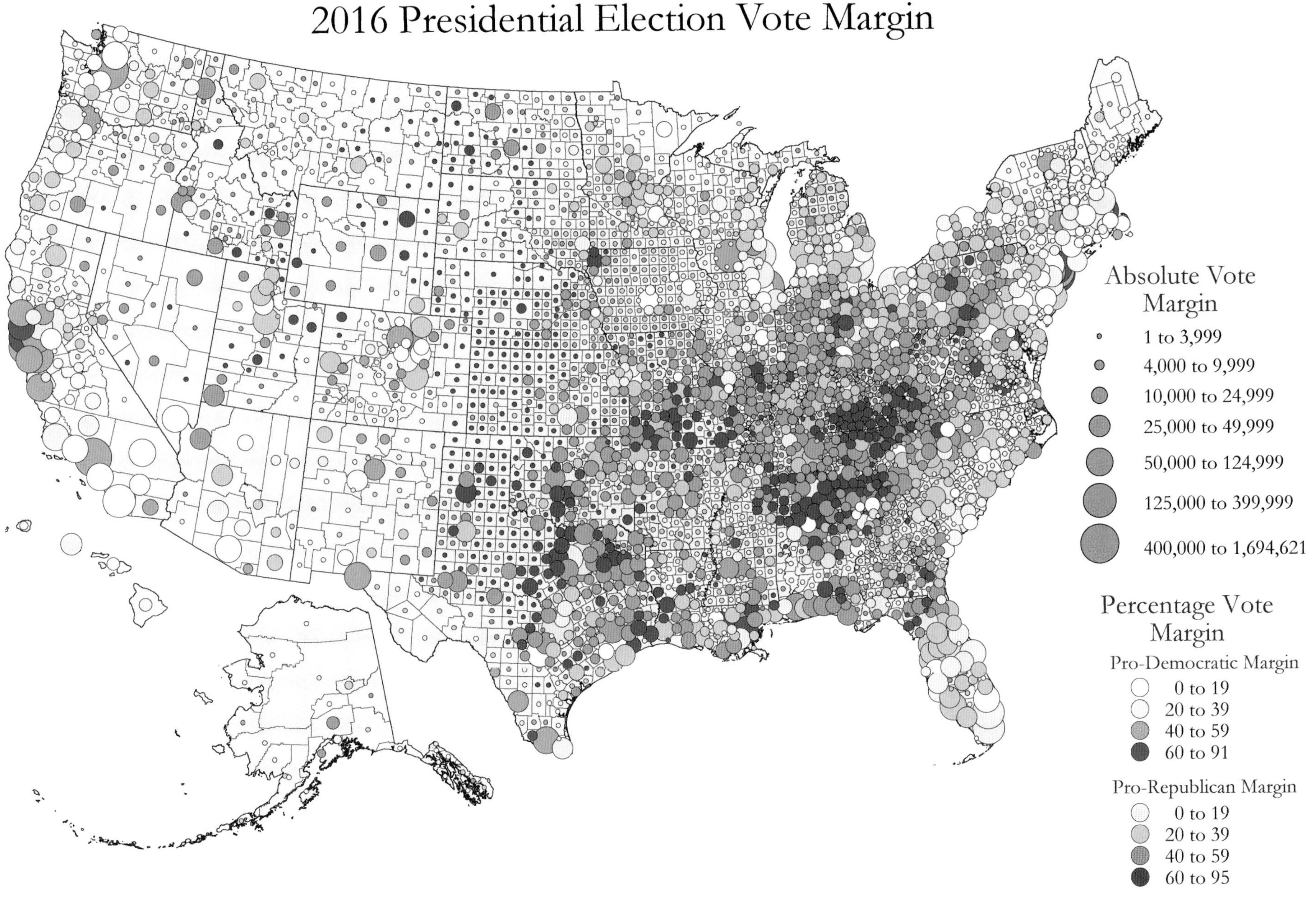
2016 Presidential Election Vote Margin
Absolute Vote Margin
1 to 3,999
4,000 to 9,999
10,000 to 24,999
25,000 to 49,999
50,000 to 124,999
125,000 to 399,999
400,000 to 1,694,621
Percentage Vote Margin
Pro-Democratic Margin
0 to 19
20 to 39
40 to 59
60 to 91
Pro-Republican Margin
0 to 19
20 to 39
40 to 59
60 to 95

FIGURE 4.7

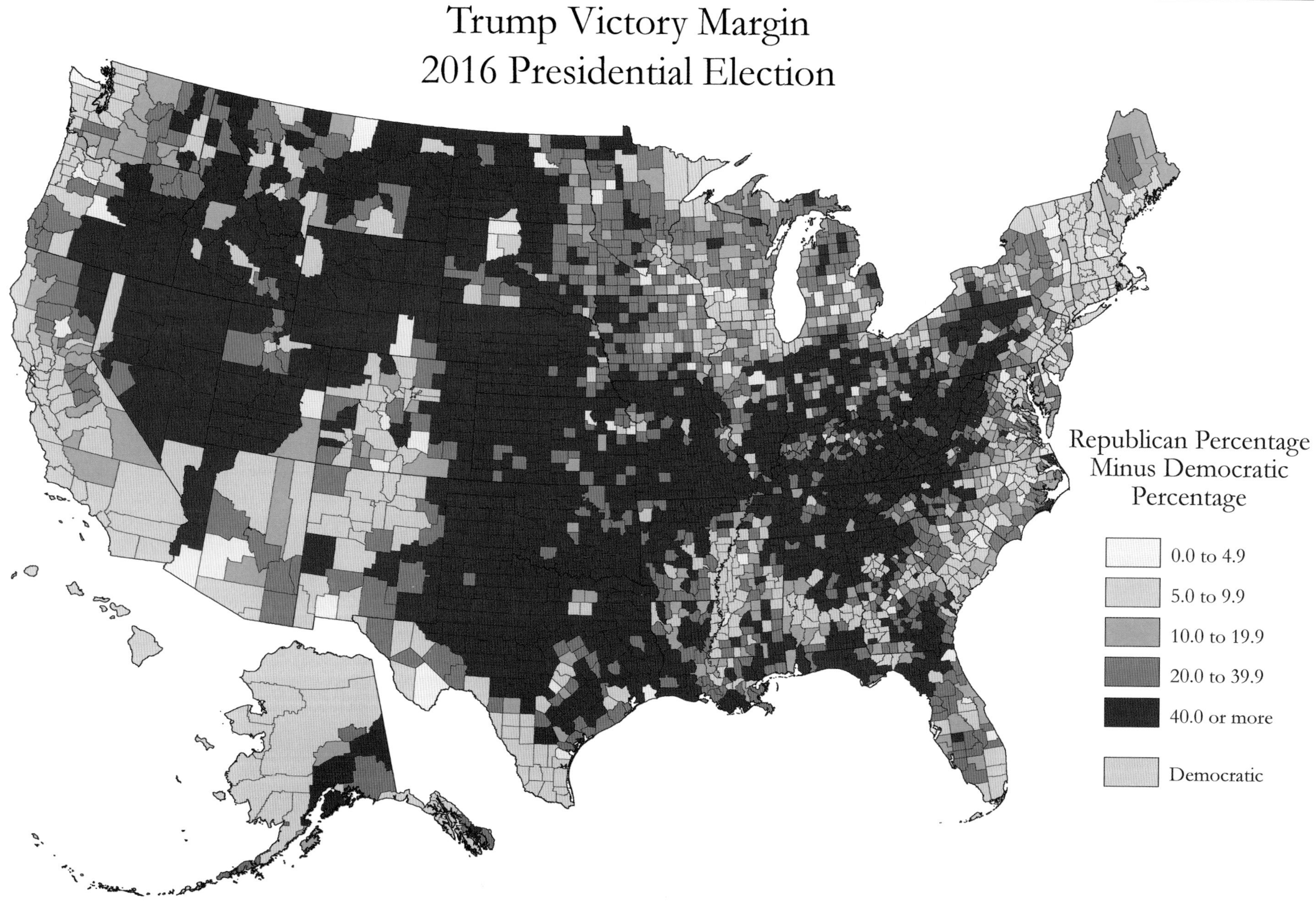
Trump Victory Margin
2016 Presidential Election
Republican Percentage
Minus Democratic
Percentage
0.0 to 4.9
5.0 to 9.9
10.0 to 19.9
20.0 to 39.9
40.0 or more
Democratic

and Oklahoma with margins of more than 40 percent. The other broad area of very high margins for Trump extends across the Great Plains and into the interior of the Rocky Mountain West, including much of Wyoming, Idaho, Utah, and Nevada.

Trump's margins in the swing states of Wisconsin, Michigan, Iowa, Ohio, and Florida tended to be lower than was the case in Appalachia, the Great Plains, and the Mountain West. However, he won counties in rural areas of these states by large enough margins to offset Clinton's support in urban areas. Note that Trump's margins of victory tended to be lower in more urbanized counties in these states, for example, in counties containing Knoxville, Wichita, Oklahoma City, and Cheyenne. But because these counties have larger populations, Trump's absolute margin of victory tended to be greater in these counties, adding to his lead in the states in which they are located.

As indicated, third-party candidates earned about 5 percent of the vote nationwide (see figures 4.8, 4.9, 4.10, and 4.11). The three most significant third-party candidates were former New Mexico governor Gary Johnson, running on the Libertarian ticket, Green Party candidate and physician Jill Stein, and Evan McMullin, a former Central Intelligence Agency agent running as an independent. Several other minor candidates also ran for the presidency. The states containing counties with the highest percentages of third-party votes included Utah and New Mexico, the home states of McMullin and Johnson, respectively. Generally speaking, third-party candidates did best in the West and in New England, which was Stein's strongest region. On the other hand, third-party candidates did poorly in the Deep South. It should be noted that laws regarding ballot access by third parties vary from state to state. In some states, it is difficult for a third party to gain ballot access. Third-party votes are thus reduced in states in which third-party candidates are not listed on the ballot.

Johnson's name appeared on the ballot in all fifty states. He and his running mate, former governor William Weld of Massachusetts, earned 3.28 percent of the popular vote nationwide. Not surprisingly, his strongest state was his home state of New Mexico, in which he won 9.3 percent of the popular vote. Elsewhere, he did best in states with strong antiestablishment and individualistic traditions. In addition to New Mexico, Johnson exceeded 5 percent of the popular vote in Alaska, Colorado, Maine, Montana, North Dakota, Oklahoma, South Dakota, and Wyoming. Except for Oklahoma and South Dakota, all of these states have relatively weak ties to organized religion. In these and other states, his support levels were strongest in rural areas such as outlying areas of coastal Alaska. Johnson's weakest levels of support were in the South and the Northeast. He earned less than 2.5 percent of the popular vote in seven states, including the Southern states of Alabama, Florida, Louisiana, Mississippi, and South Carolina, and the mid-Atlantic states of New Jersey, New York, and Pennsylvania.

Advocating an unabashed progressive platform, Stein earned 1.07 percent of the popular vote across the country. Her strongest areas were among the most liberal areas of the country, including New England and coastal areas of northern California, Oregon, and Washington. During the campaign, Stein actively supported protests against the Dakota Access Pipeline, a proposed oil and gas pipeline that would pass near the Standing Rock Reservation in North Dakota and cut across land that members of the tribe regard as sacred ground. She was arrested after spray-painting a bulldozer during a protest of the pipeline. Her actions in support of the Standing Rock protesters may have helped her gain support among Native Americans in North Dakota, Alaska, New Mexico, and elsewhere. Note that the Green Party was not on the ballot in either South Dakota or Oklahoma, both of which contain relatively large Native American populations.

McMullin's platform was very conservative, but he regarded Trump as unfit for the presidency and opposed the Democrats' liberal platform strenuously. McMullin earned 0.53 percent of the popular vote nationwide, but he earned about 21 percent of the vote in his native Utah. In fact, he outpolled Clinton in several Utah counties. McMullin is a Mormon, and his strong support in his native state may also reflect many Mormons' coolness toward Trump's candidacy. Mormon skepticism toward Trump may be the result of concerns about Trump's personal morality, his opposition to immigration, and his lack of an international vision. As well, Mormons have faced a long history of discrimination and many are therefore sensitive to intolerance of other religious groups. Elsewhere, McMullin's strongest areas include southeastern Idaho, which also contains a significant Mormon population, and Minnesota, which also has a long history of religious tolerance. It is possible that McMullin could have cut slightly into Trump's lead in other states, especially states in the northern Plains and the Mountain West, if he had been listed on these states' ballots.

As indicated, Trump won the 2016 presidential election by winning the electoral votes of Florida, Iowa, Michigan, Ohio, Pennsylvania, and Wisconsin, all of which had given their electoral votes to Barack Obama in 2012 and 2008. In the

FIGURE 4.8

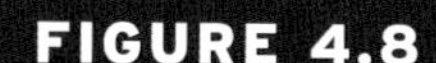

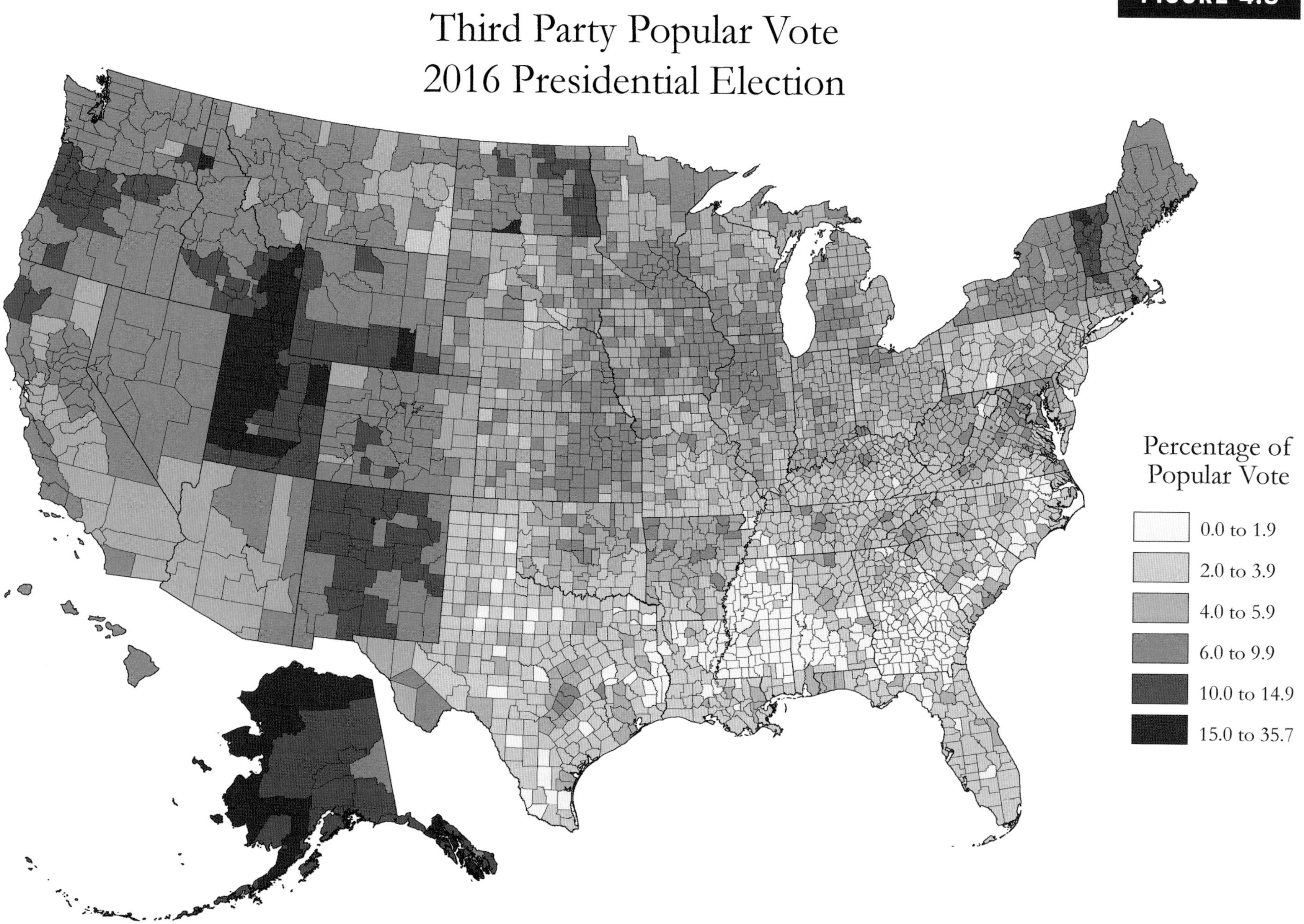
Third Party Popular Vote
2016 Presidential Election
Percentage of Popular Vote
0.0 to 1.9
2.0 to 3.9
4.0 to 5.9
6.0 to 9.9
10.0 to 14.9
15.0 to 35.7

FIGURE 4.9

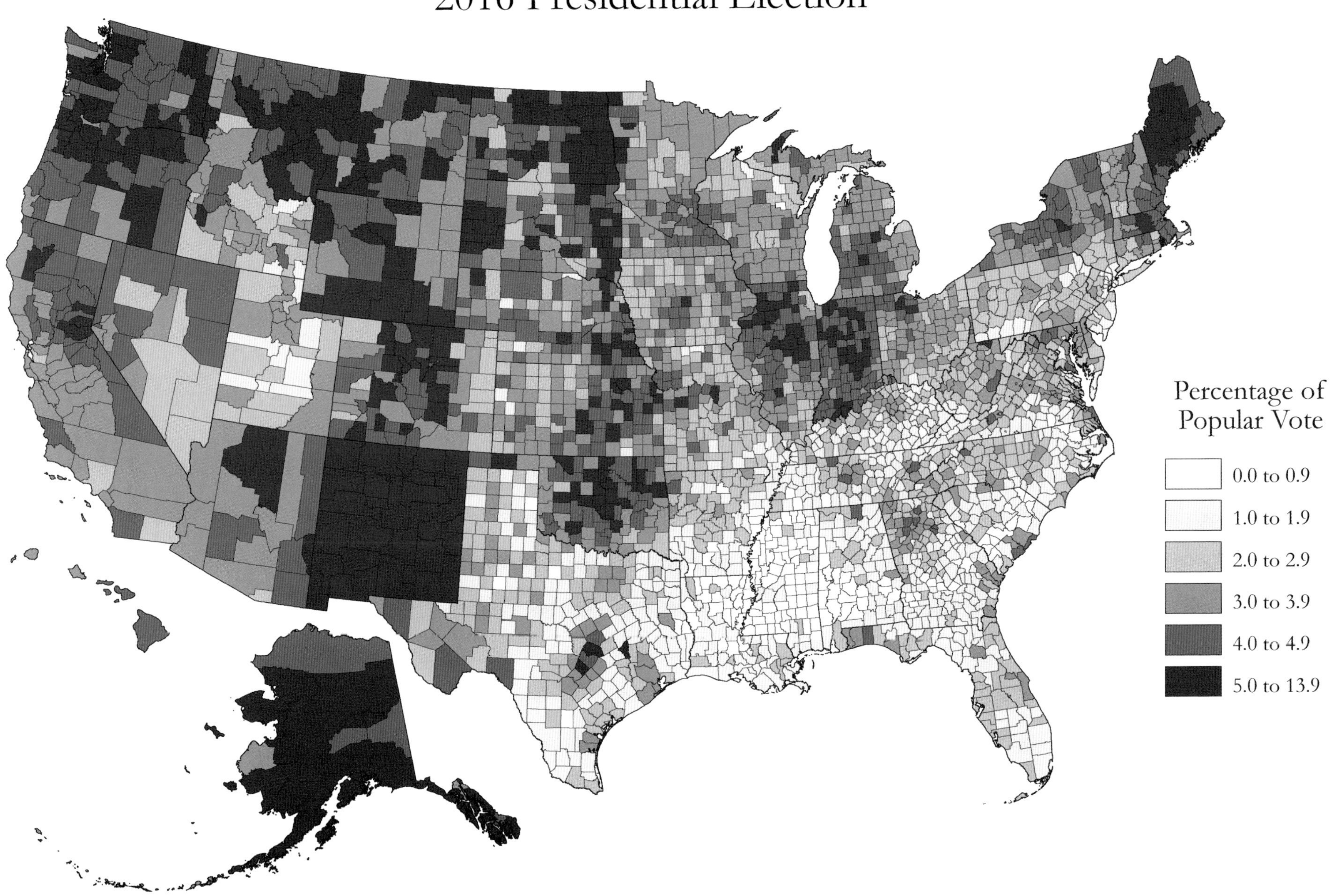

Gary Johnson, Libertarian Party Popular Vote
2016 Presidential Election
Percentage of Popular Vote
0.0 to 0.9
1.0 to 1.9
2.0 to 2.9
3.0 to 3.9
4.0 to 4.9
5.0 to 13.9

FIGURE 4.10

Jill Stein, Green Party Popular Vote 2016 Presidential Election

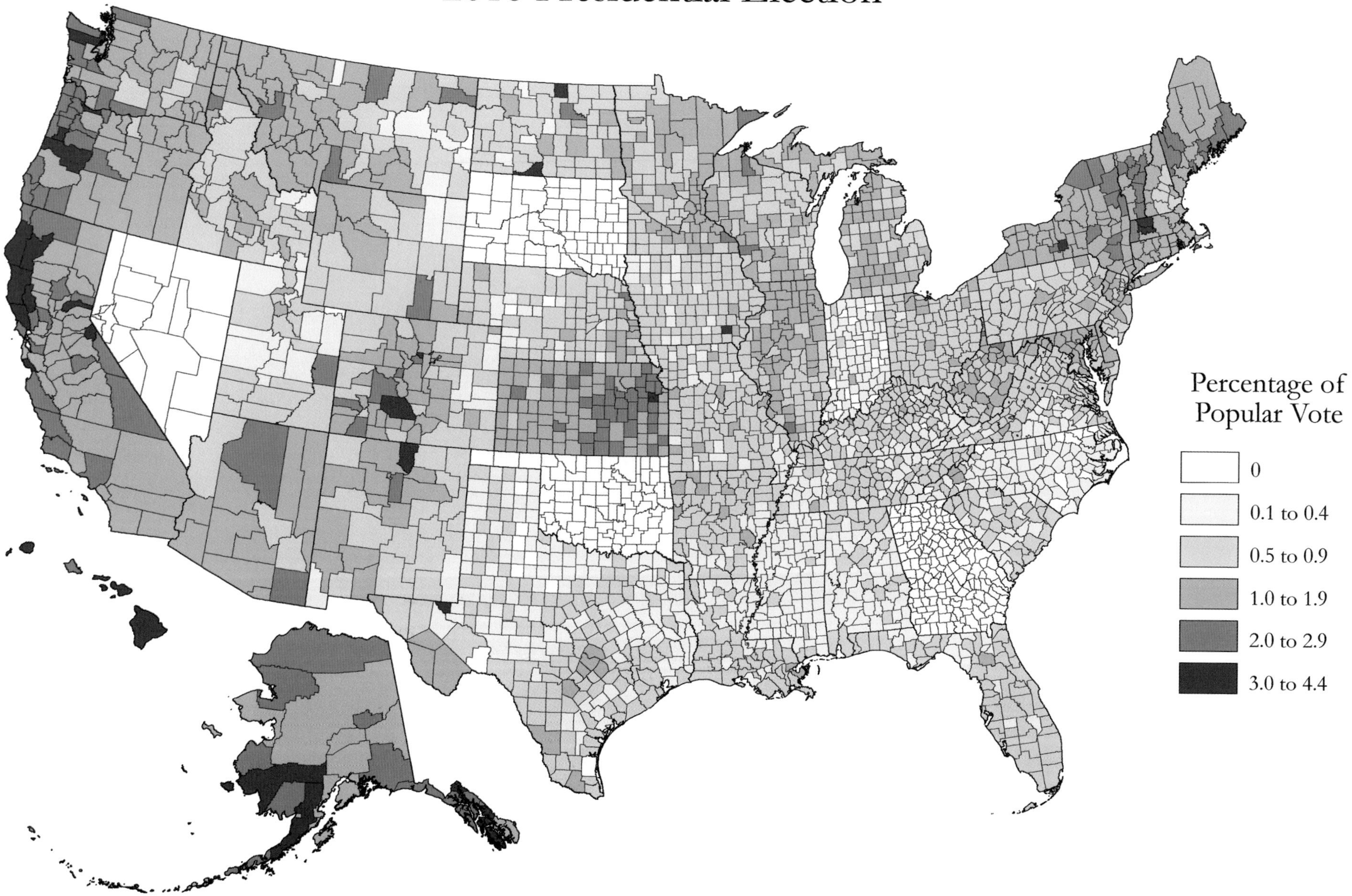

FIGURE 4.11

Evan McMullin, Independent Candidate Popular Vote 2016 Presidential Election

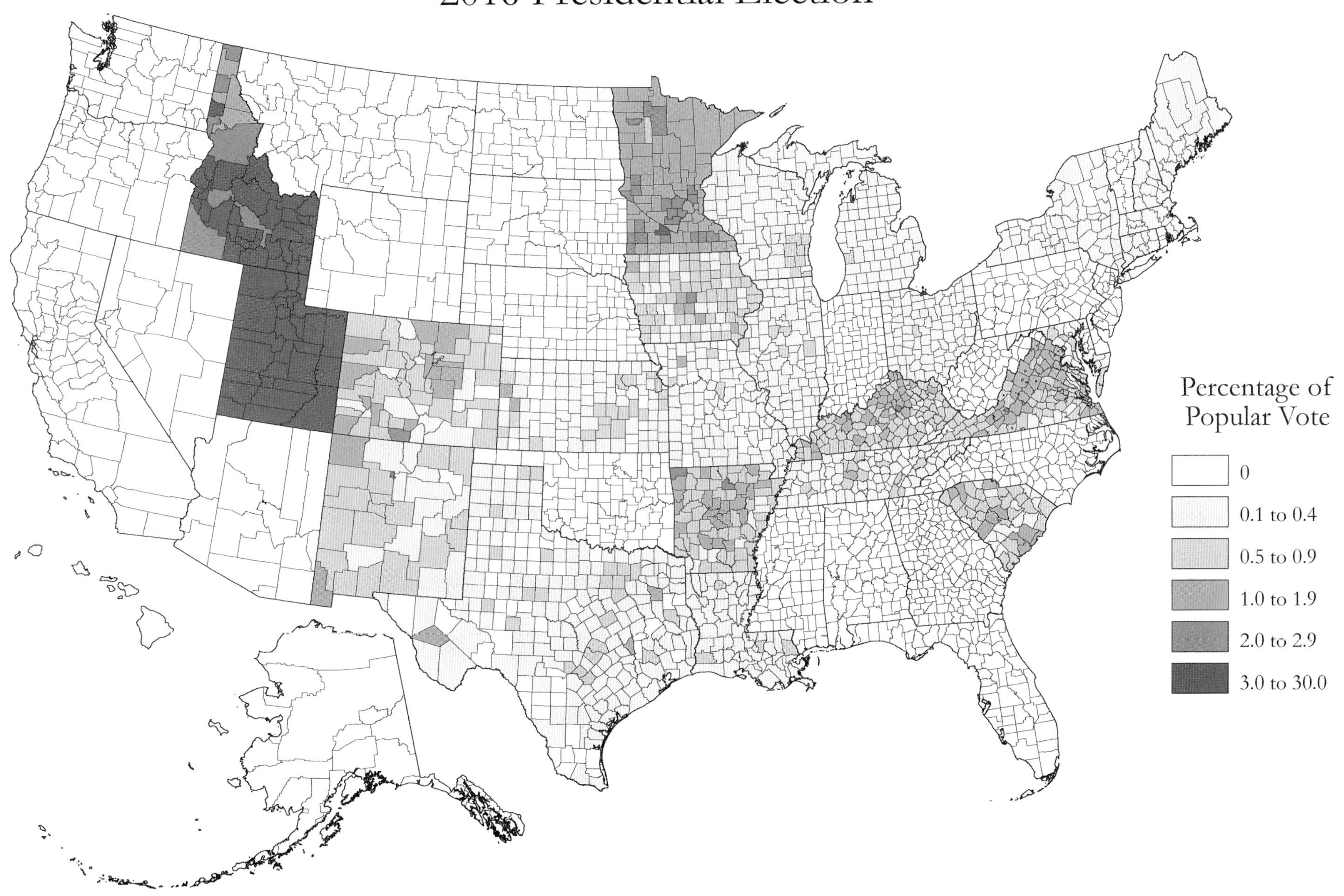

FIGURE 4.12

Change in the Republican Vote from the 2012 Election to the 2016 Election

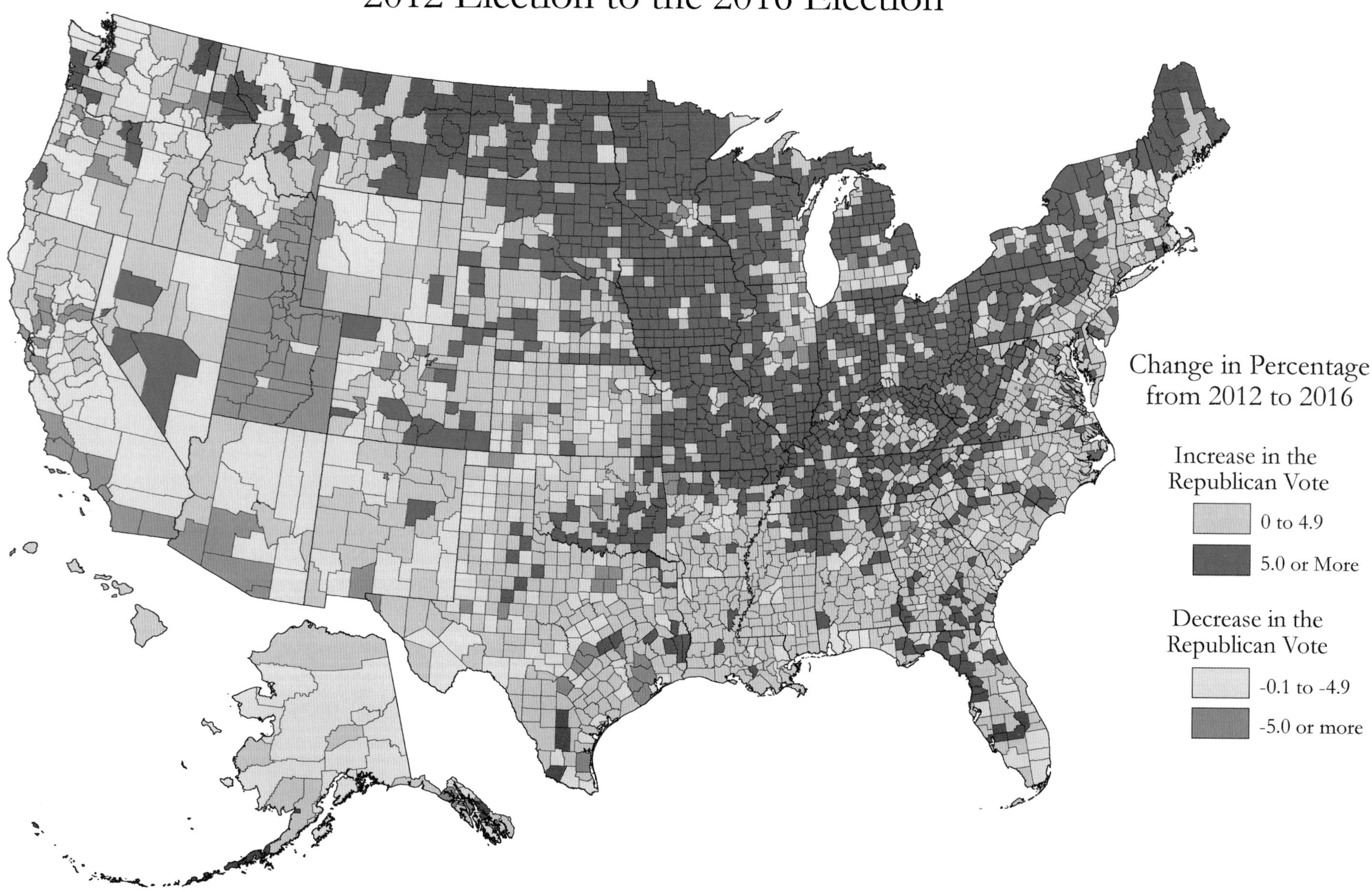

FIGURE 4.13

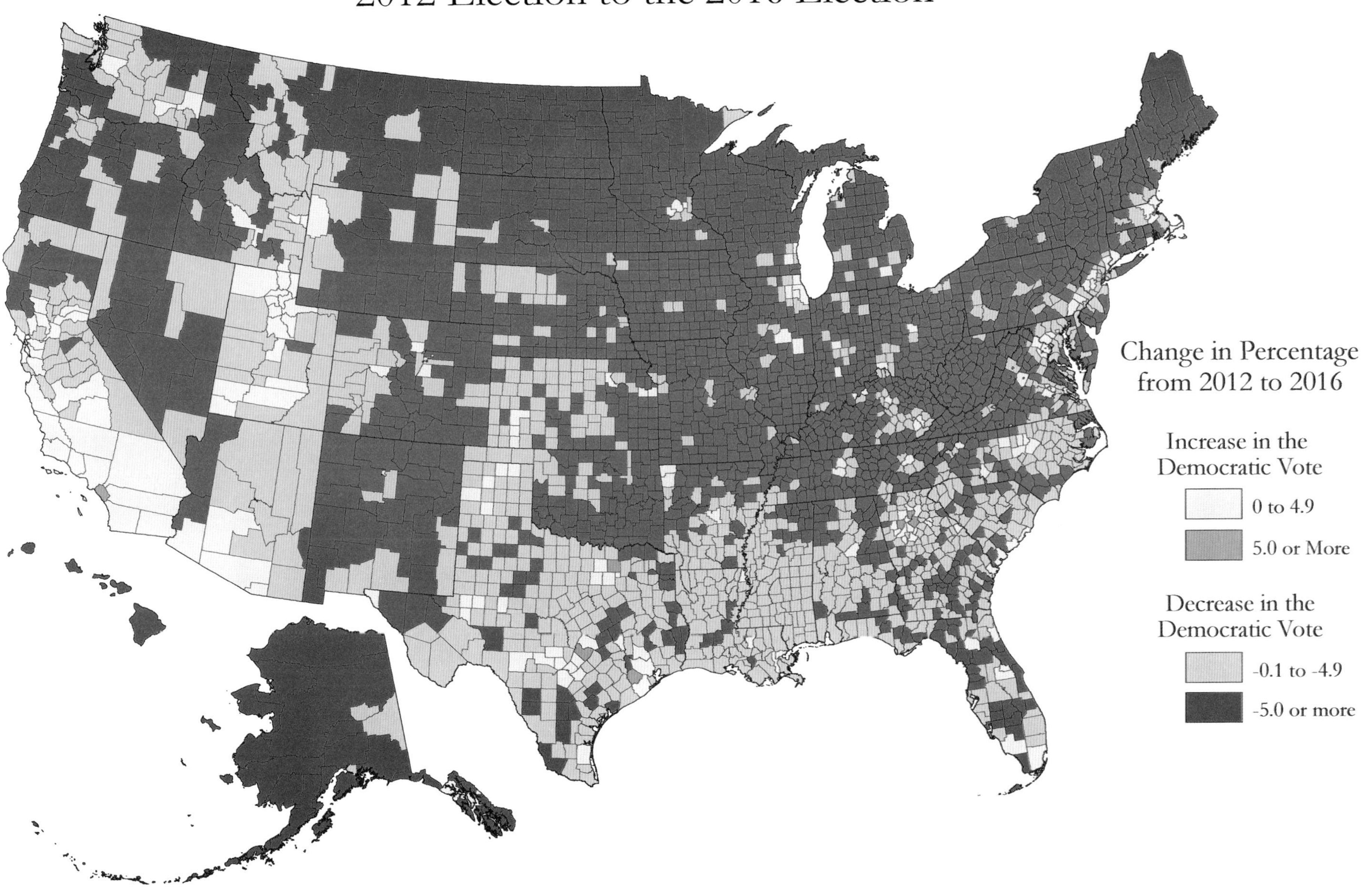
Change in the Democratic Vote from the 2012 Election to the 2016 Election
Change in Percentage from 2012 to 2016
Increase in the Democratic Vote
0 to 4.9
5.0 or More
Decrease in the Democratic Vote
-0.1 to -4.9
-5.0 or more

FIGURE 4.14

Persistence and Change
2012 and 2016 Presidential Elections

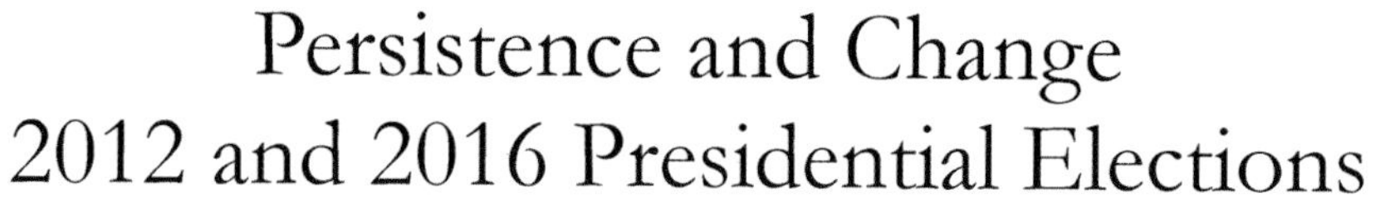

Persistence
Democratic in 2012 and 2016 (469)
Republican in 2012 and 2016 (2,403)
Change
Republican in 2012 to Democratic in 2016 (17)
Democratic in 2012 to Republican in 2016 (219)

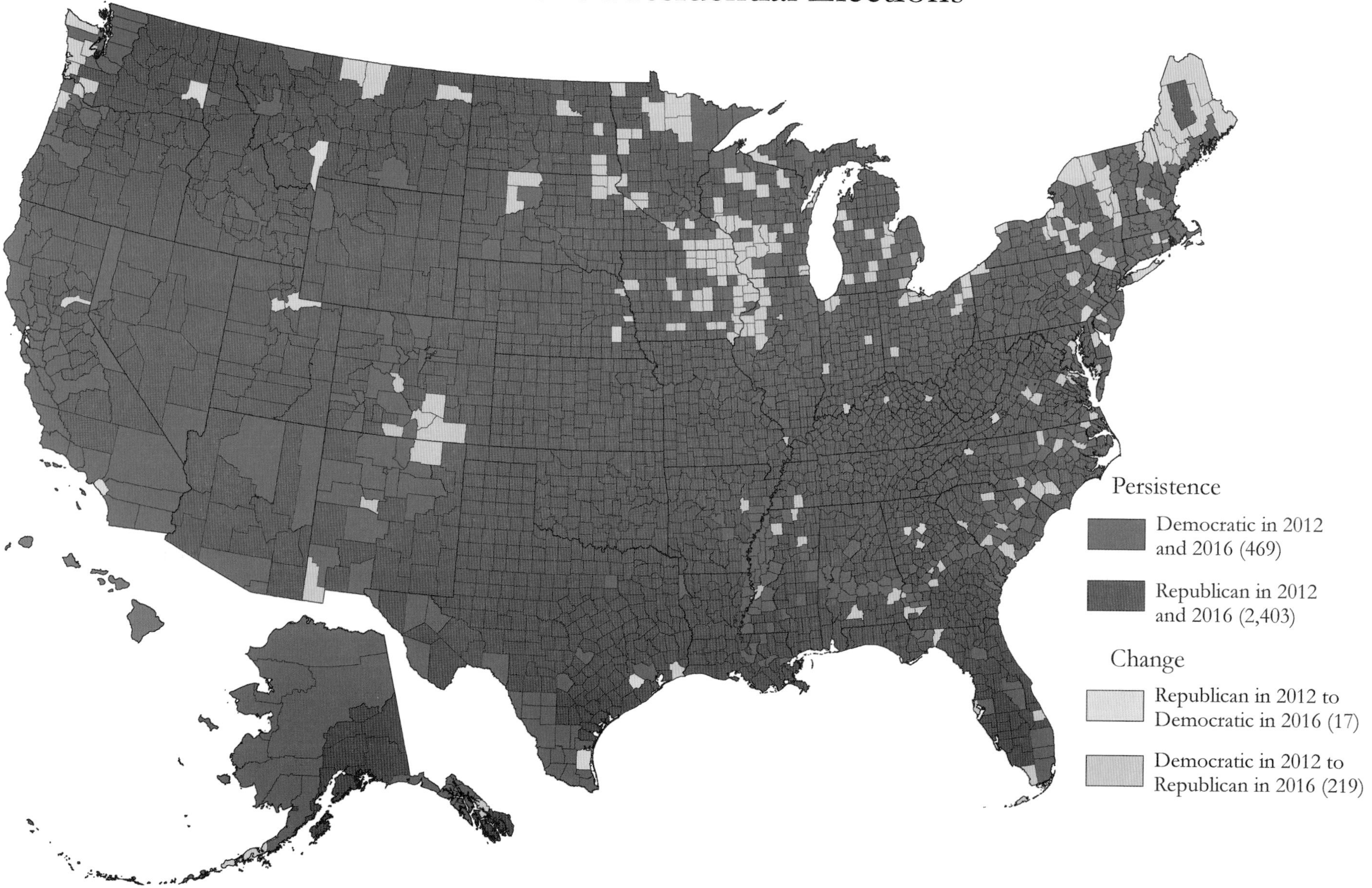

majority of counties in each of these states, Trump won at least 5 percent more of the popular vote than had his Republican predecessor, Mitt Romney, in 2012 (see figure 4.12). The Midwestern states that flipped from Obama in 2012 to Trump in 2016 are at the core of a large swath of counties in which Trump's popular vote percentage relative to Romney's percentage exceeded 5 percent. These counties extend in an arc from North Dakota and Montana southeastward to Missouri and Kentucky, and northeastward to upstate New York and Maine. Trump's margin increased by less in many counties of the South, the Great Plains, and the Rocky Mountain states in part because Romney's margins in these counties had been very large also.

Note, however, that these large increases in the Republican margin of victory in 2016 as compared to 2012 are concentrated in less urbanized counties. In Minnesota, for example, Trump's margins increased by more than 5 percent throughout the state except for the Minneapolis–St. Paul metropolitan area, in which Democratic support increased between 2012 and 2016. Similarly, Democratic margins increased in Philadelphia, Pittsburgh, Columbus, Cincinnati, Indianapolis, and Chicago, although Republican margins increased in rural areas throughout their respective states.

Meanwhile, most of the places in which Democratic support increased by more than 5 percent between 2012 and 2016 were counties that were already heavily Democratic (see figure 4.13). These include the Boston, New York, Washington, Chicago, Denver, Los Angeles, San Francisco, and Seattle metropolitan areas. Democratic margins increased substantially also in otherwise Republican states, for example, in the Austin–San Antonio corridor along with the Houston and Dallas–Fort Worth areas of Texas, the Atlanta metropolitan area, Nashville, Kansas City, and Oklahoma City. Thus, figures 4.12 and 4.13 illustrate the degree to which polarization of the American electorate continues to intensify; Republican areas become more Republican and Democratic areas became more Democratic. Moreover, the urban-rural split characterizing recent American presidential elections also increased in that the large majority of counties in which Clinton's vote share was higher than that of Obama in 2012 are metropolitan counties. The Democratic share of the vote also increased in several counties throughout the country containing college towns, including those containing Washington State University, Kansas State University, Texas A&M University, and the Universities of Kansas, Oklahoma, Colorado, and Idaho. Thus the college-town effect was especially evident in the western half of the country.

The conspicuous exception to this pattern is found in heavily Mormon counties throughout Utah and southeastern Idaho. As indicated, in these counties many Mormons were unenthusiastic about Trump's candidacy and many may have voted for McMullin rather than Trump. Thus, Trump's vote share decreased relative to that of Romney, who is himself a Mormon, in 2012.

Another perspective of the changes between 2012 and 2016 is shown in figure 4.14, which shows counties that shifted from one major party to another between the two elections. Not surprisingly, most of the counties that switched from Obama in 2012 to Trump in 2016 are located in the Upper Midwest states of Iowa, Wisconsin, and Michigan that helped secure enough Electoral College votes for Trump's victory.

Examination of maps of county-level votes for Trump, Clinton, and third-party candidates in 2016 provides insights into the outcome of the election and the possible motivations of individual voters within places throughout the country. The results illustrate the increased degree of polarization within the electorate, the deepening divide between urban and rural areas, and the degree to which outcomes are correlated to patterns of race and ethnic identity.

VOTER PARTICIPATION

CHRIS MAIER

How many people voted and how did voter turnout impact the outcome of the 2016 US presidential election? Figure 4.15 and figure 4.16 show levels of voter turnout as a percent of the overall voting age population on a statewide and county-by-county basis throughout the country. According to the US Elections Project, roughly 60.2 percent of eligible voters cast a ballot in the 2016 presidential election (US Elections Project 2016). Turnout was up from 2012, when 57.5 percent of eligible voters participated, but the turnout was down slightly from 2008, when 62.3 percent of eligible voters participated in the election (Shelley 2014).

Voter turnout rates varied considerably across the United States. Historically, northern states, especially the Upper Midwest states of Minnesota, Wisconsin, and Iowa, have produced higher voter participation rates than states in the South (Shelley 2014). The 2016 presidential election saw a continuation of that pattern with a few exceptions. Figure 4.15 compares voter turnout in the 2012 election with voter turnout in the 2016 election. Many of the states with high voter turnout in 2012, including Colorado, Iowa, Maine, Michigan, Minnesota, Montana, New Hampshire, North Carolina, Ohio, and Virginia, had high voter turnout in 2016 as well. With the exception of Montana, most of these states were relatively competitive swing states in both the 2012 and 2016 presidential elections. The state with the highest voter participation rate in the 2016 presidential election was Maine. Maine was the only state to cross the 70 percent threshold, while Iowa, Minnesota, Wisconsin, and Colorado, a non-northern state with a relatively high voter participation rate, saw voter participation rates between 65 to 69.9 percent. While the highest voter participation rates were in the northern part of the country, the lowest participation rates were generally in Appalachia and the South.

With the exception of North Carolina and Virginia, both of which were competitive swing states in the 2016 election, no state in the South had a voter participation rate above 60 percent. Five states—Arkansas, Arizona, Oklahoma, Texas, and West Virginia—had voter participation rates below 50 percent. At the county level, lower-than-average turnout rates were found in a band stretching from West Virginia south through much of Appalachia into Oklahoma and Texas. Even though Arizona, Oklahoma, and West Virginia had some of the lowest voter participation rates in the country, they actually grew in voter participation from 2012 to 2016, as evidenced by figure 4.16. Growth in voter participation in these three states may be explained by the campaign run by Donald Trump, the Republican nominee for president. Trump made the coal industry and coal jobs a focal point of his campaign, which could have resonated with voters in West Virginia and driven more of them to the polls. In Arizona, Trump's proposed immigration policies may have encouraged Latinos to get out and vote in greater numbers than in years past. Finally, Pennsylvania, which had not voted for a Republican nominee for president since 1988, saw increased voter turnout in the 2016 election. Figure 4.16 shows elevated voter turnout in many of its rural counties, especially the counties that make up the Pennsylvania T, which extends along Pennsylvania's northern border with New York and south through the central part of the state. Increased voter turnout in the Pennsylvania T, which voted heavily for Trump, helped turn Pennsylvania red and propelled Mr. Trump to the White House.

REFERENCES

McDonald, Michael P. 2017. 2016 November General Election Turnout Rates. United States Elections Project, University of Florida. http://www.electproject.org/2016g (last accessed June 28, 2017).

Shelley, Fred. 2014. Results of the 2012 Presidential Election at the State and County Levels. In J. Clark Archer, Robert H. Watrel, Fiona Davidson, Erin H. Fouberg, Kenneth C. Martis, Richard L. Morrill, Fred M. Shelley, and Gerald R. Webster, eds., *Atlas of the 2012 Elections*, 77–98. Lanham, MD: Rowman & Littlefield.

FIGURE 4.15

2012

2016

Percentage of Voting Age Population Who Voted

2012	2016
39.9 to 49.9	39.1 to 49.9
50.0 to 54.9	50.0 to 54.9
55.0 to 59.9	55.0 to 59.9
60.0 to 64.9	60.0 to 64.9
65.0 to 69.9	65.0 to 69.9
70.0 to 71.5	70.0 to 71.9

Change in Voter Turnout 2012 to 2016

Percent Change

- -7.0 to -2.0
- -1.9 to -0.1
- 0.0 to 1.9
- 2.0 to 3.9
- 4.0 to 5.9
- 6.0 to 8.3

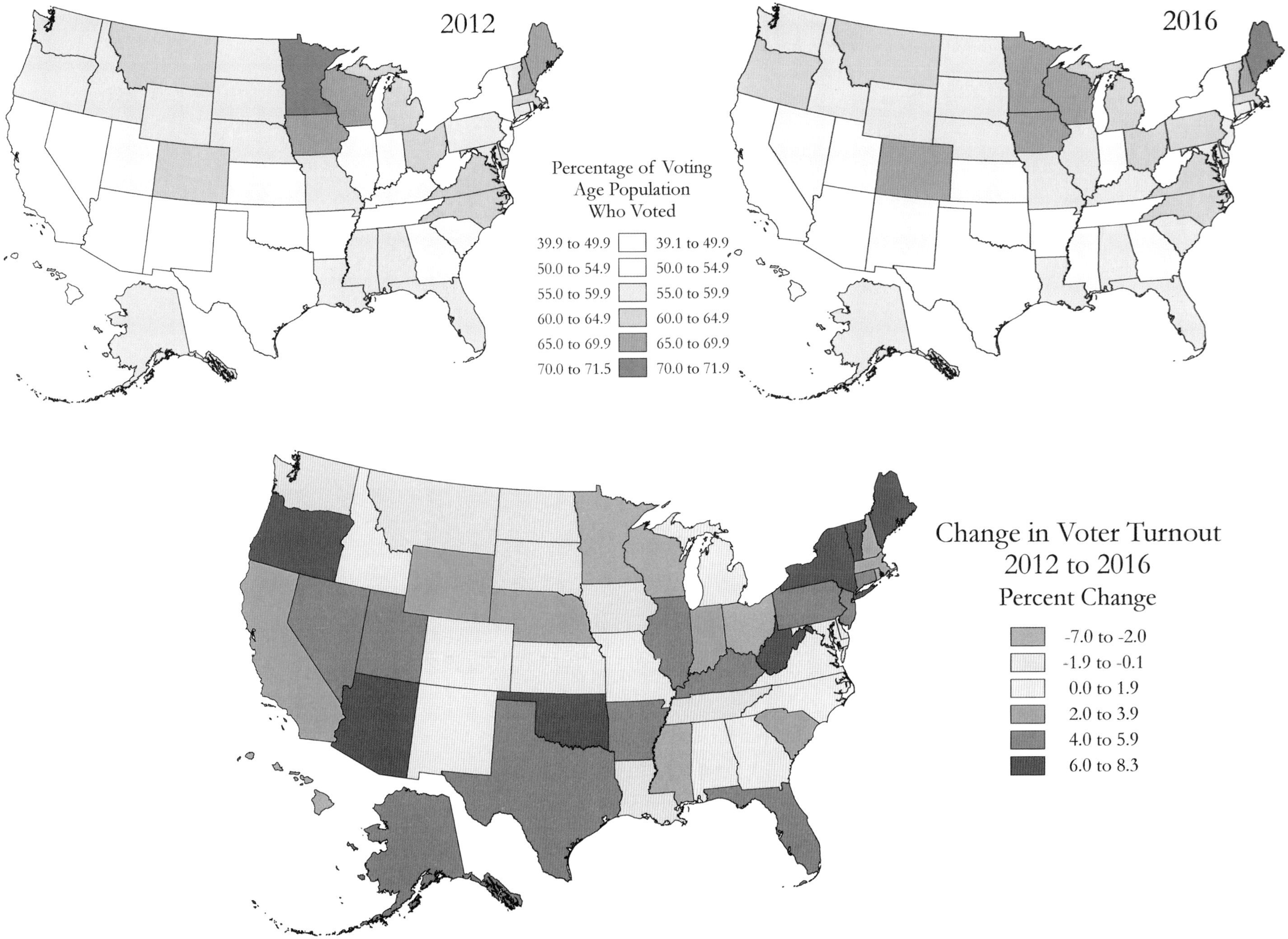

FIGURE 4.16

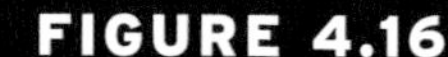

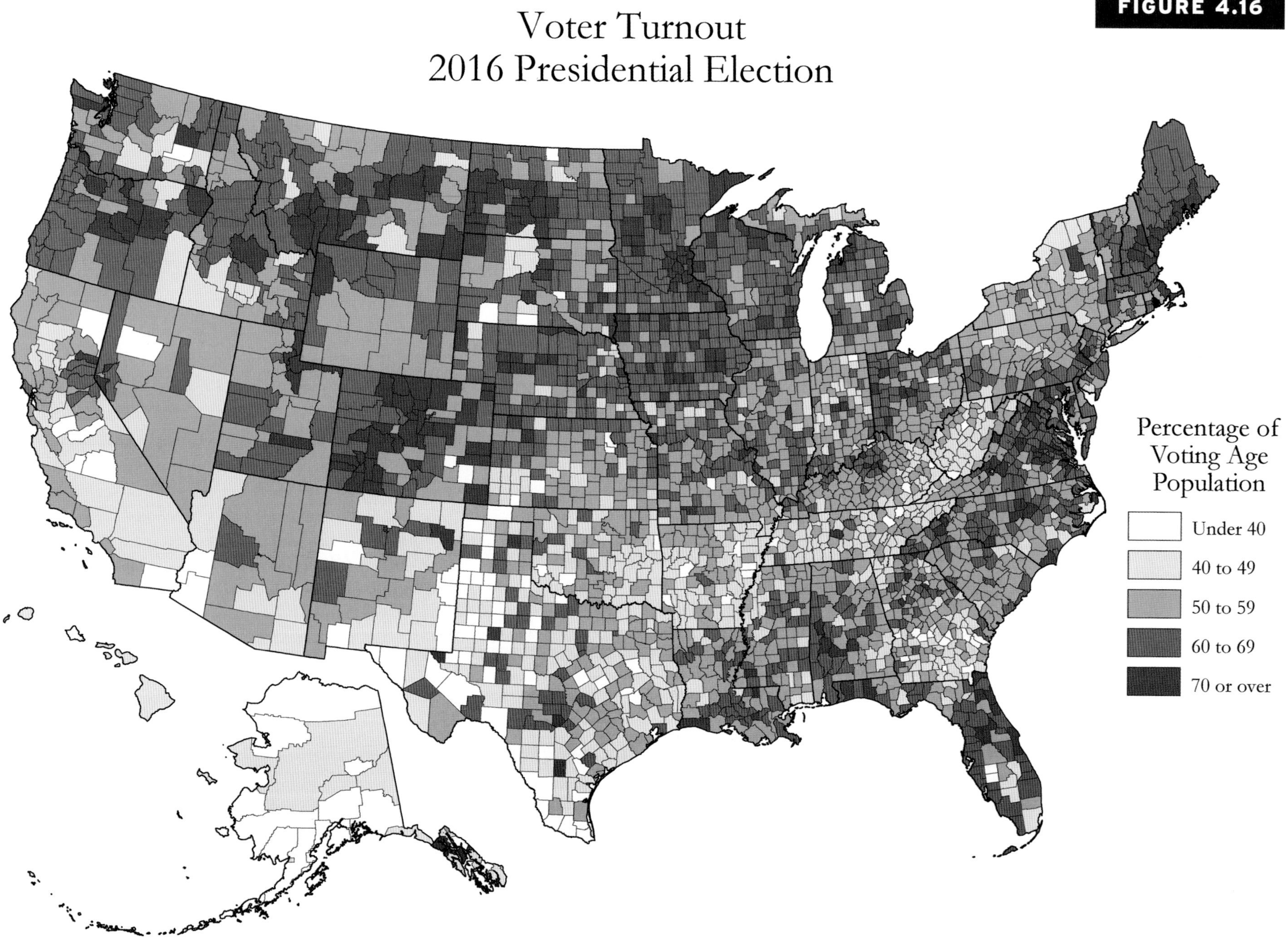
Voter Turnout
2016 Presidential Election
Percentage of Voting Age Population
Under 40
40 to 49
50 to 59
60 to 69
70 or over

STATISTICAL ANALYSIS OF THE 2016 ELECTION IN HISTORICAL PERSPECTIVE

FRED M. SHELLEY, ROBERT H. WATREL, AND J. CLARK ARCHER

Republican Donald Trump won a majority of Electoral College votes in 2016 after winning several states whose electoral votes had been cast for Democrat Barack Obama in 2012, including Florida, Iowa, Michigan, Ohio, Pennsylvania, and Wisconsin. Yet, as illustrated by maps presented elsewhere in this volume, the overall pattern of popular vote in 2016 was not much different from that of the 2012 election. With a very few exceptions, Hillary Clinton's popular vote percentages on a state-by-state basis were highest in those states in which Obama recorded his highest percentages in 2012. Similarly, Trump's popular vote percentages in 2016 were generally highest in those states that had given Republican Mitt Romney his highest popular vote percentages in 2012.

In other words, the overall geographical pattern of popular votes in 2016 varied little from the pattern of popular votes in 2012, 2008, and other recent presidential elections. Yet the geography of the 2016 popular vote varies radically from earlier elections. Before World War II, the "Solid South" was uniformly Democratic and the northern tier of states was strongly Republican. Today, this pattern has been reversed. Vermont, for example, was a solidly Republican state for more than a century after the Republican Party was founded in the 1850s. Between 1856 and 1988, Democrats carried Vermont only during Lyndon Johnson's landslide victory in 1964. Now, Vermont is one of the most solidly Democratic states in the country.

How can the geography of the 2016 presidential election be placed in long-run historical perspective? Statistical analysis of data from sequences of elections allows researchers to identify electoral epochs, or sets of consecutive elections, whose patterns of popular votes are relatively similar to one another and relatively different from earlier or later epochs. In order to achieve this goal, a statistical technique known as T-mode factor analysis was applied to electoral data.

T-mode factor analysis is a method by which maps showing the distribution of values on a particular variable can be compared over time. Conceptually, one can visualize a sequence of maps that in this case show the percentage of votes for candidates of one party at each election. If one were to look at each map in sequence, one would find that maps showing these data from many pairs of consecutive elections look quite similar. Such was the case comparing 2016 and 2012, for example. Over the larger sweep of history, however, the changes are dramatic, as the example of Vermont illustrates.

In this project, we examined the sequence of elections from 1872 through 2016, for a total of thirty-seven consecutive elections. We chose 1872 as the starting point because the two major parties in the United States had been established firmly, and because by that time most of the Southern states that had seceded before the Civil War had been readmitted to the Union and were once again participating in presidential elections. For each of these thirty-seven elections, we mapped the percentage of vote won by the Republican presidential candidate. Figure 4.17 shows the percentage of the vote won by Republican nominees in each election. Note that in a few cases such as 1892, 1912, 1968, and 1992, some voters who might otherwise have cast their ballots for Republican nominees voted instead for third-party candidates James Weaver, Theodore Roosevelt, George Wallace, and Ross Perot, respectively. In these cases, the Republican vote percentage was somewhat less than might have been the case in a two-party race.

Large, long-run changes in the county-level electoral geography of the United States are illustrated by maps showing the county-level results of the elections of 1880 (figure 4.18), 1900 (figure 4.19), 1936 (figure 4.20), 1952 (figure 4.21), 1964 (figure 4.22), 1988 (figure 4.23), and 2016 (figure

FIGURE 4.17

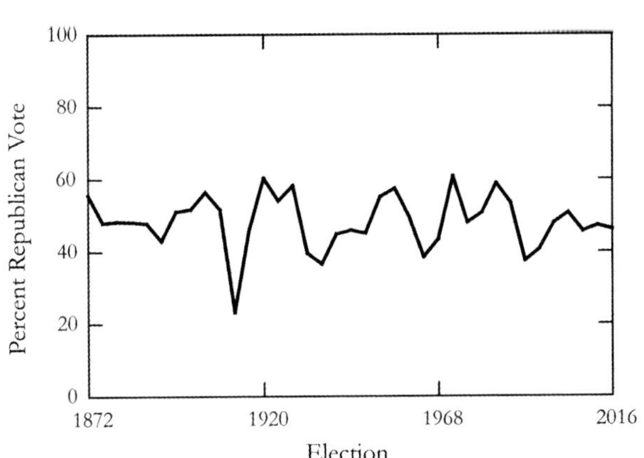

FIGURE 4.18

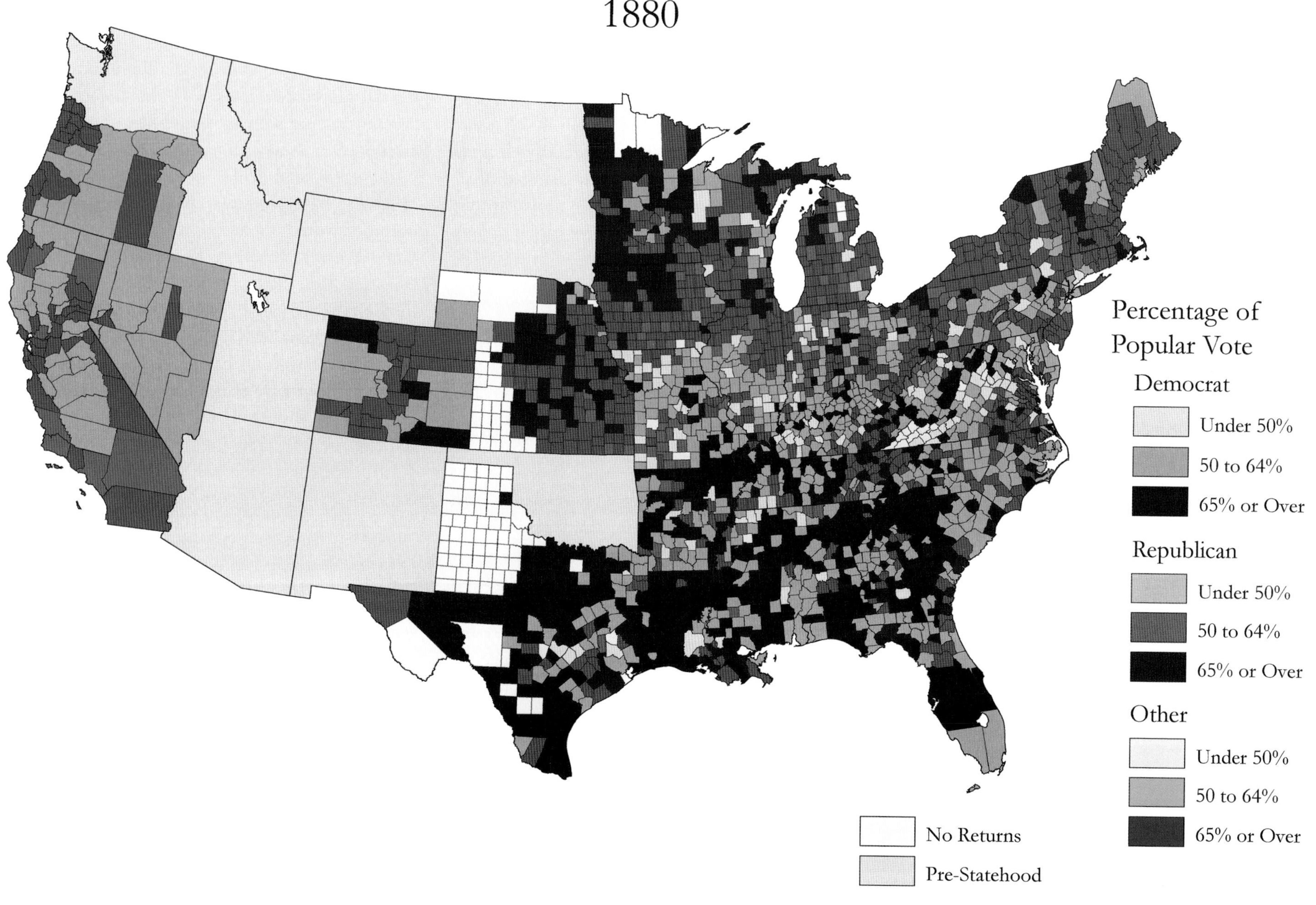
Presidential Election Popular Vote
1880
Percentage of
Popular Vote
Democrat
Under 50%
50 to 64%
65% or Over
Republican
Under 50%
50 to 64%
65% or Over
Other
Under 50%
50 to 64%
65% or Over
No Returns
Pre-Statehood

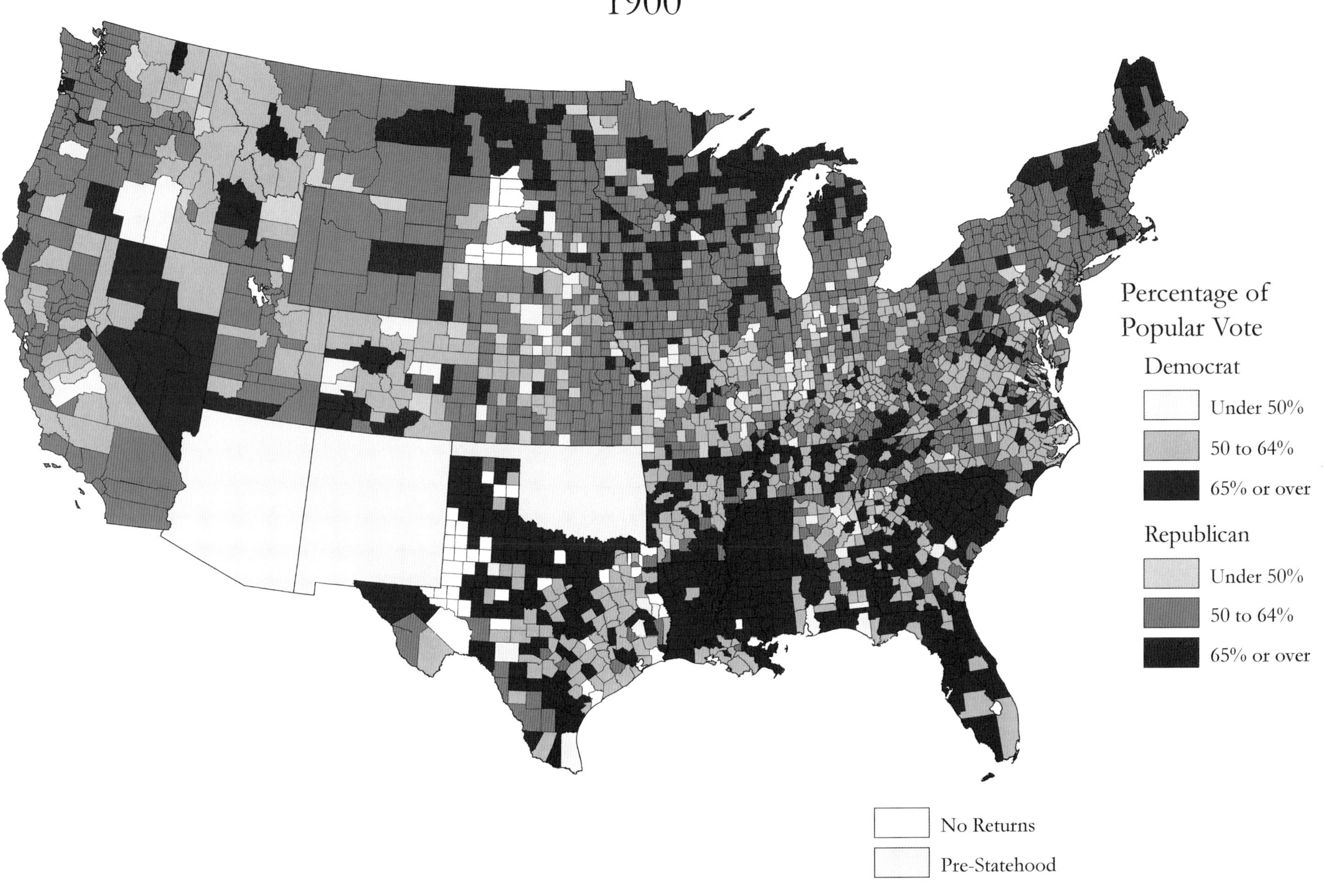
FIGURE 4.19
Presidential Election Popular Vote
1900
Percentage of
Popular Vote
Democrat
Under 50%
50 to 64%
65% or over
Republican
Under 50%
50 to 64%
65% or over
No Returns
Pre-Statehood

FIGURE 4.20

Presidential Election Popular Vote 1936

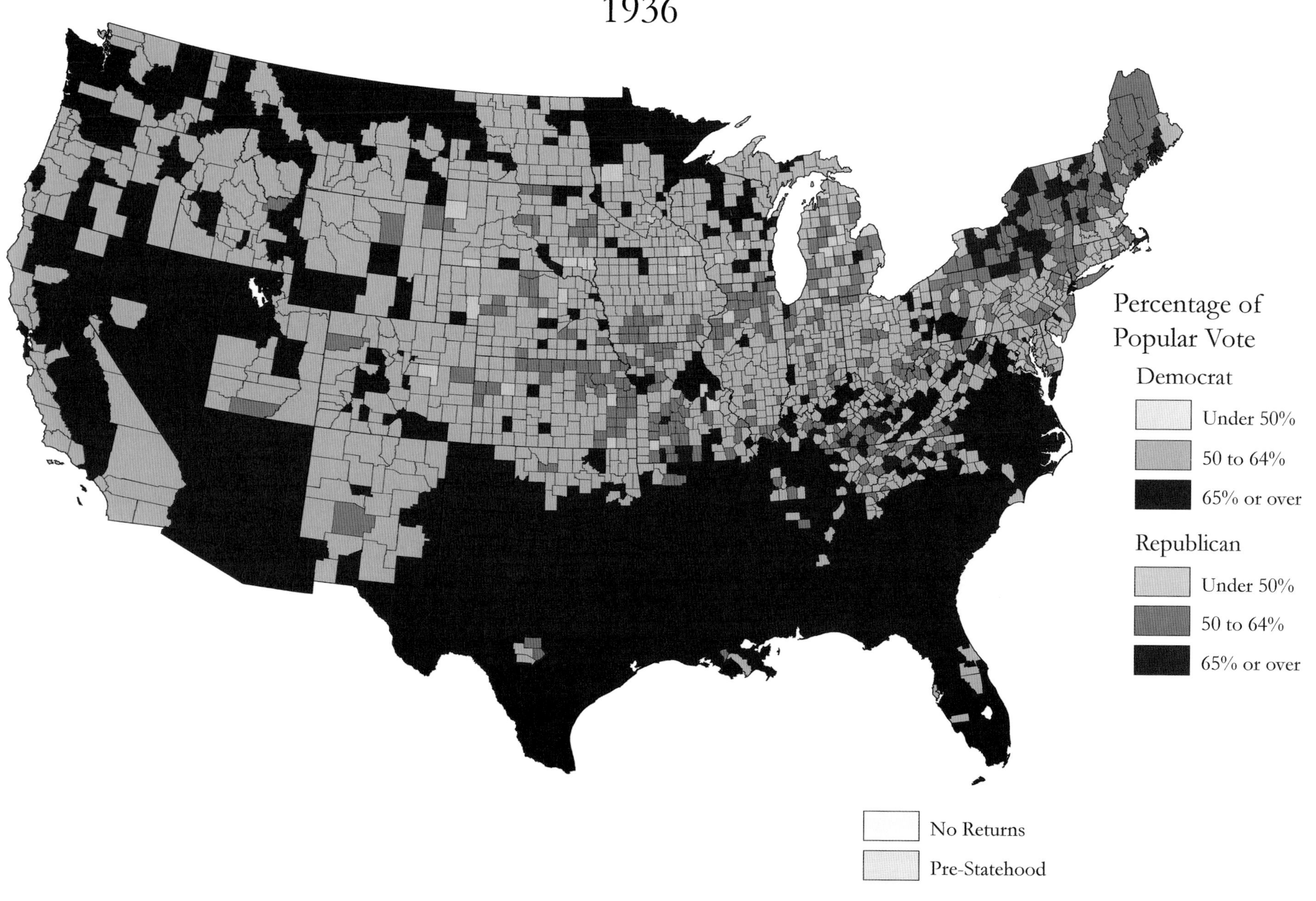

FIGURE 4.21

Presidential Election Popular Vote 1952

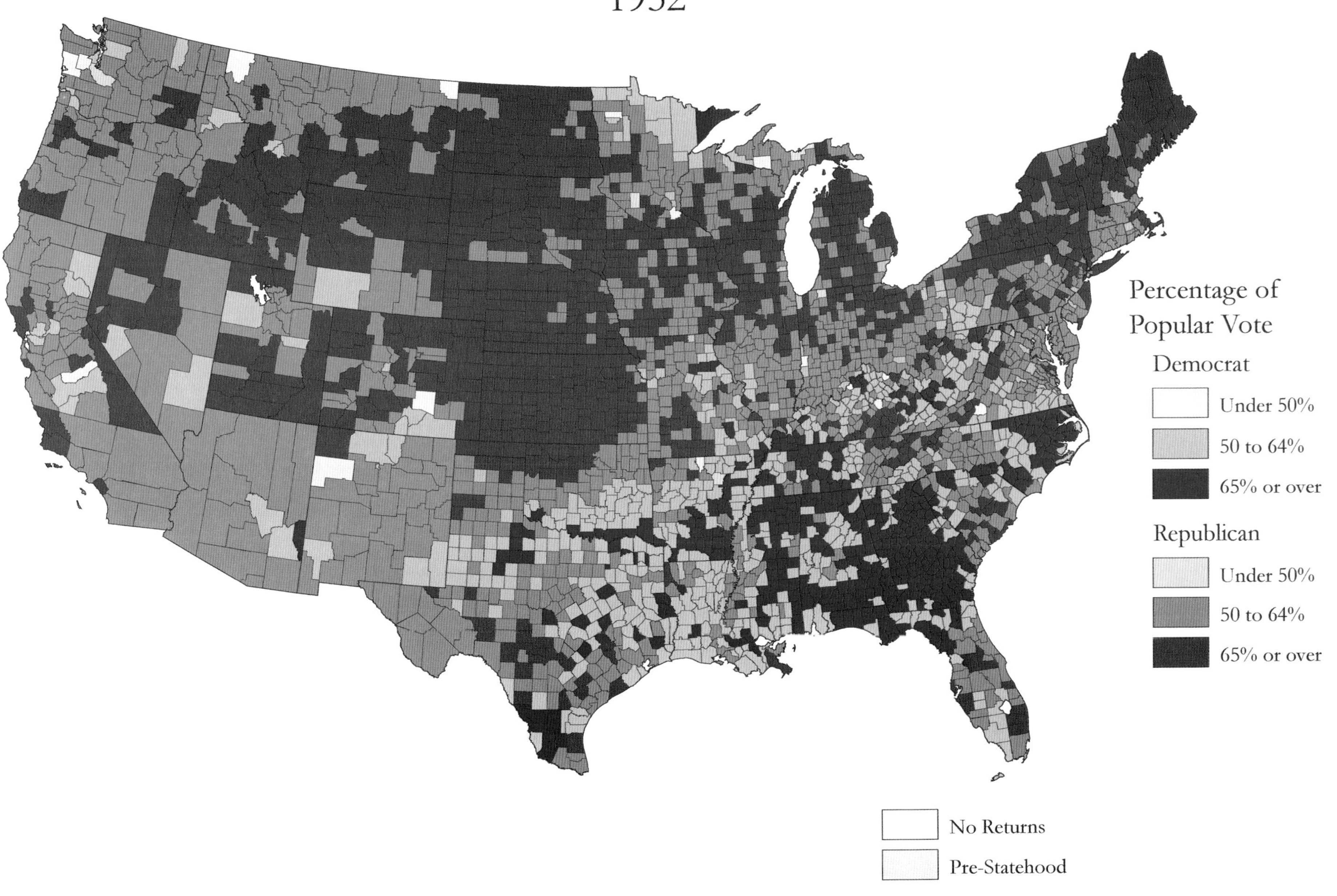

FIGURE 4.22

Presidential Election Popular Vote 1964

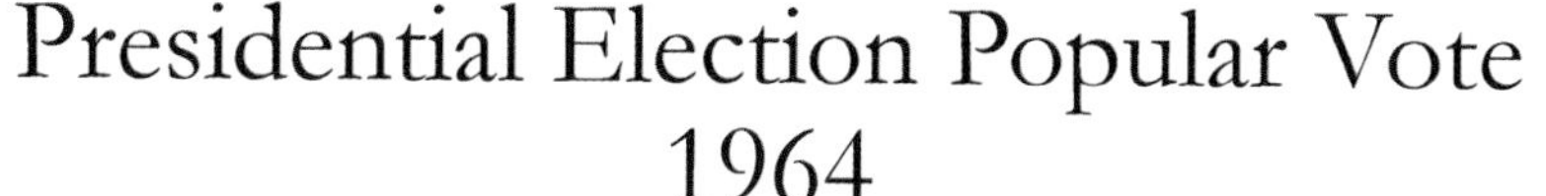

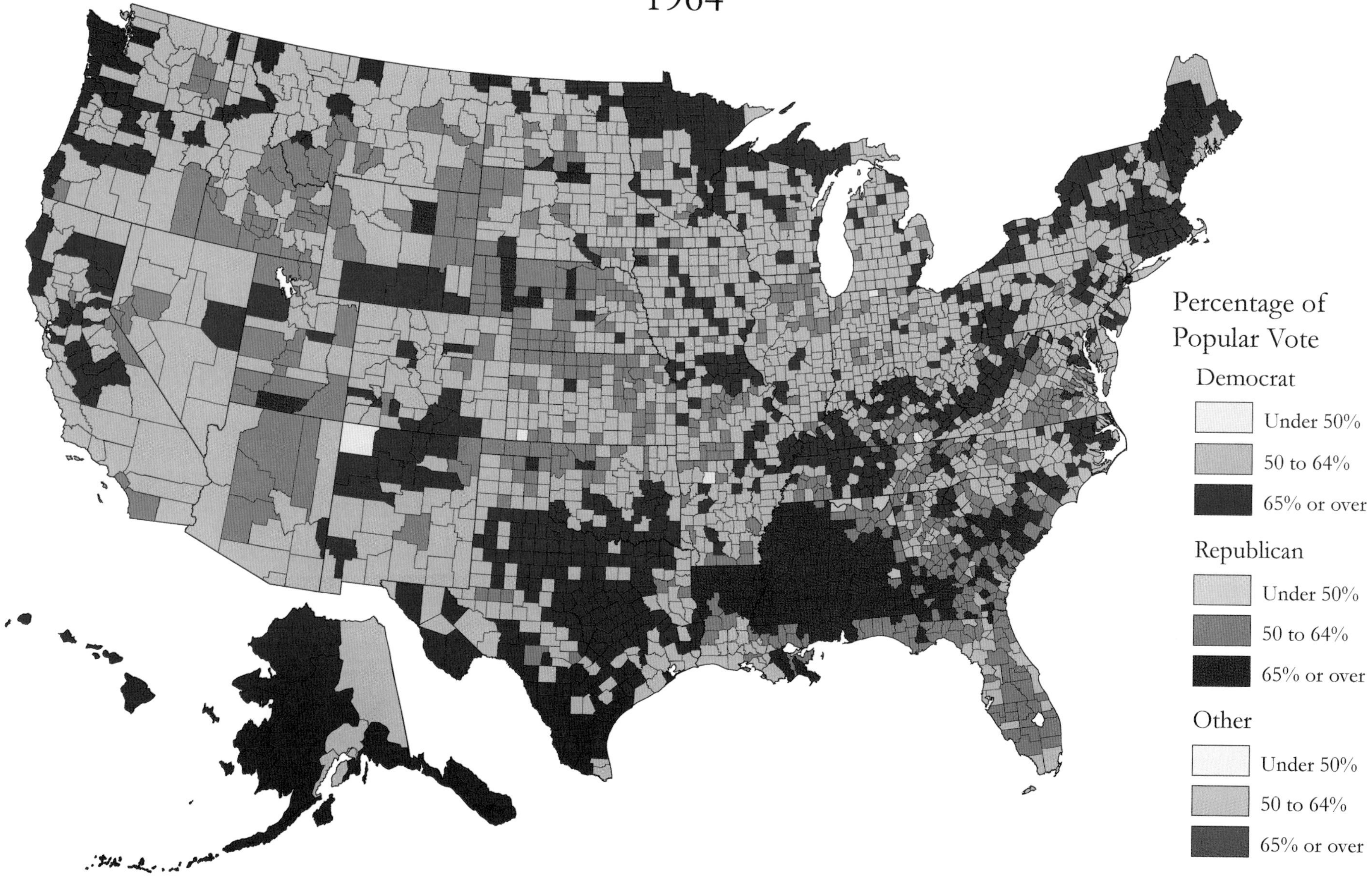

Percentage of Popular Vote
Democrat
Under 50%
50 to 64%
65% or over
Republican
Under 50%
50 to 64%
65% or over
Other
Under 50%
50 to 64%
65% or over

FIGURE 4.23

Presidential Election Popular Vote 1988

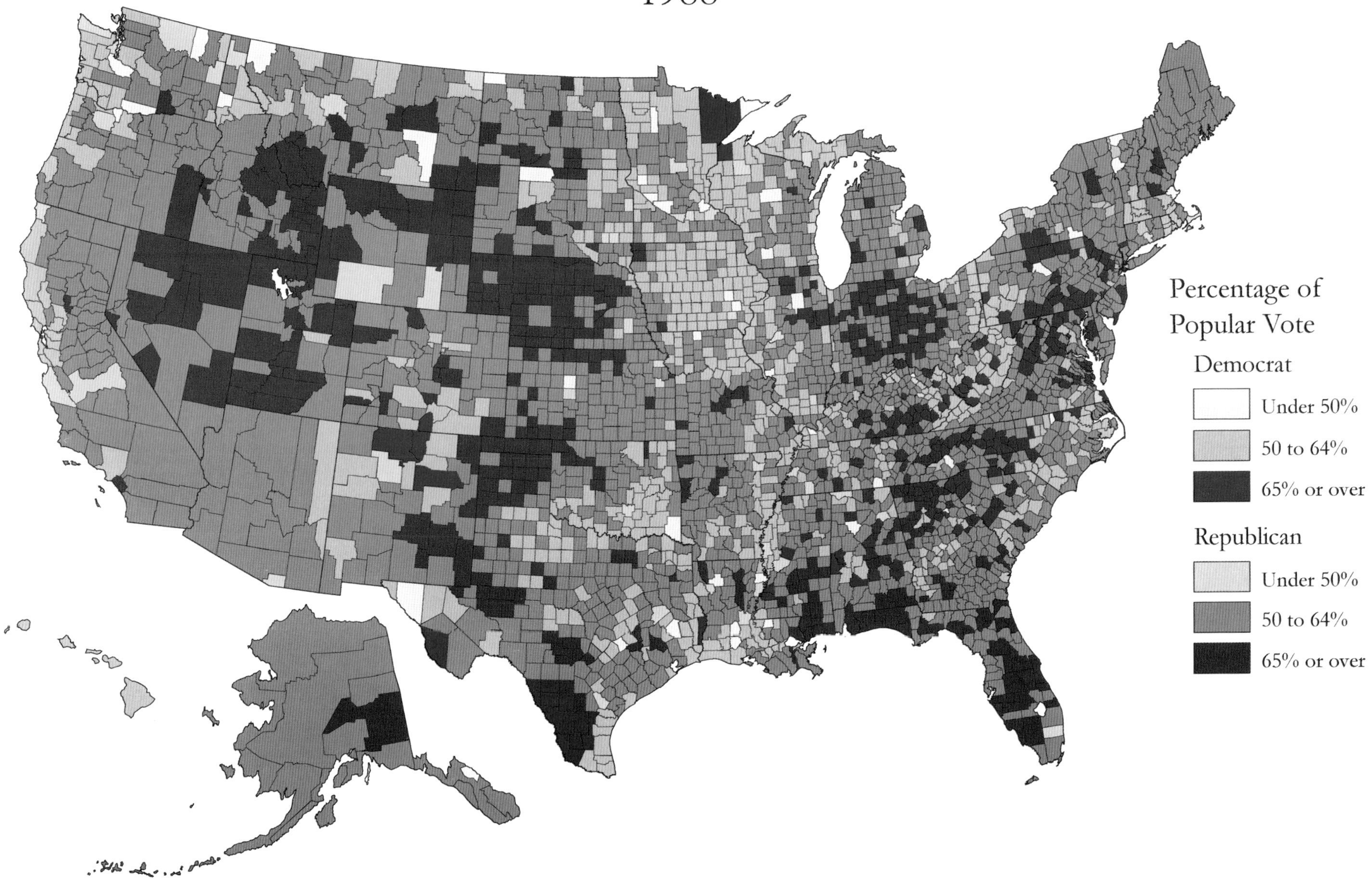

Percentage of Popular Vote

Democrat

- Under 50%
- 50 to 64%
- 65% or over

Republican

- Under 50%
- 50 to 64%
- 65% or over

FIGURE 4.24

Presidential Election Popular Vote 2016

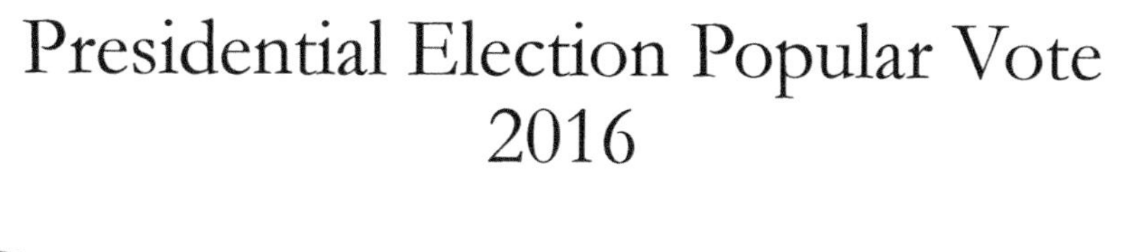

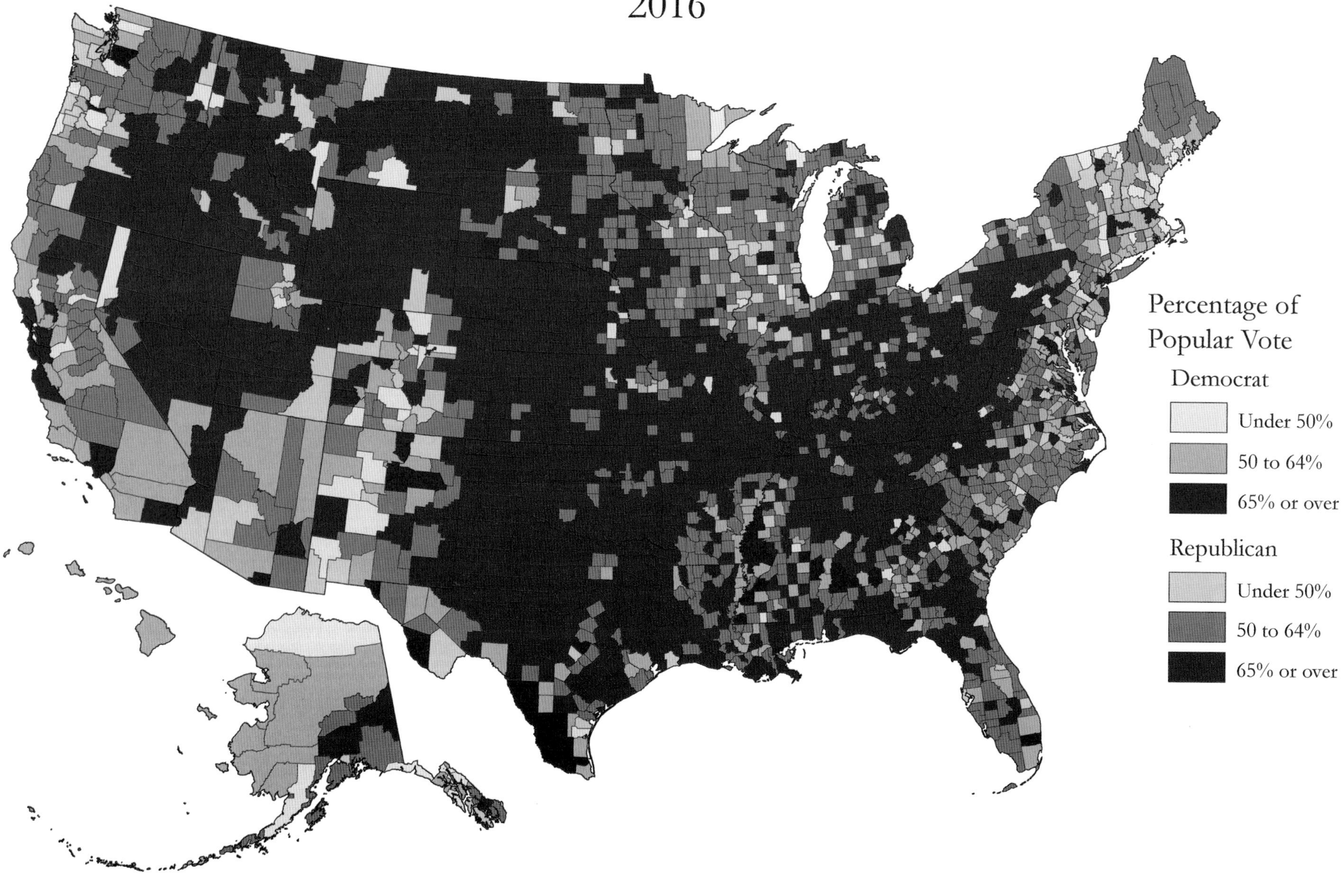
Percentage of Popular Vote
Democrat
Under 50%
50 to 64%
65% or over
Republican
Under 50%
50 to 64%
65% or over

4.24). By 1880, an electoral pattern that typified the late nineteenth and early twentieth centuries had begun to emerge. Republicans dominated much of the North, in particular those places along the northern fringe of the country stretching from northern New England to the Upper Midwest. The 1900 map shows this pattern even more clearly. The Republican nominee, William McKinley, won every county in New England and nearly every county in Michigan, Wisconsin, Minnesota, and Iowa. He won many of these counties with more than two-thirds of the vote on his way to a comfortable reelection over his Democratic opponent, William Jennings Bryan. In 1936, however, the Republicans suffered their worst defeat in US history, winning the electoral voters of Maine and Vermont only. However, the nineteenth-century pattern evident in 1880 and 1900 was still evident in 1936. Many of the counties carried by Republican Alf Landon in his unsuccessful bid for the presidency are located in the Northeast while Democratic incumbent Franklin Delano Roosevelt carried almost every county in the South.

This pattern began to break down after World War II. In 1952, Republican Dwight D. Eisenhower carried a significant number of Southern counties and won the electoral votes of a few Southern states. Increased Democratic support in the North and along the Pacific Coast, along with increased Republican support in the South, had become clearly evident by 1988. Indeed, unsuccessful Democratic nominee Michael Dukakis carried only ten states, and none of these states is located in the South where Dukakis carried only those Southern counties which are predominantly African American, including the Mississippi Delta and the Black Belt of Alabama. The trend continued in the 2016 election as shown elsewhere in this atlas.

Through T-mode analysis, one can identify time periods in which particular geographies of election results become evident (Archer and Taylor 1981; Archer and Shelley 1986). The T-mode procedure begins with the calculation of correlation coefficients between the results of each pair of elections. A correlation coefficient represents the degree of similarity between each pair of elections. The value of a correlation coefficient can range from −1 to 1. A correlation coefficient of 1 means that the pattern of votes in one election can be predicted perfectly by the pattern in another election, whereas a correlation coefficient of −1 means that the pattern in the first election is exactly the reverse of that in the second election. A correlation coefficient of 0 means that the two election patterns are entirely dissimilar. Thus, a 37 X 37 matrix of correlation coefficients was created and analyzed in order to identify groups of elections whose results are correlated highly with one another, but relatively uncorrelated or correlated negatively with other groups of elections.

Figure 4.25 shows correlation coefficients between the geography of the 2016 election and those of each previous election. Note the high degree of correlation between the elections of 2016 and 2012. Although Trump won in 2016 whereas Mitt Romney lost in 2012, the degree to which Trump improved upon Romney's performance was relatively uniform throughout the country. The 2016 election was correlated closely also with the elections of 2000, 2004, and 2008. Earlier in time, the 2016 outcome was correlated only weakly with the outcomes of most elections in the late twentieth century, very little with elections in the early twentieth century, and negatively with elections in the nineteenth century. A few exceptions can be noted, for example in 1976 in which Democrat Jimmy Carter swept the South whereas Republicans have been the dominant party in presidential elections there ever since.

The T-mode analysis of the election matrix yielded seven factors, each of which can be interpreted as an historical electoral epoch. Figure 4.26 shows each of these electoral epochs in chronological order. The first epoch consists of elections taking place from 1872 to 1888, and the second includes elections between 1892 and after World War I. Although Republicans dominated the North in both of these epochs, two key differences between them are that many of the Western states had not been admitted to the Union before 1888, and that the Populist Party arose in this region in protest of the domination of the US economy by Eastern-based capital interests. The third electoral epoch emerged after World War I and continued until after World War II.

FIGURE 4.25

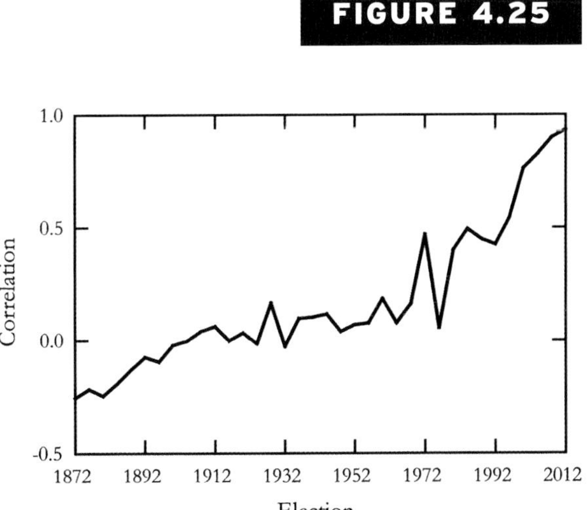

FIGURE 4.26

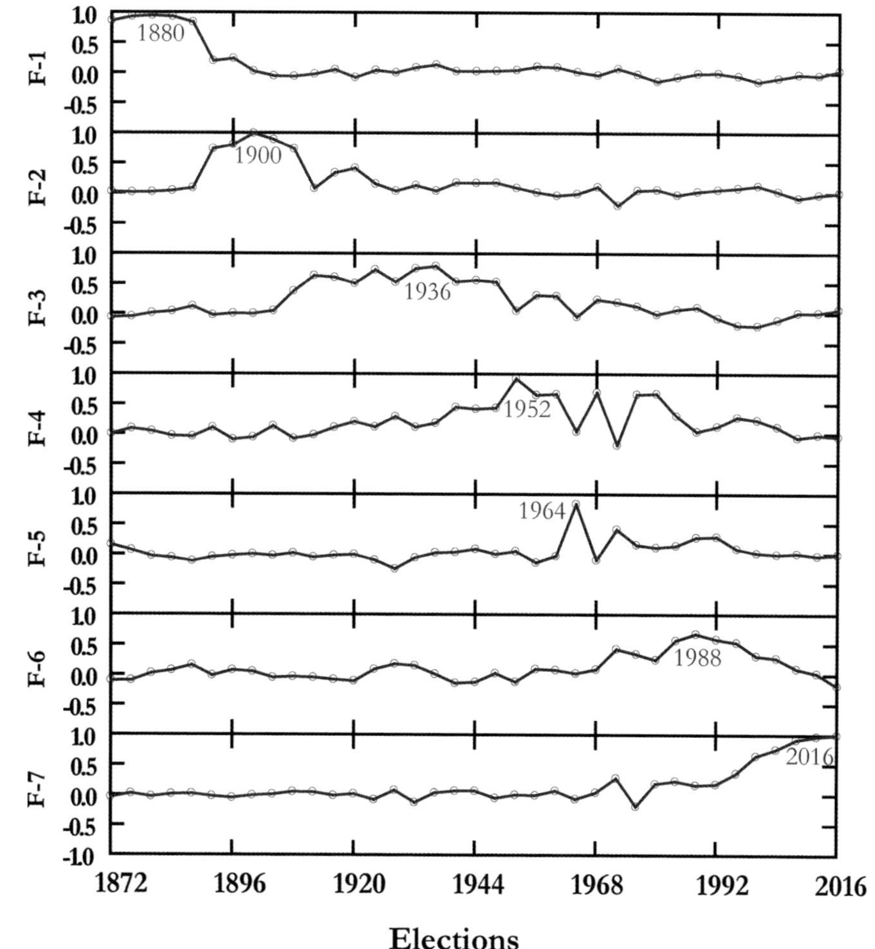

T-Mode Oblimin Factor Pattern Loadings Profiles: Percent Republican Vote by County, 1872 to 2016 Presidential Elections

Highest Loading Election Labeled in Red

The 1950s and 1960s can be identified as a transition period between World War II and today. Within this transition, 1964 was an anomaly in that Democrat Lyndon Johnson won the North by very large majorities in contrast to previous elections that were dominated in this region by Republicans. After the 1970s, the electoral patterns began to resemble those evident today. The final two electoral epochs arose during this time, with the first spanning the last two decades of the twentieth century and the second covering the elections that have occurred since 2000. Three key differences between these two epochs are evident, including the movement of Appalachia to the Republicans, the movement of the Pacific Coast to the Democrats, and, more generally, the increasing polarization between urban and rural areas. Thus Trump, Romney, and McCain each carried the large majority of counties across the United States, although their Democratic opponents won popular vote pluralities in each case because of their strength in large metropolitan areas.

The seven maps presented in this essay are the elections most typical of each epoch. Each of the graphs shows strong commonalities between these elections and the factor that represents that epoch statistically. Over the long run, the 2016 election represented a geographical continuation of a trend that had emerged in 2000. Whether this trend will continue in 2020 and beyond, of course, remains to be seen.

REFERENCES

Archer, J. Clark, and Fred M. Shelley. 1986. *American Electoral Mosaics.* Washington, DC: Association of American Geographers.

Archer, J. Clark, and Peter J. Taylor. 1981. *Section and Party: A Political Geography of American Presidential Elections, from Andrew Jackson to Ronald Reagan.* Chichester, UK: Wiley.

SPATIAL ANALYSIS OF THE 2016 ELECTION

JOHN HEPPEN

The 2016 presidential election continued a trend of increased spatial autocorrelation or polarization at the state and county levels. Both global and local techniques at measuring spatial autocorrelation highlight that trend. Global techniques give a measure of the overall level of spatial autocorrelation. Moran's *I* is a global indicator of spatial autocorrelation (Moran 1948; Moran 1950). As Moran's *I* approaches 1.0, the level of spatial autocorrelation of similar values clustering next to each other increases. A measure of 0.0 indicates randomness and no spatial autocorrelation. As Moran's *I* approaches –1.0, the pattern would expect to resemble a checkerboard or negative spatial autocorrelation.

The analysis was of the Democratic vote for president from 1892 to 2016 at the state level. Eighteen hundred ninety-two was the first year of the analysis since that was the first election where the United States was contiguous by state from coast to coast; Hawaii and Alaska are not included. The Democratic vote was paired with a spatial weights matrix, which recorded each state's neighbors, and entered into specialized software to calculate the global level of spatial autocorrelation. The election of 2016 continued in a trend of increasing spatial autocorrelation of polarization at the state level as shown in figure 4.27. The country is in an era of increased spatial autocorrelation in contrast to the previous trend from 1980 to 1992, which was an era of lower spatial polarization following a trend beginning in 1952. The era before World War II was an era in which the Democratic Party dominated the South resulting in higher levels of spatial autocorrelation. As the Republican Party became competitive in the South, the level of spatial autocorrelation decreased in a steady sawtooth pattern.

The pattern changes beginning in the 1990s as Moran's *I* takes a sharp increase beginning with the Clinton years after bottoming out in the 1980s. This coincides with the discussion among political observers that the country is becoming more

FIGURE 4.27

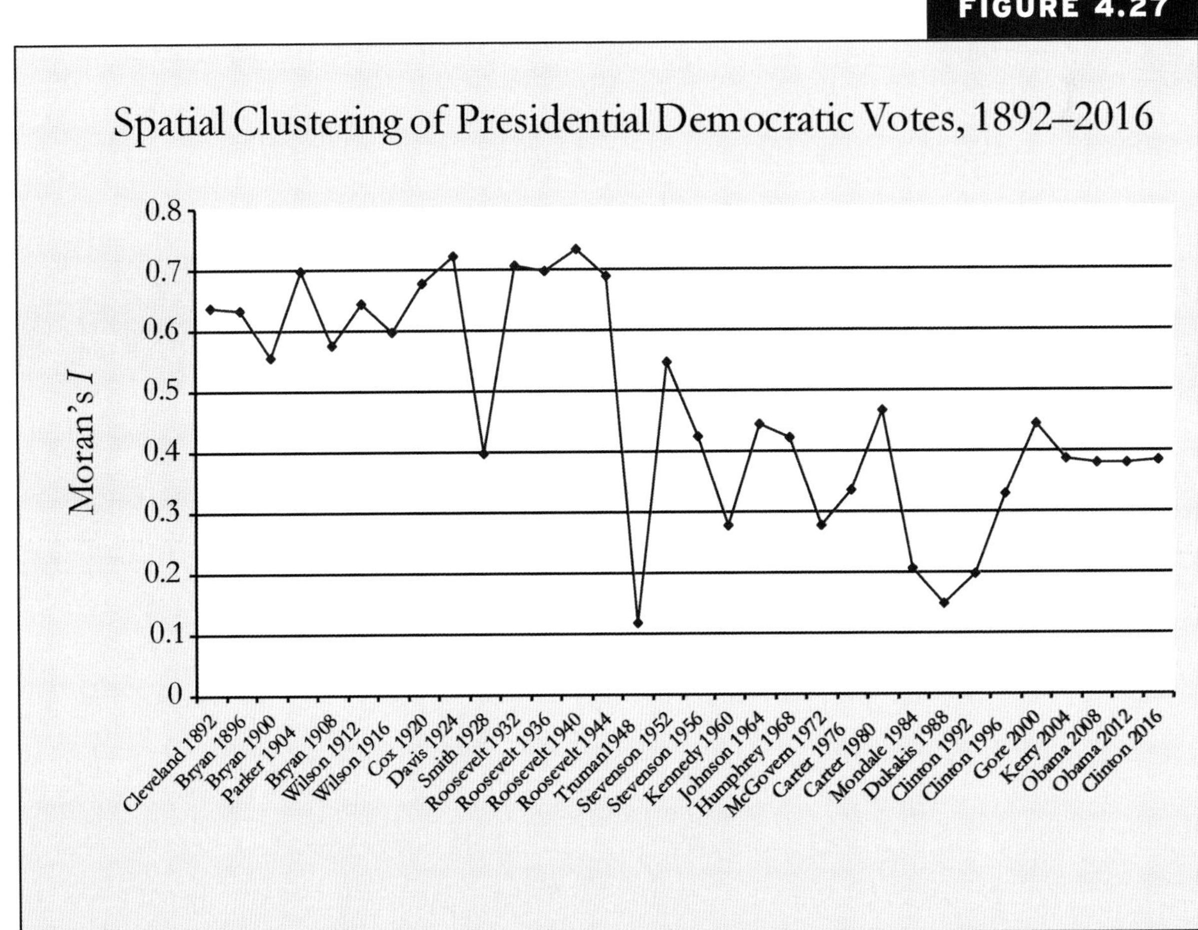

FIGURE 4.28

Trump Voting Clusters, 2016

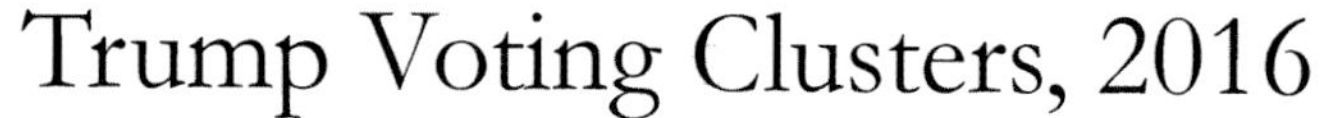

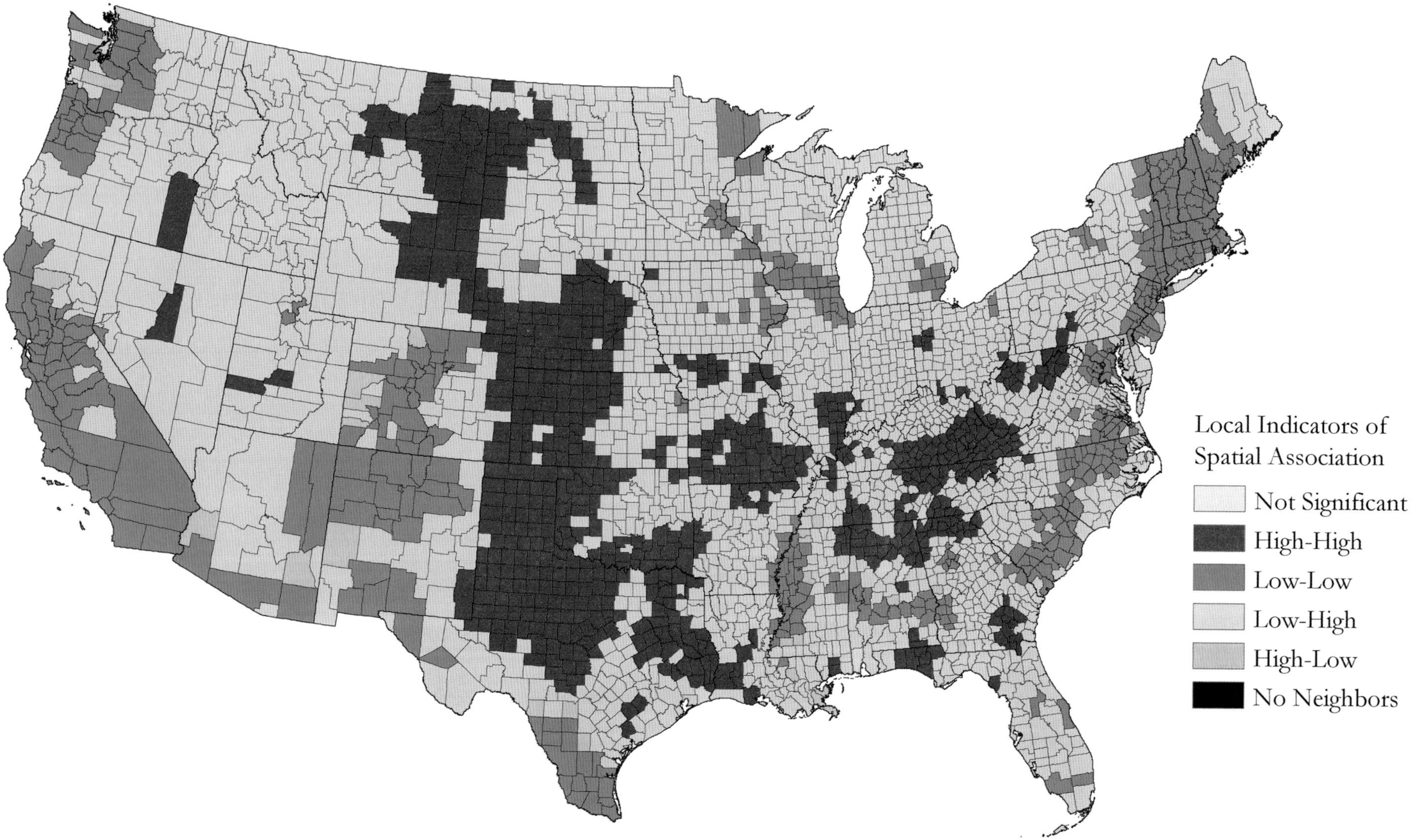
Local Indicators of Spatial Association
Not Significant
High-High
Low-Low
Low-High
High-Low
No Neighbors

FIGURE 4.29

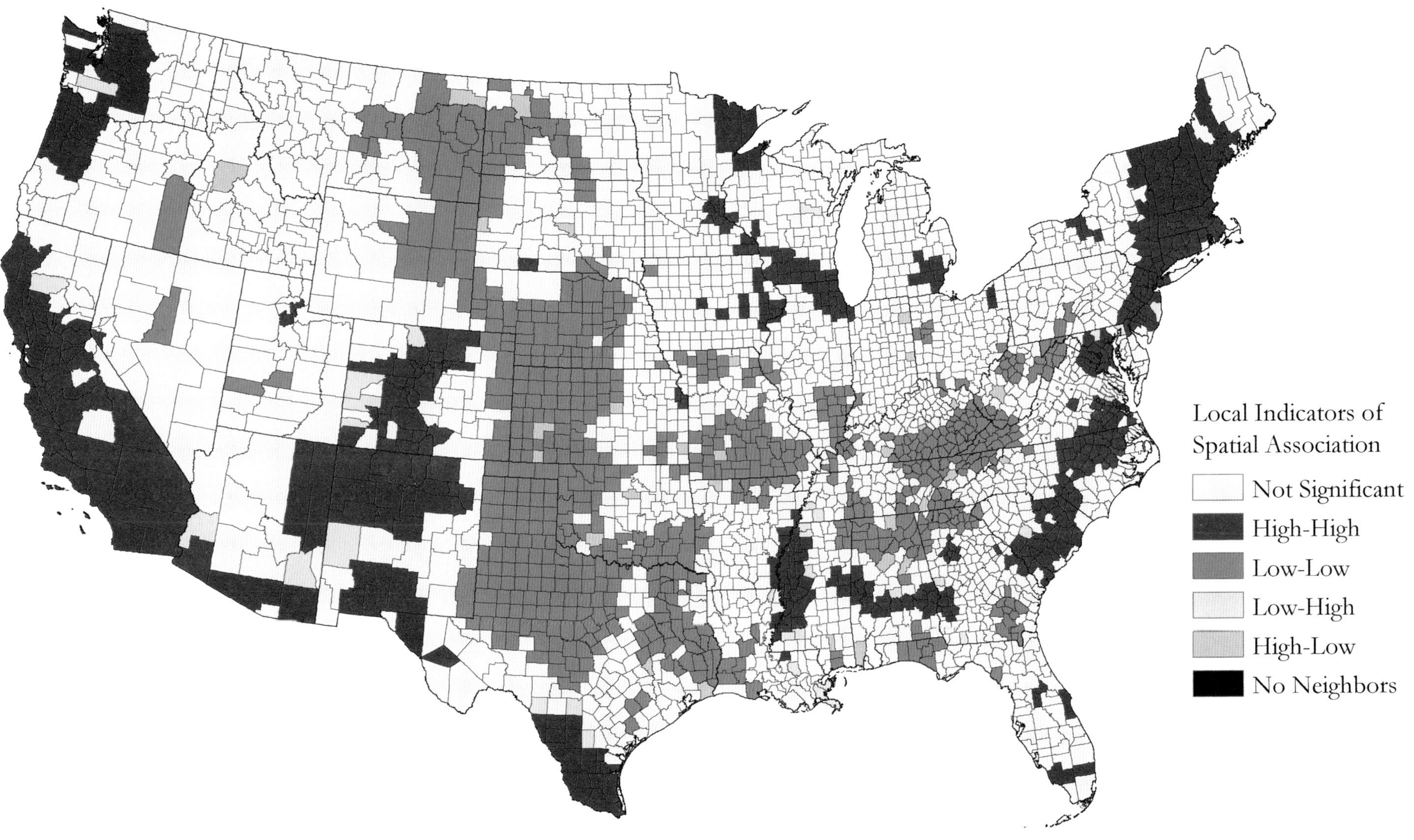
Clinton Voting Clusters, 2016
Local Indicators of Spatial Association
Not Significant
High-High
Low-Low
Low-High
High-Low
No Neighbors

divided both socially and geographically into a Red and Blue America, but the trend clearly began before the adoption of the Red and Blue America rhetoric after the 2000 election. Though it might have peaked in 2000, the level of spatial autocorrelation has remained remarkably consistent the last four presidential elections. No other era in our study period has remained so consistent, suggesting that we are in a period of stable and pronounced electoral division, with the South and Interior West voting Republican and the Northeast, Pacific, and Great Lakes leaning Democratic at the state level.

Moran's *I* at the county level for the 2012 and 2016 elections for both parties shows further evidence of a Red and Blue America. The data were the percentage of the vote at the county level for each candidate once again paired with a spatial weights matrix, which recorded each county's neighbors exactly as it was for the state level. Trump measured at 0.60 and Clinton measured at 0.60. Romney in 2012 measured 0.62 and Obama was 0.62 as well. The country at the county level is more divided and polarized than at the state level. One way to map and display the increased level of political division and polarization is at the county level using the local Moran's *I*, which is a local indicator of spatial association.

The local Moran's *I* is a local indicator of spatial association or LISA (Anselin 1995, 2016, 2017). Each unit of observation has a measure of how it contributes to the global level of spatial autocorrelation, allowing mapping of counties in our case. The local Moran's *I* tested to see if the vote in a county was spatially and statistically significant in relation to that of its neighbors. The same data and methods were used in calculating the local Moran's *I* as in calculating the Moran's *I* at the county level. Counties that are High-High are counties of high vote percentage bordered by counties of similar, high values. These are counties of high levels of support clustered together. Low-Low counties are counties of lower vote percentages bordered by similar counties. These are counties of low support clustered together. Those two cases represented clustering of similar values. High-Low counties are counties where a higher vote percentage is bordered by counties of low support. Low-High counties are counties of low votes with neighbors of high votes. Those last two categories represent outliers and are often only one county in size.

A comparison of both maps, shown in figures 4.28 and 4.29, reveals that High-High counties for Clinton tended to be Low-Low counties for Trump. By comparing both maps, the pattern emerges of Trump strength in Texas, the Great Plains, Appalachia, and the Upland South, which coincides with Clinton weakness. Areas of Clinton strength and Trump weakness include New England, Upstate New York and urban places of the Northeast Corridor, Appalachia, the Ozarks, and the Pacific Coast. Clinton was strong in the Black Belt of the South and Mississippi Delta areas of high African American populations. Counties of high Latino populations in South Texas and New Mexico registered as clusters of high support for Clinton. Greater Detroit and Northern Illinois, and counties of Wisconsin and Minnesota of the Upper Midwest, were also strong places of support. Of interest is that Clinton was weak in Utah, but Utah was not strong for Trump, showing the impact of the Evan McMullin campaign. McMullin, a Mormon and native of Utah, ran an independent conservative campaign for president.

Outlier counties in presidential elections are few, but interesting. Counties of High-Low support for either candidate tend to be next to clusters of counties of low support and counties of Low-High support are counties of low support next to counties of high support. High-Low counties for Clinton tend to be counties home to universities, American Indian reservations, and large minority populations. High-Low counties for Trump tend to be counties with large white populations next to counties with high minority populations. Low-High counties for both candidates tend to be High-Low counties for his or her opponent. In summary, at the state or county level, the election of 2016, while highly contentious, was not that much different spatially from the last few elections.

REFERENCES

Anselin, Luc. 1995. Local Indicators of Spatial Association—LISA. *Geographical Analysis* 27:93–115.

———. 2016. GeoDa Workshop Part 2. Center for Spatial Data Science. University of Chicago. https://s3.amazonaws.com/geoda/software/docs/geoda_1.8_2.pdf.

———. 2017. GeoDa 1.8. Center for Spatial Data Science. University of Chicago.

Moran, P. A. P. 1948. The Interpretation of Statistical Maps. *Journal of the Royal Statistical Society Series B* 10:245–51.

———. 1950. Notes on Continuous Stochastic Phenomena. *Biometrika* 37:17–23.

METROPOLITAN CONCENTRATION OF THE DEMOCRATIC VOTE

RICHARD L. MORRILL AND JASON COMBS

The urban-rural polarization in recent elections became even more pronounced in 2016. In the rural-urban pattern, established in the 1950s and 1960s, nonmetropolitan and rural areas tend to support Republican presidential candidates and larger metropolitan regions support Democratic presidential candidates. The rural-urban pattern was a major element in the 2016 election (Kurtzleben 2016).

Figure 4.30 depicts the percentage of votes won by Hillary Clinton versus Donald Trump for each metropolitan county. Republican Donald Trump won an overwhelming number of metropolitan and rural counties, but Hillary Clinton won many large metropolitan areas in decisive fashion (Wallace 2016). Of the 1,166 metropolitan counties, Trump carried 863 counties (74.01 percent). At the county level, even in the metropolitan category, Trump carried this category in dramatic fashion but Clinton actually won the percentage of votes casts—51.20 percent for Clinton (59,559,166 metropolitan votes) compared to 43.30 percent for Trump (50,365,663 metropolitan votes). Of the one hundred largest counties, Clinton won eighty-five of these counties, garnering 59.29 percent of the votes compared to Trump's 35.42 percent.

The largest metropolitan areas are important, as they counted for over 75 million votes of the 139 million in the 2016 election. Note that Democrat domination of the largest metropolitan areas is not complete—Clinton did best on the Atlantic coast, the Pacific coast, along with Chicago, Denver, Detroit, and Minneapolis–Saint Paul, but did not fare as well in most of the South and interior. Trump carried thirteen major metropolitan areas, with two in the west (Phoenix and Salt Lake City), five in the northeast (Cincinnati, Grand Rapids, Indianapolis, Kansas City, and Pittsburgh, with the latter two both switching to the Republican camp from the last election). Trump won nine in the South (Birmingham, Dallas, Jacksonville, Louisville, Nashville, Oklahoma City, San Antonio, and both Charlotte and Tampa Bay, which switched to the Republicans in 2016). A significant sub-pattern is Clinton's support in metropolitan areas with major universities and technology jobs, including Austin and Raleigh-Durham, for example.

Figure 4.31 shows the percentage of votes won by Hillary Clinton, Donald Trump, and other candidates in the largest populated areas where more than 500,000 votes were cast. In total, thirty-seven counties met this threshold for all presidential candidates, thirty-five when considering the two-party vote. Of those thirty-five, Hillary Clinton won thirty-two counties that cast more than 500,000 votes, compared to Donald Trump with only three (Maricopa County, Arizona; Suffolk County, New York; and Tarrant County, Texas). Clinton easily carried these thirty-five counties, capturing 19,514,376 (65.92 percent) while Trump garnered 10,084,749 (34.07 percent) votes.

Consider the top five metropolitan counties with overwhelming support for either Democrat or Republican. The top five for Clinton in order were the District of Columbia (90.86 percent), Bronx County, New York (88.52 percent), Prince George's, Virginia (88.13 percent), Petersburg, Virginia (87.20 percent), and New York, New York (86.56 percent). The top five totals for Trump are Armstrong, Texas (90.50 percent), Oldham, Texas (89.66 percent), Blount, Alabama (89.33 percent), Brantley, Georgia (88.48 percent), and Archer, Texas (88.40 percent). Each candidate captured a number of metropolitan counties by a landslide. Winning larger metropolitan counties is significant for Democratic presidential candidates because of the number of votes involved. The five counties with the highest percent support for Democrat Hillary Clinton equaled 1,571,559 more votes for Clinton. The five counties with the highest percent support for Republican Donald Trump equaled only 33,986 more votes for Trump. Compared to the 2012 election, Trump did well in the West, but nowhere near what Romney did. In 2012, Romney captured the Mormon West, with three of his top five counties in Idaho and Utah.

Clinton enjoyed success on both the East and West Coasts, especially in California, Oregon, and Washington in the West, and the District of Columbia, Massachusetts, and New York in the East. Trump, on the other hand, enjoyed limited success in many of the largest metropolitan areas but was still able to achieve victory by capturing the micropolitan and rural vote segments, offsetting Clinton's advantage in larger metropolitan

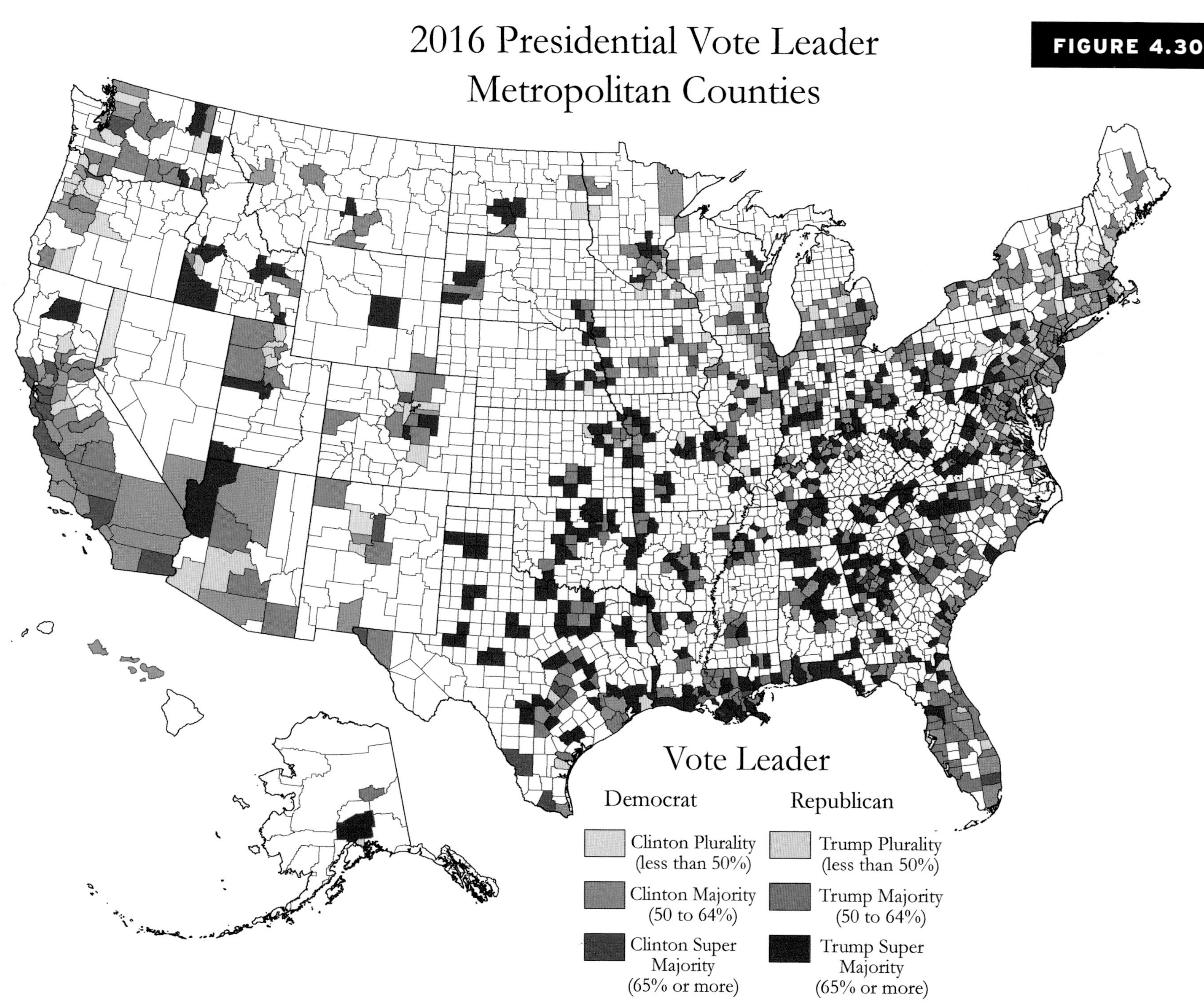
2016 Presidential Vote Leader
Metropolitan Counties
FIGURE 4.30
Vote Leader
Democrat
Republican
Clinton Plurality (less than 50%)
Trump Plurality (less than 50%)
Clinton Majority (50 to 64%)
Trump Majority (50 to 64%)
Clinton Super Majority (65% or more)
Trump Super Majority (65% or more)

FIGURE 4.31

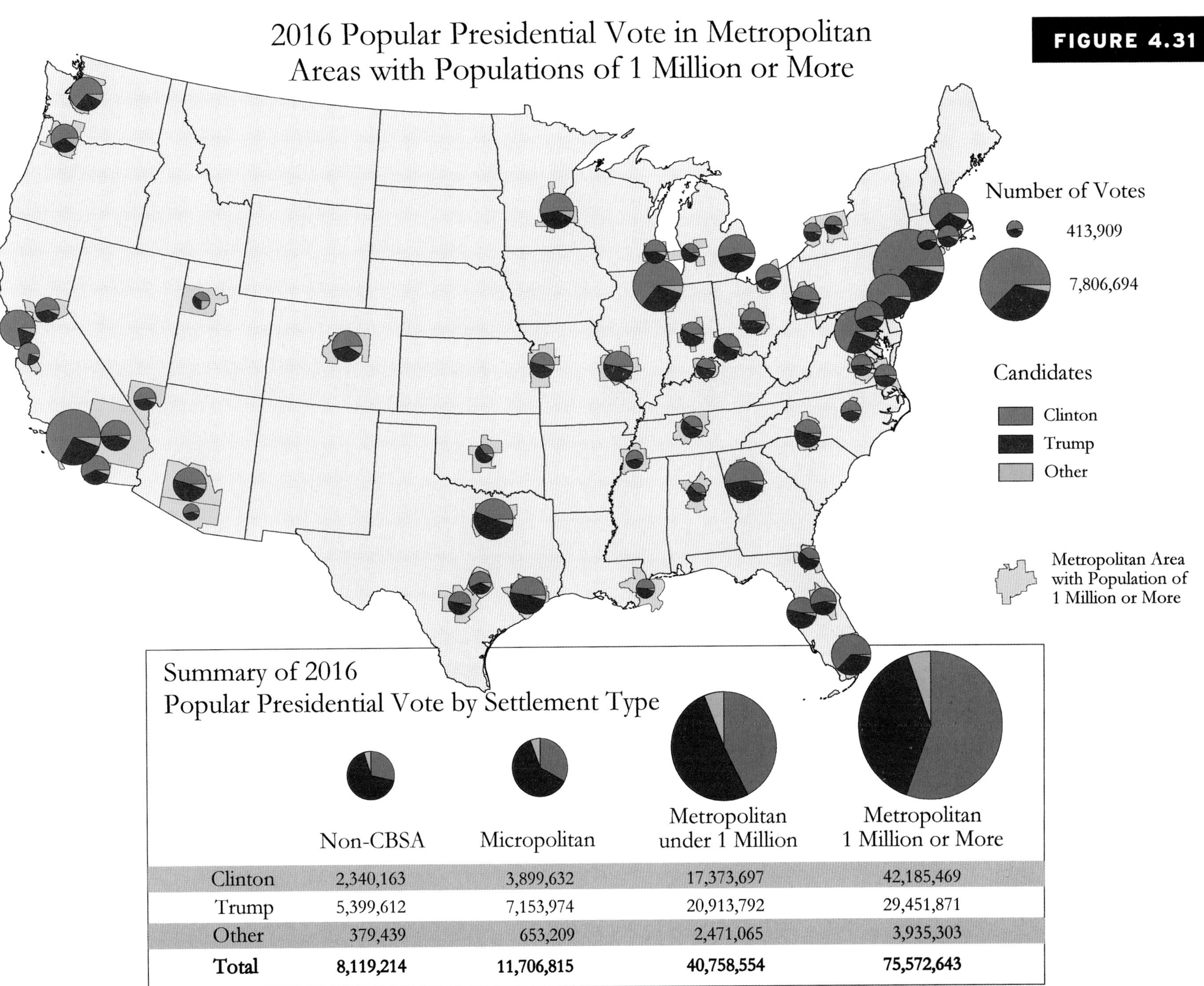

	Non-CBSA	Micropolitan	Metropolitan under 1 Million	Metropolitan 1 Million or More
Clinton	2,340,163	3,899,632	17,373,697	42,185,469
Trump	5,399,612	7,153,974	20,913,792	29,451,871
Other	379,439	653,209	2,471,065	3,935,303
Total	**8,119,214**	**11,706,815**	**40,758,554**	**75,572,643**

areas (Kirk, Scott, and Graham 2016). Trump carried fifteen of the one hundred most-populated counties, including five in Florida, three in Texas, two in Michigan, and one each in Arizona, Colorado, Kansas, New Jersey, and New York. As the United States becomes more urban and rural counties continue losing population, philosophical and political differences will most likely become more pronounced.

REFERENCES

Kirk, Ashley, Patrick Scott, and Chris Graham. 2016. US Election Results: The Maps and Analysis That Explain Donald Trump's Shock Victory to Become President. *The Telegraph*. November 15, http://www.telegraph.co.uk/news/0/us-election-results-and-state-by-state-maps (last accessed May 19, 2017).

Kurtzleben, Danielle. 2016. Rural Voters Played a Big Part in Helping Trump Defeat Clinton. *Politics*, NPR. November 14, http://www.npr.org/2016/11/14/501737150/rural-voters-played-a-big-part-in-helping-trump-defeat-clinton (last accessed May 19, 2017).

Wallace, Tim. 2016. The Two Americas of 2016. *The New York Times*. November 16, https://www.nytimes.com/interactive/2016/11/16/us/politics/the-two-americas-of-2016.html (last accessed May 19, 2017).

THE 2016 PRESIDENTIAL VOTE: THE RURAL VOTE

JEFF CRUMP

In the 2016 presidential election, rural voters strongly supported Republican Donald Trump. Trump's surprise victory was boosted by a strong showing in rural America. Trump won 1,202 of 1,317 (91.3 percent) rural counties. As figure 4.32 shows, widespread rural support made for very vivid maps wherein Trump's victory engulfs the United States in red. President Trump is very proud of such maps and has handed them out to reporters and other luminaries visiting the White House (Ryan 2017).

Trump received 66.5 percent of the rural vote while Clinton only garnered 28.8 percent. And even though rural voters accounted for just 5.96 percent of all US votes in the 2016 presidential election, Trump's rural strength proved especially important in the key states of Michigan, Pennsylvania, and Wisconsin (Brown and Monnat 2017). With razor-thin margins in each state, his strong rural showing helped him to victory in these critical states.

Among rural counties, Trump's margin of victory was greatest in Roberts County, Texas, where 95.9 percent of the voters chose Donald Trump. Reflecting the racial divisions of the 2016 presidential election, Roberts County is overwhelmingly white and has voted strongly Republican for many years. Electors in Roberts County, Texas, even vanquished Texan Lyndon Baines Johnson in 1964, giving their nod to deeply conservative Republican candidate Barry Goldwater.

Hillary Clinton was strongest in rural places such as Jefferson County, Mississippi, where she garnered 86.45 percent of the vote. In Jefferson County, Mississippi, African Americans comprise 85.7 percent of the population and it is the poorest county in Mississippi, with a median household income of $18,447 and a poverty rate of 32.5 percent.

Another rural county where Clinton did well is Oglala Lakota, South Dakota. Located on the Pine Ridge Reservation, the site of the notorious Wounded Knee massacre, Oglala Lakota County has a Native American population of 94.2 percent, where Clinton won 86.4 percent of the vote.

Trump increased the Republican share of the presidential vote in the Rust Belt, New England, and Appalachia (Monnat 2016). Trump was especially strong in rural counties suffering long-term economic distress. In areas with high unemployment, Trump outperformed the previous Republican candidate Mitt Romney (Monnat 2016). These results were especially evident in counties with a large white working-class population (Monnat 2016). Clearly Trump's message resonated with rural whites.

Many rural places are significantly impacted by the opioid crisis. As Monnat (2016) notes, in the last ten years, 400,000 people in the United States died from drug overdoses, an additional 400,000 committed suicide, and another 250,000 died due to alcoholism and alcohol-related diseases. Under the Obama administration, the response to the growing opioid epidemic was anemic. Before he was appointed US Attorney General, Eric Holder defended the major producer of OxyContin, Purdue Pharma, against charges of deceptive practices concerning the addictive qualities of the drug (Frydl 2016). As Frydl (2016) notes, once he became US Attorney General, Holder continued to protect Purdue Pharma, which paid a $634.5 million fine while making a profit of $31 billion. Rural voters cannot be faulted for thinking they were ignored by Democrats who did not seriously address the opioid epidemic.

In rural counties with increasing mortality due to drug use, alcoholism, and suicide, there is a strong relationship between these conditions and the Trump vote (Monnat 2016). In rural counties where "deaths of despair" were highest, Trump flipped many counties that had voted for Obama in 2012.

Trump's anti-immigrant rhetoric resonated especially well in rural places where opioid addiction and drug overdoses brought many communities to their knees. Rural residents in opioid counties are angry because most heroin comes from Mexico. Therefore, even in places with few immigrants, frightened residents blame their drug problem on Mexico. When Trump promised to build a wall to keep drugs out, his statements found a ready audience.

There is a crisis in rural America that has not been adequately addressed by either party. In his campaign, Trump did recognize these problems and offered solutions, however simplistic and nativist, to the scourge of opioid addiction (Quinones

2016). As Quinones (2016) states, "*that* states crucial to Trump's victory—Ohio, North Carolina and Pennsylvania . . . largely *rural, religious and white*—are now our heroin beltways amount[s] to a stunning change in our national culture." Rural places have deep problems that need to be addressed. It remains to be seen whether Trump or his opponents have the willingness to do so.

REFERENCES

Brown, David L., and Shannon Monnat. 2017. Rural Voters and the Rural Vote in 2016. *American Sociology Association: Community & Urban Sociology Section Newsletter* 29(2).

Frydl, Kathleen. 2016. The Oxy Electorate. *Medium.* November 16, https://medium.com/@kfrydl/the-oxy-electorate-3fa62765f837 (last accessed June 28, 2017).

Monnat, Shannon. 2016. Deaths of Despair and Support for Trump in the 2016 Election. Department of Agricultural Economics, Sociology, and Education Research Brief, Pennsylvania State University. December 4, http://aese.psu.edu/directory/smm67/Election16.pdf (last accessed June 28, 2017).

Quinones, S. 2016. Donald Trump & Opiates in America. *Dreamland . . . a Reporter's Blog from Author/Journalist Sam Quinones*. November 21, http://samquinones.com/reporters-blog/2016/11 (last accessed 28 June 2017).

Ryan, J. 2017. Journalist: Trump Brought Electoral Map Handouts of His Wins to Interview. *CNN.* April 28, http://www.cnn.com/2017/04/28/politics/trump-brought-printed-map-handouts-cnntv/index.html (last accessed June 28, 2017).

MICROPOLITAN COUNTY VOTING

JASON COMBS

In comparison to the 2012 election, the percentages of micropolitan and rural votes declined while the metropolitan votes actually increased. In the 2012 presidential election, micropolitan voters accounted for 9.9 percent of the vote, and in 2016, the proportion of micropolitan voters had fallen to 8.6 percent of the electorate. Rural voters similarly declined in proportion to the electorate. Rural voters accounted for 6.4 percent of the presidential vote in 2012 compared to 5.96 percent in 2016. Despite the fact that both categories accounted for a smaller proportion of the electorate, Republican candidate Donald Trump won both by landslide margins (Gamio and Keating 2016). The micropolitan and rural margins of victory helped Trump flip six key states that voted Democrat in 2012—Florida, Iowa, Michigan, Ohio, Pennsylvania, and Wisconsin.

A relatively new term, micropolitan areas include a central city with a population of 10,000 to 49,999 in addition to surrounding counties economically linked to the central city. Currently 658 counties in the United States are classified as micropolitan, as shown in table 4.1. Of the two-party vote, which represents more than 94 percent of all micropolitan votes, Republican candidate Donald Trump garnered 61.11 percent of the votes (7,153,974) compared to Democratic candidate Hillary Clinton's 33.31 percent (3,899,632). Trump carried rural counties by an even wider margin, capturing 66.5 percent (5,399,612 votes) compared to Clinton's 28.82 percent (2,340,163).

Trump in 2016 captured 61.11 percent of the micropolitan vote, mapped in figure 4.32, which equaled a tremendous advantage at the county level. The Republican candidate won 571 micropolitan counties (86.78 percent) in comparison to Clinton's 87, a meager 13.22 percent of the total. Trump enjoyed success across the country and found significant micropolitan support in the Great Plains, Midwest, Mountain West, parts of the South, and across the Ohio River states of Indiana, Ohio, and Pennsylvania. Trump carried 62 micropolitan counties with at least 80.0 percent of the vote and another 335 with at least 70.0 percent.

TABLE 4.1. Core-Based Statistical Area Voting Results by County, 2016

CBSA Level	Clinton Total Votes	Trump Total Votes	Total Other Votes	Total Vote	% Clinton	% Trump	% Other
Metro	59,559,166	50,365,663	6,406,368	116,331,197	51.20	43.30	5.51
Micro	3,899,632	7,153,974	653,209	11,706,815	33.31	61.11	5.58
Rural	2,340,163	5,399,612	379,439	8,119,214	28.82	66.50	4.67

Trump fared much better than the previous two Republican candidates, Romney (2012) and McCain (2008) in comparison. Trump's top five counties included one that was also in Romney's top five (Gray County, Texas, with 87.78 percent in 2016), but the similarities stopped there. Three counties in the Mormon West were in Romney's top five; none were in Trump's. Trump replaced three Idaho and Utah counties with three in Nebraska in the top five ranking—Glasscock, Texas (91.56 percent), McPherson, Nebraska (89.55 percent), Banner, Nebraska (88.81 percent), Logan, Nebraska (88.30 percent), and Gray, Texas (87.78 percent).

Clinton did not have widespread support at the micropolitan level but did enjoy isolated success, primarily along the West Coast, along the Rio Grande border, in the Mississippi Delta, and in the far northeastern United States. Numerous counties in Oregon and California, along with several counties in New Mexico and Texas—especially along the border with Mexico—favored Clinton over Trump. Additionally, several counties in Mississippi along the river supported Clinton, as did numerous micropolitan counties in Massachusetts, New Hampshire, and Vermont. In contrast to Trump, Clinton carried a single micropolitan county with at least 80.0 percent of the vote—Claiborne, Mississippi (86.8 percent)—and only five additional counties with at least 70.0 percent of the vote. In addition to Claiborne, Mississippi, the top five

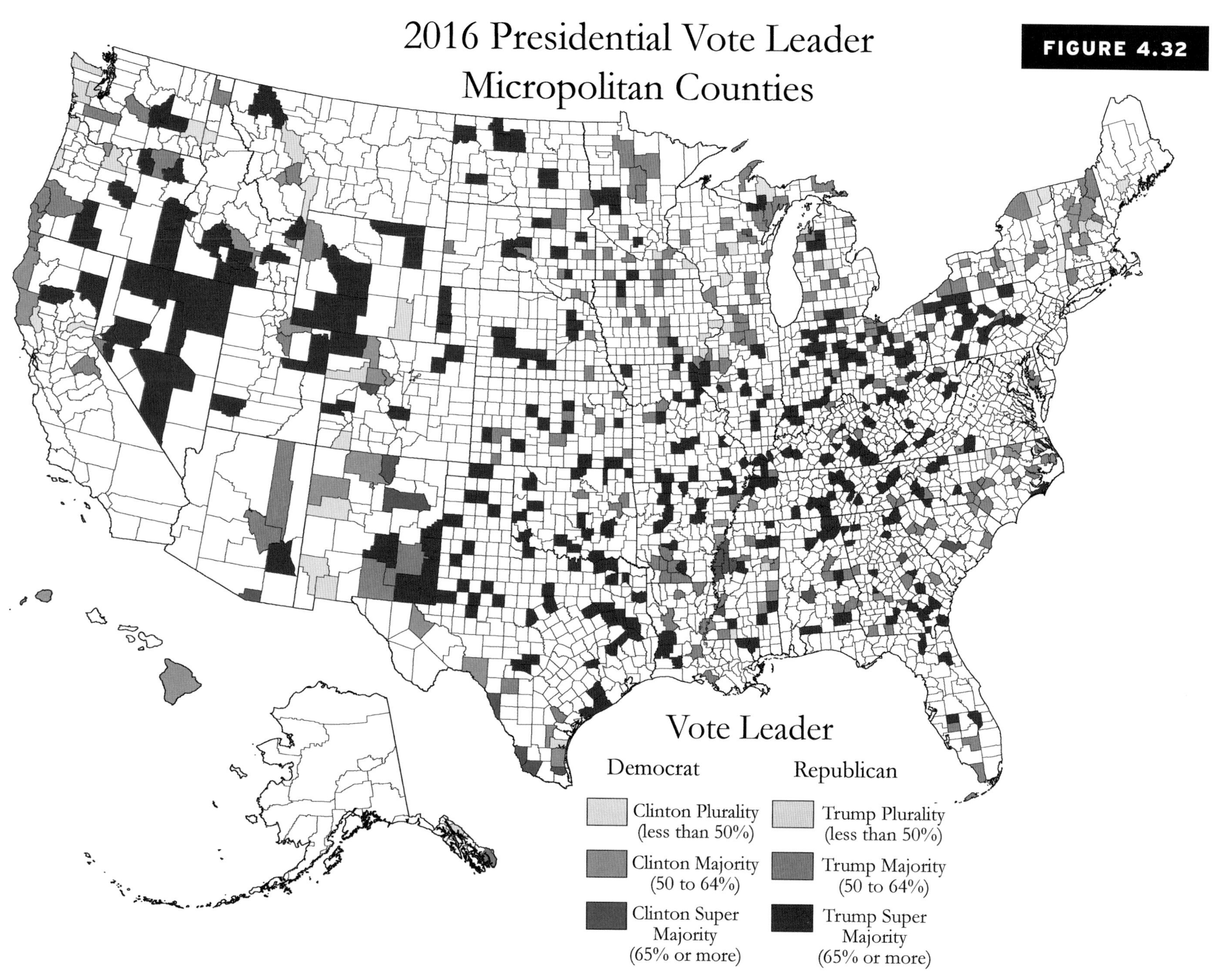
2016 Presidential Vote Leader
Micropolitan Counties
FIGURE 4.32
Vote Leader
Democrat
Republican
Clinton Plurality (less than 50%)
Clinton Majority (50 to 64%)
Clinton Super Majority (65% or more)
Trump Plurality (less than 50%)
Trump Majority (50 to 64%)
Trump Super Majority (65% or more)

include Starr, Texas (79.12 percent), Menominee, Wisconsin (76.61 percent), Maverick, Texas (76.52 percent), and Hancock, Georgia (75.45 percent).

Overall, for the micropolitan counties, Trump (with 61.11 percent) carried the category by 3,254,342 votes. As astounding as that number is, it is still less than Clinton's vote advantage in Chicago, Los Angeles, New York, and Seattle—3,869,347. This fact points to Trump's key election strategy of ceding to Clinton some of the most-populated metropolitan regions but overcoming those losses with key wins in micropolitan and rural counties that swayed the Electoral College. In previous elections, the candidate who carried key metropolitan areas enjoyed success in the Electoral College, which was not the case in 2016.

The 2016 election demonstrated voting cleavages between more liberal metropolitan areas and more conservative micropolitan and rural counties that are likely to continue (Brownstein 2016). The polarization of the electorate and these voting patterns are not new, but ideological divisions in the United States are clearly becoming more pronounced.

REFERENCES

Brownstein, Ronald. 2016. How the Election Revealed the Divide Between City and Country. *The Atlantic*. November 17, https://www.theatlantic.com/politics/archive/2016/11/clinton-trump-city-country-divide/507902 (last accessed May 19, 2017).

Gamio, Lazaro, and Dan Keating. 2016. How Trump Redrew the Electoral Map, From Sea to Shining Sea. *The Washington Post*. November 9, https://www.washingtonpost.com/graphics/politics/2016-election/election-results-from-coast-to-coast (last accessed May 19, 2017).

FLIPPED COUNTIES IN THE 2016 ELECTION

JASON COMBS

In the 2016 presidential election, "flipped" counties proved to be critical for Donald Trump's victory. Republican candidate Donald Trump flipped 221 counties that Barack Obama won in the 2012 contest—92 rural, 75 metropolitan, and 54 micropolitan counties. In comparison, Democratic candidate Hillary Clinton flipped a meager 17 counties that Republican candidate Mitt Romney carried in 2012—11 metropolitan and 6 micropolitan counties.

Clusters of counties that Trump brought to the Republican fold in 2016 are highlighted in figure 4.33. Several counties in Oregon and Washington in the Pacific Northwest, along with multiple counties in Colorado and New Mexico, flipped for Trump. Trump also flipped a number of counties in the Northeast, specifically in Maine, New Hampshire, and New York. Only one Electoral College vote (Maine had one of its four shift to the Republican ticket) in these seven states transitioned to the Republican camp. Trump flipped a number of counties stretching in an arc from the Mississippi Delta through Alabama, Florida, Georgia, North Carolina, South Carolina, and Virginia. Of all these states, only Virginia voted Democrat in 2016—in 2012 both Florida and Virginia supported Obama.

Many states that were home to a number of flipped counties played central roles in campaign spending and were critical battleground states (Pearce 2016). *NBC News* tracked spending in thirteen key battleground states that contained several flipped counties. Clinton doubled Trump's campaign budget in the thirteen states and won six of the states—Maine's Electoral College votes were split 3–1 in 2016 (Dann 2016). The six states Clinton carried were in the Democrat column in 2012, representing 40 Electoral College votes. Trump, however, carried seven of these thirteen states by flipping many strategic counties in Florida, Iowa, Michigan, North Carolina, Ohio, Pennsylvania, and Wisconsin that proved to be a tremendous advantage in the Electoral College. Six of these seven states supported Obama in 2012 and flipped to Trump in 2016, representing 96 Electoral College votes—the final tally in the Electoral College was Trump 306 to Clinton 232.

In addition to campaign spending, campaign visits concentrated on flipped counties and states (Schoen 2016). Consider public campaign events by major party nominees. Twelve states held at least ten public events in the latter half of 2016—Arizona, Colorado, Florida, Iowa, Michigan, Nevada, New Hampshire, North Carolina, Ohio, Pennsylvania, Virginia, and Wisconsin—which equaled 94 percent of all campaign events. Trump won eight of these states (125 Electoral College votes) and Clinton captured four (32 Electoral College votes). Moreover, Trump spent an abundance of time in Iowa and Wisconsin, two states in which Obama won in 2012 but that received little attention from the Clinton campaign in 2016 (Schultheis 2016). Together they hosted thirty-five public campaign events (Iowa 21 and Wisconsin 14) and were home to fifty-five Republican flipped counties (Iowa 32 counties and Wisconsin 23).

Ultimately, flipped counties were pivotal in the 2016 presidential election. Trump held a tremendous advantage over Clinton regarding flipped counties both in terms of quantity (221 to 17) and strategic location, which resulted in a decisive Electoral College victory.

REFERENCES

Dann, Carrie. 2016. Pro-Clinton Battleground Ad Spending Outstrips Trump Team by 2–1. *NBC News*. November 4, http://www.nbcnews.com/politics/first-read/pro-clinton-battleground-ad-spending-outstrips-trump-team-2-1-n677911 (last accessed May 19, 2017).

Pearce, Adam. 2016. Trump Has Spent a Fraction of What Clinton Has on Ads. *The New York Times*. October 21, https://www.nytimes.com/interactive/2016/10/21/us/elections/television-ads.html (last accessed May 19, 2017).

Schoen, John. 2016. Here's What Clinton, Trump Spent to Turn Out Votes. *CNBC*. November 7, http://www.cnbc.com/2016/11/07/heres-where-clinton-trump-spent-on-their-ground-games.html (last accessed May 19, 2017).

Schultheis, Emily. 2016. Where Have Donald Trump and Hillary Clinton Spent Their Time? *CBS News*. October 27, http://www.cbsnews.com/news/analysis-where-have-donald-trump-and-hillary-clinton-spent-their-time (last accessed May 19, 2017).

FIGURE 4.33

"Flipped" Counties between the 2012 and 2016 Presidential Elections

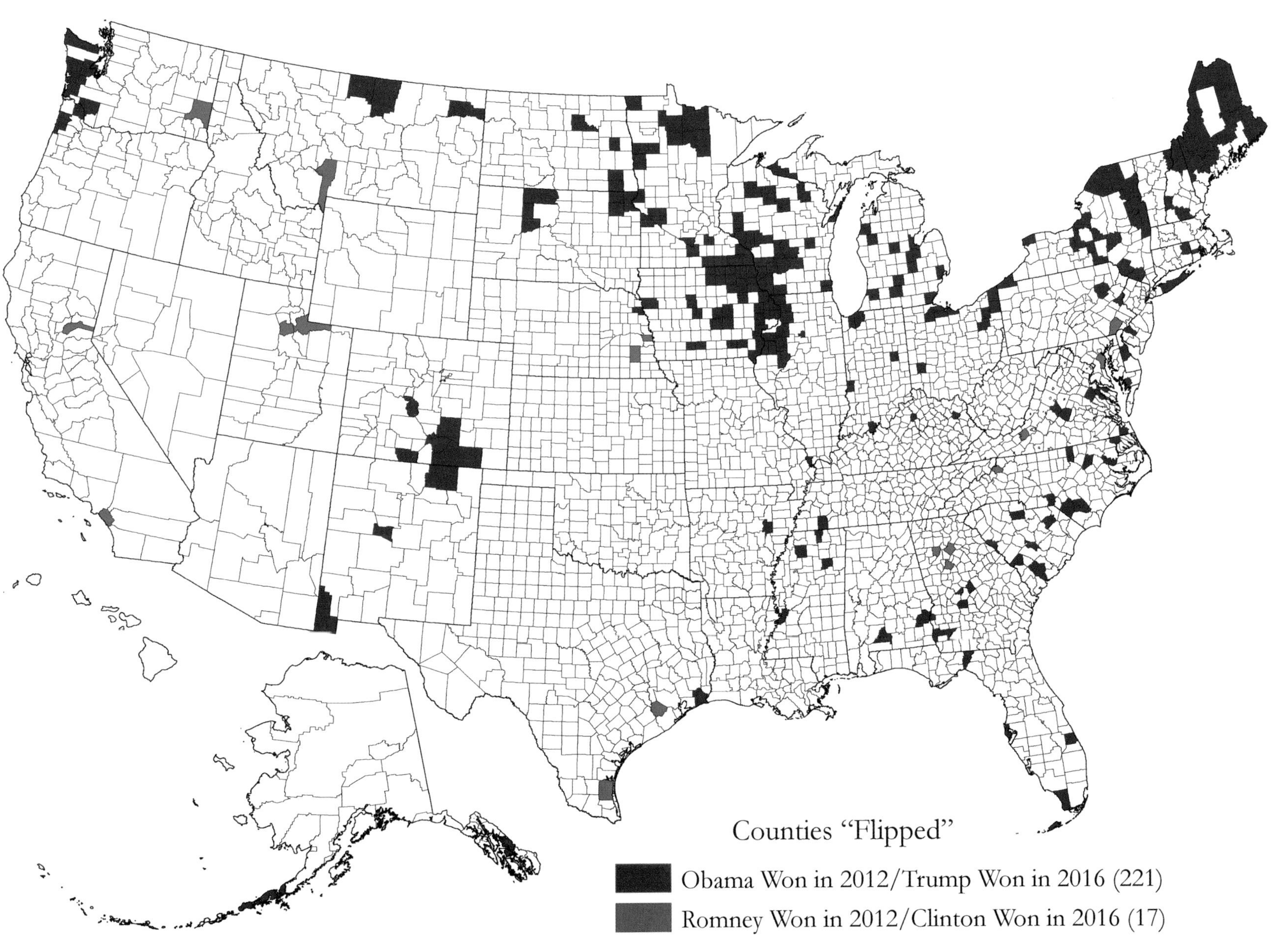

AN INCREASINGLY POLARIZED AMERICA?

RON JOHNSTON, KELVYN JONES, AND DAVID MANLEY

Donald Trump's victory in 2016 was heralded by some as initiating a major change to the country's electoral geography because he appealed to groups that had not previously given much support to Republican candidates. He also alienated others with his comments about, for example, women, immigrants, and Muslims. However, he won all of the "red states" that have traditionally voted Republican in recent decades, and Hillary Clinton won all of the Democrats' stronghold "blue states." Trump also gained sufficient additional support in several "swing states," where Obama prevailed in 2008 and 2012, to gain Electoral College victory, despite winning three million fewer votes than Hillary Clinton overall. So did the country's electoral geography change markedly in 2016?

SPATIAL POLARIZATION

It is frequently claimed that the United States has become a more divided nation recently—ideologically across the population and in Congress, and geographically. The case for increased geographical polarization was made in Bishop's (2009) argument that supporters of both Republican and Democratic presidential candidates had become spatially more concentrated. Counties won by a margin of more than 20 percentage points—termed *landslide counties*—had been increasing in number.

This argument was criticized by Abrams and Fiorina (2012) but later multilevel modelling, shown in figure 4.34, provided strong statistical evidence that polarization had increased at three separate spatial scales—census division, state, and, especially, county—over the six presidential elections between 1992 and 2012 (Johnston et al. 2016). This chapter updates that analysis to 2016, using data for 3,077 counties (or county-equivalents in some states); Alaska and the District of Columbia are excluded because they are not subdivided into equivalent sub-state areas.

To measure spatial polarization, we use the median odds ratio (MOR), which is interpreted as the average difference between, say, one state and another in the ratio of observed to expected votes for the Democratic candidate. The larger the MOR, the greater the polarization or the greater the concentration of its supporters into particular divisions, states, and counties; a full description of the method is given in Jones et al. (2015) and Johnston et al. (2016). Because the analysis excludes voters for "third-party" candidates (i.e., those representing other than the Republican and Democratic parties), the MORs are the same whichever of the two parties' votes are analyzed.

If the *Big Sort* argument is correct, the MORs should increase over time. For a firm conclusion that polarization has increased, they should significantly differ from each other using standard probability levels. That is indeed what the modelled results show, as the graphs of the MOR values and their credible intervals in figure 4.35 demonstrate.

There was an upward trend in the MOR values at each scale—from 1.18 in 1992 to 1.67 in 2016 at the divisional scale (an increase of 42 percent); from 1.25 to 1.46 at the state scale (a smaller increase of 17 percent); and from 1.48 to 1.83 at the county scale (a 24 percent increase). Polarization clearly increased: each party's voters were more concentrated in particular divisions, states within divisions, and counties within states within divisions, in 2016 than in 1992. We can be particularly confident in this conclusion at the county scale; from 1996 on, the credible intervals for each election do not overlap. This is not the case at the largest scale, not surprisingly as there are just nine divisions, and there is no significant difference between each pair at the state scale—although there is between the two end dates. The trend in all three is consistently upward, however; this is anything but trendless fluctuation—it comprises patterns of clear, multiscale spatial polarization.

THE GEOGRAPHY OF POLARIZATION: LANDSLIDE COUNTIES

The US electorate has become geographically more polarized over the last quarter of a century, therefore; but has that polarization occurred to the same

FIGURE 4.34

U.S. Census Divisions and States

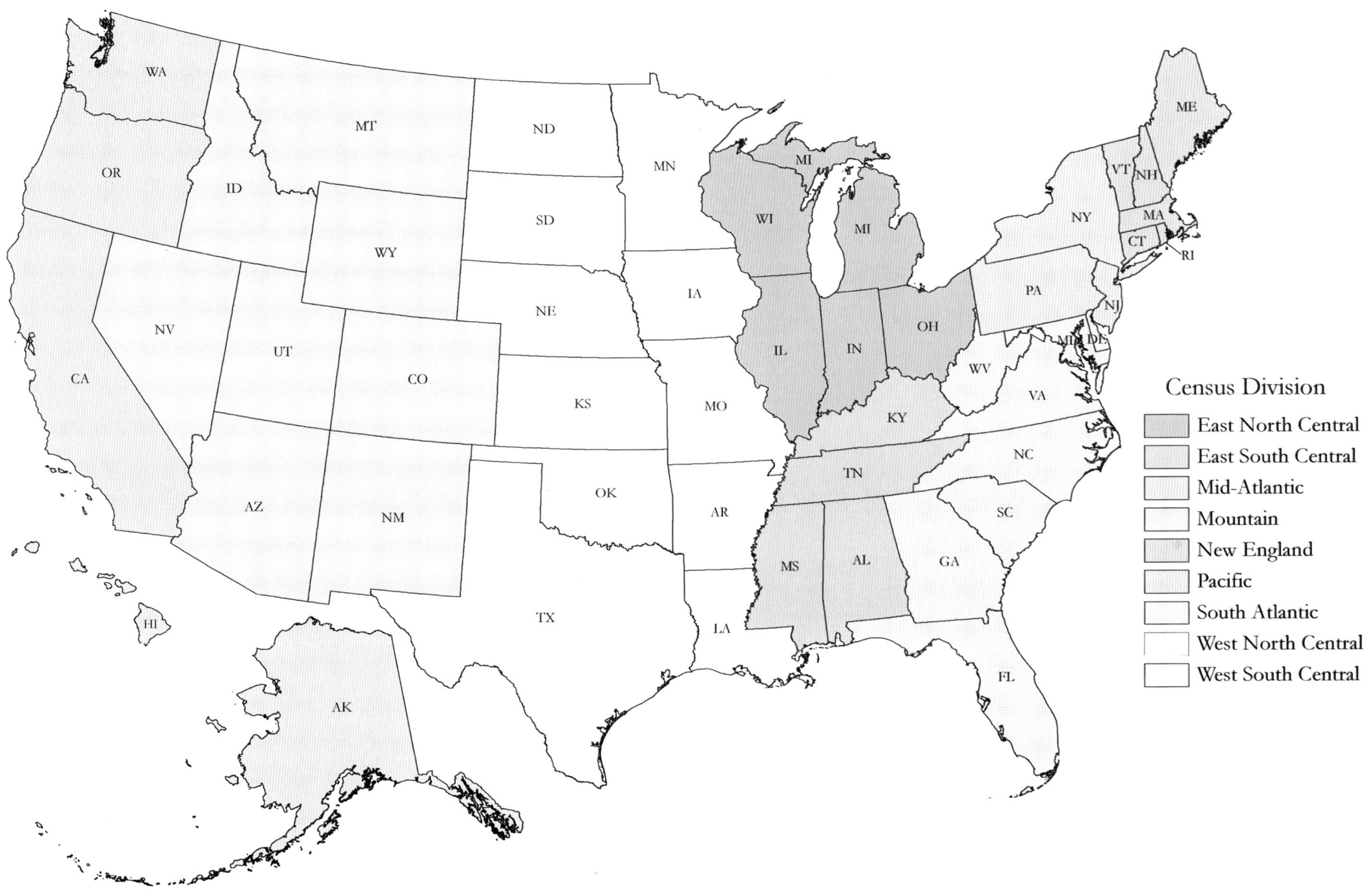

FIGURE 4.35

The MOR Values, with their Credible Intervals, at each Scale, 1992-2016

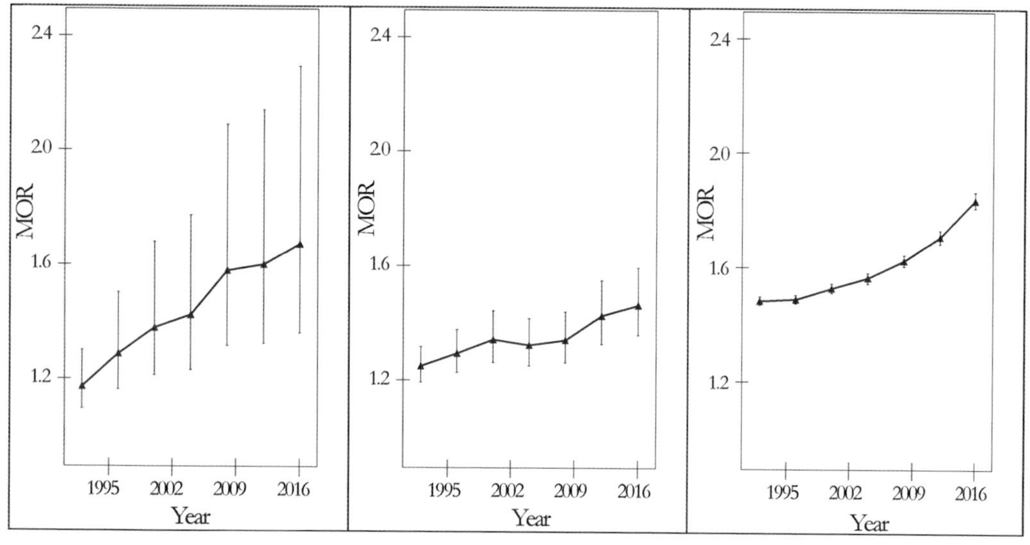

TABLE 4.2. The Number of "Landslide Counties" by Census Division, 1992 and 2016

	1992			2016			
	Neither	Rep.	Dem.	Neither	Rep.	Dem.	Total
New England	51	0	16	42	2	23	67
Mid-Atlantic	108	24	18	55	78	17	150
South Atlantic	385	72	97	149	349	56	554
East North Central	308	66	63	103	320	14	437
West North Central	373	96	56	68	445	12	525
East South Central	210	61	93	46	289	29	364
West South Central	261	89	120	52	396	22	470
Mountain	166	176	31	59	291	23	373
Pacific	101	4	32	57	47	33	137
Total	1,963	588	526	631	2,217	229	3,077

extent across the country? The four maps in figure 4.36 show the changing geography of the landslide counties, where one party gained at least 20 percent more of the (Republican plus Democrat) votes than its opponent. The number increased from 1,114 (out of 3,077) in 1992 through 1,154 and 1,620 in 1996 and 2000, respectively; 1,855 and 1,723 at the next two contests; to 1,986 in 2012 and 2,446 in 2016—an increase between the first and last contests of 120 percent. As the country's electorate became spatially more polarized so, with a slight blip in 2008 (Barack Obama's first victory), voting for presidential candidates became dominated by one of them only in an increasing proportion of the country's counties (36 percent in 1992 and 79 percent in 2016—more than doubling in just 24 years).

Those landslide counties were not evenly distributed across the United States, however, as table 4.2 shows for the nine divisions. In 1992, for example, very few counties were dominated by the Republicans in either New England or the Pacific; this hardly changed for the former division by 2016 but in the Pacific division, whereas the number of Democratic landslide victories hardly changed, those with a Republican hegemony increased from just four to forty-seven. In 1992 only the Mountain division had a majority of its counties delivering a landslide majority: 207 of its 373 returned a landslide for the Republican, George H. W. Bush, then; twenty-four years later, over three-quarters gave Donald Trump a landslide victory.

There was also variation by states within divisions. In the Mountain division, for example, in 1992 none of Arizona's counties delivered a Republican landslide, compared to seventy-four of Nebraska's ninety-three and twenty-one of Utah's twenty-nine. In 2016, Trump won a landslide

FIGURE 4.36

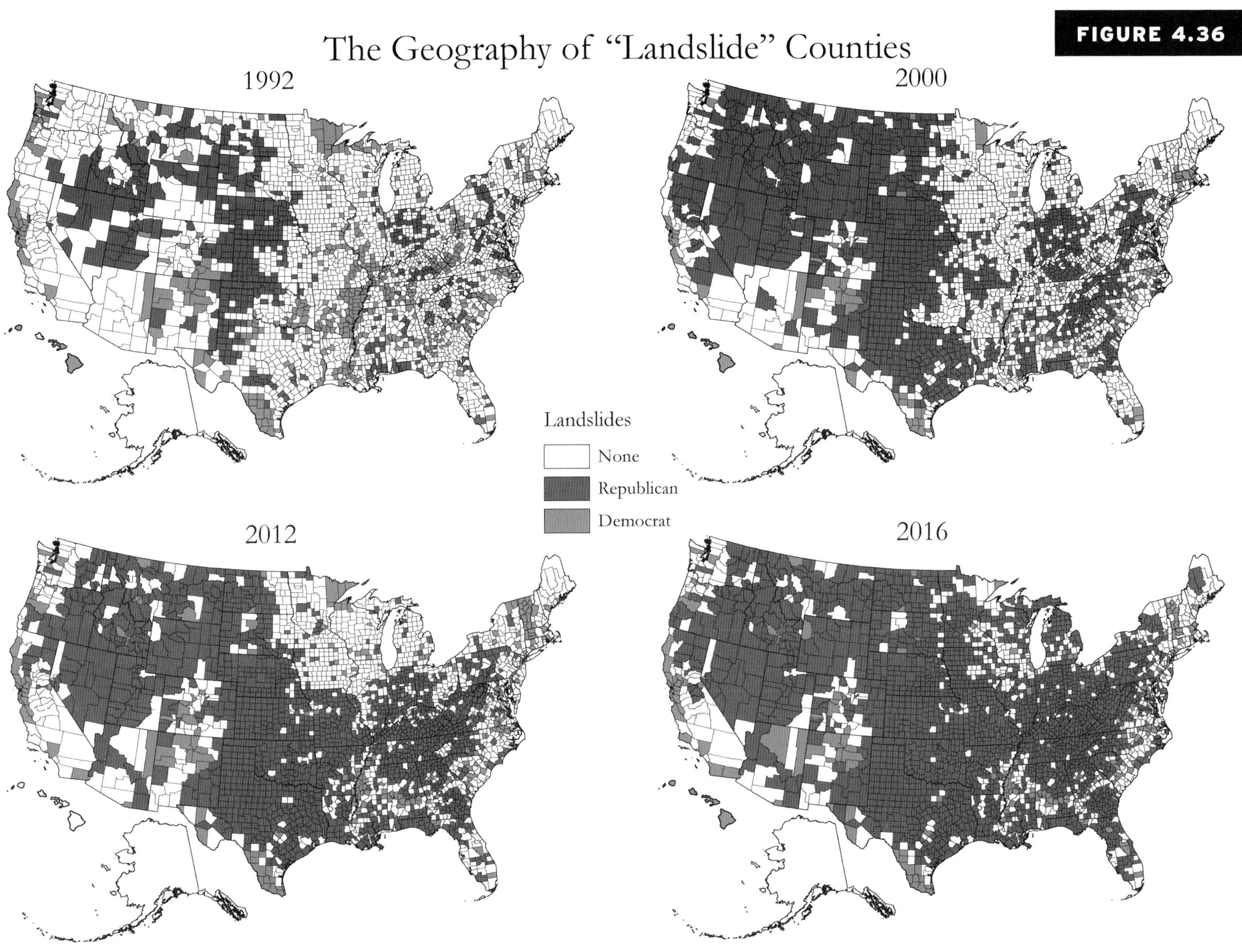

The modelled probability of a county delivering a Republican landslide, by US Census Division, 1992–2016.

in eight of Arizona's fifteen counties, ninety in Nebraska, and twenty-five in Utah (where an independent candidate won 21.5 percent of the votes cast but nevertheless Trump beat Clinton by more than 20 percentage points in all but four of the state's counties). Only New Mexico failed to deliver a Republican landslide in at least half of its counties.

The dominant feature of table 4.3, however, reflecting the geographies in figure 4.36, is the quadrupling in the number of Republican landslide counties over the twenty-four years. This growth was concentrated in a north-south belt through the country's center, extending eastward into the South Atlantic division. Fully 1,799 of the 2,050 counties in those five divisions gave Donald Trump a landslide victory; add the 291 of the 373 Mountain division counties, and 86 percent had Republican landslides. This was in marked contrast to the New England and Mid-Atlantic divisions, where 45 percent of the counties lacked a landslide majority for either party in 2016 (although the figure was 73 percent in 1992).

The result has been a fracturing of the country. Figure 4.37 shows the modelled probability of counties delivering a Republican landslide, by division. With the exception of the Mountain division, the remaining eight all had probabilities c.0.1–0.2 in 1992. By 2016 that probability had more than quadrupled in three, and had doubled in another two; in six of the nine divisions, the probability that a county returned a Republican landslide was very high. Three divisions stood out against this trend, however: the increase was much less in the Mid-Atlantic and Pacific divisions, and there was a decrease in New England.

The Modelled Probability of a County Delivering a Republican Landslide, by U.S. Census Division, 1992-2016.

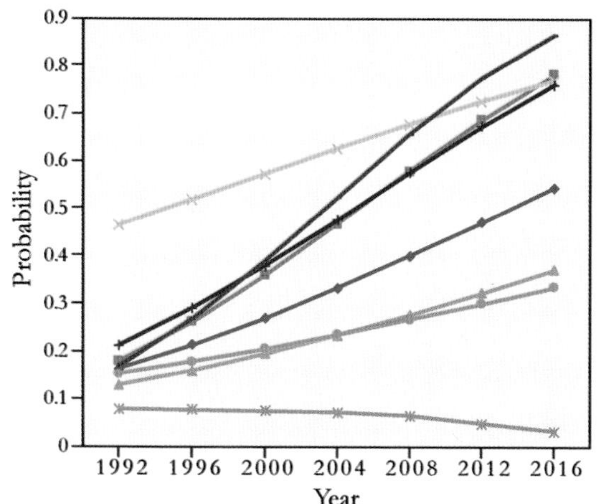

FIGURE 4.37

The average percentage voting Republican, 1992–2012 and 2016, by county.

TABLE 4.3. The Number of Voters in "Landslide Counties," 1992-2016

	Neither	Republican	Democrat	Total
Mean number of voters				
1992	26,093	14,473	44,604	27,036
1996	25,859	13,067	51,682	27,888
2000	38,253	15,329	121,524	32,809
2004	51,462	19,412	152,053	39,167
2008	49,185	15,776	123,136	41,852
2012	57,168	16,424	131,888	41,002
2016	79,938	17,281	169,872	41,487
Total number of voters				
1992	51,220,295	8,510,223	23,462,140	83,192,568
1996	49,726,147	7,971,081	28,115,946	85,813,174
2000	55,733,983	21,889,521	23,332,700	100,956,204
2004	62,886,776	32,845,280	24,784,729	120,516,785
2008	66,596,774	22,038,784	40,142,371	128,777,929
2012	62,368,779	28,184,145	35,609,789	126,163,713
2016	50,441,178	38,312,901	38,900,702	127,654,781

WHICH PARTY PREDOMINATES THE MOST?

The maps in figure 4.36 show that the Republicans now predominate across much of the country, with the Democrats concentrated in small pockets only—the 2016 map has large swaths of red and only small concentrations of blue. But to infer that Republicans predominate across the voting population would be a misinterpretation. They recorded a landslide majority in 451 counties at all seven elections, compared to just 109 for the Democrats, for example, and 1,164 delivered a Republican landslide at five or more elections, compared to just 183 for the Democrats. But most of the Republican landslide counties were small in population if not area, with the reverse for those with Democrat landslides.

The first block of data in table 4.3 shows the mean population in counties, according to whether they had a landslide for one of the parties at each of the seven elections. There was a clear, and growing, difference between those with Republican and Democrat landslides: in 1992 the latter were on average three times larger than the former; in 2016 they were almost ten times larger. The Republicans won many more landslides than the Democrats, but those victories were overwhelmingly in small counties. This is borne out by the table's second block of data, which shows the number of voters living in the various categories. At all but George W. Bush's victory in 2000, more voters lived in counties with a Democratic than with a Republican landslide. The difference was stark at the two twentieth-century elections, when three times as many voters lived in Democratic than in Republican landslide counties; it narrowed over the next five contests and in 2016 almost exactly the same number (some 31 percent of the voting population) lived in each type.

A NEW ELECTORAL MAP IN 2016?

Some commentators both before and after the 2016 election argued that Donald Trump was redrawing the US electoral map, that a new electoral geography was emerging reflecting his appeal to groups that had not voted Republican before, indeed may not have voted at all—those left behind by globalization who were concentrated in certain areas.

The analyses reported here suggest otherwise; Trump's victory merely accentuated patterns that had grown clearer over the previous two decades. Figure 4.38 relates the 2016 vote to the mean support for Republican candidates over the preceding six elections. The diagonal line indicates the pattern that would have been revealed if Trump performed as well in each county as the average for his predecessor Republican candidates. The vertical line divides counties into those where on average one party gained more votes than the other at the previous elections; the horizontal line divides them according to whether Trump obtained more or fewer votes than Clinton. Most counties to the right of the vertical line are also above the diagonal line: where Republicans won at the previous elections Trump performed on average even better, as he also did in many of those where the Republican average exceeded 40 percent of the two-party vote between 1992 and 2012. Where the Republicans were traditionally strong, therefore, Trump did even better. Where they were relatively weak (to the left of the vertical line), in many places he performed even more poorly than his predecessors. The map tilted even more, therefore, toward the Republicans in their heartlands.

FIGURE 4.38

The Average Percentage Voting Republican 1992-2012 and in 2016, by County

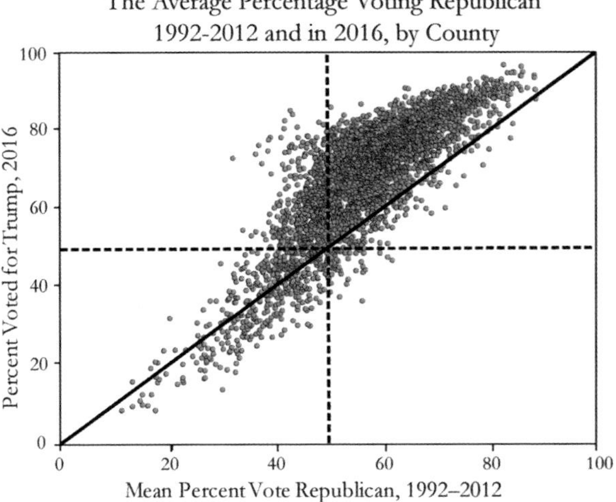

The electoral geography of the United States has been modified along a clear trend since the 1990s, therefore, which Trump's victory accentuated. Increasingly, Republicans have become the dominant party of small-town America (outside the country's Northeast), gaining an increasing number of victories in those small counties by margins of 20 percentage points or more. Countering that, the Democrats dominate much of metropolitan America, especially on the Northeast and West Coasts. Many fewer counties now deliver Democratic, as opposed to Republican, landslides but as many voters live in those pro-Democrat counties as in the much larger number that deliver Republican landslides. The United States has become increasingly, and equally, polarized—a pattern that Trump did not change but merely accentuated (or exacerbated).

REFERENCES

Abrams, Samuel J., and Morris Fiorina. 2012. "The Big Sort That Wasn't": A Skeptical Reexamination. *PS: Political Science and Politics* 45(2): 203–10.

Bishop, Bill. 2009. *The Big Sort: Why the Clustering of Like-Minded America Is Tearing Us Apart*. Boston: Houghton Mifflin.

Johnston, Ron J., David Manley, and Kelvyn Jones. 2016. Spatial Polarization of Presidential Voting in the United States, 1992–2012: The "Big Sort" Revisited. *Annals of the American Association of Geographers* 106(5): 1047–62.

Jones, Kelvyn, Ron J. Johnston, David Manley, Dewi Owen, and Chris Charlton. 2015. Ethnic Residential Segregation: A Multilevel, Multigroup, Multiscale Approach Exemplified by London in 2011. *Demography* 52(10): 1995–2019.

ELECTION OUTCOMES: ABSOLUTE AND RELATIVE

RICHARD L. MORRILL AND KIMBERLY K. JOHNSON

Three bivariate maps (figures 4.39, 4.40, and 4.41) display both absolute volume of votes, represented by the size of the circle, as well as percentage of the vote, represented by the color of the circle. Two additional maps (figures 4.42 and 4.43) show the percent change for the Democratic candidate in 2012 and 2016 and the margin of victory for the Democratic candidate in the 2016 presidential election. This is particularly useful in the 2016 election because of the radically different geography of their areas of strength: Clinton in the metropolitan cores, Trump across much of the less densely populated parts of the country.

The first two maps, for Clinton (figure 4.39) and Trump (figure 4.40), reveal a size difference in absolute votes county by county. On the Clinton map, the dark blue circles are in large metropolitan core counties, which she dominated. Additionally, these circles are much larger than the pink circles for Trump for the same counties. Conversely, the much larger number of dark pink circles for Trump dominate smaller counties across the South and the North-South borderlands as well as the Plains states. For the same regions, we can see Clinton's vote was smaller, indicated by the light blue circles in these counties. The same is true for the dark pink Trump majority counties, larger than the same counties on the Clinton map, indicating a minority vote. Quite noticeable are the larger pink circles for suburban counties, and for some core metropolitan counties in the South, and the many pink Trump-dominated small suburban counties, especially, but not just located in the South (see Minneapolis, St. Louis, and Pittsburgh).

The map for Other/Third Party candidates (figure 4.41) reveals higher shares for third-party candidates in much of the West and New England. Furthermore, we can see larger, dark brown circles in Mormon areas (i.e., Utah) and in the mountain states (i.e., Colorado and New Mexico).

The margin percentage map is like that for 2012, and effectively summarizes the huge but many fewer concentrations of large margins for Clinton in big metropolitan cores, and the far wider, more diffuse spread of margins for Trump across most of the eastern half of the country (figure 4.42) beyond those blue cores! For example, Trump has larger percentages in the Great Plains, which matches the small, dark pink circles in figure 4.40. Furthermore, we can see the margin of victory increase for Democrats in states along the West Coast. For example, in parts of California, the margin of victory for Democrats increased from 50.1 to 86.8 percent. However, a few large areas have closer votes and less dramatic margins: Harris and Bexar Counties in Texas, Orange County in California, Monroe and Erie Counties in New York.

The final map, figure 4.43, shows change in the percent for the Democrat, Obama in 2012 and Clinton in 2016. Declines for Democrats are overwhelming across perhaps 90 percent of the country, and much greater across the North, from Maine to Montana. This is especially significant in traditionally Democratic-leaning areas in Iowa, Minnesota, Michigan, Ohio, and Pennsylvania, where the electorate likely felt left behind by globalization and social change. Areas of Democratic gain are Megalopolis, southern California, and areas of Hispanic populations from California to Texas, and Utah in reaction to Trump as the GOP candidate.

FIGURE 4.39

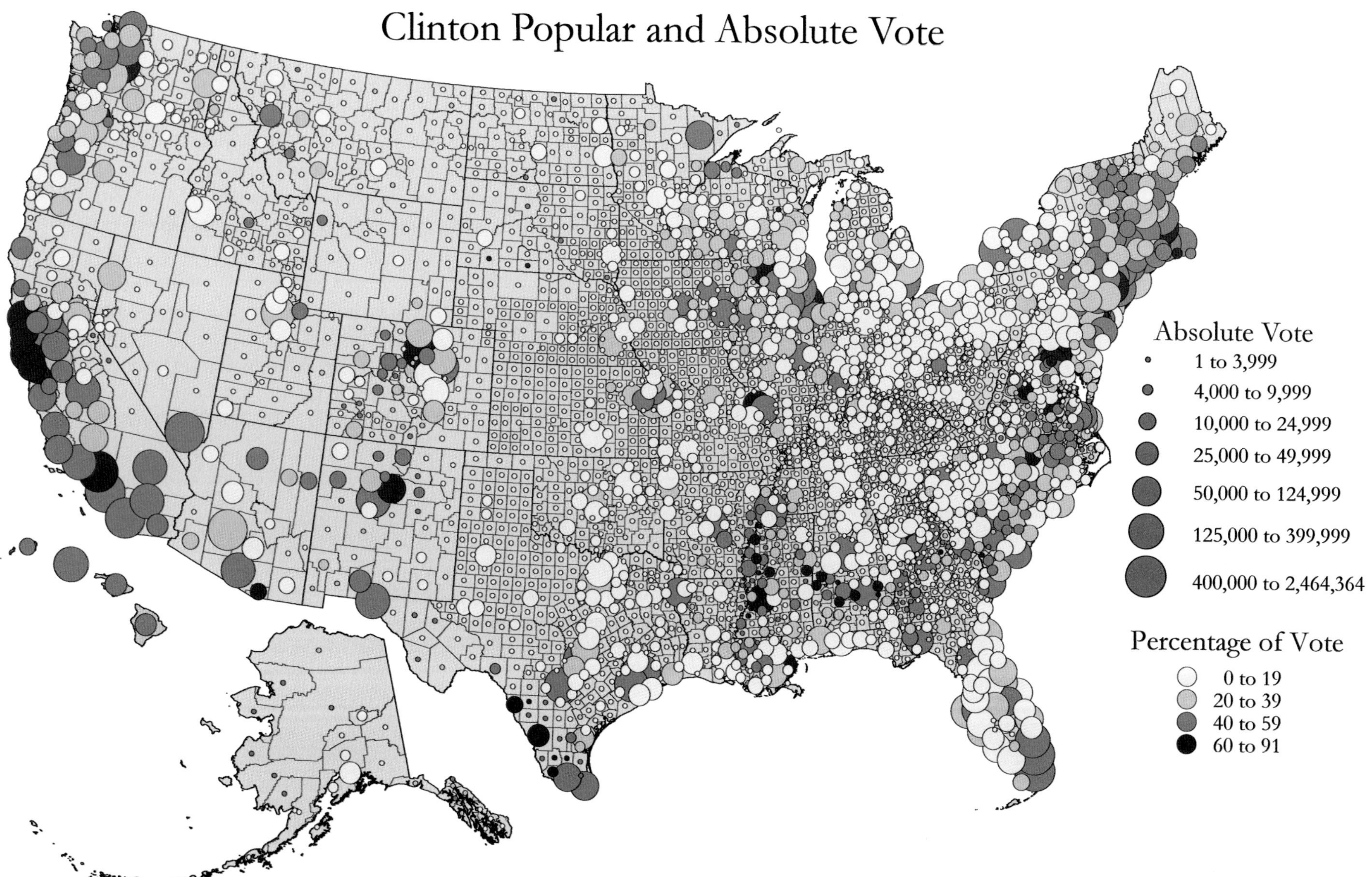
Clinton Popular and Absolute Vote
Absolute Vote
1 to 3,999
4,000 to 9,999
10,000 to 24,999
25,000 to 49,999
50,000 to 124,999
125,000 to 399,999
400,000 to 2,464,364
Percentage of Vote
0 to 19
20 to 39
40 to 59
60 to 91

FIGURE 4.40

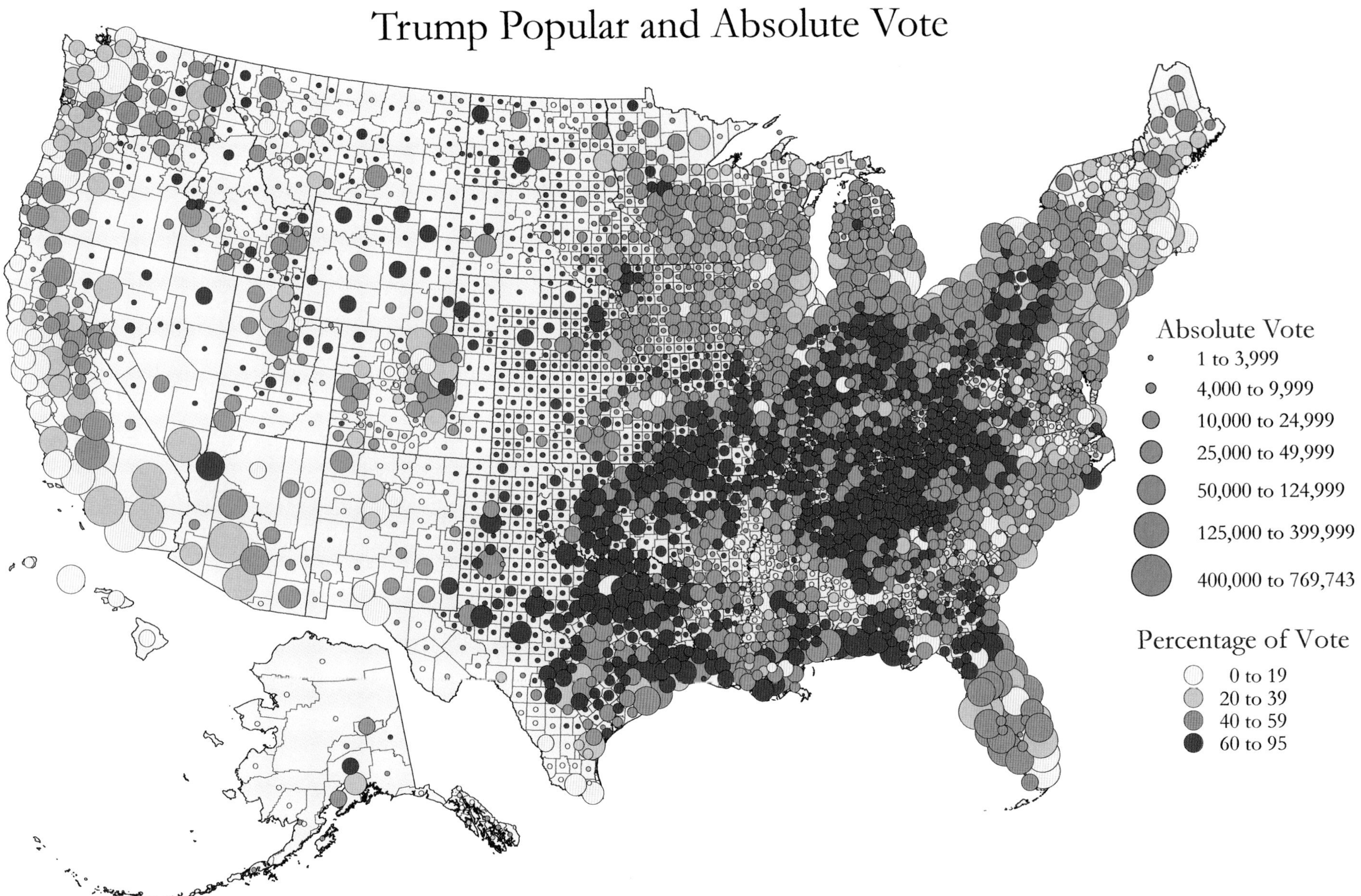
Trump Popular and Absolute Vote
Absolute Vote
1 to 3,999
4,000 to 9,999
10,000 to 24,999
25,000 to 49,999
50,000 to 124,999
125,000 to 399,999
400,000 to 769,743
Percentage of Vote
0 to 19
20 to 39
40 to 59
60 to 95

FIGURE 4.41

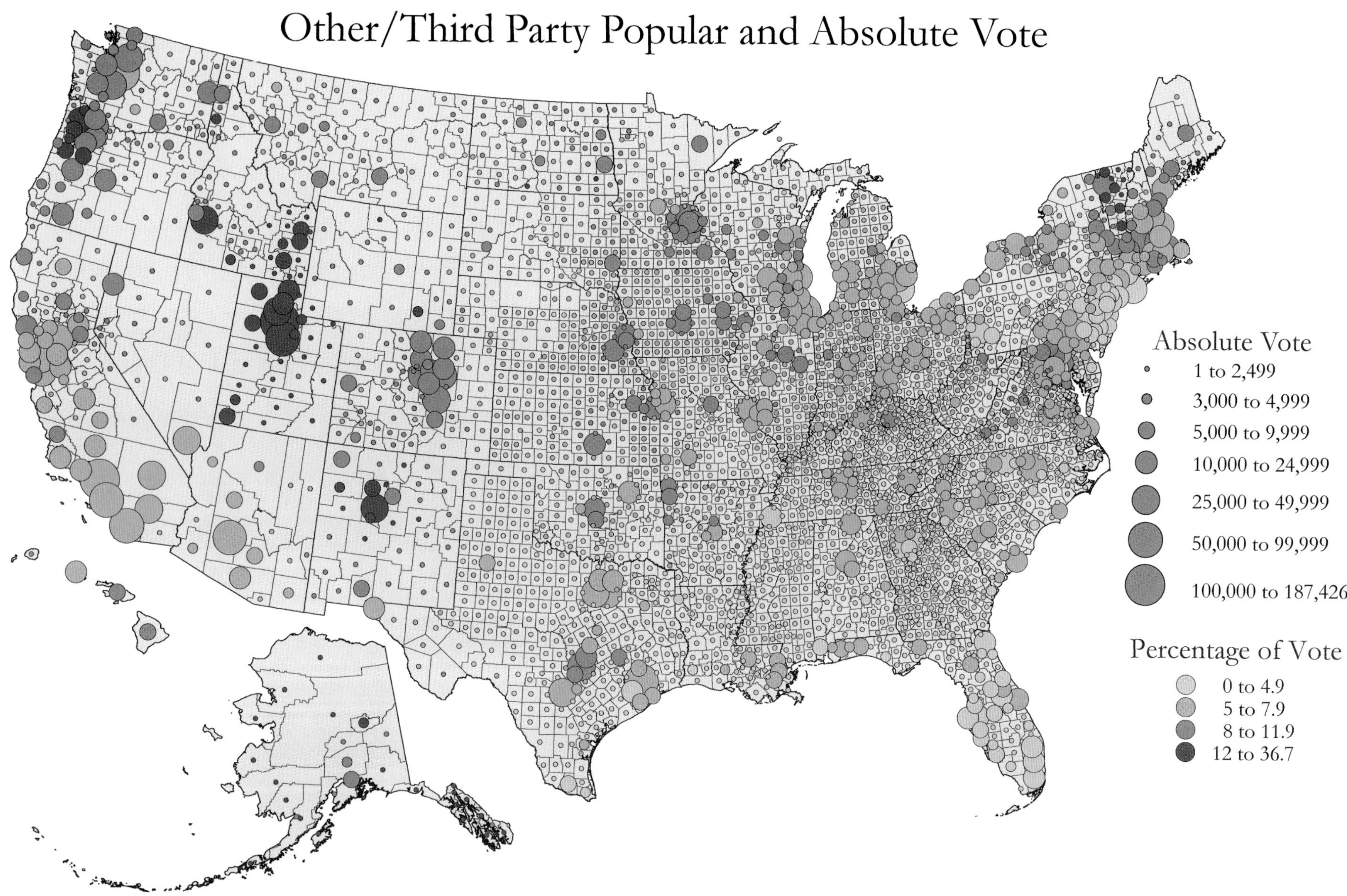
Other/Third Party Popular and Absolute Vote
Absolute Vote
1 to 2,499
3,000 to 4,999
5,000 to 9,999
10,000 to 24,999
25,000 to 49,999
50,000 to 99,999
100,000 to 187,426
Percentage of Vote
0 to 4.9
5 to 7.9
8 to 11.9
12 to 36.7

FIGURE 4.42

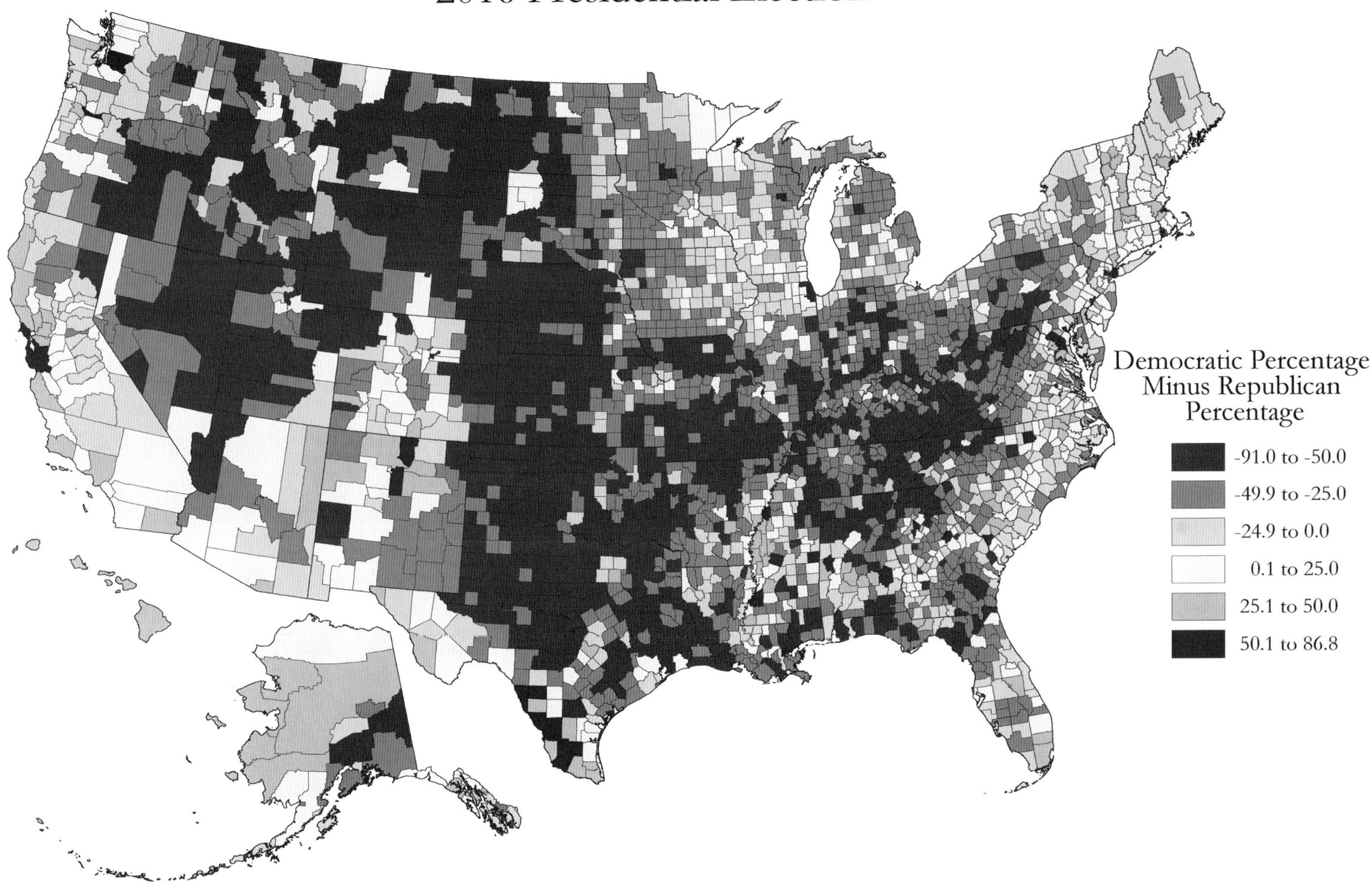
Margin of Victory
2016 Presidential Election
Democratic Percentage
Minus Republican
Percentage
-91.0 to -50.0
-49.9 to -25.0
-24.9 to 0.0
0.1 to 25.0
25.1 to 50.0
50.1 to 86.8

FIGURE 4.43

Percentage Change for the Democratic Candidate from the 2012 Election to the 2016 Election

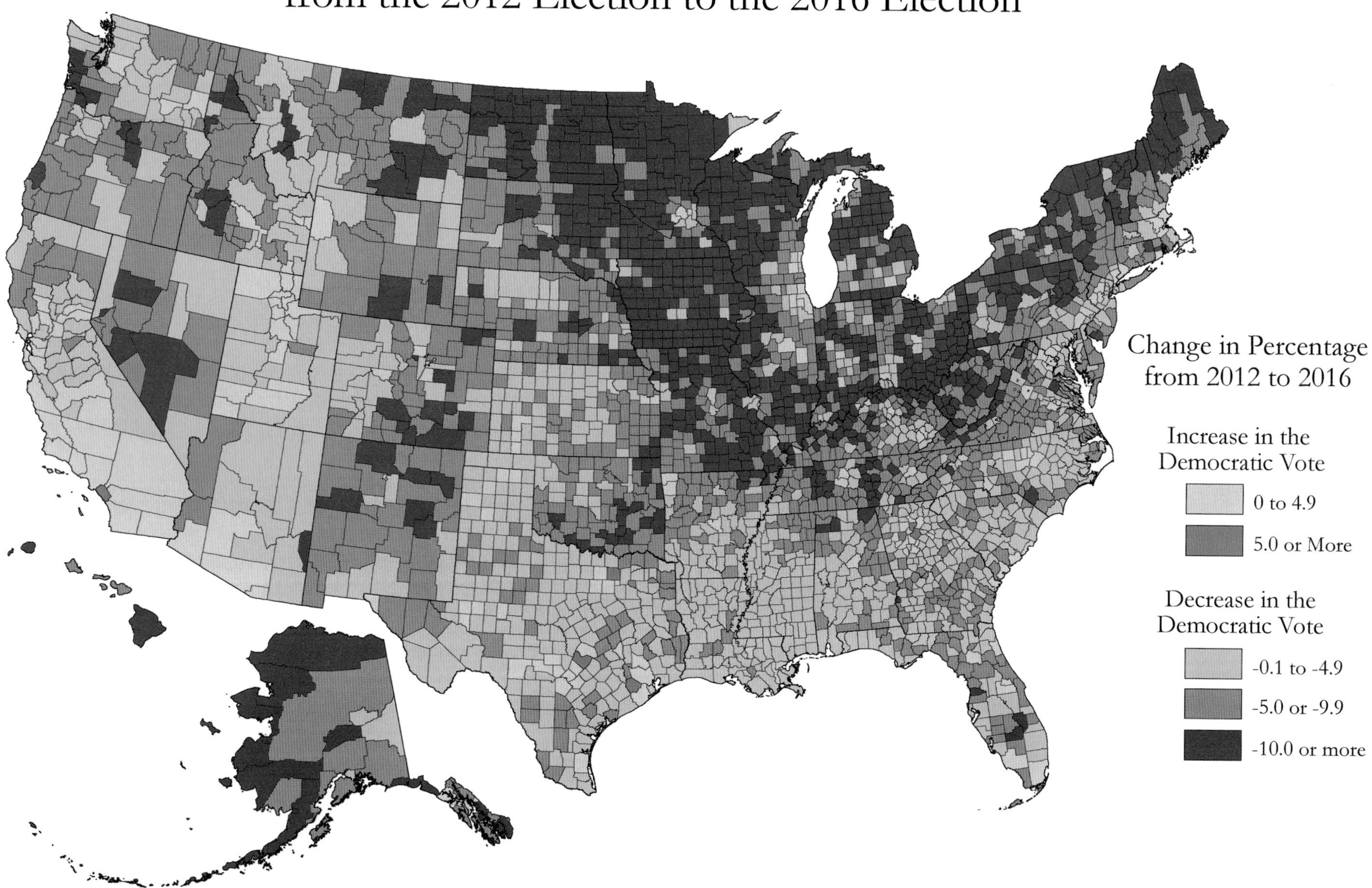

5 REGIONS

NORTHEAST

WILLIAM BERENTSEN

Though less dramatic than for the country as a whole, outcomes in the 2016 presidential elections in the Northeast states were impactful and also possibly indicate more dual-party electoral competitiveness to follow in the region in the 2020 election. For only the second time since the 1988 presidential election, when George H. W. Bush won eight states and 77 electoral votes, candidate Donald Trump won a Northeastern state (Pennsylvania, along with one of Maine's four electoral votes), thus attaining by far the largest Republican electoral vote cache in the Northeast (21) in nearly thirty years. George W. Bush won four electoral votes in New Hampshire in the 2000 election, a small but crucial win in an election when a loss of any state by Bush (271 votes) would have swung the election to Al Gore (266 votes). Hillary Clinton needed to wrest 39 electoral votes to win in 2016—the loss in Pennsylvania represented more than half of her shortfall.

Though a seldom-occurring outcome given recent electoral history in the Northeast, roots of potential Republican electoral gains date back at least eight years—especially in Maine, New Hampshire, and electoral-rich Pennsylvania. Unlike in populous southern New England, where Democrats have completely dominated presidential and congressional elections since 1992, the Northeast's Mid-Atlantic states have in recent elections experienced more competitive outcomes between Democrats and Republicans—and especially in Pennsylvania:

> There was a clear trend toward Republican presidential vote gains between 2008 and 2012 across much of the Northeast (except in and near New York City and in parts of upstate New York). While these gains in 2012 in much of the Northeast only modestly reduced still very large statewide percentage gaps between Republican and Democratic candidates (in most cases, a gap of two to six percentage points), in Pennsylvania and New Hampshire, especially, the trend could indicate concerns for Democrats in the 2016 presidential election. (Berentsen 2014)

Recent congressional election outcomes reflect the GOP's struggles in New England, where in the 115th Congress, Senator Susan Collins from Maine is the sole Republican, along with thirty Democrats and two independents. Patrick Toomey (PA) is the sole Republican senator in the Mid-Atlantic states, but in Pennsylvania the

GOP also has thirteen US Representatives (to five Democrats). In New Jersey (5/7 party split) and New York (9/18) there are also clear indications of greater GOP competitiveness in elections that impact national-level politics than in other parts of the Northeast.

In the 2016 election, as in most other parts of the USA, a further increased share in the total popular vote total by Republican candidate Trump in the Northeast allowed him to win Pennsylvania, and also to win an electoral vote in northern Maine, and very nearly to win New Hampshire, where Clinton won by less than one-half percentage point and less than 3,000 individual votes (see table 5.1). Trump's win in Pennsylvania was also close, and contested following the election, but was a less shocking outcome than it should have been for the Clinton campaign.

Contrary to immediate post-election estimates, voter turnout across the USA was higher in the November 2016 presidential election (59.3 percent) than in 2012 (58.0 percent). In New England, turnout increases were also often higher than the US average increase, especially in New York and Pennsylvania. Given that African American voter turnout dropped nationwide, it seems likely that sharp increases in the Republican proportion of the vote in central and western Pennsylvania and many areas in upstate New York could well be the white, rural and small-town voters who appear to have had a major role in propelling Trump into the presidency. Voting in these areas could well have been impacted by Trump voters with lower educational levels (less than a BA) and facing related poor economic prospects in a changing economy that especially rewards educational achievement and technological skills. Those factors may also help explain, to some extent, the increased Republican vote totals elsewhere in the Northeast, notably in Pennsylvania and northeastern Maine, but seven of the USA's most educationally accomplished (BA or better) state populations (25 years and older) are in the Northeast region—as well as eight of the ten highest advanced degree proportions of state adult populations. Nationwide in the 2016 election, Clinton won a majority of more highly educated voters, and this factor almost certainly helped her carry most of the Northeast. If this relationship between level of education and presidential vote persists, further electoral inroads by Republican presidential candidates in future elections in the Northeast could be constrained in most parts of New England. Such an effect might have lesser impacts in parts of the Mid-Atlantic region, New Hampshire, and Maine, where, despite the relationship, Republicans have historically often been more competitive than elsewhere in the Northeast (table 5.1).

The geographic patterns in the accompanying maps well illustrate election outcome differences between much of New England, on the one hand, and the Mid-Atlantic states on the other (figure 5.1). Less obvious yet still evident patterns include the success of Clinton and the Democratic Party in populous urban and inner-suburban metropolitan area counties. Clinton won all counties with

TABLE 5.1. Selected State-Level Variables Related to the 2016 Presidential Election, Northeast Region

State	% Trump Vote	% Clinton Vote	Change % Registered Voter Turnout, 2012-16	% Population ≥ 25 with BA (avg. 2011-15)
PA	**48.2**	47.5	**4.1**	28.6
NH	46.5	**46.8**	1.2	34.9
ME	44.9	**47.8**	2.3	29.0
DE	41.7	**53.1**	2.1	30.0
NJ	41.0	**55.0**	2.6	36.8
CT	40.9	**54.6**	2.9	37.6
RI	38.9	**54.4**	1.0	31.9
NY	36.5	**59.0**	3.7	34.2
MD	33.9	**60.3**	0.0	37.9
MA	32.8	**60.0**	2.3	**40.5**
VT	30.3	**56.7**	3.0	36.0
USA	46.1	**48.2**	1.3	29.8

Sources: Leip 2017; McDonald 2017; United States Census Bureau 2017.

Note: **Bold** represents the highest value within a comparison—between the first two columns, and within the last two.

FIGURE 5.1

Northeast Region Presidential Elections

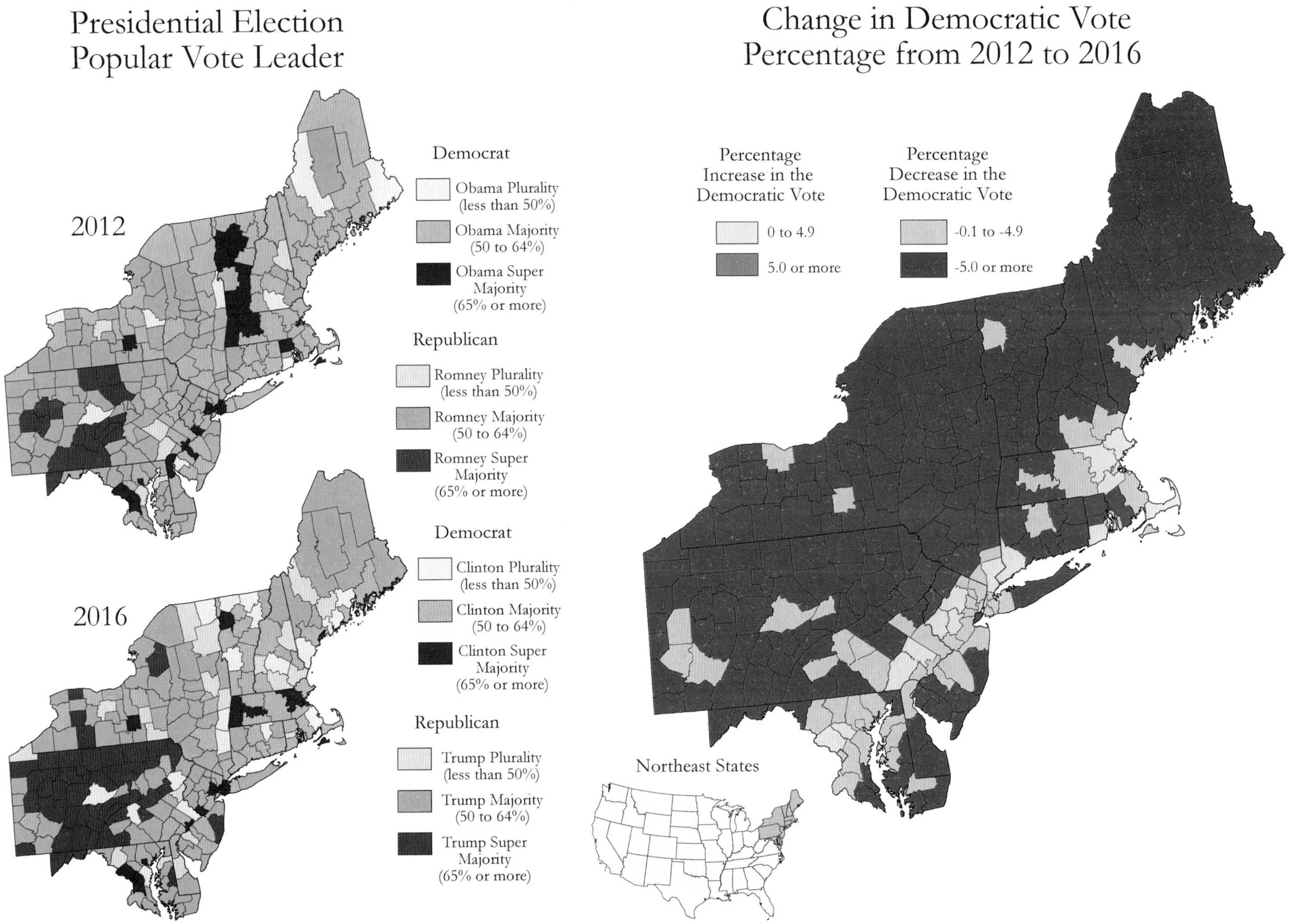

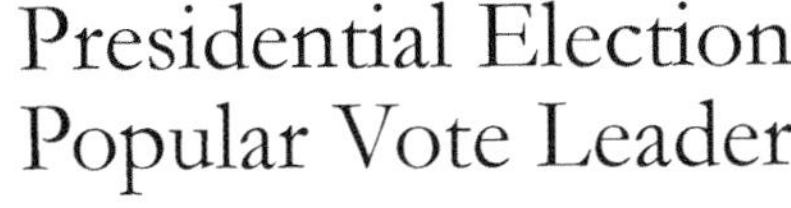

Presidential Election Popular Vote Leader

Change in Democratic Vote Percentage from 2012 to 2016

major cities in Megalopolis, from Portland, Maine, southeastward to Washington, DC, and counties with the largest cities in upstate New York. On the other hand, Trump and the Republican Party did well in smaller metro and especially nonmetro counties in thinly populated northern New England, upstate New York, Pennsylvania, Maryland, and Delaware. Trump also did relatively well, or won outright, in a number of the distant suburban counties of large metro areas (e.g., several within a ring 40–50 miles out from New York City). This larger Democratic/Republican urban/smaller urban and metro/nonmetro differentiation is, of course, generally consistent with the party outcome differences by levels of county minority populations—and to some extent the educational differences noted earlier.

In the Northeast, both the Democrat Clinton and the Republican Trump can claim some achievements in the 2016 presidential election. Geographic electoral patterns in the most recent elections were also underlain by basic, rather unsurprising socioeconomic and related political differences and voting trends. While lagging badly in presidential and congressional elections for decades in most of New England, and to a somewhat lesser extent in the Mid-Atlantic region and New Hampshire, the Republican Party has made some gains across the region in the past two presidential elections. These could be held or built upon in near-future elections, more likely in elections for Congress rather than the presidency. A substantial majority of the most populous regions in the Northeast, especially in southern New England and Vermont, are home to well-educated, historically moderate and liberal voters. Barring evolution of more surprising, new trends in national politics—such as the surprising national-level electoral success of the Republican-chosen, self-proclaimed "outsider," Donald Trump in 2016—the conservative platforms and actions of the Republican Party seem likely to continue to be an unpopular option for the majority of voters in the Northeast. This seems well exemplified by relatively large numbers of Northeast Republican congressional representatives who were neither willing to vote for, nor enthusiastically back, the House of Representatives' bill to replace Obamacare during spring 2017. Like the populous, mainland US West Coast, the majority of Northeast voters have not embraced current national-level Republican Party policies.

REFERENCES

Berentsen, William H. 2014. Northeast. In J. Clark Archer, Robert H. Watrel, Fiona Davidson, Erin H. Fouberg, Kenneth C. Martis, Richard L. Morrill, Fred M. Shelley, and Gerald R. Webster, eds., *Atlas of the 2012 Elections*, 127–30. Lanham, MD: Rowman & Littlefield.

Leip, David. 2017. United States Presidential Election Results. In *Dave Leip's Atlas of US Presidential Elections*. http://uselectionatlas.org (last accessed May 15, 2017).

McDonald, Michael P. 2017. Voter Turnout. United States Elections Project, University of Florida. http://www.electproject.org/home/voter-turnout/voter-turnout-data (last accessed May 2, 2017).

United States Census Bureau. 2017. Educational Attainment: 2011–2015 American Community Survey 5-Year Estimates. American Fact Finder. https://factfinder.census.gov/faces/tableservices/jsf/pages/productview.xhtml?pid=ACS_15_5YR_S1501&prodType=table (last accessed May 12, 2017).

APPALACHIA

KENNETH C. MARTIS

The Appalachian region stretches southwestward from southern New York State to northern Alabama and Georgia and northeastern Mississippi. Appalachia can be defined in three ways. First, it is a physiographic region containing the rolling hills of the Piedmont, mountain peaks of the ridge and valley, and dendritic drainage pattern and complex incised topography of the plateau. Appalachia is also a long-recognized cultural region characterized by: a high percentage rural white population; large areas with low rankings in educational, social, and economic indicators; high reliance on agriculture and extractive industries such as coal, timber, and natural gas; distinctive music and food heritage; and high adherence to fundamentalist Protestant and nonaffiliated Christian churches. Appalachia is also a rare phenomenon in American geography in that it is a precisely politically defined region by the United States Congress. In 1965 the Appalachian Regional Commission (ARC) was created to promote economic development in this lagging region. In order to funnel the assistance, a map was created to define the Appalachian region by county. Today the expanded ARC area encompasses 420 counties in thirteen states, the entire state of West Virginia, and the Appalachian portions of Alabama, Georgia, Kentucky, Maryland, Mississippi, New York, North Carolina, Ohio, Pennsylvania, South Carolina, Tennessee, and Virginia. The ARC boundary lines are used in the electoral analysis for this region.

HISTORICAL POLITICAL PARTY SUPPORT

Since it includes parts of northern states like New York and Pennsylvania, and parts of southern states like Georgia and Alabama, Appalachia has a complex political party voting history. During the Civil War, large areas of the upcountry South remained loyal to the Union and thereafter to the Republican Party. Throughout the Great Depression years, the Democrats gained support because of New Deal programs, such as the Tennessee Valley Authority, and the unionization efforts of the United Mine Workers. This support was sustained by Democratic president Lyndon Johnson with his "War on Poverty" programs, much of it aimed at this region (such as the ARC). As late as the 1996, Democratic presidential candidate Bill Clinton received support throughout Appalachia (see figure 6.2, *Atlas of the 2012 Elections*).

The turning point in modern Appalachian voting history came in the 2000 presidential contest between Republican George W. Bush and Democrat Al Gore. Gore had a history of promoting the ideas of fossil fuel–induced global warming and gun control, two issues that conflicted with the economic base and cultural traditions of the region. These issues, plus a plethora of socially conservative "family values" concerns, which the Republican Party championed, facilitated the rapid decline of the Democrats in Appalachia. The Democrat Obama administration's perceived "War on Coal" all but solidified the shift to the Republicans.

West Virginia is the only state wholly within the Appalachian Regional Commission boundary. This state is a textbook example of voter realignment. Table 5.2 shows the Democrat presidential vote percentage and national Democrat support ranking of West Virginia from the late twentieth century to 2016. West Virginia was reliably one of the top Democratic states since the Great Depression. As the table numbers illustrate, beginning in 2000, there was a rapid and sharp departure from the Democrats. In 2016 Hillary Clinton received

TABLE 5.2. West Virginia Presidential Vote, 1988–2016

Election	% Democrat Vote	State Rank in Democrat Support
1988	52.2	6
1992	48.4	5
1996	51.5	13
2000	45.6	25
2004	43.2	31
2008	42.5	37
2012	35.5	46
2016	26.5	49

Note: In 1992, Democratic candidate Bill Clinton won the electoral vote in a three-way race by a 13 percent margin.

only 25.6 percent of the vote in West Virginia, her second lowest percentage. West Virginia trailed only Wyoming as the most Republican state in the Union.

THE 2016 ELECTION

The candidacy and statements of Hillary Clinton only deepened Appalachian voter suspicion of the Democratic Party. In March 2016 candidate Clinton made a statement at a town hall meeting that would reverberate throughout Appalachia, "we're going to put a lot of coal miners and coal companies out of business." Throughout the presidential campaign this quote was repeated over and over in campaign speeches and on radio and television ads throughout the region. Later Clinton apologized for the statement and noted that sentence was taken out of context. The full quote is:

> Instead of dividing people the way Donald Trump does, let's reunite around policies that will bring jobs and opportunities to all these underserved poor communities. So for example, I'm the only candidate which has a policy about how to bring economic opportunity using clean renewable energy as the key into coal country. Because we're going to put a lot of coal miners and coal companies out of business, right? And we're going to make it clear that we don't want to forget those people. Those people labored in those mines for generations, losing their health, often losing their lives to turn on our lights and power our factories.

Nevertheless, the damage was done, and the statement reinforced in the voters' minds the Gore/Obama/Clinton/Democrat view of coal, a declining, but still influential economic force in the region.

Donald Trump, on the other hand, exploited this Democratic policy with a litany of promises to revive the coal industry, including abolishment of the Obama administration's clean energy policies. However unlikely the idea of bringing coal back to its dominance in the American energy system was, Appalachian voters, especially in heavily hit coal counties, saw the Republican candidate evoking hope out of despair. In addition, Trump's other "Make America Great Again" populist policies also resonated with the rural, mostly white, socially conservative population.

Candidate Clinton added to her misstatements in September 2106 by declaring that half of Trump supporters were "a basket full of deplorables," accusing them of being, among other things, racist, sexist, and homophobic. In their own minds, most in Appalachia felt their support of Trump was based upon the economic well-being of the region, Second Amendment rights, and saving American industry. Sensitive to the stereotypes of Appalachians throughout American history, the region's voters perceived one candidate as accusatory and elitist and the other as plain-speaking and espousing hope. All this in spite of a long list of misstatements, false statements, and contradictory statements made by candidate Trump, his refusal to reveal his tax history, and revelations of questionable moral behavior. In the end Trump used the Clinton "deplorables" quote the rest of the campaign, beginning by tweeting immediately after, "While Hillary said horrible things about my supporters, and while many of her supporters will never vote for me, I still respect them all!"

The maps in figure 5.2 show the Republican dominance in the Appalachian region. The 2012 map illustrates Mitt Romney's massive victory over President Obama in the vast majority of counties. The 2016 map shows the same results, but an even more dominating Republican victory—an overwhelming sea of red. Although candidate Clinton won the majority of votes nationwide, she lost the vast majority of Appalachian counties by a supermajority, that is, 65 percent plus for Trump. Astonishingly, of the 400-plus counties, Clinton won only six not on the fringe of Appalachia; Allegheny and Lackawanna in Pennsylvania (Pittsburgh and Scranton), Athens in Ohio (home of Ohio University), Buncombe in North Carolina (Asheville), Clay in Mississippi (majority African American), and Jefferson in Alabama (Birmingham). In historically Democrat West Virginia, Republican Trump not only won every county, but by a supermajority in fifty of the fifty-five.

Since the Democrats were soundly defeated in Appalachia in 2012, the 2012 to 2016 "change in vote" map is truly incredible. The vast majority of counties voted a 5 percent or more trend toward the Republicans. The only area showing a Democrat increase was a number of suburban Atlanta counties in northern Georgia. In West Virginia the continued movement to the Republicans was massive, with Trump gaining a 5 percent-plus swing in all counties except one, Monongalia (home of West Virginia University).

It cannot be emphasized enough that Donald Trump's protection of American manufacturing and reindustrialization promises were also well received in the historically Democratic union Rust Belt steel and manufacturing cities of western

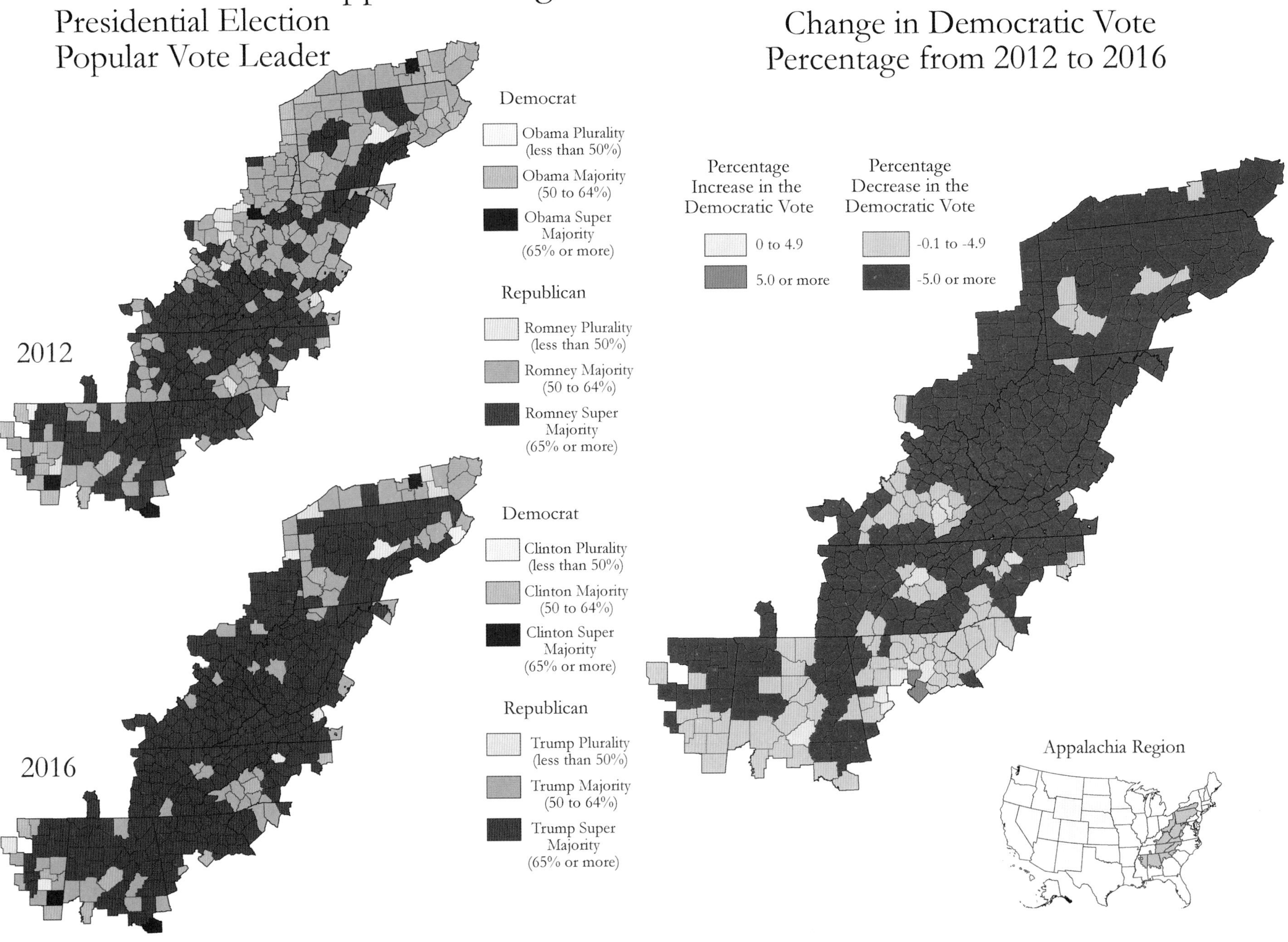
FIGURE 5.2
Appalachia Region Presidential Elections
Presidential Election
Popular Vote Leader
2012
Democrat
Obama Plurality (less than 50%)
Obama Majority (50 to 64%)
Obama Super Majority (65% or more)
Republican
Romney Plurality (less than 50%)
Romney Majority (50 to 64%)
Romney Super Majority (65% or more)
2016
Democrat
Clinton Plurality (less than 50%)
Clinton Majority (50 to 64%)
Clinton Super Majority (65% or more)
Republican
Trump Plurality (less than 50%)
Trump Majority (50 to 64%)
Trump Super Majority (65% or more)
Change in Democratic Vote
Percentage from 2012 to 2016
Percentage Increase in the Democratic Vote
0 to 4.9
5.0 or more
Percentage Decrease in the Democratic Vote
-0.1 to -4.9
-5.0 or more
Appalachia Region

Pennsylvania and southeastern Ohio. As it turned out Ohio and, unexpectedly, Pennsylvania, were key to determining the 2016 presidential election. In the Appalachian portion of these states, both rural and urban, there was a large movement toward the Republicans, helping push these critical swing electoral votes into the Trump column, facilitating his surprising victory.

REFERENCES

Archer, J. Clark, et al. 2014. *Atlas of the 2012 Elections*. Lanham, MD: Rowman & Littlefield.

Archer, J. Clark, Stephen J. Lavin, Kenneth C. Martis, Fred M. Shelley. 2006. *Historical Atlas of US Presidential Elections: 1788–2004*. Washington, DC: Congressional Quarterly Press.

Bump, Philip. 2016. Why Putting Coal Miners Out of Work Is a Very Bad Thing to Say in West Virginia. *Washington Post*, May 10.

Phillip, Abby, and Jose A. DelReal. 2016. Clinton Says She Regrets Labeling "Half" of Trump Supporters "Deplorable." *Washington Post*, September 10.

Trump, Donald J. 2016. Twitter account @realDonald Trump. September 10, 2016, 11:18 a.m., https://twitter.com/realdonaldtrump.

Webster, Gerald R., and Richard L. Morrill. 2015. Spatial and Political Realignment of the US Electorate, 1988–2012: Regional Realignment: Appalachia and the Upper South. *Political Geography* 48:93–107.

SOUTHEAST

JONATHAN I. LEIB

While the 2016 presidential election saw dramatic change in various regions of the United States when compared to 2012, the Southeast stood out for its electoral stability. In 2016, the Republican candidate, Donald Trump, won a majority of the vote in the twelve-state region. In terms of the two-party vote, Trump won 54.4 percent of the region's vote, the same percentage as Mitt Romney in 2012.

Overall, Republican dominance in the Southeast in the 2016 election can be demonstrated in several ways. First, Trump won the electoral votes of eleven of the region's twelve states, losing only Virginia. Trump's eleven states in the region was one better than Mitt Romney in 2012, as Trump won Florida for the Republicans. However, only a one percentage point change in the popular vote flipped Florida, a highly contested state in recent presidential elections. Whereas Romney lost Florida in 2012 with 49.6 percent of the two-party vote, Trump won the state in 2016 with 50.6 percent of the two-party vote. Second, the percentage point margin of victory for Trump increased over that for Romney in ten of the region's twelve states; only Virginia and Georgia saw a swing toward the Democrats in 2016. Third, at the state legislative level, with the Republicans winning control of Kentucky's House of Representatives, the 2016 election gave Republicans a majority of seats in every state House and Senate in the Southeast, giving them control of every state legislature in the region (Kromm 2016).

While Republicans strengthened their electoral hold on the region in 2016, there were several Democratic bright spots. The first is the state of Virginia. For the third election in a row, Democrats won the state at the presidential level, with Clinton defeating Trump by 5.6 percentage points of the two-party vote, an increase in the two-party victory margin of 1.6 percentage points from 2012. Indeed, recent elections suggest that Virginia may be moving from being a "toss-up" to a "leaning Democratic state," at least in statewide elections. Along with winning three presidential elections in a row, Democrats, as of mid-2017, hold the three highest statewide elected offices (governor, lieutenant governor, and attorney general) and both US Senate seats. While off-year elections in November 2017 for statewide offices may change the state's partisan balance of power, vote numbers from Virginia's June 2017 primary elections point to Democrats having a good chance of maintaining control in statewide elections. Indeed, Virginia's move toward the Democrats, while other states in the region tilt more Republican, led one of the state's leading political observers, *Richmond Times-Dispatch* columnist Jeff Schapiro (2016), to argue that the outcome of the 2016 election showed that Virginia voted "to secede—from the South."

While Virginia may be moving more toward the Democrats in statewide elections, North Carolina and Georgia may be joining Florida as "toss-up" states in presidential elections. In North Carolina, Trump won with 51.9 percent of the two-party vote. North Carolina's status as the region's newest swing state is demonstrated in that, of the eleven statewide elections on the November 2016 ballot, the winning candidate received less than 53 percent of the total vote in ten of the eleven contests. Indeed, Democratic candidates won the governor's race and state auditor's race by approximately ten thousand and six thousand votes, respectively, out of over 4.5 million cast. At the same time, the closeness of North Carolina's 2016 vote may have been impacted by recent attempts by that state's legislature to restrict voting access, which had a disproportionate effect on minority voters.

Along with Virginia, Georgia was the only state in the region in which the Democrats increased their percentage of the two-party presidential vote. In 2012, Barack Obama won 46.0 percent of Georgia's two-party vote while, in 2016, Hillary Rodham Clinton won 47.3 percent, a 1.3 percentage point increase. While Clinton still lost Georgia by over five percentage points, the shift toward the Democrats stands out in a region where most states saw their Republican share of the vote increase. While still losing the state, the shift toward the Democrats in Georgia may be indicative of two trends impacting the region's electorate. First is the widening partisan gap between urban/suburban and rural voters in the region. Second is the impact of recent immigrant voters on the electorate.

One factor often noted in the partisan divide nationwide in the 2016 election was the widening split between Democratic urban/suburban areas

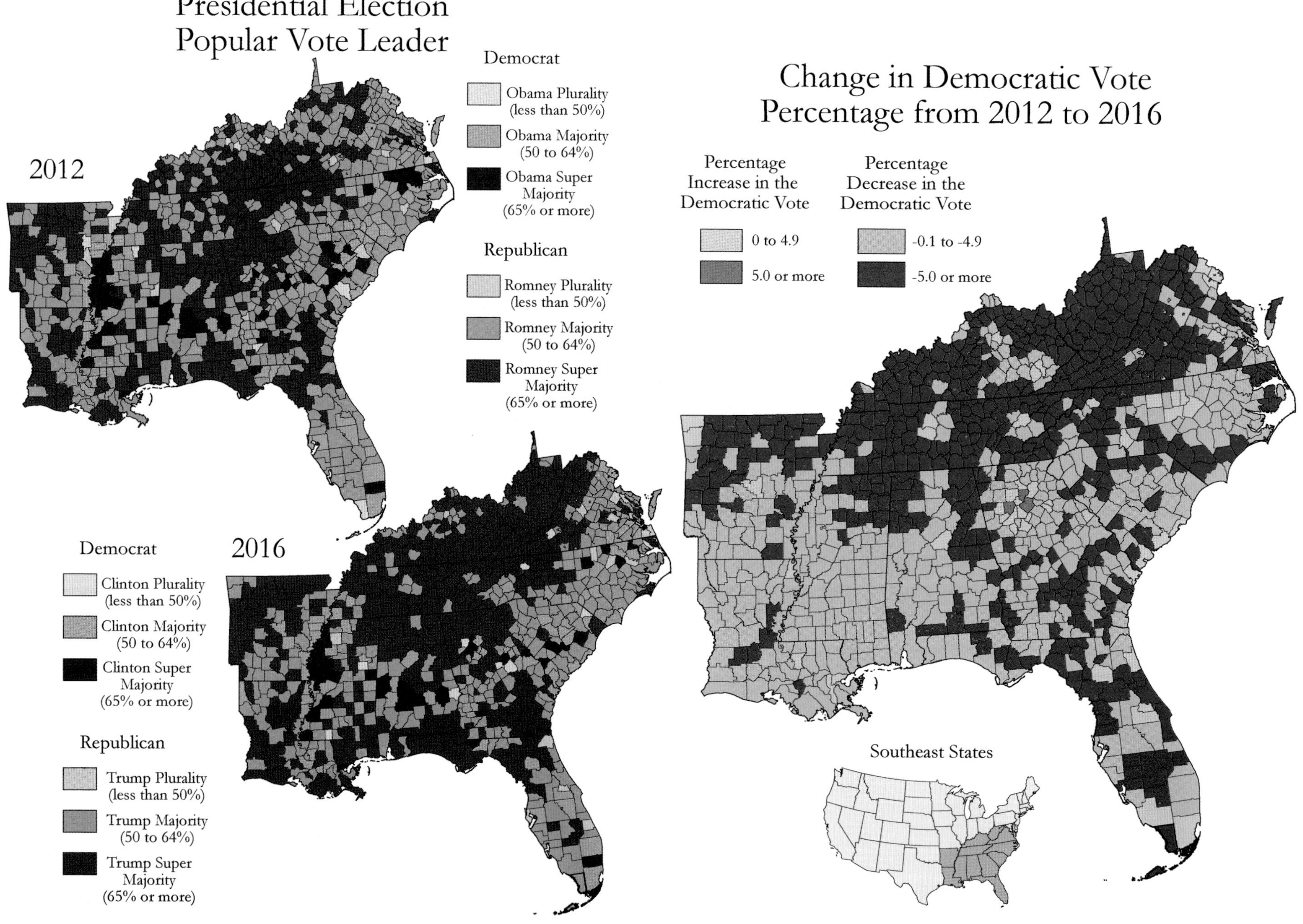
FIGURE 5.3
Southeast Region Presidential Elections
Presidential Election
Popular Vote Leader
2012
Democrat
Obama Plurality
(less than 50%)
Obama Majority
(50 to 64%)
Obama Super
Majority
(65% or more)
Republican
Romney Plurality
(less than 50%)
Romney Majority
(50 to 64%)
Romney Super
Majority
(65% or more)
2016
Democrat
Clinton Plurality
(less than 50%)
Clinton Majority
(50 to 64%)
Clinton Super
Majority
(65% or more)
Republican
Trump Plurality
(less than 50%)
Trump Majority
(50 to 64%)
Trump Super
Majority
(65% or more)
Change in Democratic Vote
Percentage from 2012 to 2016
Percentage
Increase in the
Democratic Vote
0 to 4.9
5.0 or more
Percentage
Decrease in the
Democratic Vote
-0.1 to -4.9
-5.0 or more
Southeast States

and Republican rural areas. With the exception of rural African American areas (especially in the Georgia-Alabama-Mississippi "Black Belt" and the Mississippi Delta), this trend was evidenced in the Southeast (figure 5.3). Whereas Trump won the vast majority of rural counties in the region, Clinton won most of the major urban areas, including the northern Virginia suburbs of DC and Richmond, and counties including urban centers such as Raleigh-Durham, Charlotte, Atlanta, Tampa, Orlando, Miami–West Palm Beach–Fort Lauderdale, Birmingham, New Orleans, Little Rock, Nashville, and Louisville.

In Atlanta, one of the fastest-growing urban areas of the region, not only did Clinton win the city of Atlanta but she also won many of the suburban counties surrounding Atlanta. Two of Clinton's more surprising victories were in the northern suburban counties of Cobb and Gwinnett, previously seen as solid Republican areas (the northern Atlanta suburbs served as part of Newt Gingrich's political base when he served in Congress). In both Cobb and Gwinnett Counties, Trump received nine percentage points less of the vote in losing the two counties in 2016 than Mitt Romney did in winning both in 2012.

Results in the Atlanta metropolitan area reflect changes occurring throughout the South. As figure 5.3 shows, the split between urban and rural areas continued to widen. That is, Republican rural areas became more Republican in 2016, while urban/suburban areas became more Democratic. For example, in the northern part of the rural Southeast, in places such as West Virginia, the western half of Virginia, rural parts of Kentucky, Tennessee, and northern Arkansas, the movement toward the Republicans was most pronounced, with many rural counties increasing their percentage of the Republican vote by more than five percentage points. The extent to which the rural/urban electoral divide continues in the region, in combination with differential growth rates between rural and urban areas, may impact the shape of the region's future elections. For example, West Virginia, once a reliably Democratic state in presidential elections, was most pronounced in its shift toward the Republicans. While constituents voted for Democrats, often by wide margins, in fourteen of seventeen presidential elections from 1932 to 1996, in 2016 Trump won the state with 72.2 percent of the two-party vote, an 8.6 percentage point increase from Mitt Romney in 2012. Indeed, this increase was uniform across the state, as all but one county saw a Republican vote increase of five percentage points or more.

A second issue potentially impacting regional voting patterns is in-migration to the Southeast. As Stepler and Lopez (2016) noted, over the past fifteen years, the Latino population in the United States has grown faster in the American South than in any other region. While recognizing that Latinos are not a monolithic group, and that great cultural and political diversity among Latinos exists, the increasing Latino population may have future electoral impacts both in urban and rural areas of the Southeast.

One example of the impact of Latino voters on the electorate can be found in Osceola County, Florida, south of Orlando. Over the past fifteen years, Osceola County has become a main center for immigrants coming from the island of Puerto Rico. Between 2000 and 2014, according to the Pew Research Center, the Hispanic population in Osceola County tripled from approximately 50,000 to over 150,000, with the Hispanic share of the county's population increasing from 29 percent to 50 percent. As US citizens, voting-age migrants from Puerto Rico are, of course, immediately eligible to vote, and the impact of this new electorate has been apparent in presidential election results in Osceola County. Between 2000 and 2016, the Democratic share of the presidential vote increased by ten percentage points, while the Republican share declined by nearly twelve.

The main conclusion, then, is that the 2016 presidential election results in the Southeast were quite similar to those of 2012. At the same time, trends in urban/rural voting patterns and regional migration suggest that change may be coming to Southeastern elections in the not-too-distant future.

REFERENCES

Kromm, Chris. 2016. Trump Helps Republicans Strengthen Power in Southern State Legislatures. *Facing South*. November 11, https://www.facingsouth.org/2016/11/trump-helps-republicans-strengthen-power-southern-state-legislatures (last accessed June 18, 2017).

Schapiro, Jeff. 2016. Virginia Votes to Secede—from the South. *Richmond Times-Dispatch*. November 13, http://www.richmond.com/news/virginia/government-politics/jeff-schapiro/schapiro-virginia-votes-to-secede---from-the-south/article_0a644cd2-0024-5fb6-a102-b9ac21d048c0.html (last accessed June 18, 2017).

Stepler, Renee, and Mark H. Lopez. 2016. US Latino Population Growth and Dispersion Has Slowed Since Onset of the Great Recession. Pew Research Center, Hispanic Trends. September 8, http://www.pewhispanic.org/2016/09/08/latino-population-growth-and-dispersion-has-slowed-since-the-onset-of-the-great-recession (last accessed June 18, 2017).

MIDWEST

JOHN HEPPEN

The Midwest proved to be a battleground in the autumn of 2016 as it was in 2012. Fighting for Midwest electoral votes is an entrenched feature of twenty-first-century electoral geography. George W. Bush back in 2004 even visited Marquette, Michigan, in the Upper Peninsula (Heppen 2007). Despite Trump's summer-long attacks, Hillary Clinton had an advantage going into the election. Despite fighting Donald Trump for Ohio, Clinton counted on Illinois, Iowa, Michigan, Minnesota, and Wisconsin. Minnesota had not backed a Republican in forty-four years, Wisconsin has voted Democratic since 1988, and Michigan last swung Republican in 1988. Ohio remained close according to polls right up to Election Day and Iowa was in the same boat. Donald Trump had hoped to swing Ohio, Michigan, Wisconsin, and Iowa to the Republican column by appealing to economic populism with a call for more manufacturing jobs, the end of NAFTA and the Trans-Pacific Partnership (TPP), a wall on the Mexican border, and questioning the ethics of Hillary Clinton. Trump was successful in all four states. He even visited the reliably Democratic state of Minnesota on the Sunday before Election Day.

The switch of Ohio, Michigan, Wisconsin, and Iowa contributed to his Electoral College victory. He repeatedly stated his opposition to NAFTA, which he blamed for costing manufacturing jobs and promised to bring them back. That siren call proved fruitful on Election Day. Coming on the heels of the Brexit vote in the United Kingdom, Trump claimed to be speaking for working-class Americans who lost good-paying jobs. Trump hammered on Clinton's support for NAFTA and China's entry in the World Trade Organization. During the fall campaign, Trump had hoped to make Michigan and Wisconsin competitive as well, though they were not battleground states in 2012. Trump won Michigan in the primary, as did Bernie Sanders, giving hope to his campaign. Trump's choice of Indiana governor Mike Pence solidified the conservative Christian base of the Republican Party and Indiana. Indiana had voted for Obama in 2008 before swinging solidly to Romney in 2012. Northern Indiana is part of the North American Manufacturing Belt or Rust Belt, which has suffered from deindustrialization exacerbated by globalization and neoliberal economic policies, and the winning of the Rust Belt and rural counties was the main story of Trump's victories in the Midwest. Trump based his victory on majorities among white, working- and middle-class, traditional Republican voters, and decreased turnout of Democratic voters in the urban giants of the Midwest.

Once again, the urban giants of Cleveland, Detroit, Chicago, Milwaukee, and Minneapolis–St. Paul were the home of much Democratic support, but they could not overcome the landslide in the suburbs, smaller towns, and rural places of the Midwest, and reduced turnout in Detroit and Milwaukee and Cleveland. Huge swaths of the Midwest went from blue to red. Another story of the transition of Michigan, Ohio, and Wisconsin from blue to red is the lower turnout among African American populations in the inner cities. Trump switched Iowa, Michigan, Ohio, and Wisconsin while holding on to Indiana and Missouri.

Clinton lost Michigan since voter turnout in Wayne County, home to Detroit, was down as Clinton received over 40,000 votes less than Obama did in 2012. She would have won the state if she had received the same number of votes as Obama with about 20,000 votes to spare, even with the loss of Macomb County to Trump. Macomb County is home to "Reagan Democrats" who are generally white and working-class voters. Macomb County flipped from Obama to Trump in 2016. Trump gained over 32,000 votes while Clinton lost about 31,000 votes compared to 2012. Clinton made a trip late in the campaign to Allendale, Michigan, close to Grand Rapids and the second largest metro area in the state, and then to Detroit, but to no avail.

Ohio presents a similar picture. A big prize in the Midwest due to its electoral votes and battleground status, Ohio proved pivotal. The vote in Ohio for Democrats from 2012 to 2016 decreased by over 400,000 votes, while Trump gained a little over 13,500 votes over Romney. Clinton's majorities in Cleveland, Cincinnati, Columbus, and Toledo could not overcome her losses in counties hosting Dayton and suburban collar counties around Columbus and Cincinnati. In

Midwest Region Presidential Elections

FIGURE 5.4

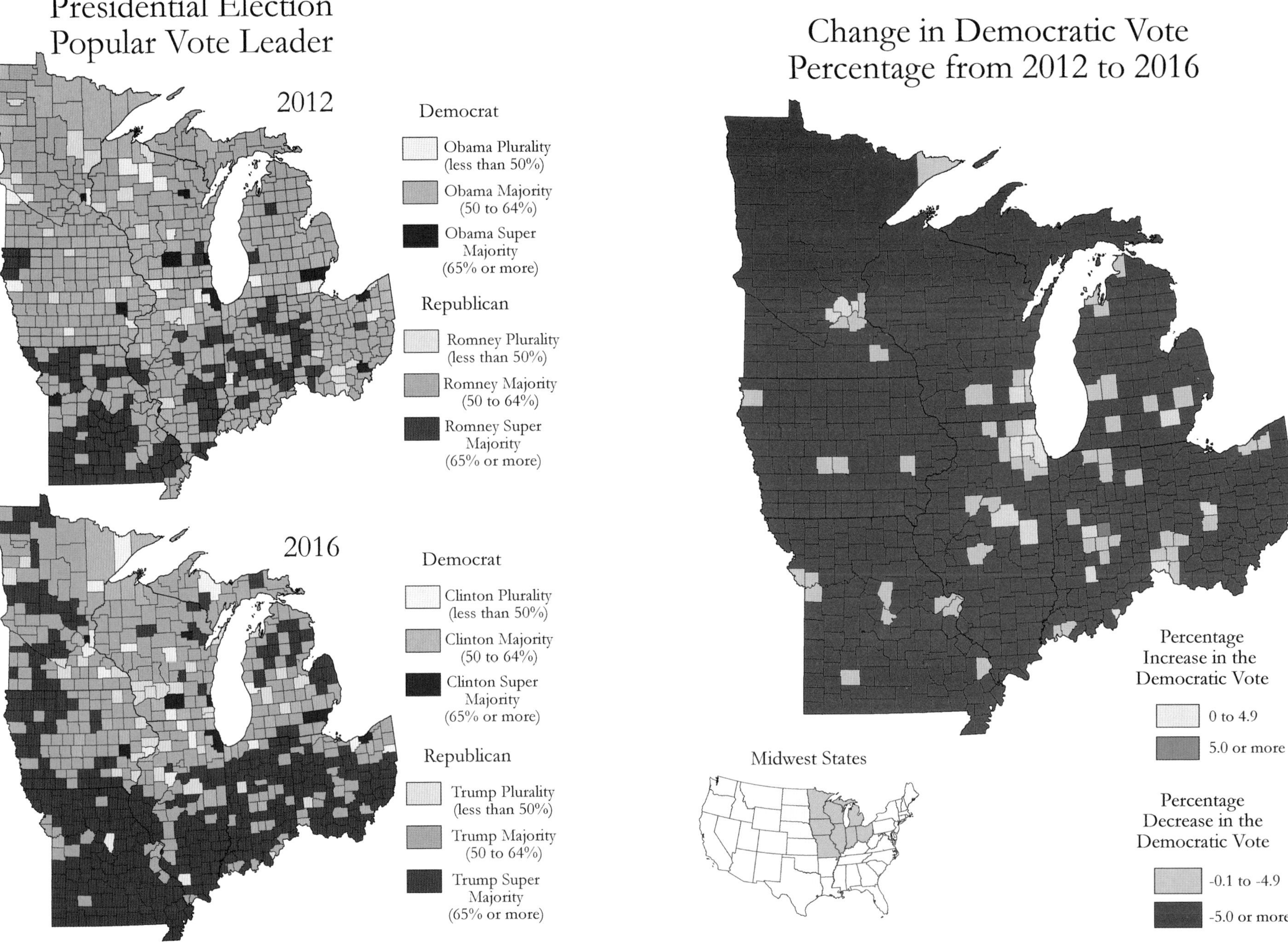

all but two counties, Clinton lost votes compared to Obama. Only in counties home to Cincinnati and Columbus did Clinton increase her vote total over Obama's in 2012. Counties in northeastern and northwestern Ohio switched from Obama to Trump. Clinton lost Stark, Portage, Trumbull, and Ashtabula in the northeast corner.

Wisconsin was another Midwestern triumph for Trump. Although it only has ten electoral votes, Wisconsin was a prime target of the Trump campaign. Trump won the state by 22,748 votes despite receiving about 2,000 fewer votes than Romney. As in other states, the urban giants of Milwaukee and Dane (Madison) Counties went for Clinton, but Trump managed to pick up the medium-sized urban counties of Racine and Kenosha in southeastern Wisconsin and took many counties with rural populations in western Wisconsin along the Mississippi River. The southwestern third of the state along the Mississippi and Wisconsin river valleys saw switches of medium- to small-sized counties. Clinton received close to 238,000 fewer votes than Obama as more Democrats than Republicans stayed home in more than just Milwaukee County. The Democratic vote in Milwaukee County was down by about 44,000 votes. In very liberal Dane County, home of the University of Wisconsin, the Democratic vote was down by about only 1,000 votes as Clinton won over 217,000 votes but, nevertheless, it was a bad year for Democrats as the Green Party vote increased by almost 3,000 votes from 2012.

Trump took Iowa away from the Democrats in 2016. He performed strongest in rural and medium-sized urban places in a familiar pattern across the Midwest. In every single Iowa county, Clinton lost votes. The vote losses were only less severe in four counties. Two counties were part of the Des Moines area. The eastern county, Johnson, is home to the University of Iowa, and the western county of Sioux was the other anomaly showing an increase in Democratic votes. Missouri was considered safe Republican territory going into the election and the prevalent urban/rural divide was at its most extreme with only three counties giving Clinton majorities. Counties housing St. Louis, Columbia, and Kansas City were the counties won by Clinton as she lost the state by over 500,000 votes. The familiar red and blue pattern with associated anomalies has become entrenched in the Midwest (Morrill, Knopp, and Brown 2011).

The one bright spot for Clinton was Illinois, her native state and home to President Obama. Chicago and Cook County was her anchor but even with the win, she showed massive losses in rural and medium-sized urban counties of downstate Illinois. Another win was Minnesota, but Minnesota was dangerously close for Clinton and also a metaphor as to how far Clinton had fallen compared to Obama, Kerry, Gore, and her husband in the Midwest. Minnesota was never competitive from 1992 to 2012 and yet Trump was relatively close in losing by about 44,000 votes, the closest presidential election in Minnesota in over a generation.

The maps in figure 5.4 highlight that Clinton suffered from widespread losses in support across the Midwest. In only a few counties, most notably counties with universities like the University of Michigan and the University of Illinois, and some urban counties home to Cincinnati, Indianapolis, Columbus, Minneapolis–St. Paul, and Chicago, did she maintain or increase upon the Obama vote in 2012. Those gains were rare as the geographic story of the election in the Midwest is the massive loss of Democratic votes. Huge swaths of rural and medium-sized urban counties in the Midwest saw a drop in Democratic support of greater than 5 percentage points. In addition, many suburban counties of Cincinnati, Cleveland, Columbus, Detroit, Chicago, Milwaukee, Minneapolis–St. Paul, Kansas City, and St. Louis saw losses of Democratic support ranging from 0.1 to 4.9 percent. The Midwest, like the rest of the country, became increasingly polarized following a trend beginning in 1992 (Johnston, Manley, and Jones 2016). In this election, the polarization trend benefited the Republican Party, much to the surprise of the pollsters and the Democrats.

REFERENCES

Heppen, John. 2007. Continuity, Change, and Campaign Visits in the Midwest during the 2004 Presidential Election. *Wisconsin Geographer* 22:3–26.

Johnston, Ron, David Manley, and Kelvyn Jones. 2016. Spatial Polarization of Presidential Voting in the United States, 1992–2012: "The 'Big Sort' Revisited." *Annals of the American Association of Geographers* 106(5): 1047–62.

Morrill, Richard, Larry Knopp, and Michael Brown. 2011. Anomalies in Red and Blue II: Towards an Understanding of the Roles of Setting, Values, and Demography in the 2004 and 2008 US Presidential Elections. *Political Geography* 30(3): 153–68.

GREAT PLAINS

ROBERT H. WATREL

The 2016 elections in the Great Plains region was another landslide win for the Republican Party at all levels of government. Running north to south, the Great Plains states consist of North Dakota, South Dakota, Nebraska, Kansas, Oklahoma, and Texas. These states have long been supporters of Republican presidential candidates and the last time a state gave all of its electoral votes to a Democratic candidate was in 1976. Not only have these states been strong supporters of Republican presidential candidates, but over the last ten to fifteen years, the Republican Party has come to dominate state politics as well (Hurt 2011).

At the state level, Great Plains voters have never been too friendly to Democratic candidates, and 2016 was no exception. Republican candidate Donald Trump's vote returns for the six Great Plains states continued a pattern that Republican presidential candidates have enjoyed for several decades. No state gave less than 52 percent (Texas) of the popular vote to Trump, and three states gave returns greater than 60 percent (North Dakota, Oklahoma, and South Dakota). Five of the six Great Plains states had a margin of victory greater than 20 percent, while Texas had the lowest margin of victory at 9 percent. Oklahoma led both categories, with a 65.3 percent popular vote and a 36.4 percent margin of victory for Trump. Democratic candidate Hillary Clinton's largest popular vote for any state was Texas with 43 percent, with all the other states giving less than 36 percent of the popular vote, and North Dakota polling the lowest at 27 percent. Third-party and write-in candidates polled well, with five states polling more than 5.75 percent and Texas at 4.5 percent. North Dakota polled the highest at 9.8 percent for third-party and write-in candidates.

The wave of Republican support was even more impressive when observed at the county level. Of the 648 counties that comprise the Great Plains states, 599 counties returned 50 percent or more for Republican candidate Donald Trump or 92.4 percent of all counties gave Trump a majority. Granted many of these counties have small populations, but it shows the popularity of the Republican Party in these mostly rural areas. If you include the additional counties where Trump received a plurality, he carried a total of 610 counties. On the other hand, Hillary Clinton received a majority in thirty-five counties and a plurality in three.

Although Democratic candidate Hillary Clinton experienced a drubbing from voters in the Great Plains, there were pockets of counties where voters have consistently supported Democratic candidates (figure 5.5). Counties where voters gave Hillary Clinton a majority or plurality of votes are counties that have long been bastions of support for Democratic candidates over the last several election cycles. These Democratic-majority counties roughly fall into four categories: counties with larger Native American populations, counties with larger Hispanic populations, several metropolitan counties mainly in Texas, and several counties with colleges.

In the northern Great Plains, almost all the counties with Democratic majorities have large Native American populations, which have historically been strong supporters of the Democratic Party (Wishart 2004). In North Dakota, Rolette County (Turtle Mountain Reservation) and Sioux County (Standing Rock Reservation) gave Democrat majorities. This pattern also holds true for South Dakota. Counties with larger Native American populations, such as Dewey (Cheyenne River Reservation), Oglala Lakota (Pine Ridge Reservation), Todd (Rosebud Reservation), and Buffalo (Crow Creek Reservation), gave a majority to Hillary Clinton. However, when comparing the 2012 and 2016 Popular Vote Leader maps (figure 5.5), some counties with larger Native American populations did flip and gave a majority or plurality to Donald Trump.

Another area of traditional Democratic support is located in the southern Great Plains, close to or along the United States–Mexico border. These are counties with historically large Hispanic populations. Some of these counties have given strong support to the Democratic Party for many decades. In fact, Brooks and Jim Hogg Counties have never given a Republican presidential candidate a majority of their votes. All of these counties have Hispanic populations over 75 percent (Barcus and Simmons 2013). Not all counties with large Hispanic populations vote Democratic, but these counties have a long history of Democratic support. Counties such as Zavala, Dimmit, Jim Hogg, Starr, Brooks, and Duval gave supermajorities (65 percent or more) to Hillary Clinton in 2016.

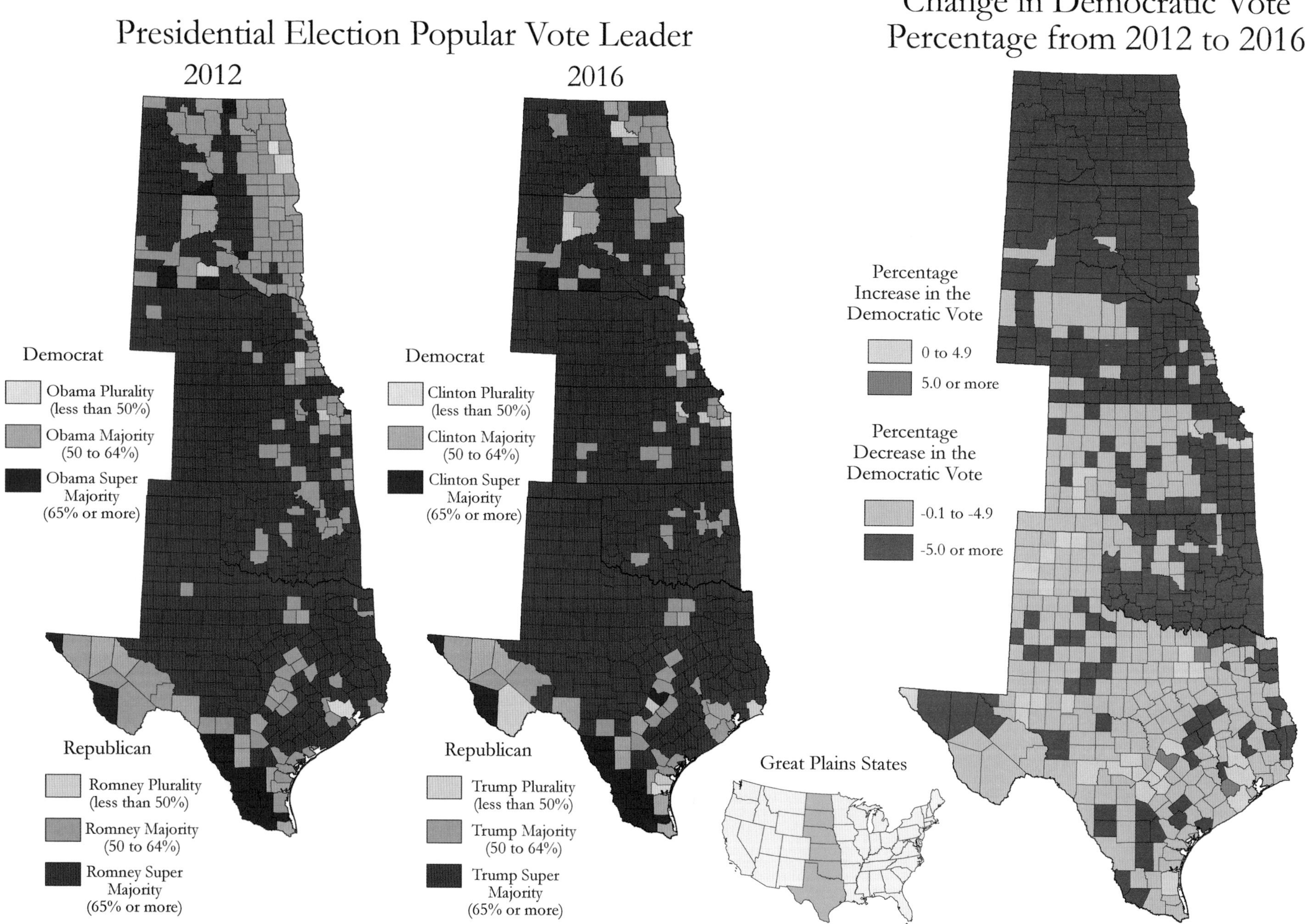

Great Plains Region Presidential Elections
FIGURE 5.5
Presidential Election Popular Vote Leader
2012
2016
Democrat
Obama Plurality (less than 50%)
Obama Majority (50 to 64%)
Obama Super Majority (65% or more)
Republican
Romney Plurality (less than 50%)
Romney Majority (50 to 64%)
Romney Super Majority (65% or more)
Democrat
Clinton Plurality (less than 50%)
Clinton Majority (50 to 64%)
Clinton Super Majority (65% or more)
Republican
Trump Plurality (less than 50%)
Trump Majority (50 to 64%)
Trump Super Majority (65% or more)
Change in Democratic Vote Percentage from 2012 to 2016
Percentage Increase in the Democratic Vote
0 to 4.9
5.0 or more
Percentage Decrease in the Democratic Vote
-0.1 to -4.9
-5.0 or more
Great Plains States

Larger urban counties, where Clinton received majorities or pluralities, include: Douglas County, Nebraska (Omaha); Lancaster County, Nebraska (Lincoln); Wyandotte County, Kansas (Kansas City); and Dallas County (Dallas), Harris and Fort Bend Counties (Houston), and Bexar County (San Antonio) in Texas. The remainder of counties that gave Clinton majorities or pluralities, have universities: Clay County, South Dakota (University of South Dakota); Lancaster County, Nebraska (University of Nebraska–Lincoln); Douglas County, Kansas (University of Kansas); and Travis County, Texas (University of Texas–Austin).

When comparing the vote returns between the 2012 and 2016 elections, a shift in the electorate is not readily apparent (figure 5.5). However, when looking over changes in the percentage of the Democratic votes from the 2012 to 2016 elections by county, the scale of the swing toward the Republican candidate becomes clearer. If there was any representation of how unpopular Hillary Clinton was in the Great Plains region, this map shows it. In all of the counties in North Dakota, South Dakota, Nebraska, and Oklahoma there was an increase in the vote for the Republican candidate. In only two states, Kansas and Texas, are there counties that saw an increase in Democratic support between 2012 and 2016. Counties with an increase of 5 percent of more for Clinton were in urban counties in Texas (Dallas, Houston, and Austin). The remainder of counties that saw a Democratic increase of 4.9 percent or less are a smattering of urban, suburban, and rural counties.

Not only has the Republican Party dominated presidential politics in the Great Plains states but also, over the last ten to fifteen years, the Republicans have increased their hold over state governments and delegations to the US Congress, so much so that several of these states can now be considered one-party states. For example, currently, in all six of the Great Plains states, Republicans hold a majority of executive offices (e.g., governor, lieutenant governor, attorney general, etc.). In four states, North Dakota, South Dakota, Kansas, and Oklahoma, Republicans have supermajorities—more than 66 percent representation—in both houses of the legislature. Nebraska has a nonpartisan unicameral legislature, but it would be misleading to say it is not dominated by conservative legislators; it can essentially be thrown into the ranks of the supermajority category. Only Texas does not hold Republican supermajorities, although Republicans enjoy a little over 63 percent representation in both legislative bodies.

This trend in Republican popularity is also evident in US congressional delegations. As of the 2016 election, there are no Democratic members in the US House of Representatives from the five Great Plains states north of Texas. Although this does not equate to very many House seats (for example, North and South Dakota only have an at-large member, Nebraska 3, Kansas 4, and Oklahoma 5), many of these seats were competitive for Democratic candidates just ten years ago. Texas is the only Great Plains state that has Democratic members in its US House of Representatives delegation with eleven members out of a total of thirty-six for the state.

In the US Senate, as of the 2016 election, there is only one Democratic senator out of twelve from the six Great Plains states. Currently, Heidi Heitkamp of North Dakota, who won in a surprise upset in 2012, is the lone Democratic senator from the Great Plains. There were four senatorial elections during the 2016 election and incumbent Republican candidates reclaimed all four seats.

The prospect for future Democratic presidential candidates in the Great Plains states looks bleak. There are a few metropolitan counties and pockets of counties with some ethno-cultural diversity (e.g., Native Americans, Hispanics, and African Americans) in the region that support the Democratic Party, but most of the remaining counties are rural, lightly populated, and predominantly white with conservative political values.

Although the Great Plains states of North Dakota, South Dakota, Nebraska, Kansas, and Oklahoma will probably not cast their electoral votes for a Democratic presidential candidate anytime soon, there is one glimmer of hope for Democrats. The state of Texas was the only state where the percentage of the total vote for the Democratic candidate increased from 2012 to 2016, 41.38 percent to 43.25 percent. This may seem like a small increase, but when comparing the margin of victory of the Republican candidates from 2012 and 2016, the margin was reduced from 15.78 percent in 2012 to 9 percent in 2016. If Hispanic, African American, and urban populations become more mobilized to Democratic presidential candidates in the near future, Texas will become the only battleground in the Great Plains and, with its thirty-six electoral votes, that would be a big boon for the Democrats.

REFERENCES

Barcus, Holly R., and Laura Simmons. 2013. Ethnic Restructuring in Rural America: Migration and the Changing Faces of Rural Communities in the Great Plains. *Professional Geographer* 65(1): 130–52.

Hurt, R. Douglas. 2011. *The Big Empty: The Great Plains in the Twentieth Century*. Tucson: University of Arizona Press.

Wishart, David J. 2004. *Encyclopedia of the Great Plains*. Lincoln: University of Nebraska Press.

MOUNTAIN WEST

TONY ROBINSON

The 2016 election victory of Donald Trump upended conventional thinking on how the Democratic Party was on the right side of demographic change. With Trump's victory in the face of a diversifying electorate thought to be more liberal, many analysts concluded that perhaps demography was not destiny after all. Though strong with increasingly populous non-white voters, Democrats faced profound problems with heartland voters in 2016—especially the white working class—who demonstrated their strength through electoral upheaval. An examination of 2016 electoral results in the Mountain West—a region long dominated by the "white working class" but also rapidly diversifying—shows evidence of the same upheaval of white working-class voters that benefited the GOP nationwide. However, a more detailed analysis of voting patterns in the West shows even stronger evidence of a continued tectonic reshaping of demographic patterns in ways that are beneficial to the Democratic Party, especially in national-level elections.

A bird's-eye examination of results across the Mountain West reveals evidence that Trump's strength in rural and white communities helped propel his presidential victory. The maps in figure 5.6 reveal that although Trump's vote share grew across most of the West (as compared to Romney), his vote shares were only high enough to claim victories in mostly rural and white counties. The "change in vote" map reveals vast swaths of red or pink Trump counties—mostly sparsely populated rural areas—surrounding islands of blue Clinton counties. This small number of blue, Democratic counties are either relatively large cities (e.g., Denver, Colorado; Missoula, Montana; Las Vegas, Nevada; Salt Lake City, Utah) or are minority-majority counties where Native Americans or Latinos make up a sizable share of the population (e.g., the Navajo/Hopi Reservations and the Blackfeet Reservation largely coincide with the blue counties in the north of Arizona and Montana).

A study of enduring Democratic strength in these urban and diverse counties points toward the tectonic uplift of the Democratic Party across the West, when measured at the presidential election level. Though these maps suggest that the Democratic party lost ground almost everywhere across the West in 2016, actual election results mean that for the third presidential election in a row, Democrats actually won three of the five most-populated states in the West (Colorado, New Mexico, and Nevada—collectively worth twenty electoral votes), whereas they had previously lost ALL eight Western states in EVERY election since 1968 (excepting Colorado, Montana, and New Mexico in Clinton's 1992 victory). Between 1968 and 2004, Democrats won just 4 percent of all possible electoral votes in the Mountain West. In the last three presidential elections, Democrats have won 43 percent of all electoral votes. Furthermore, the maps also show that in addition to the three predictably Democratic states, Arizona (the most populated state in the Mountain West) did not perform well for Trump. Election returns from Arizona show that while Romney won the state by 208,422 votes in 2012, Trump won the state by only 91,234 votes. As Republican strength wanes in Arizona, there is a good chance that four of the five most heavily populated states in the Rocky Mountain West may go Democrat in 2020.[1]

The fact that Clinton won three of the most heavily populated states in the Mountain West can be hidden in maps of vote-performance by county, which suggest absolute Republican dominance across the region. The "change in vote" map reveals a sweep of red and pink GOP counties across the Mountain West that add up to 81 percent of all counties. Moreover, the deep red of many of these counties—showing areas of Trump supermajorities—helps explain the landslide victories Trump notched in several states (Trump won Wyoming by 46.3 percent, Idaho by 31.7 percent, Montana by 20.2 percent, and Utah by 17.9 percent). However, the three states with the biggest landslides are also the least-populated states in the region. In fact, though Democrats only won 18.9 percent of the counties in the Mountain West, those counties accounted for 45 percent of all votes cast in the region. This is why the Democrats won Nevada, though the 2016 map shows that only two counties in the state voted Democrat (Las Vegas' Clark County and Reno's Washoe County).

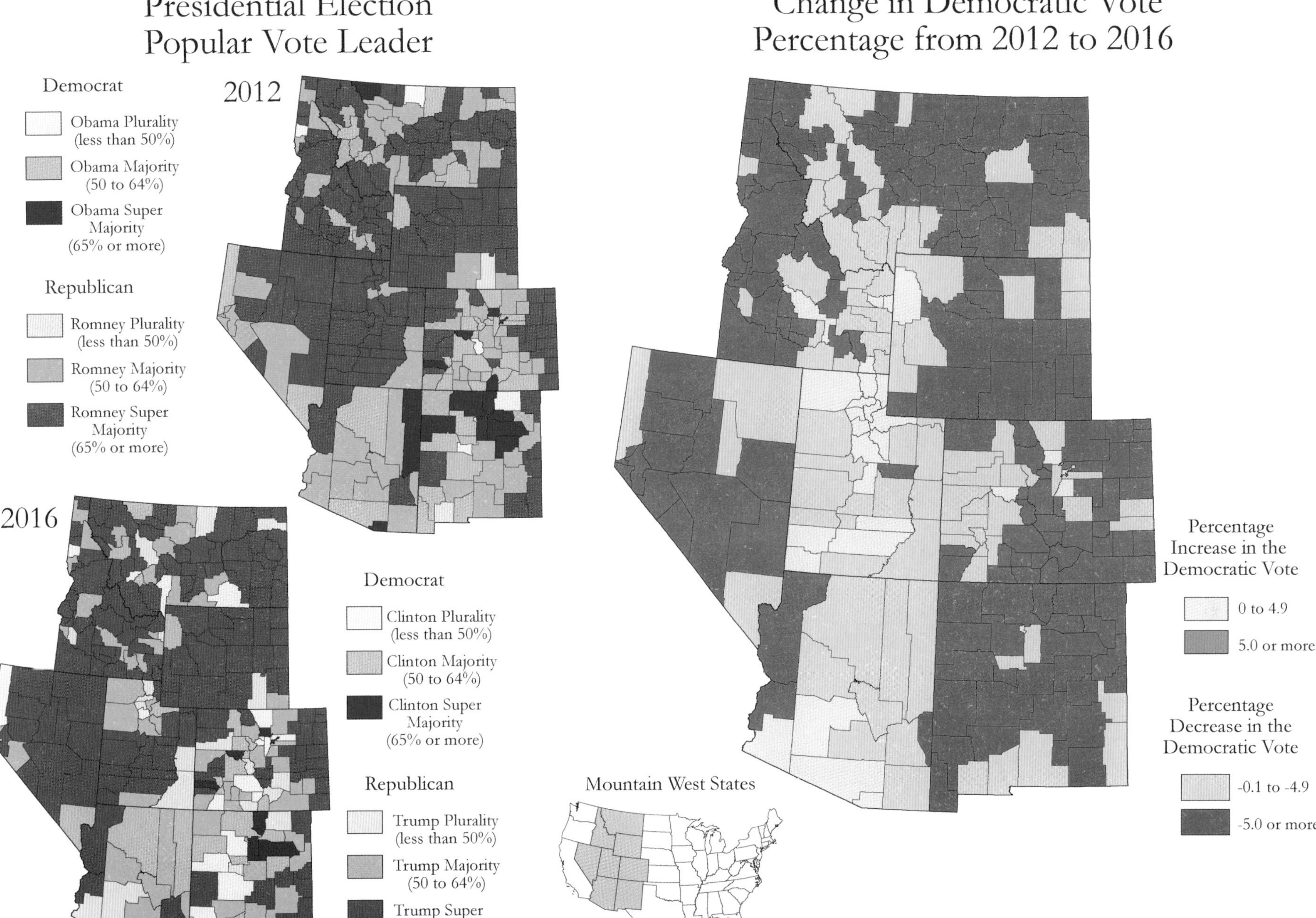
FIGURE 5.6
Mountain West Region Presidential Elections
Presidential Election
Popular Vote Leader
2012
Democrat
Obama Plurality (less than 50%)
Obama Majority (50 to 64%)
Obama Super Majority (65% or more)
Republican
Romney Plurality (less than 50%)
Romney Majority (50 to 64%)
Romney Super Majority (65% or more)
2016
Democrat
Clinton Plurality (less than 50%)
Clinton Majority (50 to 64%)
Clinton Super Majority (65% or more)
Republican
Trump Plurality (less than 50%)
Trump Majority (50 to 64%)
Trump Super Majority (65% or more)
Change in Democratic Vote
Percentage from 2012 to 2016
Percentage Increase in the Democratic Vote
0 to 4.9
5.0 or more
Percentage Decrease in the Democratic Vote
-0.1 to -4.9
-5.0 or more
Mountain West States

These heavily populated, pro-Democrat counties have common characteristics: They are either urbanized or largely non-white. What's more, many of these urban counties are rapidly growing, while the population in rural, socially conservative counties (the swaths of deep red in these maps) is shrinking as a percentage of the Mountain West. Census data show that since 2010, the Mountain West has been the fastest growing region in the country. Most of this growth has been concentrated in urban areas like the Colorado Front Range, where Democrats are finding improved prospects. In Nevada, a growing Democratic stronghold, the urban percentage of the population has grown by almost 7 percent in the last fifteen years, to over 94 percent today.

These rapidly growing areas tend to have a high percentage of white-collar jobs held by well-educated professionals or are classified as "recreation-destination" counties, such as mountain ski towns or environmental amenity communities. These areas are populated by a more liberal demographic than the resource-extraction and agriculture economy of the older Mountain West. The 2016 map shows this geography well, with a patch of Democratic blue counties defining the urbanized Front Range in the middle top of Colorado, and in Nevada's Las Vegas and Reno areas. The map also shows a blue peppering of "recreation-destination" counties across the Rocky Mountain spine, such as Jackson Hole in northwest Wyoming, Blaine County in south-central Idaho (home of the Sun Valley ski resort), and Colorado's mountain ski-town communities along the Democratic-blue summits of the Rockies. As the Mountain West continues to urbanize, the foundation of Democratic strength in this region—the urban blue islands revealed in the "change in vote" map—will continue to swing around half of all regional presidential electoral votes to the Democratic Party.

A final relevant aspect of the demographic patterns in the Mountain West is racial/ethnic diversity, which contributes to Democratic strength. For example, Native American reservation boundaries closely match several county boundaries that Democrats won in 2016 (for example, Montana's Blackfeet Reservation to the north, and New Mexico's Navajo Reservation). Still, Native Americans make up only about 2 percent of the overall Western electorate—and this population is not growing.

Latinos, however, are a different story. Latinos make up 45 percent of New Mexico's population, for example, and the swath of blue Democratic counties across that state testifies to the electoral impact of about 60 percent of those Latinos voting Democratic. Similarly, heavy Latino concentrations are present along Arizona's southern border, in Nevada's southern Clark County, and in Colorado's southwest, all areas of Democratic strength.

Census data show Latino populations growing by 34 percent in the Mountain West in the last decade—more than twice the region's overall population growth. Latinos accounted for 40 percent of New Mexico voters, 18 percent of Nevada voters, and 12 percent of Colorado voters in 2016—and it is no coincidence that Democrats won these same three states in 2016. Changing racial composition in the Mountain West will continue in future election cycles, as the Census Bureau predicts that by 2040, three states in the Mountain West (Arizona, New Mexico, and Nevada) will have minority-majority populations, which will, under current voting behavior patterns, make these states reliably Democratic in presidential elections.

An important counterweight must be offered to this analysis of likely-to-grow Democratic strength in the once reliably Republican Rocky Mountains. The previous analysis focuses on state-level presidential election results and prospects. However, the United States is a federal system with dispersed local districts sending legislators to Congress and to their state legislatures. On these governmental levels, patterns are troubling for the Democrats. The concentration of large numbers of Democrats in a small number of highly populated counties means that US House of Representative delegates and state legislators in the Mountain West (both elected by geographically dispersed local districts) tilt strongly toward the Republican Party. In terms of the US House of Representatives, the 2016 elections sent seventeen Republicans and ten Democrats to Congress. This party imbalance is even more dramatic in state legislative seats. Because state legislators are elected out of geographically dispersed and mostly red counties across the region, the 2016 elections in the Rocky Mountains sent a total of 204 Democrats to state legislatures (33 percent of all seats), in comparison to 396 Republicans (66 percent of all seats).

In these ways, the 2016 election in the West has confirmed two long-enduring, and seemingly conflictual, political adages. "Demography is destiny," many have said—and although the Trump election seemed to upend this adage with the upheaval of white, working-class voters, a closer look at election results in the Mountain West shows that underlying demographic patterns remain a force and will likely prove definitive in future presidential elections. "All politics is local," others have oft observed, and the reality of Republican strength across sprawling localities of the Mountain West has manifested itself in Republican-dominated state legislatures across the region. In these parallel and somewhat competing results, the capacity of US federalism to produce self-contradicting checks and balances is again on display.

NOTE

1. The change in the vote map also shows Trump losing substantial ground in Utah compared to Romney in 2012. However, this result stems from the coincidence of Mitt Romney (a Mormon) running for president with the Republican Party in 2012, which was popular with Utah's heavily Mormon voters. In addition, Trump's well-documented moral dalliances seemed to cause him trouble with Utah's religiously conservative voters—who voted in sizable numbers for favorite son, third-party Mormon candidate Evan McMullin. Even so, Trump won Utah's voters by almost 18 percent, demonstrating that this state is not contestable in the near future.

PACIFIC REGION

JOHN AGNEW

Until the Great Depression of the 1930s, the three contiguous West Coast states (California, Oregon, and Washington) were reliably Republican in presidential elections. Since then, but particularly since the 1990s, they have become equally reliably Democratic. This drift toward the Democratic Party in the Pacific Region is part of the national story of the geographic "flipping" of the parties as the Republican Party pursued a "southern strategy" beginning with the Nixon presidency and the Democrats have become the party of metropolitan areas and minority groups that once either leaned to or strongly supported Republican presidential candidates, but are now a reservoir of votes for the Democratic Party. At the same time, the two main parties have become very ideologically polarized nationally (Thurber and Yoshinaka 2016). To some extent this polarization is also geographical (Johnston et al. 2016), even though the polarization probably has more to do with the rightward trend of winning candidates in Republican primaries as much as anything else. It can be exaggerated when you consider that margins of victory at the district or county level are often of less than landslide proportions (Abrams 2017). In the Pacific Region, except for Alaska, the Republicans see declining registration rates as the numbers of registered Democrats and independents, particularly the latter, have increased (e.g., PPIC 2016). These days, presidential candidates rarely put in campaign appearances in the region after the primaries except in pursuit of campaign funding, mainly among wealthy donors in Hollywood and Silicon Valley.

In 2016, the Republican candidate, Donald J. Trump, someone with a mixed personal history of party registration and proclaiming many policies well away from mainstream Republican ones on trade and national security, for example, performed much better in relative terms across the region than the Republican candidates in the previous two presidential elections. He still lost heavily to Hillary Clinton in all of the states save Alaska. But he did so by establishing large margins in the most rural areas with declining shares of the region's overall population. He picked up some votes among traditionally Democratic constituencies such as timber workers in towns that had not voted Republican since the 1920s (Yardley 2016). Beyond that, and famously, Clinton's huge margin of victory in California, the most populous state, a historic high 61.7 percent of the vote, accounts for why she won the national popular vote even as Trump was winning in the Electoral College.

County-level returns in figure 5.7 tell a somewhat more complex story. They show that there is enormous variation across the region that is not well captured by the well-known stereotype since the 1990s of the "left coast." California, for example, the state of the region with easily the largest number of Electoral College votes—although as a whole it went heavily for Hillary Clinton in 2016, as it had for Barack Obama in 2008 and 2012—is divided in political complexion between its interior and coastal counties. Donald Trump captured many of the same counties in the interior as had Mitt Romney in 2012 and John McCain in 2008. Much of this interior-to-coastal contrast can be put down to rural-urban differences in ethnic composition and religious traditions, with the largely agribusiness-valley and rural-mountainous counties breaking for Republican candidates and the urban-metropolitan counties in southern California and the Bay Area going for Democrats. This is now a well-established pattern in California and in Oregon and Washington as well.

Much of the geographical polarization throughout the Pacific Region, significantly spiking in 2016, can be seen in much greater swings to Trump from Romney in rural areas and strong support for Clinton in the coastal counties (except for Orange County south of Los Angeles swinging to a Democratic candidate for the first time since 1936). These trends can be ascribed to the rightward drift of the Republican Party, narrowing the appeal of the party in the region to very specific cultural-geographical constituencies (evangelical Christians, Mormons, farmers, small-town conservatives) and producing candidates in state and congressional elections who are so extreme, particularly on cultural issues, that they cannot appeal to moderate voters (Fiorina and Abrams 2008). The strident, southern-style, white Christian nationalism of the Republican right (Jones 2016) does not sell well across California as a whole.

FIGURE 5.7

Pacific Region Presidential Elections

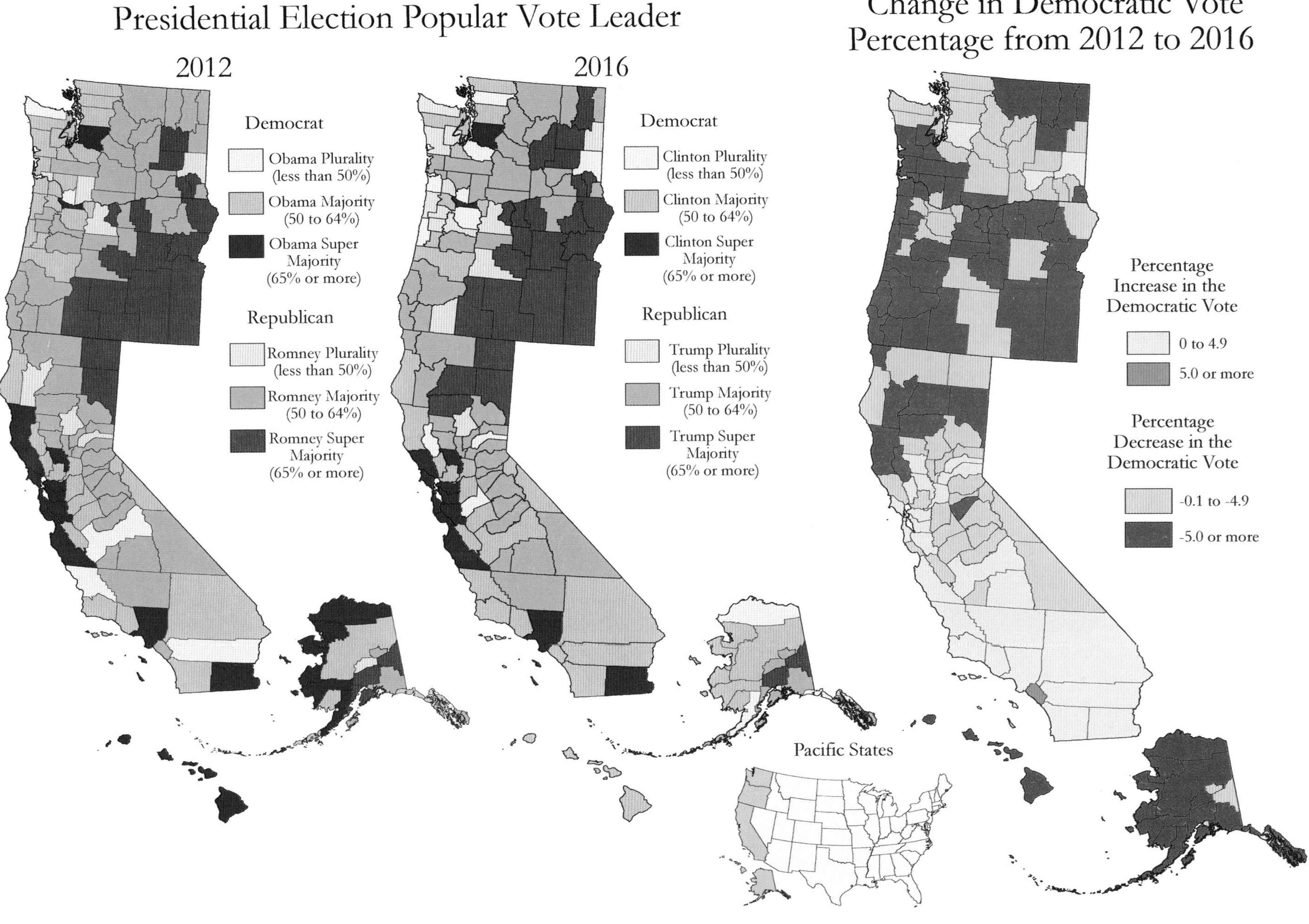

Donald Trump made no serious inroads with urban voters in coastal-urban California, Oregon, and Washington. So, the swing of votes his way in interior California and rural Oregon and Washington was nowhere near enough to make a dent in the final outcome. The Republican "fortresses" are—with the historic exception of suburban Orange County to the south of Los Angeles, finally lost in 2016—in rural areas of low population density without the numbers of voters needed to command statewide majorities. Paradoxically, given the historic business image of the party, it is typically poorer areas that now vote predominantly Republican while the richer areas support the Democrats. More specifically, Trump's economic protectionism did not play well in the more cosmopolitan and trans-Pacific-oriented coastal economies.

Even those counties in the Bay Area and southern California most affected by the 2008 economic crisis, including massive numbers of mortgage foreclosures and several municipal bankruptcies, remained firmly in the Democratic column notwithstanding Trump's open appeal to those most affected. These counties are also those with increasing numbers of Latino voters relative to the state as a whole. Though still only at 18 percent of the eligible voting age population, Latinos are, as of 2016, estimated to be 34 percent of the total population of California. Over the next twenty years, the former number will undoubtedly increase at a faster rate than the latter. As is well known, the Latino vote in California and other Pacific Region states tends, partly because of Republican positions on immigration and economic issues, increasingly Democratic. This was an important factor in 2016, given Trump's campaign was based from the beginning on antipathy not only to undocumented immigrants but to all people of Mexican descent, a large share of the Latino population in California with citizenship. Trump's bizarre and unsubstantiated claim that he lost the national vote because of "illegal" voters in California fits into this picture (Bump 2017). Whatever Trump does as president, 2016 may not have been the so-called last white election as anticipated in 2012 (Davis 2013) but in California particularly the electoral die seems cast.

If anything, the rural-urban divide, particularly between the sparsely populated southeast of the state on the one hand and Portland and the population centers of the Willamette Valley on the other, is even more extreme in Oregon than in California and Washington State. In 2016, Trump did as well in southeast Oregon as had Bush Jr. in 2004 and he improved in several counties over subsequent Republican candidates. Even though it still went for Clinton in 2016 as it did for Obama in 2012, Oregon remains more competitive in presidential elections than either California or Washington. This perhaps reflects the fact that it is generally more rural than the other two, with only one metropolitan area of any size. If Clinton could be characterized as "hanging on" in Oregon in 2016, Washington tells a less dramatic story. The basic west-east pattern there is entrenched but the Seattle-Tacoma metropolitan area exerts such a strong overall effect on the statewide outcome that, even with declining turnout by Democrats and independents for Clinton in 2016, she still managed to win the state relatively easily.

Hawaii and Alaska represent opposite ends of the political spectrum as far as the 2016 and other recent presidential elections are concerned. Ever since coming to statehood, they have been dominated respectively by the Democratic and Republican parties in just about all types of elections. In Hawaii in 2016 Clinton failed to match the success of Obama, born in the state, yet still acquired a substantial majority of the vote. Hawaii remains a difficult state for Republican candidates. With most of the population of native Hawaiian and Asian heritage, Hawaii has a completely different ethnic profile from the other states in the region. In Alaska, Trump managed to return the state to the margin that McCain achieved in 2008 with his running mate, the former governor of Alaska, Sarah Palin, after a drop-off in 2012. Perhaps Trump brought back reminders of the former governor's free-association speaking style to voters in the more populous parts of a largely rural state who had turned out previously to some extent for the ticket as her "friends and neighbors." Alaska still remains the anomaly in the Pacific Region as the one state where Republicans are the ticket to beat.

REFERENCES

Abrams, Samuel J. 2017. That Impossibly Divided California You've Read About? Actually It's Far More Politically Diverse and Competitive. Hoover Institution, Stanford University. *Eureka: California's Policy, Economics, and Politics* 1701, January 19.

Bump, Philip. 2017. The Problem with Thinking That California Went for Clinton Thanks to Illegal Votes. *The Washington Post*, January 25.

Davis, Mike. 2013. The Last White Election? *New Left Review* 79:5–52.

Fiorina, Morris P., and Samuel J. Abrams. 2008. Is California Really a Blue State? In Frederick Douzet, Thad Kousser, and Kenneth P. Miller, eds., *The New Political Geography of California*, 291–308. Berkeley: Berkeley Public Policy Press.

Johnston, Ron, Kelvyn Jones, and David Manley. 2016. The Growing Spatial Polarization of Presidential Voting in the United States, 1992–2012: Myth or Reality? *PS: Political Science and Politics* 49(4): 766–70.

Jones, Robert P. 2016. *The End of White Christian America.* New York: Simon and Schuster.

PPIC. 2016. California Voter and Party Profiles. Sacramento: Public Policy Institute of California, September.

Thurber, James A., and Antoine Yoshinaka. 2016. *American Gridlock: The Sources, Character, and Impact of Political Polarization.* Cambridge: Cambridge University Press.

Yardley, William. 2016. This Northwest Timber County Hadn't Voted GOP Since Herbert Hoover. But Times Have Changed. *Los Angeles Times*, December 11.

6 DEMOGRAPHICS AND IDENTITY

POPULATION SUBGROUPS

RICHARD L. MORRILL

America's counties differ greatly on many demographic, social, economic, and geographic characteristics. Many of these differences can be associated with levels of support for Donald Trump or Hillary Clinton in the 2016 election. In this chapter, contributors examine a variety of demographic, social, and economic characteristics. Each characteristic is first mapped for all counties, for example, the share of the population under eighteen. In a second map, a smaller subset of more extreme counties is identified by level of support for Hillary Clinton. A graph is also included comparing the Democratic and Republican shares for 2012 and 2016.

The political researcher is fascinated by the relation of the geography of voting and the underlying character of the national geography. We also know that it is behaviorally invalid to correlate the presidential race (or other races) outcome with county average values, since we know nothing about how individuals voted. Thus, at best, we can treat the correlations only as suggestive. If the correlations are very high, we can conclude that people of a particular kind in county Y are more likely than not to vote as suggested. At least the values can be helpful in interpreting political outcomes, and they give us a relative ranking of the likely importance of the variables. Please see table 6.1, Correlations of Presidential Outcomes in 2016 and Selected Characteristics of US Counties.

The table is arranged by sets of variables, in approximate order of relative strength. There are three outcome variables: The Democratic share of the votes, change in the Democratic share, and the margin percent—the percent difference between the Democratic and Republican shares. The variable most predictive of electoral outcomes, by far, is the share of non-Hispanic white males who, as endlessly discussed in the media, were the backbone of the Trump victory. In the same ethnic set of variables, the percentages of African Americans and of Asian Americans in the population are strongly related, inversely, to the non-Hispanic white male numbers. For African Americans and Asian Americans, the relation to change in percentage Democrat was lower than that for the percentage Democrat and the percentage of change in the margin, suggesting that Clinton's claim was weaker than Obama's. Although less important to the percentage Democrat or the percentage of change in the margin, the share of Hispanics was, in fact, more positively related to the change in the percentage Democrat.

Educational achievement was the next most predictive. For the variables of the percentage of voters with a BA degree or higher and the percentage of those with high school only, the former was predictive of high shares of the vote for Clinton,

TABLE 6.1. Correlations of Presidential Outcomes in 2016 and Selected Characteristics of US Counties

Variable	% Democrat	Change % Democrat	Margin % Change
Population	0.35	0.28	0.30
Log of Population	0.48	0.43	0.48
Non-Hispanic White Male	-0.60	-0.49	-0.57
BA plus	0.43	0.44	0.46
HS only	-0.42	-0.58	-0.45
Rate of International Migration	0.43	0.39	0.44
Foreign Born	0.39	0.46	0.35
African American	0.50	0.37	0.46
Asian American	0.42	0.31	0.42
Agricultural, Forestry, Mining, etc.	-0.38	-0.30	-0.40
Managerial-Professional	0.24	0.33	0.27
Age 25-44	0.31	0.32	0.25
Age 65 and over	-0.32	-0.30	-0.33
Pop. Change	0.16	0.35	0.13
Non-Family Households	0.29	0.15	0.30
Hispanic	0.18	0.32	0.18
Unemployed	0.34	0.06	0.31
Females in Labor Force	0.25	0.07	0.29
Unmarried Partners	0.28	-0.05	0.30
Pop. Under 18	-0.08	0.16	-0.03
In Poverty	0.20	0.20	0.17
Pop. Density	0.27	0.15	0.27
Construction	-0.23	-0.06	-0.24
Manufacturing	-0.09	-0.24	-0.09
Median Income	0.15	0.27	0.18
Families with Children	-0.20	-0.21	-0.17
Veterans	-0.23	-0.21	-0.27
Domestic Migrants	-0.09	0.14	-0.09
Female	0.16	0.10	0.14
Non-Movers	-0.11	-0.22	-0.21

the latter was predictive of high shares for Trump and was also highly related to the share of non-Hispanic white males (indeed it is the second highest of all calculated correlations).

The foreign born and the rate of international migration variables are similar and strongly predictive of outcomes—foreign born with a 0.46 correlation with positive change in the percentage Democrat, and international migration also more strongly related to the Clinton share and the margin percentage. On the economic side, the share of workers in agriculture, forestry, mining, etc. is predictive of an anti-Clinton vote and a negative Democrat margin percentage, while the share in managerial-professional jobs is moderately related to a higher percentage Democrat. Higher unemployment also is supportive of higher Clinton shares.

Age is moderately related to electoral outcomes, with a lower share of the elderly voting for Clinton but a higher share of those age 25–44 supportive of her. Finally, population density itself is significantly predictive, especially of the percentage for Clinton, as has been widely analyzed given the metropolitan concentration of the Democratic vote and overall majority in the 2016 election.

In the analysis of county voting patterns and population variability, we begin with demographic characteristics, population, age, and ethnicity. These are followed by a discussion of social and economic characteristics.

In this section, we map and examine demographic characteristics of counties: population size and density, percentage population change, percentage born in the state, percentage foreign born versus native born, and percentage not moving in the preceding year.

FIGURE 6.1

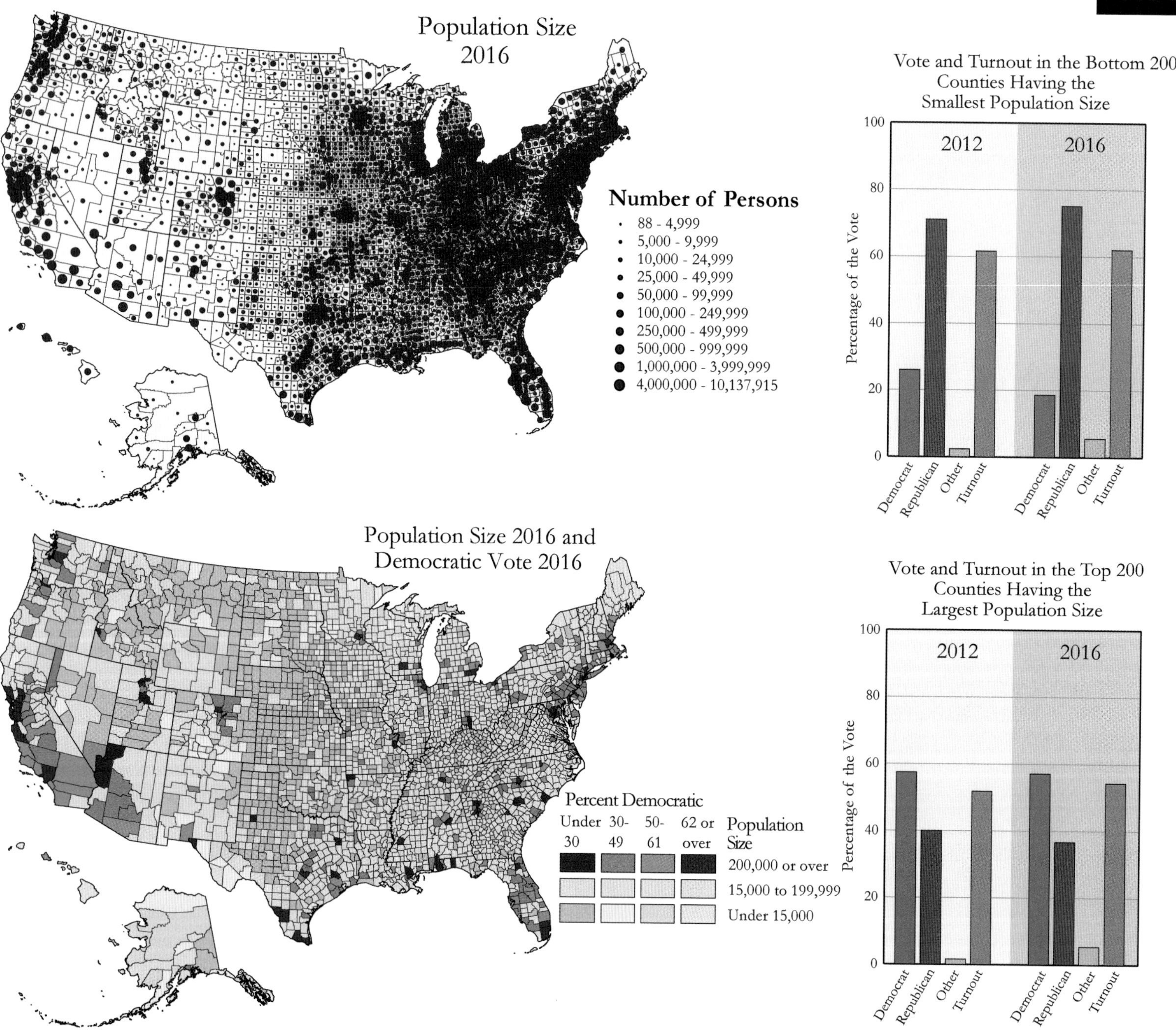
Population Size
2016
Number of Persons
88 - 4,999
5,000 - 9,999
10,000 - 24,999
25,000 - 49,999
50,000 - 99,999
100,000 - 249,999
250,000 - 499,999
500,000 - 999,999
1,000,000 - 3,999,999
4,000,000 - 10,137,915
Population Size 2016 and
Democratic Vote 2016
Percent Democratic
Under 30
30-49
50-61
62 or over
Population Size
200,000 or over
15,000 to 199,999
Under 15,000
Vote and Turnout in the Bottom 200
Counties Having the
Smallest Population Size
Vote and Turnout in the Top 200
Counties Having the
Largest Population Size
2012
2016
Percentage of the Vote
0
20
40
60
80
100
Democrat
Republican
Other
Turnout

POPULATION SIZE, 2016

Maps for population show counties under 15,000, and 15,000 to 50,000 for smaller counties, and over 200,000 for larger counties (figure 6.1). Smaller counties cover the large majority of the country, territorially, and in number of counties—2,158 of 3,142 are dominantly red, for Trump, except for the Black Belt in the South, a few Hispanic border areas, some environmental amenity areas, and Native American reservation areas. Included for Trump are most of the Interior West and the Great Plains, and about three-quarters of the Border South, much of the farm and ranching parts of the country, and mining areas, as in Appalachia. Counties under 15,000 voted 67 percent for Trump, but total votes were only 3.7 million. The least populous counties include Loving, Texas, population 113, voting only 6 percent for Clinton; King, Texas, 289 and 3 percent; Arthur, Nebraska, 469 and 5 percent; but Kalawao, Hawaii, population 88, voted 66 percent for Clinton. Populations in counties under 15,000 had extreme shifts from Democrat to Republican, the Democratic share dropping 9 percent, the Republican share rising 7 percent, for an increase in the Republican margin of 15 percent.

In contrast, the larger counties supporting Clinton include Megalopolis, the Pacific Coast and Hispanic areas, and many large metropolitan core counties in all areas, even many in the South, but Trump did well in many southern smaller metropolitan and suburban areas and greater Appalachia. The two most striking pro-Clinton realms were the entire California coast and greater Megalopolis. The moderately large counties—50,000 to 200,000—in fact voted for Trump, 58 to 36 percent, so only the largest counties preferred Clinton, 56 to 39 percent. But these housed over 90 million voters, compared to half that number in all the less-populous sets of counties. The extreme large county was Los Angeles, voting 72 percent for Clinton; then Cook, Illinois, 75 percent for Clinton; and Harris, Texas, still Democratic at 54 percent. Even these largest counties showed a slight dip in the Democratic percentage, but the Republican share dropped more, for a relative gain of 3.2 percent (both lost to "other").

POPULATION CHANGE

Overall counties that gained population significantly, 2010–2016, had larger populations and voted moderately for Clinton, while the most heavily losing counties were generally smaller and more strongly voted for Trump (figure 6.2). For all US counties, the correlation of population change and change in percentage Democrat was a significant 0.35 (see table 6.1).

The losing counties (925, more than –2.5 percent) voted 63 percent for Trump (33 for Clinton), while the gaining counties (over 4 percent) voted 51.4 to 42.6 for Clinton over Trump. The gaining counties included many small, energy development areas, but many large counties, such that the total voters in the gaining counties were ten times those in the losing areas, 63 million to 6.3 million. Counties with higher population gains and that supported Clinton were in California and Washington, and suburban Washington, DC, but in the Interior West, except for environmental and some university areas, Trump prevailed. Concentrations of Trump voters included the Bakken oilfield region, Mormon areas, and Texas energy development areas. The highest growth counties, McKenzie and Williams, North Dakota, were only 14 and 15 percent for Clinton, and the fastest growth county Clinton won was Fort Bend, Texas, at 51 percent. The gaining counties were a rare bright spot for Democrats, with the share rising from 51.2 to 51.4, while the Republican share dropped by 4.5 percent (to "other").

Counties with population losses were more prevalent and more strongly for Trump, perhaps a third or more of counties across the entire US interior, while Clinton won population-losing counties that were mainly in the Black Belt and near Native American reservations (New Mexico). Most of these counties were small, with a total vote of only 6.3 million, but voting 63 to 33 percent for Trump. The single largest concentration of counties with high population loss was in eastern Kentucky into West Virginia, suffering from declines in mining. But the highest population losses were for Alexander, Illinois, –21 percent, but 45 percent for Clinton, and Blaine, Montana, –19 percent, and only 19 percent for Clinton. These counties with population losses were *THE* extreme category of bad news for the Democrats, with the Democratic share dropping from 47 to 32 percent, leading to a huge margin increase for Republicans of 26.5 percent.

POPULATION BORN IN THE STATE

The map for shares of the population born in the state of residence shows high shares (>78 percent) mainly in the belt of states from Missouri to western New York and Pennsylvania, and from the Dakotas to northern Michigan, with people who have aged in place, despite often severe economic change (figure 6.3). They voted strongly for Trump, by 60 to 35 percent, but held only

FIGURE 6.2

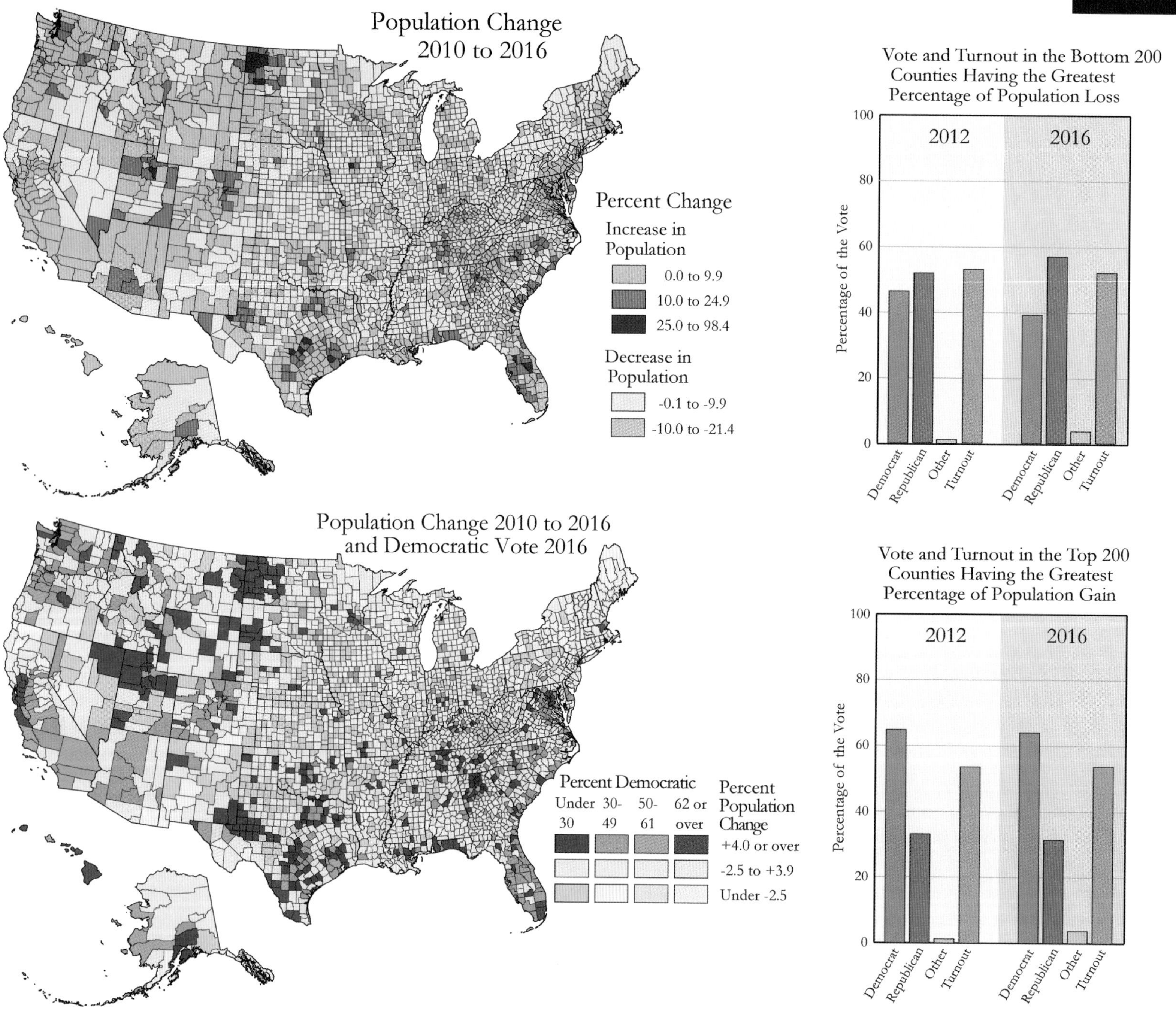

Population Change
2010 to 2016

Percent Change

Increase in Population

0.0 to 9.9

10.0 to 24.9

25.0 to 98.4

Decrease in Population

-0.1 to -9.9

-10.0 to -21.4

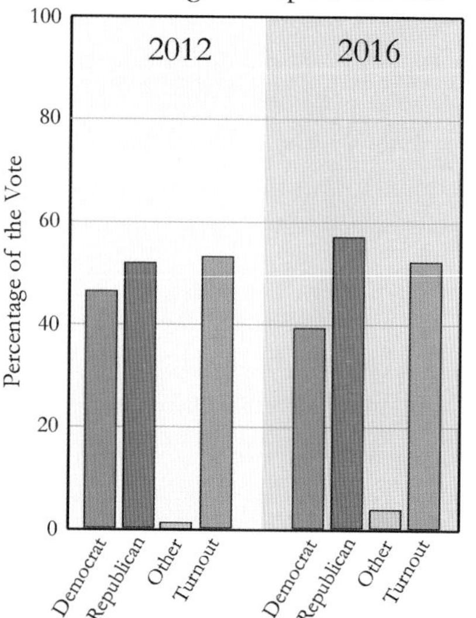

Population Change 2010 to 2016
and Democratic Vote 2016

Percent Democratic				Percent Population Change
Under 30	30-49	50-61	62 or over	
				+4.0 or over
				-2.5 to +3.9
				Under -2.5

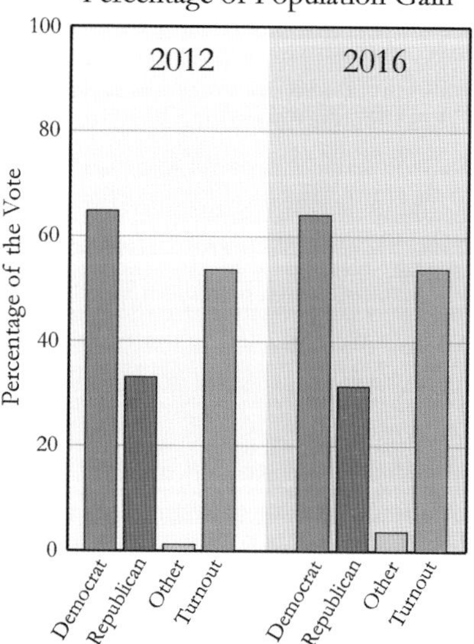

FIGURE 6.3

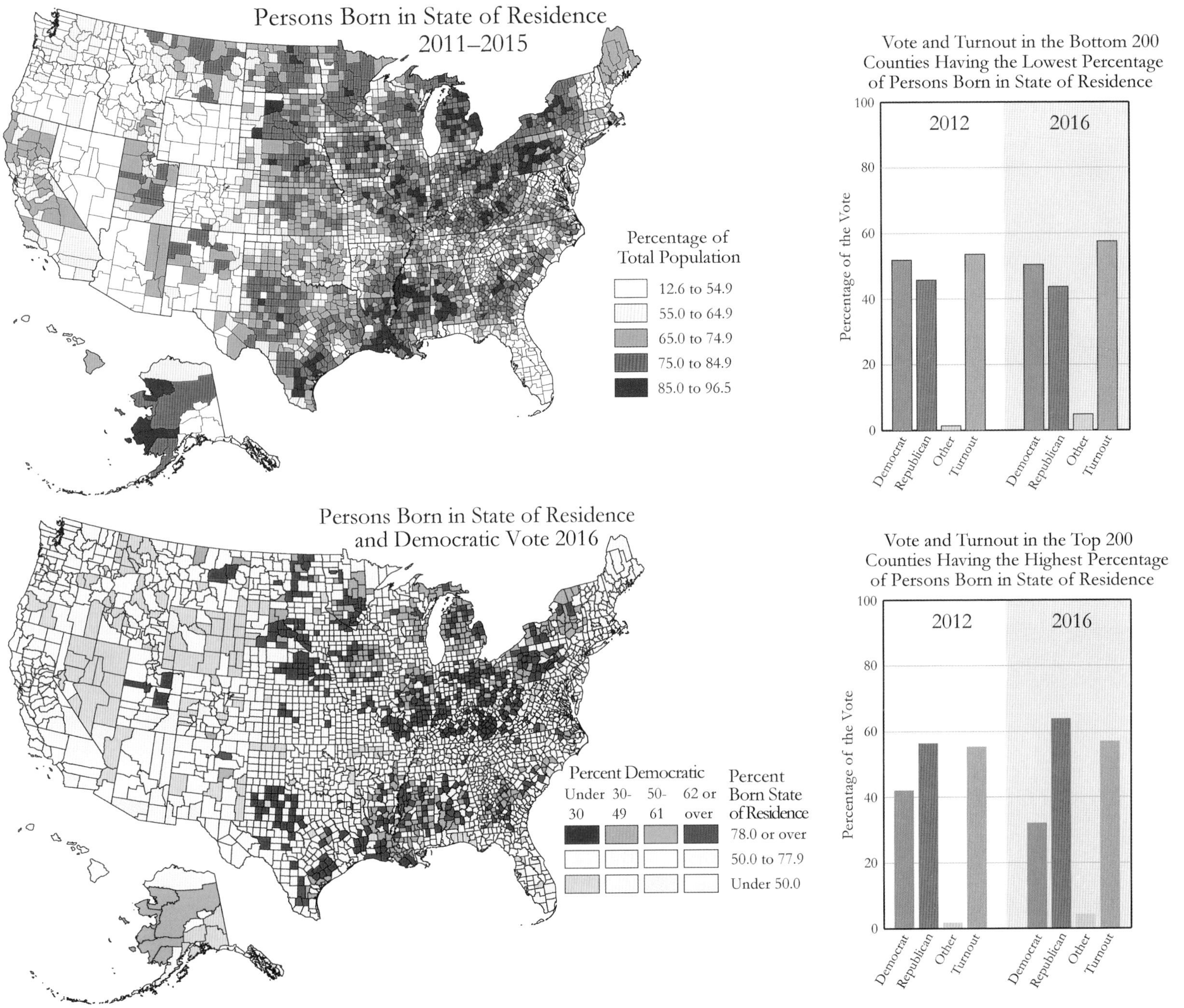

Persons Born in State of Residence 2011–2015

Percentage of Total Population

- 12.6 to 54.9
- 55.0 to 64.9
- 65.0 to 74.9
- 75.0 to 84.9
- 85.0 to 96.5

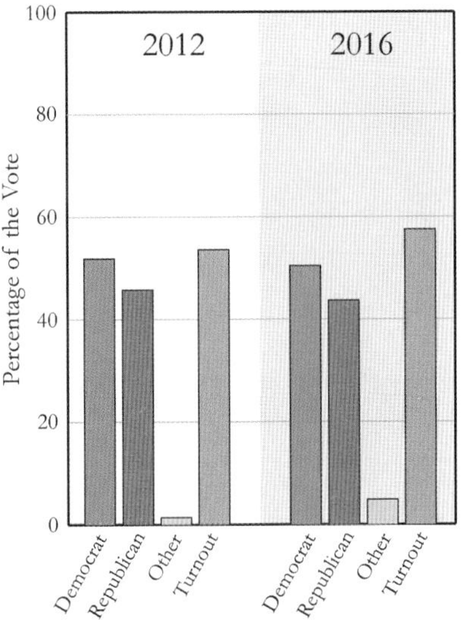

Persons Born in State of Residence and Democratic Vote 2016

Percent Democratic: Under 30	30-49	50-61	62 or over	Percent Born State of Residence
				78.0 or over
				50.0 to 77.9
				Under 50.0

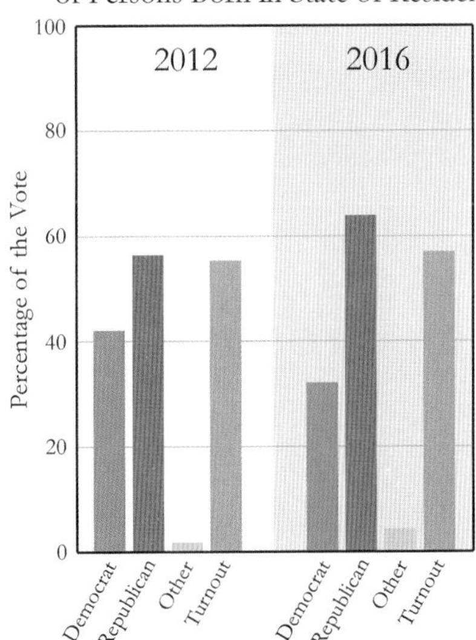

14 million voters. Clinton was strong only in the Black Belt, and on a few Native American reservations, while Trump prevailed in much of the plains, and especially the north-south borderlands. Example counties include Blaine, Montana; Leslie, Kentucky; Haakon, South Dakota; and Greene, Alabama; with 100 to 96 percent born in the state, and voting 9 percent, 9 percent, 7 percent, and 82 percent for Clinton (Greene is mainly African American, the others white). These counties experienced a big reduction in the Democratic share of 8.7 percent for a Republican margin increase of 14.5 percent.

Areas with a low share born in the state (under 50) were mainly in the West, and include strong Trump territory in Nevada, Wyoming, Montana, and Idaho, but these are offset by votes for Clinton in Los Angeles, the San Francisco area, and in King County (Seattle). As a consequence, despite all that pink, Clinton carried this set 55 to 39 percent, with a total vote of 46 million, compared to 14 million in the high born-in-state counties. Douglas, Nevada, is the extreme county at only 18 percent local born, which voted 52 percent for Clinton. These counties showed a small increase in the Democratic margin of 4.5 percent, and even a small rise in the Democratic share.

FOREIGN-BORN AND NATIVE-BORN POPULATIONS

The foreign-born population was of course a major theme in the election, with the Trump majority bemoaning immigration and distrustful of the foreign born, who indeed voted strongly for Clinton, 56 to 39 percent in the counties with the highest shares, over 6 percent of the population. For the whole United States, the correlation of the foreign-born share with the Clinton share was a respectable 0.39 and with change in the Democratic share a high 0.46, highest for all our measures (see table 6.1).

The map shows a dual America, with high foreign-born shares in the greater Southwest and Northwest, and on the Atlantic Coast, Megalopolis, and major inland metropolitan areas (figure 6.4). Within these areas, Clinton did best in the metropolitan and environmental amenity West, along the border with Mexico, and in the big metropolitan East, while Trump did well in the Interior West, including Mormon and Hispanic areas of older immigration. A few extreme counties include Miami, Florida, 52 percent foreign born and 64 percent Democratic; then Aleutians East Borough, Alaska, 50 percent, but only 33 percent for Clinton; Queens, New York, 48 and 75 percent; and Hudson, New Jersey, 42 and 75 percent.

The map of the share of population native born is the opposite end of this same variable, and these counties were dominantly Trump-supporting, and most common across the northern plains, the north-south borderlands, with a few Black Belt counties with high shares of native born and support for Clinton. These counties, >99 percent native, voted for Trump by an astounding 69 to 27 percent, but the total number of voters was only 4.2 million, compared to a stupendous 88 million in the high-share foreign-born counties. Two examples are Powder River, Wyoming, and Loving, Texas, with zero foreign born, voting 12 and 6 percent Democratic, respectively. These counties experienced a dramatic increase in the Republican margin of 1.9 percent, from a 10 percent decline in the Democratic percentage and a 7.9 percent increase in the Republican share.

NON-MOVERS IN THE PRECEDING YEAR

The map of the percentage of the population not moving in the preceding year is similar to others which relate to the populist voting trend—rural, small town, native born, white, and often declining in population (figure 6.5). High shares are most prevalent in the north-south borderlands, Appalachia and the Great Plains, where voting for Trump dominated. But since the Trump margin was modest, 52 to 44 percent, there were offsetting areas for Clinton, as in New Mexico Native American reservations and Black Belt counties. The extreme cases of not moving were King, Texas; Wheeler, Georgia; and Sioux, Nebraska; with 99 to 96 percent not moving, and voting 3, 31, and 11 percent for Clinton, respectively.

MIGRATION

Counties with migration gains over 5 percent were most obviously in energy development areas in North Dakota, Montana, and Texas, all for Trump, but also in the Bay Area, King County (Seattle), and southern Florida, voting for Clinton, so that overall the set voted marginally for Clinton (48 to 47 percent), with 21 million votes (figure 6.6). Counties with 5 to 10 percent gains were scattered across the West, in many suburban areas across the South, and the south Atlantic Coast. These counties voted slightly more for Clinton, 50 to 44 percent. Example counties are Williams and McKenzie, North Dakota (see population gains), with the highest Clinton county, Osceola, Florida, 20 percent and 61 percent Democratic, and Loudoun, Virginia, 24 and 55 percent.

FIGURE 6.4

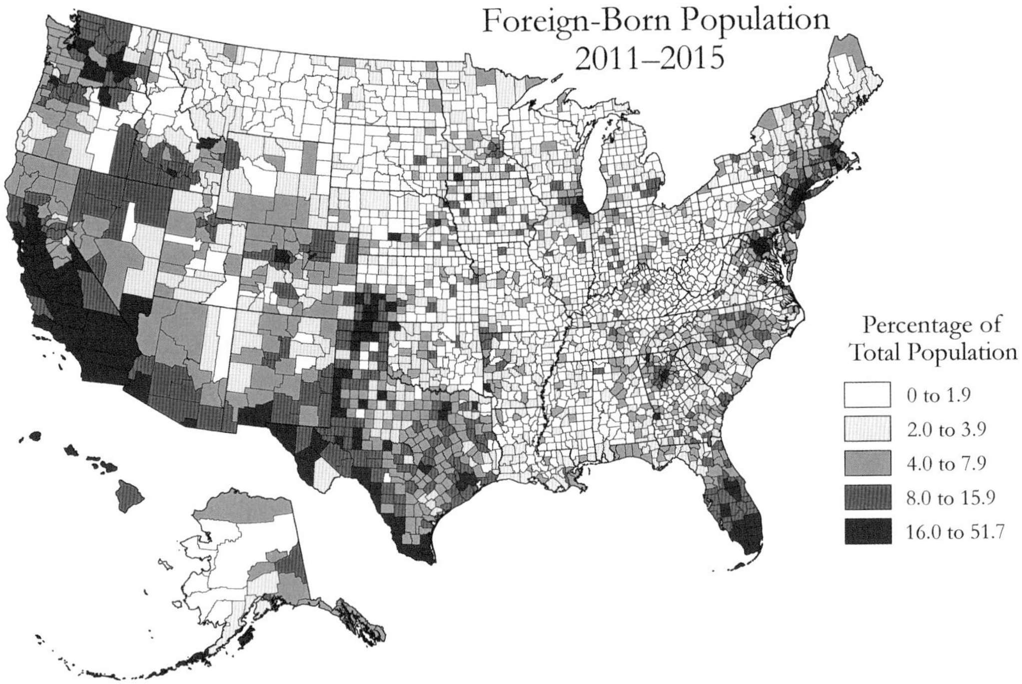

Foreign-Born Population 2011–2015

Percentage of Total Population

- 0 to 1.9
- 2.0 to 3.9
- 4.0 to 7.9
- 8.0 to 15.9
- 16.0 to 51.7

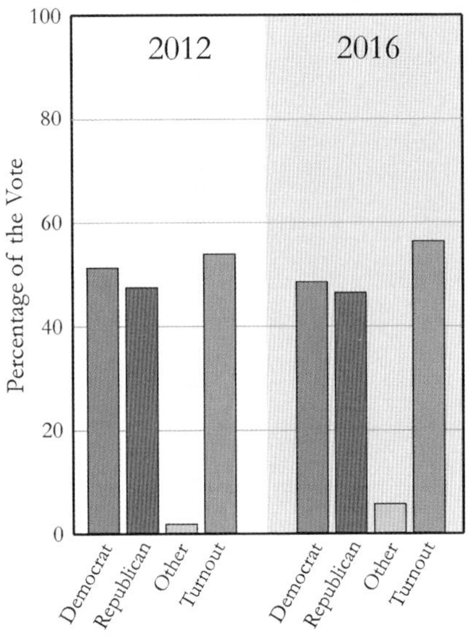

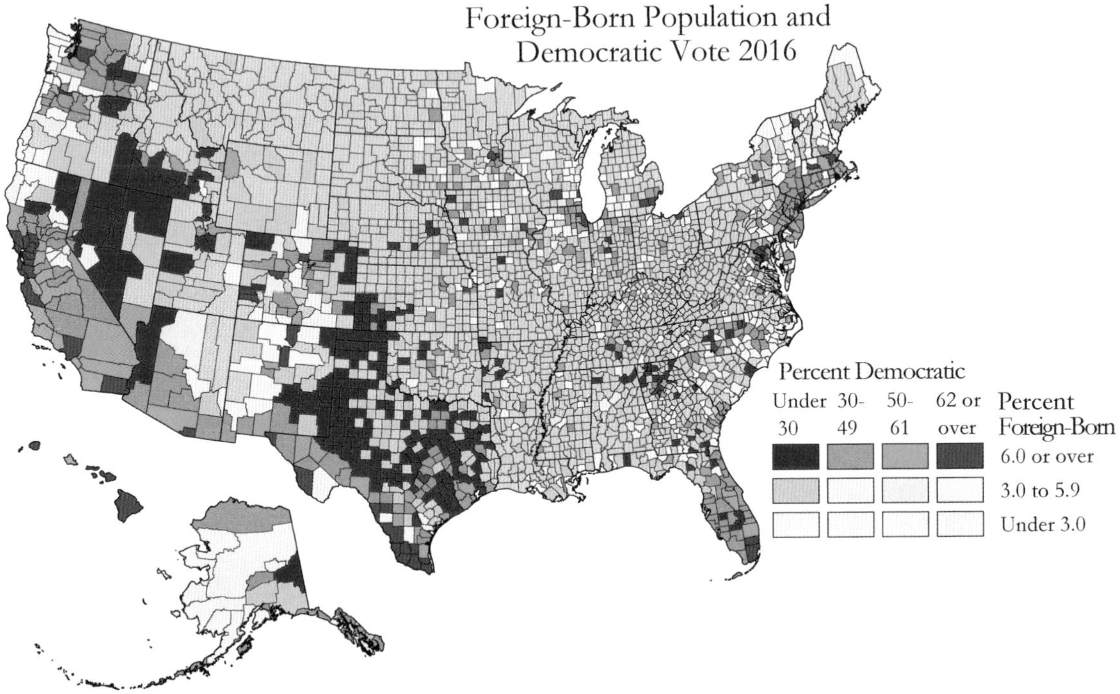

Foreign-Born Population and Democratic Vote 2016

Percent Democratic				
Under 30	30-49	50-61	62 or over	Percent Foreign-Born
				6.0 or over
				3.0 to 5.9
				Under 3.0

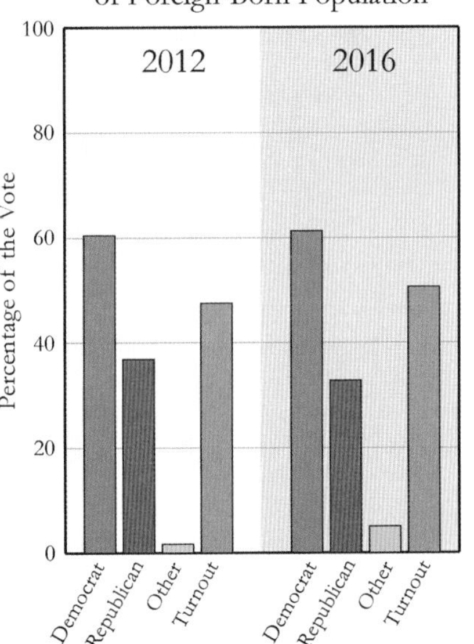

FIGURE 6.5

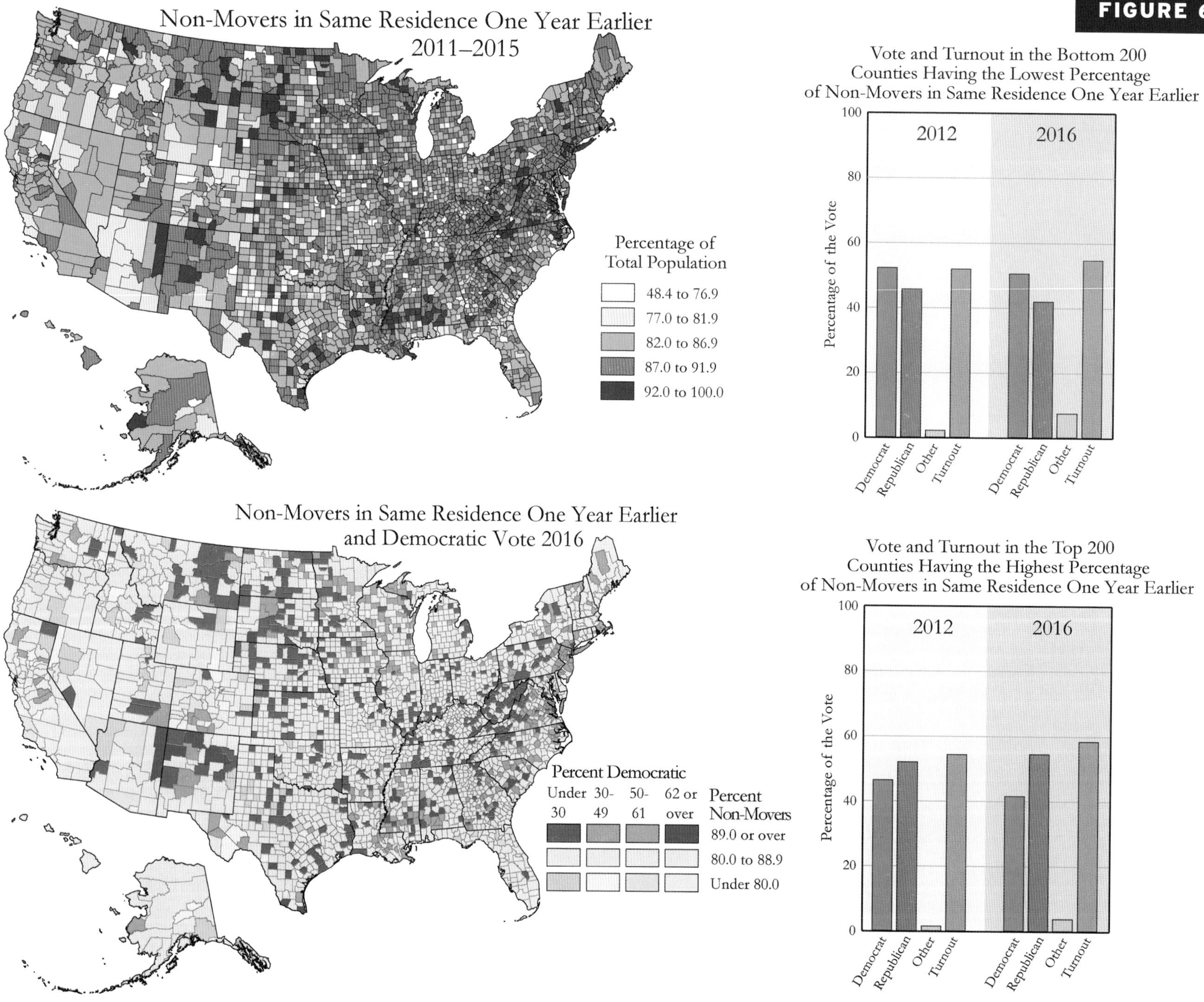

Non-Movers in Same Residence One Year Earlier 2011–2015

Percentage of Total Population

- 48.4 to 76.9
- 77.0 to 81.9
- 82.0 to 86.9
- 87.0 to 91.9
- 92.0 to 100.0

Vote and Turnout in the Bottom 200 Counties Having the Lowest Percentage of Non-Movers in Same Residence One Year Earlier

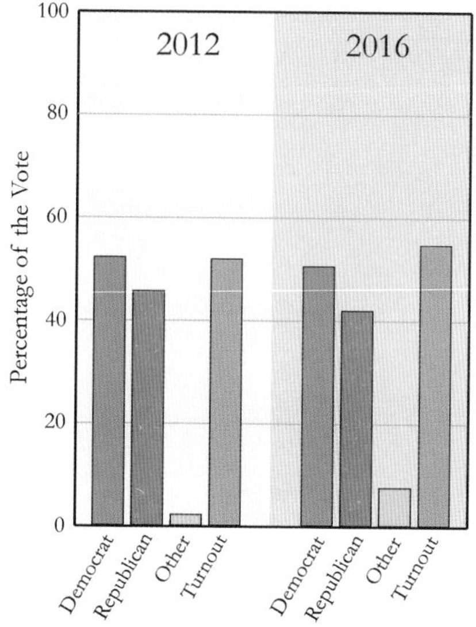

Non-Movers in Same Residence One Year Earlier and Democratic Vote 2016

Percent Democratic				
Under 30	30-49	50-61	62 or over	Percent Non-Movers
				89.0 or over
				80.0 to 88.9
				Under 80.0

Vote and Turnout in the Top 200 Counties Having the Highest Percentage of Non-Movers in Same Residence One Year Earlier

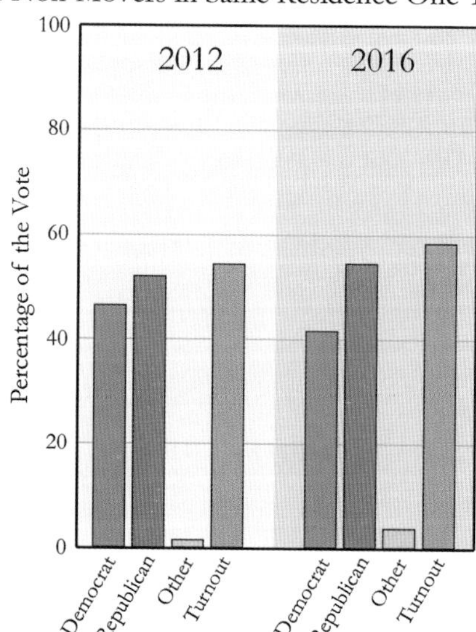

FIGURE 6.6

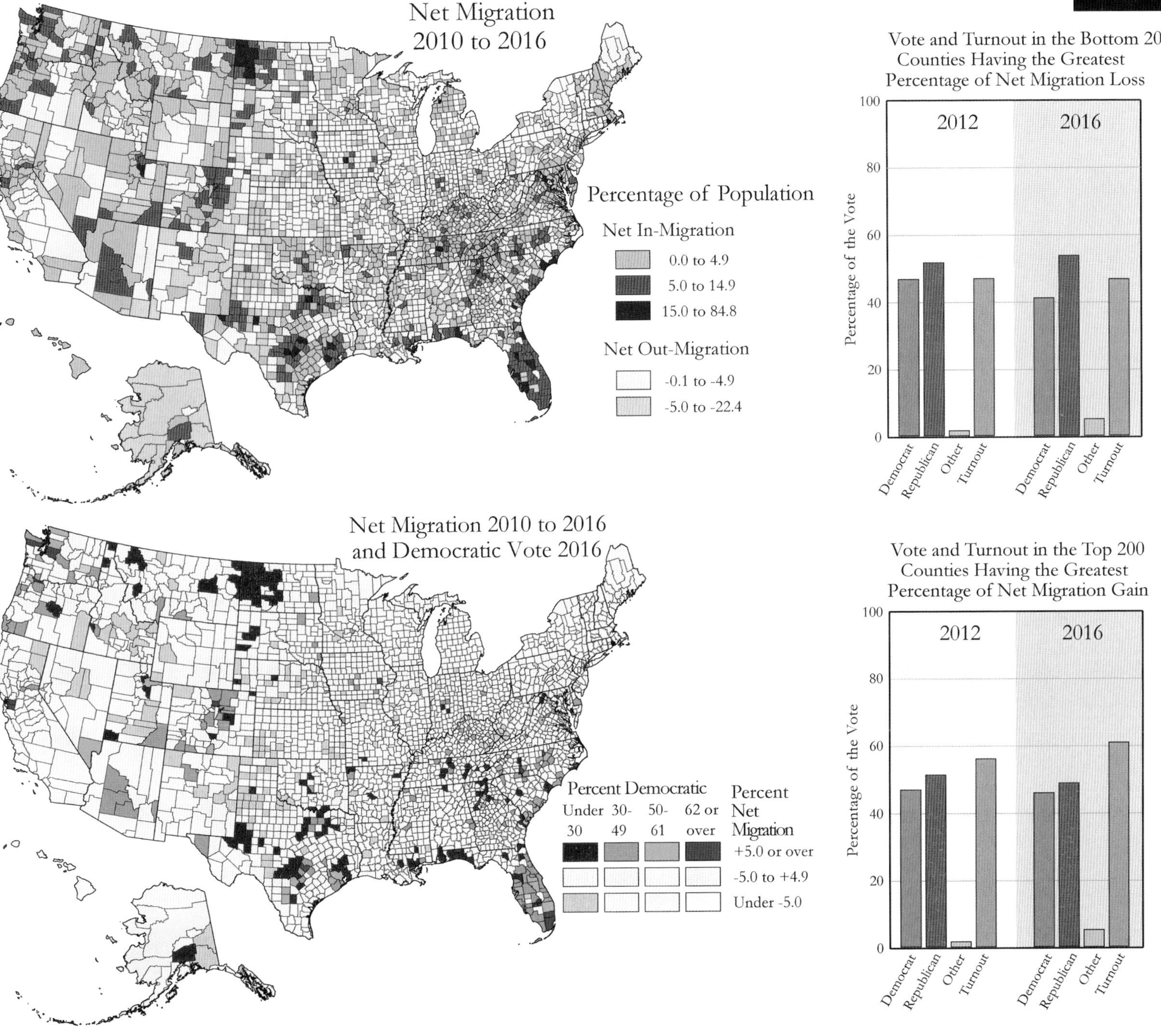

Net Migration
2010 to 2016
Percentage of Population
Net In-Migration
0.0 to 4.9
5.0 to 14.9
15.0 to 84.8
Net Out-Migration
-0.1 to -4.9
-5.0 to -22.4
Vote and Turnout in the Bottom 200
Counties Having the Greatest
Percentage of Net Migration Loss
2012
2016
Percentage of the Vote
100
80
60
40
20
0
Democrat
Republican
Other
Turnout
Net Migration 2010 to 2016
and Democratic Vote 2016
Percent Democratic
Under 30
30-49
50-61
62 or over
Percent Net Migration
+5.0 or over
-5.0 to +4.9
Under -5.0
Vote and Turnout in the Top 200
Counties Having the Greatest
Percentage of Net Migration Gain

Counties with migration losses included about one-third of counties in the Interior West and Great Plains that voted strongly for Trump, and Black Belt counties in the South that supported Clinton as strongly. Counties with the highest losses, over 10 percent, voted only marginally for Trump, 49 to 47 percent, but counties losing by 5 to 10 percent were more strongly Republican, 54 to 41 percent (the Black Belt counties tended to have the higher losses). These losing counties are small, with only 10 million voters compared to 49 million in the gaining sets. Example losing counties include Alexander, Illinois, -21 and 45 percent for Clinton; and Presidio, Texas, -18 but 66 percent for Clinton. These losing counties showed over a 20 percent increase in the Republican margin.

AGE

This section looks at patterns of voting for president for sets of counties with high shares of three age groups: those under eighteen, people twenty-five to forty-four, and those over sixty-five.

The quarter of counties with the highest shares of those under eighteen, all with over 19 percent young people, in all voted more for Trump than for Clinton, but perhaps surprising to many, only marginally so, 45 to 41 percent (figure 6.7). Also, there was a small correlation with change in the percentage Democrat and a small reduction in the Republican margin of 3 percent, unusual for 2016. The reason for this is the disparity in the populations with young children. On the one hand are some counties in the Black Belt, many more strongly Hispanic along the US-Mexico border, and a few Native American reservations, which voted moderately for Clinton, but these are outweighed by the large and cohesive Mormon realm, and by younger workers, including many Hispanics, in the energy development areas across the Great Plains, from Texas to Canada, which voted more strongly for Trump. As expected, these counties also tend to be high in shares of family households with children. Counties with low shares of the population under eighteen are common in the Northeast, Florida, the Upper Midwest, and the Pacific Northwest that do not have Hispanic immigrant populations. A few example counties with the highest share under eighteen include Todd and Buffalo, South Dakota, and Kusilvak, Alaska, with 40 percent under eighteen, all of which supported Clinton as they were also high in Native American populations, while Sumter, Florida, and Forest, Pennsylvania, with only 5 and 8 percent under eighteen, respectively, voted strongly for Trump.

The one-quarter of counties with the highest shares of those aged twenty-five to forty-four, over 25 percent, were moderately strong for Clinton, while the next quarter, with 23 to 25 percent aged twenty-five to forty-four, were as significantly for Trump (figure 6.8). For all US counties, there was a moderate correlation (0.36) with the percent for Clinton and with the percent change in the Democratic vote. There were over 81 million voters in the highest group, compared to only 30 million in the next, indicating that the reason for the high Democratic group was that the highest share counties tended to be large, metropolitan, and with greater numbers of minorities, immigrants, and the foreign born. Shares of professional jobs, higher incomes, and non-family households also tended to be higher in these counties. These also were often fast-growing regions, with in-migration. The map does not look so different from that for the under-eighteen population, with the Mormon, energy growth, and Gulf Coast areas high in both, but the difference is the much larger populations in larger metropolitan counties, especially in Megalopolis and Florida. Example counties with high shares of those twenty-five to forty-four include Bent, Colorado (39 percent), 62 percent for Trump, but then Arlington and Alexandria, Virginia, and San Francisco, California, with 44 to 39 percent aged twenty-five to forty-four, were very strong for Clinton (76, 76, and 86 percent). Low-share counties included Sumter, Florida, and Catron, New Mexico, at 12 percent aged twenty-five to forty-four, voting only 30 and 21 percent for Clinton. For the high-share group there was a small rise in the Democratic margin, mainly from a decline in the Republican share, to "others."

The counties with high shares of the elderly were far more strongly and consistently Trump voters—overall by a margin of 60 to 35 percent (figure 6.9). For all US counties, there was a modest negative correlation between the Democratic vote and the share of those over sixty-five years of age, -0.32 (table 6.1). Except for a few counties as in Florida and Arizona, these counties were mostly rural or small town, low density, often with population losses and out-migration. They are especially prevalent in the Great Plains, the non-Mormon Interior West, and in Appalachia. The only areas carried by Clinton were a few Native American reservations, as in New Mexico, and selected, often environmentally attractive counties in northern New England, the Mountain and Coastal West, and Minnesota (reservations). Only 10.5 million voted in the highest counties with over 21 percent over age sixty-five. Example extreme counties are Sumter, Florida, and Catron, New Mexico, again, plus Charlotte, Florida, with 55, 38, and 38 percent over sixty-five, voting for Clinton at 30, 21, and 35 percent. At the other extreme is Chattahoochee, Georgia, with only 4 percent over sixty-five, voting 43 percent

Population under Age 18
2011–2015

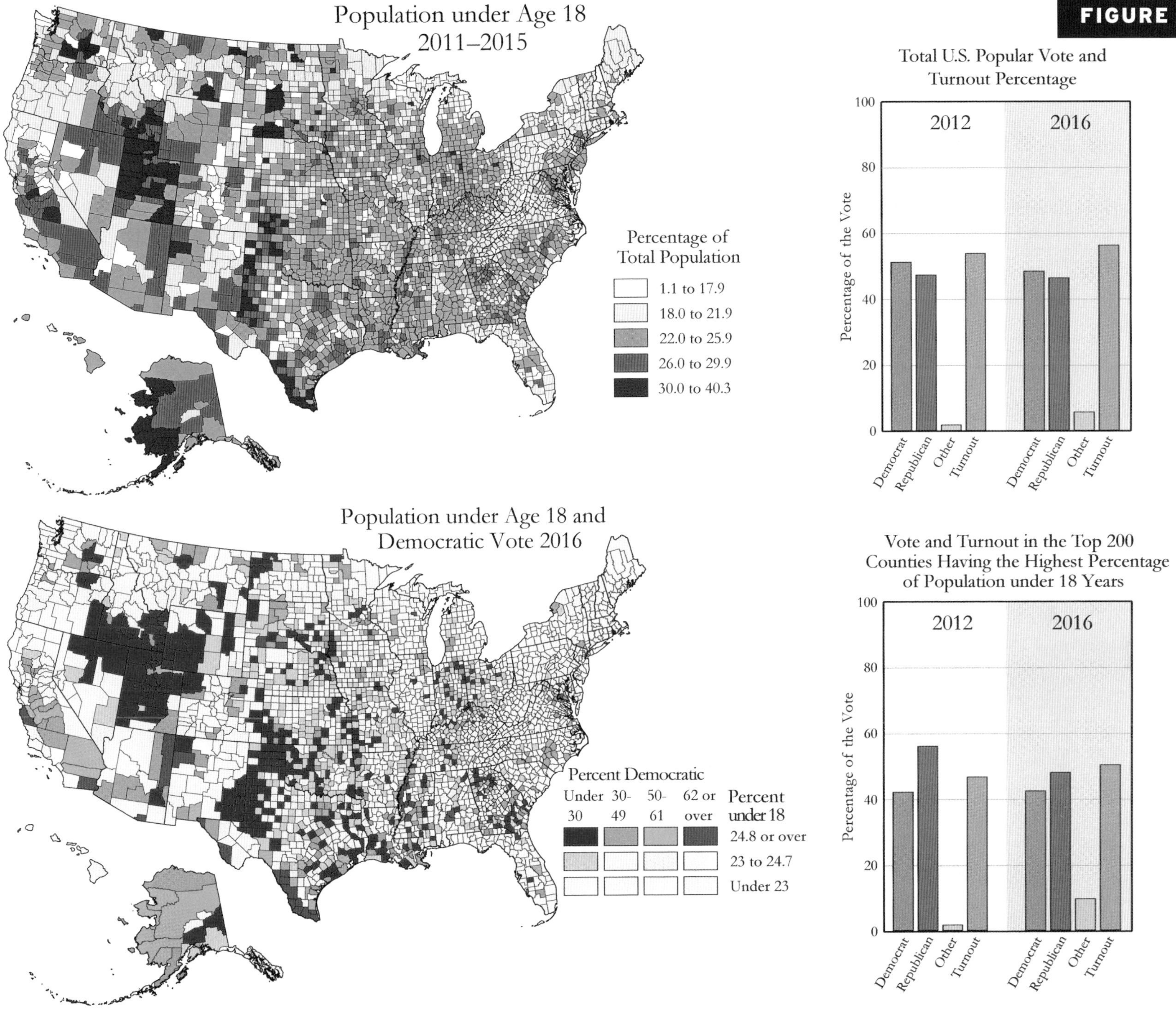

Percentage of
Total Population

1.1 to 17.9
18.0 to 21.9
22.0 to 25.9
26.0 to 29.9
30.0 to 40.3

Total U.S. Popular Vote and
Turnout Percentage

2012
2016
Percentage of the Vote
100
80
60
40
20
0
Democrat
Republican
Other
Turnout
Democrat
Republican
Other
Turnout

Population under Age 18 and
Democratic Vote 2016

Percent Democratic

Under 30	30-49	50-61	62 or over	Percent under 18
				24.8 or over
				23 to 24.7
				Under 23

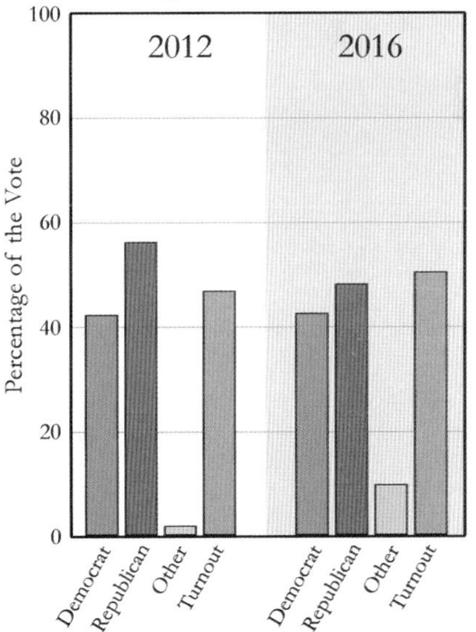

FIGURE 6.8

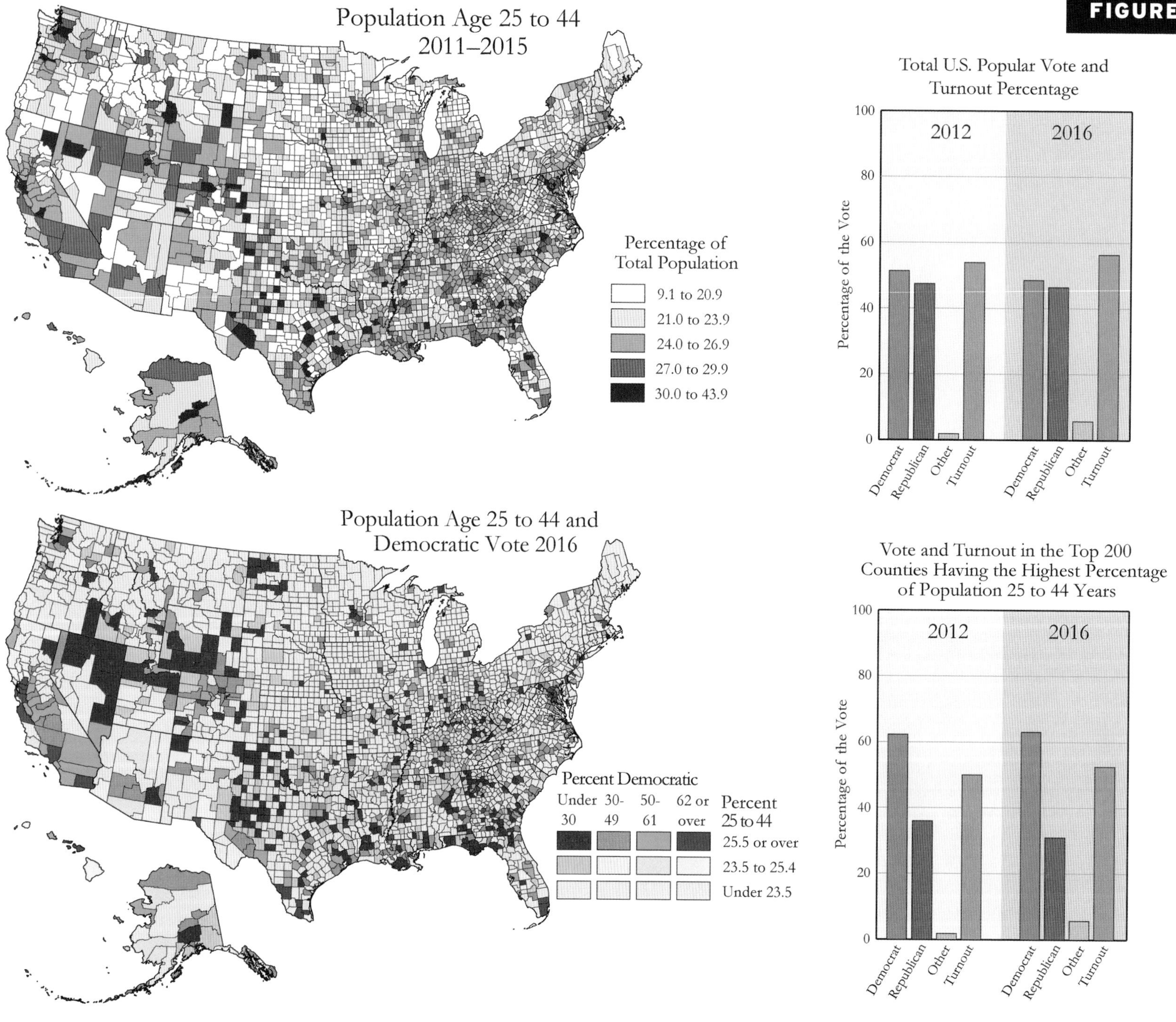

Population Age 25 to 44 2011–2015

Percentage of Total Population

- 9.1 to 20.9
- 21.0 to 23.9
- 24.0 to 26.9
- 27.0 to 29.9
- 30.0 to 43.9

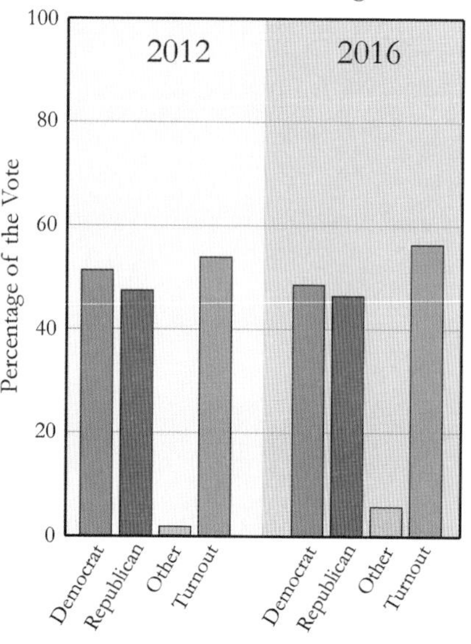

Population Age 25 to 44 and Democratic Vote 2016

Percent Democratic: Under 30	30-49	50-61	62 or over	Percent 25 to 44
				25.5 or over
				23.5 to 25.4
				Under 23.5

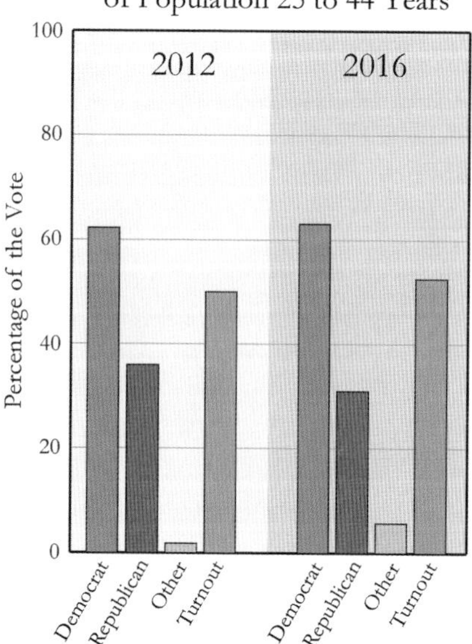

FIGURE 6.9

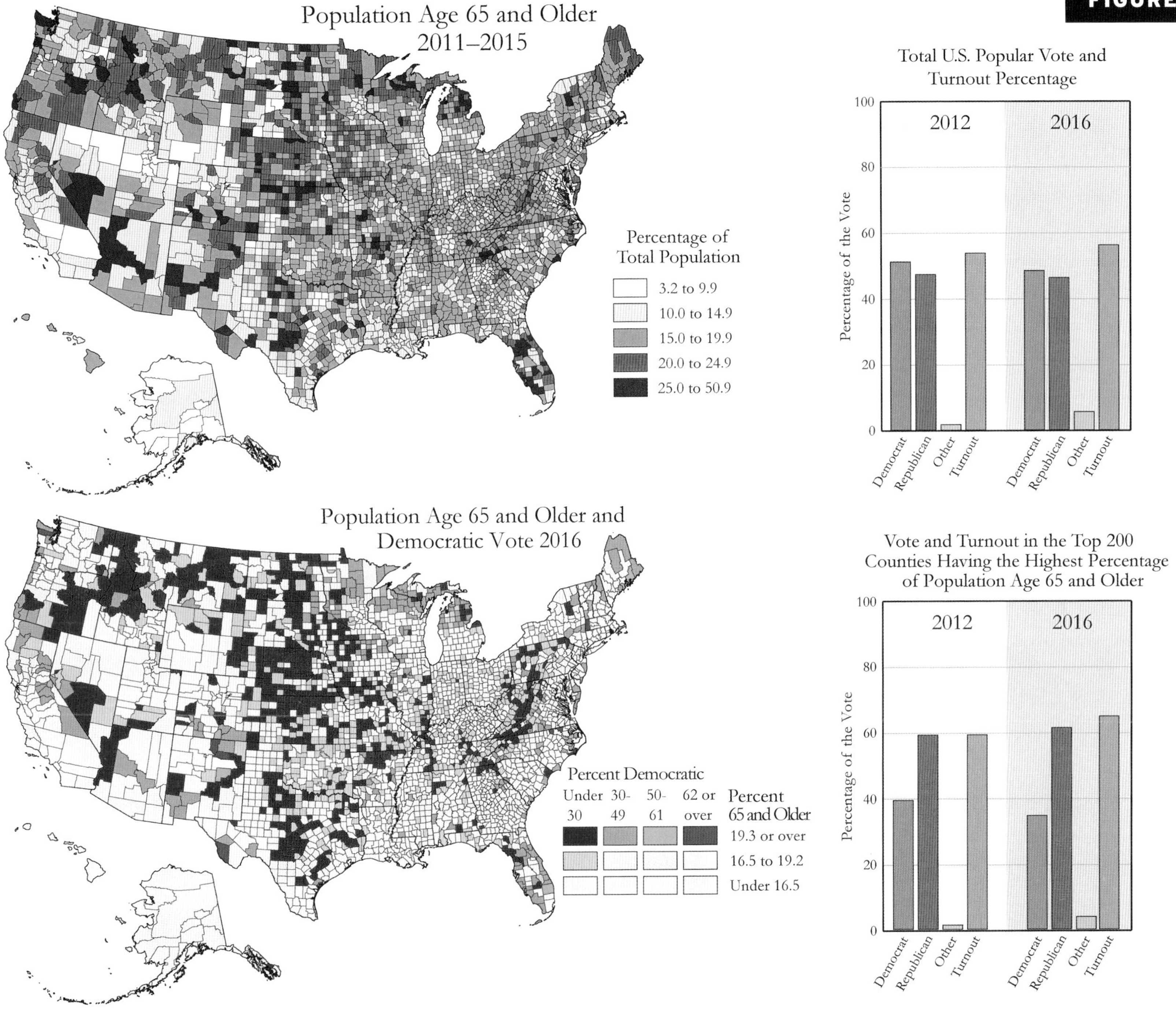

Population Age 65 and Older 2011–2015

Percentage of Total Population

- 3.2 to 9.9
- 10.0 to 14.9
- 15.0 to 19.9
- 20.0 to 24.9
- 25.0 to 50.9

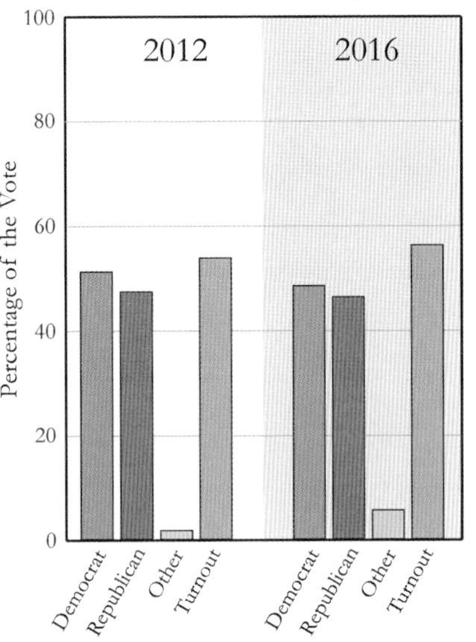

Population Age 65 and Older and Democratic Vote 2016

Percent Democratic: Under 30	30-49	50-61	62 or over	Percent 65 and Older
				19.3 or over
				16.5 to 19.2
				Under 16.5

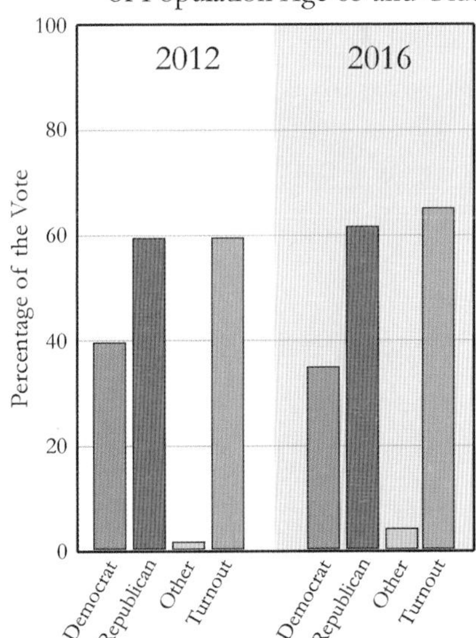

for Clinton. There was a serious increase in the Republican margin between 2012 and 2016, from a Democratic drop of 7.4 percent and a Republican increase of 4.1 percent.

RACE AND ETHNICITY

The 2016 election revealed the fundamental importance of race and ethnicity, with the share of African Americans, Asian Americans, and Hispanics highly correlated with the vote for Clinton, and the share of non-Hispanic white males even more highly predictive of the vote for Trump—indeed the single most important variable distinguishing a Democratic or a Republican vote. In this subsection, we look at maps and data for the African American population, for Native Americans, and for the highest and lowest shares of non-Hispanic white males, the lowest values of which are, of course, the highest shares of a combination of all minorities and of women. Discussion of the voting patterns of the Asian American and Hispanic populations is dealt with in separate sections of this chapter.

AFRICAN AMERICAN POPULATION

Even 160 years after the Civil War, the map of concentrations of African Americans looks remarkably historic, but a careful examination reveals two worlds: one is the map of the slave population of 160 years ago, the other of the impact of the many great migrations to the northern city ghettos—usually marked as carried by Clinton 50–62 percent—and housing millions in big cities in the North and West, and also increasingly the South (figure 6.10). Overall the correlation of percentage African American and percentage for Clinton was a high 0.51 (the second highest), and counties over 10 percent African American voted Democratic by 55 percent to 41 percent Republican for Trump. In the North, Clinton carried most of the higher share African American counties. In the South, the important feature is that the core, really high percentage of African American counties, voted strongly Democratic, while large bands of adjacent counties voted just as strongly Republican, illustrating the continuing massive power of racial difference in political behavior. Between 2012 and 2016, both the Democratic and Republican shares dropped to a rise in the vote for "others," but the Republican vote dropped more. Extreme counties included Leflore, Claiborne, and Holmes counties, all in the Mississippi Delta Black Belt, at 85, 85, and 82 percent African American, and voting for Clinton at 86, 87, and 83 percent.

NATIVE AMERICANS

Counties with over 4 percent Native American populations are remarkably few, and only thirty-six counties had as many as 32 percent or more Native Americans (figure 6.11). Because of such low numbers, the high Native American share counties voted Republican 53 to 40 percent. The only really high Democratic support was from New Mexico–Arizona (Navajo, the Diné), and South Dakota. Extreme counties were Oglala Lakota and Todd, South Dakota, 91 and 86 percent Native American, and 86 and 71 percent for Clinton. But the story overall was poor for Democrats, with a Democratic share drop of 7.7 percent and a Republican increase of 2.5 percent, for a Republican margin increase of 10 percent for these counties.

NON-HISPANIC WHITE MALES

As noted above, the non-Hispanic white male population was the most extreme in support for Trump, with Trump winning 67 to 28 percent among the highest quarter of counties, with shares over 46.2 percent, and even the second highest quarter by 60 to 33.4 percent (figure 6.12). However, the total numbers of voters were 7.9 and 17 million for those subgroups, compared to 64 million in the quarter of counties with the lowest shares (thus highest in minorities and women, who voted 59 to 36 percent for Clinton). For all US counties, this variable had the highest correlation with the percent Democrat, a serious -0.60 (table 6.1).

High shares of non-Hispanic white men extend from Idaho and Utah, but not Colorado, east to Maine, and the entire northeast to the Appalachians, creating a remarkably cohesive and continuous region, but with concentrations highest in Missouri to western Pennsylvania—areas seemingly left out in the shift to globalization and growth on the coasts—and in the northern plains, beyond the core energy growth areas. The extreme high counties for non-Hispanic white males were Petroleum, Montana, and Noble, Ohio, at 54 percent, and Powell, Montana, at 57 percent, and which voted only 4, 20, and 8 percent for Clinton. The Republican margin rose over 18 percent, from a Democratic percentage decline of 10.6 percent and a Republican rise of 7.3 percent.

Low shares of non-Hispanic white males equal high shares of all minorities and women together.

FIGURE 6.10

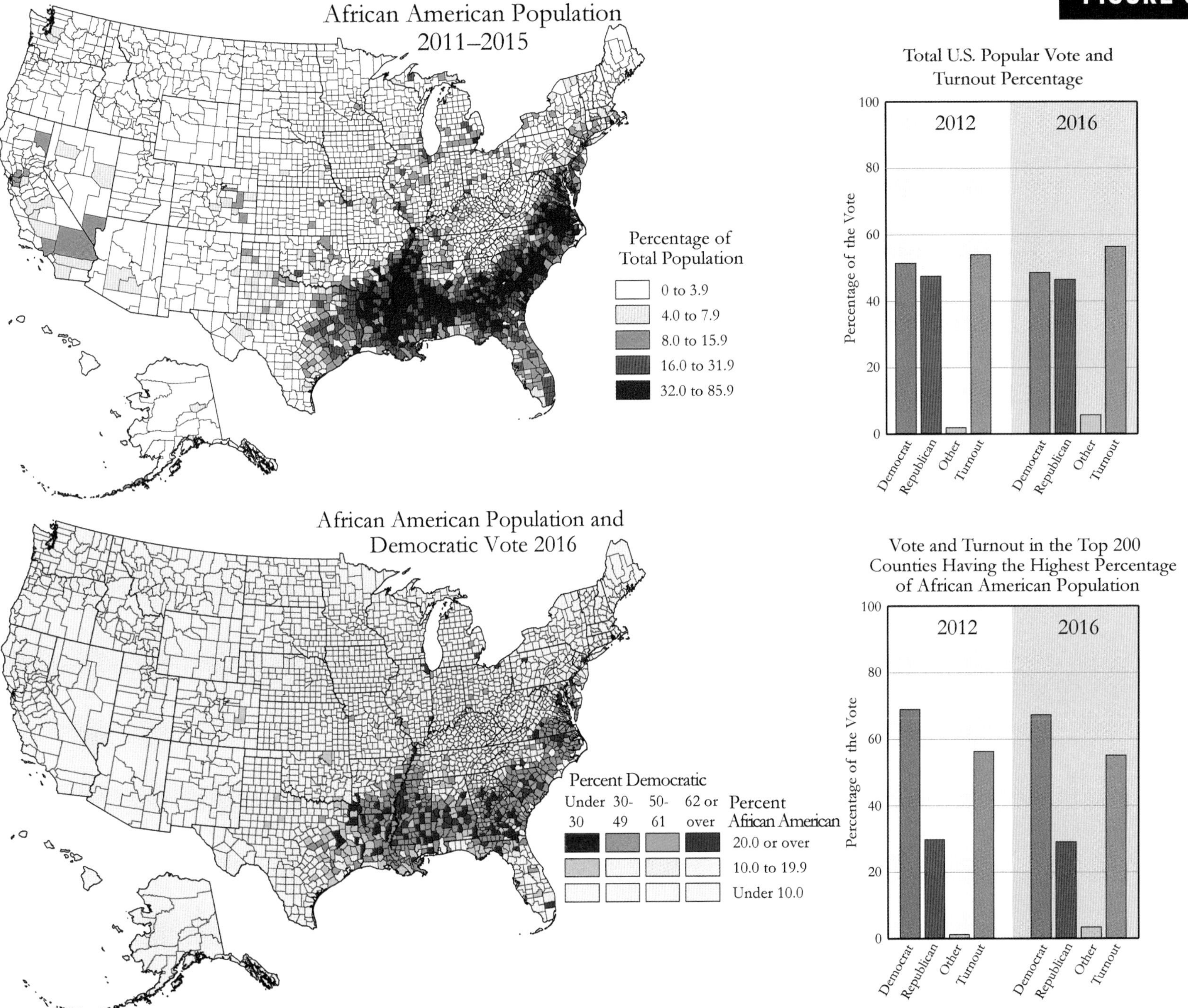
African American Population
2011–2015
Percentage of
Total Population
0 to 3.9
4.0 to 7.9
8.0 to 15.9
16.0 to 31.9
32.0 to 85.9
Total U.S. Popular Vote and
Turnout Percentage
2012
2016
Percentage of the Vote
0
20
40
60
80
100
Democrat
Republican
Other
Turnout
African American Population and
Democratic Vote 2016
Percent Democratic
Under 30
30-49
50-61
62 or over
Percent African American
20.0 or over
10.0 to 19.9
Under 10.0
Vote and Turnout in the Top 200
Counties Having the Highest Percentage
of African American Population

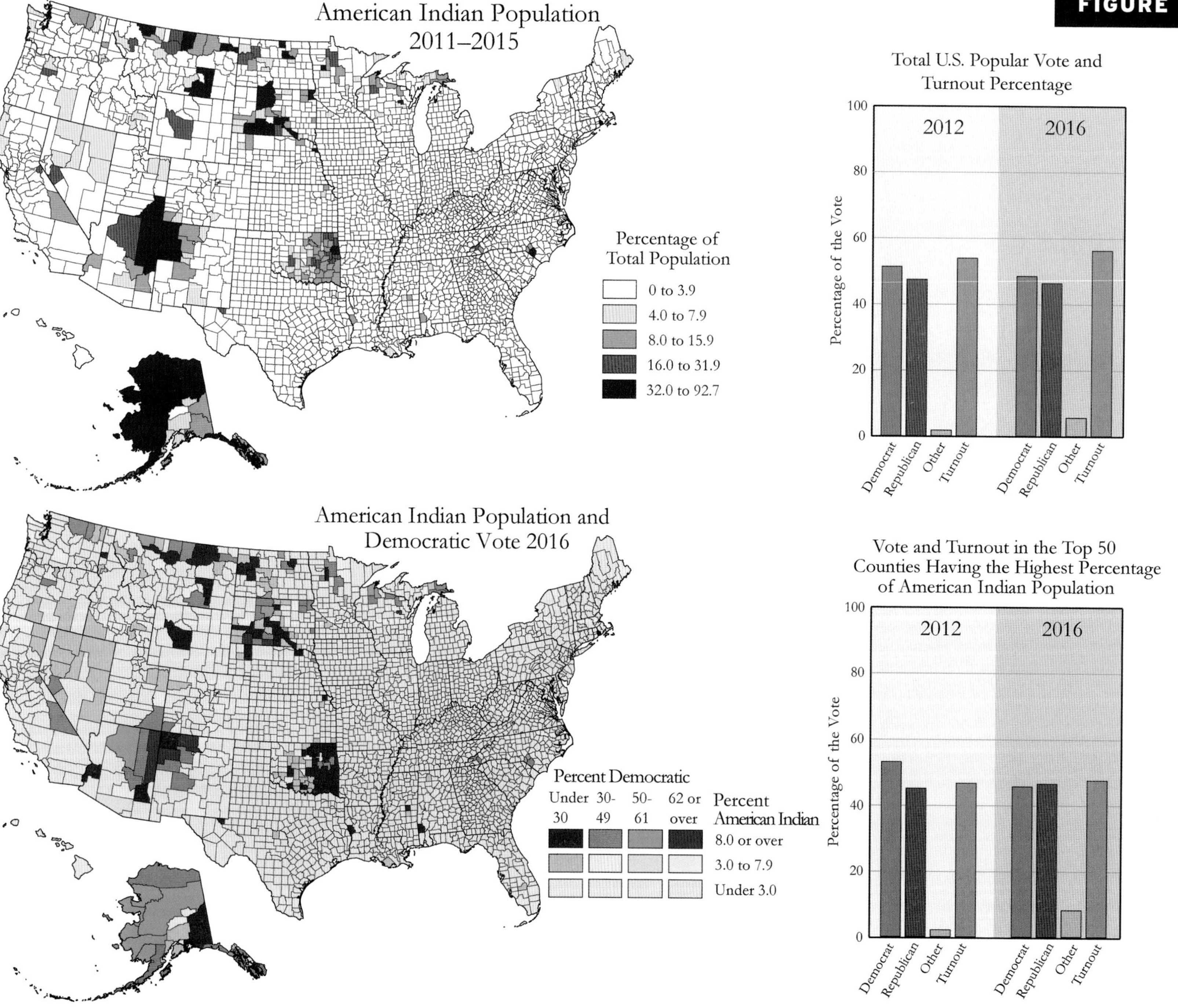
FIGURE 6.11
American Indian Population
2011–2015
Percentage of
Total Population
0 to 3.9
4.0 to 7.9
8.0 to 15.9
16.0 to 31.9
32.0 to 92.7
Total U.S. Popular Vote and
Turnout Percentage
2012
2016
Percentage of the Vote
100
80
60
40
20
0
Democrat
Republican
Other
Turnout
Democrat
Republican
Other
Turnout
American Indian Population and
Democratic Vote 2016
Percent Democratic
Under 30
30-49
50-61
62 or over
Percent
American Indian
8.0 or over
3.0 to 7.9
Under 3.0
Vote and Turnout in the Top 50
Counties Having the Highest Percentage
of American Indian Population
2012
2016
Percentage of the Vote
100
80
60
40
20
0
Democrat
Republican
Other
Turnout
Democrat
Republican
Other
Turnout

FIGURE 6.12

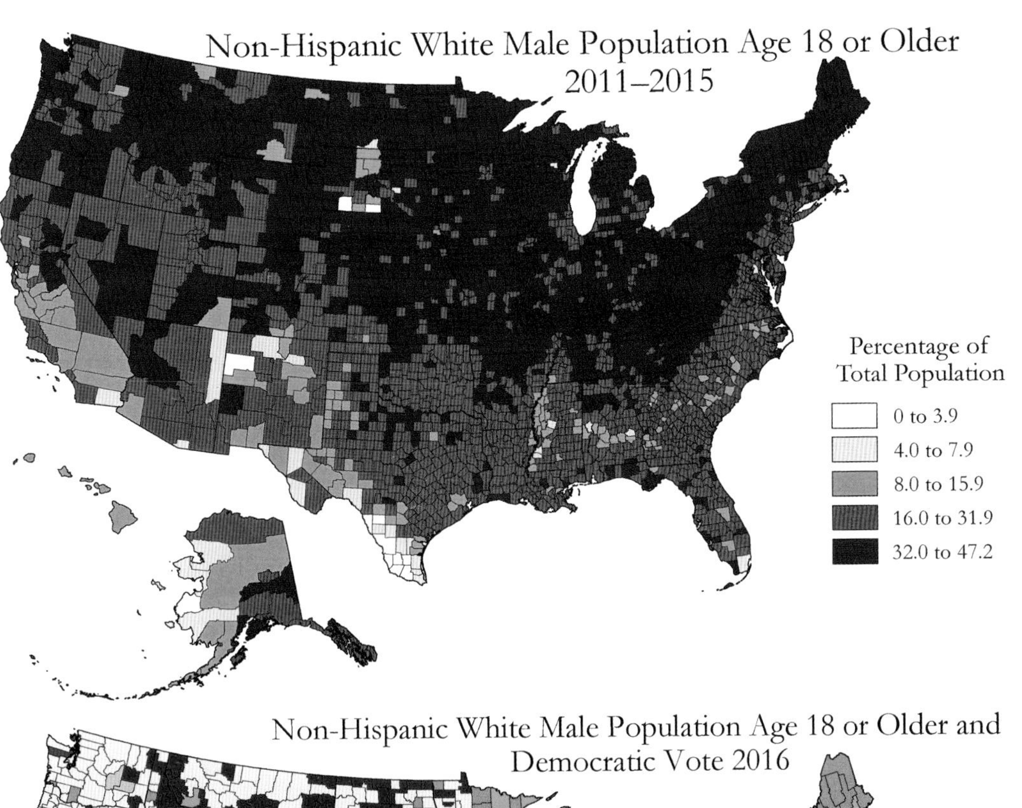

Non-Hispanic White Male Population Age 18 or Older
2011–2015
Percentage of
Total Population
0 to 3.9
4.0 to 7.9
8.0 to 15.9
16.0 to 31.9
32.0 to 47.2

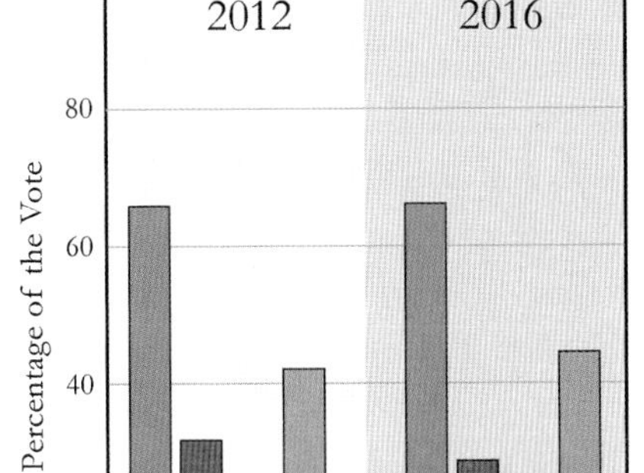

Vote and Turnout in the Bottom 200 Counties Having the Lowest Percentage of Non-Hispanic White Male Population
2012
2016
Percentage of the Vote
100
80
60
40
20
0
Democrat
Republican
Other
Turnout
Democrat
Republican
Other
Turnout

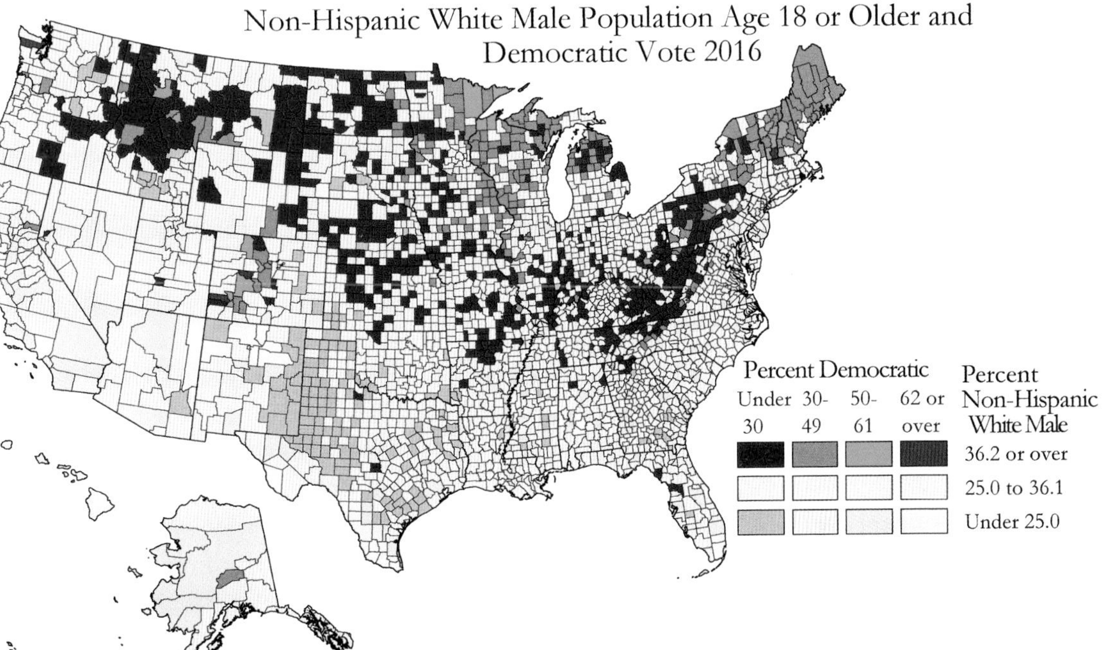

Non-Hispanic White Male Population Age 18 or Older and
Democratic Vote 2016
Percent Democratic
Under 30
30-49
50-61
62 or over
Percent Non-Hispanic White Male
36.2 or over
25.0 to 36.1
Under 25.0

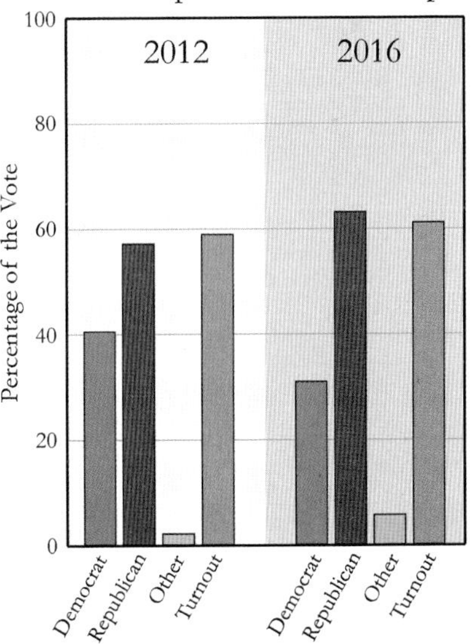

Vote and Turnout in the Top 200 Counties Having the Highest Percentage of Non-Hispanic White Male Population
2012
2016
Percentage of the Vote
100
80
60
40
20
0
Democrat
Republican
Other
Turnout
Democrat
Republican
Other
Turnout

This is a map that was supposed to be the future and the key to a Clinton victory but became instead a rallying cry for a traditional, white, male-led nation. But the model is flawed, perhaps an uneasy coalition, a statistical artifact. The map appears mainly as one of the location of minorities across the southern United States from California to Virginia, plus the largest metropolitan regions. Not surprisingly, the highest shares are along the Mexico-Texas border—Maverick, Starr, and Webb Counties, Texas—with only 2 percent non-Hispanic white males. For Democrats, the margin increased 4.6 percent, from a Democratic share rise of 0.7 and a Republican drop of 4.6 percent.

EDUCATION

Level of educational achievement is also a very strong indicator of voting for Clinton or Trump. Here we look at the share of those over twenty-five years of age with only a high school education, and the share of those with a BA degree or higher. Shares with a BA or more correlated strongly with the percent for Clinton, 0.47, and with change in the percent voting Democratic, 2012 to 2016, 0.45. Conversely, the correlation of the vote for Clinton was a negative 0.38 with the share of people with a high school degree only, and an amazing -0.58 with change in the Democratic percent, the highest correlation among available variables.

In counties where educational attainment was a BA or higher degree, a quarter of counties with over 24 percent supported Clinton 54 to 40 percent, with more than 94 million voting (of a total of 136 million) (figure 6.13). The map indicates another voting dichotomy, with high shares along the Pacific Coast leaning Democratic and fairly high shares across the high plains and northern Rocky Mountain states leaning just as heavily Republican, except for environmental amenity areas. Most of the East has lower shares of those with a BA, except for greater Megalopolis and the Atlantic Coast, and into northern New England, and which housed high shares of Democratic voters in large metropolitan counties, including example areas with high shares, such as Falls Church, Alexandria, and Arlington, Virginia, with 75, 64, and 72 percent with BAs, and voting 75 to 76 percent for Clinton. Other high BA counties include Howard, Maryland, and Los Alamos, New Mexico, with 60 and 64 percent with BAs, and 62 and 51 percent voting for Clinton.

Counties with high shares of high school graduates only are not surprisingly almost the opposite of those with high shares with a BA or higher degree (figure 6.14). The quarter of counties with the highest shares voted 66 percent Republican to 29.7 Democratic, but the total vote in these generally much smaller counties was only 9 million, compared to over 94 million in the more-educated and much larger on average counties. This map is fascinating as it displays the areas with the greatest shift from Democrat to Republican, in the North from the Dakotas to Kansas east to the Appalachian crest, in the large majority of counties, for example, in Ohio, West Virginia, Pennsylvania, Wisconsin, and even Iowa. Example counties include Loving, Texas, 64 percent high school only and 6 percent for Clinton; Dallas, Alabama, 49 percent high school only and 42 percent for Clinton; Linn, Missouri, 47 and 22 percent; then Juniata and Elk, Pennsylvania, at 47 percent high school only, and 17 and 27 percent for Clinton. Unfortunately for Democrats, there was a huge increase in the Republican margin of 18.7 percent, from a Democratic decline of 10.7 percent and a Republican gain of 8 percent.

INCOME AND POVERTY

The story here is strange to a longtime political observer because, while it is the case that the one-quarter of counties with the highest poverty did vote for Clinton over Trump by 52 to 44 percent, the one-quarter of counties with the highest median incomes over $52,000 also voted 52 to 42 percent Democratic, a seemingly impossible conundrum. But the explanation is that many of the highest income counties are now core metropolitan counties, filled with educated households, including immigrants, and part of the drastic realignment of politics in the last twenty years. The correlation of each variable with the vote for Clinton is positive but weak, indicating the new complexity of well-being and voting.

The duality may be seen on the map for median household income (figure 6.15). The high votes for Clinton are indeed the metropolitan cores, most obviously Megalopolis and the Pacific Coast, Miami, Chicago, and even Houston, but in numbers of counties, they are greatly outnumbered by the many Trump-voting counties in the Great Plains and Mountain states, often in energy development areas. And while suburban counties in the far west often voted Democratic, the larger number along the east often voted Republican. On the other hand, both in the Northeast and the West, many environmental amenity counties voted Democratic. The number of votes in the highest income counties exceeded 76 million. The highest median household income example areas include Loudoun and Fairfax, Virginia, at $124,000 and

FIGURE 6.13

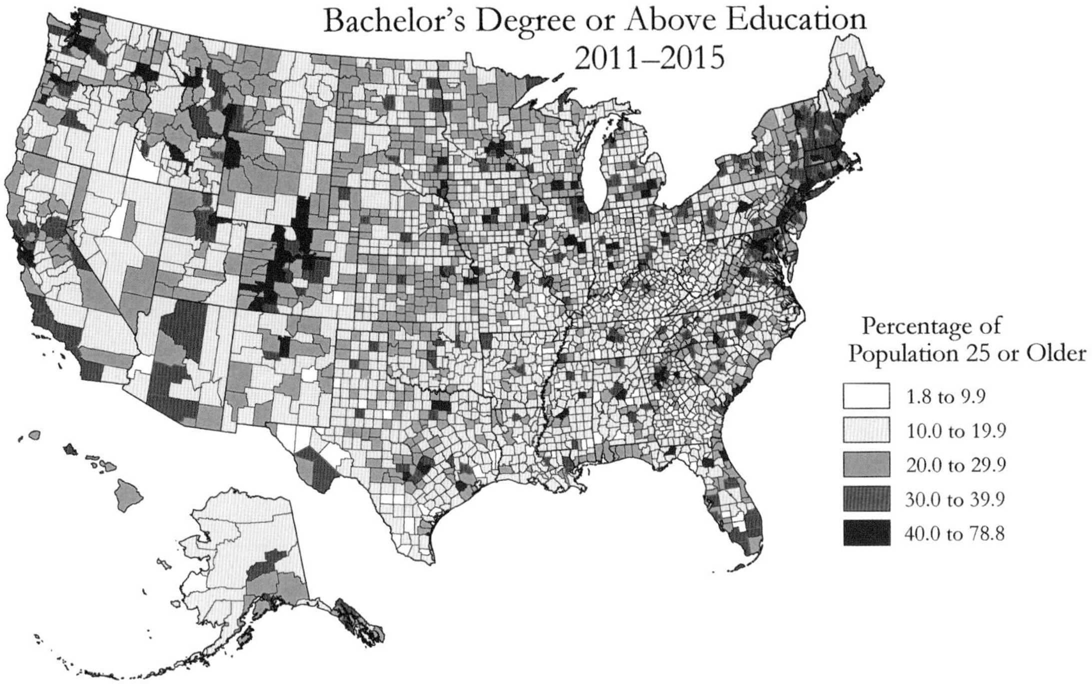

Bachelor's Degree or Above Education 2011–2015

Percentage of Population 25 or Older

- 1.8 to 9.9
- 10.0 to 19.9
- 20.0 to 29.9
- 30.0 to 39.9
- 40.0 to 78.8

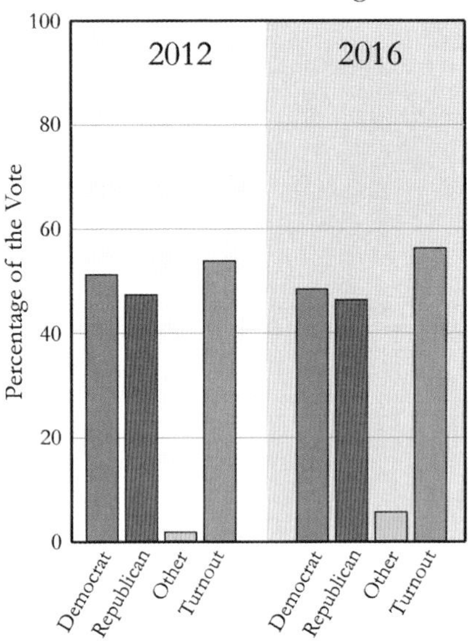

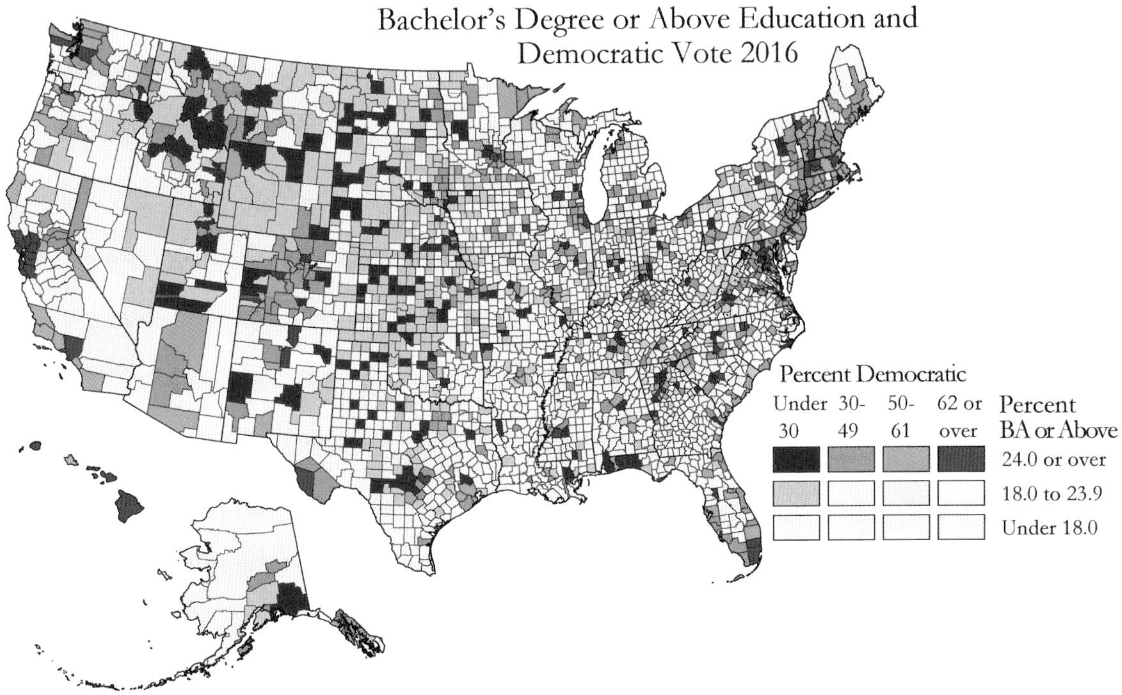

Bachelor's Degree or Above Education and Democratic Vote 2016

Percent Democratic: Under 30	30-49	50-61	62 or over	Percent BA or Above
				24.0 or over
				18.0 to 23.9
				Under 18.0

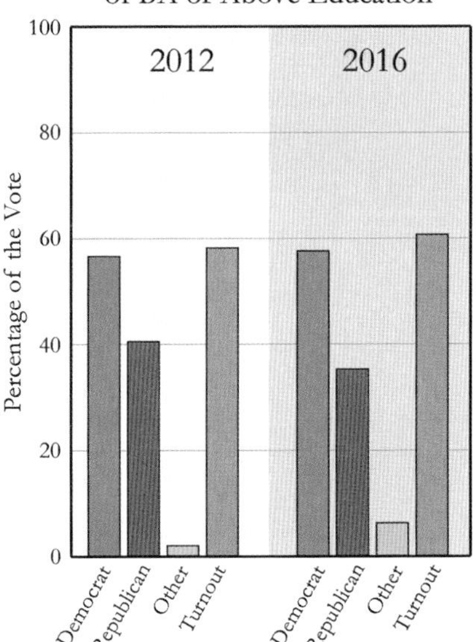

FIGURE 6.14

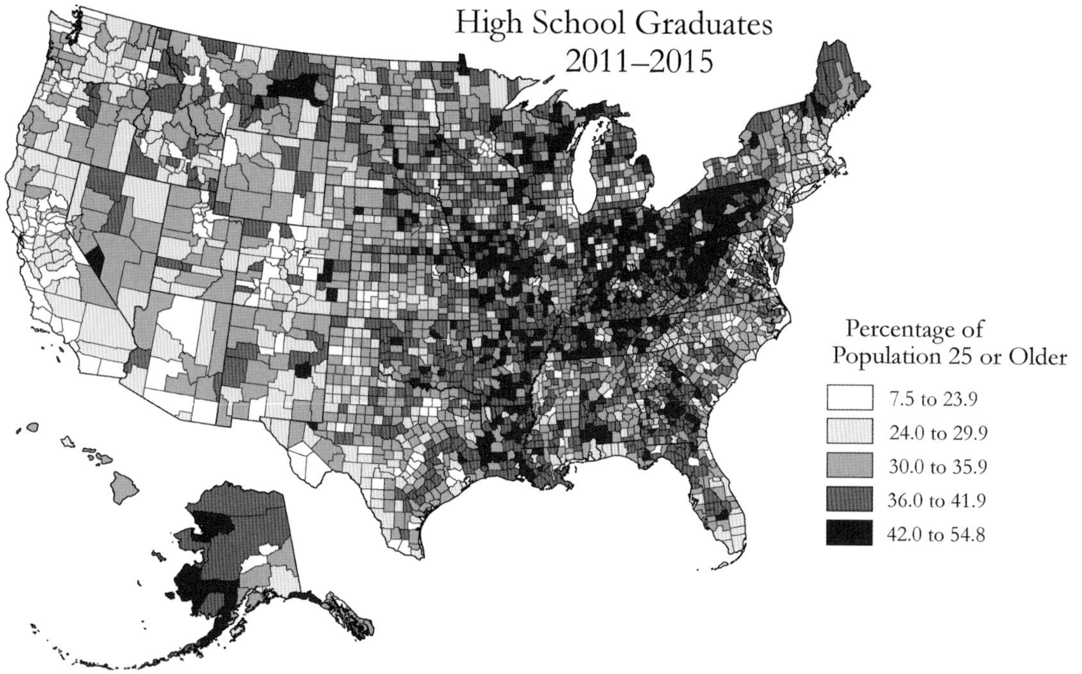

High School Graduates
2011–2015

Percentage of
Population 25 or Older

7.5 to 23.9
24.0 to 29.9
30.0 to 35.9
36.0 to 41.9
42.0 to 54.8

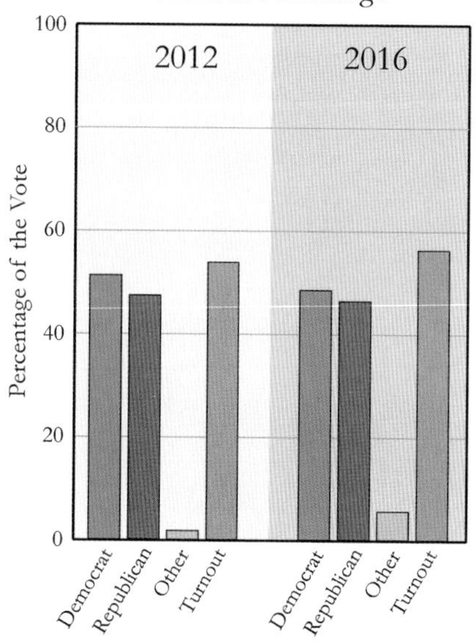

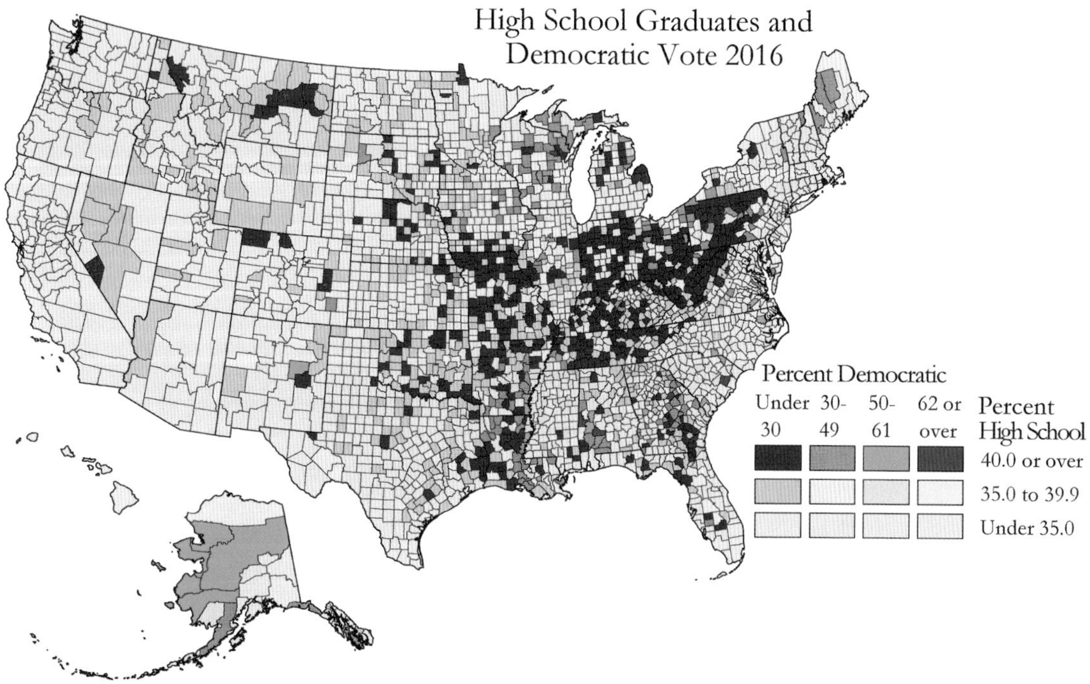

High School Graduates and
Democratic Vote 2016

Percent Democratic
Under 30
30-49
50-61
62 or over
Percent High School
40.0 or over
35.0 to 39.9
Under 35.0

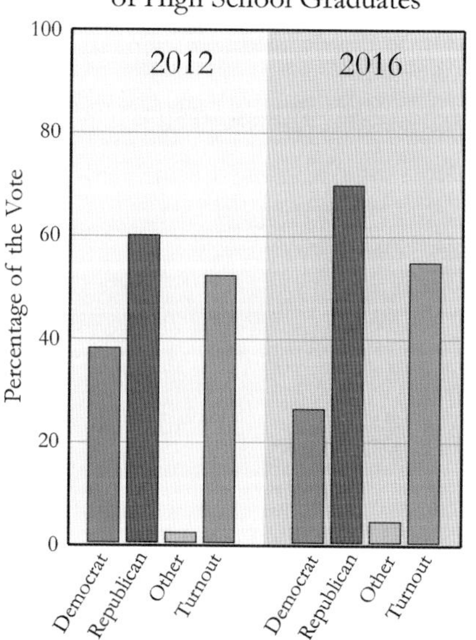

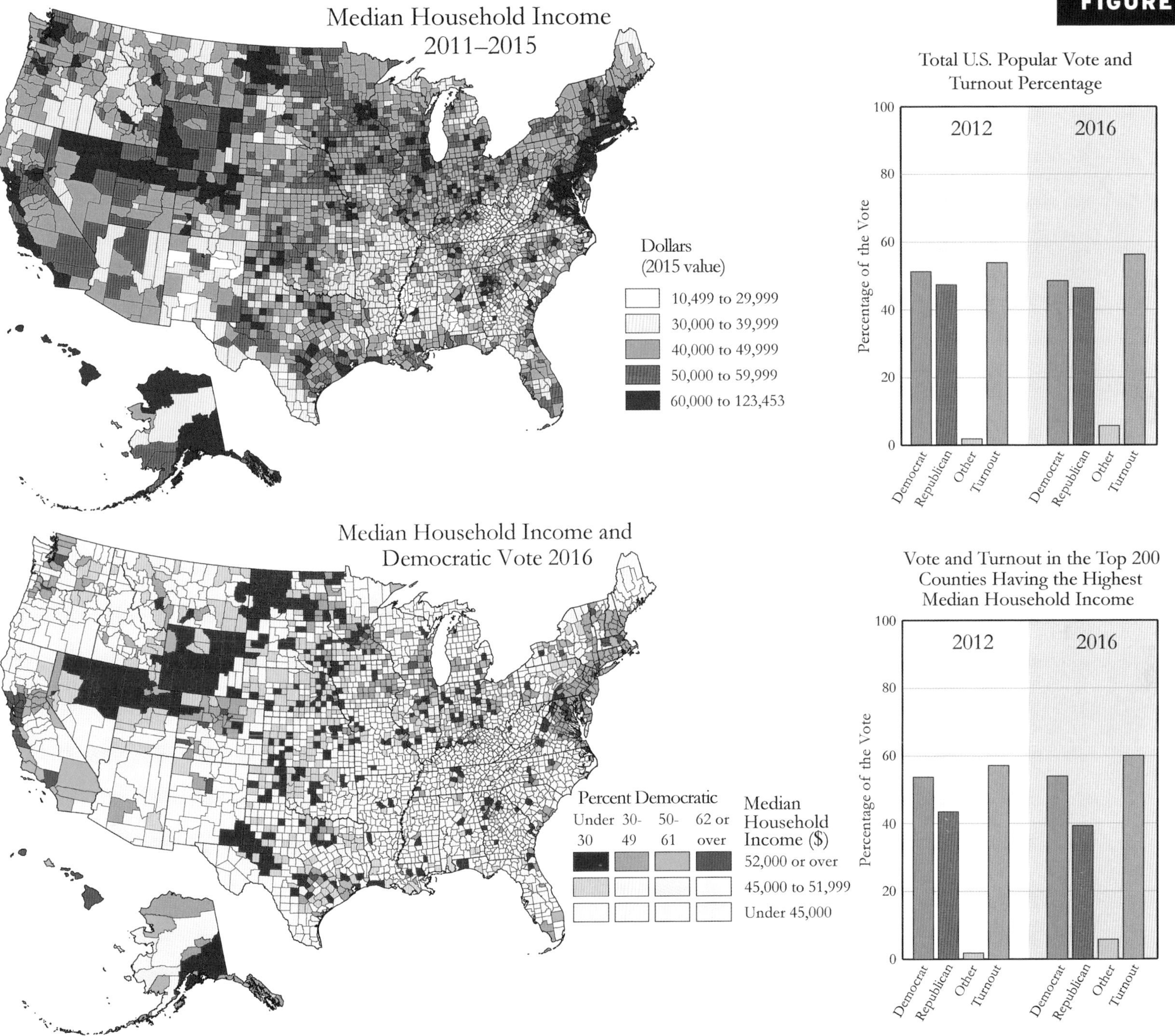

FIGURE 6.15
Median Household Income 2011–2015
Dollars (2015 value)
10,499 to 29,999
30,000 to 39,999
40,000 to 49,999
50,000 to 59,999
60,000 to 123,453
Total U.S. Popular Vote and Turnout Percentage
2012
2016
Percentage of the Vote
100
80
60
40
20
0
Democrat
Republican
Other
Turnout
Median Household Income and Democratic Vote 2016
Percent Democratic
Under 30
30-49
50-61
62 or over
Median Household Income ($)
52,000 or over
45,000 to 51,999
Under 45,000
Vote and Turnout in the Top 200 Counties Having the Highest Median Household Income

FIGURE 6.16

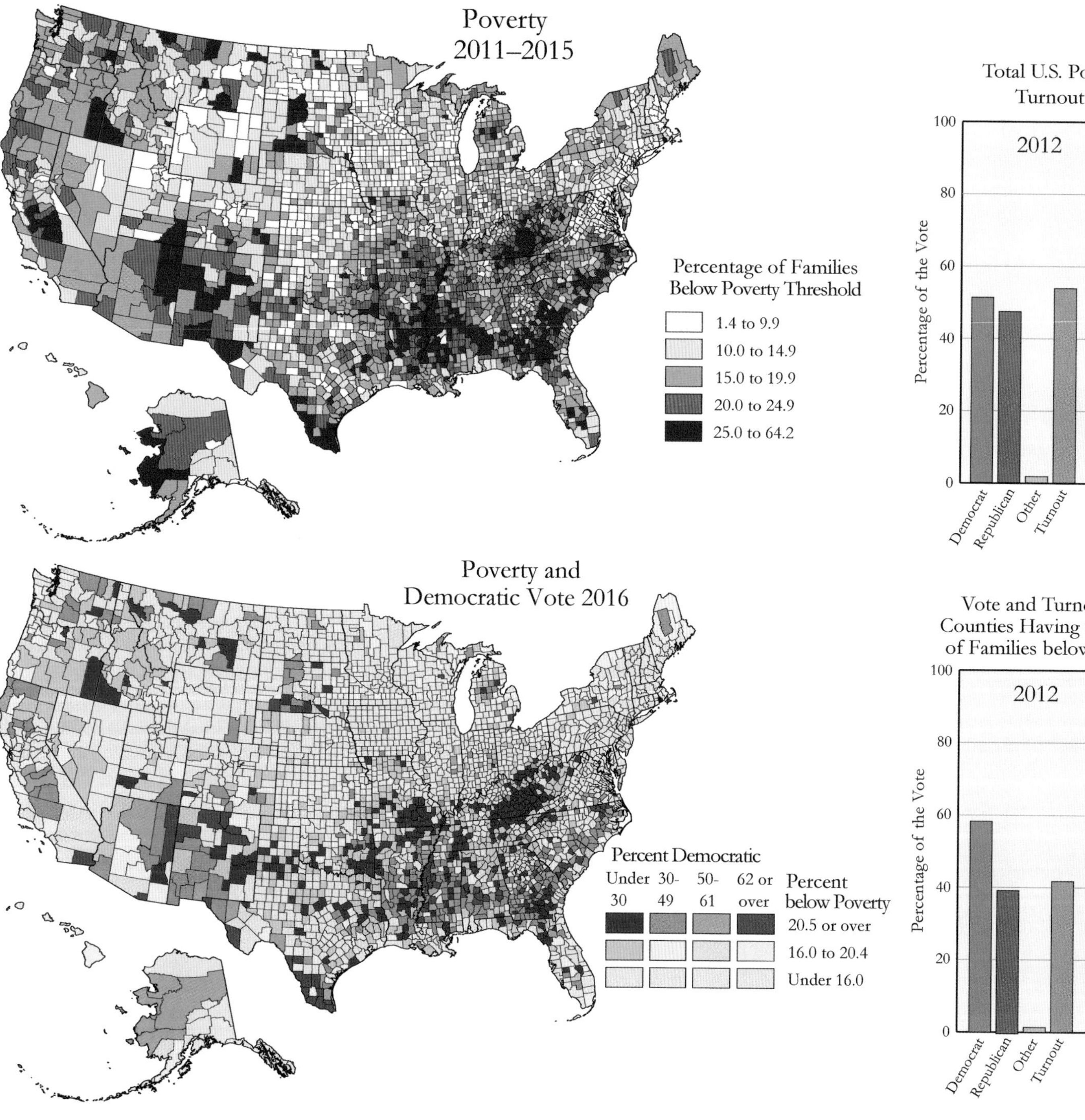
Poverty
2011–2015
Percentage of Families
Below Poverty Threshold
1.4 to 9.9
10.0 to 14.9
15.0 to 19.9
20.0 to 24.9
25.0 to 64.2
Poverty and
Democratic Vote 2016
Percent Democratic
Under 30
30-49
50-61
62 or over
Percent below Poverty
20.5 or over
16.0 to 20.4
Under 16.0
Total U.S. Popular Vote and
Turnout Percentage
2012
2016
Percentage of the Vote
0
20
40
60
80
100
Democrat
Republican
Other
Turnout
Vote and Turnout in the Top 200
Counties Having the Highest Percentage
of Families below Poverty Threshold
2012
2016
Percentage of the Vote
0
20
40
60
80
100
Democrat
Republican
Other
Turnout

$110,000, which voted 55 and 64 percent Democratic, then Howard, Maryland, and Hunterdon, New Jersey, at $110,000 and $107,000, voting 65 and, more traditional, 41 percent Democratic. There was a slight Democratic margin gain, despite a drop in the percentage Democrat of 0.4 due to a larger Republican decline of 3.9 percent, from the increase in votes for "others."

The map for poverty is a little more traditional, at least in the East, with Black Belt counties voting Democratic, but other southern and Appalachian counties voting Republican (figure 6.16). In the West, high Hispanic or Native American share counties tended to vote Democratic, but Northwestern counties with declining forest and other industries switched to Republican. In contrast to income, the number of voters in the poorest counties was 17 million, far less than for metropolitan, high-income counties. Poverty is lowest across the Northeast of the country, perhaps surprisingly high in the far Southwest, probably because of high shares of Hispanics. Overall, high rates of poverty did not mean high votes for Clinton, another indicator of the complexity of social change in the 2016 election. Examples of high poverty counties include Jefferson, Mississippi, 48 percent poor and 86 percent for Clinton (and overwhelmingly African American); Todd, South Dakota, 47 percent poor and 71 percent for Clinton (and Native American); East Carroll, Louisiana, 47 percent poor and 62 percent for Clinton (also high African American share); and Clay, Georgia, 46 percent poor and 55 percent for Clinton.

HISPANIC VOTING TRENDS AND ISSUES IN THE 2016 PRESIDENTIAL ELECTION

RYAN WEICHELT

Hispanics are currently the fastest growing minority group and now comprise 17.13 percent of the total US population, equating to a voting bloc of nearly 27.3 million eligible voters for the November 8, 2016, presidential election (Lopez et al. 2016). Hispanic populations, however, are far from uniform, spatially or ethnically. Figure 6.17 shows Hispanic populations are largest in the South and Southwest United States, as well as in major urban centers. The battleground states of New Mexico (40.4 percent), Arizona (21.5 percent), Florida (18.1 percent), Nevada (17.2 percent), and Colorado (14.5 percent) have a higher proportion of Hispanic eligible voters than the 11.3 percent national average. Other battlegrounds states, like Wisconsin, Pennsylvania, Ohio, and Virginia, are all below 5 percent. Texas and California, however, have large Hispanic voting populations (both at 28 percent), but since both are relatively uncompetitive in the Electoral College and state elections, they received little attention by the major presidential candidates.

Hispanic populations, either those that immigrated or were born in the United States, come from three major areas and display unique geographic patterns. According to 2014 US Census ACS (American Community Survey) data, Hispanics who claim to be of Mexican ancestry comprise nearly 63.9 percent of all Hispanics, followed by Puerto Rican (9.5 percent), Salvadoran (3.8 percent), and Cuban (3.7 percent). The "Other Hispanic" category comprises groups, such as "Tejano" or "Hispano," that claim no connections to foreign countries. Mexican populations dominate the map, but unique pockets of Puerto Ricans are found in and around New York City and in central Florida, with Cuban populations largest in the Miami area, and the large "Hispano" populations (denoted as Other Hispanic) throughout New Mexico and southern Colorado.

Most surveys continue to treat Hispanics as a uniform voting bloc; therefore, surveys for individual Hispanic heritage groups are rare. The few individual surveys of the three largest (Mexican, Puerto Rican, and Cuban) find Mexican voters most likely to vote Democratic. Puerto Rican and Cuban (especially older Cubans) tend to vote Republican, but Cuban populations have been trending more Democratic over the past few decades (Krogstad and Flores 2016). Pew has offered similar surveys to Hispanic populations as a whole over a number of election cycles. In a Pew research poll of registered Hispanic voters conducted in the fall of 2014, respondents ranked, in order, education (92 percent), jobs/economy (91 percent), health care (86 percent), immigration (73 percent), and conflicts in the Middle East (66 percent) as either extremely important or very important issues for the midterm elections (Pew 2014). By 2016, in a similar survey done by Pew, registered Hispanic voters stated, in order, the economy (86 percent), health care (82 percent), terrorism (80 percent), immigration (79 percent), and education (78 percent) as the top five very important issues (Lopez et al. 2014).

Leading up to the 2016 presidential election, Democrats felt confident that the growing population of Hispanic voters would greatly favor their cause. The 1996 presidential election saw the largest Democratic support by Hispanics for Bill Clinton at 76 percent, and in 2008 and 2012, Hispanic voters heavily favored Obama with 67 percent and 71 percent, respectively. With history and demographics on their side, perhaps the biggest help would come from the Republican candidate, Donald Trump, himself. On June 16, 2015, Republican candidate Donald Trump fired off the first of many shots at immigrants, in his presidential announcement speech, "When Mexico sends its people, they're not sending their best. . . . They're sending people that have lots of problems, and they're bringing those problems with us. They're bringing drugs. They're bringing crime. They're rapists. And some, I assume, are good people" (Lee 2015). In a similar line of thought Trump would later proclaim, if elected, he would a "build a wall" and make Mexico pay for it, thus capitalizing on his populist rhetoric of keeping immigrants out of the United States and protecting American jobs. Finally, Trump's comments questioning the legitimacy of Hispanic US District judge Gonzalo Curiel because of his Mexican heritage, combined with earlier comments, provided Democrats cautious optimism that Hispanic voters would turn out in record numbers to support Hillary Clinton.

FIGURE 6.17

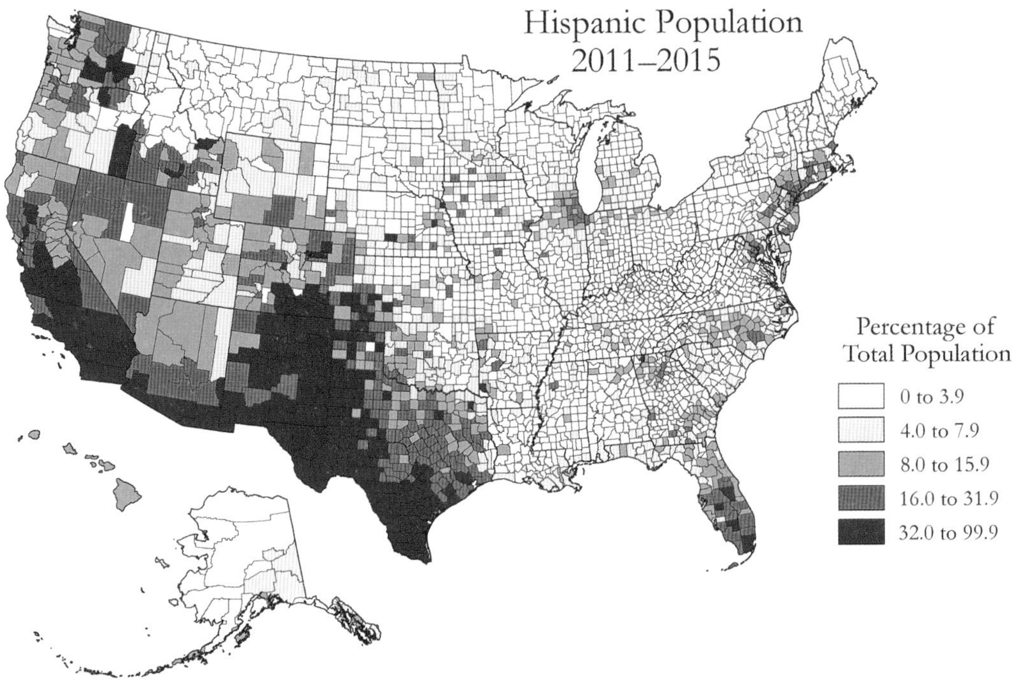

Hispanic Population
2011–2015

Percentage of
Total Population

0 to 3.9
4.0 to 7.9
8.0 to 15.9
16.0 to 31.9
32.0 to 99.9

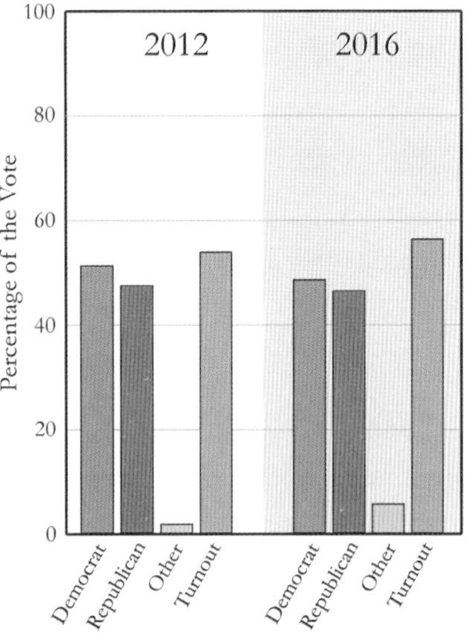

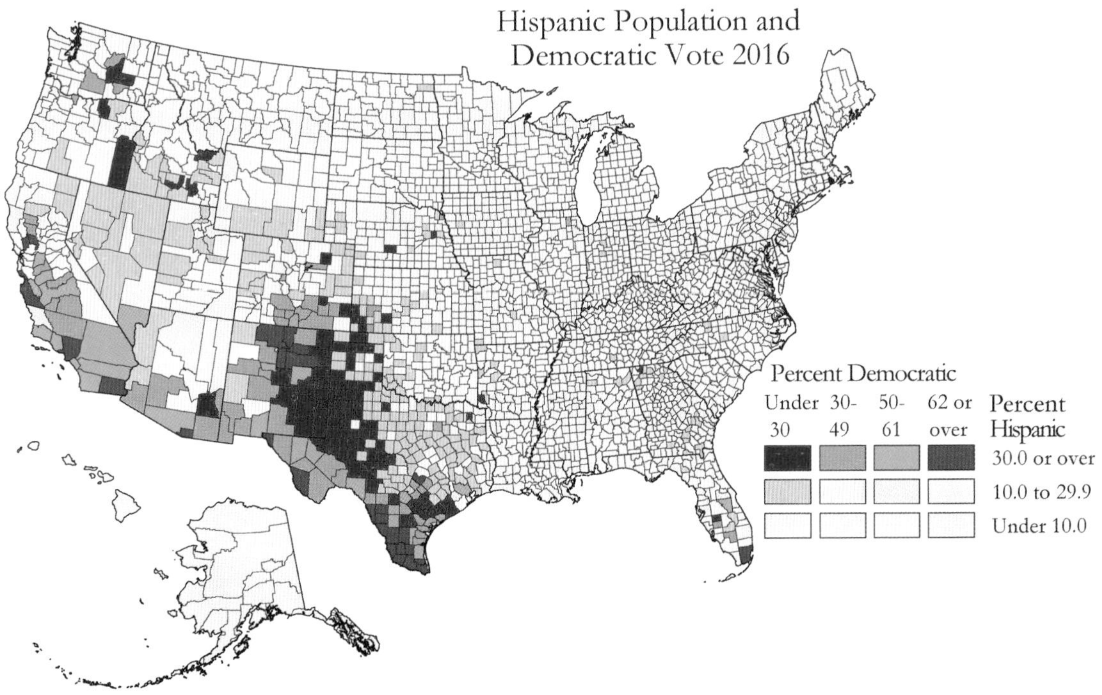

Hispanic Population and
Democratic Vote 2016

Percent Democratic

Under 30	30-49	50-61	62 or over	Percent Hispanic
				30.0 or over
				10.0 to 29.9
				Under 10.0

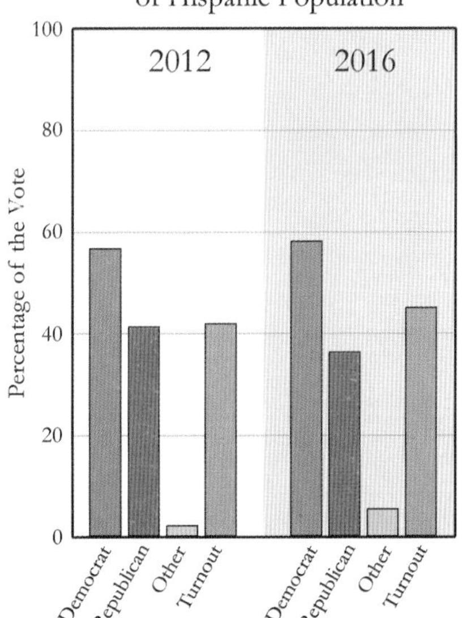

Beyond Donald Trump's campaign rhetoric, Democrats hoped the growing Hispanic population would also be helpful in electing a number of candidates to the US Senate and US House of Representatives. Key races in California and Nevada included Hispanic candidates for the US Senate and a close house race in Nevada featured a Hispanic candidate against an incumbent Republican. In Arizona, national attention focused on a Maricopa county sheriff election featuring hardline conservative sheriff Joe Arpaio. Local efforts hoped to increase Hispanic voters to help defeat the staunch anti-immigration sheriff and aid Hillary Clinton's efforts in winning Arizona. Other similar stories played out across the United States, highlighting the growing potential of the Hispanic electorate. Additionally, the Clinton campaign utilized vice presidential candidate Tim Kaine's bilingual skills to campaign across the country and on Spanish-speaking TV.

By October, according to a Pew poll (Lopez et al. 2016) of 804 Hispanics, 58 percent of Hispanic registered voters said they would vote for Hillary Clinton, compared to only 19 percent for Trump. Clinton saw less support among younger voters (18 to 35) at 48 percent, compared to older voters at 66 percent. Related to Trump's comments regarding Hispanics, 75 percent said they discussed Trump's comments regarding immigration with others and of those 75 percent, 74 percent said they were "absolutely certain" they would vote. For the 804 respondents, the Pew survey did signal a decline in the percentage of Hispanics saying they were "absolutely certain" they would vote compared to 2012, dropping from 77 percent to 69 percent. Additional questions about issues supported early surveys that education, the economy, and health care were the most important issues for Hispanics.

After the *Access Hollywood* tape of Donald Trump dropped on October 7, all polls signaled Clinton was easily going to win the election. Due to the presence of Hispanic voters in states like Arizona, Florida, and Texas, polls indicated Trump's support was dwindling. The Clinton campaign began shifting limited resources, running ads in Texas, increasing funding and their presence in Arizona and continued heavy spending in Florida and North Carolina to drum up support. Yet, due to Trump's anti-Hispanic rhetoric, his campaign spent nearly nothing on Spanish-speaking ads, and the Clinton campaign spent only $2 to $3 million on Spanish-speaking ads, compared to Obama's $20 million in 2012 (NPR 2016).

In the end, Democrats saw mixed results. According to Pew Research, compared to 2012, 4 million additional Hispanics registered to vote, increasing the number to 27.3 million. These increases were largest in the battleground states of Florida, Nevada, and Arizona, yet only one of those states, Nevada, went for Clinton. Exit polls suggested 66 percent of Hispanics supported Clinton, only 1 percent off from 2008, but 5 percent off the recent high for Obama in 2012. Trump gained an estimated 28 percent of the Hispanic vote, 1 percent higher than Romney in 2012, but 3 percent lower than McCain in 2008. On the issues, exit polls suggested 68 percent of Hispanic voters opposed to building a wall, compared to 46 percent of white voters and 82 percent of African American voters (Lopez et al. 2016). Yet, 78 percent believed undocumented immigrants should be offered some sort of chance toward citizenship. US Census estimates suggest turnout for Hispanic voters nationwide was 44.9 percent. While this was the lowest of all groups, it was an increase from 2012 (43.1 percent), but lower than 2008 at 46.5 percent (US Elections Project 2016). Yet, since more Hispanics were eligible to vote in 2016 than any other election, a turnout of 44.9 percent suggests that over 12 million Hispanic voters cast ballots.

There is no doubt that the increase in Hispanic voters was key to victories in states like Colorado, New Mexico, and Nevada. The increase of Hispanic voters in Texas, coupled with a somewhat unexcited electorate, brought Trump's victory to single digits at 9 percent, a result Democrats haven't achieved since 1996. This may signal the growing strength of the overwhelmingly Democratic Hispanic population of the Lone Star State. In Arizona, where many believed Hispanic support could provide a Democratic upset, precinct-level results estimated nearly 80 percent of Hispanics supported Clinton (Nuño and Wilcox-Archuleta 2016), and the US Elections Project (McDonald 2017) suggested voter turnout among Hispanics grew from 53 percent in 2012 to 56 percent in 2016. Research using precinct-level data found nearly similar results for Hispanic voters in Texas, Nevada, and New York, and even suggests, due to county-level exit polls suffering from "ecological fallacy," that Hispanic support for Clinton is much higher than exit polls suggest (Pedraza and Wilcox-Archuleta 2017). Florida provides a unique case due to the large variability in Hispanic heritage groups of Cubans, Puerto Ricans, and Mexicans. According to a similar voting district–based study done by Ali Valenzuela and Tyler Reny (2016), Clinton held the support of all Hispanic groups across the state. Precinct-level analysis showed Clinton won heavily Cuban Miami-Dade 48.7 percent to Trump's 46.7 percent. Obama only took 44 percent in 2012 to Romney's 55.2 percent. Outside of the Miami-Dade area, Clinton was estimated to win combined Hispanic groups 84.2 percent to Trump's 6.4 percent. Slightly contrasting this study, NBC exit polls (2016) at the county level suggested Trump won 54 percent of the Cuban vote to Clinton's 41 percent, while among all non-Cuban Hispanics Clinton won 71 percent to Trump's 26 percent, and when all Hispanics are combined Clinton took 62 percent to Trump's 5 percent.

For Democrats, the overall 2016 election cycle was a disaster, but Hispanics exhibited increased turnout and inspired key Democratic victories. This was clear in Nevada where increased Hispanic support not only won Hillary Clinton the state, but also sent the first female Hispanic to the US Senate (Catherine Cortez Masto) and provided Democrats one of the few victories over an incumbent Republican (Cresent Hardy) by Ruben Kihuen. Outside of Nevada, Democrats saw Hispanic firsts in the US House as Darren Soto became the first person of Puerto Rican heritage to represent Florida and Adriano Espaillat was the first Dominican American to be elected to Congress. Likewise, the overall increasing Hispanic electorate was key to Clinton's victories in a number of states, but certainly no more than in Nevada, Colorado, and New Mexico. As the Hispanic electorate continues to grow and traditional party politics seem to be fading, 2016 should provide Democrats some solace moving forward. Hispanic gains throughout the South and Southwest provide a key demographic for Democrats to cater to moving forward. Unfortunately, changes to voter ID laws and the rise of anti-immigration rhetoric may only hinder the already historically low voter turnout of Hispanic voters. In the end, Trump and the Republicans seem to be hinging their bets on disenfranchised white voters, pivoting Hispanics as key voters for Democrats in the coming elections.

REFERENCES

2016 Campaign: Strong Interest, Widespread Dissatisfaction. 2016. Pew Research Center. http://assets.pewresearch.org/wp-content/uploads/sites/5/2016/07/07-07-16-Voter-attitudes-release.pdf (last accessed April 15, 2017).

Florida Results. 2016. *NBC News*. NBC. March 15, http://www.nbcnews.com/politics/2016-election/primaries/FL (last accessed April 21, 2017).

Florido, Adrian. 2016. Spanish-Language Campaign Outreach Falls Short of Previous Years. NPR. http://www.npr.org/2016/10/29/499899388/spanish-language-campaign-outreach-falls-short-of-previous-years (last accessed May 3, 2017).

Hispanic Roots. 2014. United States Census Bureau. July 1, https://www.census.gov/content/dam/Census/newsroom/facts-for-features/2015/cb15-ff18_graphic.pdf (last accessed April 2017).

Krogstad, Jens M., and Antonio Flores. 2016. Unlike Other Latinos, About Half of Cuban Voters in Florida Backed Trump. Pew Research Center. November 15, http://www.pewresearch.org/fact-tank/2016/11/15/unlike-other-latinos-about-half-of-cuban-voters-in-florida-backed-trump (last accessed March 24, 2017).

Krogstad, Jens M., and Mark H. Lopez. 2016. Hillary Clinton Won Latino Vote but Fell Below 2012 Support for Obama. Pew Research Center. November 29, http://www.pewresearch.org/fact-tank/2016/11/29/hillary-clinton-wins-latino-vote-but-falls-below-2012-support-for-obama (last accessed April 18, 2017).

Lee, Michelle Ye Hee. 2015. Donald Trump's False Comments Connecting Mexican Immigrants and Crime. *Washington Post*. July 8, https://www.washingtonpost.com/news/fact-checker/wp/2015/07/08/donald-trumps-false-comments-connecting-mexican-immigrants-and-crime/?utm_term=.872648389ce5 (last accessed March 23, 2017).

Lopez, Mark H., Ana Gonzalez-Berrera, and Jens M. Krogstad. 2014. Latino Support for Democrats Falls, but Democratic Advantage Remains. Pew Research Center, Hispanic Trends. October 29, http://www.pewhispanic.org/2014/10/29/latino-support-for-democrats-falls-but-democratic-advantage-remains (last accessed February 27, 2017).

Lopez, Mark H., Ana Gonzalez-Berrera, Jens M. Krogstad, and Gustavo Lopez. 2016. Democrats Maintain Edge as Party "More Concerned" for Latinos, but Views Similar to 2012. Pew Research Center, Hispanic Trends. October 11, http://www.pewhispanic.org/2016/10/11/democrats-maintain-edge-as-party-more-concerned-for-latinos-but-views-similar-to-2012 (last accessed March 23, 2017).

Mapping the Latino Electorate by State. 2016. Pew Research Center, Hispanic Trends. January 19, http://www.pewhispanic.org/interactives/mapping-the-latino-electorate-by-state (last accessed March 1, 2017).

McDonald, Michael P. 2017. Voter Turnout Demographics. United States Elections Project, University of Florida. http://www.electproject.org/home/voter-turnout/demographics (last accessed April 27, 2017).

Nuño, Stephen A., and Bryan Wilcox-Archuleta. 2016. Viewpoints: Why Exit Polls Are Wrong about Latino Voters in Arizona. *AZ Central*. November 26, http://www.azcentral.com/story/opinion/op-ed/2016/11/26/exit-polls-wrong-latino-voters-arizona/94288570 (last accessed May 5, 2017).

Pedraza, Francisco I., and Bryan Wilcox-Archuleta. 2017. Precinct Returns Prove Exit Polls Wrong on Latino Vote. *The Nevada Independent*. January 21, https://thenevadaindependent.com/article/precinct-returns-prove-exit-polls-wrong-latino-vote (last accessed April 24, 2017).

Schmidt, Samantha. 2016. A "Silver Lining" on Election Night: First Latina Elected to US Senate. *The Washington Post*. November 9, https://www.washingtonpost.com/news/morning-mix/wp/2016/11/09/a-silver-lining-on-election-night-first-latina-elected-to-u-s-senate/?utm_term=.25a4c3c7d051 (last accessed March 18, 2017).

Stepler, Renee, and Mark H. Lopez. 2016. US Latino Population Growth and Dispersion Has Slowed Since Onset of the Great Recession. Pew Research Center, Hispanic Trends. September 8, http://www.pewhispanic.org/2016/09/08/latino-population-growth-and-dispersion-has-slowed-since-the-onset-of-the-great-recession (last accessed March 6, 2016).

US Elections Project. 2016. Voter Turnout Demographics. http://www.electproject.org/home/voter-turnout/demographics (last accessed April 27, 2017).

Valenzuela, Ali, and Tyler Reny. 2016. Study: Trump Fared Worse Than Romney in Florida Hispanic Vote. *The Hill*. December 16, http://thehill.com/blogs/pundits-blog/presidential-campaign/310760-study-finds-trump-faired-worse-than-romney-with (last accessed May 5, 2017).

ASIAN AMERICAN VOTE

DANIEL A. MCGOWIN

In 2015, the estimated Asian American population in the United States was just over 17 million. This number ranks Asian Americans fourth among ethnic/racial groups in the United States, behind whites, Hispanics, and African Americans. And at just 5.4 percent of the total US population, Asian Americans are a distant fourth; Hispanics, for example, account for 17.6 percent of the population.

However, despite their relatively small population size, Asian Americans in the United States rank as the fastest-growing ethnic/racial group in the country. The population increased from 6.9 million in 1990 to 10.2 million in 2000 to 14.7 million in 2010. In terms of percentage change, the Asian American population grew by 43.8 percent between 2000 and 2010, and 113.2 percent between 1990 and 2010. According to the US Census Bureau (2016a), the Asian American population is the fastest-growing ethnic group in the country. Additionally, the Pew Research Center (2012) notes that more immigrants arriving to the United States are Asian rather than Hispanic, led primarily by Chinese immigrants. These trends point toward a growing influence for the Asian community in the United States.

Yet, the Asian American vote is often overlooked, taking a back seat to interests in other ethnic groups. To be sure, the Asian American electorate is still relatively small. The Census Bureau (2016b) estimates that the Asian American voting population accounts for only 4.1 percent of all voters, which is half that of Hispanic voters and one-third of the African American vote. The only state with a large Asian American voting population is Hawaii (37.6 percent of the state's electorate, a plurality of the state); coincidentally, Hawaii is the only US state with an Asian American majority population. In California, home to the largest total population of Asian Americans, the voting population is 13.5 percent of the total voting roll, which ranks ahead of African Americans (6.9 percent) but behind whites (65.2 percent) and Hispanics, who can be of any race (28.6 percent).

Before continuing, it is important to note that as a minority group, Asian Americans are perhaps the most diverse and contrasting of all such groups. Using the definition developed by the United States Census Bureau, "Asian" includes Northeast Asia (e.g., China, Japan, South Korea), South Asia (e.g., India, Pakistan, Sri Lanka), and Southeast Asia (e.g., Indonesia, Thailand, Vietnam). This definition includes numerous different and mutually unintelligible languages, as well as countries home to the four largest religions—Christianity, Islam, Hinduism, and Buddhism. Asian Americans also differ greatly in terms of social indicators such as education attainment (44.6 percent of Taiwanese hold a graduate degree compared to 4.2 percent of Cambodians), median household income ($74,548 for Japanese versus $49,515 for Bangladeshi), and occupation (19.1 percent of Vietnamese are involved in manufacturing compared to 8.5 percent of Filipinos). Suffice it to say that as a cultural group, Asian Americans are not a monolithic group. However, in terms of voting, Asian Americans of all backgrounds do tend to exhibit many similarities.

In terms of how Asian Americans tend to vote, there are two reports that offer insight to preferences—the Asian American Voices in the 2016 Election (Ramakrishnan et al. 2016) and the Asian American Vote 2016 (Asian American Legal Defense and Education Fund 2017). The former survey was conducted prior to the election while the latter was conducted as an exit poll on Election Day. Both reports provide a comprehensive profile of the Asian American vote.

Going into the elections, Asian Americans were twice as likely to identify as Democrat than as Republican, with 55 percent favoring Hillary Clinton compared to 14 percent for Donald Trump. However, it is worth noting that 41 percent of Asian Americans identify as "independent." Nonpartisan Asian Americans are decreasing in number as more voters begin to gravitate toward the Democratic Party. These numbers translated into resounding support for Secretary Clinton as she received 79 percent of the Asian American vote; Mr. Trump received just 18 percent. Additionally, Hillary Clinton received more crossover votes from registered Republicans (20 percent) compared to Asian American Democrats who voted for Mr. Trump (5 percent); unregistered Asian American voters overwhelmingly supported the Democratic candidate (73 percent).

A closer examination of different ethnic groups reveals that while Asian Americans in general supported Secretary Clinton, there was variance in that level of support. For example, prior to the election, 67 percent of Asian Indians favored Hillary Clinton compared to just 41 percent of Vietnamese Americans; Cambodians were the only other group to provide Secretary Clinton with only a plurality of support. In terms of support for Donald Trump, the largest support came from Filipinos (25 percent) and Japanese (20 percent). These numbers played out in the exit polls as Hillary Clinton received 84 percent of the Asian Indian vote compared to 65 percent of the Vietnamese vote; Mr. Trump received 32 percent from the latter and just 8 percent from the former. It is also worth noting that Asian Americans from predominantly Muslim countries overwhelmingly supported Secretary Clinton (96 percent of Pakistanis; 96 percent of Bangladeshis; and 86 percent of Arabs).

In terms of issues, many Asian Americans side with those issues that are at the forefront of the Democratic Party's agenda. Sixty percent of Asian Americans supported the Affordable Care Act while 66 percent supported increased federal assistance for college. Asian Americans overwhelmingly supported doing more to create equality among African Americans and whites (72 percent), as well as addressing climate change (76 percent). Immigration issues tend to be a bit more contentious. Only 44 percent of Asian Americans supported accepting Syrian refugees compared to 35 percent opposing. Filipinos were the only group to be more opposed (41 percent) than supportive (36 percent) to allowing Syrian refugees to enter the United States, while Asian Indians (55 percent), Cambodians (57 percent), and Hmong (74 percent) were the only groups to offer majority support. That Hmong overwhelmingly support Syrian refugees should not be a surprise, given their own history as refugees. Concerning a ban on Muslims entering the United States, 62 percent opposed such a measure, though Vietnamese were a bit more split on the issue (40–31, with 29 percent undecided). Finally, that Asian Americans generally oppose the legalization of marijuana (56 percent) reflects the contentiousness of the topic. Indeed, the Democratic Party only added a "pathway" to legalization of marijuana to its platform in 2016 (Democratic Party 2016). In the end, Asian Americans stated that the economy was the most important factor influencing their vote, followed by immigration, health care, and education.

Geographically mapping the Asian American vote can be somewhat challenging given their relatively small population. However, there are two ways to get a sense of this geography—exit polls and geographic concentrations of Asian American populations. The aforementioned Asian American Vote 2016 report conducted exit polls of Asian American voters in fifteen locations—California, Florida, Georgia, Louisiana, Maryland, Massachusetts, Michigan, Nevada, New Jersey, New Mexico, New York, Pennsylvania, Texas, Virginia, and Washington, DC. Hillary Clinton received tremendous support from Asian Americans in DC (93 percent), Michigan (89 percent), and Pennsylvania (87 percent). Secretary Clinton's lowest support came from Texas (59 percent), New Mexico (57 percent), and Louisiana (46 percent). In fact, Louisiana was the only state in the survey in which Donald Trump won the Asian American vote (50 percent), which is likely due to the state's large Vietnamese population and their propensity to vote Republican. However, Democrats made gains among Asian Americans in each of these states with the exception of Nevada. The Republican candidate was more supported in Louisiana in 2008 (85 percent) and 2012 (81 percent) than in 2016.

Examining county-level data (figure 6.18), Asian Americans are the leading ethnic group in only two locations—Honolulu County, Hawaii (43 percent), and Aleutians East Borough, Alaska (35.4 percent). In total, there are twelve counties (or equivalent) where the Asian American population accounts for at least 20 percent of the population. Among those counties, eleven voted in favor of Hillary Clinton; only Aleutians East Borough voted for Donald Trump (53.7 percent versus 32.8 percent). Like most Asian American Alaskans, Aleutians East Borough's Asian American population is mostly Filipino, which was noted above to be the most likely to support Mr. Trump. While difficult to suggest that Asian Americans greatly influence the vote in these places, it is worth noting that several of these counties tend to be ethnically diverse, with whites failing to constitute a majority in any of these twelve counties. On average, the more heterogeneous the ethnic composition of a location is, the more likely its constituents are to vote for a Democratic candidate over a Republican one.

Over the course of two-plus decades, the Asian American vote shifted. According to 1992 exit polls, president George H. W. Bush received 55 percent of the Asian American vote compared to 31 percent for Bill Clinton; independent candidate H. Ross Perot received 15 percent. While this pattern held in 1996, Asian Americans began voting for the Democratic candidate in 2000. Beginning with Al Gore (55 percent), the percentage of Asian Americans voting for the Democratic

FIGURE 6.18

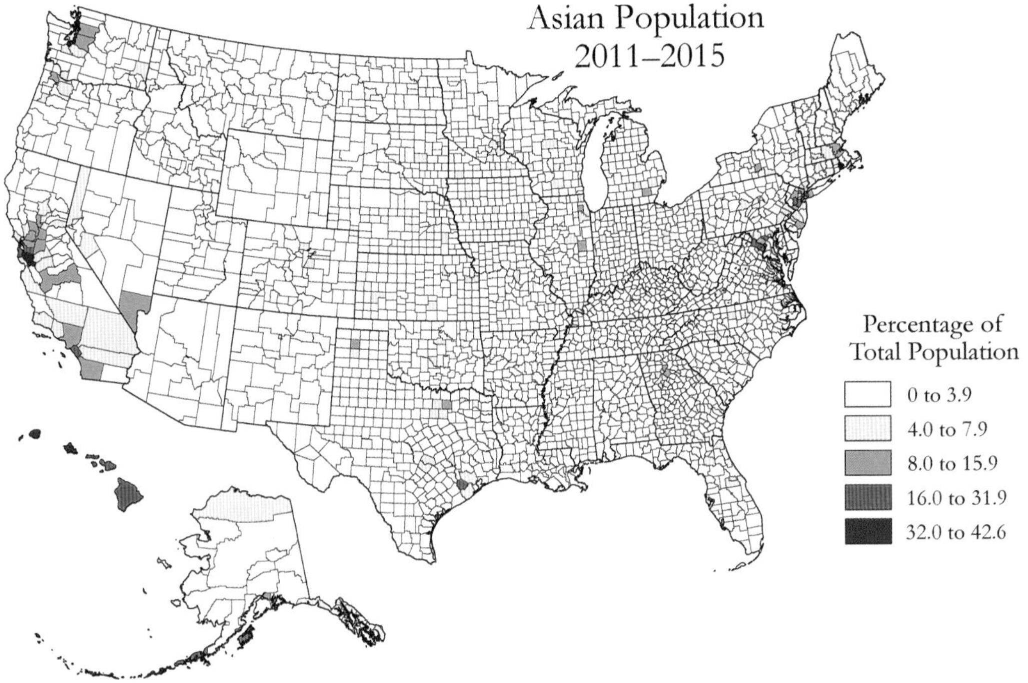

Asian Population 2011–2015

Percentage of Total Population

- 0 to 3.9
- 4.0 to 7.9
- 8.0 to 15.9
- 16.0 to 31.9
- 32.0 to 42.6

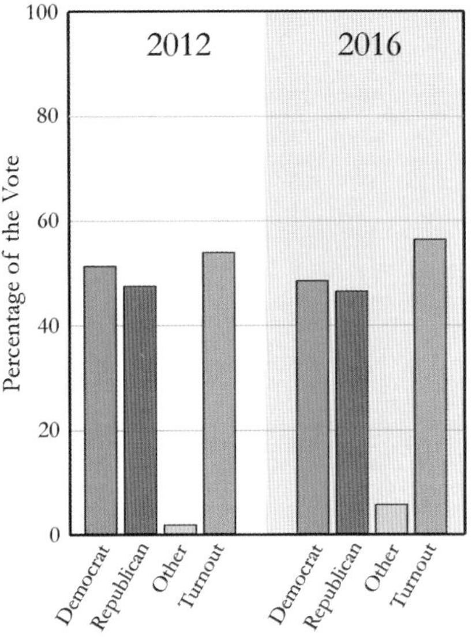

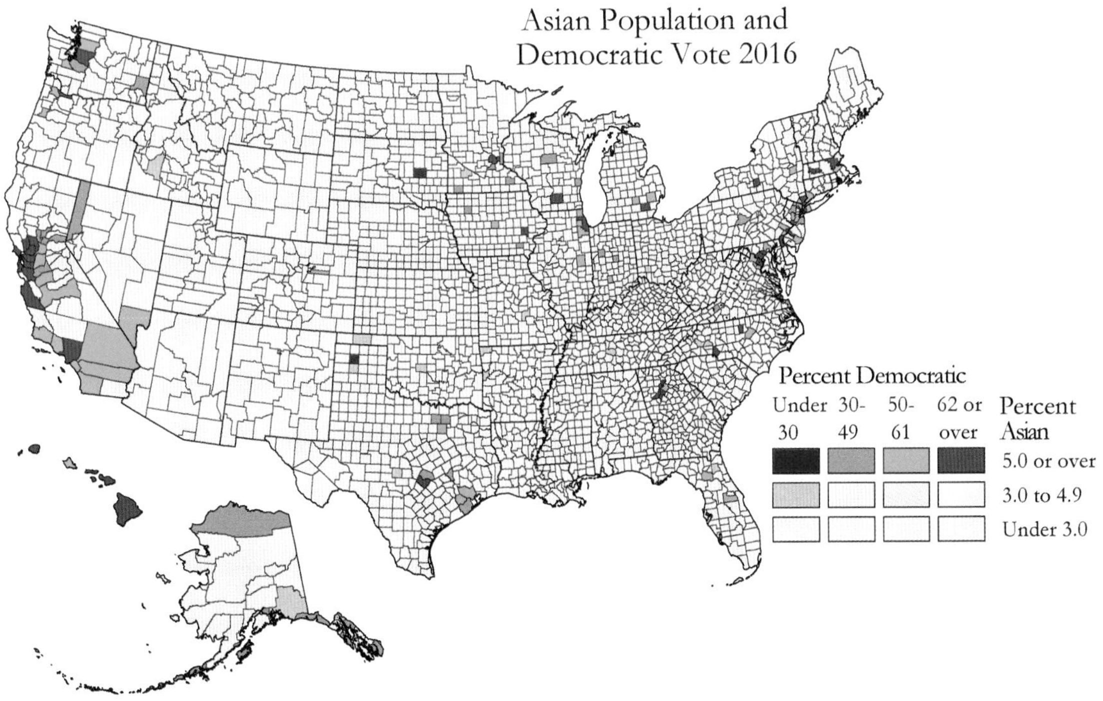

Asian Population and Democratic Vote 2016

Percent Democratic: Under 30	30-49	50-61	62 or over	Percent Asian
				5.0 or over
				3.0 to 4.9
				Under 3.0

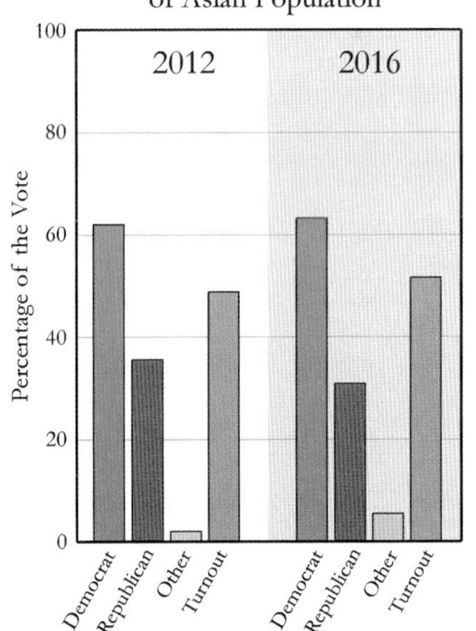

candidate increased with every election (Roper Center 2017).

There are several possible reasons for this shift. As indicated above, Asian Americans tend to be progressive and their positions tend to coincide with that of the Democratic Party. There are also changing attitudes among Asian American voters. For example, many Vietnamese arriving in the United States in the 1980s were staunchly anti-Communist, which coupled nicely with the rhetoric of President Ronald Reagan and the Republican Party. Now, the economy and affordable health care are of greater concern (Khalid 2015). There is also sentiment that the Republican Party is less inclusionary than the Democratic Party, especially given the former's stance on immigration (Mo 2015). Indeed, the Republican Party's strong sense of Christian conservatism may work as a "push factor" for many Asian Americans who are not Christian (Ramakrishnan 2016).

Though Asian American voters constitute a small percentage of the total electorate, their influence will continue to grow. Currently, Asian Americans are the least politically engaged racial/ethnic group in the United States. This could be in part due to the lack of courting from either major political party (Ramakrishnan 2014; Baik 2016). However, that many Asian Americans are unaffiliated with a major political party suggests that their vote is untapped and could be an important "swing vote" as the Asian American population grows in the United States and their political engagement increases.

REFERENCES

Asian American Legal Defense and Education Fund. 2017. The Asian American Vote 2016. The Asian American Legal Defense and Education Fund. http://aaldef.org/TheAsianAmericanVote2016-AALDEF.pdf (last accessed April 18, 2017).

Baik, Jennifer. 2016. Will Asian Americans Vote? *The American Prospect*. September 26, http://prospect.org/article/will-asian-americans-vote.

Democratic Party. 2016. The 2016 Democratic Platform. Democratic National Committee. https://www.democrats.org/party-platform.

Khalid, Asma. 2015. How Asian-American Voters Went from Republican to Democratic. *Morning Edition*, NPR. September 16, http://www.npr.org/sections/itsallpolitics/2015/09/16/439574726/how-asian-american-voters-went-from-republican-to-democratic.

Mo, Cecilia H. 2015. Why Asian Americans Don't Vote Republican. *The Washington Post*. November 2, https://www.washingtonpost.com/news/monkey-cage/wp/2015/11/02/why-asian-americans-dont-vote-republican.

Pew Research Center. 2012. The Rise of Asian Americans. Pew Research Center, Social & Demographic Trends. June 19 (updated April 4, 2013), http://www.pewsocialtrends.org/asianamericans-graphics.

Ramakrishnan, Karthick. 2014. Asian Americans Turn Out for What? Asian American Youth Voters in 2014. APIA Vote. October 23, http://www.apiavote.org/sites/apiavote/files/asianam-youthvote-oct23.pdf.

———. 2016. How Asian Americans Became Democrats. *The American Prospect*. July 26, http://prospect.org/article/how-asian-americans-became-democrats-0.

Ramakrishnan, Karthick, Janelle Wong, Taeku Lee, and Jennifer Lee. 2016. Asian American Voices in the 2016 Election. National Asian American Survey. October 5, http://naasurvey.com/wp-content/uploads/2016/10/NAAS2016-Oct5-report.pdf.

Roper Center. 2017. United States Presidential Elections. Roper Center for Public Opinion Research, Cornell University. https://ropercenter.cornell.edu/polls/us-elections/presidential-elections.

United States Census Bureau. 2016a. Sumter County, Fla., Is Nation's Oldest, Census Bureau Reports. June 23, https://www.census.gov/newsroom/press-releases/2016/cb16-107.html.

———. 2016b. Citizen Voting-Age Population. November 15, https://www.census.gov/library/visualizations/2016/comm/citizen_voting_age_population.html.

GENDER AND VOTING IN THE 2016 ELECTION

FIONA M. DAVIDSON

A record 73 million women voted in the 2016 presidential election, representing 61.3 percent of the eligible female voters. Turnout increased from 2012, when only 59.6 percent of women voted, and was 2.4 percent higher than turnout for men. The tendency for women to vote at higher rates than men has been a constant in every election since 1980. For most of the twentieth century, women turned out to vote at much lower rates than men did and, in fact, in the wake of the passage of the Nineteenth Amendment, voter turnout dropped dramatically in 1920 and 1924 as the number of eligible voters doubled. However, the number of people actually voting increased much more slowly; in 1916 turnout was a respectable 61.6 percent, but in 1920 it dropped to 49.2 percent and then again to 48.9 percent in 1924.

There is no national data on turnout by gender until exit polling began in 1952 (Gallup Presidential Election Center), but small-scale, local studies have indicated that depressed turnout was a function largely of women fearing repercussions (both domestic and work-related) if they voted, or holding anti-suffragist positions (Allen 2009). By the early 1960s women's participation in presidential elections had increased to over 67 percent, but this was still lower than the turnout rate for men (71.9 percent). For the next three election cycles, turnout fell for both groups but fell much faster for men than for women so that, by 1980, the voting percentages were reversed and for the last nine presidential elections women have consistently outvoted men by an increasing margin (a difference of less than 2 percent in 1984; but over 4 percent in 2012).

Women's increased influence at the polls has been magnified by the tendency for gender differences in voting behavior to also vary over time. Discussed as the "gender gap," the difference in male and female partisan voting is first captured by exit polls in 1952 (Gallup Presidential Election Center) when 5 percent more women than men voted Republican. This Republican bias continued through the next two election cycles until 1964, when women favored Johnson over Goldwater by 24 points, and for the first time had a higher Democratic vote than men by 2 percent. In every election since 1964—with the exception of the Carter/Ford election of 1976 and the 1992 Clinton/Bush election, when substantially more men voted third party than women—women have been more likely to vote Democrat than men, with margins ranging from 1 percent (1972) to 12 percent (2016). While there have been fluctuations in the size of the gap over time, overall it has increased steadily, averaging around 4 percent in the 1970s, and 11 percent over the last two elections. In 2016, 54 percent of women voted for Hillary Clinton, an increase of 1 percent over the female vote for Obama in 2012, and the gender gap reached an historic 12 percent or 24 points (the sum of the difference between the female/male Republican and Democratic votes).

Women, however, are not a monolithic voting group either demographically or geographically. When women's voting patterns are disaggregated by race, it is apparent that white women are marginally more likely to vote Republican than Democrat. In 2004, the first year for which there is exit polling data for gender and race, there was a 31 percent gap between white female and non-white female votes for John Kerry. By 2008 that had increased to 37 percent, although the percent of white women voting Republican had declined by 2 points; and by 2016 the gap was again 37 percent with a further reduction, to 52 percent, of white women voting Republican.

State exit polls are particularly useful for understanding geographic differences in the voting patterns of different demographic groups and, while the number of states conducting exit polls dropped sharply in 2016, results from the twenty-seven states polled illuminate several important gender-related voting patterns in the 2016 election (figures 6.19 and 6.20).

Overall, the 2016 election saw an expansion of the number of "split" states, where the majority of women voted differently (always more Democratic) than most men. In 2012, there were twelve states where women voted for Obama and men voted for Romney and, in all but one (North Carolina), those female votes were sufficient to win the state. By 2016 there were seventeen split states, in eight the female Democratic vote carried the state and in nine it was the overwhelming male vote

FIGURE 6.19

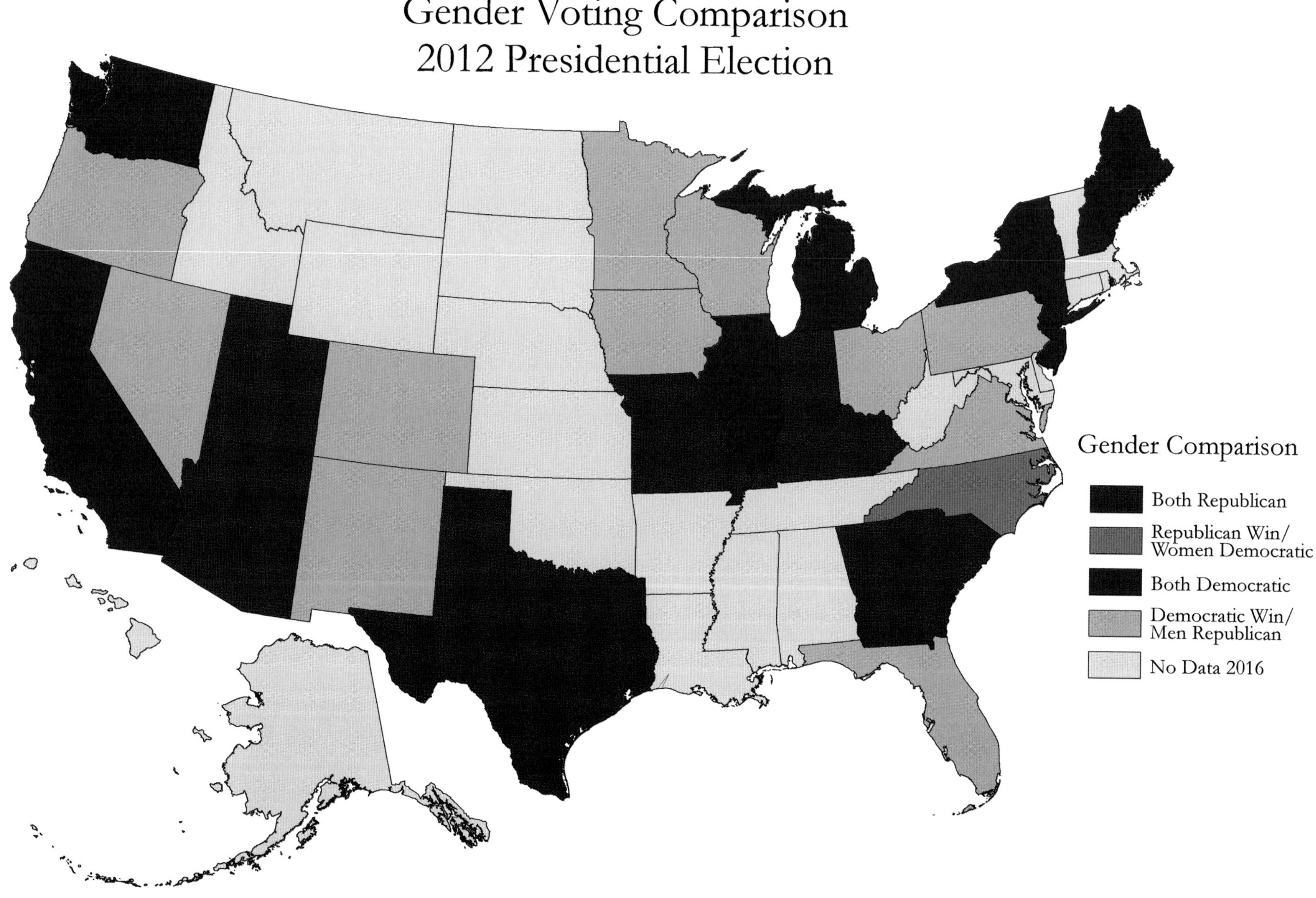
Gender Voting Comparison
2012 Presidential Election
Gender Comparison
Both Republican
Republican Win/
Women Democratic
Both Democratic
Democratic Win/
Men Republican
No Data 2016

FIGURE 6.20

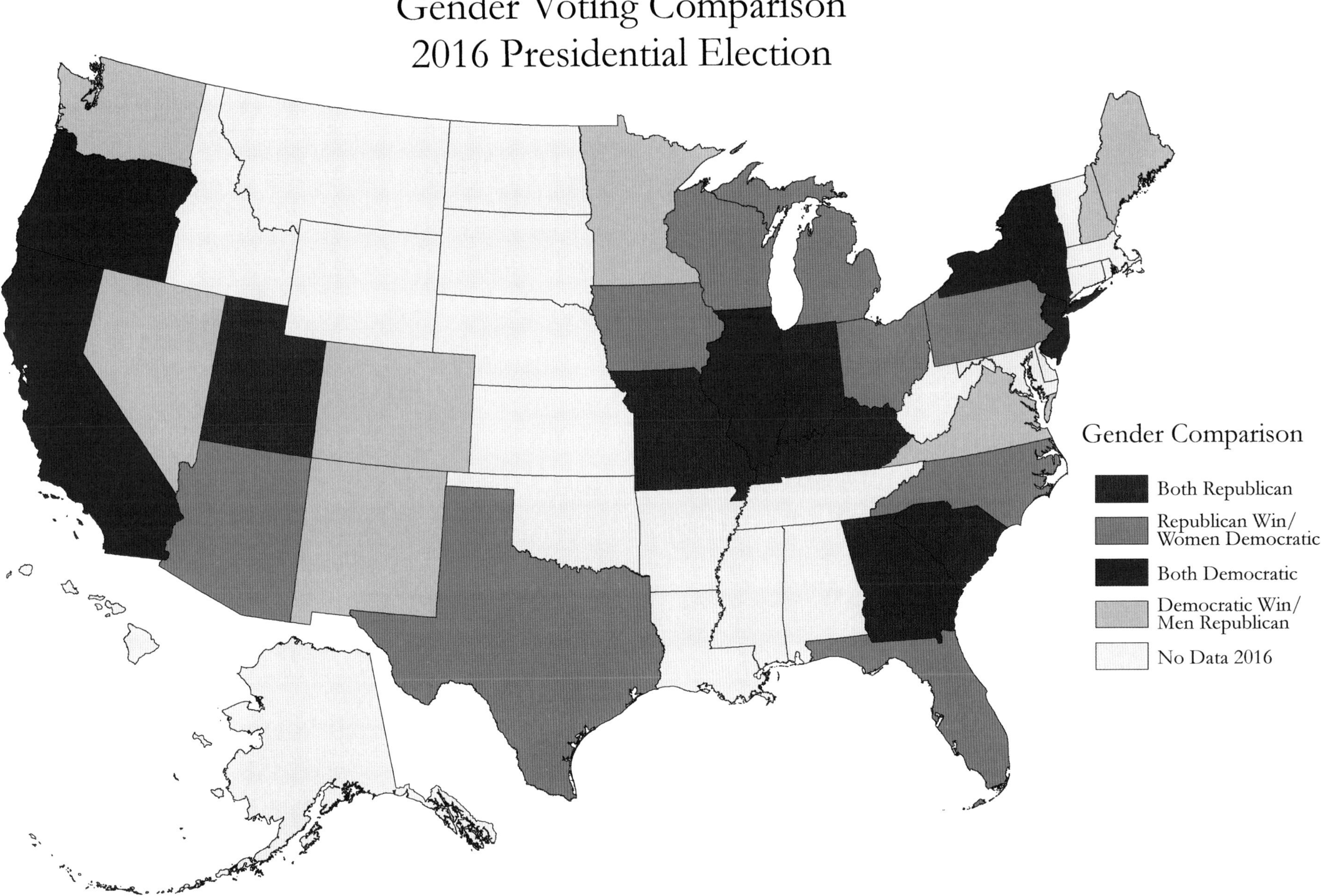
Gender Voting Comparison
2016 Presidential Election
Gender Comparison
Both Republican
Republican Win/
Women Democratic
Both Democratic
Democratic Win/
Men Republican
No Data 2016

that carried the state for Donald Trump. Four of these states were "battleground" states where relatively small electoral majorities resulted in Electoral College wins for the Republican. In Ohio, Pennsylvania, Michigan, and Wisconsin, male voters swung Republican at much higher percentages than female voters, and female Democrats stayed home, increasing the gender gap by as much as 13 points in Pennsylvania. Only in Florida, where the Republican vote remained static for both men and women, and the Democratic vote declined by 3 points for both groups, did the gender gap remain unchanged as third-party voting shifted the state from a marginal Democratic win in 2012 to a marginal Republican one in 2016. There are two other states that moved into the "split" category. Both Arizona and Texas shifted from safe Republican states, where both men and women favored Republican candidates, to Democratic female/Republican male states.

FEMALE VOTING BY COUNTY

Unlike many other demographic variables such as ethnicity, family composition, or religious preference, there is not a great deal of variation in gender distribution at the county level. However, voting behavior in counties in which women are overrepresented (greater than 51.1 percent of the population) or underrepresented (less than 49 percent of the population) provides an interesting microcosm of the national trends in gender divergence in voting.

Counties in which women make up less than 49 percent of the population are, unsurprisingly, overwhelmingly rural, reflecting the gendered makeup of resource extraction and other primary industries that are largely rural-based (figure 6.21). Equally unsurprising, given the national trends in gendered voting, these same counties show an overwhelming tendency to vote Republican. Only 53 of them saw a 50 percent or higher vote for the Democratic candidate while over 200 of them voted Republican, most of them by more than 70 percent. Even in states where the overall vote favored the Democratic candidate, often overwhelmingly so, for example in the Pacific Coast states, most of the male-dominated counties trended Republican. Those that didn't were all in California and had high percentages of Hispanic populations. Similarly, in Texas, New Mexico, and Southern states from Mississippi to North Carolina, the rural counties with an underrepresentation of women, and that voted Democratic, all had minority populations (either African American or Hispanic) of 32 percent or higher. Only in Colorado, where there is a north/south strip of counties with high Democratic voting and low female percentage, is the relationship between male/rural/Republican voting disturbed. Except for some high-percentage Hispanic counties in the south, it appears that a higher-than-average median household income (see figure 6.15), and populations with a BA degree or higher (see figure 6.13) increased the Democratic vote in these counties.

Counties where women are overrepresented (51.1 percent of the population or higher) are rarer in the West, most them occurring along the Lower Mississippi Valley, Gulf, and Atlantic Coast states. These counties are much more evenly split between Democratic and Republican voting. Except for counties with high Hispanic, Native American, and African American populations (in the South and Southwest), most of the female-dominated counties that trended Democratic are metropolitan areas; South Florida, the New England/Mid-Atlantic conurbation, and Chicago and smaller cities such as St. Louis, Kansas City, Cleveland, and Atlanta. Once again, the rural areas, outside the African American–dominated counties of the Mississippi Delta and central Alabama/Georgia, are dominated by Republican voters, reflecting the 53 percent of white women who voted Republican in this election.

Somewhat similar patterns are evident when we examine the distribution of voting behavior relative to the percentage of women in the labor force. Overall, counties with the highest percentages of economically active women had a higher Democratic vote than those with the lowest percentages, and the Democratic vote in high–female participation counties increased between 2012 and 2016. Predictably, these clusters of high female participation/Democratic voting occur on the East and West Coasts and in larger metropolitan areas where service and white-collar jobs dominate. Interestingly, however, these counties also often have high percentages of husband/wife households with young children. Since husband/wife households with minor children overall trend Republican, this suggests that whether it is for economic necessity, or personal fulfillment, households where mothers work outside the home trend Democratic.

However, there is also a swath of higher-than-average female participation throughout the Great Plains and parts of the Mountain West. Here high female labor force participation occurs in those counties in which there is a low percentage of husband/wife households with children under eighteen. In fact, a comparison of the two maps (figure 6.22 and figure 6.23) shows almost an inverse relationship between females in the labor

FIGURE 6.21

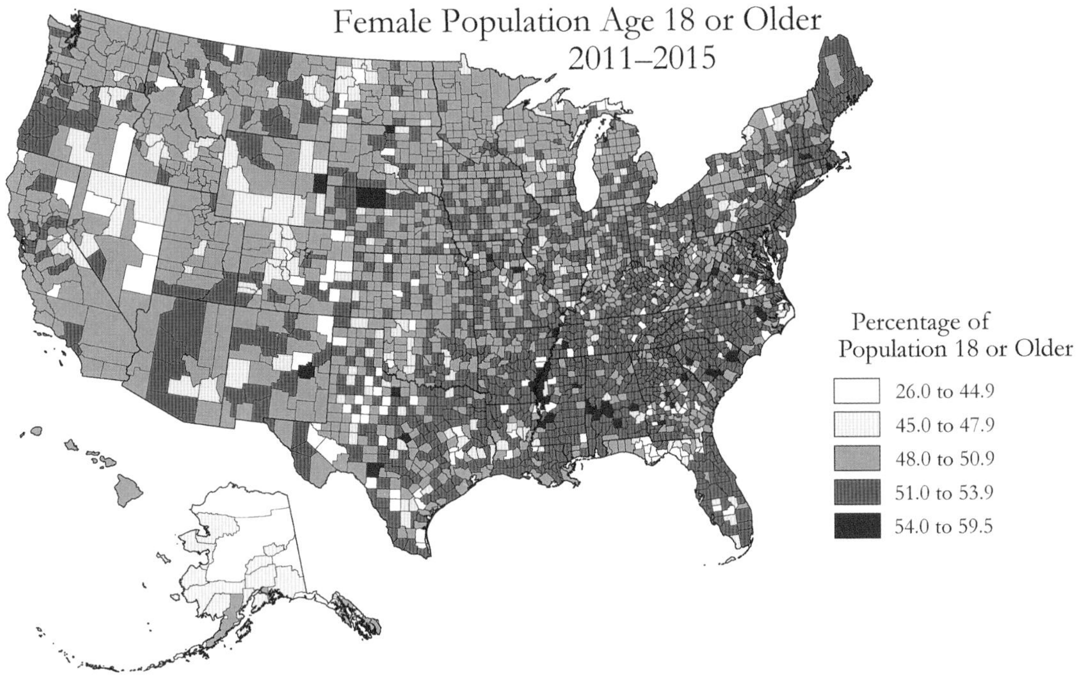

Female Population Age 18 or Older 2011–2015

Percentage of Population 18 or Older

- 26.0 to 44.9
- 45.0 to 47.9
- 48.0 to 50.9
- 51.0 to 53.9
- 54.0 to 59.5

Vote and Turnout in the Bottom 200 Counties Having the Lowest Percentage of Female Population 18 or Older

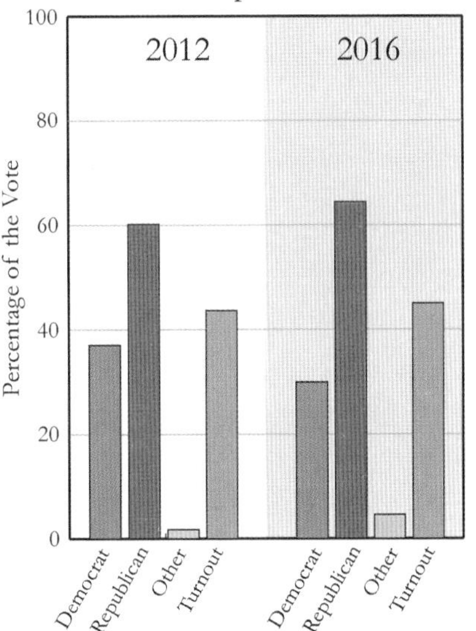

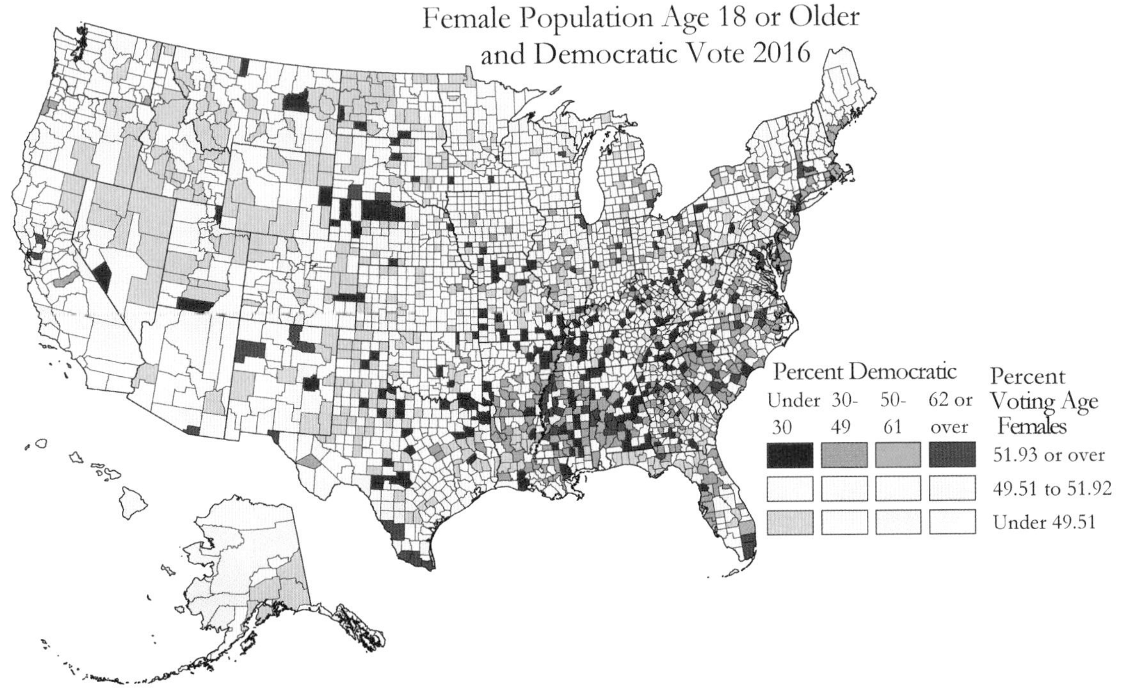

Female Population Age 18 or Older and Democratic Vote 2016

Percent Democratic: Under 30	30-49	50-61	62 or over	Percent Voting Age Females
				51.93 or over
				49.51 to 51.92
				Under 49.51

Vote and Turnout in the Top 200 Counties Having the Highest Percentage of Female Population 18 or Older

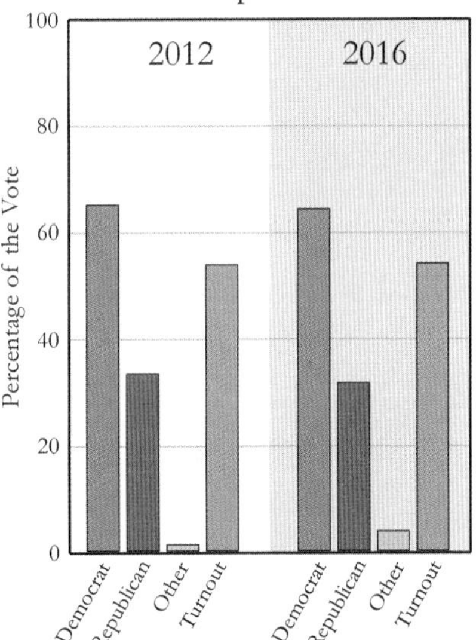

FIGURE 6.22

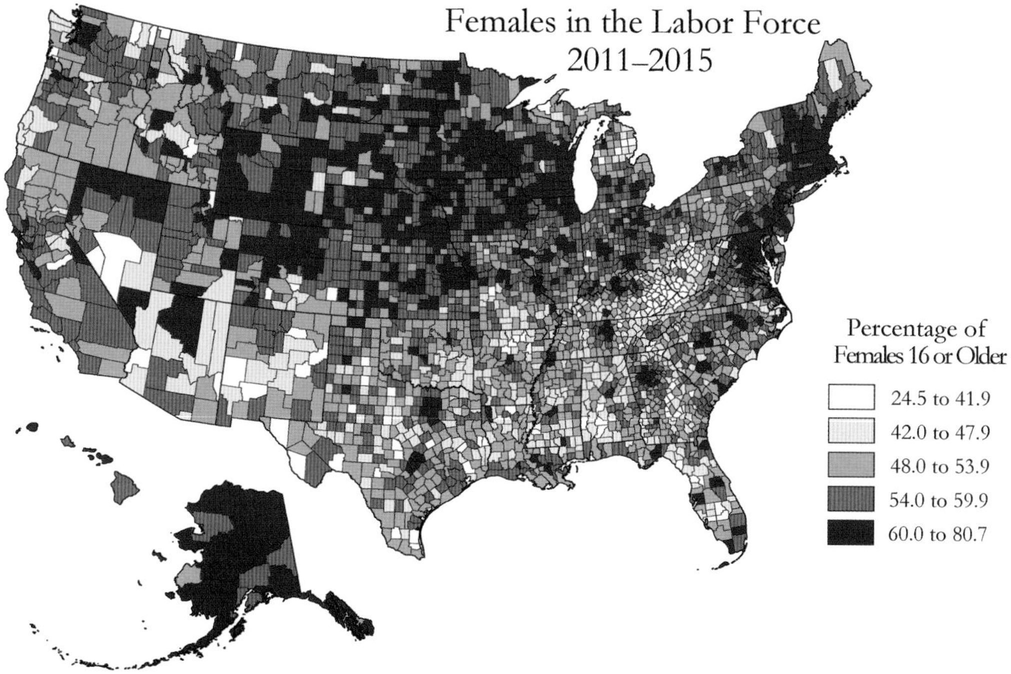

Females in the Labor Force 2011–2015

Percentage of Females 16 or Older

- 24.5 to 41.9
- 42.0 to 47.9
- 48.0 to 53.9
- 54.0 to 59.9
- 60.0 to 80.7

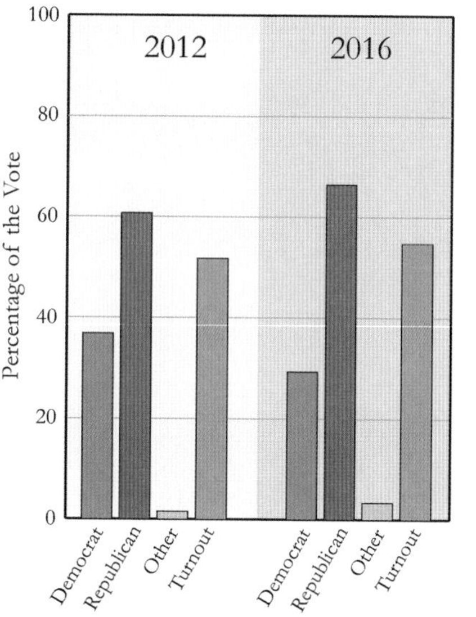

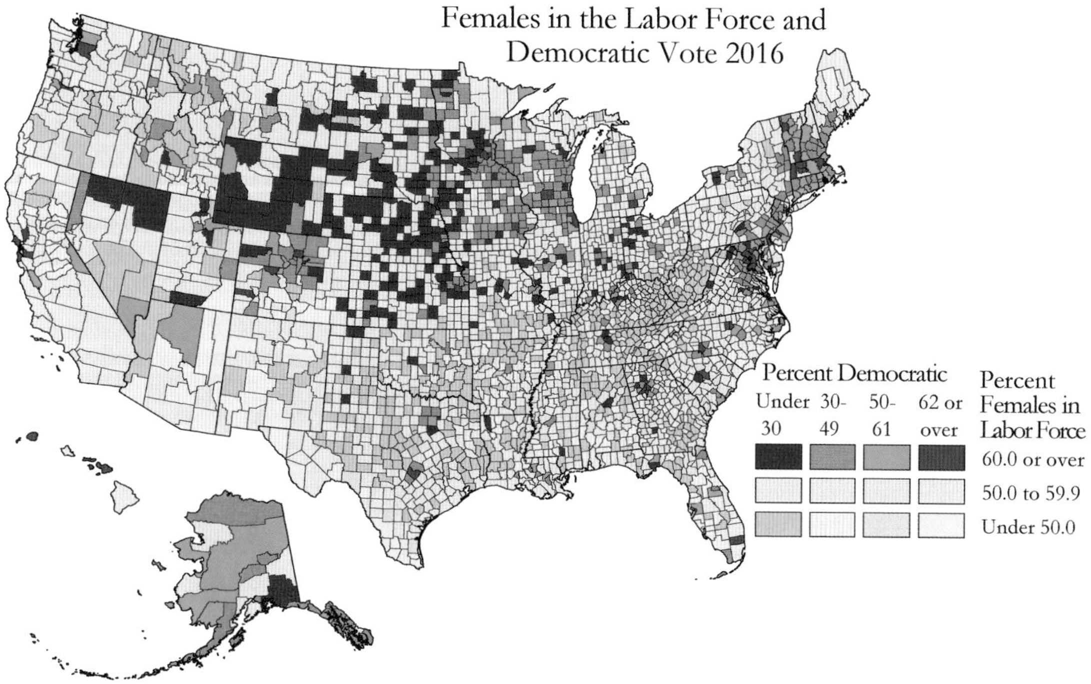

Females in the Labor Force and Democratic Vote 2016

Percent Democratic: Under 30	30-49	50-61	62 or over	Percent Females in Labor Force
				60.0 or over
				50.0 to 59.9
				Under 50.0

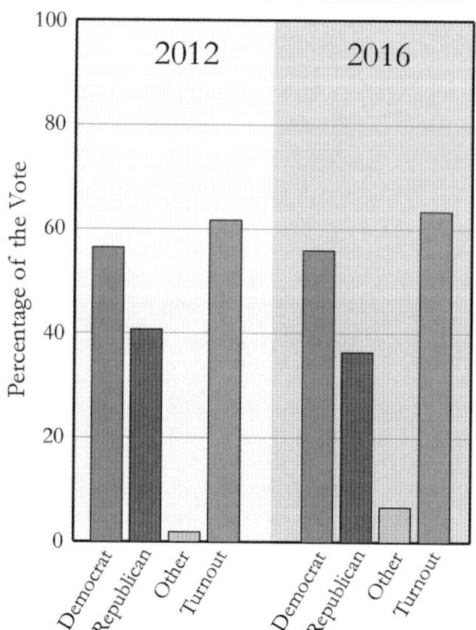

FIGURE 6.23

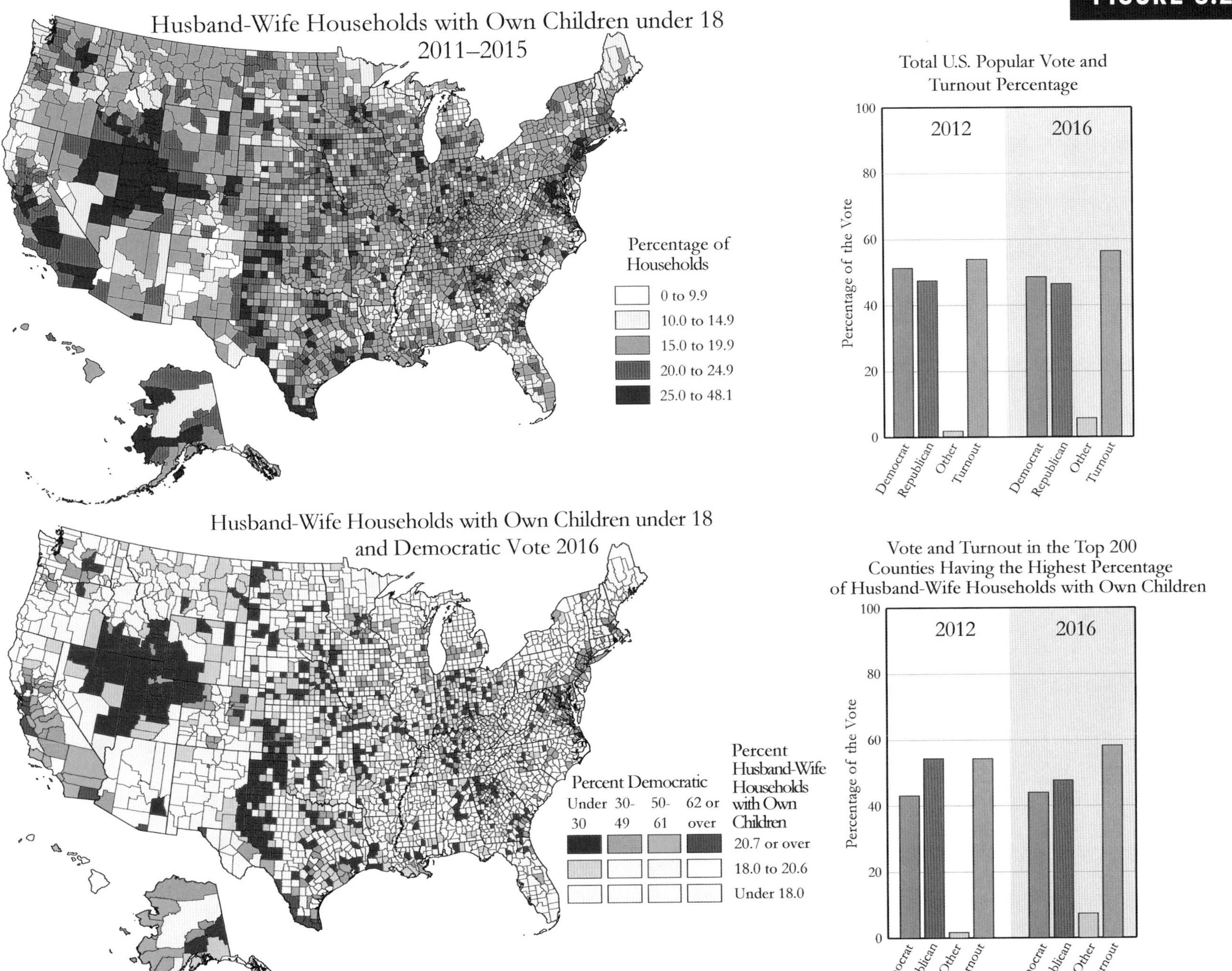
Husband-Wife Households with Own Children under 18
2011–2015
Percentage of Households
0 to 9.9
10.0 to 14.9
15.0 to 19.9
20.0 to 24.9
25.0 to 48.1
Total U.S. Popular Vote and Turnout Percentage
2012
2016
Percentage of the Vote
100
80
60
40
20
0
Democrat
Republican
Other
Turnout
Husband-Wife Households with Own Children under 18 and Democratic Vote 2016
Percent Democratic
Under 30
30-49
50-61
62 or over
Percent Husband-Wife Households with Own Children
20.7 or over
18.0 to 20.6
Under 18.0
Vote and Turnout in the Top 200 Counties Having the Highest Percentage of Husband-Wife Households with Own Children

FIGURE 6.24

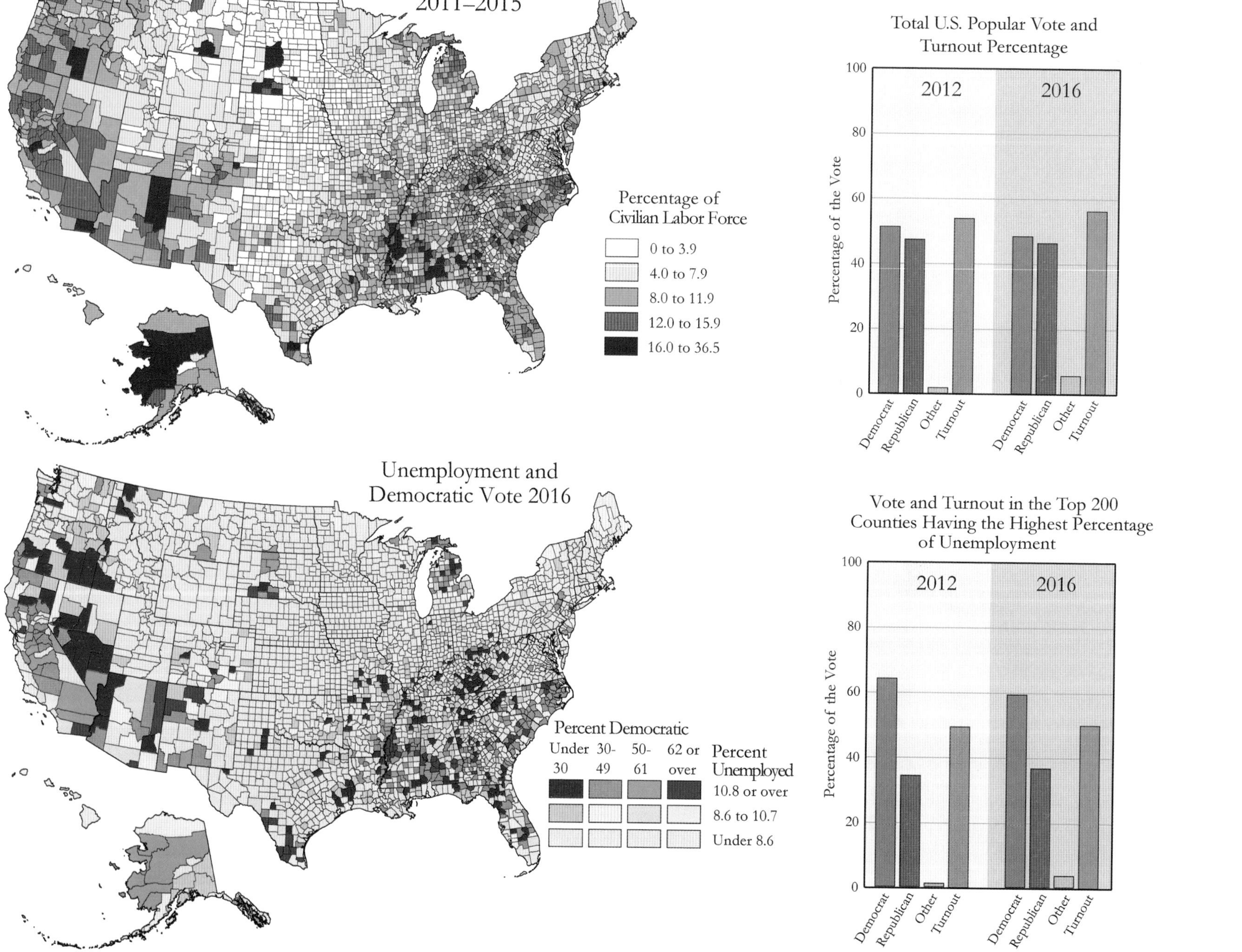

Unemployment 2011–2015

Percentage of Civilian Labor Force

0 to 3.9

4.0 to 7.9

8.0 to 11.9

12.0 to 15.9

16.0 to 36.5

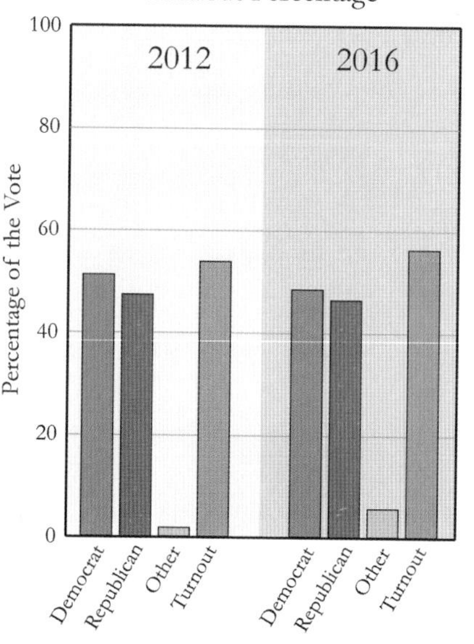

Unemployment and Democratic Vote 2016

Percent Democratic

Under 30	30-49	50-61	62 or over	Percent Unemployed
				10.8 or over
				8.6 to 10.7
				Under 8.6

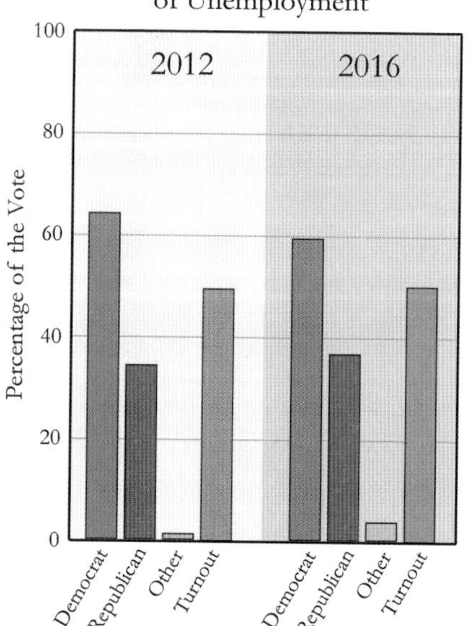

force and husband/wife households with children under eighteen. In the Great Plains, the transition line between high and low female participation in the labor force appears in southwest Nebraska/northwest Kansas, almost exactly where we see the transition from below-average traditional families to above average. Rural, and with economies based heavily on primary, particularly extractive, industries, these counties voted overwhelmingly Republican, indicating a not-unexpected relationship between traditional family roles and Republican voting.

The final area of higher-than-average female labor force participation is in the Midwest from Ohio to central Minnesota, counties with higher-than-average employment in manufacturing. Hit hard by the 2008 recession, these counties do not have particularly high unemployment (figure 6.24) but this area was targeted by much of the anti-globalization Trump campaign rhetoric in the 2016 election. Consequently, counties with high levels of female engagement in the economy, outside the major metropolitan areas, largely voted Republican, although not by as large a percentage as the counties west of the Mississippi.

With the exception of a few counties in southern Texas, the Southwest, and the Deep South, counties with low female labor force participation trend definitively Republican, and an examination of the 200 counties with the lowest female participation rates indicates increased Republican preference over time. From a gap of just over 20 points in 2012, these counties voted 65/30 in favor of the Republican candidate in 2016, indicating that both high and low female participation rate counties became more partisan between the two elections.

Overall, the female vote in the 2016 presidential election reinforced the ongoing gender divisions that have been apparent in US elections since the 1980s. Women continue to be more likely to vote than men, and more likely to vote for the Democratic candidate, with even the percentage of white women voting Republican down by 1 percent from 2012. Eight million more women than men cast votes in November 2016, and over 13 million more women than men cast their votes for Hillary Clinton. However, as the state and county vote disaggregations indicate, these millions of votes were not sufficient to overcome the inherent geographic bias in the US presidential election system.

REFERENCES

Allen, Jodie. 2009. Reluctant Suffragettes: When Women Questioned Their Right to Vote. March 18, http://www.pewresearch.org/2009/03/18/reluctant-suffragettes-when-women-questioned-their-right-to-vote (last accessed June 14, 2017).

CAWP. Gender Differences in Voter Turnout. Center for American Women and Politics (CAWP), Eagleton Institute of Politics, Rutgers University. July 20, http://www.cawp.rutgers.edu/sites/default/files/resources/genderdiff.pdf (last accessed May 30, 2017).

Gallup. US Presidential Election Center. http://www.gallup.com/poll/154559/us-presidential-election-center.aspx (last accessed June 14, 2017.).

McDonald, Michael P. 2017. Voter Turnout Demographics. United States Elections Project, University of Florida. http://www.electproject.org/home/voter-turnout/demographics (last accessed June 5, 2017).

RELIGION AND THE 2016 US PRESIDENTIAL ELECTION

FRED M. SHELLEY

Since the late 1970s, religion has been a significant predictor of voting decisions in US presidential elections. Persons who identify themselves as highly religious and who attend religious services regularly have been much more likely to vote for Republican candidates, whereas those who are not religious are more likely to vote for Democrats. The 2016 election was no exception. Religious voters were much more likely to vote for Donald Trump than for Hillary Clinton. State-level maps showing intensity of religious feeling show strong correlations with maps showing support for Trump.

Between the Civil War and World War II, religious affiliation played a major role in determining the outcome of presidential elections. Generally speaking, Protestants supported Republicans while Roman Catholics supported Democrats. In 1884, for example, Presbyterian minister Samuel D. Burchard described the Democratic Party as the party of "rum, Romanism, and rebellion." Burchard's remark offended many Catholics, who turned out in large numbers to vote for Democrat Grover Cleveland, especially in New York. As a result, Cleveland won New York narrowly and thereby defeated his Republican opponent, James G. Blaine, in the election.

During this time, the "Solid South" was dominated by Democrats and therefore it was largely ignored in national politics. This began to change in the 1960s and 1970s, however, when many white Southerners began to support Republican candidates. Many Southern evangelical Protestants had begun to regard the national Democratic Party as too liberal and too secular. Democrat Jimmy Carter, a Southern Baptist and the first major-party presidential nominee from the South since before the Civil War, won ten of the eleven former Confederate states in 1976, losing only Virginia. Four years later, however, Republican Ronald Reagan won ten of these states in defeating Carter, losing only Carter's home state of Georgia. Reagan's support for issues of concern to evangelical voters, including opposition to the Supreme Court's decision in *Roe v. Wade* legalizing abortion, encouraged many religious conservatives to support his candidacy. White religious voters, especially evangelicals, have supported Republican nominees in large numbers ever since. Many African Americans also identify themselves as evangelical Protestants but most remain steadfastly loyal to the Democratic Party.

RELIGION AND PRESIDENTIAL POLITICS IN 2016

In 2016, the Gallup organization conducted a survey of nearly 175,000 Americans concerning the importance of religion in their lives. Persons were asked whether they felt that religion is important to them and to report whether they attend religious services "every week or almost every week." Those who answered yes to both questions were categorized as "very religious." Those who answered yes to one of the questions and no to the other were categorized as "moderately religious" and those who answered no to both questions were categorized as "not religious." On this basis, the percentage of respondents in each category in each state was determined. Overall, on the basis of this survey, 38 percent of Americans were categorized as "very religious," 30 percent as "moderately religious," and 32 percent as "not religious." The complete results of the survey can be accessed at http://www.gallup.com/poll/203747/mississippi-retains-standing-religious-state.aspx.

Perhaps not surprisingly, many of the states containing the highest percentages of "very religious" people were found in the South. Mississippi led the country with 59 percent, followed by Alabama at 56 percent, and predominantly Mormon Utah at 54 percent. The eighteen states containing the highest percentages of "very religious" persons were all carried by Donald Trump in the 2016 election. Vermont had the lowest percentage of "very religious people" at 21 percent, followed by Maine at 23 percent, and Massachusetts at 25 percent. Of the fourteen states with the lowest percentage of "very religious" people, thirteen were carried by Hillary Clinton, with Alaska as the only exception. This pattern held with the percentage of persons who identified themselves as "not religious." Vermont had the highest percentage of "not religious"

FIGURE 6.25

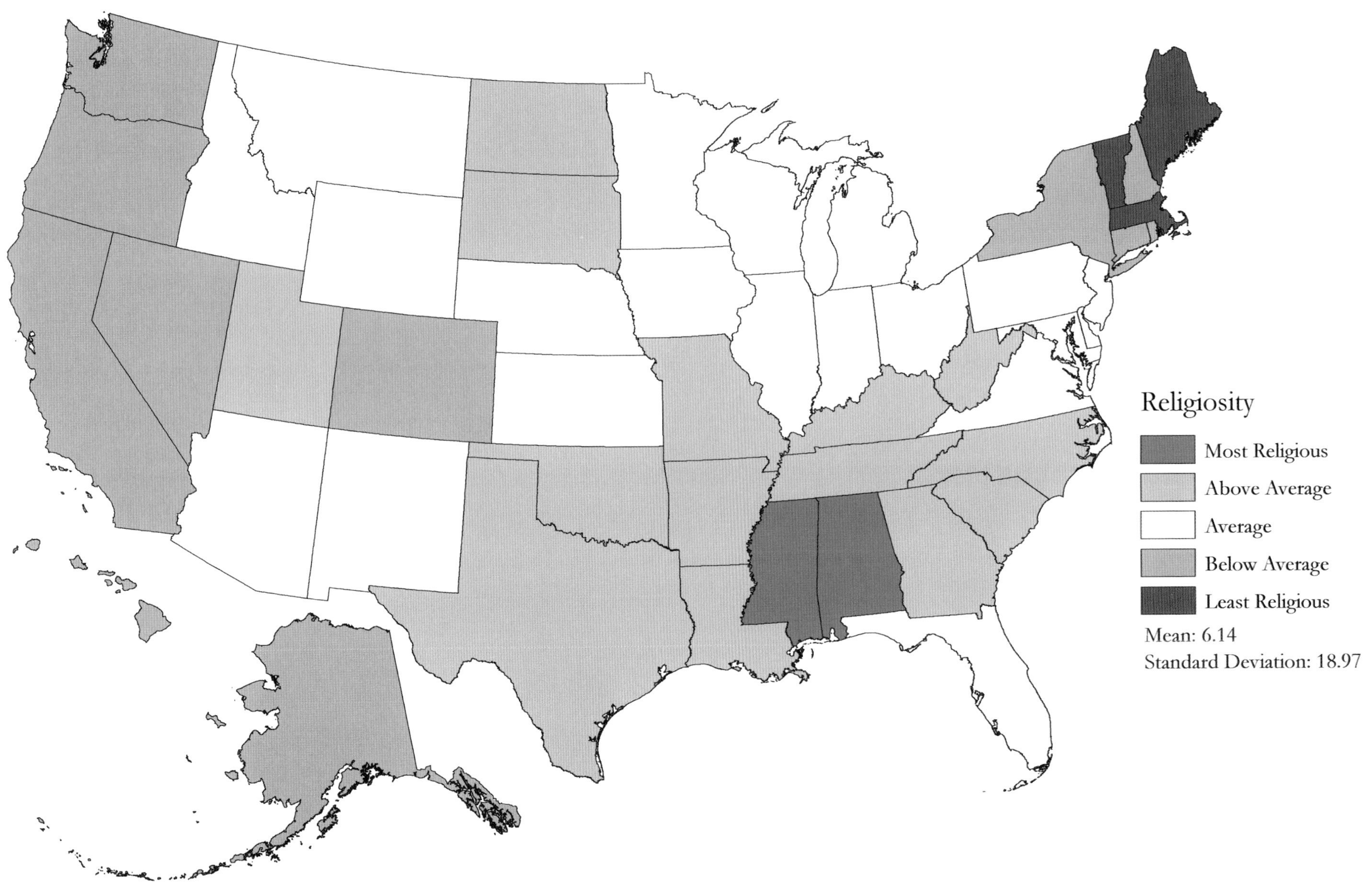
Index of Religiosity
Religiosity
Most Religious
Above Average
Average
Below Average
Least Religious
Mean: 6.14
Standard Deviation: 18.97

people with 58 percent, and Mississippi had the lowest percentage with 12 percent.

A crude index of religiosity by state can be calculated by subtracting the percentage of "not religious" people from the percentage of "very religious" people. For example, Mississippi with 59 percent "very religious" and 12 percent "not religious" has an index value of +47, while Vermont with 21 percent "very religious" and 58 percent "not religious" has an index value of –37 (figure 6.25). The southern "Bible Belt" has the highest scores on this index, whereas the lowest scores come from New England, the Pacific Northwest, Nevada, Alaska, and Hawaii. Comparison of this map with the state-level map of election outcomes illustrates the strong relationship between religiosity and support for Trump in the 2016 election. States with high religiosity indices also reported high vote percentages for Trump, and vice versa.

OUTLIERS AND CONCLUSION

The overall correlation between the Trump vote percentage and the religiosity index by state was r = 0.71. However, some states reported Trump vote percentages higher than would be expected on the basis of the religiosity index. These states included Alaska, Montana, Wyoming, Idaho, West Virginia, and Oklahoma. All of these states have relatively low percentages of non-white voters, histories of dependence on mineral extraction and the energy industry, and in some cases a history of libertarian political views. On the other hand, in states such as Maryland, Virginia, North Carolina, and South Carolina, the Trump vote was less than might be expected on the basis of religiosity. Here, as well as in the Deep South, large numbers of African American evangelical Protestants voted for Clinton. The correlation between religiosity and Trump support would likely be even clearer if it could be measured only for white evangelicals.

Utah represents another exception. A majority of Utah's residents are Mormons, and Salt Lake City is the international headquarters of the Mormon church. Although Utah has been a reliably Republican state for many years, many Mormon voters were unenthusiastic about Trump's candidacy. In the Utah Republican caucuses prior to the Republican National Convention, Trump got only 14 percent of the vote while Senator Ted Cruz, the caucus winner, got 69 percent. Mormon opposition to Trump has been attributed to concerns about Trump's personal morality, his anti-immigration policies along with his anti-internationalist outlook, and concern about Trump's intolerance toward other religions. Evan McMullin, a Mormon from Utah running as a third-party candidate, got 21.5 percent of Utah's popular vote in the general election. More generally, Mormons are recognized as having a high degree of community orientation and were less likely than expected to support Trump, whereas persons with a more libertarian, self-interested outlook on life were more likely to support him. This difference along with race seems to help explain geographical differences in support for Trump on the basis of religiosity, controlling for the basic relationship between party affiliation and religious orientation.

Overall, religion remained an important predictor of the outcome of the 2016 election at a state level and the trend seems unlikely to change at this point. However, younger voters tend to be less interested in formal religion and more oriented to their communities as opposed to themselves relative to their elders. Over the long run, this trend may help to bode well for the Democrats looking toward the future.

BIBLE BELT

DANIEL A. MCGOWIN AND GERALD R. WEBSTER

According to the *New York Times* exit poll following the 2016 presidential election (Huang et al. 2016), Donald Trump won the votes of 81 percent of white evangelical or white born-again Christians. This marked a 3 percent increase for the Republican nominee from 2012 and the highest since the newspaper included the question in its exit poll. Furthermore, Mr. Trump collected 55 percent of the votes from individuals who attend religious services on a weekly basis (CNN 2016; Fox News 2016). Given Mr. Trump's success nationally among white evangelicals, it should not be surprising the pattern that emerged with voters in the Bible Belt.

The term "Bible Belt" was first coined in 1925 by journalist H. L. Mencken following his coverage of the Scopes "monkey trial" in Dayton, Tennessee (Webster et al. 2015). Though ill-defined geographically by Mencken, the term is most often used in reference to the religiously conservative area of the southeastern quarter of the United States. While many attempts to geographically define the Bible Belt exist, we utilize Brunn, Webster, and Archer's (2011) updated geographic definition of the Bible Belt initially published by Charles Heatwole in the *Journal of Geography* (1978). Heatwole based the spatial location of the Bible Belt on the distribution of twenty-four Protestant denominations that believe in the literal interpretation of the Bible. Here we use 2010 data from the Glenmary Research Center to examine the top 200 counties in terms of their proportion of adherents (with a minimum threshold of 43.3 percent) belonging to such denominations. In total there were 29 million members of Bible Belt denominations in 2010, with nearly 20 million being members of the Southern Baptist Convention (Webster et al. 2015). The other large denominations include the Lutheran Church–Missouri Synod (2.2 million), Christian Churches and Churches of Christ (1.4 million), Seventh-day Adventists (1.2 million), and Church of God (Cleveland, Tennessee) (1.1 million) (Webster et al. 2015). While counties with high proportions of members of Bible Belt denominations are located in western North Carolina to northern Florida and west to the Texas panhandle, the Bible Belt's core would today appear centered on the Oklahoma-Texas borderlands.

The Republican Party's platform is one that evolved over the past few decades to focus on cultural issues such as abortion, same-sex marriage, school prayer, and immigration. For example, Mr. Trump's focus on immigration, refugees, and a border wall with Mexico helped him gain votes nationwide among those concerned with immigration (CNN 2016). This focus serves as a means to court the religious conservative vote. Indeed, these issues and the Republican Party's position tend to resonate well with Bible Belt voters. Thus, it is no surprise that Donald Trump won 73.4 percent of the votes in the top 200 Bible Belt counties. And this is despite the fact that Mr. Trump only garnered 46.1 percent of the national popular vote, 2.1 percent less than opponent Hillary Clinton. Secretary Clinton only managed to gain 23.4 percent of Bible Belt votes, a 6 percent decrease from President Barack Obama's proportion in 2012. While this is a major drop, it reflects a continuing trend among Bible Belt voters. Since 2004, Democrats have witnessed a 9.3 percent decrease in votes in this region, while Republicans gained 6.8 percent; Mr. Trump himself accounted for a 4.1 point increase from Republican nominee Mitt Romney in 2012.

In terms of the individual counties (figure 6.26), Mr. Trump won more than 80 percent of the vote in 59 of the 200 top Bible Belt counties. In four counties—Armstrong, Borden, Motley, and Shackelford, in Texas—he won over 90 percent of the vote; these counties are located near the core of the Bible Belt. By contrast, Secretary Clinton managed less than 10 percent of the vote in sixteen counties, receiving less than 7 percent in four counties—Armstrong, Motley, and Shackelford in Texas, and Cimarron in Oklahoma. Mr. Trump won at least 75 percent of the vote in over half (120) of all Bible Belt counties, and at least 60 percent in 182 counties. Secretary Clinton did win two Bible Belt counties—Marengo County, Alabama (51.1 percent), and Fredericksburg, Virginia (59.5 percent)—though this is three fewer than President Obama won in 2012. It is noteworthy that Marengo County is the only Bible Belt county with an African American majority population; Fredericksburg is 22.1 percent African American and 10.1 percent Hispanic.

FIGURE 6.26

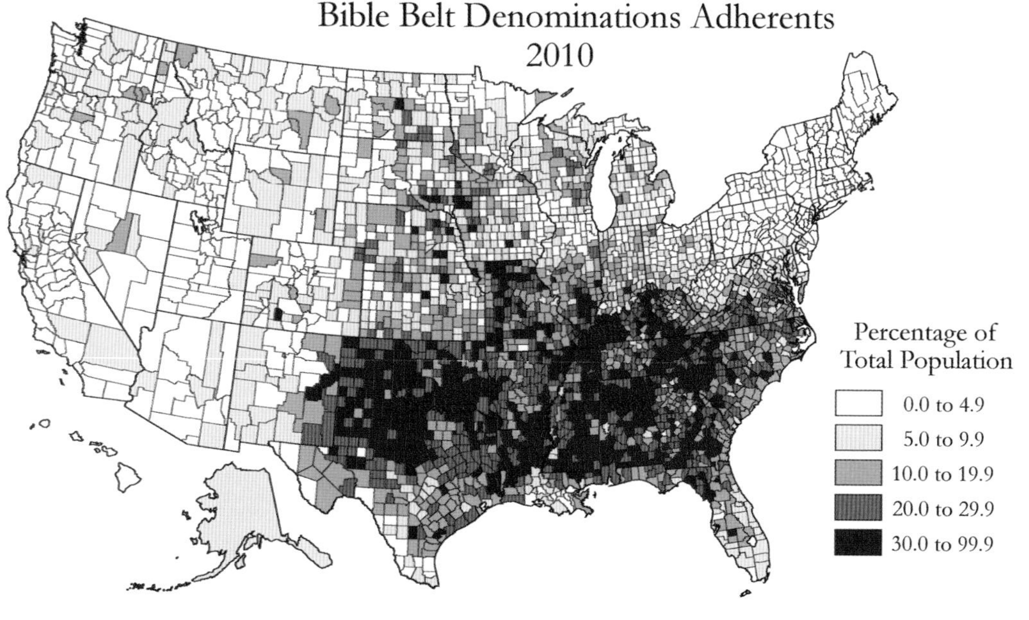

Bible Belt Denominations Adherents
2010
Percentage of
Total Population
0.0 to 4.9
5.0 to 9.9
10.0 to 19.9
20.0 to 29.9
30.0 to 99.9

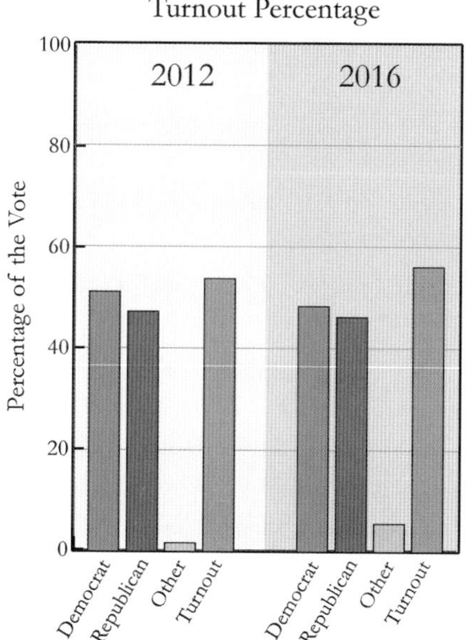

Total U.S. Popular Vote and
Turnout Percentage
2012
2016
Percentage of the Vote
0
20
40
60
80
100
Democrat
Republican
Other
Turnout

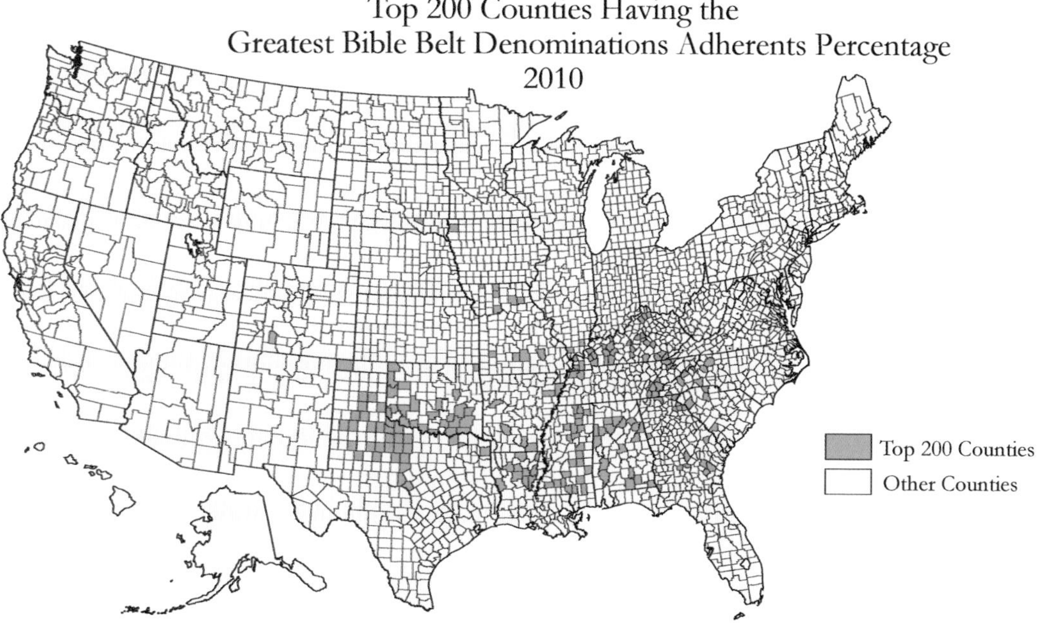

Top 200 Counties Having the
Greatest Bible Belt Denominations Adherents Percentage
2010
Top 200 Counties
Other Counties

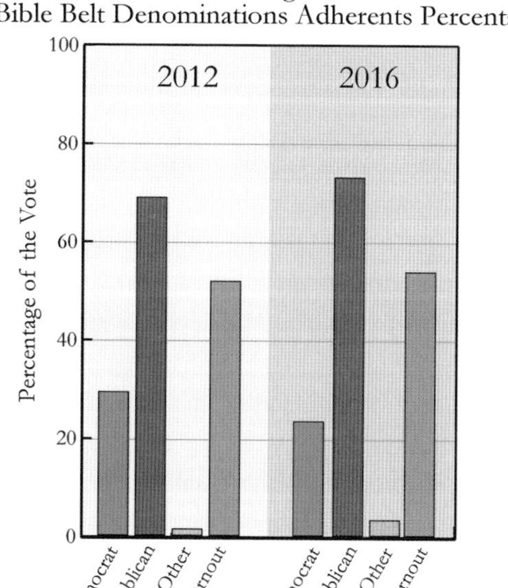

Vote and Turnout in the Top 200
Counties Having the Greatest
Bible Belt Denominations Adherents Percentage
2012
2016
Percentage of the Vote
0
20
40
60
80
100
Democrat
Republican
Other
Turnout

Bible Belt counties display several notable demographic tendencies. For example, Bible Belt counties have an average population of just over 25,000 people compared to approximately 100,000 residents for the average county in the United States. Bible Belt counties also tend to be less densely populated versus the rest of the United States—forty people per square mile versus the national average of eighty people per square mile. In terms of voting, counties with a higher percentage of votes for the Republican Party's nominee tend to have small populations. Indeed, seven of the ten Bible Belt counties with the highest percentage of votes for Mr. Trump have populations of less than 10,000 people, and six of those have a population of fewer than 5,000 people. The populations of Bible Belt counties also tend to include fewer minority group members. Sixty-six percent of the US population is non-Hispanic white, but non-Hispanic whites constitute over 80 percent of the population in the top 200 Bible Belt counties. Finally, education levels lag in the top 200 Bible Belt counties, with less than 15 percent of the adult population having a college degree compared with more than 25 percent nationally. Thus, these religiously conservative counties tend to be sparsely populated, largely composed of white residents with lesser levels of educational attainment, and they strongly support the Republican Party in presidential elections. As an example, of the fifty Bible Belt counties with the highest percentage of votes for Mr. Trump, forty-one have populations at least 80 percent white, and eighteen are more than 90 percent white.

Finally, third-party candidates won 3.2 percent of the vote in Bible Belt counties. While this is still a relatively minuscule number, it also represents a nearly 2 percentage point increase from 2012, or a 159 percent increase in the raw numbers. In 2012, no county in the Bible Belt had more than 5 percent of its vote go to third-party candidates, with Worth County, Missouri, being the only one to crack 4 percent (4.1 percent). In 2016, eight counties exceeded 5 percent while thirty-two counties were above 4 percent. Mineral County, Colorado, witnessed the highest percentage of third-party votes (10.9 percent), followed by Lynchburg, Virginia (8.1 percent), and Fredericksburg, Virginia (7.2 percent). One possible explanation could be dissatisfaction with the two major party candidates. The rise in third-party votes in Bible Belt counties reflected a nationwide increase, with third-party candidates receiving just over 5 percent of the total vote, up from 1.6 percent in 2012.

REFERENCES

Brunn, Stanley D., Gerald R. Webster, and J. Clark Archer. 2011. The Bible Belt in a Changing South: Shrinking, Relocating, and Multiple Buckles. *Southeastern Geographer* 51(4): 513–49.

CNN. 2016. Exit Polls: National President. *Politics*, CNN. November 23, http://www.cnn.com/election/results/exit-polls.

Fox News. 2016. Fox News Exit Polls: 2016 National President Exit Poll. Fox News. http://www.foxnews.com/politics/elections/2016/exit-polls.

Heatwole, Charles. 1978. The Bible Belt: A Problem in Regional Definition. *Journal of Geography* 77:50–55.

Huang, Jon, Samuel Jacoby, Michael Strickland, and K. K. Rebecca Lai. 2016. Election 2016: Exit Polls. *The New York Times*. November 8, https://www.nytimes.com/interactive/2016/11/08/us/politics/election-exit-polls.html.

Webster, Gerald R., Robert H. Watrel, J. Clark Archer, and Stanley D. Brunn. 2015. Bible Belt Membership Patterns, Correlates and Landscapes. In Stanley D. Brunn, ed., *The Changing World Religion Map: Sacred Places, Identities, Practices and Politics*. New York: Springer.

TRUMP, BREXIT, AND THE GLOBAL REVOLT OF THE "LEFT BEHIND"

RON JOHNSTON, DAVID MANLEY, AND KELVYN JONES

To many commentators, Trump's success in the 2016 primary and presidential elections was a further example of an emerging pattern of revolt against the established political order across much of the developed world. Political parties—such as Alternative für Deutschland (Alternative for Germany), Partij voor de Vrijheid (Party for Freedom, the Netherlands), Front National (National Front, France), True Finns/Finns Party, Golden Dawn (Greece), Jobbik (Hungary), Sweden Democrats, Freedom Party (Austria), Pauline Hanson's One Nation Party (Australia), and the United Kingdom Independence Party (UKIP)—promote similar programs, often identified as right-wing populist and nationalist/isolationist/protectionist. Their particular focus varies with national circumstances but all emphasize the negative impacts: of globalization on working-class communities, as manufacturing and other jobs are exported to lower-wage economies; of large-scale immigration (especially of low-wage workers and their dependents) that impacts employment prospects, wage levels, and welfare state demands; and of the loss of sovereignty to supranational institutions. They also contest the impacts of multiculturalism on societal cohesion and distrust the political elites who are accused of being out of touch with the concerns of those "left behind" and who feel alienated from the established political parties, with many rarely if ever voting in elections. (There are many books on the rise of these parties and their class base. See, for example, Standing (2016) on the changing class structure; Gest (2016) for a US-UK comparative study; and Evans and Tilley (2017) on the electoral implications.)

Trump explicitly associated his campaign to "make America great again"—through industrial revival, restricting immigration, and asserting white culture—with UKIP, which he applauded for gaining a referendum on whether the United Kingdom should leave the European Union (EU) and then successfully campaigning with a large segment of the country's Conservative Party to win that poll. Nigel Farage, UKIP's then leader, campaigned for Trump, who welcomed the British reassertion of sovereignty as a paradigm he wished the United States to follow.

UKIP, BREXIT, AND THE POPULIST RIGHT GEOGRAPHIES

UKIP's initial following was largely among right-wing pro-Conservatives who opposed the loss of sovereignty over much economic and social policy to the European Union as well as the United Kingdom's subservience to EU laws and courts. (On UKIP's history, see Goodwin and Milazzo (2015).) Increasingly, however, it focused on large-scale immigration, unregulated under the EU's freedom of movement principle. Large numbers of workers moved to the United Kingdom after 2004, many taking low-paid, low-skilled jobs that employers found hard to fill with local workers, but were presented by UKIP as depressing wages for unskilled and semi-skilled workers and putting pressure on housing, education, and health services. This argument, promoted by large segments of the national print media, attracted increasing support in communities that traditionally strongly supported the social democratic Labour Party but whose promotion of globalization and multiculturalism when in government from 1997 to 2010 alienated its politicians from many of its working-class core supporters, a situation exacerbated by most of its MPs' support for retaining membership in the European Union, contrary to the majority views in many working-class towns.

UKIP's best performance was as the largest party (with 26.6 percent of the votes) at the 2014 European Parliament elections (conducted using proportional representation); its greatest support came from those with no or few educational qualifications, especially whites, and from older voters, especially males. Similar patterns occurred at the 2015 general election (UKIP came in third with 12.7 percent of the votes) and the 2016 referendum, when 51.9 percent, on a high turnout, voted to leave the European Union.

Figure 6.27 shows a consistent geography of support for UKIP and Brexit across the local authorities in which the votes were counted. Two British regions stand out with majorities for Remain and low percentages voting for UKIP two years previously. Scotland—the local authorities

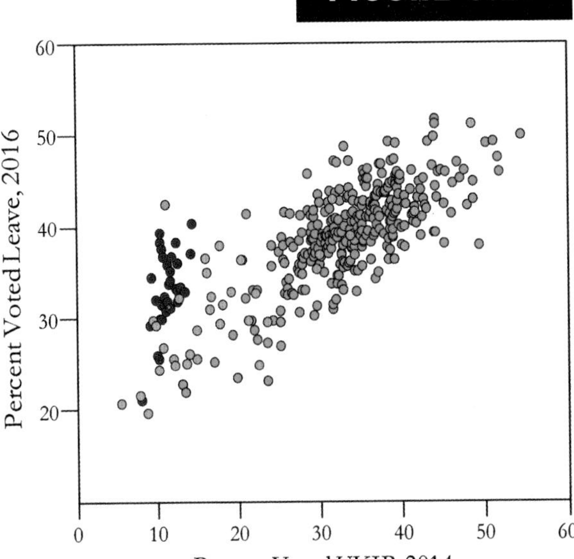

Local authorities in Scotland are shown in red and those in London are shown in blue.

shown in red—voted 62 percent for Remain, reflecting the dominant Scottish National Party's view that Scotland's future would be better in an independent country within the European Union rather than outside it in a newly independent United Kingdom.

London, by far the most cosmopolitan part of the United Kingdom, voted 59.9 percent Remain. Greater support for staying within the European Union characterized not only London's local authorities (shown in blue in figure 6.27) and major metropolitan cities—Birmingham, Leeds, Liverpool, Manchester, Newcastle, and Sheffield—when compared with their conurban hinterlands, but also many other places with concentrations of well-educated young people, such as Cambridge and Oxford. Figure 6.28, for England and Wales, shows a strong negative relationship between the

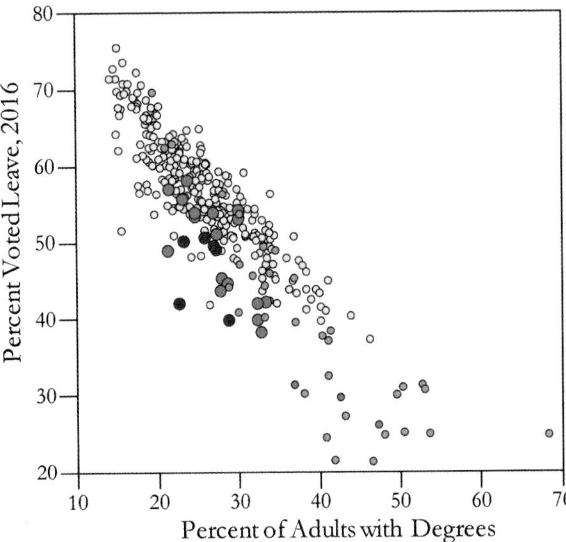

Local authorities in London are shown in blue; the six main metropolitan cities are shown in red; and the major university cities are in green.

percentage of an area's population with degrees and support for leaving the European Union;[1] the six metropolitan centers (Birmingham, Leeds, Liverpool, Manchester, Newcastle, and Sheffield) shown in red, all had lower percentages voting Leave than other places with comparable percentages of their populations having degrees, as did most of the other major university cities (shown in green) as well.

In many parts of Great Britain there was a disjuncture between the party supported at the 2015 general election and voting in the 2016 referendum. This is illustrated by the equal-area cartogram in figure 6.29, which shows the constituencies won by the two major parties—Conservative and Labour—in 2015 according to the referendum majority. Of Labour's 232 seats, 148 returned a majority for Leave, including the great majority of those in northern England and Wales (Labour's traditional heartlands, along with Scotland where the SNP won all but three of the seats in 2015); only in London and several major cities (Birmingham, Leeds, Liverpool, Manchester, Newcastle, and Sheffield) did some Labour seats return majorities for Remain. Similarly, the great majority of Conservative constituencies outside London and the relatively affluent parts of the southeast voted to leave the European Union.

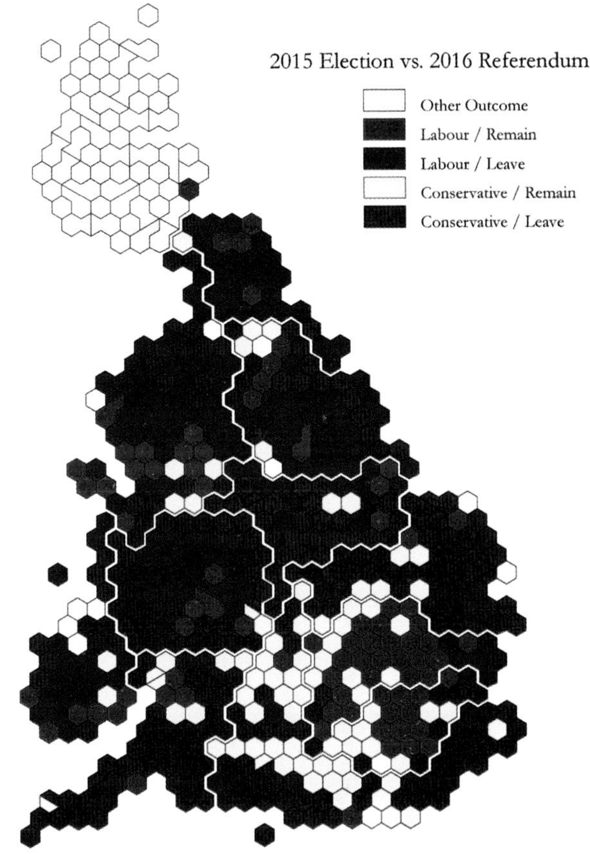

These patterns of voting in the United Kingdom are paralleled by similar geographies of voting for populist, right-wing parties across Europe. Support for their protectionist/nationalist policies is weakest in the capital cities and strongest in the declining industrial regions. In France, for example, voting for the Front National has been lowest in départements with relatively large well-qualified populations, and lower still in Paris, especially in the banlieues with large immigrant (many of them Muslim) populations.

WHO VOTED FOR TRUMP, WHERE?

So, did voting for Trump follow similar patterns? Was his support also greatest among the "left behind"—the poorly qualified older voters—and less among immigrant populations, plus African Americans? Figure 6.30 suggests a similar, but much less clear-cut, pattern to that found in England and Wales. The separate regression lines for counties with more and less than 20 percent of their population either African American or Hispanic converge in places with large percentages of their adult populations having degrees, but they are some 17 percentage points apart in their support for Trump where few have such qualifications. On average, for any percentage of the adult population with a degree, counties with relatively large African American and Hispanic populations gave less support to Trump than similar counties with relatively small non-white populations.

One reason for the greater spread of counties in figure 6.30 than in figure 6.28 is that whereas UKIP, and most comparable European parties, have had to develop support bases and geographies

FIGURE 6.30

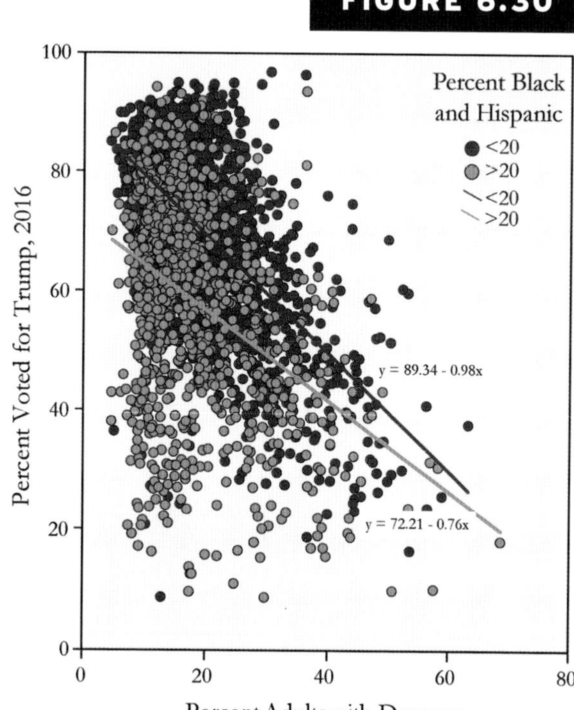

de novo, Trump's victory was built on the Republican Party's pre-2016 deep electoral foundations, as illustrated in chapter 4 of this atlas; any analysis of the socio-geographical base for his success has to take that into account.

Figure 6.31 repeats the graph in chapter 4 (see figure 4.38) and divides the counties into six groups on three criteria (table 6.2): whether mean

FIGURE 6.31

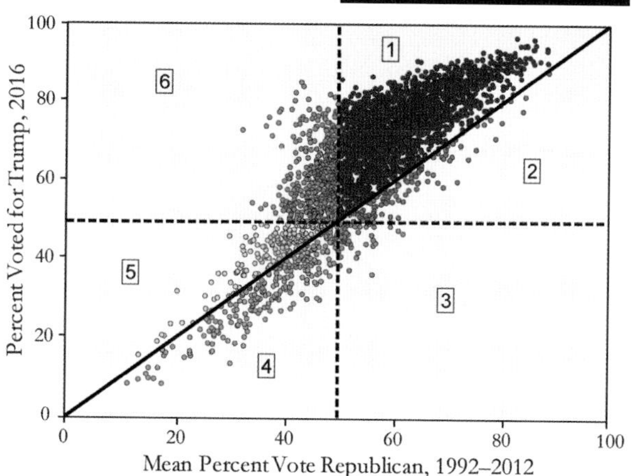

For key, see table 6.2.

support for Republican candidates (1992–2012) was greater or less than 50 percent of the two-party total; whether Trump won greater or less than 50 percent of votes there; and whether Trump's support was greater or less than the mean for 1992–2012. Counties in type 1 are where Trump both gained a majority of votes in Republican strongholds and outperformed the mean; those in type 2 are similar on the first two criteria but Trump underperformed relative to earlier Republican candidates. Types 2, 3, and 4 are counties where Trump performed more poorly than anticipated from the previous six presidential contests, whereas

TABLE 6.2. The Typology of Counties in Figure 6.31

Type	1	2	3	4	5	6
Mean Republican Vote, 1992-2012	>50	>50	>50	<50	<50	<50
Vote for Trump	>50	>50	<50	<50	<50	>50
Trump : Mean	T>M	T<M	T<M	T<M	T>M	T>M
Number of Counties	2,074	113	49	224	190	427

TABLE 6.3. Population Characteristics of Counties According to the Classification in Table 6.2

Type	1	2	3	4	5	6
Percent Hispanic	7.7	13.7	11.7	16.9	12.7	3.7
Percent African American	6.1	8.5	14.0	19.7	18.1	7.7
Percent African American/Hispanic	13.9	22.2	25.7	36.6	30.7	11.4
Percent Non-Hispanic White	82.9	73.1	68.1	54.4	63.0	84.8
Percent 65<	16.7	12.2	10.7	12.1	14.6	16.9
Percent Degree	16.7	27.3	32.5	30.9	21.0	15.8
Percent Unemployed	6.3	5.9	6.3	8.0	8.7	7.5
Percent in Poverty	15.0	12.0	11.5	16.9	18.1	15.6
Median Family Income	40,379	51,232	57,011	49,910	42,268	40,881
Factor 1	-0.25	-0.02	0.33	0.86	0.72	-0.04
Factor 2	-0.22	1.14	1.76	1.14	0.14	-0.28
Factor 3	-0.10	0.46	0.43	0.91	0.48	0.40

TABLE 6.4. Principal Components Factor Analysis of the Population Characteristics: Rotated Factor Loadings

Rotated Factor	1	2	3
Percent African American	0.83	-0.04	0.08
Percent Hispanic	0.01	0.02	0.96
Percent Non-Hispanic White	-0.71	-0.03	-0.77
Percent Degree	-0.14	0.85	0.05
Percent 65<	-0.48	-0.52	-0.39
Percent in Poverty	0.67	-0.62	0.30
Median Family Income	-0.23	0.93	-0.08

types 1, 5, and 6 are where he out-performed his predecessors. The latter group of counties, where Trump gained more support than other recent Republican candidates, outnumber the former by 2,691 to 386.

Nine variables were selected to represent population groups according to their anticipated propensity of voting for Trump. Areas with large percentages of Hispanics and African Americans were expected to give him weak support and be concentrated in types 2–4; degree-holders and younger sections of the population should also be concentrated there. The unemployed, those in poverty, and those with low incomes (the groups targeted by Trump) should be concentrated in types 1, 5, and 6, on the other hand.

Many of these expected relationships are there (table 6.3). Median family incomes were substantially lower in counties where Trump outperformed his predecessors (types 1, 5, and 6), for example, and on average there were many more degree-holders in types 2–4, where African Americans and Hispanics were also relatively more numerous. In general, areas that shifted toward Trump (types 1, 5, and 6) had slightly more older people but there were no differences in the unemployment levels.

One reason for that last finding is that the selected variables are intercorrelated; areas with large African American populations also tend to have high unemployment levels. A principal components factor analysis reduced the variables to three common patterns (table 6.4): the first component combines African American percentages with poverty levels—the more African Americans in a county, the more people living in poverty; the second combines degree-holding with incomes—the more degree-holders in a county, the higher the median income; and the third focuses on the percentage who are Hispanic.

The counties' standardized scores on each factor have a mean of 0.0 and a standard deviation of 1.0, so the mean positive scores for factor 1 in types 4–5 indicate that counties with many African Americans and people living in poverty tend to deliver majorities for Democrat candidates, with the lower mean score for type 5 indicating that there were fewer African Americans and people living in poverty where Trump improved on the average Republican performance than in the type 4 counties where he fell further behind the Democrats.

The greatest difference between types was on factor 2. Counties where Trump performed below the average Republican percentage—types 2–4—had large positive scores: places with large, affluent, degree-holding populations were where he fell back relative to previous Republican presidential candidates. Type 4 counties in particular were also those with high positive scores on the third factor—Republicans have traditionally not performed well in areas with relatively large Hispanic populations, but Trump did even worse than his predecessors.

Table 6.5 replicates table 6.3 with the counties classified according to the difference between Trump's percentage of the two-party vote in 2016 and the Republican mean over the previous six contests. There are some very clear gradients across the five groups, from the 331 counties where Trump underperformed relative to predecessor candidates to the 139 where his vote share was more than 15 points larger. The better his relative performance, the smaller a county's African American and Hispanic percentages, the lower the median family income, and the smaller the percentage of adults with degrees. Again, however, there was little variation in the percentages unemployed and in poverty. But the factor scores clarify the situation: high positive scores on all three in the left-hand columns show Trump performing relatively badly where there were large African American and Hispanic populations, relatively high poverty and low incomes; relatively high negative scores in the right-hand columns show that he performed best, in relative terms, where there were few African Americans, few Hispanics, few degree-holders, and few affluent families.

Although there are similarities in the populations who supported Brexit in the UK and those who voted for Trump in the USA, those parallels must not be carried too far when comparing the two geographies. In Britain supporters of the two main parties were divided about Brexit—Labour supporters more so than the Conservatives—and this is reflected in a map that differs markedly from the country's long-established electoral geography. Trump's victory, on the other hand, was firmly built on his predecessors' foundations, losing ground to the Democrats mainly in areas with large minority populations and/or those with substantial young, well-educated groups. His vote share increased by over 10 percentage points relative to his predecessors' average in 679 counties, of which only 121 were won by Obama in 2012. Of those 121 counties, most—as figure 6.32 shows—were concentrated on New England's northern borders and in the far west of the Rust Belt: 26 were in Iowa, 15 in Wisconsin, 14 in Minnesota, 10 in Illinois, 9 in New York, and 6 in Ohio; they had relatively small African American and Hispanic populations but above average percentages unemployed and living in poverty.

How did Trump increase the Republicans' share of the vote, especially in the party's strongholds? Did he convert more who voted Democrat in 2012 than Clinton converted former Republicans? Did more former Democrats abstain in 2012 than former Republicans? And did more of those who previously abstained, and more first-time voters, turn out for him rather than for Clinton? For answers, we need detailed survey data, but the exit polls suggest that there was little pro-Trump movement overall among those who voted in 2012 so the most likely answers are to be found among those who did not vote in 2012 and those who voted then but not in 2016.

Some interpret the 2016 election and referendum results as harbingers of widespread major changes in political life. Across much of Europe, as clearly illustrated by the French presidential

TABLE 6.5. The Population Characteristics of Counties according to the Change in the Republican Share of the Vote between the 1992–2012 Average and 2016

Change	Decrease	0-5	5-10	10-15	15<
Percent Hispanic	17.7	10.8	6.2	3.1	2.2
Percent African American	10.2	15.1	6.2	1.9	1.0
Percent African American/Hispanic	27.8	26.0	12.4	5.0	3.2
Percent Non-Hispanic White	65.7	70.4	83.4	90.9	94.8
Percent 65<	12.0	15.4	16.7	17.7	18.2
Percent Degree	32.2	19.0	16.5	14.7	13.0
Percent Unemployed	6.3	7.1	6.9	6.9	6.9
Percent in Poverty	12.8	16.5	15.7	14.5	14.8
Median Family Income	54,284	41,272	39,992	40,355	38,818
Factor 1	0.16	0.32	-0.16	-0.41	-0.50
Factor 2	1.49	0.02	-0.27	-0.40	-0.59
Factor 3	0.80	0.26	-0.20	-0.53	-0.64
Number of Counties	331	1,075	993	539	139

FIGURE 6.32

Counties That Provided Majority Support for Obama in 2012 and Trump in 2016

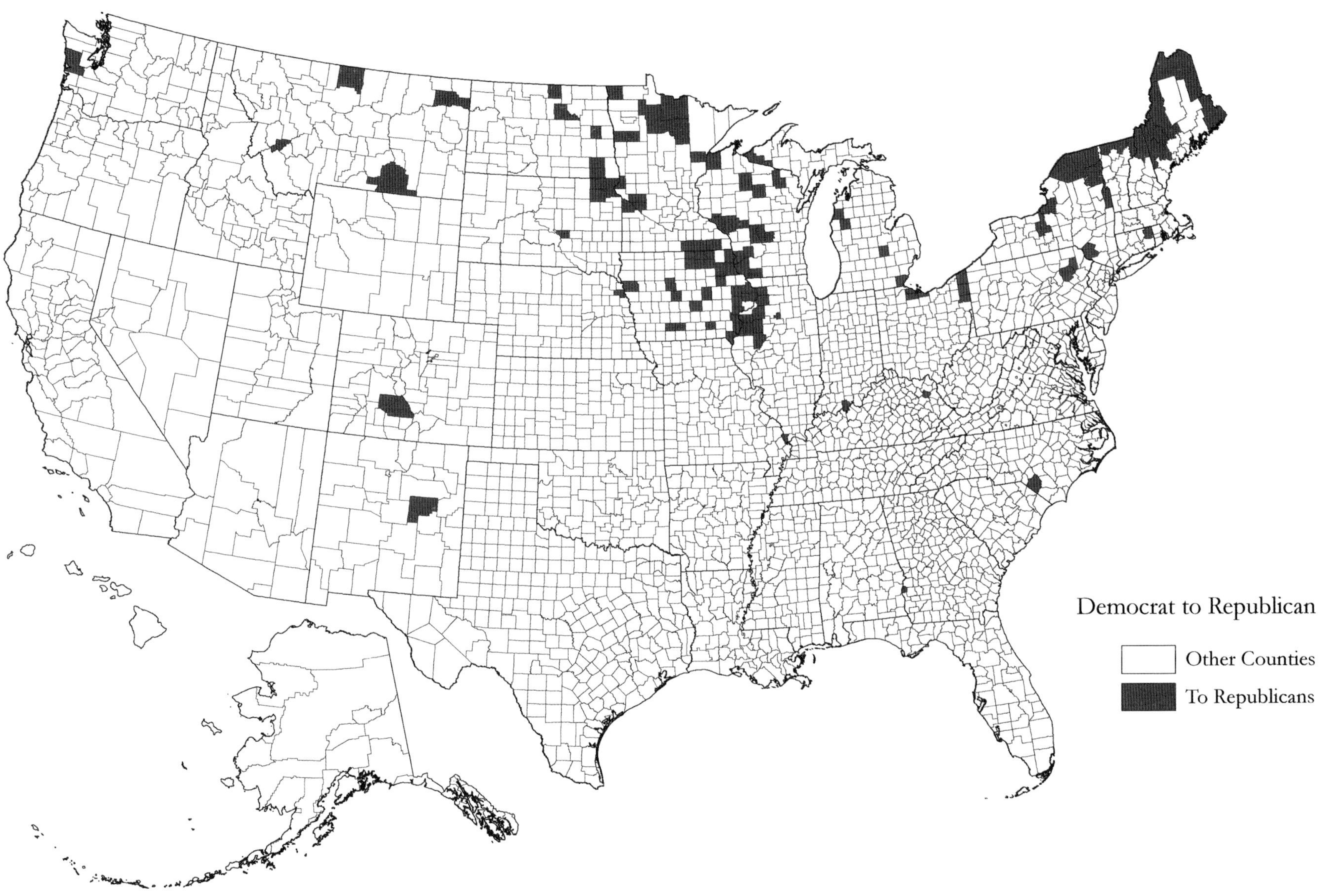

election of May 2017, the established parties of right, center, and left are fighting to retain their traditional support against new parties, candidates, and movements that challenge the beliefs that underpinned several decades of liberalism, globalization, and multiculturalism. Nationalist and protectionist arguments are gaining ground, and new electoral geographies are being sketched out if not yet firmly drawn. According to a commentary on the then upcoming French presidential election:

> Ms Le Pen's nationalist, protectionist, anti-immigrant populism . . . [challenged] Mr Macron's defence of open markets and European integration. It is the same choice that was offered in last year's US presidential election and the UK's EU referendum. In all three cases, it cuts across conventional party lines. (Anne-Sylvaine Chassany, *The Financial Times*, March 4, 2017)

Trump's victory appears to fit that mold in many respects, but the geography of his support does not suggest that his victory cut across conventional party lines. The country's political landscape had become increasingly fractured over recent decades, and he accentuated that trend. Whether it continues . . . ?

NOTE

1. In Northern Ireland, for which comparable data are not available, 56 percent favored staying in the European Union—reflecting the closeness of ties with the Republic of Ireland; support for Remain was greatest in the areas with large Roman Catholic populations, most of whom vote at elections for parties favoring a united Ireland.

REFERENCES

Evans, Geoffrey, and James Tilley. 2017. *The New Politics of Class: The Political Exclusion of the British Working Class*. Oxford: Oxford University Press.

Gest, Justin. 2016. *The New Minority: White Working Class Politics in an Age of Immigration and Inequality*. Oxford: Oxford University Press.

Goodwin, Matthew, and Caitlin Milazzo. 2015. *UKIP: Inside the Campaign to Redraw the Map of British Politics*. Oxford: Oxford University Press.

Standing, Guy. 2016. *The Precariat: The New Dangerous Class*. London: Bloomsbury.

7 CONGRESSIONAL ELECTIONS AND ROLL-CALL VOTES

MEMBERSHIP, PARTY, AND CAUCUSES IN THE 114TH CONGRESS

ERIN H. FOUBERG

The 114th Congress was in session during the contentious Republican and Democratic presidential primaries as well as the US presidential election. Starting on January 3, 2015, and ending on January 3, 2017, the 114th Congress included the last two full years of Barack Obama's presidency. Republican primary candidate Senator Ted Cruz was the first to enter the Republican race within months of the convening of the 114th Congress, on March 3, 2015, and Democratic Party nominee Hillary Clinton was the first to enter the Democratic race on April 12, 2015. All of the Republican and Democratic primaries took place between the Iowa Caucus on February 1 and the District of Columbia primary on June 14, 2016. The election of President Donald Trump and the transition toward his inauguration occurred during the last two months of the 114th Congress.

Figure 7.1 shows the party affiliation in the US House of Representatives during the 114th Congress. Elections for the 114th Congress reflected a growing dissatisfaction with both the ineffectiveness of the 113th Congress and the progressive politics of President Barack Obama in some parts of the country. Congressional approval in the first year of the 113th Congress was at a record low of 14 percent, and at the end of the 113th Congress was not much better, at 15 percent among all voters (Riffkin 2014).

Republicans controlled the House and Democrats controlled the Senate in the 113th Congress. Elections for the 114th Congress voted in several more Republicans, leading to Republican control of both the House and Senate. Democrats began the 113th Congress with fifty-three Democratic Senators plus two independents who caucused with Democrats. After the 2014 elections, at the start of the 114th Congress, Democrats held only forty-four Senate seats plus two independents, and Republicans had the majority with fifty-four seats. Republican control of the House increased after the 2014 elections. At the beginning of the 113th Congress, Republicans held 240 seats in the House, and after the 2014 elections, Republican majority in the House increased to 247 seats to kick off the 114th Congress.

The 114th Congress had a record number of women, with eighty-eight in the House (including four delegates) and twenty in the Senate, a record number of Hispanic or Latino members, and an average age "among the highest of any congress in recent US history" (Manning 2015). The average length of service of members of the House, 8.8 years (4.4 terms) was low in the 114th Congress compared to an average of 10.3 years in the 110th Congress. "At the beginning of the 114th

FIGURE 7.1

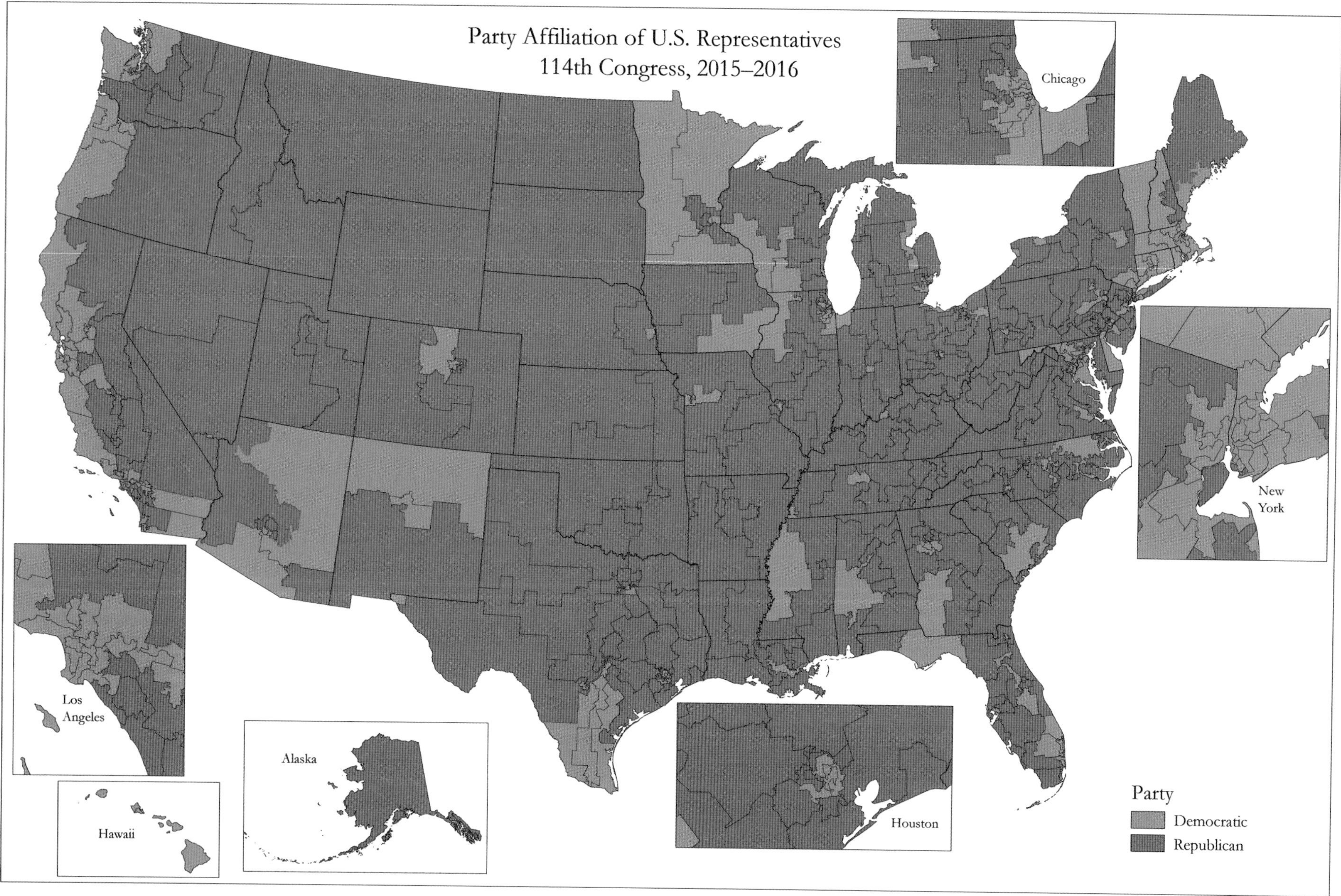
Party Affiliation of U.S. Representatives
114th Congress, 2015–2016
Chicago
New
York
Los
Angeles
Alaska
Hawaii
Houston
Party
Democratic
Republican

FIGURE 7.2

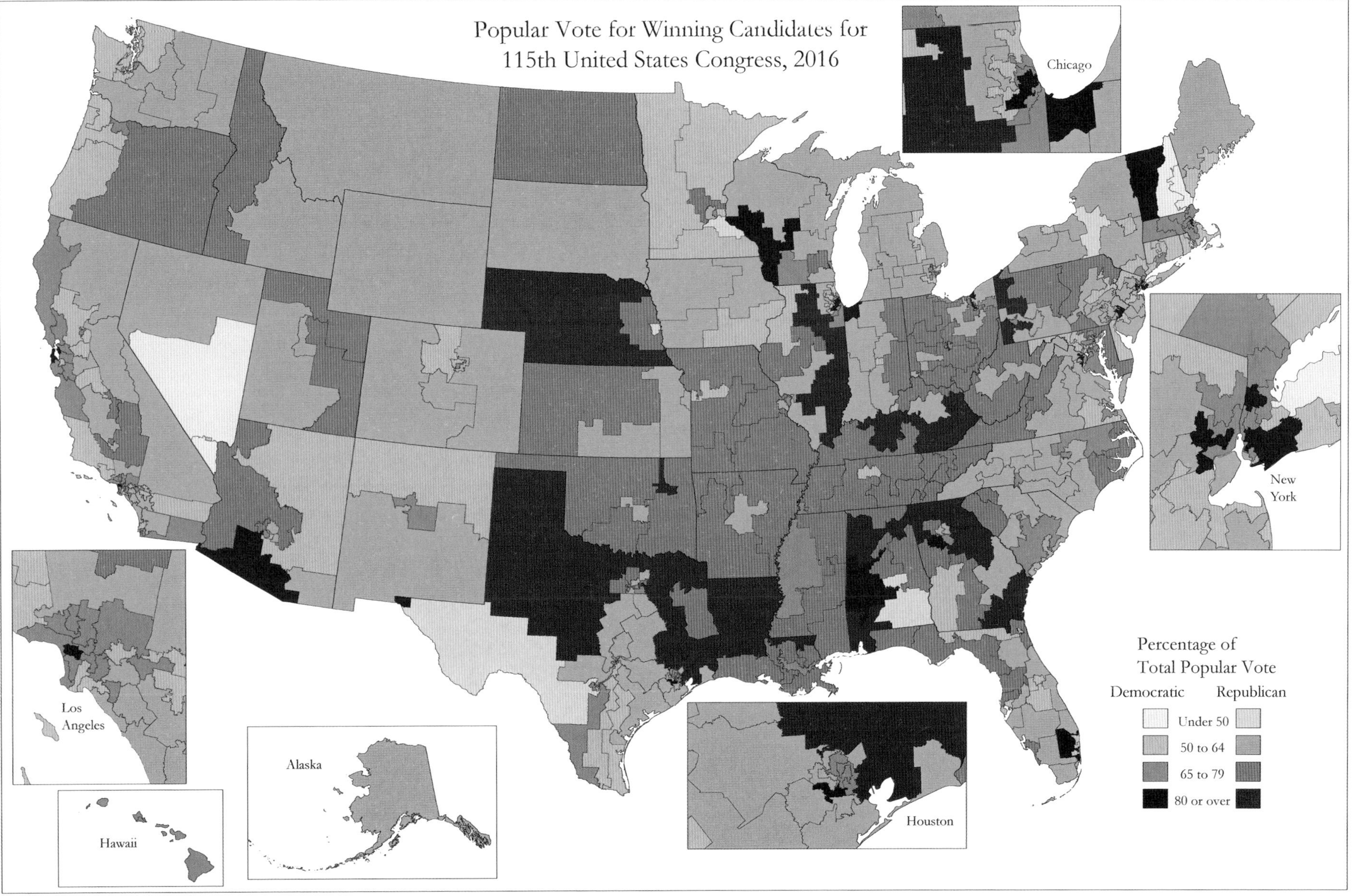

Popular Vote for Winning Candidates for
115th United States Congress, 2016
Chicago
New
York
Los
Angeles
Alaska
Hawaii
Houston
Percentage of
Total Popular Vote
Democratic
Republican
Under 50
50 to 64
65 to 79
80 or over

Congress, 131 Representatives, including 2 Delegates (30.4 percent of House members), had no more than 2 years of house experience" (Manning 2015).

Many of the newest Republican members of the House had an immediate impact on legislation by banding together to form the Freedom Caucus. Caucuses are fluid in the House, reflecting political and philosophical concerns of the country. The Blue Dog Democrats, formed as a strong moderate voice in 1995, peaked in membership in 2008 with fifty-four members but were relatively weak by the 114th Congress (fourteen members). The Tea Party, which rose to prominence by influencing redistricting following the 2010 Census and had sixty members in the House in the 112th Congress (Mehta 2014), had also weakened by the 114th Congress to between twenty-four and thirty-six members (Fuller 2015). Regardless of the Congress or caucus, members associate voluntarily, and a caucus is generally comprised of members of one political party.

The demise of the Tea Party Caucus occurred both because the popularity of the Tea Party among Republican voters declined quickly between 2010 and 2014 (from 48 to 33 percent among Republican voters) and because, in many ways, the Tea Party accomplished what they set out to do: shift the Republican Party to positions that are more conservative. "Over the long term, the House Republican caucus has gotten consistently more conservative" according to the DW-NOMINATE score, which measures roll-call votes "centered on the role of government in the economy; higher scores show more opposition to that overlap" (Bump 2015). The DW-NOMINATE scale ranges from –1 (most liberal) to +1 (most conservative).

Representative Jim Jordan and eight other founders formed the Freedom Caucus at the beginning of the 114th Congress. Membership in the Freedom Caucus is by invitation only, and the caucus does not publish a list of who belongs. Pew Research Center "confirmed the identities of 36 Freedom Caucus members through representatives' public statements, their comments to the media or their offices' direct responses" (DeSilver 2015). Many members of the group were previously active in the Tea Party Caucus. Using the DW-NOMINATE score of these thirty-six members of the Freedom Caucus, DeSilver found they are among the most conservative members of Congress with an average score of 0.691, compared to the average score of all other Republicans at 0.457. The average of Democrats is –0.409. Freedom Caucus members are also less senior than average Republican or Democrat members. "Of the 36 identified members, 26 (72 percent) were first elected in 2010 or later, compared with 54% of other House Republicans" (DeSilver 2015).

Freedom Caucus members affected the 114th Congress by voting as a bloc. Freedom Caucus districts are spread across twenty-five states with many in Appalachia, the South, and the Southwest. Although relatively few Republicans belong to the Freedom Caucus, when they vote as a bloc against Republican leadership initiatives, they drop Republican votes below a majority. One of the immediate and far-reaching impacts the Freedom Caucus had on the 114th Congress was removing Rep. John Boehner (Ohio) as Speaker of the House and replacing him with Rep. Paul Ryan (Wisconsin) in October 2015.

As figure 7.2 shows, the darker red House districts had large majority votes for Republican candidates, and the darker blue House districts had large majority votes for Democrat candidates. Elections for the 115th Congress occurred with the 2016 presidential election. Freedom Caucus members fared well in the elections, outperforming support for President Trump in their own districts by an average of 7.5 percent (Kelly and McMinn 2017). President Trump will need the support of the Freedom Caucus to use the House Republican majority to pass legislation in his agenda and to keep his campaign promise to repeal and replace the Affordable Care Act.

REFERENCES

Bump, Phillip. 2015. Tea Party Support Hits a New Low—Because the Tea Party Already Won. *Washington Post*. October 26, https://www.washingtonpost.com/news/the-fix/wp/2015/10/26/tea-party-support-hits-a-new-low-because-the-tea-party-already-won/?utm_term=.60a675992336 (last accessed June 15, 2017).

DeSilver, Drew. 2015. What Is the House Freedom Caucus, and Who's in It? Pew Research Center. October 20, http://www.pewresearch.org/fact-tank/2015/10/20/house-freedom-caucus-what-is-it-and-whos-in-it (last accessed June 15, 2017).

Fuller, Matt. 2015. New Tea Party Caucus Chairman: DHS Fight Could Break the GOP. *Roll Call*. February 26, http://www.rollcall.com/news/home/new-tea-party-caucus-chairman-dhs-fight-could-break-the-gop (last accessed June 15, 2017).

Kelly, Ryan, and Sean McMinn. 2017. Members Who Vote With Freedom Caucus Did Better Than Trump in Elections. *Roll Call*. March 31, http://www.rollcall.com/news/politics/members-vote-freedom-caucus-better-trump-elections (last accessed June 15, 2017).

Manning, Jennifer. 2015. Membership of the 114th Congress: A Profile. Congressional Research Service. October 31, https://archive.org/details/R43869MembershipoftheI14thCongressAProfile-crs (last accessed June 15, 2017).

Mehta, Dhrumil. 2014. The Age of Tea Party Members in Congress. *Five Thirty Eight*. May 5, https://fivethirtyeight.com/datalab/the-age-of-tea-party-members-in-congress (last accessed June 15, 2017).

Riffkin, Rebecca. 2014. 2014 US Approval of Congress Remains Near All-Time Low. Gallup. December 15, http://www.gallup.com/poll/180113/2014-approval-congress-remains-near-time-low.aspx (last accessed June 15, 2017).

114TH CONGRESS HOUSE ROLL-CALL VOTES

ERIN H. FOUBERG

The 114th Congress was in session during the last two years of President Barack Obama's second term. Republicans held the majority in both the House and Senate in the 114th, having taken control of the Senate in the 2014 midterm elections. The 114th Congress was marked with continued political partisanship, enhanced by a contentious presidential election.

To gauge partisanship in Congress, political scientists Keith Poole and Howard Rosenthal developed the DW-NOMINATE metric to measure roll-call votes by members of Congress on a two-dimensional grid. "One dimension represents the traditional liberal-conservative spectrum; the second picks up regional issue differences, such as the split between Northern and Southern Democrats over civil rights in the 1950s and 1960s" (DeSilver 2014). Poole and Rosenthal's data set includes every member of Congress who has served since 1789. Each member has a score between -1 (liberal) to +1 (conservative), with 0 being moderate.

An analysis of the DW-NOMINATE scores of members of the House of Representatives by party over time confirms "formerly significant regional distinctions have declined in importance—or, more precisely, merged into the overall liberal-conservative divide" (DeSilver 2014). In 1973–1974, members of Congress had overlapping ideologies. Using DW-NOMINATE scores, DeSilver (2014) found that in 1972–1973, 240 members of the House fell between the most conservative Democrat and the most liberal Republican, creating a large moderate voice in Congress. By 2011–2012, there was "no overlap" in political ideologies in either the House or Senate, meaning that every Republican scored more conservative than every Democrat did on the metric.

Based on Poole and Rosenthal's findings, the 114th Congress was no different than previous Congresses. Partisanship in the House is evident in the five roll-call votes mapped and discussed in this entry. At the end of the 114th Congress (2015–2016), the House of Representatives had 247 Republicans, 187 Democrats, and one vacancy. Both the Democrat and Republican presidential primaries took place during the 114th Congress. The Republican-led House took on several issues central to President Obama's agenda, against which Republican presidential primary candidates were running. In three roll-call votes analyzed here, the House voted on issues raised in the primaries and presidential campaigns: Repeal of the Affordable Care Act, Sanctuary Cities, and LGBT Anti-Discrimination.

REPEAL OF THE AFFORDABLE CARE ACT

On February 2, 2016, Republicans in the House and Senate used the reconciliation process to circumvent a Democratic filibuster in the Senate and pass H.R. 3762, dismantling much of the Affordable Care Act. Republican members of Congress saw the vote as symbolic, knowing President Obama would veto it. Reconciliation requires only a simple majority in the Senate, instead of sixty votes. The vote was significant because it was the first of more than fifty bills repealing all or part of the Affordable Care Act that made it to the president's desk (Fabian 2016). On January 8, President Obama vetoed the bill. Figure 7.3 maps the House vote to overturn the president's veto of H.R. 3762 on February 2, 2016. Following party lines almost perfectly, 240 Republicans and 1 Democrat voted in favor of overturning the veto and 3 Republicans and 183 Democrats voted against, falling short of the two-thirds required.

SANCTUARY CITIES

Dozens of US cities passed sanctuary city ordinances in the 1980s, protecting undocumented migrants from deportation when reporting crimes to police. During the Republican presidential primary, Donald Trump called Mexican immigrants rapists and criminals in a June 2015 speech. On July 1, 2015, conservatives in the House had an example of a Mexican criminal to hold up to rally against sanctuary cities. The bill was a response to the July murder of Kathryn Steinle, a San Francisco native, who was killed by Juan Francisco Lopez-Sanchez, an undocumented immigrant from Mexico and convicted felon (Colbern 2015).

FIGURE 7.3

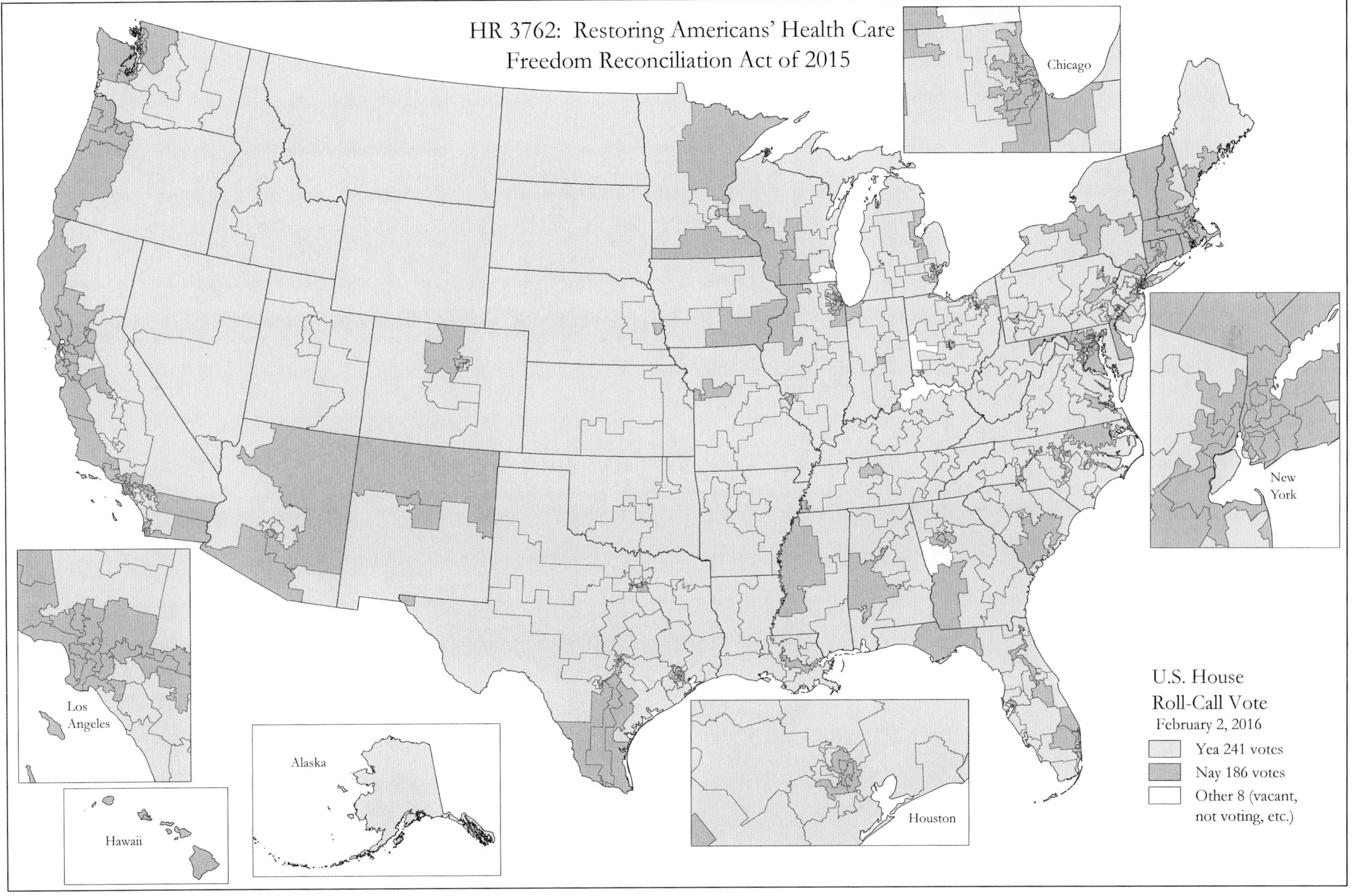

HR 3762: Restoring Americans' Health Care
Freedom Reconciliation Act of 2015
Chicago
New
York
Los
Angeles
Alaska
Hawaii
Houston
U.S. House
Roll-Call Vote
February 2, 2016
Yea 241 votes
Nay 186 votes
Other 8 (vacant,
not voting, etc.)

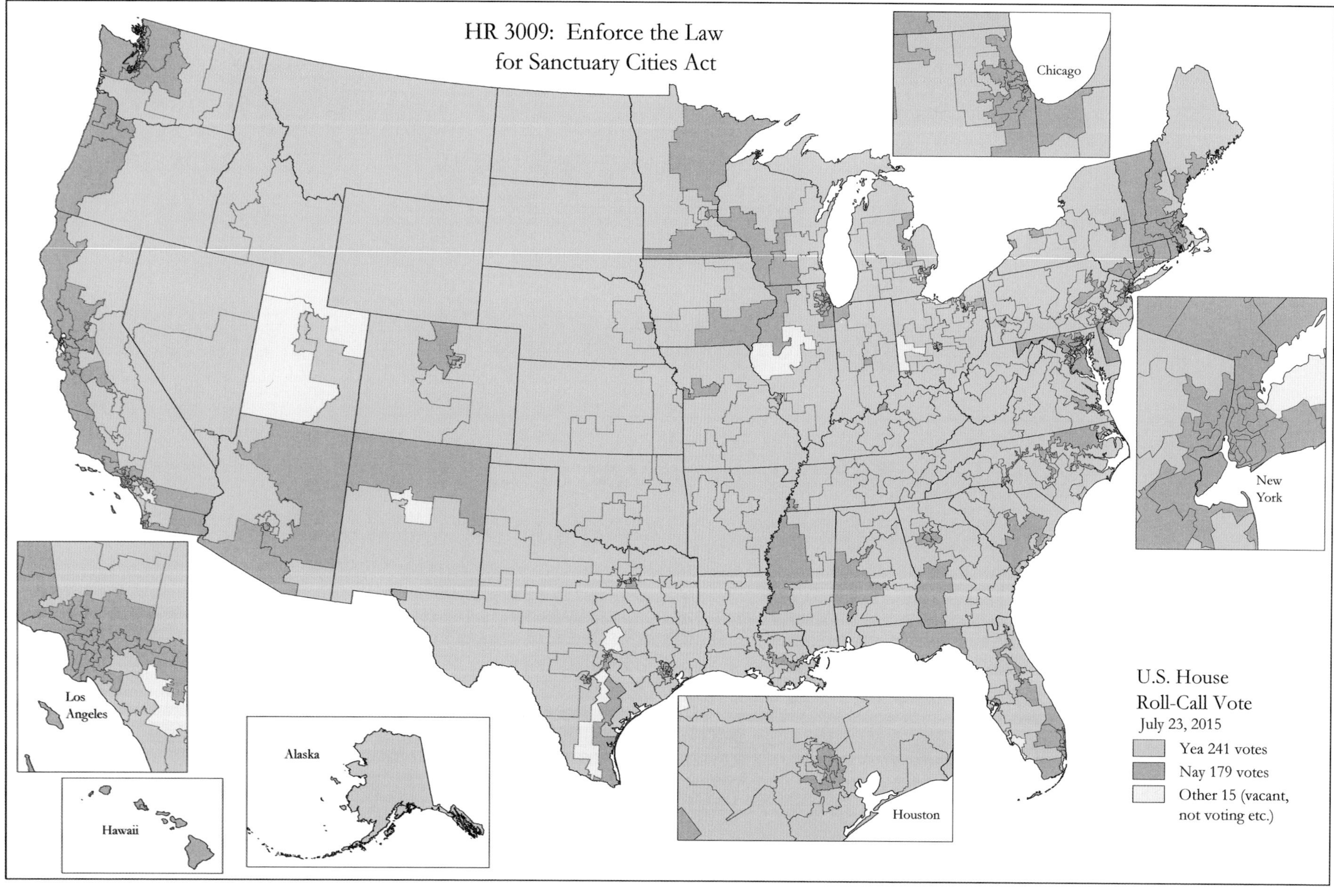
HR 3009: Enforce the Law
for Sanctuary Cities Act
Chicago
New
York
Los
Angeles
Alaska
Hawaii
Houston
U.S. House
Roll-Call Vote
July 23, 2015
Yea 241 votes
Nay 179 votes
Other 15 (vacant,
not voting etc.)

San Francisco became a sanctuary city in 1989. The San Francisco police released Lopez-Sanchez, held on marijuana charges, a month before the murder. The US Immigration and Customs Enforcement (ICE) had an immigration detainer to deport Lopez-Sanchez after his release from prison, but the San Francisco police did not inform ICE of his release. In response, Republicans introduced H.R. 3009, a bill to deny federal funds for policing to sanctuary cities. Figure 7.4 maps the House roll-call vote to withhold federal police funds from sanctuary cities. The vote followed party lines with a few detractors from each party. Two hundred and thirty-five Republicans and six Democrats voted in favor, and five Republicans and 174 Democrats voted against. The House referred the bill to the Senate, but the bill did not receive a vote in the Senate. The US Conference of Mayors and the National League of Cities "opposed H.R. 3009 on the grounds that sanctuary policies 'strengthen police-community relations and build trust'" (Colbern 2015).

MALONEY AMENDMENT

In July 2014, President Obama signed an executive order to extend protection against discrimination regardless of sexual orientation or gender identity in hiring by federal contractors. Looking to codify the executive order, Democratic Representative Sean Maloney (New York) attached an amendment to a Department of Veterans' Affairs spending bill in May 2016 that barred "the government from paying federal contractors that discriminate based on gender identity or sexual orientation" (Snell 2016). Figure 7.5 shows the vote on the amendment, which failed with 212 in favor and 213 opposed. Just before the vote, it looked as though the amendment would pass, but seven Republican members changed from their expected vote at roll call. "Democrats booed and shouted as the amendment failed, and party leaders unleashed a wave of criticism" (Snell 2016). One week later, the House voted 223–195 to approve the Maloney Amendment attached to an Energy Department spending bill "after 43 Republicans joined all Democrats in support" (Marcos 2016). The entire energy bill, including the Maloney Amendment, collapsed before having the chance to become a law. These two roll-call votes on the Maloney Amendment are particularly interesting to uncover the divide within the Republican Party in the House during the 114th Congress. The forty-three Republicans included representatives from all regions except the South and Great Plains. Republican Representatives from Florida, New York, New Jersey, the West, and the Midwest voted in favor of the Maloney Amendment. On June 12, 2016, a gunman targeted the LGBT community in an attack, killing forty-nine people at the Pulse Nightclub in Orlando, Florida. Three days after the Orlando attack, Rep. Maloney attached his amendment to a Defense Department spending bill in the House, but the House Rules Committee, led by the Republican leadership, blocked a vote on the amendment.

THE KEYSTONE PIPELINE AND IRAN

The House also considered economic, environmental, and international issues during the 114th Congress. Democrats framed the Keystone pipeline as an environmental issue, and Republicans framed it as an economic issue. Democrats considered the question of sanctions on Iran a test of allegiance to President Obama, and Republicans framed it as a way to constrain President Obama.

Figure 7.6 maps a key vote in the House to move forward the Keystone XL pipeline project. Framed by supporters as an issue of energy independence and job creation, the House voted on January 9, 2015, to approve the construction of a more than 1,000-mile pipeline with some bipartisan support. The House voted 266 in favor and 153 against, with all voting Republicans and 28 Democrats approving construction by TransCanada Corporation. Projected cost of the Keystone XL pipeline is upward of $10 billion. The pipeline will transport oil from tar sands of Alberta, Canada, to the Gulf Coast of the United States (McCarthy 2017). In the waning days of President Obama's second term, members of the Standing Rock Sioux tribe and supporters waged a more than eight-month protest over the Dakota Access pipeline in North Dakota. The US Army Corps of Engineers denied an easement to Energy Transfer Partners on December 4, 2016, halting construction. On January 24, 2017, three days after taking office, President Donald Trump issued executive orders authorizing construction of the Keystone XL pipeline and the Dakota Access pipeline.

The Obama administration, working with the United Kingdom, France, Russia, China, and Germany, negotiated a nuclear agreement with Iran during Obama's second term in office. The agreement gradually lifted sanctions against Iran in exchange for Iran limiting its nuclear program to nuclear energy and cooperating with the International Atomic Energy Agency (IAEA). Republican leadership in the House put forward H.R. 3460 in 2015 to "suspend until January 21, 2017,

FIGURE 7.5

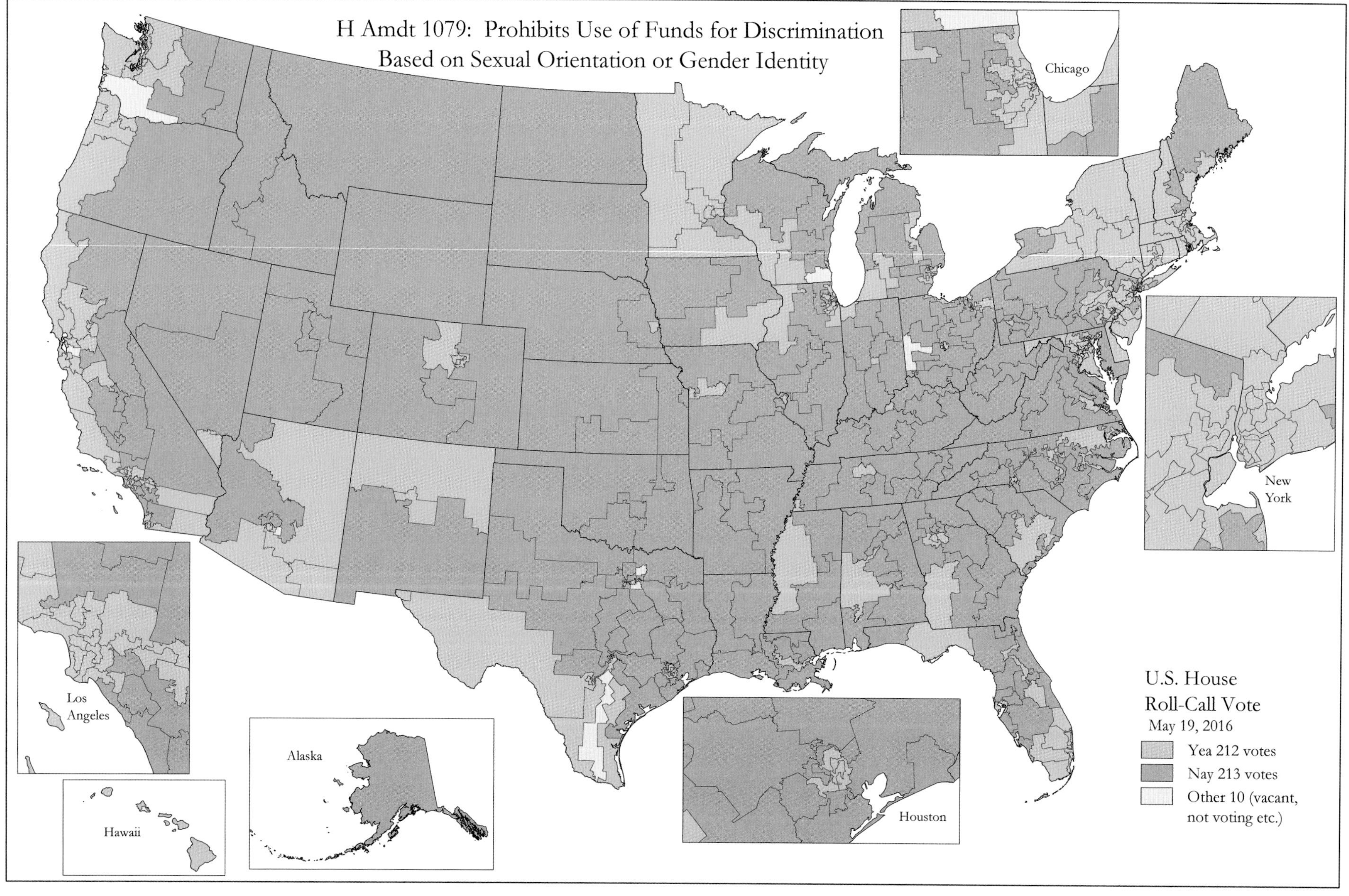
H Amdt 1079: Prohibits Use of Funds for Discrimination
Based on Sexual Orientation or Gender Identity
Chicago
New
York
Los
Angeles
Alaska
Hawaii
Houston
U.S. House
Roll-Call Vote
May 19, 2016
Yea 212 votes
Nay 213 votes
Other 10 (vacant,
not voting etc.)

FIGURE 7.6

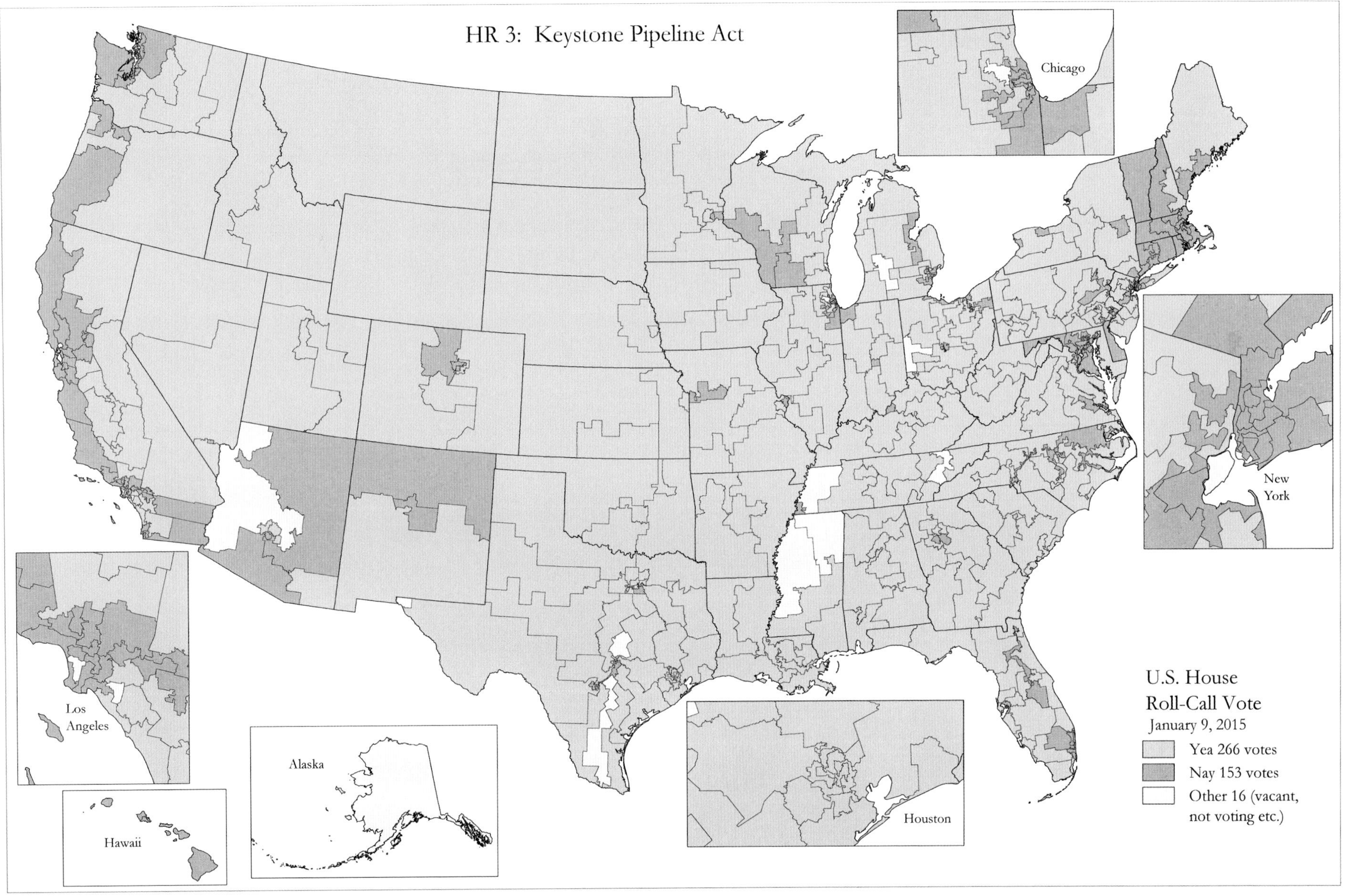
HR 3: Keystone Pipeline Act
Chicago
New
York
Los
Angeles
Hawaii
Alaska
Houston
U.S. House
Roll-Call Vote
January 9, 2015
Yea 266 votes
Nay 153 votes
Other 16 (vacant,
not voting etc.)

FIGURE 7.7

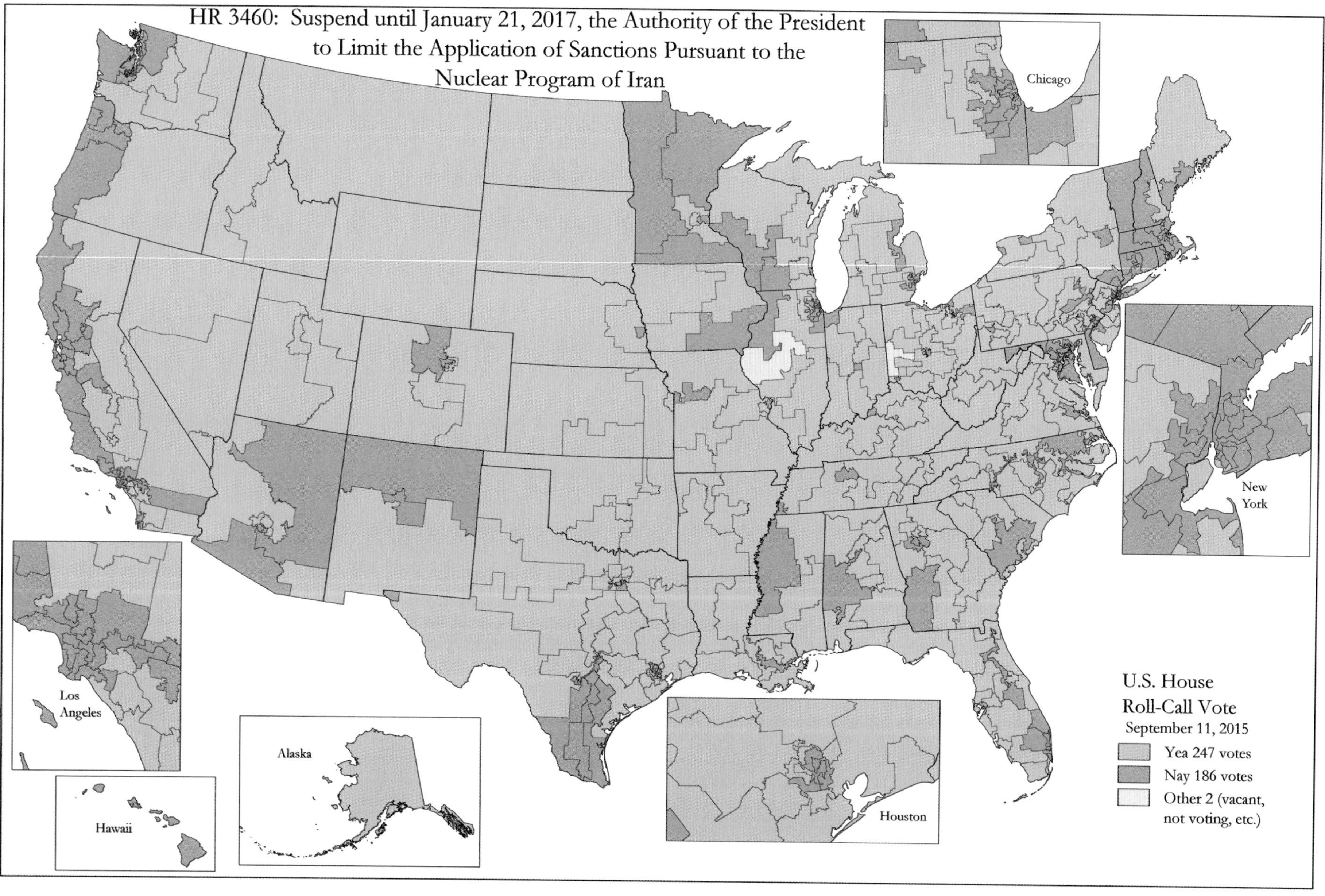
HR 3460: Suspend until January 21, 2017, the Authority of the President to Limit the Application of Sanctions Pursuant to the Nuclear Program of Iran
Chicago
New York
Los Angeles
Alaska
Hawaii
Houston
U.S. House
Roll-Call Vote
September 11, 2015
Yea 247 votes
Nay 186 votes
Other 2 (vacant, not voting, etc.)

the authority of the President to waive, suspend, reduce, provide relief from, or otherwise limit the application of sanctions pursuant to an agreement related to the nuclear program of Iran" (CBO 2015). Members voted to pass H.R. 3460 on September 11, 2015. The distribution of votes, shown in figure 7.7 again followed party lines with 247 voting in favor (including 2 Democrats) and 186 voting against (all Democrats). The Senate received the House bill in September 2015 and referred it to the Committee on Foreign Relations in July 2016.

Concern with President Obama's legacy and issues brought forward through presidential primaries and campaigns had direct impact on legislation considered by the House in the 114th Congress. Among the five roll-call votes considered here, three were nearly completely along partisan lines, reflecting the increasing political polarization in Congress since the 1970s. Among these five votes, the Keystone pipeline vote and the Maloney Amendment vote received some support across the aisle, which was significant, at least in the context of a partisan Congress.

REFERENCES

BBC. 2016. Iran Nuclear Deal: Key Details. *BBC News*. January 16, http://www.bbc.com/news/world-middle-east-33521655 (last accessed 21 June 2017).

CBO (Congressional Budget Office). 2015. H.R. 3460, A Bill to Suspend until January 21, 2017, the Authority of the President to Waive, Suspend, Reduce, Provide Relief from, or otherwise Limit the Application of Sanctions Pursuant to an Agreement Related to the Nuclear Program of Iran. September 11, https://www.cbo.gov/publication/50823 (last accessed June 21, 2017).

Colbern, Allan. 2015. The House Is Picking a Fight with "Sanctuary City" Ordinances. How Is This Like the Fugitive Slave Laws? *Washington Post*. August 13, https://www.washingtonpost.com/news/monkey-cage/wp/2015/08/13/the-house-is-picking-a-fight-with-sanctuary-city-ordinances-how-is-this-like-the-fugitive-slave-laws/?utm_term=.4065c0aa1ce4 (last accessed June 21, 2017).

DeSilver, Drew. 2014. The Polarized Congress of Today Has Its Roots in the 1970s. Pew Research. June 12, http://www.pewresearch.org/fact-tank/2014/06/12/polarized-politics-in-congress-began-in-the-1970s-and-has-been-getting-worse-ever-since (last accessed June 21, 2017).

Fabian, Jordan. 2016. Obama Vetoes Health Bill Repeal. *The Hill*. January 8, http://thehill.com/homenews/administration/265078-obama-vetoes-healthcare-bill-repeal (last accessed June 21, 2017).

Marcos, Christina. 2016. House GOP Leaders Block LGBT Vote after Orlando Shooting. *The Hill*. June 14, http://thehill.com/blogs/floor-action/house/283531-house-gop-leaders-block-lgbt-vote-after-orlando-shooting (last accessed June 21, 2017).

McCarthy, Tom. 2017. How Keystone XL and Dakota Access Went from Opposition to Resurrection. *The Guardian*. January 24, https://www.theguardian.com/us-news/2017/jan/24/keystone-xl-dakota-access-pipeline-explainer (last accessed June 21, 2017).

Snell, Kelsey. 2016. House Approves LGBT Anti-Discrimination Measure. *Washington Post*. May 25, https://www.washingtonpost.com/news/powerpost/wp/2016/05/25/house-to-vote-again-on-lgbt-anti-discrimination-measure/?utm_term=.89c48070bcbb (last accessed June 21, 2017).

OVERVIEW OF THE 2016 SENATE ELECTIONS

RYAN WEICHELT

Heading into the 2016 election cycle, Democrats felt cautiously optimistic they would be able to regain control of the US Senate after their humiliating loss of nine seats during the 2014 midterm elections. Many Democrats believed since Donald Trump was leading the Republican Party and a handful of "Tea Party" senators faced reelection, they could win back the Senate, retain the presidency, and possibly win the House. While unlikely that Democrats would take a large lead in the Senate, polls indicated that seats in Florida, Indiana, Missouri, New Hampshire, Nevada, North Carolina, Pennsylvania, Indiana, and Wisconsin, all either held by Republicans or open seats, were toss-ups. Furthermore, polls clearly showed that Illinois would be an easy victory for the Democrats and Senator Michael Bennet of Colorado was likely to win. If all toss-up seats were to go to the Democrats, it would nearly erase the loss of nine seats they had suffered in 2014. In the end, Democrats were only able to win two toss-up seats in Nevada and New Hampshire. A number of Senate races across the country, however, capture the unique election atmosphere of 2016 as a whole.

SPATIAL PATTERNS

Figure 7.8 shows the results of the 2016 Senate races across the country. Democratic senatorial candidates remained in traditional safe states on the East and West Coasts, including Hawaii. In those races, Democratic candidates won by large margins, with incumbent Chuck Schumer of New York winning by 43 percentage points over his rival. Due to election rules, California had two female Democratic candidates square off to fill the vacancy of longtime senator Barbara Boxer. In the end, Kamala Harris easily defeated Loretta Sanchez, 62 percent to 38 percent. For Republicans, incumbents in traditionally red states also easily won reelection with similarly large victories in many places. For example, incumbent John Hoeven of North Dakota defeated his Democratic rival, Eliot Glassheim, by 61 percent (78.4 percent to 17 percent). The lone exception to this was the surprisingly busy ballot in Alaska. Former Gulf War veteran Joe Miller ran an ambitious campaign on the Libertarian ticket and won 29 percent of vote, but incumbent Lisa Murkowski won by a plurality at 44 percent. Remaining votes were split between an independent and a Democrat (13 percent and 12 percent, respectively).

TEA PARTY SENATORS

While many of the incumbent races were rather uneventful affairs, the toss-up states did provide plenty of intrigue. The Tea Party movement of 2010 ushered in social and fiscally conservative ideas aimed at debt reduction with strong connections to the Christian Right movement. During the 2010 midterms, Tea Party candidates provided Republicans with key victories in the Senate as well as some upsets in traditionally blue states. The four candidates most connected to the Tea Party running for reelection in 2016 were Rand Paul of Kentucky, Mike Lee of Utah, Jerry Moran of Kansas, and Ron Johnson of Wisconsin. Given the sudden success of the Tea Party in 2010 and the subsequent decline of Tea Party members in the House of Representatives in the following years, Tea Party senators had the benefit of six years between elections, leaving only one, Ron Johnson (Wisconsin), in the hot seat in 2016. Running against former Democratic senator and opponent in 2010, Russ Feingold, Johnson lagged behind in the polls during the entire election season. Wisconsin was eyed as a likely pickup for Democrats. By November 8, Johnson would join his Tea Party brothers in victory as he easily defeated Feingold 50.2 percent to 46.8 percent. Though Johnson clearly benefited from Trump's late success, he did campaign on key Tea Party promises of lowering debt, repealing Obamacare, and job creation. On the other hand, Feingold ran a rather lackluster campaign promoting progressive reforms, but with a depressed voter turnout due in part to a lack of enthusiasm for Hillary Clinton and excitement over Trump in rural areas, Feingold decisively lost to the incumbent for a second time.

FIGURE 7.8

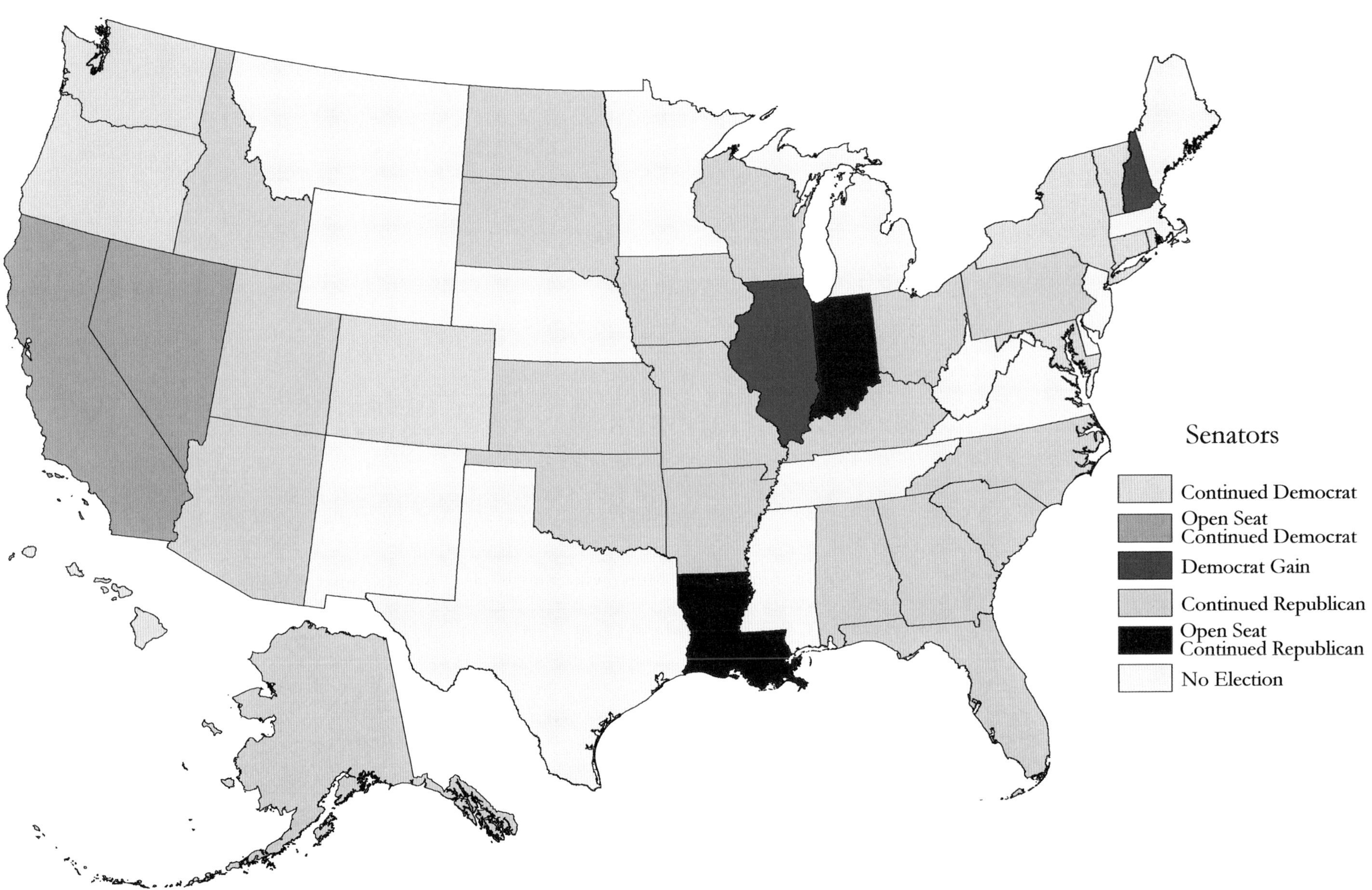

2016 Senate Elections
Senators
Continued Democrat
Open Seat Continued Democrat
Democrat Gain
Continued Republican
Open Seat Continued Republican
No Election

YOUTHFUL CANDIDATES

Missouri and Florida also demonstrated close elections, but for different reasons. Incumbent Roy Blunt faced a unique challenger in Democrat Jason Kander. Blunt, considered an establishment Republican with ties to free trade, led polling comfortably until a September Emerson College poll showed Kander with a two-point lead. Kander, a former army captain who served in Afghanistan, ran a simple but effective commercial showing him assembling an assault rifle blindfolded while delivering a monologue defending himself against Blunt's assertions that he was weak on gun control. It became an instant Internet sensation, leaving the *Washington Post* to declare this as "the best ad of the election so far" (Stevenson 2016). However, polls remained tight up to November and Blunt won the election by 78,000 votes. In a surprisingly close election in a generally red state, Kander's age (35) and veteran status could represent a moderate tactic for Democrats to utilize in future elections.

Though the Florida Senate race featured, perhaps, a contest of the youngest candidates, the election was more about Marco Rubio (age 45) than his opponent, Democrat Patrick Murphy (age 32). Young and Hispanic (of Cuban descent), Rubio became a rising star in the Senate after his victory in 2010. After announcing he would run for president in June 2015, Rubio stated he would not seek reelection (Florida law prohibits being on the ballot for two seats). After a surprisingly strong start in the Iowa Caucus, many saw Rubio as the likely Republican presidential candidate come fall. Yet, after a series of poor debates and a surging Donald Trump, Rubio dropped out of the race on March 16 after losing his home state of Florida in the Republican primary. Deciding to reverse his pledge not to run for reelection after running for president, Rubio announced he would seek reelection on June 22, days before the filling deadline. Because of Rubio's late entry, Murphy questioned his commitment to the Senate and attacked his "connections" to Donald Trump. Fighting back, Rubio attacked Murphy as young, inexperienced, and too closely tied to his father's wealth (Alvarez 2016). Ultimately, Rubio proved correct. Murphy refused to debate the Republican, baffling Democrats, and also, this rookie mistake slowed much-needed donations from Democrats locally and nationwide (Caputo and Robillard 2016). Though polls tightened in the end, Rubio easily won. Rubio even gained a higher percentage of Republican votes than Donald Trump did. Rubio's connection to the Cuban community and conservative views contrasted with Murphy's pro-choice stance and support of the Affordable Care Act, and softening relations with Cuba combined for Rubio's simple victory. Though youth was abundant in this election, Rubio's popularity and Murphy's "rookie mistakes" kept the seat in Republican hands.

HIGH-COST CAMPAIGN

Pennsylvania was the site of the most expensive Senate race in 2016, between incumbent Republican Pat Toomey and Democratic challenger Katie McGinty. When accounting for all money spent for this election, it totaled over $118 million. McGinty was a former environmental advisor to Bill Clinton, while Toomey once ran the free-market advocacy group Club for Growth (Stolberg 2016). Like many incumbent Republicans, Toomey avoided supporting Trump throughout the entire campaign, with the exception of Election Day, where he finally relented and stated, unenthusiastically, that he supported Trump. McGinty, capitalizing on her connections to Bill Clinton, joined Hillary Clinton at a final Election Day rally in Philadelphia in hopes of gaining last-second votes. Much like Feingold in Wisconsin, many thought McGinty would win due to her positive and consistent showing in the polls, but Trump won the Keystone State and Toomey most likely benefited from the "Trump Bump" with a 1.6 percent victory (48.9 percent to 47.3 percent). Unlike Clinton, McGinty lost to Toomey in key suburban counties like Chester and Bucks counties, and the interior counties of Dauphin and Centre (home to Penn State).

HISPANICS, GENDER, AND TRUMP

Not all was lost for Democrats on November 8 in the Senate. Democrats were able to win two elections in the toss-up states of Nevada and New Hampshire. Nevada elected the first Hispanic female to the US Senate, Catherine Cortez Masto, over Joe Heck (47.1 percent to 44.7 percent) to replace outgoing Senate Minority Leader Harry Reid. While Trump provided support to Republicans in some states, his influence had the opposite effect in both these races. Masto was able to capitalize on the growing influence of Hispanic voters in Nevada by attacking Trump on immigration and his plan to build a wall. Joe Heck, at first critical of Donald Trump, later supported him but flipped back again by suggesting Trump should step down after the release of the *Access Hollywood* tapes, which certainly impacted his support at the polls. In the end, Masto won 47.1 percent to 44.7 percent.

In New Hampshire, Governor Maggie Hassan narrowly defeated Republican incumbent Kelly Ayotte by only 743 votes in the closest election in the country. While Ayotte attempted to distance herself from Trump during much of the campaign, one key gaffe, in support of Donald Trump, most likely cost her the election. At a campaign stop Ayotte was asked if she saw Trump as a role model for kids; she stated "absolutely" (Seelye 2016). In a fit of bad luck, days later, the misstep was further exacerbated by the release of the *Access Hollywood* tapes. New Hampshire is unique for the large number of independent voters and Hassan was able to gain the support of just enough to claim victory, while most likely, Ayotte's gaffe about Trump lost her precious votes.

In the end, the US Senate elections mirrored many of the themes from the entire 2016 election cycle, mainly the role of Trump, health care, gender issues, youthful candidates, and diversity. Solid blue and red states delivered strong and predictable victories for their respective senators, but polls turned out to be rather poor indicators predicting victors in many toss-up races. Democrats hoped to gain eight toss-up seats, but in the end, only won two. In the toss-up states lost by Democrats, both parties had to carry the burden of the presidential candidates. Florida, Pennsylvania, Nevada, and New Hampshire illustrate the challenge of subtly distancing candidates from Donald Trump without driving away their Republican base. In the states of Pennsylvania, Missouri, and Wisconsin, Clinton's unpopularity drove down voter turnout, most likely costing McGinty and Feingold victories. Trump's name on the ballot certainly helped Johnson in Wisconsin, Toomey in Pennsylvania, and Rubio in Florida, but hurt Ayotte in New Hampshire and Heck in Nevada.

While Democrats had a poor showing in this election cycle, there were some positive outcomes for them. In the four states in which Democrats either defeated an incumbent or fell into the toss-up category, all victors were women and, in the case of Nevada, the first Hispanic female was elected to the US Senate. Nevada also illustrated the impact of a united Hispanic voting bloc in the state. Finally, Democrats also had strong showings with younger candidates in Missouri and Florida, despite their losses. For Republicans, many can argue they "eked out" victories. The main issue moving toward 2018 will be the impact of Donald Trump on the Republican Party and how closely candidates attach themselves to his policies. As seen in 2016, while Trump had a positive impact for some, aligning with him can have devastating effects.

REFERENCES

Alvarez, Lizette. 2016. Marco Rubio Wins Re-election in Florida Senate Race. *The New York Times*. https://www.nytimes.com/2016/12/09/us/politics/marco-rubio-florida-senate.html (last accessed March 24, 2017).

Caputo, Marc, and Kevin Robillard. 2016. How DC Democrats Are Killing Murphy—and Helping Rubio. *Politico*. October 7, http://www.politico.com/states/florida/story/2016/10/how-dc-democrats-are-killing-murphy-and-helping-rubio-106208 (last accessed March 16, 2017).

Seelye, Katharine Q. 2016. Maggie Hassan Unseats Kelly Ayotte in New Hampshire Senate Race. *The New York Times*. November 9, https://www.nytimes.com/2016/11/09/us/politics/new-hampshire-senate-hassan-ayotte.html (last accessed March 24, 2017).

Stevenson, Peter W. 2016. This May Be the Best Ad of the Election So Far. *The Washington Post*. September 15, https://www.washingtonpost.com/news/the-fix/wp/2016/09/15/this-campaign-ad-might-be-the-biggest-mic-drop-of-2016/?utm_term=.c380cca2cc1e (last accessed April 12, 2017).

Stolberg, Sheryl G. 2016. Patrick Toomey Wins Re-election in Pennsylvania Senate Race. *The New York Times*. November 9, https://www.nytimes.com/2016/11/09/us/politics/pennsylvania-senate-patrick-toomey.html (last accessed March 23, 2017).

2016 WISCONSIN SENATE ELECTION

KENNETH FRENCH

The 2016 Wisconsin senatorial race was a rematch of the 2010 senatorial election between two rivals: Republican Ron Johnson and Democrat Russ Feingold. The incumbent, Senator Ron Johnson, a former business leader from Oshkosh, served on the foreign relations, budget, and commerce committees in his first term. He notably served as chairman of the Committee on Homeland Security and Governmental Affairs since 2015. Former three-term senator Russ Feingold (served from 1993 to 2011) resigned as United States Special Envoy for the Great Lakes Region of Africa for the opportunity to take back his seat. As senator, he was a champion for campaign finance reform and helped shape the 2002 Bipartisan Campaign Reform Act with Republican senator John McCain of Arizona. The 2016 Wisconsin senatorial race was tensely contested between candidates with diametrically opposing ideologies. Senator Johnson rode the Tea Party wave (Williamson, Skocpol, and Coggin 2011) to victory in 2010 and former senator Feingold represented the progressive side of the Democratic Party.

The issues leading up to the 2016 Wisconsin senatorial election mirrored that of the nation as a whole. The issues of health care, Supreme Court Justice nominee, national security, and economy were debated by Mr. Feingold and Mr. Johnson. Similar to Republicans nationally, Senator Johnson wanted to repeal and replace the Affordable Care Act, also known as Obamacare. Former senator Feingold favored the idea that more Americans received health insurance, while conceding that Obamacare needed modifications to decrease deductibles and premiums. Mr. Feingold expressed frustrations over Senate Republicans for not holding a Supreme Court confirming vote for Judge Merrick Garland, while Mr. Johnson noted that he would confirm a judge who favored conservative values. For example, Mr. Johnson favored protecting the Second Amendment and Mr. Feingold wanted common sense background checks on gun purchases. National security, focusing on terrorism and the Islamic State, was a popular issue for many Wisconsinites and Senator Johnson had the advantage of being chair of Homeland Security. The economic issue of job growth pitted a former CEO of a plastic sheet manufacturing company (PACUR) against a progressive Democrat in favor of raising the federal minimum wage to fifteen dollars an hour. Early public polling data suggested that Mr. Feingold would easily win in a state that also heavily leaned toward the Democratic presidential candidate, Hillary Clinton. The race tightened considerably as November 8, 2016, approached and the final result went against the earlier public polling numbers.

In the 2016 Wisconsin senatorial general election, Senator Ron Johnson received 50.2 percent of the popular vote, former senator Feingold 46.8 percent, and Libertarian candidate Phillip Anderson had 3.0 percent of the vote. From 2010 to 2016, Senator Johnson's percentage of the popular vote declined by 1.7 percent (51.9 percent to 50.2 percent, respectively) and Feingold's percentage declined by only 0.2 percent (47.0 percent to 46.8 percent, respectively). As expected, given the rematch resulted in the same outcome, the geographic patterns were very similar between 2010 and 2016 (see figure 7.9). Only two counties switched between the elections, as Lafayette and Richland (both increased by 1.9 percent Democratic vote from 2010 to 2016) actually went from Johnson to Feingold. Previous research (Morrill, Knopp, and Brown 2007) indicated there could be anomalies to the standard "red" nonmetropolitan and "blue" metropolitan areas. However, the typical geographic patterns of Republican success in suburban and rural counties versus more Democratic support in urban counties persisted in this 2016 election. Mr. Johnson won the Milwaukee suburban counties (such as 67.9 percent of the vote in Waukesha County), while Mr. Feingold won 71.8 percent of the votes in Dane County (city of Madison) and 63.7 percent of Milwaukee County (city of Milwaukee). Nonetheless, these suburban and urban counties increased their Democratic vote from 2010 to 2016. Senator Johnson made up those declines from rural counties in the northern and central areas of the state as the proportion of Democratic vote significantly declined from 2010 to 2016. Voters from places that lost manufacturing jobs, in both urban (Kenosha and Racine) and rural areas, favored Senator Johnson. The growing political diversity of rural areas, including both

FIGURE 7.9

Wisconsin U.S. Senate Election Popular Vote Leader, 2016

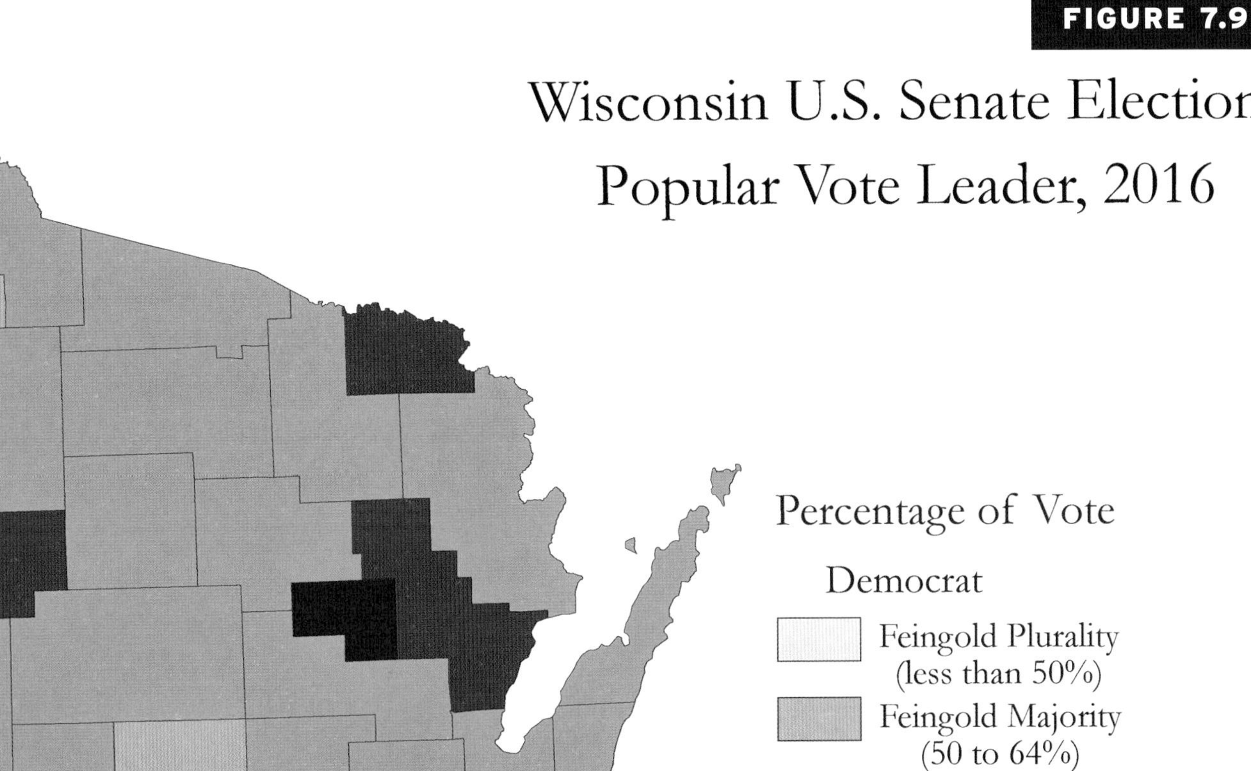

farming and recreational counties (Scala, Johnson, and Rogers 2015), should include the rural manufacturing areas. Are unemployed union workers shifting their allegiances from the Democrats to the Republicans?

This 2016 Wisconsin senatorial race between Mr. Feingold and Mr. Johnson was an upset. However, it was not as surprising as Republican presidential candidate Donald Trump winning the state. Senator Johnson outperformed Mr. Trump in Wisconsin, as the former won 50.2 percent of the vote and the latter won 47.2 percent. Mr. Johnson did better than Mr. Trump in the Milwaukee suburbs—67.9 percent of Waukesha County voted for Mr. Johnson and 60.0 percent voted for Mr. Trump. Future analytical research would be needed to see if Senator Johnson helped Mr. Trump in the suburbs, in a "reverse coattails effect" (Ames 1994), to narrowly win Wisconsin. Mr. Johnson may have ridden Mr. Trump's coattails in central and northern Wisconsin—which could explain the dramatic decline in Democratic votes from the 2010 to 2016 Senate election. The future will tell if the victory of Republican senator Johnson over former Democratic senator Russ Feingold is yet another recent example of Wisconsin quickly transitioning from a "blue" to a "red" state.

REFERENCES

Ames, Barry. 1994. The Reverse Coattails Effect: Local Party Organization in the 1989 Brazilian Presidential Election. *American Political Science Review* 88:95–111.

Morrill, Richard, Larry Knopp, and Michael Brown. 2007. Anomalies in Red and Blue: Exceptionalism in American Electoral Geography. *Political Geography* 26:525–53.

Scala, Dante, Kenneth Johnson, and Luke Rogers. 2015. Red Rural, Blue Rural? Presidential Voting Patterns in a Changing Rural America. *Political Geography* 48:108–18.

Williamson, Vanessa, Theda Skocpol, and John Coggin. 2011. The Tea Party and the Remaking of Republican Conservatism. *Perspectives on Politics* 9:25–43.

2016 MINNESOTA SECOND CONGRESSIONAL DISTRICT ELECTION

SAMUEL LOFTSGAARDEN

When seven-term Republican representative John Kline announced his decision to forgo running for reelection, Democrats (better known in Minnesota as the Democratic-Farmer-Labor Party or DFL) saw an opportunity to flip the Second Congressional District in their favor. A number of media outlets reported on the competitive nature of this election, with one even suggesting this race would "likely be one of the most-watched congressional races in the country" (Stassen-Berger 2015). The DFL selected Angie Craig, who if elected, would be Minnesota's first openly gay member of Congress, while Republicans selected a controversial conservative talk radio host and political neophyte, Jason Lewis. After Lewis's primary victory, he was far behind in fundraising due in part to Craig's backing from the Democratic Congressional Campaign Committee's Red to Blue Program (DCCC 2016). To the shock of academia and media around the state however, Lewis scored an upset victory with 46.95 percent of the total vote compared to Craig's 45.16 percent. Although the Democrats were defeated in a contest they hoped to win, this race was won by the closest of margins in more than a decade.

The Republican Party and John Kline have long held control on the Second District, with Kline consistently retaining power since his first election in 2002. The district's boundaries have undergone multiple iterations over the years due to redistricting. In its current form, dating back to 2012, this district (see figure 7.10) occupies southeastern Minnesota along the Mississippi River and stretches into the suburbs of the Minneapolis–St. Paul metro area. According to American Community Survey 2015 five-year estimates, 681,358 people live in the Second District. Of that total population, 79.7 percent live inside 114 census tracts that are within twenty miles of the Twin Cities. Comprised of mainly white (86 percent), middle aged (median age 37.2), and affluent (median household income of $75,564), the Second District resembles a perceived quintessential Republican district. During the 2012 General Election, Republicans had a strong advantage in most areas of the Second District. Democrats only won 86 out of 292 precincts in the district, with 62 of these precincts within twenty miles of the Twin Cities. These 62 precincts accounted for 77.5 percent of all DFL votes in the district. Kline therefore dominated many of the remaining precincts found in generally rural areas outside of the Twin Cities, winning the election by 8 percent. These patterns remained similar in the 2014 election, with Kline increasing his victory to 17 percent. Yet, with the incumbency advantage erased and with Donald Trump dominating headlines, the DFL hoped they could steal the district.

With hope high that Craig would win, money flowed in. By the election's end, Craig was able to amass $3,832,195 in contributions, with over 59.5 percent of these donations coming from individual supporters (FEC 2016). Along with this large amount of money, Craig loaned herself $975,000. Lewis's contributions, on the other hand, never topped a million and he provided $0 in loans to himself. As the election drew near, Trump's negative influence on all Republicans was felt with the release of the *Access Hollywood* tapes. Lewis was attacked on all fronts based on his previous inflammatory rhetoric espoused on his radio program. A reliable KSTP-TV poll on October 17, 2016, showed Craig with a 5 percent lead. However, the poll also indicated that 12 percent of eligible voters were still undecided with a little over three weeks to Election Day (Survey USA 2016). By election night, in a shocking twist, Jason Lewis, like many Republicans across the country, scored an upset victory, retaining Republican control of the Second District.

The two previous election cycles resulted in Republican victories of 8.16 percent (2012) and 17.17 percent (2014) over their DFL competitors. Yet, compared to 2012, the Second District saw an increase in total voter turnout (358,442 in 2012 to 365,474 in 2016). In 2016, however, the margin of victory for the Republican shrank to 0.79 percentage points. Lewis's campaign saw the Republican garner 18,706 fewer votes in the 2016 study area compared to 2012. Republicans also saw the percentage of Republican-affiliated voters in the study area decrease by 7.63 percent compared to 2012.

Two factors can be attributed to a change in voting patterns in the Minnesota Second. The first factor is that the DFL increased its support in the areas outside the Minneapolis–St. Paul

FIGURE 7.10

2016 U.S. House of Representatives Election 2nd Congressional District, Minnesota

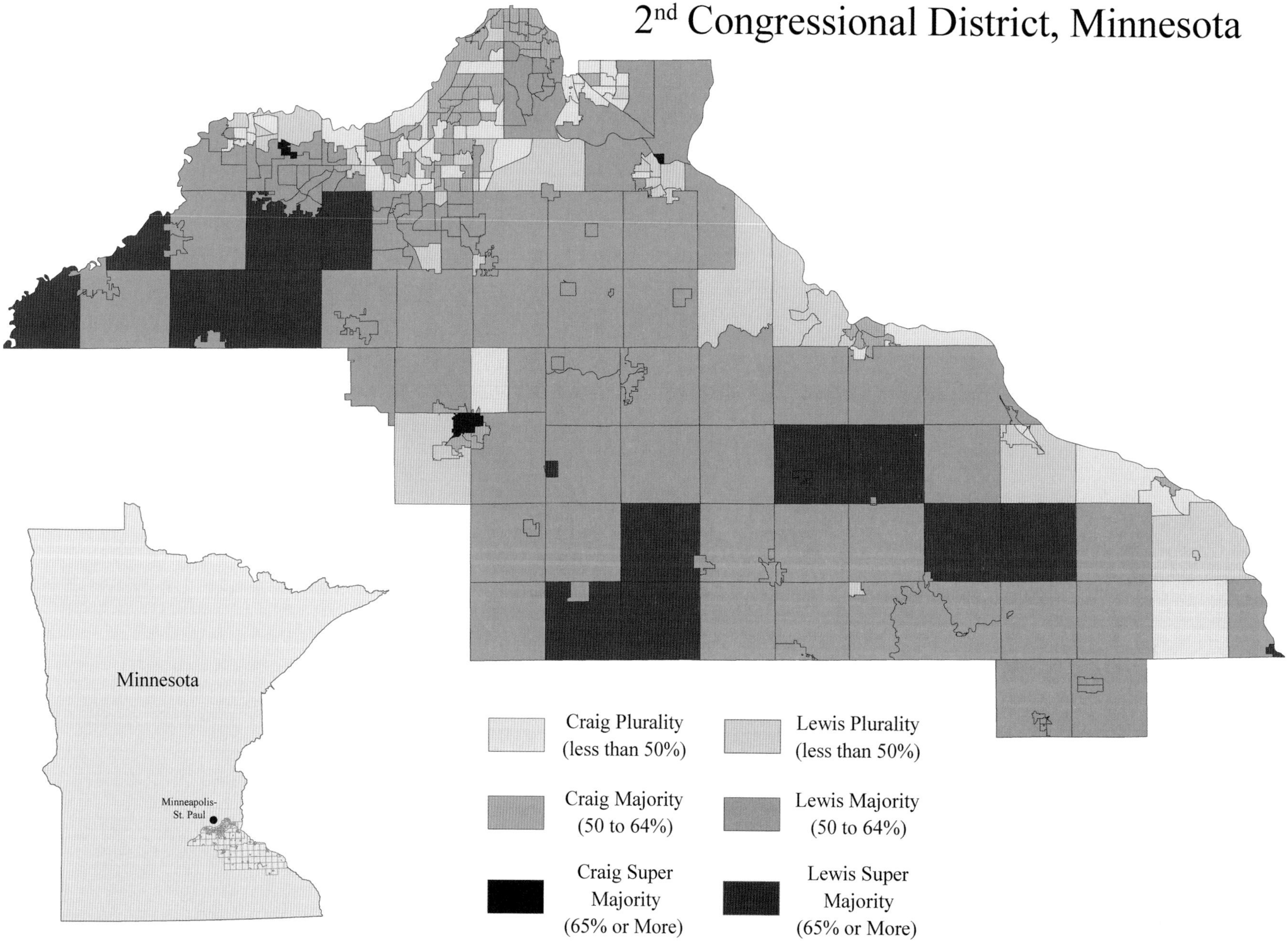

Minnesota

Minneapolis-St. Paul

Craig Plurality (less than 50%)

Lewis Plurality (less than 50%)

Craig Majority (50 to 64%)

Lewis Majority (50 to 64%)

Craig Super Majority (65% or More)

Lewis Super Majority (65% or More)

metropolitan area. As figure 7.10 illustrates, Craig was able to garner support, compared to previous elections, in voting precincts along the Mississippi River, especially in the cities of Red Wing and Wabasha, and in the central areas of the district. The second factor related to the influence of the Progressive Party vote. In 2012, the two major parties garnered 99.85 percent of the vote, including write-ins. The DFL in that year had 45.85 percent of all votes. However, in 2016 the vote was more evenly divided, but the two major parties only controlled 92.11 percent of total voters. The cause for the decrease in major party support this election cycle was the appearance of independent candidate and progressive-minded Paula Overby. Her results took away 28,869 voters who most likely would have voted for Craig.

With a huge advantage in campaign spending, a strong lead in the polls, and a political climate favoring Democratic candidates across the country, all indications were that Angie Craig would coast to victory. In the end that would not be. Some Republicans claimed the victory was due in part to Donald Trump (Montgomery 2016). Trump won the district 46 percent to Clinton's 45 percent. Yet, looking at the numbers, the loss can be contributed more to the spoiler effect of the Progressive, Overby. Lewis's slim 6,655 vote victory most likely would have been erased had Overby not been on the ballot. Overby's highest vote totals were in voting precincts in the MSP metropolitan areas surrounded by areas that supported Craig. Though disappointing for the DFL, the decrease in the number of Republican voters and the increase in liberal-minded voters in the district will place Lewis back in the hot seat in 2018, most likely making the Minnesota Second ripe for the taking.

REFERENCES

DCCC. 2016. DCCC Chairman Luján Announces First 31 Districts in Red to Blue Program. Press Release. Democratic Congressional Campaign Committee. February 11, http://dccc.org/dccc-chairman-lujan-announces-first-31-districts-red-blue-program (last accessed April 11, 2017).

FEC. Disclosure Data Search. Campaign Finance Data. Federal Election Commission. http://www.fec.gov/finance/disclosure/disclosure_data_search.shtml (last accessed February 15, 2017).

Montgomery, David. 2016. GOP's Jason Lewis Wins MN 2nd Congressional District; Incumbent Democrats Narrowly Hold Seats. *Twin Cities*. http://www.twincities.com/2016/11/08/minnesotas-congressional-races-2nd-district-early-results (last accessed April 17, 2017).

Office of the Minnesota Secretary of State. 2016. *Minnesota Secretary Of State*. http://www.sos.state.mn.us/elections-voting/election-results (last accessed April 1, 2017).

Stassen-Berger, Rachel. 2015. Another Democrat Files for 2nd Congressional District. TwinCities.com. *Pioneer Press*. March 24, http://blogs.twincities.com/politics/2015/03/24/another-democrat-files-2nd-congressional-district (last accessed April 17, 2017).

Survey USA. 2016. DFL Candidate Craig Has Advantage in Minnesota's 2nd Congressional District; Seat Would Be "Pick-Up" for Democrats in US House. SurveyUSA Election Poll #23236. October 13–16, http://www.surveyusa.com/client/PollReport.aspx?g=8f733c88-bd4b-4ea3-8267-bfc8046fb37f (last accessed January 7, 2017).

United States Census Bureau. 2010. American Fact Finder: Advanced Search. https://factfinder.census.gov/faces/nav/jsf/pages/searchresults.xhtml?refresh= (last accessed April 1, 2017).

SYMBIOTIC ELECTIONS: THE 2016 ARIZONA SENATE AND FIRST CONGRESSIONAL DISTRICT

LEVI JOHN WOLF

In the 2016 election cycle, Arizona played a notable, yet ultimately predictable, role in presidential, senatorial, and congressional elections. Indeed, in an election where the popular vote swung toward the Democrats, Republicans generally did well in the state but saw mixed results in ballot propositions. It is difficult to disentangle the eventual fortunes of the Senate and the First Congressional District campaigns, given their common thread in Representative Ann Kirkpatrick, the northern Arizona congresswoman whose resignation from her home district of Arizona First to run against John McCain opened up a competitive House seat with no incumbent. Relatedly, the eventual state of the race in the Arizona First spoke to the strength of accrued incumbency advantage and the cultivation of a personal vote, with one of the most competitive House seats in the past two cycles.

SENATE

In the spirit of widespread concerns about the impact Donald Trump might have on important down-ballot races, many wondered whether Senator John McCain would be "dragged down" by an unpopular presidential ticket. Whereas McCain was a widely supported incumbent senator with a long-standing base of support, goodwill, and name recognition, McCain's age and tepid messaging about a controversial Republican presidential candidate made an upset easily within reach. This upset was not to be, however. McCain ended up outperforming the presidential candidate in a race that was essentially about the national issues in the presidential campaign.

While the presidential election landscape may have seemed favorable to Kirkpatrick, a few structural factors made it difficult to grow her base of support. Critically, she had to address historical softness in her home district support while attempting to build up statewide name recognition. Before running for the Senate, Kirkpatrick had been a representative for Arizona's First Congressional District, a district that covers nearly all of the sparsely populated northern and eastern portions of the state, includes the Navajo and Hopi nations, and also incorporates the outskirts of Arizona's two most populous metropolitan areas, Phoenix and Tucson. Kirkpatrick was first elected to the Arizona First District before the contentious 2010 redistricting of House seats. Yet, Kirkpatrick's electoral successes came under structurally favorable conditions: she first won in the Democratic wave election of 2008 after the Republican incumbent, Rick Renzi, retired. While the 2010 midterms were a typical midterm election in that the president's party lost ground, Kirkpatrick saw her sixteen-point win turned into a six-point loss during the 2010 midterms. The district was then redrawn before the 2012 election and was widely viewed as more favorable toward Democrats. In addition to increasing the district's Democrat base, the redistricting also encouraged Paul Gosar, to whom she lost in 2010, to move from the Arizona First District to the newly drawn and heavily Republican Fourth District. In the new favorable First District with no incumbent, Kirkpatrick won by a three-point margin against state representative Jonathan Paton. In 2014, Kirkpatrick won reelection on a five-point margin over Arizona House Speaker Andy Tobin.

On this record, Kirkpatrick challenged McCain in the 2016 Senate race. In the primary election, McCain faced a significant challenge from state legislator Kelli Ward. McCain's longevity in the increasingly tumultuous political climate in Arizona had garnered him significant negative attention from the Tea Party movement, and Ward's challenge from the right focused precisely on McCain's age and long tenure in the Senate. In contrast, the Democrats were fully united behind Kirkpatrick, who faced no significant primary challenger. Throughout the campaign, McCain's tepid statements about President Trump's campaign drove many to believe McCain felt he could not run against the presidential ticket but did not want to run close to the presidential ticket, either. This was complicated by comments made by Trump calling into question the heroism of John McCain's time as a POW in Vietnam. In addition, a few polls showed Clinton up in the state, and both Clinton and Trump held many rallies in the state to bolster early voting and get-out-the-vote efforts. According to the US Elections Project, early voting was up by 8.9 percent, meaning about 60 percent of all ballots cast in Arizona were cast before November 8 (McDonald 2016). Early voting and positive marks in the polls for Clinton all boded well for Kirkpatrick (Nowicki 2016), Likewise, Trump's apparent continued antipathy toward McCain in many Arizona rallies also seemed to sap enthusiasm from him (Sanchez 2016).

In the end, the statewide race ended up breaking toward Trump as Election Day drew near. McCain ended up outperforming the Republican presidential ticket by nearly 100,000 votes, and defeating Kirkpatrick by over 12 percentage points. Thus, McCain's apparent personal vote (Cain et al. 1987) provided a more-than-comfortable margin. Kirkpatrick's relative electoral weakness in her home district was never addressed; while the northern Navajo and Coconino counties split toward Kirkpatrick as expected, many of the other counties she represented in the Arizona First went to McCain instead (see figure 7.11). High Hispanic turnout in the state, with around 70 percent of eligible Hispanic voters casting a ballot, broke strongly to Clinton (Nuño and Wilcox-Archuleta 2016), reflecting a mobilized, coherent ethnic voting bloc. However, McCain's strong support base in the Phoenix metropolitan area overwhelmed the votes Kirkpatrick earned elsewhere in the state, especially in Coconino and Apache counties in the Arizona First. McCain built a lead of nearly 200,000 votes in Maricopa, which is an order of magnitude larger than the net margin over all counties Kirkpatrick won. Kirkpatrick only narrowly carried the areas outside of Tucson, the second-most populous metropolitan area in the state, and her margin was hardly improved with overwhelming wins in the two sparsely populated counties in her northern base of support. Thus, by maintaining his strong historical base of support in the most populous areas of Arizona, McCain won the race in spite of historic Hispanic voter mobilization and an aloof relationship with the Republican presidential candidate.

ARIZONA FIRST

Kirkpatrick's run also affected the race for her replacement. The seat in Arizona's First Congressional District, vacated by Ann Kirkpatrick to pursue John McCain's Senate seat, was rated by most agencies as a race that leaned Democrat or was a toss-up. Despite its rating, Republicans had been successful in the district in the past. However, after the 2010 redistricting empowered incumbent Paul Gosar to move to a newly created safe Republican Fourth District, Kirkpatrick won both in 2012 and in 2014. The new design of the Arizona First District added exurban areas of Tucson from the Eighth District and combined the Navajo and Hopi nations into a single district, increasing the propensity for the First District to lean Democrat. In both the 2012 and 2014 elections, Kirkpatrick's margin of victory was around 10,000 votes, or 3 percentage points in 2012 and 5 points in the lower-turnout midterm election of 2014. Both times, Kirkpatrick won against popular state legislators.

After Kirkpatrick announced her intention to vacate the First District seat to challenge McCain for the Senate, the Republican primary had many more serious candidates than the Democratic primary. Former Pinal County sheriff Paul Babeu eventually won the primary. A three-time sheriff, Babeu had run for the Republican nomination for Congress in the Fourth District in 2012. In that race, he ended up pulling out early due to a sex and abuse-of-power scandal. In the 2016 Republican Primary, many prominent candidates ran against Babeu, including former Arizona secretary of state and 2014 gubernatorial candidate Ken Bennett, former congressional candidate Wendy Rogers, and northern Arizona businessperson and rancher Gary Kiehne. The field never narrowed, and Babeu won the primary with only 30.8 percent of the vote. In contrast, the Democratic Party primary was a contest between two nominal Democrats. Former Republican state legislator Tom O'Halleran, who lost his conservative central Arizona State Senate seat after switching his registration to independent in 2014, secured most Democratic Party officials' endorsements and eventually beat former Libertarian candidate Miguel Olivas for the Democratic nomination, winning by around 17 percentage points.

During the race, Babeu ran an essentially national campaign. Babeu's tough stance on immigration fit comfortably with presidential candidate Trump's messaging on the issue, and Babeu spoke at many of the large rallies held in the Phoenix area. In addition, Babeu's close professional relationship with controversial Maricopa County sheriff Joe Arpaio heightened his focus on border issues. In contrast, O'Halleran's messaging against Babeu focused on Babeu's increasingly common presence on national television. Babeu occupied many spots on national news discussing hard-line stances on border security as a Trump surrogate, in addition to confronting President Obama during a nationally televised town hall. Thus, O'Halleran suggested, Babeu was focused on raising his own national profile while simultaneously losing touch with the people he was to represent.

FIGURE 7.11

Arizona U.S. Senate Election Popular Vote Leader, 2016

Percentage of Vote

Democrat

- Kirkpartick Plurality (less than 50%)
- Kirkpartick Majority (50 to 64%)
- Kirkpatrick Super Majority (65% or more)

Republican

- McCain Plurality (less than 50%)
- McCain Majority (50 to 64%)
- McCain Super Majority (65% or more)

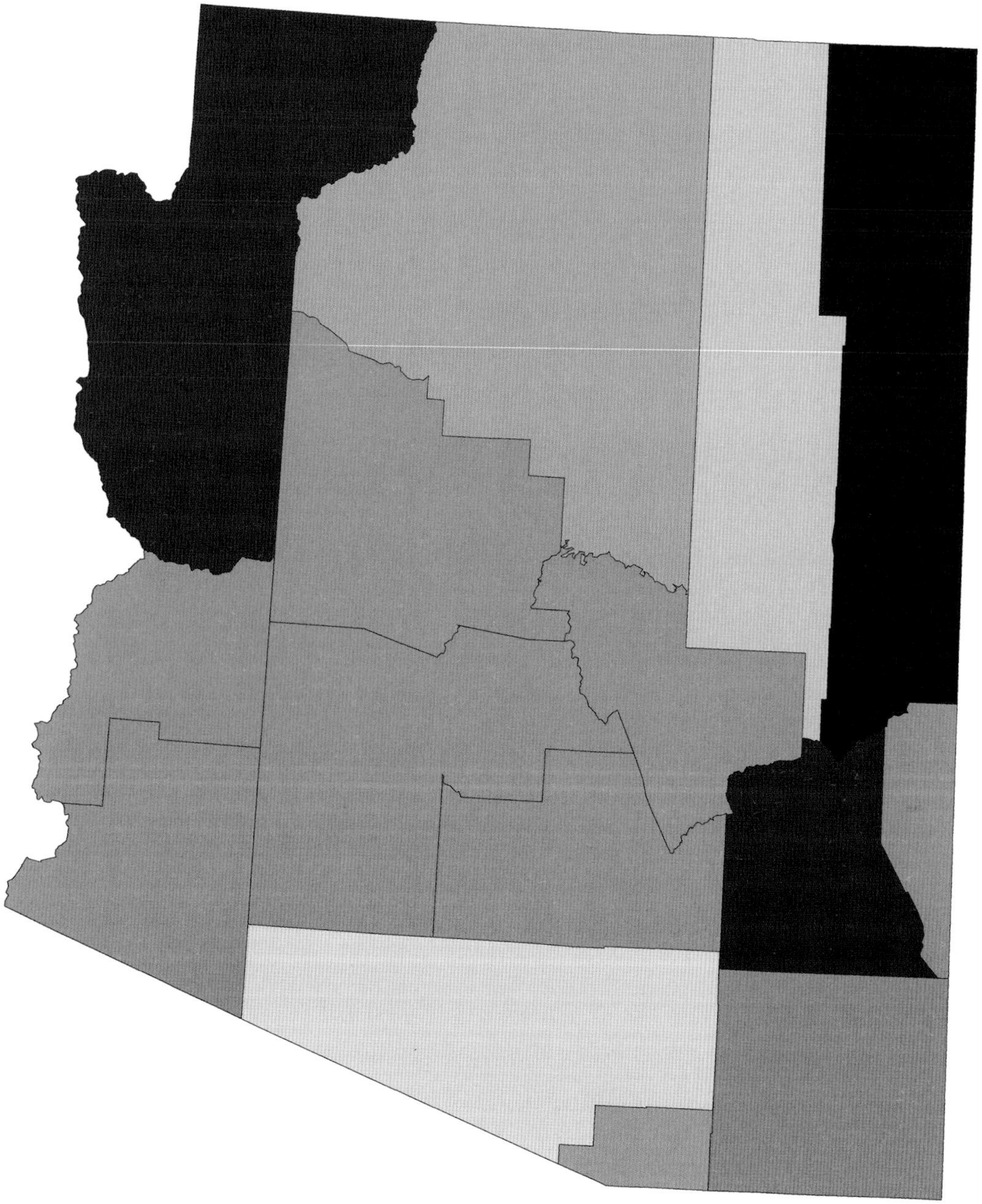

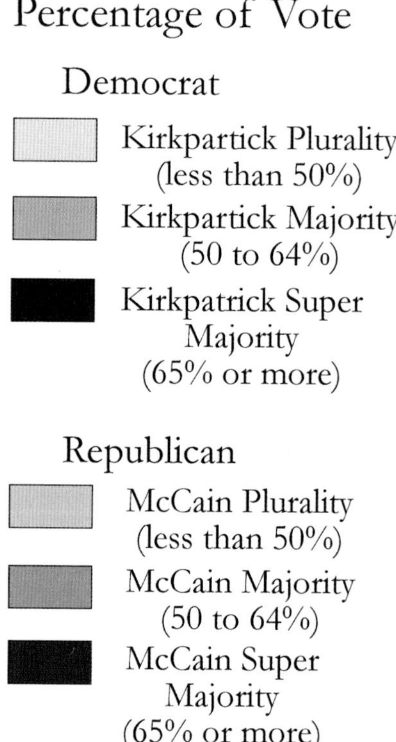

Alternatively, O'Halleran's history as a Republican state legislator led Babeu to accuse the campaign of opportunism, and that O'Halleran re-registered as a Democrat only to pick up the safe seat. O'Halleran suggested instead that he left the Republican Party due to his deep ideological convictions about the importance of public education. In addition to significant debate about education and gun control, energy policy and jobs were uniquely significant issues in the race. The First District also has a large number of coal mining employees working at the Navajo Generating Station, the third-largest single source of carbon dioxide pollution in the United States (NPR 2015). Atmospheric pollution from mining and power generation industries continually influences air quality in Grand Canyon National Park (partially located in Arizona's First) and water supplies for the entire Colorado River watershed. In addition, these industries also employ a significant number of people in the district. Thus the discussion of potential regulations about emissions, specifically on coal, loomed large in the debate about jobs, energy, and climate.

In FEC filings, fundraising in the race was approximately equal, with both candidates eventually raising around a million dollars in support of their candidacies. However, Babeu's national stature and earned media on nationally televised events far outstripped that which O'Halleran attained. Regardless of any potential disparity, O'Halleran's messaging proved effective: O'Halleran won by nearly 20,000 votes, around 7 percentage points. Surprisingly, despite his work, public appearances, and strong support of the candidate, Babeu significantly underperformed relative to President Trump in the district. Fourteen thousand voters in Arizona's First District cast votes for Trump but not Babeu. Thus, despite Trump's general success and insurgent power in the closing days of the campaign, Babeu did not benefit. Likewise, the inclusion of Kirkpatrick on the ballot, and her legacy in the Arizona First also provided O'Halleran a safety net in the election (see figure 7.11).

REFERENCES

Cain, Bruce, John Ferejohn, and Morris Fiorina. 1987. *The Personal Vote: Constituency Service and Electoral Independence*. Cambridge, MA: Harvard University Press.

McDonald, Michael P. 2016. Early Vote, Election Eve Predictions. *The Huffington Post*. http://www.huffingtonpost.com/michael-p-mcdonald/early-vote-election-eve-p_b_12853864.html (last accessed January 12, 2017).

Nowicki, Dan. 2016. Poll: Clinton Up 5 Points Over Trump in Arizona. *AZ Central*. October 20, http://www.azcentral.com/story/news/politics/elections/2016/10/19/arizona-poll-hillary-clinton-donald-trump/92339110 (last accessed January 14, 2017).

NPR. 2015. How a Historical Blunder Helped Create the Water Crisis in the West. *Fresh Air*, NPR. Aired June 25, http://www.npr.org/2015/06/25/417430662/how-a-historical-blunder-helped-create-the-water-crisis-in-the-west (last accessed January 20, 2017).

Nuño, Stephen A., and Bryan Wilcox-Archuleta. 2016. Viewpoints: Why Exit Polls Are Wrong about Latino Voters in Arizona. *AZ Central*. November 26, http://www.azcentral.com/story/opinion/op-ed/2016/11/26/exit-polls-wrong-latino-voters-arizona/94288570 (last accessed February 27, 2017).

Wingett-Sanchez, Yvonne, and Dan Nowicki. 2016. Donald Trump Returning to Arizona on Saturday for 7th Rally. *AZ Central*. October 27, http://www.azcentral.com/story/news/politics/elections/2016/10/27/donald-trumps-campaign-scouting-locations-saturday-rally/92534068 (last accessed January 14, 2017).

OBAMACARE AND THE 2016 ELECTION

RYAN WEICHELT

The Patient Protection and Affordable Care Act, also known as "Obamacare," prompted an immediate conservative backlash upon its passage in the US House on October 8, 2009, and its signing into law by President Obama on March 23, 2010. Critics of Obamacare argued that universal health care would push individuals off existing plans and dramatically increase insurance costs (particularly for small business owners), all while increasing government debt, increasing drug prices, and, perhaps in the minds of some fringe voters, ushering in a new era of socialism. Supporters of the initiative championed the increased coverage for more Americans, especially the allowing of young adults to remain on their parents' insurance for extended years, increased coverage for women's health, and the elimination of the preexisting condition clause. A March 2010 *Real Clear Politics* poll (2017) average indicated 51.4 percent "Opposed" Obamacare, with only 39.9 percent "In Favor." This divide would continue as new Tea Party Republicans campaigned on repealing the Affordable Care Act and took back the House of Representatives in the 2010 midterm elections, while also gaining a number of seats in the Senate. Though unable to repeal Obamacare in the coming years, repealing the Affordable Care Act became a key and consistent Republican campaign promise in elections to come.

In 2015 David Frum of *The Atlantic* wrote a piece titled "The Question That Will Decide the 2016 Election," in which he posed this question as "Will you take away my health insurance?" It was a crucial point. In 2015, estimates suggested that 11.2 million people were added to the Medicaid program since 2010, and another 10 million were receiving government subsidies through federal exchanges. Furthermore, another estimated 5.7 million young adults were added to their parents' plan. Subsequent analyses from the Washington Center for Equitable Growth found that eligibility for Obamacare exchange subsidies increased with poverty. Spatially, the highest beneficiaries of Obamacare are located throughout the South and in rural counties across America. Further analysis by the *New York Times* found the percentage increase in insurance coverage provided by the Affordable Care Act was largest in poor, minority, young, male, rural, and solidly Republican counties. Many of these same counties, especially in the southern United States, also included the highest rates of uninsured Americans (Quealy and Sanger-Katz 2014).

Health care remained a top concern heading into the 2016 election cycle and a July 2016 Pew poll indicated that it ranked only below the economy, terrorism, and foreign policy in importance. Presidential candidates also took notice of the issue. Every Republican candidate campaigned on repealing the Affordable Care Act and when Donald Trump won the nomination, he continued to push for a repeal and provided a weak seven-point plan to replace Obamacare solely based on "free market principles." These principles include tax deductions, encouraging competition among states, and lowering drug costs (Diamond 2016). Trump was also keen to add that enforcing immigration laws would most likely decrease health care costs, but provided little evidence to support the assertion. By November 1, Trump stated if he won the election, he would hold a special session of Congress to repeal and replace Obamacare while at the same time consistently saying it was a "catastrophe."

On the other side of the issue, Hillary Clinton was backed into a corner. Having attached herself to the legacy of Barack Obama, she could add very little to the debate beyond support for the president's legacy-defining domestic legislation. In late October, a Department of Health and Human Services report suggested that insurance rates would increase 22 percent by 2017 due in large part to the Affordable Care Act (Luhby 2016). Handcuffed, Clinton's only response was to fix the broken parts of Obamacare while simultaneously arguing that if Trump were to be elected, over 20 million Americans would lose insurance coverage. By the campaign's end, President Obama himself agreed that portions of the Affordable Care Act needed to be fixed, but criticized Trump for offering no viable solution.

Similar arguments were made in the House and Senate elections. In late 2015 Speaker of the House, Paul Ryan, declared the GOP's "First Priority of 2016" was to repeal Obamacare. A vote was held on Groundhog Day 2016, but this and all attempts to repeal Obamacare or to override the president's veto failed. While no tally was officially recorded, there is evidence that over sixty votes to repeal or override a veto on Obamacare were taken by Republican legislators during Obama's tenure (Benen 2016). By mid-October, after the Trump *Access Hollywood* tapes dominated headlines, Republicans began to prepare for the worst. Estimates suggested Republicans would most likely lose the Senate and some even suggested the House, but by late October, Republicans found unlikely support from a Democrat in Minnesota. News of the Obamacare hikes of 22 percent caused popular Democratic governor Mark Dayton to proclaim that due to increases in premiums, the Affordable Care Act was "no longer affordable to increasing numbers of people." In the same article, the author cited a KSTP survey identifying health care was either the top issue or a top-three issue in the most competitive congressional districts in Minnesota (Brodey 2016). Outside groups capitalized on Dayton's comment not only in Minnesota, but nationally. Democrats, much like Clinton, had little response other than to warn repealing Obamacare would costs millions insurance coverage.

In the end, Donald Trump and Republicans scored unlikely victories across the country. Not only did Republicans retain control of Congress, they now had a Republican president who could help effectively repeal the Affordable Care Act. *NBC News* exit polls (2016) found that 45 percent of voters believed Obamacare went too far and this same block of voters overwhelmingly broke for Donald Trump 80 percent to 13 percent. As seen throughout this atlas, Trump and Republican support generally increased in areas with increasing rates of poverty and rural populations. Ironically, these same voters were more likely to either benefit from federal subsidies under the Affordable Care Act and/or to be provided some form of coverage that would not have been possible before passage of this controversial act. Though Obamacare itself may not have been the defining issue of the 2016 election cycle, perhaps the undercurrents of the health-care controversy provided the needed populist message to push Republicans across the finish line in key elections. In a rather interesting paradox, Obama's greatest domestic victory was perhaps the Democrats' improbable curse.

REFERENCES

4 Top Voting Issues in 2016 Election. 2016. 2016 Campaign: Strong Interest, Widespread Dissatisfaction. Pew Research Center. July 7, http://www.people-press.org/2016/07/07/4-top-voting-issues-in-2016-election (last accessed May 15, 2017).

Benen, Steve. 2016. On Groundhog Day, Republicans Vote to Repeal Obamacare. *The Rachel Maddow Show*, MSNBC. February 2, http://www.msnbc.com/rachel-maddow-show/groundhog-day-republicans-vote-repeal-obamacare (last accessed May 10, 2017).

Brodey, Sam. 2016. Health Insurance News Is a Gift to Republican Candidates. *MinnPost*. October 28, https://www.minnpost.com/politics-policy/2016/10/health-insurance-news-gift-republican-candidates (last accessed May 10, 2017).

Diamond, Jeremy. 2016. Donald Trump Releases Health Care Reform Plan. *Politics*, CNN. http://www.cnn.com/2016/03/02/politics/donald-trump-health-care-plan/index.html (last accessed May 7, 2017).

Frum, David. 2015. The Question That Will Decide the 2016 Election. *The Atlantic*. April 22, https://www.theatlantic.com/politics/archive/2015/04/the-question-that-will-decide-the-2016-election/391137 (last accessed May 4, 2017).

Large Share of Voters Feel Obamacare Went Too Far. 2016. *NBC News*. NBC. http://www.nbcnews.com/card/nbc-news-exit-poll-results-large-share-voters-feel-obamacare-n680451 (last accessed April 28, 2017).

Luhby, Tami. 2016. Obamacare Premiums to Soar 22%. *Money*. CNN. October 25, http://money.cnn.com/2016/10/24/news/economy/obamacare-premiums/index.html (last accessed May 10, 2017).

Public Approval of Health Care Law. 2017. *Real Clear Politics*. https://www.realclearpolitics.com/epolls/other/obama_and_democrats_health_care_plan-1130.html (last accessed May 10, 2017).

Quealy, Kevin, and Margot Sanger-Katz. 2014. Obama's Health Law: Who Was Helped Most. *The New York Times*. October 29, https://www.nytimes.com/interactive/2014/10/29/upshot/obamacare-who-was-helped-most.html (last accessed May 7, 2017).

8 STATE ELECTIONS, LOCAL ELECTIONS, AND REFERENDA

PERSISTENCE AND CHANGE IN STATE AND LOCAL ELECTIONS, 2016

RICHARD L. MORRILL

Although most of the media and voter attention seems to have been on the presidential race, ballots across the country included vital contests for governors and state legislatures, as well as US Senators and members of the 115th House of Representatives. These elections all contribute to the distribution of power in the country and to the balance of liberal and conservative ideologies. While the outcomes across these myriad contests may not have been quite as dismal to the Democrats as the presidency loss, the outcomes were far less rosy than had been expected. This entry will look first at the gubernatorial contests, the United States Senate, a brief synopsis of the net change across the US House of Representatives, and then check the balance of Republican and Democratic control in state legislatures, concluding with the change in the "trifecta," or the partisan control over governors as well as legislatures. The story is not comforting to Democratic power and aspirations.

GUBERNATORIAL CONTESTS

Only twelve states had gubernatorial races in 2016 (see figure 8.1). The outcome story was as dismal as the presidency contest for Democrats as they lost three governors to the Republicans, in Missouri and in generally Democratic-leaning New Hampshire and Vermont. Greitens won in Missouri, Sununu in New Hampshire, and Scott in Vermont. North Carolina, after a recount, provided an offsetting gain for the Democrats, with a win by Cooper over McCrory. Democrats held onto seats in Montana, Oregon, Washington, and West Virginia, with Republicans maintaining control in Indiana, North Dakota, and Utah.

As a result of the 2016 elections, Republicans now hold thirty-three of the fifty possible gubernatorial seats, to the Democrats' sixteen seats. Spatially, Democrats' gubernatorial strength is found in the far west coast and in the northeast, but Republicans monopolized the interior and southern states of the country, a consistent theme of this entry. Even worse for the Democrats is that the Republicans now have a trifecta in twenty-five states, controlling both houses of the state legislature as well as the governor's mansion (see figure 8.3).

SENATE CONTESTS

As it relates to the United States Senate, the story for the Democrats was not as poor as that seen with governors. Democrats won twelve of

FIGURE 8.1

Persistence and Change for Gubernatorial and U.S. Senatorial Elections by State, 2016

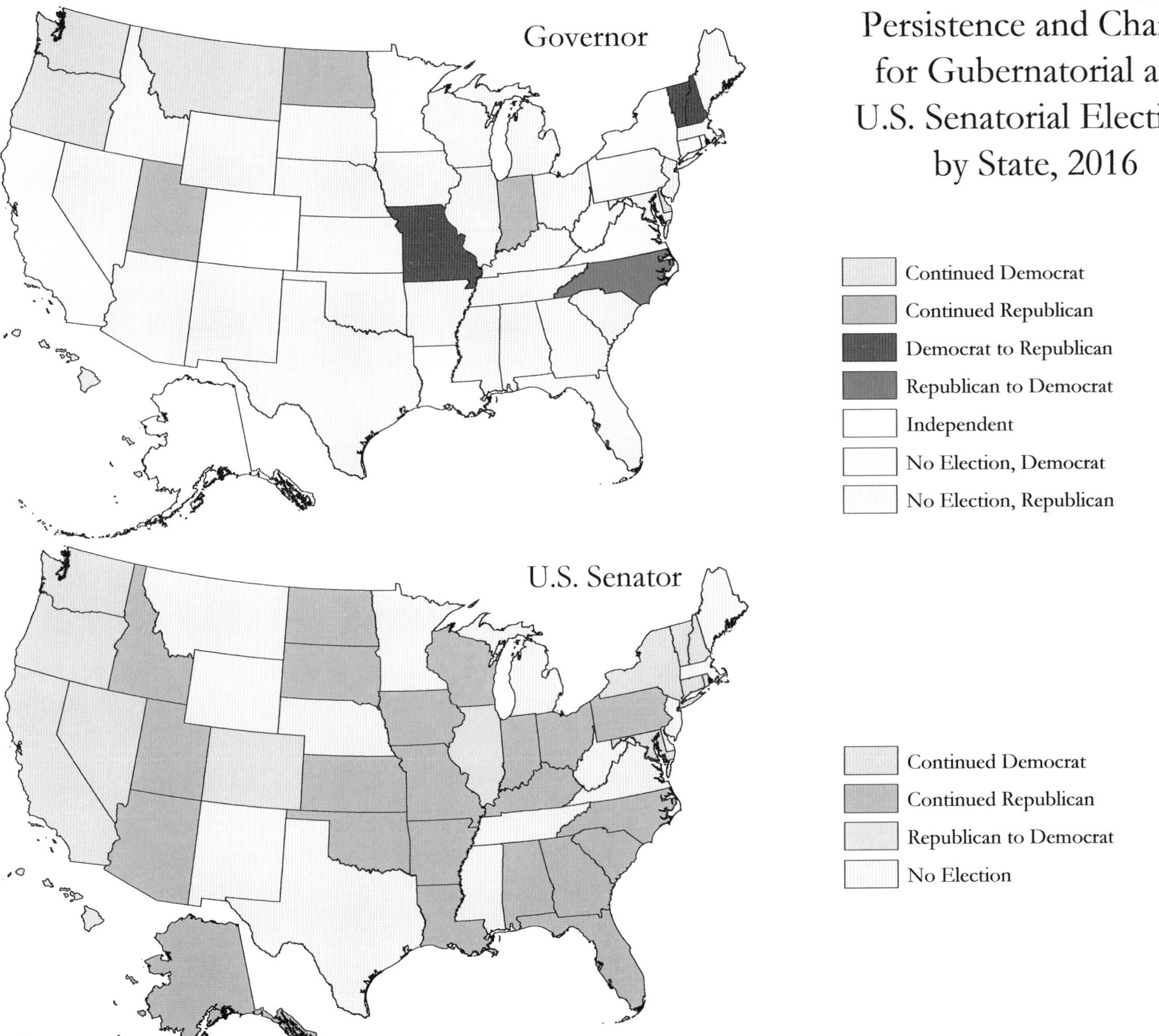

FIGURE 8.2

Persistence and Change for U.S. House and State Legislatures by State, 2016

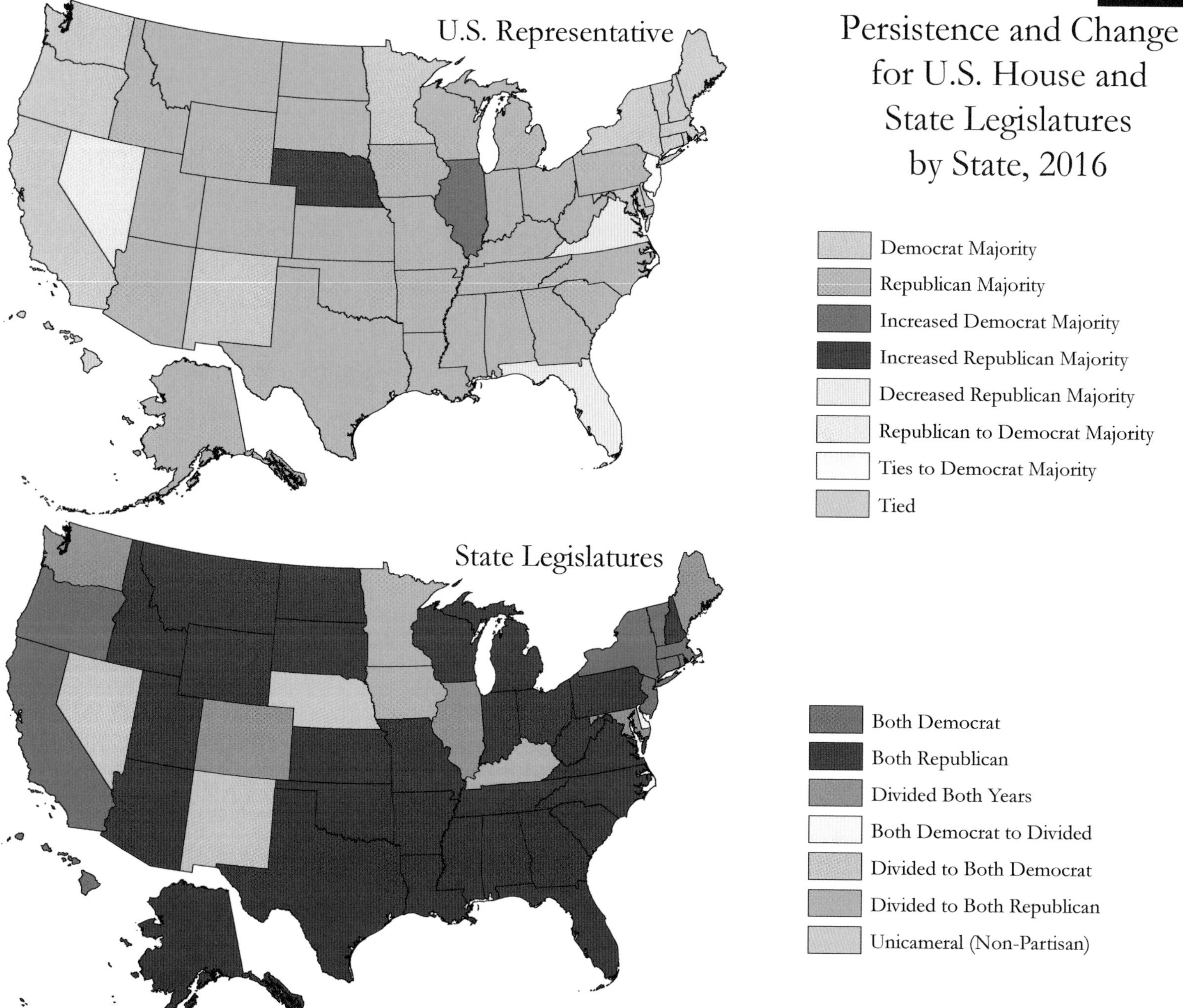

FIGURE 8.3

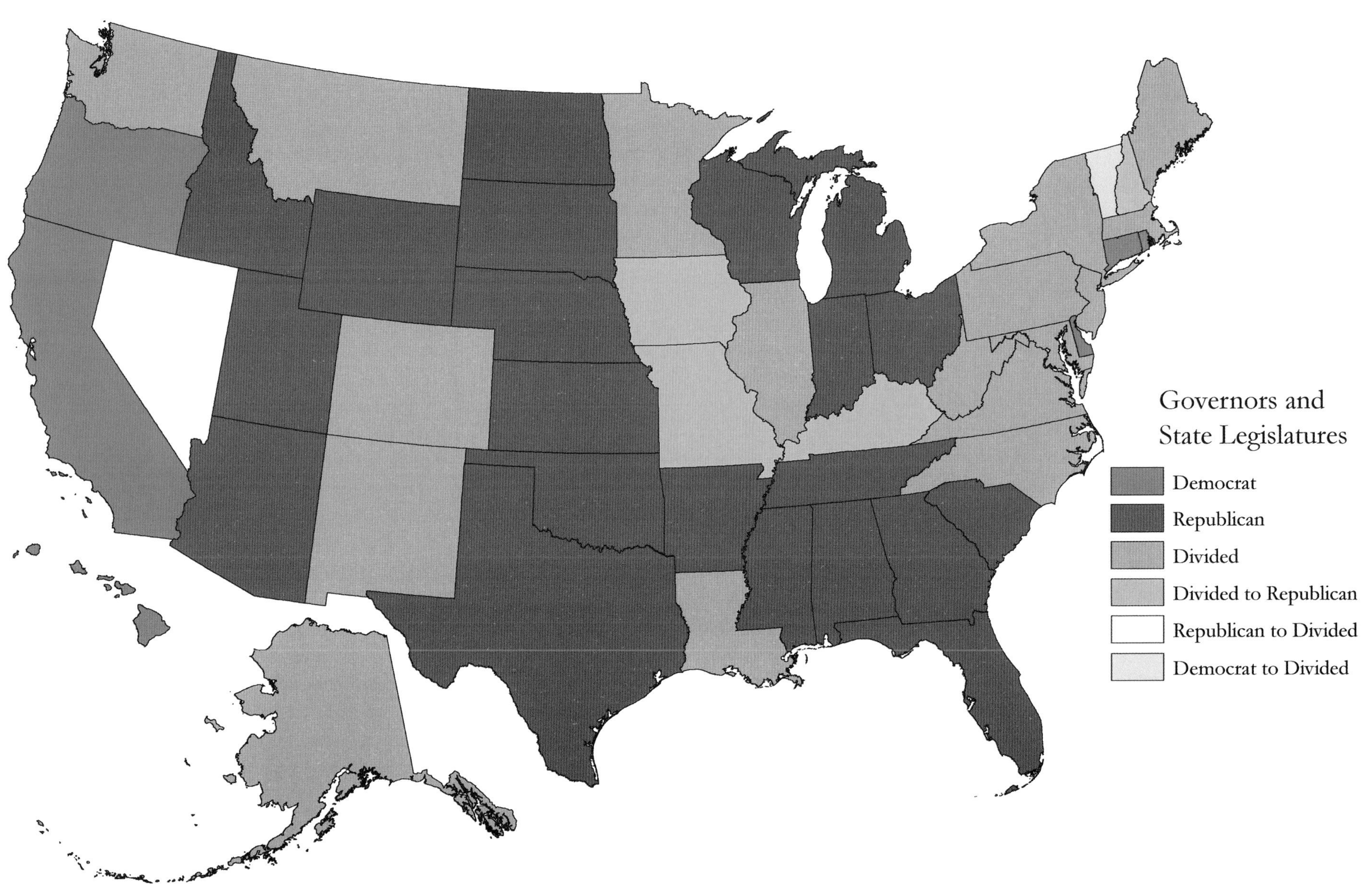
2016 Trifectas
Governors and State Legislatures
Democrat
Republican
Divided
Divided to Republican
Republican to Divided
Democrat to Divided

thirty-four contests, increasing their numbers by two, reaching forty-eight (including two independent senators who caucus with Democrats) to the Republicans' fifty-two seats. Due to a variety of reasons, this was far from what they had hoped for, given that Republicans were up for reelection in twenty-four of the contested races, compared to only ten for Democrats.

As seen in figure 8.1, Republicans held onto seats in Alabama, Alaska, Arizona, Florida, Georgia, Idaho, Indiana, Iowa, Kansas, Kentucky, Louisiana (in a December runoff election), North Carolina, North Dakota, Ohio, Oklahoma, Pennsylvania, South Carolina, South Dakota, Utah, and Wisconsin. Democrats retained seats in California, Colorado, Connecticut, Hawaii, Maryland, New York, Oregon, Vermont, and Washington.

Though success was limited, Democrats did gain two seats in Illinois (Duckworth over Kirk) and New Hampshire (Hassan over Ayotte). In 2018, Democrats will have the unenviable task of defending twenty-five seats (twenty-three Democratic and two independents who caucus with the Democrats) of thirty-three total contests, leaving Republicans only needing to defend eight seats. As was seen among governors, Democratic strength is located in the far west and northeast United States, with Republicans dominating far more territory over the interior and southern states of the country.

115TH CONGRESS, HOUSE OF REPRESENTATIVES

During the 2016 Election, Democrats picked up a net of six seats in the House of Representatives. While far fewer than many hoped, this did move the number of Democratic seats to 194, still far below the Republican total of 241. Democrats took two seats in Florida and Nevada, while gaining one seat each in Illinois, New Hampshire, New Jersey, and Virginia. For the 2016 House elections as a whole, 97 percent of all incumbents won reelection.

In tallying all House members, Republicans hold a majority of seats in thirty states. This truth is critical in the case of decisions in which each state has one vote. Democrats hold the majority in eighteen states, with two states having an equal number of Democratic and Republican representatives. Figure 8.2 illustrates the balance of Democratic versus Republican control. As is the case with senators and governors, Democratic support is strongest in the northeast and far west, with Republicans dominating the southern and interior districts.

STATE LEGISLATURES

The partisan balance in state legislatures stayed essentially the same compared to previous elections, with only moderate changes (see figure 8.2). Democrats kept control of both houses in eight states: California, Connecticut, Hawaii, New York, Massachusetts, Vermont, New Jersey, and Rhode Island. Colorado, Illinois, Maine, Maryland, and Washington remain divided, with Delaware moving from the Democratic to the divided group. Washington provides a unique example of divided government, created by a conservative Democratic senator caucusing with Republicans. Nevada and New Mexico both shifted to Democratic control of both houses, but three states—Iowa, Kentucky, and Minnesota—shifted from divided to full Republican control.

Consequently, similar patterns as described earlier can be seen in the geography of party control of state legislatures. Of the ten state houses controlled by Democrats, all but New Mexico and Nevada are found on the east and west coasts. In truly outstanding spatial patterns, Republicans hold both houses in thirty-five states (exceptions being Colorado and Illinois) in the southern and interior states of the country.

TRIFECTAS

States demonstrating one-party control of both houses of the legislature as well as the governorship (trifectas) are a key measure of political imbalance of power. Democrats hold trifectas in only six states: California, Connecticut, Delaware, Rhode Island, Oregon, and Hawaii. Nineteen states have divided control, leaving twenty-five states with total Republican control (see figure 8.3). This is an increase from the preelection total of twenty-one, having added Iowa, Missouri, Kentucky, and New Hampshire from a divided status to Republican, but losing Nevada to the divided column.

In sum, while Democrats had some important local victories, as in Nevada, Republican gains were more pervasive. Republican victories at a variety of levels in places like Iowa, Missouri, Minnesota, and Kentucky more or less eliminated Democrat control through the interior of the United States. Though Democrats controlled both coasts, New Hampshire and Vermont provide some level of political independence.

MISSOURI GUBERNATORIAL ELECTION, 2016

MATTHEW ENGEL

The 2016 gubernatorial election in Missouri has continuity with previous elections for governor in the post–World War II era, but also breaks new ground in certain respects. The Republican candidate, Eric Greitens, handily defeated the Democratic candidate Chris Koster with 51.1 percent of the vote to 45.5 percent. As seen in figure 8.4, the traditional strongholds for the Democratic Party were still solidly behind that party. The cores of the Kansas City and St. Louis metropolitan areas voted for the Democratic candidate—Jackson County, St. Louis County, and the independent city of St. Louis. The fourth and final unit that voted Democratic is Boone County in mid-Missouri, which is home to the flagship campus of the University of Missouri, and that county behaves in a similar fashion to flagship university counties in other states. The remainder of the state's 111 counties voted for the Republican candidate in varying degrees.

Although Missouri is often considered a "red" state in the media, it is more accurate to consider it a swing state (Rafferty 1983). In the post–World War II era, Missouri has elected or reelected a Democratic governor in thirteen elections and a Republican in six. For presidential election results, the reverse is the case, with the state voting for the Democratic candidate in seven instances and the Republican candidate in twelve elections. The swing state status is also reflected in the politicians elected to the US Senate, with six different Democrats and six different Republicans serving in that capacity since 1945. Although not evident on the map from 2016, volatility in elections for governor can be seen at the county level in previous elections. Some of those typically safe Democratic counties voted Republican on occasion, and many nonmetropolitan counties will vote for a Democratic candidate when the "right" person is running for office.

The 2016 election for governor had parallels to the national election. The sitting Democratic governor could not run again due to term limits, which opened the seat for competition. The eventual Republican nominee overcame a contentious primary field crowded with four candidates, two of whom were established politicians. Surprisingly, the two seasoned politicians, one of whom had twelve years' experience as lieutenant governor, received fewer votes in the primary than either of the newcomers who had never held any elected office (Missouri Secretary of State 2016a). On the Democratic side, an established politician who served eight years as the attorney general of Missouri secured the nomination. Throughout the period leading up to the November election, polls consistently showed that the Democratic candidate was favored to win the office and in many instances by an amount greater than the margins of error of those polls (Schmitt 2016). The outcome caught many people by surprise.

Interestingly, both of the candidates had switched party affiliations. Greitens left the Democratic Party in 2014, and Koster left the Republican Party in 2007 (Hancock 2016). Both dealt with accusations of being opportunistic for changing their political affiliation. This also meant that the label of "flip-flopper" did not really damage the prospects of either candidate since each had walked across the aisle to further their political careers.

A pattern that was broken was the propensity of Missourians to elect governors who have roots outside of Kansas City and St. Louis. Throughout its entire history, only four of its fifty governors had strong ties to either of the largest cities in the state (Missouri Secretary of State 2016b). Even though it is the population anchor of western Missouri, Kansas City has only produced a single governor. In contrast, tiny Birch Tree (population 679 in 2010) in the heart of the Ozarks can claim two recent governors. In 2016, all four of the candidates in the Republican primary had deep St. Louis connections. In the past, oftentimes a candidate from the largest metropolitan areas would be sifted out of the race in the primary, partially due to the aversion of nonmetropolitan voters. With all four Republican candidates having St. Louis ties, that meant the winner of that contest would have metropolitan roots by default. On the Democratic side, Koster had no serious challenger in the primary, so his birthplace of St. Louis and career as prosecutor near Kansas City did not hinder him. Thus, in the general election, Missourians were going to seat a candidate from the "big city," no matter how they voted.

FIGURE 8.4

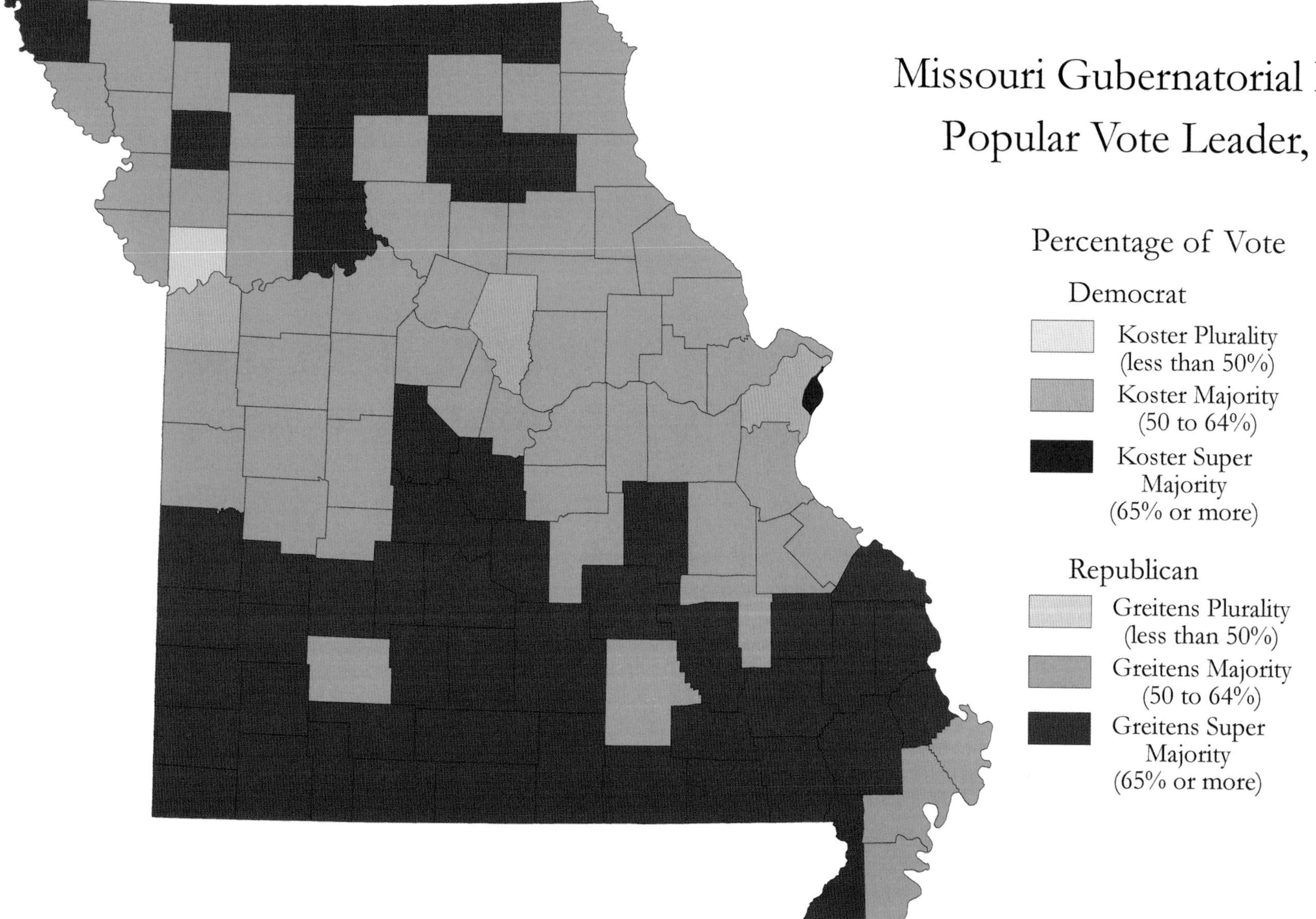
Missouri Gubernatorial Election
Popular Vote Leader, 2016
Percentage of Vote
Democrat
Koster Plurality
(less than 50%)
Koster Majority
(50 to 64%)
Koster Super
Majority
(65% or more)
Republican
Greitens Plurality
(less than 50%)
Greitens Majority
(50 to 64%)
Greitens Super
Majority
(65% or more)

On the surface, the pattern on the map might not seem to communicate much. What does stand out is even when the Republican candidate for governor wins in Missouri, typically a number of scattered nonmetropolitan counties back the Democratic candidate. The sheer number of counties carried by the Republican in this instance is far more intense than the norm. Even when a Republican governor was elected by a decent margin, such as John Ashcroft in 1984 or Matt Blunt in 2004, at least a handful of nonmetropolitan counties swung Democratic. That did not happen in 2016. In all likelihood, Greitens was able to build on his own support by riding the coattails of Donald Trump in the general election to carry all but those traditionally loyal Democratic zones.

Just as the core units of Kansas City and St. Louis, along with Boone County, went solidly Democratic, the traditional Republican strongholds are evident too. The people in the Ozark Mountains, which are in the southern third of the state, typically vote Republican. This is especially true in the southwest corner of Missouri, which consistently votes Republican no matter the candidate. Another traditional Republican stronghold is the north-central portion of the state, which is not as reliable for that party as the Ozarks, but does show up in the 2016 results in its intensity of support. The section of Missouri that best fits the definition of a "swing region" is the belt of counties in the greater Missouri River valley, which can be identified on figure 8.4 with the meandering line between the Democratic anchors. In this election, that swing district was handily won by Greitens, which contributed to his comfortable margin of victory.

REFERENCES

Hancock, Jason. 2016. Eric Greitens Wins Republican Nomination for Missouri Governor, Will Face Democrat Chris Koster. *Kansas City Star*. August 3, http://www.kansascity.com/news/politics-government/election/article93405572.html.

Missouri Secretary of State. 2016a. http://enrarchives.sos.mo.gov/enrnet (last accessed April 16, 2017).

Missouri Secretary of State. 2016b. Official Manual, State of Missouri 2015–2016. http://www.sos.mo.gov/BlueBook (last accessed April 16, 2017).

Rafferty, Milton D. 1983. *Missouri: A Geography*. Boulder, CO: Westview Press.

Schmitt, Will. 2016. With Election Six Days Away, Polls Show Toss-Up Race Between Greitens and Chris Koster. *Springfield News-Leader*. November 3, http://www.news-leader.com/story/news/politics/elections/2016/11/02/election-six-days-away-polls-show-toss-up-race-between-eric-greitens-and-chris-koster/93190370/.

SEATTLE'S 2013 VOTE ON ELECTION OF COUNCIL BY DISTRICT

RICHARD L. MORRILL AND BEN ANDERSTONE

Municipal elections, particularly those occurring during nonpresidential or midterm years, are not usually very noteworthy, but Seattle's 2013 election was unique enough to warrant further inspection. The city had traditionally elected city council members at large, but in 2013 this changed to a mixed system whereby two members were elected at large and seven were elected by district. In addition, the longtime incumbent mayor also lost his race to a self-avowed socialist. While the mayor's race is in itself interesting, here we will focus on the vote to change the council's longtime election system.

Neighborhood interests, especially those far from the city center, led the district election effort yet, ironically, much of the heaviest support was near core areas. The election is correctly seen as a revolt against the establishment, against "business as usual," but what does this really mean? In this review, we look at the geographic pattern of votes, in order to uncover how different areas of the city as well as different kinds of people voted. We provide some summary statistics, and then review the geography of the vote in two ways, at a more aggregated level using census tracts, which enable us to relate the vote to census variables, and also at the detailed precinct level.

I (Morrill) admit that this essay gives me an opportunity to report on a singular achievement not only of my career, but of my lengthy time as Seattle resident. That is, I drew the map of the district plan that was endorsed by two-thirds of voters, despite being opposed by the "establishment" and widely expected to fail, as had two earlier attempts. I drew the plan with very traditional criteria of equal population, geographic compactness, maintenance of traditional neighborhoods, and with a provision for a majority minority district. The effect of these was a map of remarkable compactness, with minimal distortion or division of communities, but with the corresponding tendency for districts to be rather heterogeneous (see figure 8.5).

We begin with a table profiling the districts by demographic characteristics and their voting in the 2013 election (see table 8.1). Variation in support for districts was actually surprisingly tiny, from 62.5 percent to 68.1 percent. The strongest support for districts was not from the areas farthest from downtown (First and Fifth), but rather from the most "left" or nonconformist Third and Sixth. Conversely, the intervening central Seventh District showed the lowest support for districts, as expected. One possible reason for the distinction is the greater dependence of the Seventh on downtown jobs, while the Sixth and even the Third have stronger ties to the University of Washington. Analysis at the census tract level of aggregation showed a moderate variation of support for districts. Results of the election saw a low of 58 percent and 59 percent in two downtown tracts as well as 59 percent in Madison Park, while other

TABLE 8.1. Profile of Seattle Districts

Variable	First	Second	Third	Fourth	Fifth	Sixth	Seventh
% Families w/children	39	50	23	27	34	28	15
% Single	35	31	48	39	38	37	56
% Minority	28	77	31	27	29	19	20
% Under 18	20	21	13	15	17	15	21
% Rent	40	48	62	54	47	46	63
% BA or More	44	29	57	73	52	64	61
% Poor Persons	9	20	15	18	10	7	14
Median HH Income	68	47	62	57	63	74	62
2013 Election Results	**First**	**Second**	**Third**	**Fourth**	**Fifth**	**Sixth**	**Seventh**
% Yes district election	65.1	65.3	67.1	66.9	65.8	68.1	62.5

FIGURE 8.5

Seattle's 2013 Vote on Election of City Council Members by District

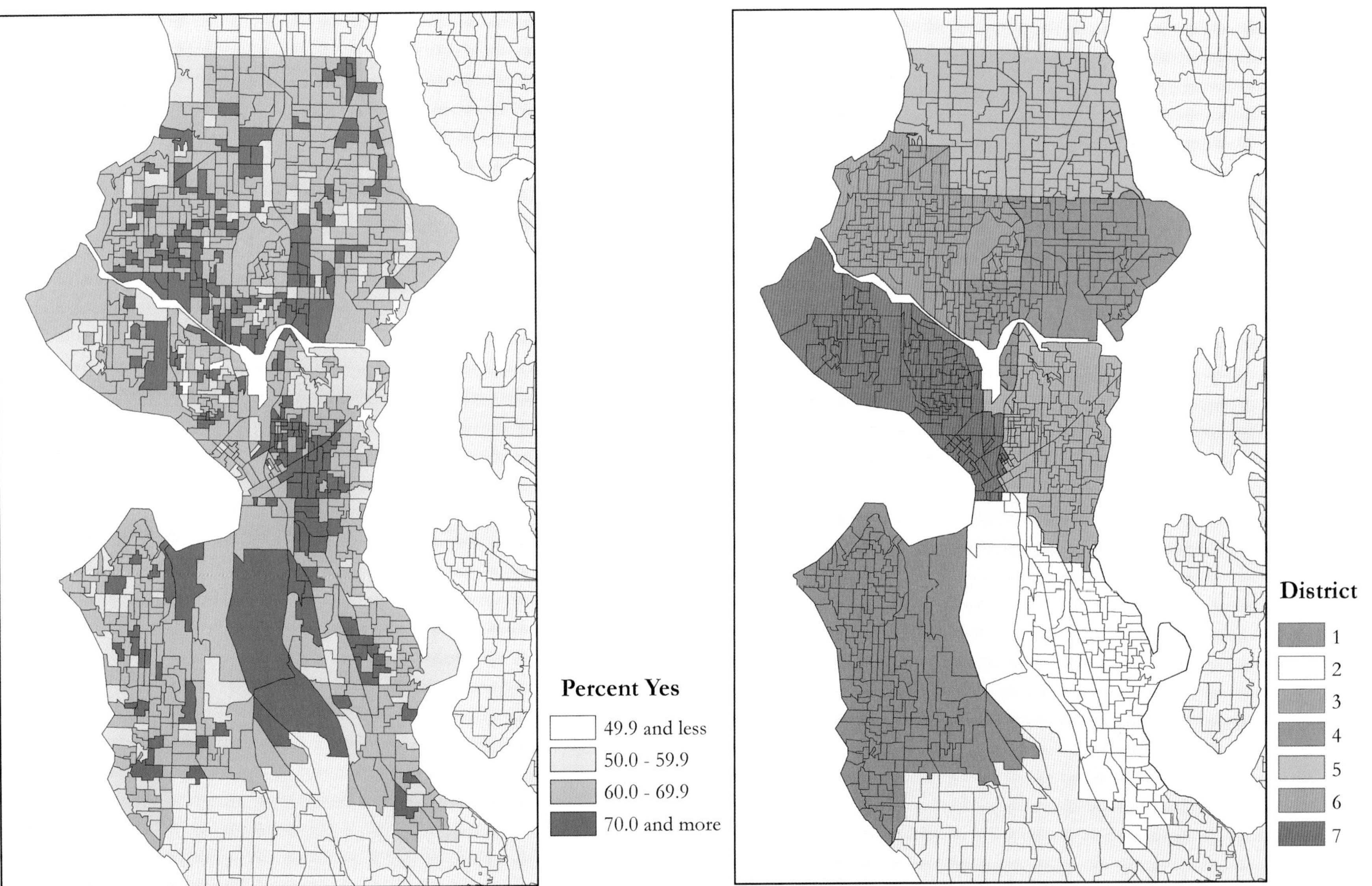

areas produced a high of 77 percent at the University of Washington, 71 percent to 75 percent in central Capitol Hill tracts, and 71 percent to 72 percent in Ballard.

We students of elections enjoy explaining the geographic differences in voting through demographic characteristics. Without exit poll data on individuals, we use a riskier "ecological" correlation, relying upon the average characteristics of census tracts. Through this we can discover likely relationships. In the case of the Seattle 2013 contests, however, the relationships are meaningful but not very robust, as demographic variables do not convincingly explain the vote. But, high support for districts does have a common pattern, correlating most strongly with those tracts with a high proportion of unmarried residents and individuals in the 20–34 years of age bracket combined with high transit use and a lower rate of home ownership. These are typically all characteristics of urban areas, with high levels of commuting to greater downtown and to the University of Washington. People in these areas are arguably idealist, or open to new ideas. Conversely, opposition to the district system is correlated with high levels of married individuals, homeownership, and greater median incomes. In other words, established traditional neighborhoods! This is a little counterintuitive for districts, for which we might have expected stronger support from the homeowning neighborhoods resisting downtown-oriented, new urbanist policies. Instead, some new urbanist neighborhoods were the most supportive, suggesting instead that idealists and seekers of change put the possibility of electing younger, more open-to-radical-change persons to the council as a high priority.

What missing variable might account for this? Very likely it is the very understandable reaction of the young to excessive inequality, the dearth of middle-class jobs, and the over-concentration of wealth and power that is the basis for strong support for districts. And we should recognize the seemingly strong influence of the Seattle weekly, *The Stranger*, and its endorsement of districts and its overt addressing of inequality.

Discussion at a finer geography will help us better understand the differences noted above. The pattern of voting at the precinct level (see figure 8.5) reinforces our observation very early that there was little or no tendency for less central single-family home neighborhoods to be the strongest supporters for districts, as had been expected. Rather patterns indicated that class and, to a degree age, was the dominant factor, with younger, less affluent, white or minority, single unmarried, LGBT, voting most strongly for district representation—while waterfront view, affluent, familial precincts were the least supportive. After the election, it was better understood that the strongest motivation for districts was the likelihood of greater representation of women, and of more radical change, and this indeed occurred. So ironically the change to districts supported the trend toward "densification" that was a strong motivation of the original and strongest supporters.

MONTANA 2016: CONSERVATISM VERSUS CONTRARIANISM?

LARRY KNOPP

The 2016 results in Montana evince a hostility toward Democrats that has been growing since the first Clinton administration (with the exception of 2008, when the presidential vote was the fourth closest in the country), moderated by a long-standing independent and contrarian streak. Hillary Clinton's support cratered compared even to Barack Obama's in 2012 (a twenty-point deficit for Clinton compared with a fourteen-point deficit for Obama), and every statewide partisan race except one was won by a Republican. The exception was a big one, however: the governor's race. In addition, Donald Trump's increased share of the vote compared with Mitt Romney's in 2012 was trivial (0.35 percent).

The hostility to Democrats was clearly driven by an antipathy toward Clinton and the national Democratic Party. Only one other Democrat running statewide performed worse (the candidate for attorney general). In that race, the incumbent Republican was very popular and the Democrat filed literally at the last minute. In the presidential race, Clinton garnered a mere 35 percent of the statewide vote, carrying only six of fifty-six counties and an outright majority in only three (see figure 8.6). Even in two of the state's three majority–Native American counties (one of which she actually lost), her vote share cratered compared with Obama's in 2012. The only bright spot for her was a surprise victory in Montana State University's Gallatin County (Bozeman), which has been trending blue for several elections. Her other county victories were in the two other majority–Native American counties, two traditionally Democratic and labor-oriented counties containing the old mining towns of Butte and Anaconda (though her shares were drastically reduced there too), and in the long-standing progressive oasis of Missoula County, home to the University of Montana.

Meanwhile the incumbent Democratic governor, Steve Bullock, outperformed Clinton by nearly 90,000 votes out of just over a half-million cast, or fifteen percentage points. Figure 8.7 shows Bullock carried seven of the ten most populous counties (compared with three out of ten for Clinton), including the bellwethers of Cascade (Great Falls, a declining industrial, railroad, and military center), Lewis and Clark (Helena, the state capital), and Lake (which includes both affluent residences on Flathead Lake and a substantial portion of the Flathead Reservation). A popular centrist, Bullock succeeded where other Democrats failed by stressing small business–focused job growth through tax incentives, fiscal responsibility, and, crucially, access to public lands—a sacrosanct issue in Montana. In this regard, he benefited from relentless attacks on his Republican opponent, Greg Gianforte, many of them by groups not formally connected to the Bullock campaign. Gianforte, a wealthy high-tech entrepreneur and creationist Christian conservative based in Bozeman, was accused of suing to eliminate a public easement through his own property and of supporting organizations dedicated to selling off public lands and weakening access to public waterways. In addition, the Montana Democratic Party continuously referred to him as a "New Jersey multimillionaire" (referencing his prior state of residence) who was out of step with Montana culture and values. Bullock, meanwhile, positioned himself as nonideological and bipartisan in his approach to government (which also contrasted with a highly partisan and conservative Republican-controlled legislature). In the end, Bullock won by 4 percentage points with a bare but absolute majority of the vote, as compared with a narrower 49 percent to 47 percent victory in 2012 (in both 2012 and 2016, a Libertarian took roughly 3.5 percent). Arguably, then, Gianforte lost the election as much as Bullock won it, as the Democratic candidate's percentage of the vote increased by 1 percent while the Republican's decreased by the same amount.

Worth noting as well is that voters solidly rejected, as they also did in 2014, an aggressive effort by conservatives to elect a state Supreme Court justice. This, despite the fact that conservatives contested the open seat on explicitly ideological grounds and in spite of the fact that the winner was publicly associated with and raised money from progressive and Democratic groups and individuals. Taken as a whole, then, the 2016 Montana election results suggest an electorate that was animated by an ongoing tension between conservative/anti-Democrat and

FIGURE 8.6

Montana Presidential Election Popular Vote Leader, 2016

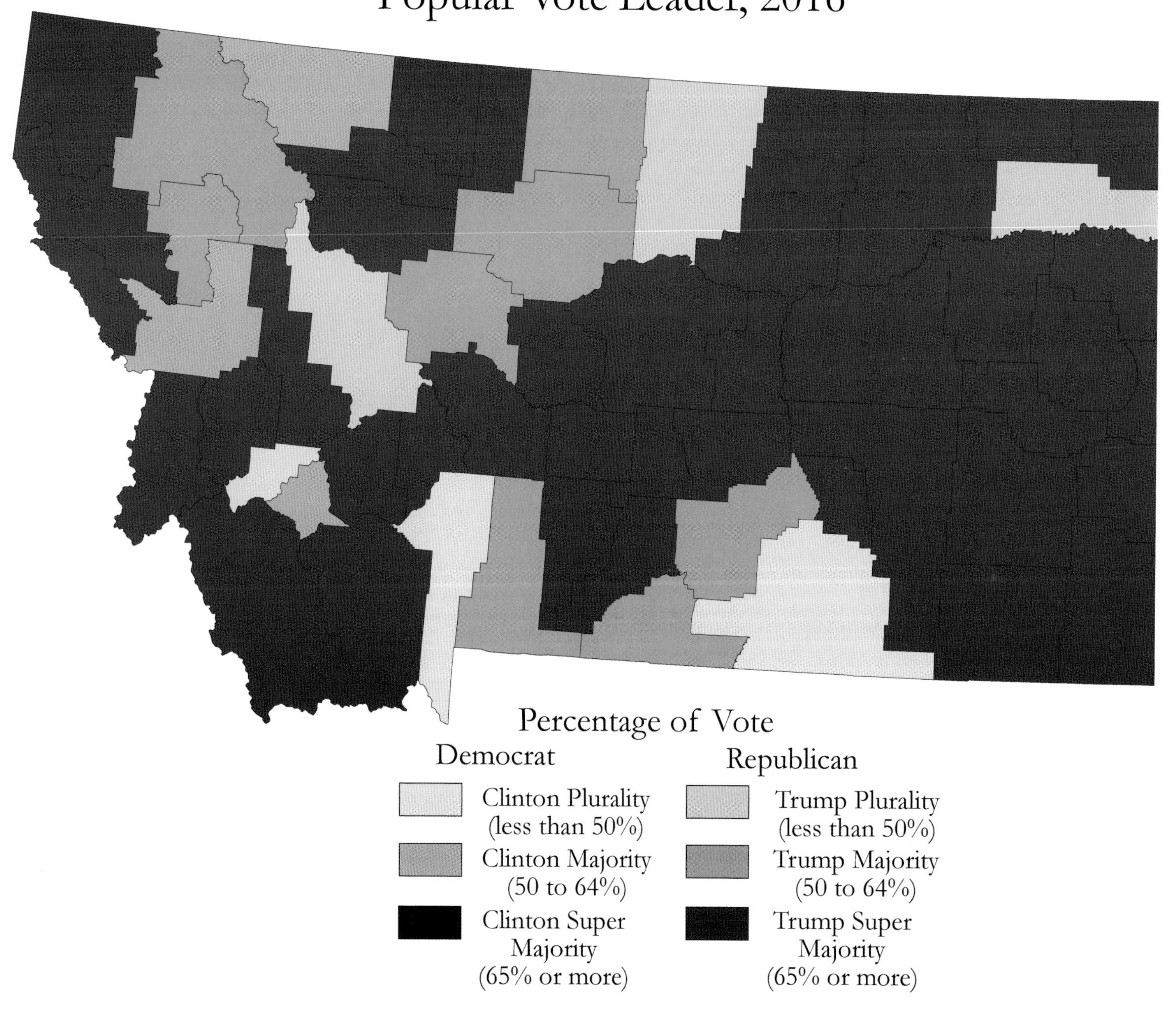

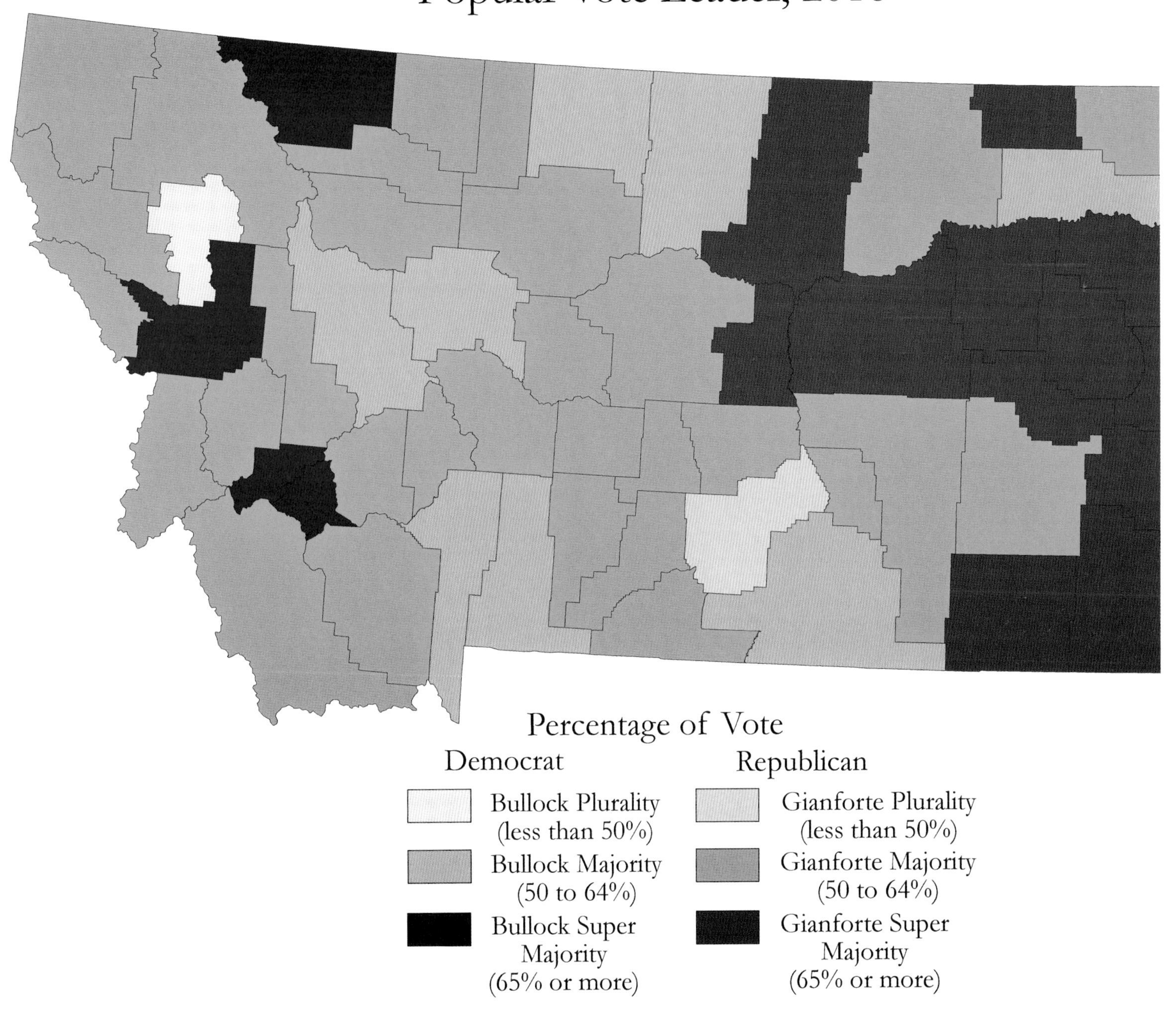
FIGURE 8.7
Montana Gubernatorial Election
Popular Vote Leader, 2016
Percentage of Vote
Democrat
Republican
Bullock Plurality
(less than 50%)
Bullock Majority
(50 to 64%)
Bullock Super
Majority
(65% or more)
Gianforte Plurality
(less than 50%)
Gianforte Majority
(50 to 64%)
Gianforte Super
Majority
(65% or more)

independent/contrarian impulses. In what was a very good year for conservatives and Republicans overall, Montana voters nonetheless rewarded candidates for two important statewide offices who presented themselves as independent of the overall trend and as either nonpartisan or bipartisan in their approaches to government. This suggests a refusal on the parts of many Montana voters to march in lockstep with any partisan or ideological agenda, even while sending a strong message overall in support of conservatism and the Republican Party.

NORTH CAROLINA GUBERNATORIAL ELECTION, 2016

KATIE WEICHELT

The North Carolina governor's election was one of the most closely watched races of the 2016 cycle. The Republican incumbent Pat McCrory's approval rating was in decline and polls showed that his challenger, Democrat Roy Cooper, mounted a serious challenge for the gubernatorial seat. The governor's popularity decreased when he caught national headlines and ignited a culture war after signing House Bill 2 (H.B. 2) into law in the spring of 2016. H.B. 2, passed by a Republican-dominated state house, required individuals seeking to use public restrooms to use the bathroom that matched the gender on their birth certificate. Though private businesses were not required to abide by this law, the local and national backlash was immediate. Ultimately, this controversy is the most likely catalyst that led to Cooper's victory.

North Carolina, a state that had voted Republican in several previous presidential election cycles, elected Barack Obama in 2008 by a margin of only 14,000 votes. Just two years later however, the Tea Party–led backlash would elect a Republican majority to the state legislature. An obvious gerrymandering plan allowed Republicans to dominate the state house over the next decade. During these years, Republicans, headlined by McCroy's election to the governor's mansion in 2012, enacted a series of conservative measures, the most famous being H.B. 2 and a 2013 push to restrict voting access through voter identification laws and slashing early voting opportunities in African American districts. The laws pertaining to the curtailing of voter opportunities were struck down in July 2016 by a federal count, but the controversies of H.B. 2 hung like a cloud over the gubernatorial election.

With the passage of H.B. 2 in March 2016, companies, artists, and other individuals initiated boycotts of the state. Lionsgate, a film production studio, canceled plans to film a series pilot. PayPal scrapped plans to open a new facility that was set to bring in 400 jobs in Raleigh, and Deutsche Bank announced a plan to freeze the expansion of 250 jobs at its Cary, North Carolina, center. In addition, various musicians such as Bruce Springsteen and Ringo Starr canceled performances in the state. In September 2016, the NCAA announced that it would move seven championship events from the state during the 2016–2017 academic year, including the first and second rounds of the Division I Men's Basketball Championship, stating that the decision was a direct result of H.B. 2.

McCrory's approval ratings began to decline over the economic fallout. In the months leading up to the election, journalists and analysts began commenting on the danger McCrory would face in the upcoming election. They noted a great deal of dissatisfaction with the legislature's actions and the economic fallout. On election night as the results rolled in, it looked like Roy Cooper would be able to unseat the governor. A large batch of voting results from Durham County, a Democratic stronghold, tipped the race into the challenger's favor. However, the margins were small. Cooper declared victory with only a lead of less than 5,000 votes. McCrory, however, refused to concede and argued that the candidates should wait until remaining military, provisional, and absentee ballots were counted. Some Cooper supporters protested outside of the governor's mansion by parking a moving truck in front of the house. As the weeks went by, McCrory filed a request for a recount, but supporters of the governor-elect moved to challenge the recount. As the absentee ballots were being counted, Cooper's margin increased.

Durham County, which pushed Cooper to the lead on election night, would again be front and center in deciding the election outcome. Durham's late reporting of vote tallies resulted from election workers' inability to read voting data from memory cards. The elections board agreed that this was enough reason to order a machine recount. McCrory and his campaign agreed that they would not seek a statewide recount if the Durham recount reproduced the election night numbers. Results stayed consistent and in the end, Roy Cooper defeated Pat McCrory by less than 5,000 votes, giving Democrats their only gubernatorial flip of the 2016 election season.

Cooper claimed victory in counties located in the north central portion of the state (see figure 8.8). Some of his largest victories were in Durham County, where he claimed 78.5 percent of the vote, and Orange County, with 74.8 percent. Both counties are part of the Durham–Chapel Hill metropolitan area and home to Duke University and

North Carolina Gubernatorial Election Popular Vote Leader, 2016

FIGURE 8.8

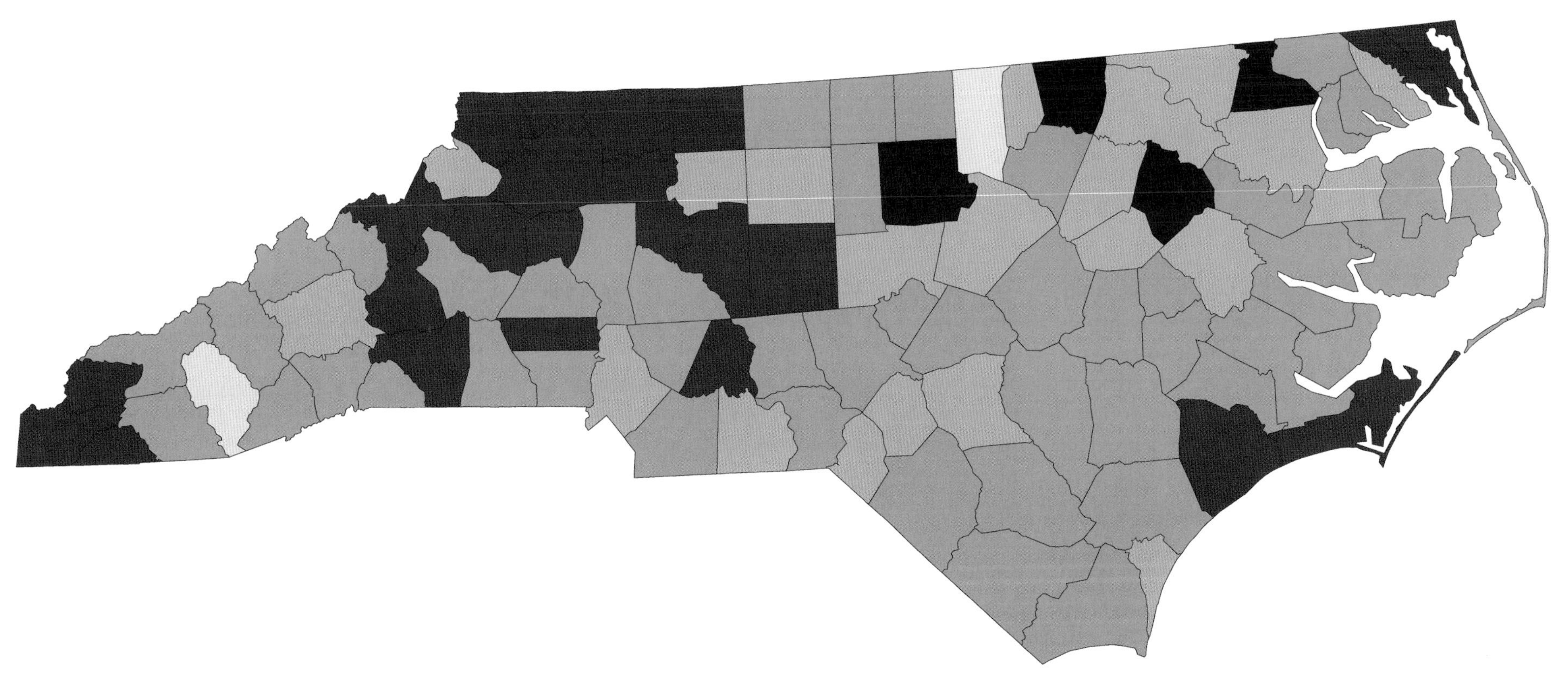

Percentage of Vote

Democrat	Republican
Cooper Plurality (less than 50%)	McCrory Plurality (less than 50%)
Cooper Majority (50 to 64%)	McCrory Majority (50 to 64%)
Cooper Super Majority (65% or more)	McCrory Super Majority (65% or more)

the University of North Carolina–Chapel Hill. Additionally, Cooper dominated in the stretch of northern counties from Granville County to Hertford County and much of the larger Research Triangle region as a whole. Beyond this region, Cooper also claimed victory in Buncombe County (Asheville) and Jackson County in the southwestern region of the state. McCrory's support was strongest in the rural and mainly white suburban areas throughout the state. Exit polls supported these patterns, illustrating native North Carolinians tended to favor McCrory over Cooper whereas the opposite was true for those who moved to the state.

In the end though, McCrory's fate seemed tied to H.B. 2. Exit polls also confirm that H.B. 2 was indeed unpopular, with nearly two-thirds of voters saying that they opposed the law. However, the results of the North Carolina election remain a mystery. Despite the low approval of H.B. 2, the legislature that drafted the bill did not suffer the consequences that McCrory did, and Donald Trump managed to win the state over Hillary Clinton. Some analysts have argued that some voters who typically lean Democrat were not excited by a Clinton presidency, particularly those living in rural or economically depressed areas. In addition, Democrats focused and spent greatly on defeating the Republican incumbent, which ultimately allowed them to deliver the only Democratic gubernatorial victory of the election cycle.

REFERENCES

Barrett, Mark. 2016. How Could McCrory Lose While Trump Wins NC? *Citizen Times*. November 9, http://www.citizen-times.com/story/news/local/2016/11/09/how-could-mccrory-lose-while-trump-wins-nc/93544174 (last accessed March 21, 2017).

Bort, Ryan. 2016. A Comprehensive Timeline of Public Figures Boycotting North Carolina Over the HB2 "Bathroom Bill." *Newsweek*. September 14, http://www.newsweek.com/north-carolina-hb2-bathroom-bill-timeline-498052 (last accessed March 21, 2017).

Campbell, Colin. 2016. Elections Board Orders Durham County Recount in Party-Line Vote. *News & Observer*. November 30, http://www.newsobserver.com/news/politics-government/election/article118035013.html (last accessed March 11, 2017).

Jenkins, Colleen. 2016. North Carolina Governor Unwilling to Concede in Tight Race. Reuters. November 9, http://www.reuters.com/article/us-usa-election-north-carolina-idUSKBN13434N (last accessed March 11, 2017).

NCAA to Relocate Championships from North Carolina for 2016–17. 2016. NCAA. September 12, http://www.ncaa.org/about/resources/media-center/news/ncaa-relocate-championships-north-carolina-2016-17 (last accessed March 21, 2017).

HOW LAQUAN MCDONALD'S SHOOTING "SHOOK UP" THE COOK COUNTY STATE'S ATTORNEY ELECTION

MEGAN A. GALL AND JENNIFER L. PATIN

The 2014 police shooting of eighteen-year-old Michael Brown in Ferguson, Missouri, began a new chapter in America's political and social movement history. Young Michael Brown's murder further exposed the unsettling fact that many communities across the United States are familiar with police killings of unarmed African Americans. One can presume that the visibility, or "viral" broadcasting, of Michael Brown's death and related circumstances brought record numbers of citizens to the streets in protest of police brutality. Organizations like Black Lives Matter, Assata's Daughters, FLY, and Black Youth Project 100 (Ross 2016) organized resistance across the nation, with some local protests making national news. Naturally, national media and socially invested organizations sought to connect the dots between these killings, the impact on communities, and the larger systemic problems in the administration of law and order. Consequently, the media attention given to localized unrest brought unusual focus on local and state officials like sheriffs and state's attorneys.

On October 20, 2014, a Chicago police officer shot seventeen-year-old Laquan McDonald sixteen times. At the time, McDonald's death went relatively unpublicized. A year later, after a judge ordered the police bodycam video of McDonald's shooting to be made public, the fatality got national attention, and communities revived demonstration on a much larger scale.

At the time, state's attorney Anita Alvarez was responsible for "the second largest prosecutor's office in the nation," including "the prosecution of all misdemeanor and felony crimes committed in Cook County, one of the largest counties in the United States" (Cook County State's Attorney 2017). Alvarez, who was privy to the McDonald video, faced fierce public criticism for waiting 400 days before charging the shooting officer with murder. Her handling of other criminal justice matters, like Chicago's overcrowded prisons among other issues, was already under public scrutiny (Rice 2016).

Tensions between community members and law enforcement were clear and present influences on the state's attorney 2016 election in Cook County, Illinois, home to the City of Chicago. Locally, advocacy groups focused on ousting Alvarez. Protests continued, using websites to organize and distribute information around well-defined objectives. Activists leveraged social media to promote memes and hashtags like #ByeAnita. As a critical part of their messaging, organizers were not promoting Kim Foxx or Donna More, but rather imploring voters to hold Anita Alvarez accountable (Ross 2016).

Alvarez, a Latina Democrat, first won her seat in 2008. She eked out a primary victory with 25.73 percent of the vote; her opponent, Tom Allen, trailed with 24.72 percent of the vote (Cook County Clerk 2017). That year, Alvarez won the general election with 60.84 percent of the vote (Cook County Clerk 2017). She enjoyed a solid Latino voter base and a substantial chunk of the African American vote (Rice 2016). Even though local dissatisfaction was brewing, Alvarez went unchallenged in the 2012 primary (Rice 2016). But by 2016, with an activated electorate and mounting political pressure, Alvarez faced two challengers in the Democratic primary: Kim Foxx, who was vying to be the first African American woman to hold the office, and Donna More.

Figure 8.9 identifies the largest racial group among Cook County Census tracts. As can be seen, African Americans comprise the largest group throughout southern Cook County, mainly the neighborhoods of South Chicago. Latino populations can be found throughout the County, but larger proportions are concentrated in the central areas of Chicago. White populations dominate remaining areas, including the neighborhoods of north central Chicago and the surrounding suburbs. With figure 8.9 in mind, and with racial politics and dynamics front and center in the 2016 Cook County election, how did Chicagoans decide their next state's attorney? Ecological inference (EI) models give us some insight (Wittenberg et al. 2007). These models allow us to draw conclusions about individual-level behavior using aggregate-level data. We estimated (see table 8.2) the voting behavior of African Americans, Latinos, and whites in the 2016 State's Attorney Democratic Primary for all of Cook County, the City of Chicago, and the Chicago Townships (or suburbs). Results show that across the county, African American voters were no longer throwing

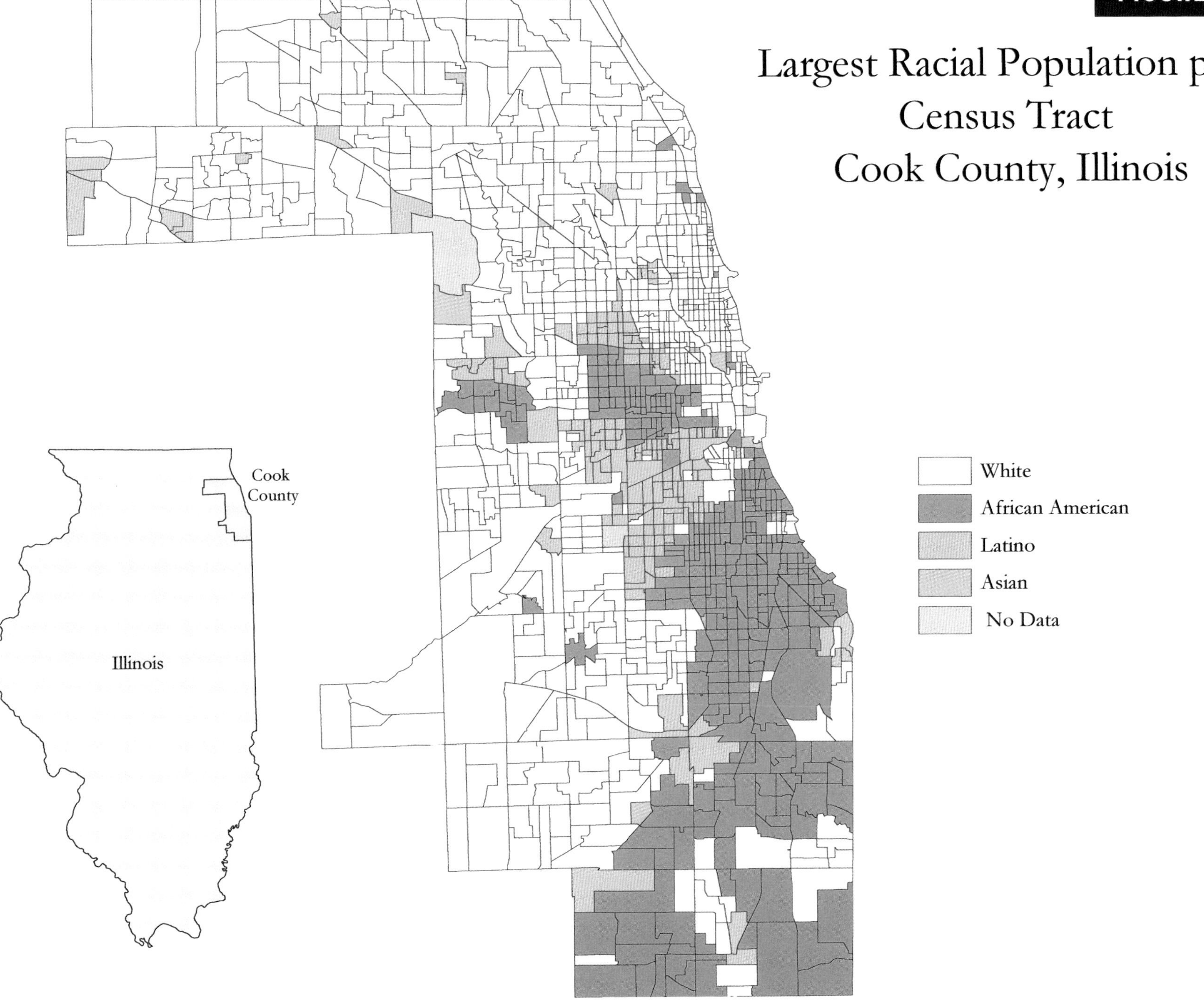
FIGURE 8.9
Largest Racial Population per Census Tract Cook County, Illinois
Cook County
Illinois
White
African American
Latino
Asian
No Data

TABLE 8.2. March 2016 Primary Election Results for State's Attorney, Cook County, Illinois

	Cook County Estimates		
	White Vote	African American Vote	Latino Vote
Kim Foxx	43%	88%	35%
Anita Alvarez	39%	5%	52%
Donna More	18%	7%	13%
	Township Estimates		
	White Vote	African American Vote	Latino Vote
Kim Foxx	41%	93%	26%
Anita Alvarez	40%	1%	62%
Donna More	19%	6%	13%
	City of Chicago Estimates		
	White Vote	African American Vote	Latino Vote
Kim Foxx	49%	87%	35%
Anita Alvarez	35%	6%	51%
Donna More	16%	7%	13%

substantive support behind Alvarez but instead, 88 percent supported Foxx. The City of Chicago and Townships supported Foxx at different levels. In the townships, African American support for Foxx was 93 percent, five points higher than estimated for the City of Chicago (87 percent). In terms of African American voter preferences, Donna More came in second with 7 percent of the county vote.

Similarly, though not as dramatically, Alvarez also lost her Latino base, with only 52 percent of Latino votes going to Alvarez countywide. Here, the differences between the Townships and the City of Chicago were more pronounced. Latino support for Alvarez in the townships was 62 percent, a full 11 points higher than the 51 percent she garnered in the city. The other 50 percent of Latino voters preferred Kim Foxx, giving her 35 percent of the vote.

Finally, support from white voters across the county split their vote primarily between Foxx and Alvarez, with each candidate securing slightly more than 40 percent of the white vote. In the end, Foxx was able to stitch together a multiracial coalition of voters and sweep the primary with 58.31 percent of the vote (Cook County Clerk 2017). Foxx went on to win the general election with 72.06 percent of the vote with a broad coalition of voters behind her.

REFERENCES

Cook County Clerk. 2017. Elections—Suburban Cook County. 2008 Election Results: Presidential General, Presidential Primary; 2016 Election Results: Presidential General, Presidential Primary. http://www.cookcountyclerk.com/elections/results/Pages/default.aspx (last accessed May 1, 2017).

Cook County State's Attorney. 2017. About the Cook County State's Attorney's Office. https://www.cookcountystatesattorney.org/about (last accessed May 14, 2017).

Rice, Josie D. 2016. Here Are More Reasons Why Chicago Should Vote Anita Alvarez Out of Office Tuesday. *Daily Kos*. March 14, http://www.dailykos.com/story/2016/3/14/1500898/-Here-are-more-reasons-why-Chicago-should-vote-Anita-Alvarez-out-of-office-tomorrow (last accessed May 1, 2017).

Ross, Janell. 2016. Black Lives Matter Won on Tuesday. Prosecutors Lost. *Washington Post*. March 16, https://www.washingtonpost.com/news/the-fix/wp/2016/03/16/black-lives-matter-won-on-tuesday-prosecutors-lost/?utm_term=.85b80dadf2a2.

Wittenberg, Jason, Ferdinand Alimadhi, and Olivia Lau. 2007. ei.RxC: Hierarchical Multinomial-Dirichlet Ecological Inference Model. In Kosuke Imai, Gary King, and Olivia Lau, eds., *Zelig: Everyone's Statistical Software*, 170–73. http://gking.harvard.edu/zelig (last accessed May 13, 2017).

COMPARISON OF 2012 AND 2016 PRESIDENTIAL RESULTS FOR WISCONSIN VOTING DISTRICTS

RYAN WEICHELT

Wisconsin has long been a Democratic stronghold for presidential elections. Given that the state had not elected a Republican since 1984, one could argue that the Badger State was the biggest surprise of November 8. Leading up to the election, Hillary Clinton held a rather comfortable lead in the polls. *Real Clear Politics* (2016) calculated a 6.5 percent lead for Clinton and the gold standard for Wisconsin polls, the Marquette Law School poll, showed a six-point lead in its final poll on October 27. Due to this perceived insurmountable lead, Clinton decided not to campaign in Wisconsin in order to consolidate resources in other battleground states. Donald Trump, in what was seen as a last gasp, decided to campaign one more time in the Badger State. The campaign headed to Eau Claire, Wisconsin, on a warm fall evening on November 1. Though the city itself is comfortably Democratic, the largest city of western Wisconsin holds a large geographic media market. The areas around Eau Claire can be categorized as mainly rural with struggling local economies steeped in dairy farming and frac sand mining. This area has also seen a fair amount of electoral volatility in state and national elections since 2008 (Weichelt 2016). In the end, Trump campaigned to an estimated crowd of 2,000 people with more waiting outside the arena and garnered the attention of local and national news outlets alike (Glauber and Carpenter 2016).

Not called until the early morning of November 9, to the shock of many, Trump narrowly won Wisconsin by an estimated 22,000 votes. Adding to the dismay for Democrats, its former senator, Democrat Russ Feingold, also lost in a surprising manner to incumbent Republican senator Ron Johnson. With such a strong lead in the polls, how did Clinton (and Feingold) lose Wisconsin? With so much emphasis on rural voting success for Trump, much of the attention was focused on north and western Wisconsin, thus the November 1 rally in Eau Claire. Figure 8.10 illustrates the change in vote between the 2012 and 2016 election at the voting district level. The greatest decline in Democratic voting can be seen in the rural areas of the state, especially the northern and western voting districts. Yet, a closer examination of the data illustrates rural voting changes were not as large as reported by media outlets. Certainly Trump's success in Wisconsin was propelled by rural voters, but when compared to 2012, most rural areas saw only minimal increases for Trump compared to Romney of about five to fifty votes. More important, Clinton's loss can be attributed more to the large decline of support in the Milwaukee area, due to a lack of enthusiasm for Clinton and the spoiler effect of Libertarian Gary Johnson on the ballot. Compared to 2012, the 2016 election saw 96,788 fewer voters in Wisconsin. The Milwaukee area alone saw a decline of nearly 52,000 votes compared to 2012, with Clinton losing 43,514 votes compared to Obama. Gary Johnson's garnering of over 102,000 votes, mainly in college towns across the state, added to her loss as well. However, Hillary Clinton, as can be seen in figure 8.10, was able to gain support, compared to Obama, in the traditionally Republican suburban counties around Milwaukee, highlighting traditional conservatives' contempt of Trump. Could one campaign stop by Clinton in late October have changed the tide? Most likely this question will long be debated, but voting district comparisons demonstrate that while rural areas provided Trump the needed votes to prevail, low Democratic support in Milwaukee and the inclusion of Gary Johnson on the ballot offer more compelling evidence as to why Trump became the first Republican to win the Badger State since 1984.

REFERENCES

Election 2016 Presidential Polls. 2016. *Real Clear Politics*. https://www.realclearpolitics.com/epolls/latest_polls/president (last accessed April 15, 2017).

Glauber, Bill, and Jacob Carpenter. 2016. Trump Upbeat about Chances in Eau Claire Visit. *Milwaukee Journal Sentinel*. November 1, http://www.jsonline.com/story/news/politics/elections/2016/11/01/uw-eau-claire-prepares-trump-visit/93137712 (last accessed April 15, 2017).

Weichelt, Ryan D. 2016. The Forgotten North: How Democrats Ignored Northern Wisconsin and Republicans Used Geography to Gain Control. *The Electorate*. November 21, http://theelectoratewi.weebly.com/home/the-forgotten-north-how-democrats-ignored-northern-wisconsin-and-republicans-used-geography-to-gain-control (last accessed March 18, 2017).

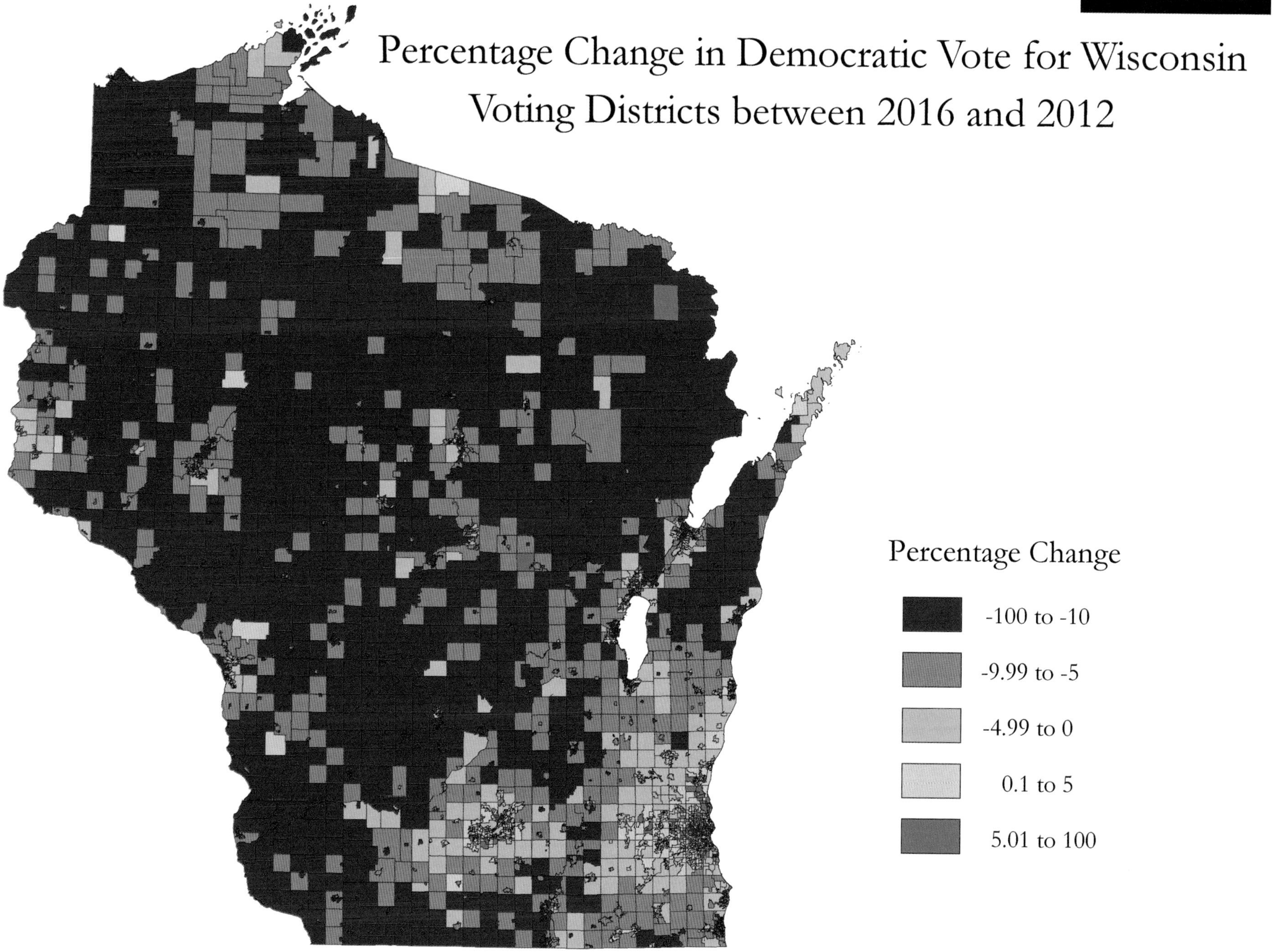

FIGURE 8.10

Percentage Change in Democratic Vote for Wisconsin Voting Districts between 2016 and 2012

Percentage Change

-100 to -10

-9.99 to -5

-4.99 to 0

0.1 to 5

5.01 to 100

MARIJUANA LEGALIZATION VOTES IN 2016

RICHARD L. MORRILL AND LARRY KNOPP

Five states—California, Arizona, and Nevada in the far southwest and Maine and Massachusetts in the far northeast—had ballot issues on legalization of recreational marijuana in 2016. Four others (Arkansas, Florida, North Dakota, and Montana) voted on measures to legalize or broaden access to medical marijuana. The recreational measures passed comfortably in California, Nevada, and Massachusetts and marginally in Maine, while the medical marijuana measures were successful in all four of the states in which they were on the ballot. Legalization failed narrowly in Arizona.

We discuss here the results of the recreational legalization measures only—by county in California, Nevada, and Arizona, and by town in Maine and Massachusetts (since in New England counties are almost entirely irrelevant to both data collection and governance).

In California legalization passed by 56 percent (figure 8.11). The most obvious pattern is the high support in most of the Pacific coast, especially in the greater San Francisco region. A second region of support was Los Angeles, San Bernardino, and Santa Barbara. Third are environment-conscious counties of the High Sierras. Levels of support were lower in some current areas of illegal production (e.g., Mendocino, Siskiyou, and Trinity Counties). Generally opposed to marijuana legalization were the state's dominant farming strongholds, the Central Valley, and Imperial County on the Mexico and Arizona borders.

In Nevada, legalization was somewhat closer, with a "yes" vote of 54.5 percent. The pattern was simple. As in the presidential race, legalization won in big metropolitan Clark and Washoe Counties (Las Vegas and Reno, respectively), and narrowly in predominantly suburban Storey and Nye Counties. Everywhere else in the state it failed, heavily in more rural areas and more narrowly elsewhere. The very low support in Lincoln County may be related to its high Mormon population share.

Arizona is the exception to the legalization juggernaut, narrowly failing (52–48 percent). Support was strongest in the two counties strongly influenced by public universities, Pima (Tucson and the University of Arizona) and Coconino (Flagstaff and Northern Arizona University). The rest of the state voted no, including Native American counties, farm counties like Yuma, and crucially, Maricopa (Phoenix), with over 3 million people. There, the measure did pass in Tempe, home to Arizona State University, but opposition elsewhere led to a narrow loss in the county overall. The strength of the Mormon Church and high shares of elderly may also have contributed to the loss in Arizona.

In Maine marijuana legalization passed only barely, with 50.2 percent of the vote (figure 8.12). As in the Southwest and in Washington, Oregon, and Colorado in earlier elections, votes in favor were highest in metropolitan cores, here Portland and its prosperous neighbors, and in coastal, tourist-oriented, and environmentally attractive areas, and lowest in most of the interior and other sparsely populated counties. The highest votes in favor of legalization were in Woodstock (73 percent), Portland (65 percent), Orono (University of Maine, 67 percent), Bar Harbor (59 percent), and Kittery (61 percent)—all either environmental amenity/tourist or metropolitan areas. The lowest votes in favor were in dozens of tiny rural areas, but also the somewhat larger towns of Caribou (37 percent), Fort Kent (33 percent), and Mars Hill (29 percent)—all in the remote and economically depressed extreme northeastern part of the state (which also voted heavily for Trump in the presidential race).

In Massachusetts, the overall percentage in favor of legalization was very similar to that in Nevada (54 percent). The highest support was in Boston-Cambridge and almost the entire western Berkshire region (also home to many prominent colleges) (figure 8.13). In addition, high levels of support can be seen in the islands of Nantucket and Dukes, on the outer reaches of Cape Cod (Truro and Wellfleet), and quite strongly in college-dominated towns and environmental-amenity towns across the state, as was also the case in Maine. Particularly high levels of support were in Cambridge (71 percent) and Amherst (75 percent). Opposition was largely concentrated in areas near older industrial towns that represent the older economy, for example, Lawrence (58 percent opposed) as well as some suburbs of Boston.

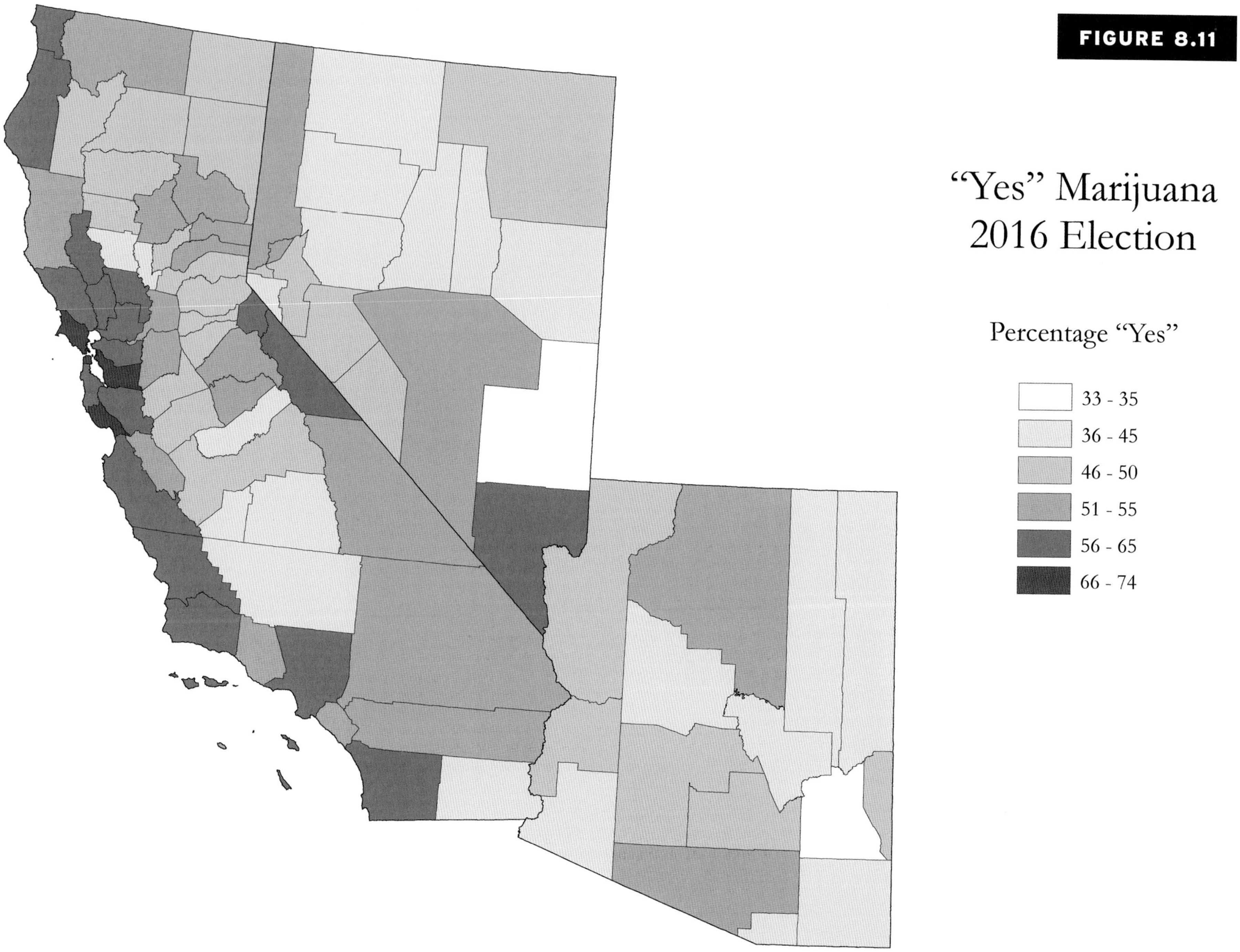

FIGURE 8.11

"Yes" Marijuana 2016 Election

Percentage "Yes"

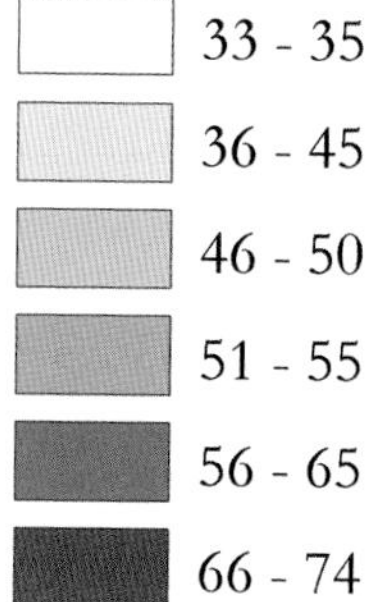

FIGURE 8.12

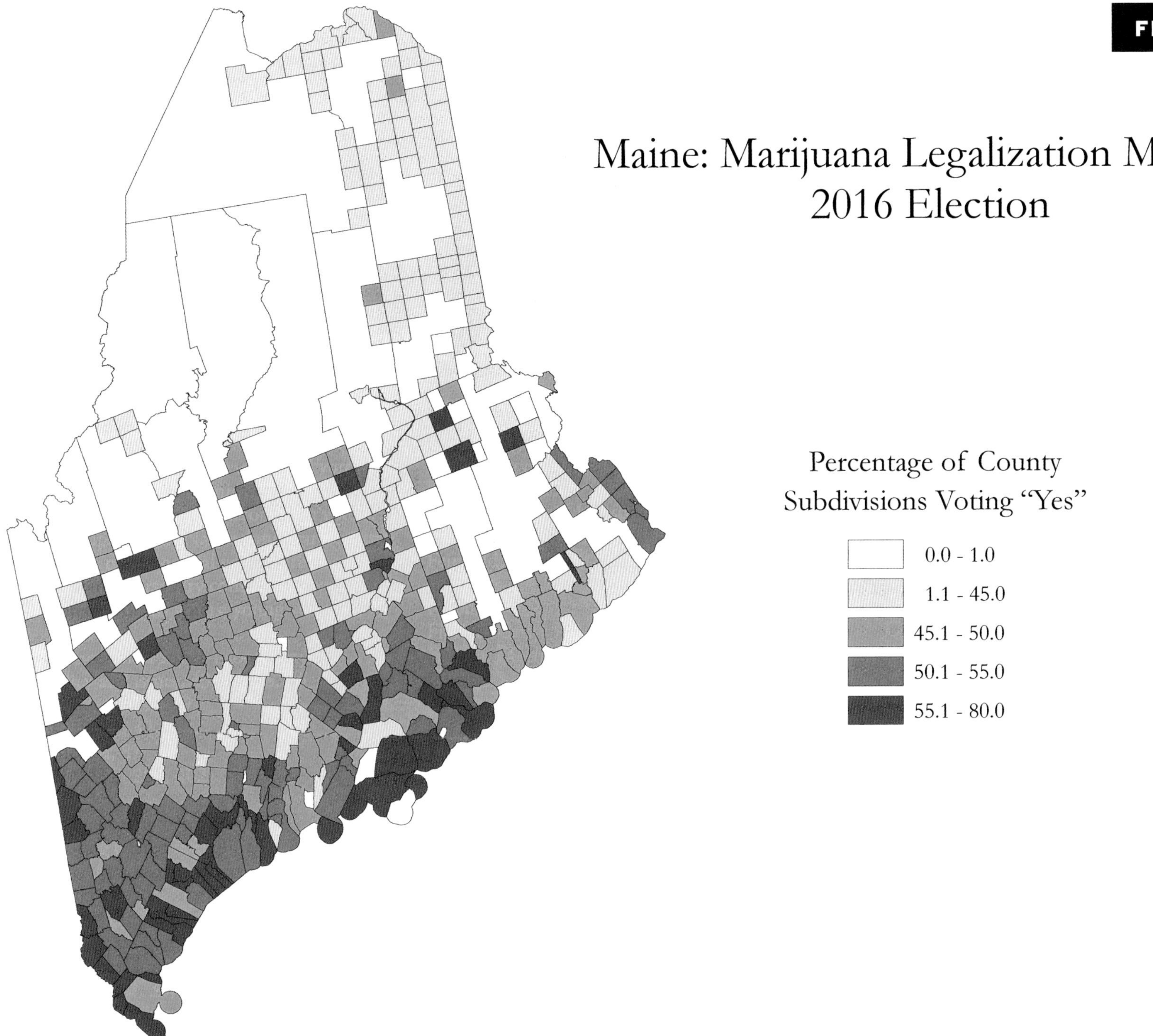
Maine: Marijuana Legalization Measure
2016 Election
Percentage of County
Subdivisions Voting "Yes"
0.0 - 1.0
1.1 - 45.0
45.1 - 50.0
50.1 - 55.0
55.1 - 80.0

FIGURE 8.13

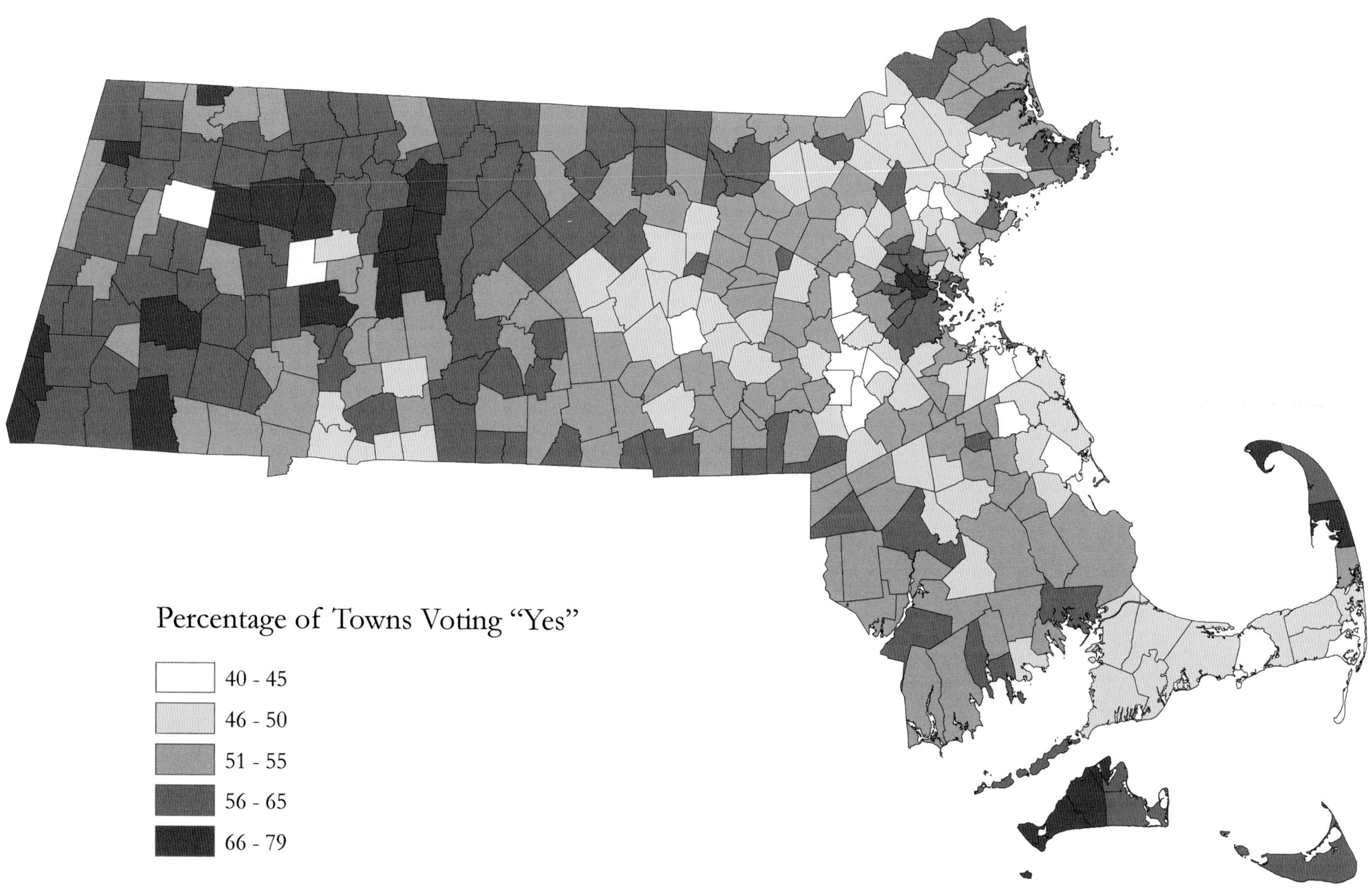
Massachusetts: Marijuana Legalization Initiative
2016 Election
Percentage of Towns Voting "Yes"
40 - 45
46 - 50
51 - 55
56 - 65
66 - 79

PRECINCT-LEVEL ANALYSIS IN WASHINGTON: MINIMUM WAGE VERSUS THE PRESIDENCY

BEN ANDERSTONE AND RICHARD L. MORRILL

Precinct-level mapping is valuable for revealing microgeographic patterns. We use precinct returns to contrast results for Democratic presidential candidate Hillary Clinton with a hard-fought ballot measure, Initiative 1433, to raise the minimum wage to $15 per hour statewide. Both Clinton and Initiative 1433 won in Washington—although neither by as much as the state's ultra-liberal reputation might suggest.

We map the results at the state level, with an inset of metropolitan Seattle, revealing the "two Washingtons": greater Seattle versus the rest of the state. Since we are also fortunate to have constructed a file cross-referencing precincts with census tracts, we are also able to provide some statistical relationships of interest.

In figure 8.14 the "two Washingtons" were certainly visible in the presidential election results. Hillary Clinton's 16-point win in Washington State was driven by a record-setting margin in King County (Seattle and suburbs), where she prevailed by 49 points. Most of her other wins were also in urban Puget Sound. She won Snohomish County (Seattle suburbs and working-class Everett) by 16 points, Thurston County (state capital Olympia) by 15, and Whatcom County (college town Bellingham) by 17.

In rural and small-town Washington, Clinton's results were considerably worse. She lost several historically Democratic working-class counties that Obama had twice carried. One of those, Grays Harbor County—which included the sawmill towns of Hoquiam and Aberdeen—had not voted Republican since 1928. Elsewhere, Clinton suffered significant losses in most rural counties. This was especially true in eastern Washington, where her only win was in Whitman County, where she dominated the college town of Pullman.

At face, the patterns for Initiative 1433 (I-1433) are similar (figure 8.15). The measure carried every county in the Puget Sound region. Elsewhere, it managed a majority in several of the working-class Obama/Trump counties—Grays Harbor, Pacific, Mason, and Skamania. Only one Clinton county, Whitman, voted against I-1433. Indeed, I-1433 outperformed Clinton's vote share in every county but King. In some, it did so by a significant stretch. The southeastern Washington county of Asotin (Clarkston) voted against Clinton by 26 points, but rejected I-1433 by only 6.

To the extent partisan crossover occurred on I-1433, it is most visible on the local level (figure 8.16). In Seattle, I-1433 passed by 63 points, significantly trailing Clinton's 76-point margin. The measure also lagged in the affluent, educated suburbs of Bellevue, Redmond, and Mercer Island. Conversely, smaller towns and cities often gave much stronger votes to the minimum wage increase. The lumber town of Pe Ell in Lewis County gave barely a fifth of the vote to Clinton, but passed I-1433.

Table 8.3 summarizes the statewide vote and presents some simple correlations of the vote, as summarized to an intermediate level of the census tract, with relevant census measures. Despite the visible differences in support for Clinton and I-1433, the correlation is a commanding 0.94. Support for Clinton is most highly associated with variables that best distinguish greater Seattle from the rest of the state—density, level of education, ethnicity, especially the concentration of Asian Americans in the Seattle area, less familial household types, young workers, and professional occupations. Support for a higher minimum wage is similar, but higher in areas with many racial minorities and nonfamily households, but is much less related to education and occupation. Differences in support are well explained by education, occupation, and income. Educated, affluent voters around Seattle were more likely to support Clinton than a higher minimum wage. In nonmetropolitan Washington, especially in areas that have seen economic decline in recent decades, the pattern was the opposite.

These results show that the classic "two Washingtons" pattern remains a force in state politics. However, it also reveals the divides—East versus West, metro versus nonmetro—as perhaps oversimplified. While the minimum wage issue was both popular and partisan statewide, comparison with the presidential results is illuminative. Some of the wealthy, educated voters in the Seattle metro—an area where many have recently begun voting Democratic—opposed the wage increase. Conversely, in rural areas and smaller cities—areas

FIGURE 8.14

Democratic Popular Vote 2016 Presidential Election

Seattle Area

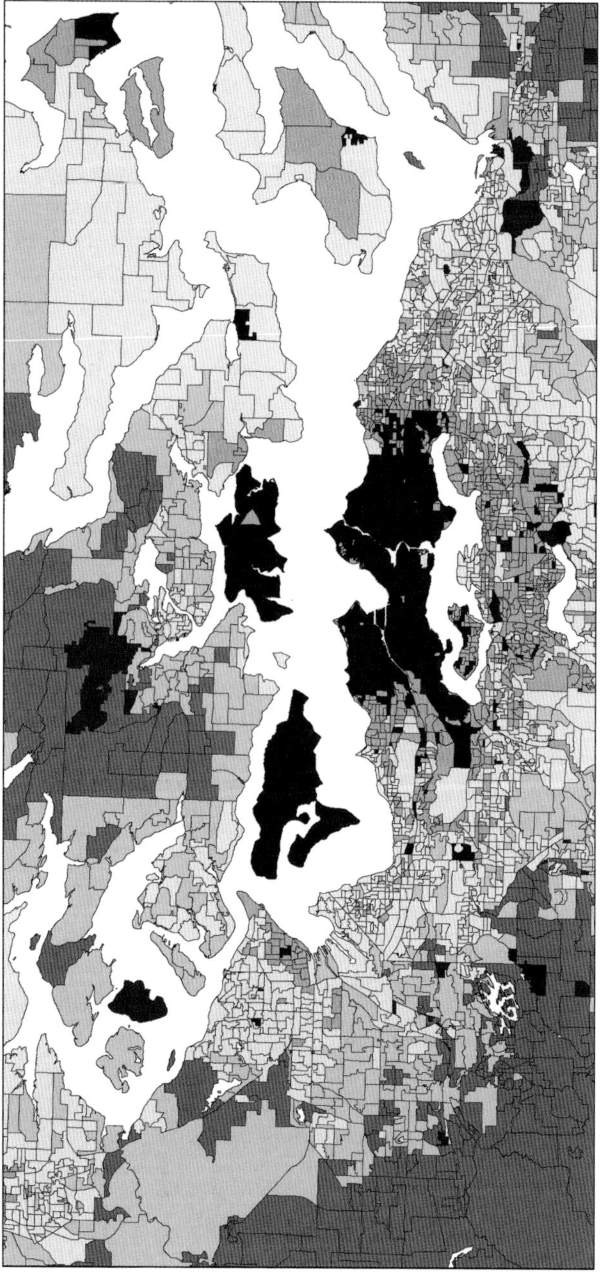

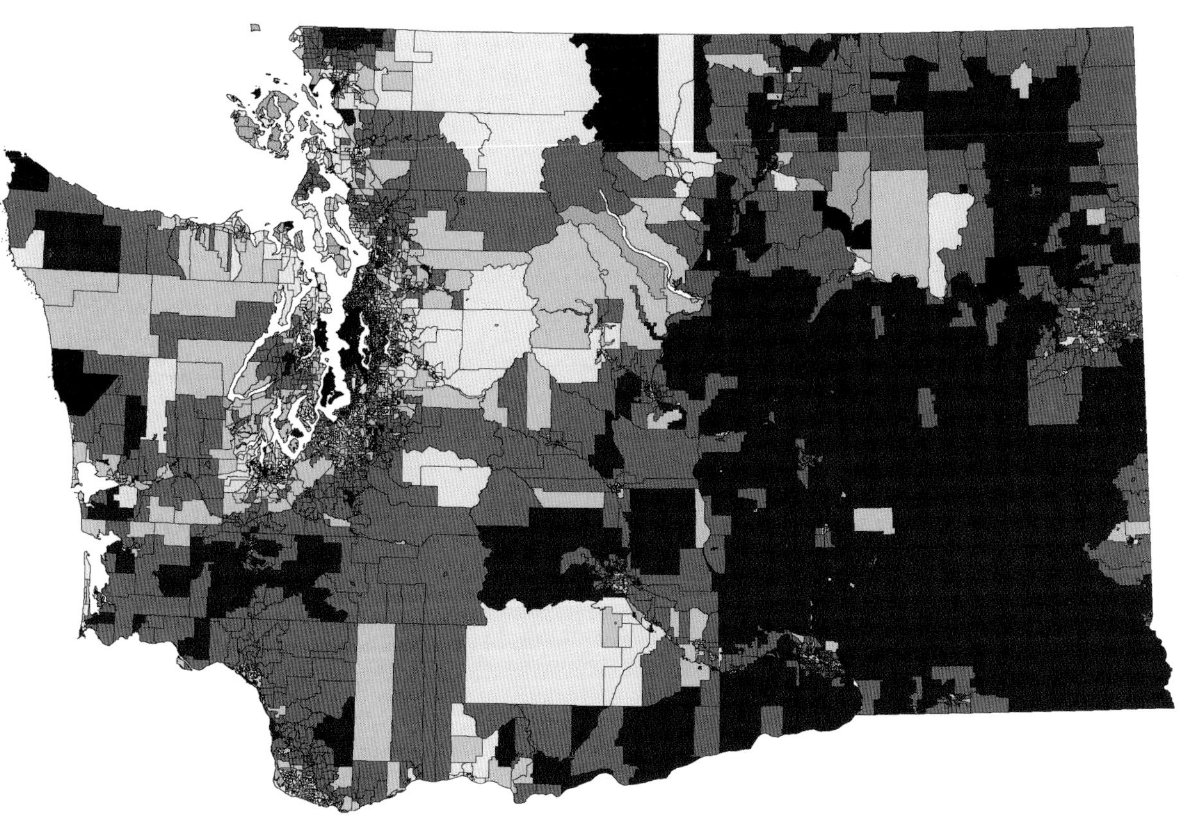

Democratic Percentage of the Popular Vote

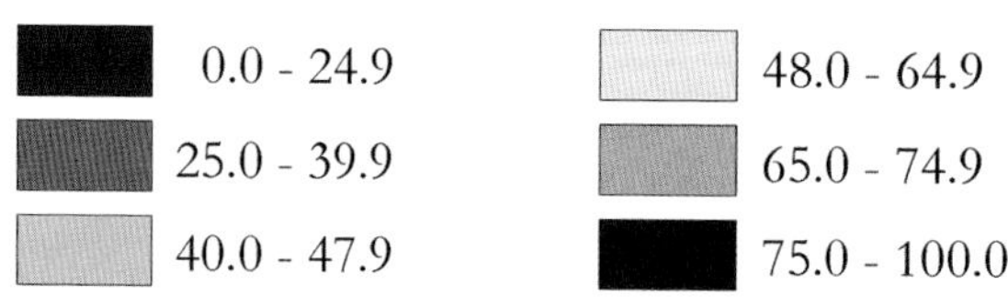

FIGURE 8.15

Initiative 1433: Increase Minimum Wage Washington 2016 Election

Seattle Area

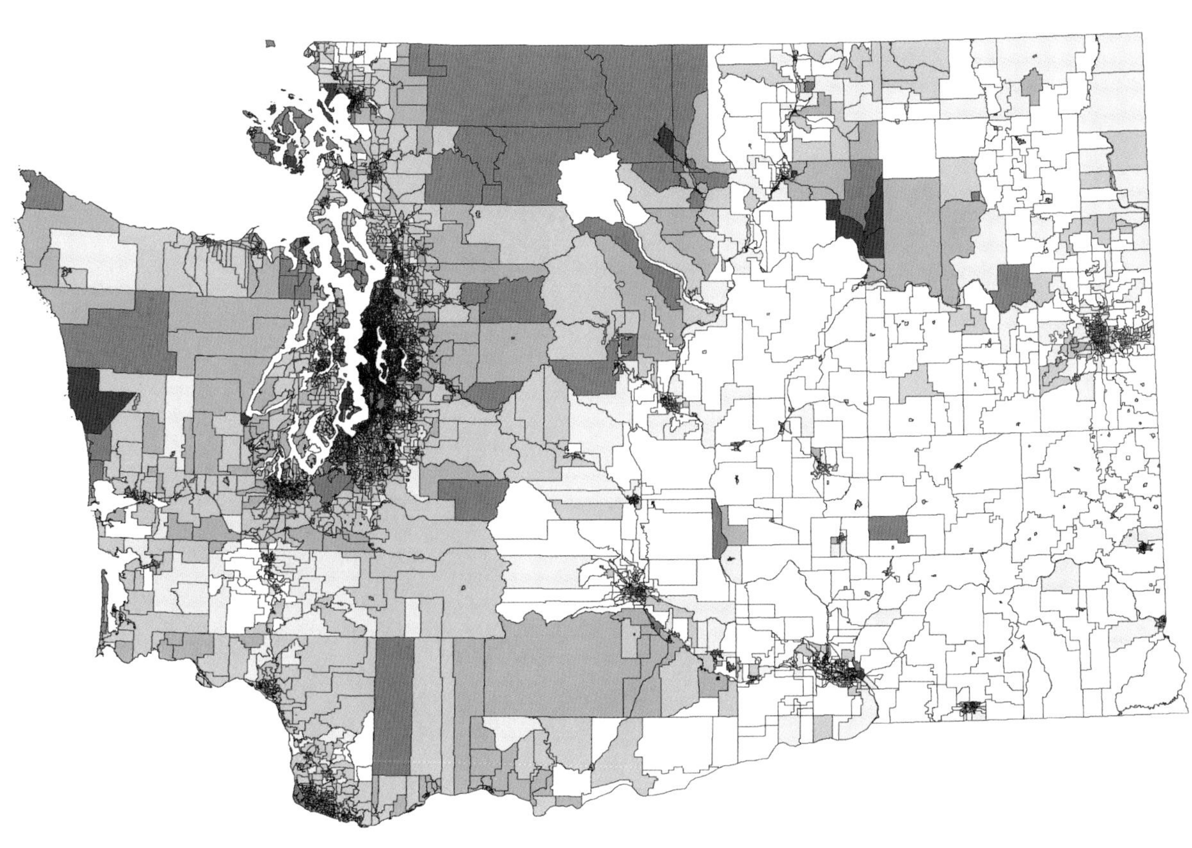

Percentage Voting "Yes"

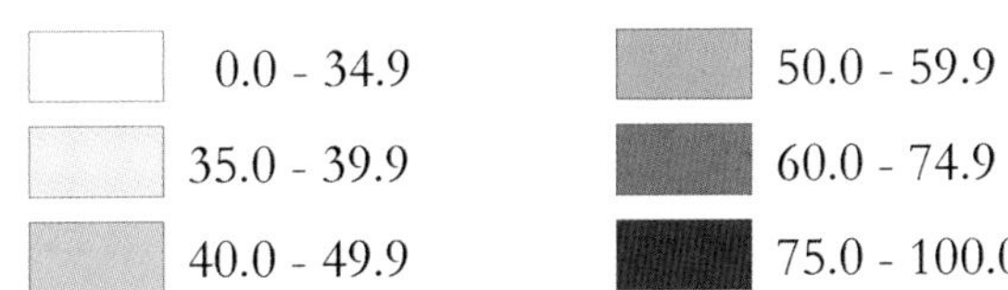

FIGURE 8.16

Percentage Difference of Clinton Vote and Initiative 1433

Seattle Area

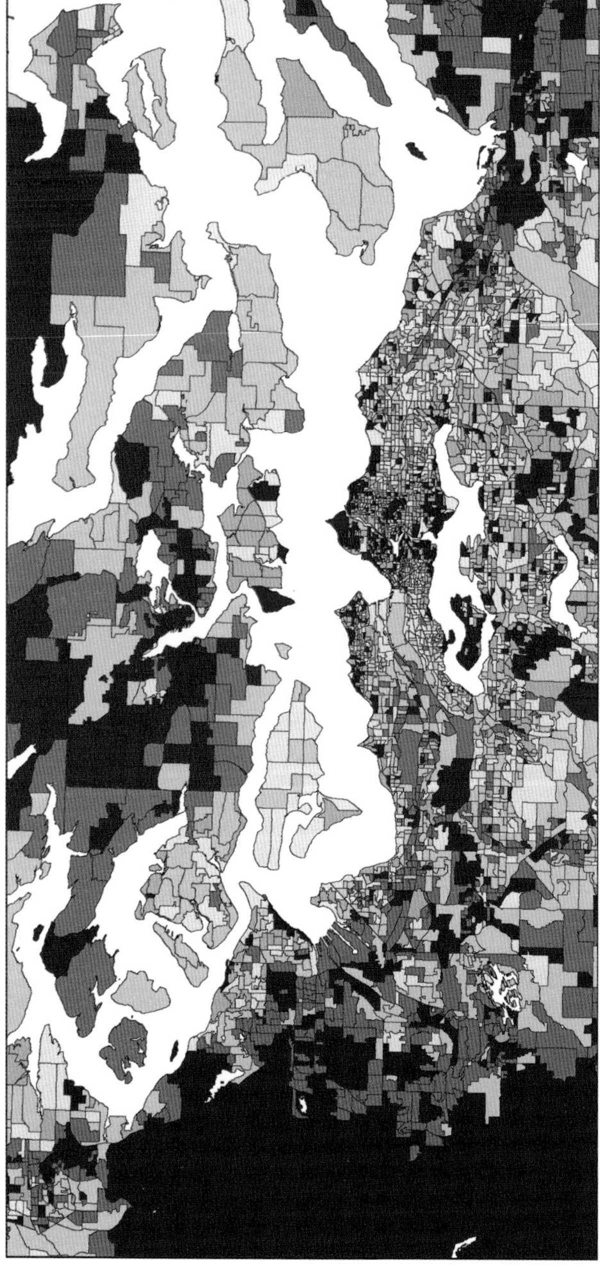

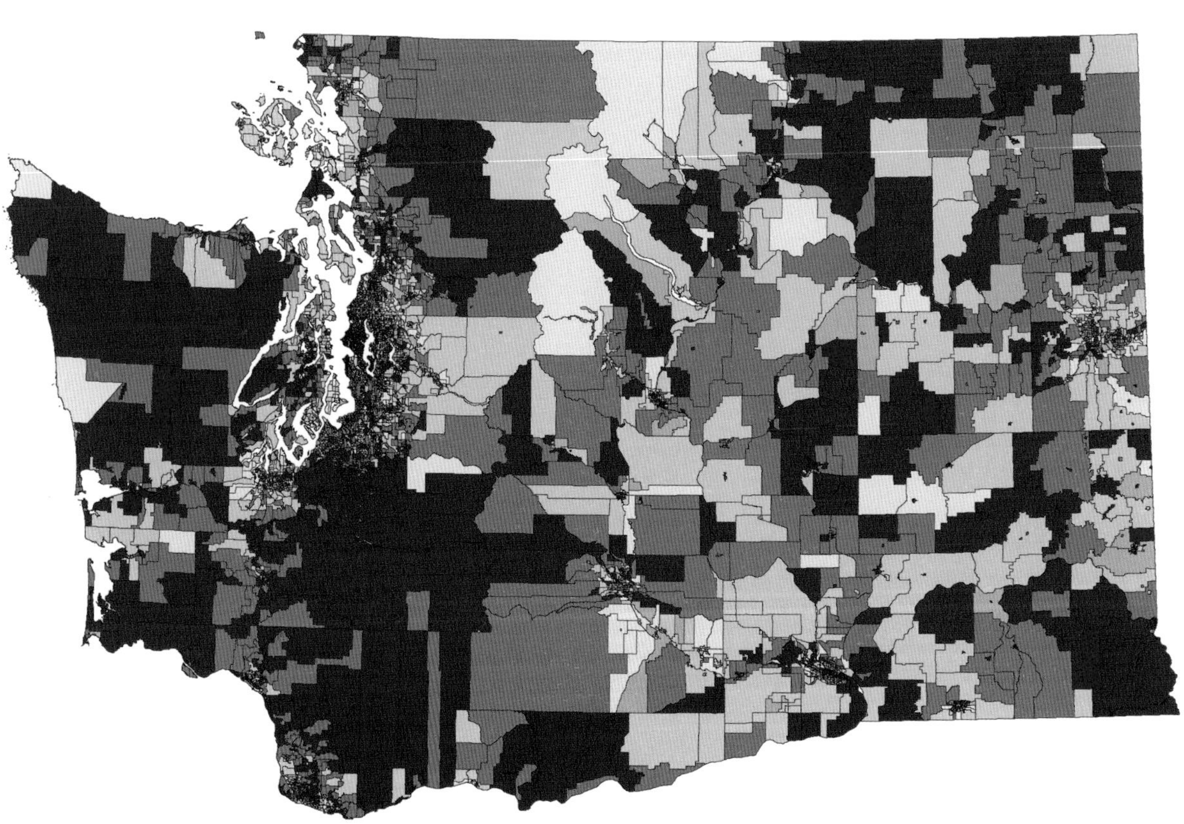

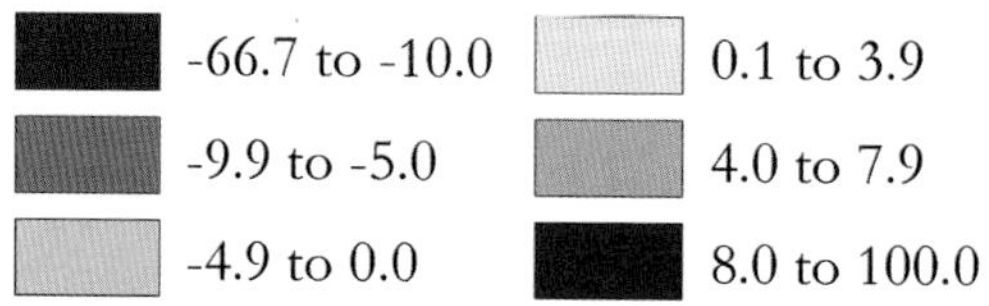

that have mostly recently "reddened"—quite a few voters voted to support Donald Trump and the wage increase. There may be "two Washingtons," but each contains multitudes.

TABLE 8.3. Correlations of Percentage for Clinton and Percentage for I-1433 Minimum Wage

		r	
Clinton %	Min. Wage	0.94	
Clinton %	Obama	0.95	
Clinton %	Difference	0.75	
	Clinton %	**Min. Wage**	**Difference**
Density	0.6	0.61	0.35
High school only	-0.57	-0.38	-0.74
BA degree or higher	0.57	0.37	0.77
% Asian American	0.54	0.56	0.4
Unmarried partners	0.51	0.57	0.31
Foreign born	0.46	0.44	
Husband, wife	-0.49	-0.51	
Families, no child			
African American	0.42	0.54	
Single	0.41	0.47	
Professional occupuation	0.41	0.36	0.66
% Age 20-34	0.4	0.42	
Construction	-0.41	-0.25	-0.54
% White	-0.38	-0.41	
Minority	0.38	0.46	
% Age <18	-0.38	-0.25	-0.29
Agricultural occupation	-0.32	-0.333	-0.52
Females in labor force	0.31	1.34	
Husband, wife, child	-0.25	-0.37	
Median income			0.42

Note: Blank cells indicate nonsignificant correlations.

9 THE 2016 ELECTION AND BEYOND

A plurality of American voters cast their ballots for Democrat Hillary Clinton in the 2016 presidential election but, in what many observers considered an upset, Republican Donald Trump won a majority of Electoral College votes and took office as the 45th President of the United States on January 20, 2017. Although he had universal name recognition from his business activities and his reality television appearances, Trump became the first person who had neither held public office nor served in a high government post nor had significant military experience to win the presidency. Trump defeated several well-known, politically experienced candidates in winning the Republican nomination before defeating Clinton, who also had substantial political experience as a US senator and secretary of state, in the general election.

Journalists and other observers have advanced many explanations of the election result. Some have focused on outright sexism and misogyny; others have criticized Clinton for ineffective campaigning; some have referred to divisions within the Democratic Party during and after the primary election campaign; some have argued that Clinton's use of a private e-mail server as secretary of state, along with FBI director James Comey's calling attention to the issue just a few days before the election, damaged her candidacy; some have stated that the Trump campaign was successful in recognizing and tapping into a strong antiestablishment mood among the electorate. No doubt historians will debate these and many other reasons underlying the outcome of the election for decades to come.

Whatever the reasons, Trump's victory, along with continuing Republican control of both houses of Congress, has changed the direction of American political discourse and American public policy. This was evident in actions that took place within the first few months after Trump took office, including his effort to issue executive orders banning immigration from selected countries, his appointment of conservative judge Neil Gorsuch to the Supreme Court, and his withdrawing of the United States from international climate change policy agreements. Trump's campaign and his actions since his inauguration have been interpreted as a rebuke against the internationalist, globalized outlook of Barack Obama's administration, replacing this outlook with an isolationist, protectionist, anti-elitist, and anti-globalist point of view.

On grounds such as these, some political scientists and journalists have referred to the 2016 presidential election as a watershed election—one that, like the elections of 1860, 1896, and 1932, and perhaps 1980, might go down in history as representing a fundamental turning point in American history. Whether the election and inauguration of Trump will come to be regarded as a watershed in American history remains to be seen. But from a geographical point of view, the 2016 election did not represent a sharp break from the recent past. Places whose voters supported Trump in 2016 were generally places whose voters have supported Republican nominees over the past few decades. Similarly, places whose voters supported Clinton in 2016 were usually places whose voters supported previous Democratic nominees in the recent past.

Trump did not win the election following a major shift in voting decisions made by the electorate. Public opinion surveys showed that a large majority of persons who voted for Obama in 2012 voted for Clinton in 2016 and that a large majority of those who voted for Mitt Romney in 2012 voted for Trump in 2016. Rather, Trump owed his victory to decisions made by a very small percentage of the voters living in what was for him the most advantageous places. Of the fifty states, forty-four gave their electoral votes to the same party in 2016 as in 2012. And, of the six states that shifted to the Republicans, three did so by only narrow margins. An additional 80,000 votes for Clinton in Wisconsin, Michigan, and Pennsylvania would have given her the Electoral College votes of these states and would have secured her the presidency.

As the maps in this atlas illustrate, Trump's increased support in the Rust Belt in 2016 relative to that for Romney in 2012 was key to his winning the election. Throughout the region, Trump won at least 5 percent more popular votes than did Romney in hundreds of counties in the region, especially in rural areas. Indeed, the election highlighted the increasing polarization between Democratic support in large metropolitan areas and Republican support in exurbs, small cities, and the rural countryside. This was evident in the two Rust Belt states carried by Clinton, Illinois and Minnesota. In these states, Clinton's strong support in the Chicago and Twin Cities metropolitan areas, respectively, outweighed Trump's strength elsewhere.

With Trump in office, both major parties are beginning to look toward the future. In order to regain the White House, Democrats must recapture enough states to shift at least thirty-eight electoral votes from the Republicans. A variety of strategies have been proposed. Some have advocated a concerted effort to recapture the Rust Belt including Ohio and Iowa as well as Wisconsin, Michigan, and Pennsylvania. On this view, the Democrats should focus on regaining the support of blue-collar workers and rural residents in these states who voted for Obama in 2008 and 2012 but voted for Trump in 2016. Other observers have recommended that the Democrats focus more on rapidly growing states with large minority populations such as Arizona, Georgia, North Carolina, and Texas. Proponents of this perspective point to demographics because the minority populations of these states are growing faster than the white populations and because these states are attracting large numbers of young in-migrants who tend to be more liberal than their elders.

Underlying these questions is ongoing tension within the party concerning its directions. Progressives, many of whom supported Bernie Sanders in the Democratic primaries, have argued that the party should move to the left. Some have criticized the 2016 Clinton campaign for paying too little attention to the concerns of progressives, especially millennials. On the other hand, some Democrats respond that a move to the left would concede the center to the Republicans. From a geographical perspective, these observers predict that moving the party in a progressive direction would reinforce Democratic support in the already liberal Northeast and Pacific Coast states, but would make it more difficult for the Democrats to recapture the purple states whose electoral votes may be critical to a Democratic victory in 2020.

Voter turnout is also a concern. Generally speaking, the Republicans have done better turning out their supporters than have the Democrats. High turnouts helped Obama win the 2008 and 2012 elections. However, Democratic turnout was relatively much lower in the 2010 and 2014 midterm elections, in which the Republicans scored significant gains in Congress and in state and local elections. Democratic turnout in the 2016 presidential election dropped relative to 2008 and 2012, to the point that this reduced turnout may have cost Clinton the election. On this basis, some Democrats have argued that the party should select a younger, more charismatic, and more inspiring candidate than Clinton in 2016. Proponents of this view point to the successes of Obama and Bill Clinton, both of whom are regarded as charismatic individuals and inspiring speakers. As well, both were in their forties when first elected to the presidency, in contrast to Hillary Clinton, who turned 69 shortly before the 2016 election.

Meanwhile, the Republicans may also face tensions within their party. Despite his success in 2016, Trump remains an outsider within the Republican establishment. During the first few months of his administration, Trump's popularity ratings among the American public were low and he reinforced his reputation for unpredictability and impulsive behavior. These concerns, should they intensify, may affect the 2018 midterm elections and especially Republican candidates who may be forced to distance themselves from the Trump administration. Of course, the Republican Party's goal will be to retain its 2016 majority, but some party leaders are expressing concern that Trump's unpopularity, if it continues, could impede the party's efforts to retain the presidency in 2020.

Overall, the patterns of voting illustrated in this atlas show that the 2016 election, when examined from a geographical perspective, represents a continuation of recent trends rather than a sharp break from the past. However, the changing nature of American political discourse in light of Trump's victory could well signal the beginning of a longer-term realignment in American elections. Perhaps only in years and decades to come will historians be able to draw conclusions as to the degree to which the 2016 contest will be regarded as a watershed election.

INDEX

Note: Page references for figures and tables are italicized.

ABOUT THE CONTRIBUTORS

John Agnew is professor of geography at the University of California, Los Angeles.

Ben Anderstone is a political consultant based in Seattle, Washington.

J. Clark Archer is professor of geography, University of Nebraska–Lincoln.

Jill A. Archer is a retired media specialist, Lincoln Public Schools, Lincoln, Nebraska.

Matthew Balentine is a graduate student of geography at the University of North Carolina, Greensboro.

William Berentsen is professor of geography at the University of Connecticut, Storrs.

Jason Combs is professor of geography at the University of Nebraska at Kearney.

Jeffrey Crump is professor in the Housing Studies Program at the University of Minnesota.

Carl T. Dahlman is professor of geography at Miami University, Oxford.

Fiona M. Davidson is associate professor of geography at the University of Arkansas.

Lisa M. DeChano-Cook is associate professor of geography at Western Michigan University.

Matthew Engel is adjunct lecturer of geography at the University of Nebraska at Kearney.

Richard L. Engstrom is professor emeritus of political science at the University of New Orleans and research associate at the Center for the Study of Race, Ethnicity, and Gender in the Social Sciences at Duke University.

Erin H. Fouberg is professor of geography at Northern State University.

Kenneth French is assistant professor of geography at the University of Wisconsin–Parkside.

Megan A. Gall is a social scientist at the Voting Rights Project, Lawyers' Committee for Civil Rights Under Law, Washington, DC.

Mark Graham is professor of Internet geography, Oxford Internet Institute, University of Oxford, and Alan Turing Institute, London.

Scott Hale is a senior data scientist at the Oxford Internet Institute, University of Oxford, and Alan Turing Institute, London.

John Heppen is professor of geography at the University of Wisconsin–River Falls.

Ashley M. Hitt is an undergraduate student in geography at the University of Oklahoma.

Kimberly K. Johnson is a graduate student in geography at the University of Oklahoma.

Ron Johnston is professor of geography at the University of Bristol, UK.

Kelvyn Jones is professor of geography at the University of Bristol, UK.

Larry Knopp is professor of geography at the University of Washington, Tacoma.

Jonathan Leib is professor of geography at Old Dominion University.

Samuel Loftsgaarden is a geography student at the University of Wisconsin–Eau Claire.

Chris Maier is adjunct professor of geography at South Dakota State University.

David Manley is professor of geographer at the University of Bristol, UK.

Kenneth C. Martis is professor of geography at West Virginia University.

Daniel A. McGowin is assistant professor of geography at Jacksonville State University.

Richard L. Morrill is emeritus professor of geography at the University of Washington.

Jennifer L. Patin is a development officer at the Voting Rights Project, Lawyers' Committee for Civil Rights Under Law, Washington, DC.

Tony Robinson is associate professor of political science at the University of Colorado at Denver.

Fred M. Shelley is professor of geography at the University of Oklahoma.

Monica Stephens is assistant professor of geography at SUNY at Buffalo.

Li Tong is a graduate student of geography at SUNY at Buffalo.

Robert H. Watrel is associate professor of geography at South Dakota State University.

Gerald R. Webster is professor of geography at the University of Wyoming.

Katie Weichelt is adjunct professor of geography at the University of Wisconsin–Eau Claire.

Ryan Weichelt is associate professor of geography at the University of Wisconsin–Eau Claire.

Lindy Westenhoff is a graduate student in geography at the University of Wyoming.

Levi John Wolf is a graduate student at the School of Geographical Sciences & Urban Planning, Arizona State University.